EZRA POUND IN CONTEXT

Long at the center of the modernist project, from editing Eliot's *The Waste Land* to publishing Joyce, Pound has also been a provocateur and instigator of new movements, while initiating a new poetics. This is the first volume to summarize and analyze the multiple contexts of Pound's work, underlining the magnitude of his contribution and drawing on new archival, textual, and theoretical studies. Pound's political and economic ideas also receive attention. With its concentration on the contexts of history, sociology, aesthetics, and politics, the volume will provide a portrait of Pound's unusually international reach: an American-born, modern poet absorbing the cultures of England, France, Italy, and China. These essays situate Pound in the social and material realities of his time and will be invaluable for students and scholars of Pound and modernism.

IRA B. NADEL is Professor of English at the University of British Columbia. He is the author of *The Cambridge Introduction to Ezra Pound* (2007) and editor of *The Cambridge Companion to Ezra Pound* (1999).

EZRA POUND IN CONTEXT

EDITED BY

IRA B. NADEL

University of British Columbia

CAMBRIDGE UNIVERSITY PRESS
Cambridge, New York, Melbourne, Madrid, Cape Town, Singapore,
São Paulo, Delhi, Dubai, Tokyo, Mexico City

Cambridge University Press
The Edinburgh Building, Cambridge CB2 8RU, UK

Published in the United States of America by Cambridge University Press, New York

www.cambridge.org
Information on this title: www.cambridge.org/9780521515078

First published 2010

Printed in the United Kingdom at the University Press, Cambridge

A catalogue record for this publication is available from the British Library

Library of Congress Cataloguing in Publication data
Ezra Pound in context / edited by Ira B. Nadel.
p.   cm.
Includes index.
ISBN 978-0-521-51507-8 (hardback)
1. Pound, Ezra, 1885–1972 – Criticism and interpretation.   I. Nadel, Ira Bruce.   II. Title.
PS3531.O82Z625   2010
811′.52 – dc22   2010035126

ISBN 978-0-521-51507-8 Hardback

Contents

Notes on contributors

BARRY AHEARN is Professor of English at Tulane University, New Orleans. His publications include *Zukofsky's "A": An Introduction* (1983), *William Carlos Williams and Alterity* (1994), and *The Correspondence of William Carlos Williams and Louis Zukofsky* (2003). He has recently completed an edition of the selected letters of Zukofsky.

MASSIMO BACIGALUPO teaches American literature at the University of Genoa, Italy, and lives in Rapallo. His family has been associated with the Pounds for several generations. He is the author of *The Forméd Trace: The Later Poetry of Ezra Pound* (1980), and of annotated Italian editions of Pound's *Hugh Selwyn Mauberley* (1982), *Homage to Sextus Propertius* (1984), and *Canti postumi* (2001). In 2008 he co-edited the volume *Ezra Pound, Language and Persona*. He is an associate of the journals *Poesia, Paideuma* and *Leviathan*, and a member of the Ligurian Academy of Sciences and Letters. His translations of Pound, Wordsworth, Dickinson, Stevens, and many others won him the 2001 Italian National Translation Prize.

GREGORY BARNHISEL is Associate Professor of English and the Director of first-year writing at Duquesne University in Pittsburgh, Pennsylvania. He is the author of *James Laughlin, New Directions, and the Remaking of Ezra Pound* (2005) and the textbook *Media and Messages: Strategies and Readings in Public Rhetoric* (2005), as well as articles in *Paideuma, Papers of the Bibliographical Society of America*, and *Modernism/Modernity*. His current scholarly work focuses on the use of modernist art in the US cultural diplomacy program in the early Cold War.

REBECCA BEASLEY is a Fellow and University Lecturer in English at The Queen's College, Oxford. She is the author of *Ezra Pound and the Visual Culture of Modernism* (Cambridge University Press, 2007), and *Theorists of Modernist Poetry: Ezra Pound, T.S. Eliot and T.E. Hulme* (2007). She is currently working on a study of the impact of Russian culture on British modernism.

GEORGE BORNSTEIN is C. A. Patrides Professor of Literature Emeritus at the University of Michigan. He has written and edited over a dozen books on modernist literature, including most recently *Material Modernism: The Politics of the Page* (2001) and, with Richard J. Finneran, *Early Essays by W. B. Yeats* (2010). His new book *The Colors of Zion: Blacks, Jews, And Irish a Century ago* will appear shortly.

PETER BROOKER is Professorial Fellow at the Centre for Modernist Studies, University of Sussex. He has written widely on contemporary writing and theory and is the author of *Bertolt Brecht: Dialectics, Poetry, Politics* (1989), *New York Fictions* (1996), *Modernity and Metropolis* (2004), *Bohemia in London* (2004, 2007), and *A Glossary of Cultural Theory* (1999, 2003). With Andrew Thacker, he is editor of *The Geographies of Modernism* (2005), co-director of the Arts and Humanities Research Council-funded Modernist Magazine Project, and co-editor of Volume 1 of *The Oxford Critical and Cultural History of Modernist Magazines* (2009). He is also co-editor of *Oxford Handbook of Modernisms* (2010).

ERIC BULSON is the author of the *Cambridge Introduction to James Joyce* (2006) and *Novels, Maps, Modernity: the Spatial Imagination, 1850–2000* (2009). He teaches at colleges in Geneva, NY.

RONAL BUSH, Drue Heinz Professor of American Literature at Oxford University, is the author of *The Genesis of Ezra Pound's Cantos* (1976) and *T.S. Eliot: A Study of Character and Style* (1983). He has published widely on Pound, Eliot, Joyce, and other modernist topics and is at work on a two-volume genetic study and critical edition of the Pisan Cantos.

MARK BYRON is a member of the Department of English at the University of Sydney. He has taught at the University of Washington and at Cambridge University, where he completed his PhD in 2001. His two current projects include a digital variorum edition of Ezra Pound's *Cantos* and a digital edition of Samuel Beckett's novel *Watt*.

PATRICIA COCKRAM was Associate Professor of English at Lehman College of the City University of New York. She published several articles on Pound and was the author of *James Joyce and Ezra Pound, a More Than Literary Friendship* (2005). Her current project had been a book to be called "The French Ezra Pound", a study of the influence of French literature on

Pound's poetry, his publication history in France, and the reception of his work and its influence in France today.

JOHN XIROS COOPER is a Professor of English at the University of British Columbia. He has published five books and a number of articles and book chapters. His publications include work on modernism, T. S. Eliot, Ezra Pound and William Carlos Williams, among other topics. He is working on a new book on modernism and he has recently been awarded a research grant for work on Lord Byron and modernity.

MICHAEL COYLE is Professor of English at Colgate University, Hamilton, NY, and founding President of the Modernist Studies Association. He serves on the boards of directors for various author societies. His *Ezra Pound, Popular Genres, and the Discourse of Culture* was published in 1995; he has subsequently edited two other Pound collections for the National Poetry Foundation: *Ezra Pound and African American Modernism* (2001) and, with Steven G. Yao, *Ezra Pound and Education* (forthcoming). Other edited collections include *Raymond Williams and Modernism* (2003) and with Debra Rae Cohen and Jane Lewty, *Broadcasting Modernism* (2009). He is currently completing *Professional Attention: Ezra Pound and the Career of Modernist Criticism*.

HELEN DENNIS is Associate Professor in the Department of English at the University of Warwick. She has published widely on American litera-ture, including Elizabeth Bishop, Willa Cather, H.D., Ezra Pound, Adri-enne Rich, and Native American literature. Major publications include: *A New Approach to the Poetry of Ezra Pound: through the Medieval Provençal Aspect* (1996) and *Native American Literature: Towards a Spatialized Read-ing* (2006). Her poetry has been published in small press publications, most recently *Bluebeard's Wives* (2007).

MARGARET FISHER, PhD, Fellow of the American Academy of Rome (2009), is a choreographer, video director, and independent scholar cur-rently writing on Futurism and radio. She is the author of *Ezra Pound's Radio Operas: The BBC Experiments, 1931–1933* (2002), *Collis O Heliconii: The Recovery of Ezra Pound's Third Opera, Settings of Poems by Catullus and Sappho* (2005), and *Ezra Pound Composer: Ego Scriptor Cantilenae* (audio CD, 2003). She co-authored, with Robert Hughes, *Paroles de Villon: Two performance Editions of Le Testament* (2008), and *Cavalcanti: A Perspective on the Music of Ezra Pound* (2003).

BENJAMIN FRIEDLANDER is the author of *Simulcast: Four Experiments in Criticism* (2004) and editor of *Robert Creeley, Selected Poems, 1945–2005* (2008). He is an Associate Professor of English at the University of Maine and a member of the editorial board for the National Poetry Foundation, USA.

JOHN GERY is a Research Professor of English at the University of New Orleans and Director of the Ezra Pound Center for Literature, Brunnenburg, Italy. He has published five volumes of poetry, including *The Enemies of Leisure* (1995) and *A Gallery of Ghosts* (2008), as well as *Nuclear Annihilation and Contemporary American Poetry: Ways of Nothingness* (1996) and (with Rosella Mamoli Zorzi, Massimo Bacigalupo, and Stefano Maria Casella) *In Venice and in the Veneto with Ezra Pound* (2007). He currently serves as Secretary of the Ezra Pound International Conference.

MIRANDA HICKMAN is an Associate Professor of English at McGill University, Montreal. Her most recent book is *The Geometry of Modernism* (2006); she has also published on Ezra Pound's publishing practices, H. D. and the body, and the legacy of Raymond Chandler in contemporary culture. She has contributed a chapter on modernist women poets in *The Cambridge Companion to Modernist Women Writers* (2009) and is currently completing an annotated edition of Ezra Pound's letters to publisher Stanley Nott and co-editing a volume of essays entitled *Rereading the New Criticism.*

MATTHEW HOFER is Assistant Professor of English at the University of New Mexico. He has published articles on modernist poetry and poetics in *American Literary Scholarship*, *Modernism/Modernity*, *New German Critique*, and other venues, and is co-editor of *Oscar Wilde in America: The Interviews* (2009).

ALEX HOUEN is a lecturer at Cambridge University. He is the author of *Terrorism and Modern Literature: from Joseph Conrad to Ciaran Carson* (2002), as well as numerous articles on modernism, the avant-garde, and twentieth-century American writers.

DANIEL KATZ teaches in the Department of English and Comparative Literary Studies at the University of Warwick. He is the author of *Saying I No More: Subjectivity and Consciousness in the Prose of Samuel Beckett* (1999) and *American Modernism's Expatriate Scene: The Labour of Translation* (2007).

FENG LAN is Associate Professor of Chinese Language and Literature at the Florida State University. He is the author of *Ezra Pound and*

Confucianism: Remaking Humanism in the Face of Modernity (2005), and has published articles in English and Chinese on Pound, translation studies, Confucianism, Chinese cinema, and diasporic literature.

ETHAN LEWIS teaches Modern and Renaissance Literature at the University of Illinois-Springfield. His published works include, with Robert Kuhn McGregor, *Conundrums for the Long Week-End: England, Dorothy L. Sayers, and Lord Peter Wimsey* (2000), winner of an Edgar Award for a critical monograph, and *Modernist Image: Imagist Technique in the Work of Pound and Eliot* (2007). He is currently writing a phenomenological critique of Shakespeare.

PETER LIEBREGTS graduated in Classics at the University of Utrecht and took his doctorate at Leiden University, where he is currently a Full Professor of Modern Literatures in English. His main research interests are modernism, the *Nachleben* of classical literature and culture, and religion and literature. Besides numerous articles on literatures in English from the Renaissance to the present, he has published *Centaurs in the Twilight: W.B. Yeats's Use of the Classical Tradition* (1993), and *Ezra Pound and Neoplatonism* (2004).

JAMES LONGENBACH is the author of three books of poems, most recently *Draft of a Letter* (2007), as well as six books of literary criticism, including *Stone Cottage: Pound, Yeats, and Modernism* (Oxford) and *The Art of the Poetic Line* (2008). He is Joseph H. Gilmore Professor of English at the University of Rochester, NY.

ALEC MARSH, Professor of English at Muhlenberg College, Allentown, PA, is the author of *Money and Modernity: Pound, Williams and the Spirit of Jefferson* (1998) and the editor of *Small Boy: The Wisconsin Childhood of Homer L. Pound* (2003), a memoir by the poet's father. He is currently at work on a study of Ezra Pound and the American right and a short biography.

CRAIG MONK is Associate Professor of English and Associate Dean in the Faculty of Arts and Science at the University of Lethbridge, Alberta. He is the author of *Writing the Lost Generation* (2008), as well as articles on modernist literary magazines published in *American Periodicals*, *Canadian Journal of Irish Studies*, *Canadian Review of American Studies*, *Journal of Modern Literature*, *Mosaic*, and *History of Photography*.

IRA B. NADEL, Professor of English at the University of British Columbia and Distinguished University Scholar, is also a Fellow of the Royal

Society of Canada. He is the author of biographies of Leonard Cohen, Tom Stoppard, and David Mamet. His life of Leon Uris will appear in 2010. He has also edited the *Cambridge Companion to Ezra Pound* (1999), *The Letters of Ezra Pound to Alice Corbin Henderson* (1993), and *Ezra Pound, Early Writings, Poems and Prose* (2005).

JOHN G. NICHOLS is Associate Professor of English and Director of Film Studies at Christopher Newport University, Newport News, Virginia. He specializes in early twentieth-century literature and film. He is currently completing a manuscript on the intersections of modernism, advice, and amateurism, entitled, "The Amateur Moderns."

WILLIAM D. PADEN is Professor of French at Northwestern University, Evanston, IL, and a specialist in medieval literature and language, especially in the poetry of the troubadours. Among other titles, he is the author of *Medieval Lyric: Genres in Historical Context* (2002) and *Troubadour Poems from the South of France* (2007).

ZHAOMING QIAN is Chancellor's Research Professor of English at the University of New Orleans and Y. C. Tang Chair Professor of Comparative Literature and Director of the Center for Modernist Studies at Zhejiang University, China. His books include *Orientalism and Modernism: The Legacy of China in Pound and Williams* (1995), *The Modernist Response to Chinese Art: Pound, Moore, Stevens* (2003), *Ezra Pound and China* (2003), and *Ezra Pound's Chinese Friends* (2008). His research has been supported by fellowships from the National Endowment of the Humanities, the American Philosophical Society, and Yale University.

TIM REDMAN is Professor of Literary Studies in the School of Arts and Humanities at the University of Texas at Dallas, where he has taught for twenty years. He has written numerous essays in the field of Pound studies and is currently at work on a biography of Pound. He is best known for his book *Ezra Pound and Italian Fascism* (1991), which has recently appeared in paperback. Aside from his work on Pound, he has an international reputation in the field of chess and education.

CATERINA RICCIARDI, Professor of American Literature at the University of Roma Tre, has written various essays on American modernism. She is the author of *EIKONEΣ. Ezra Pound e il Rinascimento* (1991), and of *Ezra Pound. Ghiande di Luce* (2006). She edited *Ezra Pound, Idee fondamentali. Meridiano di Roma (1939–1943)* (1991), and the Italian translation of *Indiscretions; or, Une Revue de deux Mondes* (2004).

VINCENT SHERRY is Professor and Chair of English at Washington University in St Louis, where he teaches and writes about modernist literature in Britain and Ireland. He is currently writing a biography of Ezra Pound and a book-length study of European Decadence and modernist literature in English. His previous publications include *The Great War and the Language of Modernism* (2003), *James Joyce; Ulysses* (1995; 2nd edn. 2004), *Ezra Pound, Wyndham Lewis, and Radical Modernism* (1993), and *The Uncommon Tongue: The Poetry and Criticism of Geoffrey Hill* (1987). He has edited the *Cambridge Companion to the Literature of the First World War* (2005) and several volumes on post-Second World War British and Irish Poets for the *Dictionary of Literary Biography* (1984, 1985).

STEPHEN SICARI is Professor of English and long-time chair of the English Department at St John's University in New York. Among his publications are *Pound's Epic Ambition: Dante and the Modern World* (1991) and *Joyce's Modernist Allegory: Ulysses and the History of the Novel* (2001). He has recently completed a study titled *A Modernist Humanism*, which includes a chapter on Pound and the Enlightenment.

ROBERT SPOO is a tenured faculty member at the University of Tulsa College of Law. He earned his MA and PhD in English from Princeton University, and his JD from the Yale Law School, where he was executive editor of the *Yale Law Journal*. Prior to his legal career, he taught for more than ten years in the English Department at the University of Tulsa, where he was editor of the *James Joyce Quarterly*, and published *James Joyce and the Language of History* (1994), and edited with Omar Pound, *Ezra and Dorothy Pound, Letters in Captivity 1945–1946* (1999).

ELLEN STAUDER is David Eddings Professor of English and Humanities and Dean of Faculty at Reed College, Portland, OR. She has recently completed a book, *Form Cut Into Time: Ezra Pound and the Poetics of Rhythm*, and has also authored essays on Pound, Pater, Loy and others.

LEON SURETTE is Professor of English (Emeritus) at the University of Western Ontario. He is the author of five books including *Light from Eleusis: A Study of Ezra Pound's Cantos* (1979), *The Birth of Modernism: Ezra Pound, T.S. Eliot, W.B. Yeats and the Occult* (1993), and *Pound in Purgatory: From Economic Radicalism to Anti-Semitism* (1999). He studied at the University of Toronto with Marshal McLuhan and Northrop Frye.

DAVID TEN EYCK is an Assistant Professor of American Literature at Nancy–Université (France). He specializes in modernism and twentieth-century poetry and is currently co-editing a critical edition of Ezra Pound's *Pisan Cantos*.

DEMETRES P. TRYPHONOPOULOS is University Research Professor at the University of New Brunswick, Canada. He is the author of *The Celestial Tradition: A Study of Ezra Pound's "The Cantos"* (1992) and co-editor of *An Ezra Pound Encyclopedia* (2005), as well as several volumes on Ezra Pound and William Carlos Williams. His latest publication is an annotated edition of *Majic Ring* (2009), an H.D. autobiographical novel.

EMILY MITCHELL WALLACE'S PhD in comparative literature is from Bryn Mawr College, Pennsylvania. She has taught literature at the University of Pennsylvania, Swarthmore, Curtis Institute of Music, and an interdisciplinary seminar in painting, poetry, and science at Yale. She is currently a research scholar in the Center for Visual Culture at Bryn Mawr. A recent essay on Pound is "'Why Not Spirits? – The Universe is Alive': Ezra Pound, Joseph Rock, the Na Khi, and Plotinus," published in *Ezra Pound and China*, ed. Zhaoming Qian (2003).

STEVEN G. YAO is the author of *Translation and the Languages of Modernism: Gender, Politics, Language* (2002), and is an Associate Professor of English at Hamilton College, Clinton, NY, where he teaches Anglo-American modernism, translation history and theory, and Asian American literature. His essays have appeared in *Textual Practice*, */LIT: Literature, Interpretation, Theory*, and *Representations*. Currently, he is completing a book-length study of Chinese American poetry entitled, *Foreign Accents: Chinese American Verse and the Counter-Poetics of Difference in the U.S., 1910-Present* (2010), which has earned fellowships from the Stanford Humanities Center and the American Council of Learned Societies. He is also co-editor of the essay collections, *Sinographies: Writing China* (2008) and *Pacific Rim Modernisms* (2009).

SERENELLA ZANOTTI, Lecturer in English Language and Translation at the University of Rome III, received her PhD from the University of Rome with a thesis on Pound's Italian writings and letters. She then specialized in modernism and translation at the Department of English and Comparative Literature, Goldsmiths College, University of London, after which she became Lecturer in English Language and Translation at the Università per Stranieri of Siena, Italy. She has published extensively on Joyce, Pound, and translation. Her articles and essays have appeared in national and international journals and books. She is the author of *Joyce in Italy / L'italiano in Joyce* (2004).

Acknowledgements

Poundians far and wide have contributed, cooperated, and confirmed the vibrant scholarship in the field during the process of preparing this volume. Generous of spirit and gracious in practice, they have uniformly supported what has been the challenge of uniting over forty critics in one collection. Whether in Italy, Australia, the UK, the USA or Canada, they have been supportive and encouraging. One of the pleasures of undertaking such a task has, in fact, been the constant sharing of knowledge among Pound critics and scholars worldwide, and I have learned a great deal in the process. The importance of context has also been reaffirmed by these essays, recalling Pound's own comment in his "Note to [the] Base Censor" written at Pisa: "The form of the poem and main progress is conditioned by its own inner shape, but the life of the D.T.C. passing OUTSIDE the scheme cannot but impinge, or break into the main flow." Context is "the life . . . passing OUTSIDE."

Warm thanks especially to Massimo Bacigalupo, George Bornstein, Ron Bush, Patricia Cockram, Margaret Fisher, Tim Redman, Robert Spoo, and Demetres Tryphonopoulos for their collective friendship and support. Special thanks to Ray Ryan of Cambridge University Press, who from the first recognized the importance of including Pound in the writers in context series. Maartje Scheltens of the Press has also provided a steady hand in the completion of the volume.

IRA B. NADEL

Chronology

1885	Ezra Weston Loomis Pound born to Homer Pound and Isabel Weston Pound on October 30 in Hailey, Idaho.
1887	Family moves to New York City, where they live with Isabel's Uncle Ezra and Aunt Frank Weston.
1889	Family moves to Philadelphia; Homer Pound accepts job as assistant assayer in the U.S. Mint. Works there until his retirement in 1928.
1890	Pounds move to Jenkintown, PA, a suburb just north of Philadelphia.
1892	Pounds settle into their long-term residence in Wyncote, PA.
1897	Ezra Pound enrolled in Cheltenham Military Academy.
1898	Aunt Frank Weston takes Pound and his mother to Europe, visiting Gibraltar, Tunisia, and Venice, later recalled in *The Cantos*.
1901–3	Pound enters the University of Pennsylvania at fifteen and meets Hilda Doolittle, William Carlos Williams.
1902	The Pounds and Aunt Frank take Pound on his second tour of Europe.
1903–5	Because of poor marks and university restrictions on language study, Pound transfers to Hamilton College, Clinton, New York, where he studies Provençal, Anglo-Saxon, Italian.
1905	Graduates from Hamilton with BA and publishes a translation from Provençal in the *Hamilton Literary Magazine*. Reads Dante and considers writing a modern epic based on *The Divine Comedy*. Begins graduate study at the University of Pennsylvania;

	meets Hilda Doolittle, for whom he forms an anthology of his early poems that he calls "Hilda's Book."
1906	MA in Romance languages from University of Pennsylvania and summer fellowship for research in Spain on the plays of Lope de Vega. Sails to Gibraltar and visits Madrid, Burgos, Paris, and London. Returns to university but fails a literary criticism course and becomes disillusioned with his professors.
1907	Learns that his fellowship will not be renewed; accepts job in Crawfordsville, Indiana at Wabash College, a small Presbyterian School, where he will teach Spanish and French. Falls in love with Mary Moore of Trenton in the summer. Will dedicate *Personae* (1909) to her.
1907–8	Instructor in Romance languages at Wabash College.
1908	Dismissed in February for harboring an actress in his rooms overnight, reported by his landladies. Spurned by both Mary Moore and Hilda Doolittle, he convinces his father to underwrite a trip to Europe to pursue a career as a poet. Sails in March and ends up in Venice publishing (at his own expense) his first collection of poems, *A lume spento* (July). Moves to London in August and begins to meet various literary figures through his publisher Elkin Mathews. Publishes *A Quinzaine for This Yule*.
1909	Delivers six lectures on literature of southern Europe to be revised and published as *The Spirit of Romance* (1910). Meets Olivia Shakespear and her daughter Dorothy, whom he will marry in 1914. Also meets Ford Madox Hueffer, who prints "Sestina Altaforte" in his *English Review*. Mathews publishes *Personae* in April. Attends meetings of the Poets' Club and that of the Secessionist Club found by T.E. Hulme and F.S. Flint. Meets Wyndham Lewis, D.H. Lawrence, and W. B. Yeats.
1910	Completes second set of lectures on medieval literature to be published with the first as *The Spirit of Romance*. William Carlos Williams visits. Leaves for Paris in March, and through the pianist Walter Morse Rummel, meets Margaret Cravens, who will become

	his patron. Works on a translation of Cavalcanti. In June returns to the United States seeking either to start a business or an academic career. In November *Provença*, an American edition of his poems, appears.
1911	Returns to London in February but immediately heads to Paris, where he works on a translation of troubadour poet Arnaut Daniel, and collaborates with Rummel on musical settings of troubadour poetry. Mathews publishes *Canzoni*. Travels to Germany to meet Hueffer, who dismisses Pound's archaic diction and urges him to concentrate on contemporary language. In London meets A.R. Orage, editor of *The New Age*, where his work will soon appear. Friendship with Yeats becomes closer. Hilda Doolittle arrives, to learn that Pound intends to marry Dorothy Shakespear.
1912	Meets Henry James through Hueffer. *Cavalcanti* appears in May, *Ripostes* in October. Finds Andreas Divus' Latin translation of the *Odyssey* in Paris important for the opening of *The Cantos*. Walking tour in southern France, June–July, cut short by news of Margaret Cravens' suicide in Paris. In London by fall, promoting his new school, imagism. Harriet Monroe, Chicago, asks Pound to contribute to her new magazine, *Poetry*. He becomes foreign correspondent, submitting work by Yeats, Aldington, himself, and Doolittle whom he renames "H.D. Imagiste." Introduces Richard Aldington to Hilda Doolittle; a romance follows.
1913	Meets Robert Frost; arranges for publication of William Carlos Williams' *The Tempers* by Mathews; publishes his manifesto on Imagism in *Poetry* (March 1913); "In a Station of the Metro" appears in April issue. Becomes literary editor of *The Egoist*; completes *Lustra*, although it is not published until 1916. Meets Henri Gaudier-Brzeska, Mary Fenollosa, widow of sinologist Ernest Fenollosa. Spends first of three winters with Yeats at Stone Cottage in Sussex. Learns of James Joyce.

1914	Marries Dorothy Shakespear, April 20, in London. Begins to work on Fenollosa's translations of Japanese drama and Chinese poems. Arranges for serial publication of *A Portrait of the Artist as a Young Man* in *The Egoist*. His anthology *Des Imagistes* appears in New York. Vol. 1 of *Blast*, edited by Pound and Lewis, appears in July, proclaiming the birth of vorticism. Introduced by Conrad Aiken to T.S. Eliot and enthusiastically recommends "Prufrock" to *Poetry*.
1915	Publishes "Exile's Letter," first of the poems drawn from Fenollosa's notes. "Imagism and England," February; "Provincia Deserta," March; "Near Perigord," December. Gaudier-Brzeska killed in France in war in June. *BLAST* vol. 2 appears. Edits *Catholic Anthology*; begins work on longish new poem which will become *The Cantos*. Mathews publishes *Cathy* in April.
1916	*Gaudier-Brzeska: A Memoir*, April. *Lustra*, London, September. *Certain Noble Plays of Japan*, September.
1917	*"Noh" or Accomplishment*, an expanded version of *Certain Noble Plays of Japan* with Fenollosa's essay on Japanese theatre; becomes foreign editor of *The Little Review*. "Three Cantos" appears in *Poetry*. T.S. Eliot's anonymous pamphlet, *Ezra Pound: His Metric and Poetry*, appears in New York. Publishes art criticism as B.H. Dias and music criticism as William Atheling in *The New Age*.
1918	Prose collection *Pavannes and Divisions* appears; meets Major C.H. Douglas, whose "Social Credit" approach to economics will have a lasting effect.
1919	Walking tour with Eliot through the Dordogne. *Quia Pauper Amavi* published with the original "Three Cantos" and full text of "Homage to Sextus Propertius." Writes Cantos V, VI, VII.
1920	Foreign correspondent for *The Dial*. *Instigations*, containing "Chinese Written Character as a Medium for Poetry," appears in April. *Hugh Selwyn Mauberley* Published. Pound meets Joyce for the first time at Sirmione in June; helps him settle in Paris in July.

1921	Settles in Paris in April. Meets Picabia, Cocteau, and Brancusi. John Quinn, New York lawyer and patron, visits Pound and Joyce. Begins opera *Le Testament de Villon* with the help of Agnes Bedford. Publishes Cantos v, vi, vii in *The Dial*. Eliot, passing through, shows Pound early version of what would become *The Waste Land*. Meets Ernest Hemingway.
1922	On New Year's Eve, meets Picasso. Eliot in January gives Pound revised draft of *The Waste Land* and within three weeks, Pound returns the manuscript with extensive comments, cuts, and changes. Canto viii appears in *The Dial*. Travels extensively in Italy, discovering the life and work of Sigismondo Malatesta, *condottiere* of Rimini. Completes rough drafts of Cantos ix–xi in Paris.
1923	*Indiscretions* published. Three Malatesta Cantos appear in *The Criterion*. Revises opening section of *The Cantos*. Meets American violinist Olga Rudge at Natalie Barney's Paris salon. Writes the Malatesta Cantos, viii–xi.
1924	In October travels with Dorothy to first Rapallo and then Sicily until they return to live permanently in Rapallo in January 1925. Begins a lifelong relationship with Olga Rudge. *Anthiel and the Treatise on Harmony* published in October. Becomes interested in economics and social theories.
1925	Deluxe edition of *A Draft of xvi Cantos* published in Paris in January by William Bird's Three Mountains Press. Decorative initials by Henry Strater. Pound concentrates on composition of cantos, translation of Confucius, and study of economics. In July, Olga Rudge gives birth to Pound's daughter Mary.
1926	*Le Testament de Villon* premieres in Paris. In September Dorothy gives birth to a son (Omar) conceived during a December 1925 trip without Pound to Egypt. *Personae*, selections from his early work, published.
1927–28	Edits and publishes his journal *Exile*, which lasts for only four issues. Begins friendship with Louis

Zukofsky, who will visit in 1933. Pound and Olga begin to spend time in Venice, where she owns a small home at 252 Dorsoduro, just off the Calle Querini. In February, Olga performs for Mussolini at his residence. Pound awarded the *Dial* prize for 1928. *A Draft of the Cantos 17–27*, with initials by Gladys Hynes, published by John Rodker in London. Eliot introduces and edits Pound's *Selected Poems*.

1929   Homer and Isabel Pound retire to Rapallo. Olga closes her Paris apartment and moves to Venice permanently. Pound refers to her "hidden nest" in Canto LXXVI.

1930   Two hundred copies of *A Draft of XXX Cantos* appear in Paris, published by Nancy Cunard at her Hours Press. *Imaginary Letters* also published. Begins to contribute literary and other commentary in Italian to *L'Indice*.

1931   *How to Read*. BBC broadcast of his opera *Le Testament*.

1933   Private audience with Mussolini in Rome, who praises *A Draft of XXX Cantos*. Recounted in Canto XLI. *ABC of Economics* published by Faber and Faber in London. *Active Anthology* appears. Zukofsky visits, as does the youthful James Laughlin, later to become Pound's publisher in America through his New Directions press.

1934   *ABC of Reading* plus *Make It New*, a collection of his literary criticism. *Eleven New Cantos* XXXI–XLI published in New York. James Laughlin spends several months with Pound in Rapallo at what he called the "Ezuversity."

1935   *Social Credit: An Impact*; *Jefferson and/or Mussolini*. Olga, Pound, and Gerhart Munch promote concerts in and around Rapallo.

1936   Founding of New Directions publishing in New York by James Laughlin.

1937   *Polite Essays*, January; *The Fifth Decad of Cantos*, June; *Confucius, Digest of the Analects*, June.

1938   *Guide to Kulchur*, July. Elected to National Institute of Arts and Letters. Travels to London for funeral of

	mother-in-law, Olivia Shakespear. Meets Yeats for the last time, his son for the first.
1939, April	Returns to the USA after twenty-eight years. Lobbies congressmen and senators in attempt to avert war in Europe. In New York meets H.L. Mencken, Marianne Moore. Honorary degree from Hamilton College. Gives public reading at Harvard. Returns to Italy in late June and begins friendship with philosopher George Santayana in Venice. *What is Money for?* appears.
1940	*Cantos LII–LXXI*, containing the so-called "Chinese Cantos." American edition adds a pamphlet with two essays: "Notes on the Cantos," by James Laughlin, and "Notes on the Versification of the Cantos," by Delmore Schwartz. Writes scripts critical of America for Rome Radio, read in English by others. Articles begin to appear in the *Japan Times* (Tokyo) often reprints from *Il Meridiano di Roma*. Work on *The Cantos* halts.
1941	Begins regular radio broadcasts on shortwave from Rome to America and to American troops in support, he claims, of the US Constitution. Remarks highly critical of Roosevelt and the war effort as well as anti-Semitic. To continue for three years except for an interval between December 1941 and February 1943: 120 broadcasts in all.
1942, February	Death of Homer Pound. Mary continues with Italian translation of the *Cantos*. Pound and family refused permission to join Americans being evacuated from Italy to Portugal. *Carte de Visita* published in Rome. English edition to appear as *A Visiting Card* in 1952.
1943, July	Indicted *in absentia* on thirteen counts of treason by a Grand Jury in Washington, DC. The day before, on July 25, 1943, Mussolini deposed from power. Pound leaves Rome on foot to begin 450-mile journey, partly by train, to visit Mary in the Tyrol, September. Italy occupied by German troops.
1944	Writes the two "Italian Cantos," LXXII–LXXIII, published in *Marina Repubblicana* in early 1945, but absent from the complete *Cantos* until 1985.

1945, May	Two Italian partisans arrest Pound at his home in Sant'Ambrogio above Rapallo on May 3 and, after some initial confusion and release, he reports to US Army authorities, who send him, accompanied by Olga, to Genoa. Arrested and sent on the Disciplinary Training Center north of Pisa on May 24, where he spends three weeks in solitary confinement in an exposed steel cage. After breakdown, transferred to medical tent, where he begins to compose what would become *The Pisan Cantos* (LXXIV–LXXXIV) and a translation of Confucius. He is sixty years old. On November 16, he is suddenly and secretly taken from the DTC to Rome, where he begins flight to Washington, DC to be re-indicted for treason. Arraigned on November 27 but trial postponed until psychiatric examination completed. December 21, Pound found mentally unfit to stand trial; committed to St. Elizabeths Hospital for the Criminally Insane, where he will stay for the next twelve and a half years.
1946	Visited by T.S. Eliot. Later guests to include Marianne Moore, Randall Jarrell, Thornton Wilder, Stephen Spender, Elizabeth Bishop, Katherine Anne Porter, and Langston Hughes. Mary Pound marries Prince Boris de Rachewiltz.
1947	Translation of Confucius, *The Unwobbling Pivot and The Great Digest.*
1948	February. Death of Isabel Pound. Visit from Robert Lowell, at the time Poetry Consultant to the Library of Congress. Marshall McLuhan and Hugh Kenner also visit. *If This Be Treason . . .* (edited by Olga Rudge) published, containing six of Pound's Rome radio broadcasts. *The Pisan Cantos* published July; *The Cantos*, first publication of the complete cantos, July.
1949, February	Awarded the Bollingen Prize for *The Pisan Cantos* by the Library of Congress amid widespread national controversy. *Selected Poems* published.
1950	*Patria Mia*, reworking of articles on America originally published in A.R. Orage's *New Age* from

	1912 and 1913. *Letters of Ezra Pound, 1907–1941*, edited by D.D. Paige. Retitled *Selected Letters* in 1971.
1952	Olga Rudge visits Pound at St. Elizabeths for the first time since his flight to the USA.
1953	Mary de Rachewiltz visits her father. *Translations* published in July. Includes "Cavalcanti Poems," "Cathay," Noh plays.
1954	*Literary Essays of Ezra Pound*, edited by T.S. Eliot. *The Classic Anthology Defined by Confucius*.
1955	*Section: Rock-Drill*.
1956	Sophocles, *Women of Trachis, A Version by Ezra Pound*.
1958, April	Robert Frost and others, including T.S. Eliot, Ernest Hemingway, and Archibald MacLeish, press for Pound's release, which is granted to the seventy-two-year-old poet on April 18. Discharged on May 7, he departs for Italy on June 30, after visiting childhood home in Wyncote, PA and then William Carlos Williams in New Jersey. Arrives in Naples, Italy on July 9 with Dorothy and Marcella Spann, artist and disciple. Tells reporters "all America is an insane asylum" and offers the Fascist salute.
1959	*Thrones: 96–100 de los cantares* published; mostly written at St. Elizabeths. Composes some of the cantos to appear in *Drafts & Fragments*.
1962	Wins Harriet Monroe Memorial Prize offered by *Poetry*.
1964	Anthology *Confucius to Cummings* appears, edited with Marcella Spann.
1965	Attends memorial service in London's Westminster Abbey for T.S. Eliot, who died in January. Visits Yeats' widow in Dublin. In summer visits the Spoleto Festival and reads poems by Robert Lowell and Marianne Moore. Outside the theatre, he reads from *The Cantos* to a crowd. Turns eighty on October 30. Travels to Paris; attends performance of Beckett's *Endgame*. Beckett visits Pound the next day at his hotel.
1966	Pound becomes nearly silent; two years later he would declare, "I did not enter into silence; silence captured

me." Depression cited as the principal cause.
Archives of Pound's papers, manuscripts, letters
deposited at Yale University.

1967   Publication of *Selected Cantos* and *Pound/Joyce* letters.
Pirated edition of *Cantos 110–116* appears in New York.
Pound visits Joyce's grave in Zurich. Allen Ginsberg
visits Pound in Sant'Ambrogio and then Venice.

1968   *Redondillas or Something of That Sort.* The poem and
Pound's notes reprinted from page proofs cut from
Canzoni 1911.

1969, June   With Olga, unexpectedly arrives in New York for
exhibition of *The Waste Land* manuscript at New
York Public Library and meeting of the Academy of
American Poets. Pound and Olga accompany
Laughlin to Hamilton College where Laughlin
receives an honorary degree. Pound, on stage, receives
a standing ovation.
Drafts & Fragments of Cantos CX–CXVII published by
New Directions.

1972   Dies at age eighty-seven in Venice on November 1.
Buried in the Protestant section of the island
cemetery of San Michele.
Paideuma, the Pound journal, founded.

1973   December 8, death of Dorothy Pound.

1996   March 15, death of Olga Rudge.

Abbreviations and note on references to The Cantos

POUND

ABCR	*ABC of Reading*. 1934. New York: New Directions, 1960.
C	*The Cantos*. Thirteenth printing. New York: New Directions, 1995.
CAV	*Pound's Cavalcanti: An Edition of the Translations, Notes and Essays*. Ed. David Anderson. Princeton: Princeton University Press, 1983.
CCEP	*The Cambridge Companion to Ezra Pound*. Ed. Ira B. Nadel. Cambridge: Cambridge University Press, 1999.
CEP	*The Collected Early Poems of Ezra Pound*. Ed. Michael John King. Intro. Louis L. Martz. New York: New Directions, 1976.
CP	*Canti postumi*. Ed. Massimo Bacigalupo. Milan: Mondadori, 2002.
CSP	*Collected Shorter Poems*. London: Faber & Faber, 1968.
CST	*The Cantos of Ezra Pound, Some Testimonies*. New York: Farrar & Rinehart, Inc. 1933.
CWC	*Chinese Written Character*, in *Instigations*. New York: Boni and Liveright, 1920.
End	H. D.[Hilda Doolittle] *End to Torment, A Memoir of Ezra Pound with Poems from "Hilda's Book" by Ezra Pound*. Ed. Norman Holmes Pearson and Michael King. New York: New Directions, 1979.
EPCH	*Ezra Pound, The Critical Heritage*. Ed. Eric Homberger. London: Routledge & Kegan Paul, 1972.
EPCP	*Ezra Pound's Poetry and Prose, Contributions to Periodicals*. 11 vols. Ed. Lea Baechler, A. Walton Litz, James Longenbach. New York: Garland, 1991.

EPDS	*Ezra Pound and Dorothy Shakespear, Their Letters 1909–1914*. Ed. Omar Pound and A. Walton Litz. New York: New Directions, 1984.
EPEC	*Ezra Pound's Economic Correspondence*. Ed. Roxana Preda. Gainesville: University Press of Florida, 2007.
EPEW	*Ezra Pound: Early Writings, Poems and Prose*. Ed. Ira B. Nadel. New York: Penguin Books, 2005.
EPJL	*Ezra Pound and James Laughlin, Selected Letters*. Ed. David Gordon. New York: W.W. Norton, 1994.
EP/JQ	*The Selected Letters of Ezra Pound to John Quinn, 1915–1924*. Ed. Timothy Materer. Durham, NC: Duke University Press, 1991.
EPLR	*Pound/ The Little Review*. Ed. Thomas L. Scott, *et al.* New York: New Directions, 1988.
EPM	*Ezra Pound and Music*. Ed. R. Murray Schafer. New York: New Directions, 1977.
EP/MC	*Ezra Pound and Margaret Cravens, A Tragic Friendship, 1910–1912*. Ed. Omar Pound and Robert Spoo. Durham, NC: Duke University Press, 1988.
EPS	*"Ezra Pound Speaking," Radio Speeches of World War II*. Ed. Leonard W. Doob. Westport, CT: Greenwood Press, 1978.
EPSP	*Ezra Pound: Selected Poems*. Ed. T.S. Eliot. London: Faber, 1928.
EPVA	*Ezra Pound and the Visual Arts*. Ed. Harriet Zinnes. New York: New Directions, 1980.
EPWB	*The Correspondence of Ezra Pound and Senator William Borah*. Ed. Sarah C. Holmes. Urbana: University of Illinois Press, 2001.
EP/WCW	*Selected Letters of Ezra Pound and William Carlos Williams*. Ed. Hugh Witemeyer. New York: New Directions, 1996.
GB	*Gaudier-Brzeska*. 1916; New York: New Directions, 1974.
GK	*Guide to Kulchur*. New York: New Directions, 1970.
IC	*I Cantos* ed., Mary de Rachewiltz. Milan: Mondadori, 1985.
IND	"Indiscretions," *Pavannes and Divagations*. Norfolk, CT: New Directions, 1958.
JM	*Jefferson and/or Mussolini*. London: Stanley Nott, 1935.
LC	Pound, Ezra and Dorothy. *Letters in Captivity, 1945–1946*. Ed. Omar Pound and Robert Spoo. New York: Oxford Univ. Press, 1999.

LE	*Literary Essays.* Ed. T.S. Eliot. New York: New Directions, 1976.
MIN	*Make It New.* London: Faber & Faber, 1934.
NPL	de Gourmont, Rémy, *Natural Philosophy of Love.* Translated with a postscript by Ezra Pound. New York: Boni and Liveright, 1922.
P, 1909	*Personae.* London: Elkin Mathews, 1909.
P, 1926	*Personae, The Collected Poems of Ezra Pound.* New York: Boni and Liveright, 1926.
P, 1990	*Personae; The Shorter Poems.* Rev. edn. Ed. Lea Baechler and A. Walton Litz. New York: New Directions, 1990.
PC	*The Pisan Cantos.* New York: New Directions, 1948.
PC, 2003	*Pisan Cantos,* Ed. Richard Sieburth. New York: New Directions, 2003
PDD	*Pavannes and Divagations.* Norfolk, CT: New Directions, 1958.
PE	*Polite Essays.* London: Faber & Faber, 1937.
P/J	*Pound/Joyce, Letters of Ezra Pound to James Joyce.* Ed. Forrest Read. New York: New Directions, 1967.
PL	*Letters of Ezra Pound and Wyndham Lewis.* Ed. Timothy Materer. New York: New Directions, 1985.
PM	*Patria Mia and The Treatise on Harmony.* London: Peter Owen, 1962.
PS	*Poems 1918–1921.* New York: Boni and Liveright, 1921.
SL	*Selected Letters of Ezra Pound.* Ed. D.D. Paige. New York: New Directions, 1971.
SP	*Selected Poems.* Ed. T.S. Eliot. London: Faber & Gwyer, 1928.
SPR	*Selected Prose, 1909–1965.* Ed. William Cookson. London: Faber and Faber, 1973.
SPS	*Selected Poems 1908–1959.* Ed. T.S. Eliot. London: Faber & Faber, 1975.
SR	*The Spirit of Romance.* Rev. edn. New York: New Directions, 1968.
TAH	*Ta Hio. The Great Learning, Newly Rendered into the American Language.* Seattle: University of Washington Book Store, 1928.
WT	*Women of Trachis.* New York: New Directions, 1956.
WTSF	*Walking Tour in Southern France.* Ed. Richard Sieburth. New York: New Directions, 1992.

OTHER

ASC	Humphrey Carpenter, *A Serious Character, The Life of Ezra Pound*. London: Faber & Faber, 1988.
EPRO	Margaret Fisher, *Ezra Pound's Radio Operas, The BBC Experiments, 1931–1933*. Cambridge, MA: MIT Press, 2002.
Moody	A. David Moody, *Ezra Pound: Poet, A Portrait of the Man and His Work* I: *The Young Genius 1885–1920*. New York: Oxford University Press, 2007.
PE	Hugh Kenner, *The Pound Era*. Berkeley: University of California Press, 1971.
Stock	Noel Stock, *The Life of Ezra Pound*. London: Routledge & Kegan Paul, 1970.

NOTE ON REFERENCES TO *THE CANTOS*

All citations from Ezra Pound's *Cantos* are from the 13th printing, published by New Directions, New York, 1995.

Introduction

Ira B. Nadel

Most of the stuff I write does not pretend to make itself intelligible to
anyone who has not done a certain quite large amount of reading.[1]

Ezra Pound, who published his first poem in 1902 and his last in 1969,
understood the necessity of context. The range, volume, and arcane nature
of his material, as impressive as it was immense, required background
which he expected of his readers. Initially, this meant knowledge of the
Provençal poets, Dante, Confucius, and a healthy dose of Greek and Latin,
as well as Chinese and American history. As editor, translator, anthologist,
essayist, and poet, he anticipated that his readers would understand as well
the sources, allusions, and origins of his work. The complex of materials
was part of being modern.

Pound worked hard to educate his peers who recognized his skills. T.S.
Eliot called him "*il miglior fabbro*," "the better craftsman." James Joyce
declared he was "a miracle of ebulliency, gusto and help." Yeats recalled
that to "talk over a poem with him" was "like getting you to put a sentence
into dialect. All becomes clear and natural." He redirected the poetry of
Yeats, discovered Robert Frost, and promoted H.D. He edited *The Waste
Land*, oversaw the publication of *Ulysses*, and created new movements
like Imagism and Vorticism. Wyndham Lewis summed him up as the
"demon pantechnicon driver, busy with removal of the old world into new
quarters."

But to understand Pound, it is necessary to understand the context of his
work and life. That is precisely what this volume presents – the placement of
his career within the social, political, historical, and literary developments
of his period, one that ranges from the Georgian Revival in poetry to
postmodern theory. The Boer War ended the year of his first publication
and Richard M. Nixon became President in his last. Braque and Picasso
painted their first Cubist paintings the year Pound published his first book
(1908) and Andy Warhol painted his "Campbell Soup Cans II" series in the

year of Pound's last publication (1969). Pound's writing encompasses two
world wars, the birth of nations, and a dramatic shift in sexual attitudes.
Women got the vote, and men got to the moon. Nationalism competed
with empire as print culture found new methods of dissemination.

Pound's work in many ways represents a shorthanded cultural history
of civilization. It begins with a revival of the classical past through Homer
and then the Roman poet Propertius, before turning to Renaissance figures, notably the *condottiere* and patron of Rimini, Sigismondo Malatesta.
Then, after an engagement with American leaders like John Adams and
Thomas Jefferson, he addresses the economic policy of "Social Credit"
and the social policies of fascism. But he also paid attention to the East,
through his encounter with Chinese poetry, Japanese drama, and Confucian thought. So convincing was his understanding of Chinese poetry that
in 1928 T.S. Eliot famously wrote that "Chinese poetry, as we know it today, is something invented by Ezra Pound" (*SPS*, xvii). What appealed so
strongly to Pound was the Confucian discipline "*to call people and things by
their names . . . to see that the terminology was exact*" (*GK*, 16). Pound reaches
widely and broadly using global culture as his canvas. It is no surprise that
the title of his 1938 prose volume, *Guide to Kulchur*, means *all* cultures.

Pound's work also represents a history of modernist publishing. From
periodical and newspaper publication of his poetry, he moved to little
magazines and then limited edition presses like John Rodker (London)
or the Hours Press (Paris). He found that these elite outlets concentrated
on small print runs of physically attractive, well-designed, expensive volumes which enlarged the distinctive, avant-garde nature of his work. But
as social and economic ideas became more prominent in his work, he
wanted greater access to readers. By the 1930s he began to publish with
more prominent university and literary trade presses: the University of
Washington Press, Faber and Faber, Farrar & Rinehart and then New
Directions. Later in his career, he turned to publishers of a more political character, notably Stanley Nott in the UK and Henry Regnery in
America. As a poet, political/economic writer, and frequent contributor
to magazines and newspapers, Pound chose publishers who reflected his
independent approaches. And whether it was Elkin Mathews in London,
Nancy Cunard in Paris, Giovanni Scheiwiller in Milan, or James Laughlin
in New York, Pound directed, cajoled, and at times interfered with the
production of his volumes. In his essay on Pound and publishing in this
volume, Gregory Barnhisel reviews the evolution of Pound and his publishers, emphasizing the tenuous balance between his artistic interests and
commercial desires.

Pound, of course, promoted others, from T.S. Eliot and Joyce to Robert Frost and Louis Zukofsky. His active role in shaping, if not defining, modernism has been often told but cannot be overlooked. His energetic support and encouragement of others remains indisputable, from editing *The Waste Land* to ensuring that Joyce's *Portrait of the Artist* appeared in *The Egoist*. His Bel Esprit project of March 1922, where thirty people would each pledge £10 per year to T.S. Eliot, providing a guaranteed income of £300, was only one of many such efforts to turn patronage into a public effort. It collapsed but not his desire to aid others, even proposing to Mussolini in the summer of 1923 that Il Duce adopt a program of cultural patronage outlined and organized by Pound.[2]

Pound strenuously worked to see that new writers received the attention they deserved, while for older writers like Yeats he redirected their style. The importance of this activity was crucial, as Hemingway acknowledged in 1925. Pound, he said, "tries to advance the fortunes, both material and artistic, of his friends . . . he defends them when they are attacked, he gets them into magazines and out of jail [and] gets publishers to take their books" (in *CCEP*, 22). He offered aesthetic advice, technical expertise, and practical support. Yeats, H.D., Eliot, and Joyce were the immediate beneficiaries but Wyndham Lewis, Basil Bunting, and Louis Zukofsky also benefited from his innovations and energy.

Editing anthologies was another means of getting people read, especially newer poets. *Des Imagistes* (1914) and *Active Anthology* (1933) are two examples of how he continued with the traditional form and yet transformed it into a vehicle for original, if not unorthodox, voices. *Blast* and *Exile*, his two magazines, were similarly part of a modernist tradition yet very different in conception and content from other periodicals.

Imagism, vorticism, the ideogram, Greek, Chinese, comparative literature – Pound's shaping of the modern was as much the repeated effort to "make it new" as it was to reignite the past. Through his writings on the troubadours, Arnaut Daniel, Dante, and Cavalcanti, he showed their importance for modernity. Similarly with Confucius and Propertius. The work of Hugh Kenner and Marjorie Perloff in restating Pound's critical influence in making the modern, even within the recent context of redefining the term, underlines the significance of his actions.[3] Pound valued the experimental and the new, claiming in 1913 that "any work of art which is not a beginning, an invention, a discovery is of little worth" ("How I Began," *EPEW*, 211).

Pound was nothing if not inquisitive. With his kind of Yankee confidence, he strode into the literary world of London, then Paris, to find out what was going on: "Ford in the afternoons and Yeats in the evenings" was his modus operandi, which he aggressively pursued (*PE*, 81; *SL*, 296). Such intellectual swaggering quickly transferred to his literary work: from researching the troubadours to studying economics, he claimed expertise in all – as well as in Greek, Latin, Chinese, Confucius, and Italian politics. More often he was right and not right, claiming that his Anglo Saxon "Seafarer" (1911) or Latin-based "Homage to Sextus Propertius" (1919) were, and were not, translations. Critics, of course, often and vocally disagreed. But he disregarded them.

His poetry, notably *The Cantos*, incorporated numerous historical and foreign sources, sometimes impeding its literary development and narrative unity. Social thought, historical incidents, and economic theory soon dominated his long poem, published in nine volumes over a fifty-two year period, its first periodical publication in 1917. The use of documents and other non-literary materials began to dominate the text until his imprisonment in Pisa where, without recourse to texts other than Confucius, he concentrated on his own past to shape his poetry through a formidable personal style. St. Elizabeths meant a return to books (he borrowed frequently from the Library of Congress) and continued engagement with translation and creativity, resulting in two additional titles for *The Cantos – Section: Rock-Drill* (1955) and *Thrones* (1959). *Drafts & Fragments* (1969), the final volume of the work ended, although it did not complete, his modern epic.

Such productivity took place within a sphere of consistent political, economic, historical, and personal conflict. Pound the journalist, teacher, editor, and broadcaster competed with Pound the poet, each identity or "persona" connecting in fractious ways with the other. For Pound, while differences may exist in genre, differences within his ideas did not. The social role of literature, for example, a reflection of economic and political conditions, was constant. Literature, he felt, had a duty to the state (*LE*, 21). At one point in Rapallo, he posted precepts on a wall for the people to follow, mixing politics with Confucius. One read: "When the archer misses the bull's eye, the cause of the error is within himself."[4] Conversely, one who knew little of economics or social progress could not know much about the process and content of poetry.

But controversy, of course, swirled around him, most notably in his economic views, his support of fascism, his anti-Semitism, and his relentless critique of America's policies during and after the Second World War. For the first, he opposed any economic system that suggested capitalistic free enterprise, which he believed only led to its supreme evil, usury. Social Credit was the only answer. For the second, he upheld Mussolini and his accomplishments in Italy from the 1920s until his death. For the third, he held the Jews responsible for exorbitant banking practices, war, and social inequality. For the fourth, he blamed Roosevelt for America's foolhardy liberal policies and decision to fight in Europe and then Japan.

His 1943 indictment for treason, renewed after his arrest and then return to the USA in 1945, increased his intolerance and disgust with America, although not his identity as an American. His radio broadcasts, in fact, stressed his Americaness and valuation of American history. It would "make any young man more American," he claimed, "if he sticks to seein' American history FIRST before swallowin' exotic perversions."[5] His broadcasts, however, created public intolerance of his ideas, which in turn diminished the importance and acceptance of his work. Winning the Bollingen Prize for poetry in 1949, awarded by the Library of Congress, only intensified his vilification. The *New York Times* headline of February 20, 1949 stated this clearly: "Pound in Mental Clinic, Wins Prize For Poetry Penned in Treason Cell." His award was an insult and outrage to the American people.

In the midst of these controversies Pound had a hero: Mussolini. Il Duce, preceded by the military lord of Rimini, Malatesta, demonstrated that right thinking and economic reform could support the arts and forward culture. Pound's enthusiasm for Mussolini, strengthened by a private meeting with him in 1933, only reinforced support for his leadership and fascism, which Pound understood as a form of cultural patronage. Pound's promotion of fascism came from his faith in the public function and utility of art, updating Shelley's belief that poets are the "unacknowledged legislators of the world." Pound believed that the artist's mission was to change the world and could guide political action: "the artist is always too far ahead of any revolution, or reaction . . . for his vote to have any immediate result . . . [but] the party that follows him wins" (*EPCP*, IV: 379–80).

Pound's fascism, anti-Semitism, and anti-Americanism naturally impeded the reception of his work, and this has persisted to this day. Several essays in the collection address these issues, notably those by Serenella Zanotti, Alex Houen, and Emily Wallace.[6] No consensus on Pound's reputation has yet emerged, but the very debate is credit to the activist poetics Pound promoted. Poets do not observe, he insisted: they engage with social and political change.

Despite his polarizing politics, Pound's influence upon modern poetry and poetic style remains. "Use no superfluous words, no adjective which does not reveal something," is only one of his many declarations reviving, if not revolutionizing, writing (*LE*, 4). "Precise terminology is the first implement, dish and container," he later wrote in Canto XCIX/731. In rejecting the rhetorical embellishments of the late Victorians and Georgians, turning instead to the "cut direct" method he observed in Gaudier-Brzeska and expressed through Imagism, Pound renewed the language of poetry for his time. Parataxis and fragmentation became the new "formula." In "A Retrospect" (1918) he predicted a poetry which would be "harder and saner." Rhetoric would not be the source of its force but energy, directness (*LE*, 12). The objective presentation of material would be the goal, rejecting symbolist, expressionist, or romantic forms. The Chinese ideogram was one way to achieve this because it "*means* the thing or the action or the situation, or quality germane to the several things that it pictures" (*ABCR*, 21). Poetry was to be made "as much like granite as it can be . . . austere, direct, free from emotional slither" (*LE*, 12).

New critical practices have generated new readings of Pound. Cultural studies, new historicism, feminism, psychological criticism, gender studies, deconstructionism, and textual criticism have all contributed to this process. And yet, interpretive methods of the past also shape our reading of Pound today. In the act of reading Pound we, like the method Malatesta used in assessing strategies of battle, evaluate the present in terms of the past to determine the future; similarly, in reading Pound one must do so in light of *his* sources and influences. Pound's actions within *The Cantos* – interpreting events as signs for telling the future – anticipate reader-response to text, reading, and history within the work. Events read through history, as Malatesta understands them, parallel reader-reaction to the unexpected structure and language of the work. Exposed to apparently random events in the work, events which contradict conventions of narrative unity and sequence, the reader must recapitulate the action or movement enacted within the text by Pound and translate it into an interpretative act in light of history presented (1) by the text itself and (2) through a shared background of knowledge established by context. The historical discourse of *The Cantos*, partly expressed through its constant citations which disrupt narrative and thematic continuity, requires contextual understanding, while the poem simultaneously undermines accepted notions of referentiality and representation. The final lines of the last canto in *Thrones* embodies this via language through its incorporation of English, Greek, Italian, and French (CIX/794). Pound himself relied on context to read his own poem, telling his Italian publisher in 1956, for example, that one cannot read the final cantos until one has read and understood the earlier.

Context is crucial for understanding *The Cantos* and Pound's other works. Contextual studies, the framing of a work within subjects beyond the text such as translation, journalism, the visual arts, the Orient, and travel – all represented in this volume – provide the grid for reading Pound's poetry. The current collection also reinterprets Pound's relationship to America, as well as to women and economics, supplemented by discussions of his influence, archives, and education.

Contextual studies shifts the line of interpretation from the text to its frame. It explores the ways external elements, whether they be events, geography, or personal incidents, contribute to a work's poetic identity. Boundaries between event, time, and the text overlap, as context assists in identifying the strategies of the text employed by the poet. Indeed, establishing the social, historical, personal, and generic context of Pound's work is the fundamental goal of *Ezra Pound in Context*. The central focus is the analysis of the interrelationships that exist between the events recounted in the works, the narratives themselves, and the situations in which the narratives were constructed. Individual chapters study these connections by combining a close formal analysis of the texts with an examination of the relationship between Pound and a particular subject, to illustrate the ways he accomplishes the "telling." Narrative action in time and place, past and present, might be another focus of this approach.

A work of art cannot be understood in isolation from the contexts in which it is created. This is the basic principle of contextual studies, which tracks how historical, social, political, and economic codes from a culture embed themselves in a text. Cultural studies might be the broad rubric but context is the immediate focus. The cultural genealogy of a text might be another aspect of this approach, as demonstrated by this sentence: "Five months after Mussolini had assumed power with the March on Rome on 20 March 1923, Ezra Pound found himself in Rimini, where he had come to reexamine the manuscript of Gaspare Broglio's memoirs, along with other materials related to Sigismondo Malatesta."[7] A frame for understanding Pound's writing the Malatesta Cantos immediately becomes clear. Identity, one of the major motifs of *The Cantos* and concerns of modernism, may best be studied through the contextual nature of the poem.

Three sections divide *Ezra Pound in Context*. Part I, "Biography and works," addresses his prose criticism and poetics, as well as his letters, radio broadcasts, and relationship with, and criticism of, the law. Other topics in this opening section consider economics, archives, and textual criticism, all three crucial to evaluating his work, yet all three posing complex issues of assessment. His role as editor and anthologist, an activity he maintained throughout his life, is also explored. Part II, "Historical and cultural context," situates Pound in varying geographic and intellectual worlds beginning with America and continuing in Venice, Provence, London, Paris, Rapallo, Pisa, and Rome. It then examines his use of the classics, and the development of concepts like imagism and vorticism, before considering music, the visual arts, education, "little magazines," and publishing. Dante and Confucius are also discussed, as well as fascism, gender, and race. One chapter analyzes Pound's anti-Semitism; another deals with Pound's influence on the making of modernism.

"Critical reception," the final section, addresses the challenges of the fluctuating response to his work, divided into three periods: before Paris (1908–20), before Pisa (1920–45), and after Pisa (1945–72). A final chapter, on his influence, examines the legacy of his work on new generations of writers. How we evaluate Pound is a further concern of the volume, especially in the context of European and American cultures and their influence on *The Cantos*.

Ezra Pound in Context pays attention, as well, to reformulations of Pound's relationship to the key figures who composed his poetic constellation and intellectual agenda. It considers the ways in which earlier poets, and his contemporaries, plus their cultures, influenced his writing. Pound understood poetry as the outgrowth of a tradition and an age. "It took two centuries of Provence and one of Tuscany to develop the media of Dante's masterwork," and "it took the latinists of the Renaissance, and the Pleiade, and his own age of painted speech to prepare Shakespeare his tools," he wrote in 1913 (*LE*, 9–10).

From the beginning, Pound broadcast his ideas in didactic, powerful ways with a manner equally insistent and declamatory: "give me a bed, a bowl of soup and a microphone" he declaimed (*EPCP*, x: 245). He was relentlessly instructive in publishing works with titles like *How to Read*, or the *ABC of Economics*. His energy and impatience demanded this form of communication, the Rome Radio broadcasts of the 1940s extensions of a style he initiated in his earliest prose.

Despite his intransigent political and economic views, Pound's influence was lasting. He may in fact be largely responsible for innovations in modern American poetry, from the Projectivists to the Objectivists and L-A-N-G-U-A-G-E poets. *The Cantos* demonstrated the possibility of a radical ideological openness, even if it had lengthy, undigested, and discontinuous sections displaying an unfocused textual heteroglossia.

But to study Pound is to discover how criticism, scholarship, biography, and bibliography constantly revise received ideas and accepted attitudes as they uncover innovative interpretations and adjust to new facts. This is synergistic and energizing for students and scholars of Pound, as the work in this volume attests. Pound excites, poetically and intellectually. Clarity is all and his definiteness is bracing: "The poet's job is to *define* and yet again define till the detail of surface is in accord with the root in justice" (*SL*, 366). One cannot be passive reading a poet who reveres the irascible and admonishes all to "cut direct" (*SL*, 111; *GB*, 19). "To break the pentameter," he reminds us, "that was the first heave" (LXXXI/538). Pound's response to the conflicts he confronted (and often generated) constitute what Baudelaire called "the heroism of modern life."[8] But context remains essential to understand Pound the artist and the critic. Pound himself recognized this. In *Patria Mia* he wrote, "it is not enough that the artist have impulse, he must be in a position to know what has been done and what is yet to do" (*PM*, 53). The same is true for Pound's readers.

NOTES

1 Ezra Pound to Viola Baxter Jordan, October 12, 1907, in "Letters to Viola Baxter Jordan," *Paideuma* 1.1. (1972): 108.

2 See Lawrence W. Rainey, *The Institutions of Modernism, Literary Elites and Public Culture* (New Haven: Yale University Press, 1998), 109.

3 See Hugh Kenner, *The Pound Era* (Berkeley: University of California Press, 1971); Marjorie Perloff, "Pound/Stevens, Whose Era?" in *Dance of the Intellect, Studies in the Poetry of the Pound Tradition* (Cambridge: Cambridge University Press, 1985), 1–32. On redefining modernism see, among others, Peter Nicholls, *Modernisms: A Literary Guide* (Berkeley: University of California Press, 1995); Lawrence Rainey, *The Institutions of Modernism* (New Haven: Yale University Press, 1998); Michael Levenson, *A Genealogy of Modernism* (Cambridge: Cambridge University Press, 1984); Daniel Albright, *Untwisting the Serpent: Modernism in Music, Literature and Other Arts* (Chicago: University of Chicago Press, 2000); David Bradshaw and Kevin J.H. Dettmar, eds., *A Companion to Modernist Literature and Culture* (Oxford: Blackwell, 2006); Michael H. Whitworth, ed., *Modernism* (Oxford: Blackwell, 2007); Peter Childs, *Modernism*, 2nd edn. (London: Routledge, 2008).

4 Anne Conover, *Olga Rudge & Ezra Pound, "What Thou Lov'st Well"* (New Haven: Yale University Press, 2001), 218–19.

5 *EPS*, 121. In the same broadcast of May 9, 1942, he added that he could write "a whole American history by implication stikin' to unknown folks" but that the "WAR" has been the same war fought by "John Adams, Jefferson, Van Buren . . . Abe Lincoln, V.P. Johnson, my Grand dad. All fighting the kikified usurers" (*EPS*, 121).

6 For earlier treatments of these subjects see Robert Casillo, *The Genealogy of Demons: Anti-Semitism, Fascism and the Myths of Ezra Pound* (Evanston, IL: Northwestern University Press, 1988) and Charles Bernstein, "Pounding Fascism," in *A Poetics* (Cambridge, MA: Harvard University Press,

1992), plus "Pound and The Poetry of Today," in *My Way: Speeches and Poems* (Chicago: University of Chicago Press, 1999) and "Rereading Pound," Poetics List Serve (Spring 1996): http://epc.buffalo.edu/authors/Bernstein/essays/poundbern.html. Also important are Marjorie Perloff's posting on the same list serve under the title "Pound and Fascism" and Wendy Flory, "Pound and Anti-Semitism," *CCEP*, 284–300.

7 Rainey, *Institutions of Modernism*, 128.

8 Charles Baudelaire, "Salon of 1846," in *Modernity and Modernism: French Painting in the Nineteenth Century*, ed. Francis Frascina *et al.* (New Haven: Yale University Press, 1993), 53.

PART I

Biography and works

CHAPTER I

Prose criticism

Vincent Sherry

Writing in November 1919, looking back from the end of the decade in which he entered (and transformed) London literary culture, Ezra Pound characterizes the state of literary criticism in England near the beginning of "the Asquith regime," close to the time of his 1908 arrival in that country, as

> deader than mutton, as I have endlessly noted, it was dead because ideas are disliked . . . Literary criticism was dead because official and accepted figures like Sir Henry Newbolt were much more concerned with an external and personal correctness than with an internal depth. They were much more anxious to look tidy and emit the seven or eight ligneous bleats required on all polite occasions than to discover international standards and stimulae. (*EPCP*, III: 354)

The heavy hand of caricature carries the extreme truth for Pound of his earlier, activist perception and program, which have by now settled into their customary antipathies. These oppositions feature on one side the dead hand of literary convention and insular hebetudes and, on the other, the fresher energies of a transatlantic intelligentsia and pan-European avant-garde, whose experimental verve and inventive temper are coincident in every practical respect with the nascent strengths of the movement we know now as "modernism." Pound's part in the triumphalist narratives of modernism is of course considerable, including his work both as poet and literary critic and his roles, severally, as contributor, chronicler, agent provocateur, and scold. Yet the larger parts of the narrative of heroic modernism were drafted *ex post facto*; what they gain in boldness of feature and attraction of animosity, they give away in circumstantial complexity, in the thickness of actual inaugural motivations. In the story of Pound as the exemplary modernist, these lost origins include his negotiations as a literary critic with the poetics and ethics of an older sensibility, a gathering of miscellaneous but companion talents, a group that stands in relation to modernism as a kind of contested precedent, one which is all too likely to slide into the cartoon formulations that Pound and his own companion talents later contrived to hide the profounder likenesses. This is the precedent tradition of "Decadence."

Decadence, it needs to be recognized first of all, is not a "movement" or "school"; it is not simply another tribe to be rivaled and ousted – in that series of gang warfares to which English literary history seems sometimes reducible. Decadence is instead a comprehensive sensibility, indeed a *weltanschauung*, one which includes a highly developed sense of its late historical day and which takes this premonition of lateness, age, or decline (de-*cad*-ere, "to *fall* away") as the basis for a broad range of artistic practices. A complementary hypothesis in scientific culture features the principle of entropy, the running down of energy in the physical universe, as one of the more novel and interesting concepts. This sensibility finds one of its strongest concentrations in mid to late nineteenth-century France, most of all in Paris, but it was coextensive through the major capitals of northern Europe. Here it coincides with apprehensions of decline in political and social history: a decaying aristocracy, an imperial outlook losing moral confidence even as it was gaining terrain, and the emergence of "the crowd" as a randomizing force in the experience of urban modernity. Taken together, these apprehensions converge in a premonition of lost dominance by a former master class which, whether or not the Decadents were actually members of it, was appropriated as an imaginative vantage for their representations of this feeling of chronic, accumulating loss. In this historically informed understanding, then, "Decadence" may comprise but exceed those classificatory categories of "wayward behavior" (ranging from excessive dietary tastes to obscure sexual practices) and recover its better, more revelatory sense as a register of change, sometimes tumultuous change, and an intimation of the anxieties that attend that condition.

The point of crisis that "Decadence" marks in this cultural chronology seems to coincide with the moment of opportunity that is usually claimed as the incentive force of artistic modernism, which, we presume, seizes the predicament of the older order as its own advantaging circumstance. If this formulation makes sense in terms of a standard cultural history, that smoothed-over story, it is lived out in a much more ragged and embattled and interesting way in the actual clinches of the literary history that Pound inscribes as journalist and scholar between 1908 and 1920, the years in which he authors many of the documents that will form the canons of critical modernism. To recover the substance of Decadence in Pound's literary criticism in these years may serve, then, to regain a greater measure of his own formative struggles and of the embedded debts of literary modernism, of its historicity. This is a historicity in which Pound's own literary biography significantly shares: Decadence, in this account, shifts from a set of literary poses that he has received from his immediate forebears (variously claimed and disclaimed) to an imaginative understanding that is being lived out as a contemporary condition, as present history, specifically in the Great War of 1914–18, which provides a historical content and depth that we may follow as the increasing burden of the narrative of his early critical career.

Two of the prose pieces Pound wrote before going to Europe in 1908 show him scanning one of the main linguistic resources of literary Decadence. This is late medieval Latin. In "Raphaelite Latin," 1906, and "M. Antonius Flamininus and John Keats," early 1908, he appreciates a Latinity that exists entirely as a scribal and archival language. Unspoken, this Latin stands in the category of "dead language" that appears so frequently as a trope in the poetics of literary Decadence, most notably perhaps in the practice of Walter Pater, who interred his English in its Latinate crypts – famously, in the characterization by Max Beerbohm, who described Pater's style as that "sedulous ritual wherewith he laid out every sentence as in a shroud – hanging, like a widower, long over its marmoreal beauty . . . its sepulcher."[1] With its emphasis on the material of aesthetic language as dead matter, this linguistic sensibility expresses some enabling sense among its practitioners of writing in a late phase of the English language; in effect, they take the life-cycle of the Latin tongue as the memento mori they inscribe in words that stir – or, rather, do not stir – around those Latin roots, those dead radicals. The morbidity of contemporary civilization, which is bound also to organic cycles in analogous models of cultural time, is the testament that waits at the end of their sentences, their dying falls. And it is this whole sensibility that Pound responds to as provocation for his own lyric poetry in prose, in the 1908 piece where he contrasts it to the full-throated vocalese of Browning's verse:

No, if you want such battle cry, or song of the day's work, go elsewhere, for here, in our classicists, whose tones are as Whistler's when he paints the mist at moth hour, is no strong, vivifying power to uphold us; for when we rest for a moment from the contest, what beauty can we find for our ease like to this evanescent yet ever returning classicism, that is warm without burning . . . a beauty that is of autumn's as Browning's is of summer and the day's heat . . . a beauty of the half-light of Hesper and Aurora, of twilight and the hours between the false dawn and the true. (*EPCP*, I: 17)

Pound's travel to England brings the sensibility of this youthful decadent into contact with a contemporary political history that he casts into the imaginative patterns he has learned as an apprentice decadent. From his reading he understands the circumstances that established the first literary decadence in Rome as a late imperial age, and he comes increasingly to represent similar conditions in present British history, paralleling the course and fate of the Roman and British Empires. In this heightened apprehension of his own moment, he finds the fall of empire as the establishing condition of his emergent identity as man of letters. "London," he writes in 1913, "is like Rome of the decadence, so far, at least, as letters are concerned. She is a main and vortex drawing strength from the peripheries." If he advantages himself in this circumstance with the livelier identity of the vital barbarian, he quickly civilizes that likeness by drawing it into company with extra-territorials of already established repute: "Thus the finest authors, in my judgment –Yeats, James, Hudson, and Conrad – are all foreigners, and among the prominent English writers vigour of thought, as in the case of Wells and Bennett, is found only in conjunction with a consummate vulgarity" (*EPCP*, I: 116).

In this imaginative configuration of political and literary history, then, Pound can take on both stances of barbarian yawper and late imperial writer-stylist. If a different set of affective possibilities attends each of those roles, the heavier emotional toll is being paid by the writer inscribing – and mourning – the fall of that imperial ideal, as in 1912, in "Patria Mia," where Pound presents the high dream of empire as always already foregone: "All the fine dreams of empire, of a universal empire, Rome, the imperium restored, and so on, came to little. The dream, nevertheless, had its value, it set a model for emulation, a model of orderly procedure, and it was used as a spur through every awakening from the eighth century to the sixteenth. Yet it came to no sort of civic reality" (*EPCP*, I: 101). This emphasis on the elegiac measure of an always falling imperial ideal is the stress of decadence, indeed of decadence as a steady state condition of Pound's literary-historical imagination. Far from having disappeared as the former aesthetic order, it reveals its ongoing and developing import as Pound negotiates it in relation to the emergent pressures of an incipient modernism.

The signal document in this exchange is the polemic he writes for the first number of *The Egoist* on January 1, 1914. He is introducing the "Men of 1914," the modernists of the teens, to a London literary society that still holds the memory of a preceding generation and decade, the English nineties, the so-called decade of Decadence. The main point of rhetorical, oppositional energy in the piece is the difference between a poetics of vital voice in Pound's people and the mortuary art of nineties poets, who are working in the writerly silence they inherited as the legacy of Pater's deathly prose. While these figurative values of vocal vitality and writerly morbidity may be reified in retrospect as the signature aesthetics of these two respective generations, they are working in the piece as subsidiary features, really as terms in a pseudo-argument, for the main imaginative energy of the polemic, as may be seen in reading it, undermines the differences he is otherwise rhetorically exaggerating.

Consider, for instance, the extraordinary contortions of rhetoric and affect as he forges a heroic poetic identity for his vital songsters: "We have attained to a weariness more highly energized than the weariness of the glorious nineties," he overtures, then expostulates: "And in the face of this [burden of the writerly nineties] are we in the heat of our declining youth expected to stretch the one word merde over eighteen elaborate paragraphs?" (*EPCP*, 1: 212). "In the heat of our declining youth," "a weariness more highly energized": this is not just a young modernism sowing its vocal oats in poetry. Pound is reinscribing one of the defining paradoxes of the English nineties, the so-called Tragic Generation. Those young men, typified by Aubrey Beardsley, seemed to hasten their early demise with the vigor of artistic creation, dying as bodies as they were born as imaginations. Granted, one may use Yeats' figure of the Tragic Generation too easily as a heuristic device, so to focus a whole historical complex in this single powerful figure of genius consuming itself young. But there was something in that age that made Beardsley and Lionel Johnson and Ernest Dowson so memorable, so representative.[2]

The last decade of the last century before the last century of the millennium, with an aging and long-dying queen holding on over an aging, long-dying empire: the sense of an ending that is the dominant feeling of the time was pointed most strongly where it touched the young. The character who captures the affect of this decade is a youth force-ripened into senescence and early death – as preserved in the signature figures of the brief candle, the sunset dawn, or the heat of Pound's declining youth. In appropriating this conceit, then, he is assembling the identikit for his modernist generation out of the materials of the decade and generation he is ostensibly rejecting, but my point is not that he is confirming an influence all the more strongly in contesting it so unsuccessfully. Rather, it is that the nineties type, whether in the figure of Yeats' dying generation or Pound's energized weariness, extends across the long turn of the century and, in bringing decay and morbidity along as the dominant conditions of cultural practice, establishes these conditions in the program and personality of modernist poetics. If decadence can be said to flourish, it is flourishing here.

And flourishing clearly as a performance piece. While the 1908 and 1914 writings express different values, they are alike in taking the attitudes of Decadence as prompts for highly rhetorical, role-playing affect. In 1908, the lyric afflatus warms in the cool evening light of the Decadent *landskip*; in 1914, in that rhetorical *topos* of "weariness more highly energized than the weariness of the glorious nineties," Pound attempts to outperform the paradox, taking the figure of a youth incinerating himself with energy and ramping up the vitalist side of the conceit in an attempt to outrun the riddle, to outdo the oppositional logic of the paradox, even though this sentence holds his sense to the all-too-elegant curve of a nineties antithesis. The earlier passage may be flattery that parodies, if inadvertently, while the second is parody that flatters, and not so inadvertently, but in both cases the histrionic energy is running very high. And in both cases the mortality motif, the late age of the world in the first passage and the late age of youth in the second, clearly establishes the main dramatic feeling.

What Pound knew about early death in early 1914 was not a great deal; he, and the rest of Europe, knew a lot about it by the end of that year, when, in the wording of the war lyrics he composed in 1919 for *Hugh Selwyn Mauberley*, the fate of "Young blood and high blood, / Fair cheeks and fine bodies" (*P*, 1990, 188) was already being broadly mourned. If this conceit formed the substance of a jauntily performed paradox in early 1914, it has been realized, made real as historical experience and so changed, changed utterly, by 1919. How the imaginative paradigms of Decadence are evolved, deepened, and seasoned through Pound's own closely realized historical experience, is the story that is told in some of the most important critical prose he wrote in the war years.

Already in early 1915, in "Affirmations VI," he expresses a relation to literary Latin that is significantly different from the appreciation he made in that long-before-war moment of 1908, when, in the gloaming of Whistler's moth hour, he had swollen on Latin words that could signify any or every thing he might make them mean. Returning in 1915 to late medieval and early Renaissance Latin, he abjures vagueness of that kind as the very cause of decline and does so in a way that says a good deal about the present historical moment, about the manipulations of political discourse in the current war, and about the real feeling of history disintegrating in the contemporary circumstance: "And in the midst of these awakenings Italy went to rot, destroyed by rhetoric, destroyed by the periodic sentence and by the flowing paragraph, as the Roman Empire had been destroyed before her. For when words cease to cling close to things, kingdoms fall, empires wane and diminish." (*EPCP*, II: 16).

Silently but unmistakably, perhaps all the more powerfully for being unheard, the historical institution of the British Empire is entering the calculation through its presumptive double, the Roman Empire, as it was doing in the contemporary record of monitions to the British public, who were being warned that the same end that the former empire had met was awaiting theirs, if resolve was not conscripted for the current war. That this end-of-empire-days feeling is a powerful coadjutor in the productions of literary decadence is borne out even in the short compass of this prose passage. In this model of cultural and political history, it may be the grandiosity of an imperial ideology that establishes grandness as the size, as the metric that measures the magnitude of the imminent fall. And in the grandiosity of Pound's own wording at the end of this 1915 passage, we can read him taking the measure of the current circumstance with an embittered eloquence which, in its grandiloquence, testifies to his apprehension of something very large at stake, something estimable really being lost. It is a loss that imposes the severer test of reality on the lexicon of literary Decadence.

Its most powerfully affective expression comes in the poetry of this moment, most notably in *Homage to Sextus Propertius*, the creative translation of the Roman poet in which Pound provides a concentrated expression of the attitudes to historical decadence that he was mapping in his critical prose. Writing of this sequence in 1931 he quips jokingly, but indicatively: "The *Homage* presents certain emotions as vital to me in 1917, faced with the infinite and ineffable imbecility of the British Empire, as they were to Propertius some centuries earlier, when faced with the infinite and ineffable imbecility of the Roman Empire" (*SL*, 231). Where the decadence of the Roman poet shows in an ingenious retreat and strategic "fall" from the mission and idiolect of high Augustan martial verse, of which he makes a masterfully playful subversion, it appears as the motive design behind the comic Latinity of Pound's poetic vocabulary, which he samples in that 1931 comment. And in the poem this verbal wit runs to one of its consummations in a prosodic comedy of strangling polysyllablics, like these: "The time is come, the air heaves in torridity, / The dry earth pants against the canicular heat" (*P*, 1990, 217).

Pound may be out-pattering Pater in the poetic sport of these antic Latinisms, but the historical import is the same as that decadent Victorian's usage. Returning the current war in his representation to a language rifted with the memory and destiny of the older empire, he is inscribing his own memento mori to the English language and the British Empire, which is a subject of coded reference throughout the sequence. This is the darker matter, the tragic backdrop to the high-jinks of the poem's verbal surface, its performative foreground, so that, all in all, in a sort of tonal chiaroscuro, where the rising rhythm of Pound's verbalist humor includes the dying fall of a former (and present) empire, that decadent presentiment of the end has been made entirely new by the modernist.

Not that Pound controls the atrocities of modern history through some Nietzschean laughter at catastrophe. The experience of fall and loss extends inevitably to the modernist generation in the war years, which, in the severe light of Pound's extreme perception, is repeating an 1890s story in the history of the 1910s. Yes, this perception confirms the bearing of the legends of *fin de siècle* on the artistic self-consciousness of the new century, but not automatically, and certainly not easily. Pound expresses this apprehension with an extraordinary pathos, at once recognizing and resisting the compliance of his decade with the narrative of the older generation's fable and fate. He concentrates this struggle into those two words, "decade" and "generation," which he repeats in augmented and cognate forms across the critical prose of the second half of the decade, leaving this *topos* as the record and trace of shifting identities, changing aims, failing campaigns. Here "generation" leaves behind the sense of productive strength and picks up the latent but ready association of life-cycles, mortality. And "decade" undergoes a shift in value so extreme that this new meaning has to mutate from a different root: *decus*, "ten" yields to *decadere*, "to fall away," thus to "decadence" and "decay." The figure of generation in this new decade is the poor, bare, forked animal of mortality, unaccommodated by the jauntier sport of prewar conceits.

"An age may be said to be decadent, or a generation may be said to be in a state of prone senility," he writes early in 1915, "when its creative minds are dead and when its survivors maintain a mental dignity – to wit, the dignity or stationariness of a corpse in its cerements. Excess or even absinthe is not the sure sign of decadence" (*EPCP*, II: 4). Where "absinthe" appears as the emblem of an artistic "decadence," Pound seeks to preserve this valorized image from the wrong sort of decay, the mortmain of an identifiably elderly generation.[3] To attach this brand to older attitudes, even in rhetorical reverse, suggests that the categories of polar opposition are no longer intact. Are the counter-conventional, "creative minds" of Pound's own "generation" also aging, also going "dead"? This is the question he asks more directly several months later – and answers, using the narrative of the first tragic generation to inscribe the fate of the *Blast* decade: "Has any one yet answered the query why is it that in other times artists went on getting more and more powerful as they grew older, whereas now they decline after the first out*burst*, or at least after the first successes?" (*EPCP*, II: 45).

He reveals this fatalism more categorically when he recycles the keywords through his private correspondence, unconstrained by the needs of literary polemic. Writing to Wyndham Lewis in May 1916, he cites "a book by me called 'This Generation' dealing with contemporary events in the woild-uv-letters, with passing reference of about 3500 words on vorticism, including my original essays on you and Edward [Wadsworth]" (*PL*, 35). A title and cast of characters that recall the volatile force of the *Blast* generation, "This Generation" was lost in manuscript in transatlantic passage, but this fate appears consistent with the several major reversals the whole story records of a once-insurgent impulse. Already at the start of the negotiation, in a letter to John Quinn in February 1916, Pound augurs the imminent downturn of his "generation" in rewording the book's subtitle. "The Spirit of the Half-Decade" plays out, in this ruefully humorous mispronunciation: "Am. humorists please copy 'half-decayed'" (*EP/JQ*, 64).

As the decade ended, Pound wrote a retrospective, round-up review of Arthur Symons, one of the hallmark poets of the English nineties. While he appreciates Symons as a representative of the best of "'decadence'" and admires him equally as the author of the "best of the Paterine prose books of the nineties," he reserves complete approbation. "Symons," he judges in April 1920, "has reappeared as if still in the land of '95, writing still of Javanese dancers... Poem after poem strikes one as not quite the thing to convince a younger audience that Symons was, in the nineties, a permanent poet." The period feeling of the nineties both prescribes and limits the validity of Symons. And what, except years, has intervened? "I am deliberately beginning this essay from memory, and in the surety that there has been no book of Symons on my shelf since some vague period 'before the war'" (*EPCP*, IV: 58–9). The dating is as definitive as it appears casual, anecdotal. For if Pound holds the war to account for his generation's outliving the appeal of the nineties myth, it is because, in that ordeal, he and they have also lived out that legend. This is no obscure testament to the ongoing power of a tradition that Pound has made new, and newly tragic, and in that accomplishment offered the basis for our understanding of it as a sensibility in which these two terms, now enriched historically, may combine significantly: modernist Decadence.

NOTES

1 Max Beerbohm, "Diminuendo," in *The Works of Max Beerbohm* (London: John Lane, The Bodley Head, 1896), 150.
2 For the dominance of this conceit, see the account of popular literary journalism sampled by Holbrook Jackson, *The Eighteen-Nineties: A Review of Art and Ideas at the Close of the Nineteenth Century* (1913; rpt. Atlantic Highlands, NJ: Humanities Press, 1976), throughout.
3 In the same passage: "There is perhaps no more authentic sign of the senility of a certain generation of publicists (now, thank heaven, gradually fading from the world) than their abject terror in the face of motive ideas" (*EPCP*, II: 4).

CHAPTER 2

Poetics

Ellen Stauder

THE LUMINOUS DETAILS OF A NEW POETICS

Despite the fact that Pound was prodigiously prolific as a poet, essayist, and letter writer, he wrote no systematic treatise on poetics. Nonetheless, his extensive writings on poetry are often memorable: "Literature is news that STAYS news" (*ABCR*, 29); "Artists are the antennae of the race" (*ABCR*, 73, 81); "Dichten=condensare" (*ABCR*, 36, 92). But the definition he repeated most often – five times – was one he borrowed from Dante: "Poetry is a composition of words set to music."[1] Simple as this definition may seem, it contains the nucleus of an entire poetics; that is, it addresses, when fleshed out fully, the essential questions of any poetics: what is the nature of the language from which a poem is made, who makes it, and for what end or purpose? In tapping Dante for this definition, Pound is not simply reaching back to a literary giant to gain authority; he goes to Dante because he believed the definition to be sound and because Dante articulated his definition at what, for Pound, was a crucial turning point in European literary history.

Pound argues that during Dante's time, poets, especially Petrarch, but even Dante himself, stopped making poems in the ancient tradition, started by the Greek lyric poets and extending up through the medieval period. That ancient practice understood poems to be a joining of music and words; neither music nor language predominated – they were simply inconceivable apart from one another. The disruption of this poetics, built around the joining of music and poetry, came when word and sound were separated. Words began to be put in service of philosophical sonnets done in the ornamental style of Petrarch while sounds became strictly the province of musical pieces such as the sonata (*LE*, 91).

Though Pound thought that some later poets had attempted to repair this rift between words and music, he felt compelled at his own historical moment to address it again. His sense of belatedness is not the result of a nostalgic antiquarianism; rather, his reaching backwards in time came as a result of his sense that the English iambic pentameter tradition – the dominant English poetic paradigm since Chaucer – had written itself to a dead end; it needed, along with the rhetorical and figurative dimensions of poetry, to be made new. "In a decent period you find: *Qui perd ses mots perd son ton*, as an axiom. Who loses his words loses his note" (*ABCR*, 159). This rejoining of words and music, Pound's making of a new poetics, was the product of a reinvention of the old, a reinvention Pound achieved initially through translation.

One of Pound's earliest and most important projects shows how he understood translation and how he used it to craft a new understanding of poetry and poetics; it includes translations along with prose commentaries. "I Gather the Limbs of Osiris" was published in twelve installments in *The New Age* from November 1911 through February 1912. The set of articles intersperse five prose essays and seven groups of translations, one from Anglo-Saxon ("The Seafarer"), one from Cavalcanti's medieval Italian, and five from the Provençal of Arnaut Daniel. The first installment, Pound's translation of "The Seafarer", appears without introduction except for a parenthetical headnote from the editor announcing that the series will consist of Pound's "expositions and translations in illustration of 'The New Method' in scholarship" (*EPCP*, 1: 43). This new method was what Pound called "luminous detail," that kernel or work or event, the knowledge of which yields insight into a field of inquiry. He distinguished the luminous detail from a mere recitation of facts, saying that luminous details govern "knowledge as the switchboard the electric circuit" (*EPCP*, 1: 44). Pound was particularly interested in those donative authors whose work lit up the switchboard of literary perception through the newness of their language, rather than simply handing down what was already known, the work of merely symptomatic authors (*EPCP*, 1: 49).

The "I Gather the Limbs of Osiris" series presents the reader with luminous details through the translations themselves but also through the arrangement of the whole and the relationship among the parts. Of his method of arrangement and selection, Pound writes, "I have, if you will, hung my gallery, a gallery of photographs, of perhaps not very good photographs, but of the best I can lay hold of" (*EPCP*, 1: 45). The series shows Pound choosing poetic objects for his gallery, framing them through his prose, and hanging them in an order designed to refigure poetic relationships in order to make a new switchboard of poetics. Notably, the series is not made for single-point viewing; rather, Pound presents his readers with a view of contiguous poetic surfaces that display the activity of poetic making, creating the possibility of evaluation, transmission, and new creation. At this large-scale level of design, the "I Gather the Limbs of Osiris" series anticipates future major work, including *Gaudier-Brzeska* (1916) and *The Cantos*, both of which are constructed from juxtaposed fragments of literary and other materials that display and test the activity of the poet-maker through their arrangement. Likewise, Pound's motivation for the series has something in common with T. S. Eliot's desire, reflected in "Tradition and the Individual Talent" (1919) as well as *The Waste Land* (1922), to foreground the present moment of the past through a poetics of fragmentation and juxtaposition that emphasizes not the personality of the poet but the poet's medium.

The "I Gather the Limbs of Osiris" series reveals two other elements essential to understanding Pound's poetics and to the unpacking of his Dantean definition of poetry, namely his practice of translation and his understanding of technique as a mark of a poet's character or sincerity. Pound's translations of members of Dante's poetic circle, especially Cavalcanti and Arnaut Daniel, follow in the footsteps of the poet and painter, Dante Gabriel Rossetti (1828–82). His translations, *The Early Italian Poets*, date from 1861 and were revised in 1874. Rossetti's study of these poets and the medieval Italian painters led him to develop a parallel aesthetic. In painting, this aesthetic featured a flattened picture plane, an emphasis on the materiality of the canvas and frame, and a use of luminous color along the lines of stained glass.[2] Following Rossetti's model, Pound's early Italian translation program also sought pre-Renaissance or pre-Raphaelite models, locating in Cavalcanti and Arnaut Daniel sources for an aesthetic of objective making on the one hand and, on the other, a poetry in which word and sound are joined.

Pound's translations often sound archaic rather than modern. Compare the opening stanza of Cavalcanti's "Chi è questa," first in Rossetti's translation and then in Pound's Osiris rendering:

> Who is she coming, whom all gaze upon,
>   Who makes the air all tremulous with light,
> And at whose side is Love himself? that none
>   Dare speak, but each man's sighs are infinite.[3]

> Who is she coming, drawing all men's gaze,
> Who makes the air one trembling clarity
> Till none can speak but each sighs piteously
> Where she leads Love adown her trodden ways?
>   (*EPCP*, 1: 47)

Pound wrote that in these translations he was not aiming, as Rossetti had, to make beautiful sound, a melodious translation, but rather to make what he called an exegetical translation (*SR*, 106) emphasizing the personality of the man, the meaning of the poems rather than the music.

But he invites the reader to engage with Cavalcanti's music which, he says, "is easily available for any one who will learn Italian pronunciation" (*EPCP*, 1: 110). In other words, the reader is not meant to stop with Pound's translation; the translation means to take the reader back to the originals and to be engaged with them directly. Pound, in effect, performs a pre-Raphaelite maneuver both on his Victorian predecessors and on the medieval poets. In sending the reader to Cavalcanti to hear the Italian, Pound wants the reader to re-hear, or hear for the first time, the freshness of the original and to allow it to stand in contrast to the longstanding English iambic pentameter tradition, including Rossetti's. Pound bends the illusionism of iambic pentameter through his "scholastic excavation" in order to create a conversation among sonic innovators whose interchanges spark the possibilities of a new poetic music, a rejoining of music and word. Arnaut Daniel, as the poet behind the poet, i.e., to whom Cavalcanti and Dante were most indebted, was especially significant to Pound because he developed a prosody that used syllable and word groupings – extended rhythm units – that could be used as units of equivalence, an innovation that is the single most important feature of what would become Pound's signature free-verse rhythm.

The results of hearing the luminous details of adjacent translations include reconceiving lost traditions as well as opening the possibilities of new poetic sound. Another result is to foreground the poet's distinctive act of making, aligning this making with the artistically essential process of discovering one's *virtù*. Pound defines *virtù* as the "one element that predominates," (*EPCP*, 1: 53) or, "the potency, the efficient property of a substance or person" (*CAV*, 13). According to Pound, when that *virtù*, or character, is adequately represented, the poem achieves absolute rhythm. In effect, absolute rhythm is the equivalent of a poetic fingerprint. As he wrote in 1912: "I believe in an 'absolute rhythm,' a rhythm, that is, in poetry which corresponds exactly to the emotion or shade of emotion to be expressed. A man's rhythm must be interpretative, it will be, therefore, in the end, his own, uncounterfeiting, uncounterfeitable" (*LE*, 9). Thus, absolute rhythm is a type of forming activity that exemplifies human states and powers in action. For Pound, the representation of this ethos is less an expression of individuality for its own sake than a display for the purposes of testing character and the individual's capacity for making the distinctions and determinations essential to creativity.[4]

Peter Nicholls has noted that Pound's translations had in common with many of the personae poems he began to write around 1909 a notion of poetry that originates "not in self-expression but in the division between the subject and its other." Weaving together different voices, Nicholls argues, puts the emphasis of modernist poetics less on the inspired maker than on the craft or medium. We "attend less to the poet as maker than to the poem as the event of making."[5] Pound's movement from his exegetical translations to his personae poems, imagism and vorticism, during the crucial years of 1909–14, is a process of increasing emphasis on the way the poems stage the dynamic process of making as their central concern. Like William Carlos Williams in his experimental *Spring and All* (1922), which included both poetry and prose, Pound's development in this period involved a rejection of symbolism and a mimetic aesthetic, as well as an assertion that works of art are the locus of the real.

The "I Gather the Limbs of Osiris" series allowed Pound to demonstrate a new method in poetics; however, the exegetical pentameter and the attendant antiquated diction of these poems could not be the mainstay of a poet bent on making himself new and modern. Pound began to write personae poems such as "La Fraisne," "Cino," or "Piere Vidal Old" in 1909, developing the tension between self and representation or self and other. Pound shared an interest in the genre and its problematics of self-representation with Eliot, whose "The Love Song of J. Alfred Prufrock" (1917) also achieves an ironic self-distancing. While Pound's translations required him to turn to the single available resource, the exegetical pentameter, the personae poems allowed him the freedom to translate or read his poet-speakers both from within, as the alter-poet speaking, and from without, making the invisible mask translucently apparent.

In "Sestina: Altaforte," for example, Pound adopts the persona of Bertran de Born, whom Dante put into hell because he stirred up strife. He chose to put de Born's speech into the form of a sestina, a form that de Born never used and that had been invented by Arnaut Daniel. The salient feature of the sestina is its repeated end words, which also act as repeated rhythmic cadences. Dante's description of de Born in the *Inferno* shows why the characteristics of the sestina as a form for this mask make it such an appropriate vehicle. In the *Inferno* de Born appears with his head in his hand, being swung like a lantern: "Of itself it made itself a lamp, and they were two in one and one in two" (*SR*, 45).

While the symbolism of having a head disjoined from a body fits de Born's crime of causing strife between fathers and sons, it also suggests a dualistic split within his own self, a sense of simultaneous identity and distinction. The successive stanzas, with their defined yet constantly moving end words, mirror this sense of identity and difference.

The sestina form also allows room for Pound's own translation of spirit by giving him a set of sonorities that trace de Born's *virtù* by transposing his sensibility into a form that renders him not by the art of approximating identity, that is, through translation, but through making an abstract aural arrangement, a set of sonic marks. In borrowing Arnaut's sestina form, Pound makes an act of appropriation that provides a distance and a necessary perspective both on de Born and on himself. The poem constructs de Born's character through something that is neither him nor his, and yet makes the rendering so intense and vivid as to be exact. Pound's process of rendering de Born's *virtù* is as much the subject of the poem as de Born himself.

Imagism, inaugurated by Pound, H. D., and Richard Aldington in 1912–13, is often heralded as the founding movement of poetic modernism. The movement enlarged the distance among the poet-maker, the persona, and the language of the poem by insisting on the presentation and objectivity of the image and by doing away with a persona altogether in favor of the presentation of an "emotional and intellectual complex in an instant of time" (*LE*, 4). The three tenets of imagism are meant to address what this complex is and how it is embodied in the poem but their laconic nature often mystifies as much as it helps: "1. Direct treatment of the 'thing' whether subjective or objective. 2. To use absolutely no word that does not contribute to the presentation. 3. As regarding rhythm: to compose in the sequence of the musical phrase, not in sequence of a metronome" (*LE*, 3).

Pound's "Vorticism" essay from 1914, though written retrospectively about imagism, contains an especially clarifying discussion of the "things". He stresses that the image is like the mathematics of analytical geometry which allows one not simply to represent space but to bring form into being. He writes:

The image is not an idea. It is a radiant node or cluster; it is what I can, and must perforce, call a VORTEX, from which, and through which, and into which, ideas are constantly rushing. In decency one can only call it a VORTEX. And from this necessity came the name "vorticism." *Nomina sunt consequentia rerum*, and never was that statement of Aquinas more true than in the case of the vorticist movement. (*GB*, 92)

Pound's Latin quote from Aquinas, meaning "names are the consequences of things," is helpful in understanding the nature of the imagist's "real." The phrase actually comes from Dante's *Vita Nuova*,[6] in which he explains that after writing the poems, Love directed him to write that he was beset with several different and conflicting ideas of love. He lists four of those views, the third being that the name of Love is sweet in accordance with the notion that there is a likeness between the thing and its name (names are the consequences of things). Here, the correspondence between language and thing is coupled with the idea that the understanding of love arises out of the exploration of conflicting, even contradictory views, much like Pound's energized vortex.

Like Dante's exploration of Love, which requires an ongoing process of constructing and dismantling ideas, the image or vortex is a provisional instance of construction open to testing by others. The testing must be performed not by looking for some object or referent that lies behind the thing but by recognizing how the patterns of language, especially rhythmic patterns, are the "thing." The patterns make a process of discovery possible. In his 1915 essay, "As for Imagisme," Pound wrote: "Energy creates pattern . . . I would say further that emotional force gives the image." He immediately clarifies his terminology: "Perhaps I should say, not pattern, but pattern-units, or units of design" (*EPCP*, II: 8–9).

Armed with this new vocabulary, he revisits the three imagist tenets, including in the process a rewrite of his Dantean definition: "Poetry is a composition or an 'organization' of words set to 'music.' By 'music' here we can scarcely mean much more than rhythm and timbre" (*EPCP*, II: 8–9). In updating his poetics here, shifting from "composition" to "organization," Pound puts his emphasis not on mimetic representation but on rhythmic pattern-units of design as themselves the locus of representation. Rhythm is a material instantiation of emotion, or the complex, or the "thing," that, through its very patterning, is at the same time an indication of the abstraction necessary to the image. In *The Pound Era*, Kenner writes that "The vortex is not the water but a patterned energy made visible by the water" (*PE*, 145). Rephrasing Kenner, we might say that the image or vortex is not the rhythm but a patterned energy made materially visible as well as audible by the rhythm.

Pound reflected the importance of this kind of patterning in the way he first published the most famous imagist poem, "In a Station of the Metro" (1913). He wrote to Harriet Monroe, editor of *Poetry* magazine, about the layout: "In the 'Metro' hokku, I was careful, I think, to indicate spaces between the rhythmic units, and I want them observed" (*SL*, 17). The poem appeared in *Poetry* like this:

IN A STATION OF THE METRO

The apparition   of these faces   in the crowd   :
Petals   on a wet, black   bough   .   (*P*, 251)

Later printings took away the extra spacing and replaced the colon at the end of the first line with a semicolon, but Pound makes the rhythm unit clear already in the title (w w s w, as in "In a Station" or "of the Metro").[7] Pound repeats this unit, at times overlapping it or employing the blank space to mark the silence of the unsounded weak syllables, e.g., at the end of the first line and carrying over into the beginning of the second.

This first printing showed how Pound thought that the organization of sound into patterned rhythm units could bring about the super-positioning of images that marked the transformative instant from outward to inward, a process of tangible abstraction. Imagist rhythm is absolute not because it renders the poet's or persona's *virtù* but because it presents directly the instantiating "thing," the energies and patterns of experience.

DECREATION AND *THE CANTOS*

Pound began to work on the so-called "Ur-Cantos" by 1915 but he had trouble getting this project under way. For his epic poem "including history" (*ABCR*, 46) that would tell "the tale of the tribe" (*GK*, 194), he needed a form that was more than just a "rag-bag" and a narrative voice that would be a "pervasive but nowhere visible register."[8] While his imagist and vorticist experiments showed him how to create pattern units of design, it was not immediately clear how these units could undergird a poem whose length and materials exceeded imagist miniatures. Moments of vision were to have their place in *The Cantos*, instances where time seems to stand still or be so fully embodied as to transport the listener to a space out of time. But to write a poem including history, he also had to make room for the contingent, the accidental, the event whose shape had yet to be fully discerned.

The two most important breakthrough moments in the process of discovering an appropriate form came in Canto IV (1919) and in the ironic
critiques of *Hugh Selwyn Mauberley* (1920). Canto IV focuses on objects as
they come into being at various cultural, social, and gender boundaries;
they are rendered not through description but through a fragmentation
that highlights their explicitly vocalized enactment (for instance, the opening twelve lines). Pound goes well beyond the imagist moment by using
phrasally defined rhythm groupings to shape an experience of time in
which it folds ply over ply back on itself, allowing an intermixing of
different temporal and cultural dimensions. This temporal interweaving
fosters an ongoing sense of anticipation and revision rather than the more
delimited imagist focus on a single moment.

The critical role that a reshaped prosody played in bringing about a
fully working model for the *Cantos* suggests that Pound never abandoned
the idea that a poem is a composition or organization of words set to
music, even if he radically reinvented that music. It was not necessary that
it be either humable or singable but rather, that it be precise. This new
music went hand in hand with a revised notion of the poet-maker. Readers
searching for structural models for the poem have usually stuck with one
or more of the analogues Pound provided: "Homer for the Odyssean
voyage toward the restoration of civic order; Dante for the pilgrim's ascent
through infernal and purgatorial regions toward Paradise; and Ovid for
transformations, one energy passing through gods and men, everything
connected with everything else, many stories woven into a single tale."[9]

Each analogue offers a model for both a protagonist and a poet figure,
each a maker or seeker whose quest is necessarily one of wandering and
error, a path of sailing "after knowledge / Knowing less than drugged
beasts" (XLVII/236). Despite the necessity of such error, the poet-wanderer
figure is also open to the transformative moments of insight that punctuate
the journey. Such a poet does not and cannot have a known *telos* and thus
cannot impose a certain order on the welter of details that confront him
along the way. Though in the fascist moments of the *Pisan Cantos* Pound
tried to insist on such an order, his linguistic organization undercut that
misguided quest.

The anti-Semitic and fascist rantings of what Charles Bernstein has
called Pound's "spouting mouth" were ultimately framed by his poetic
ear, which set these materials alongside others, creating a structure that
invited the reader to make his or her own critical judgements.[10] The *Pisan
Cantos* thus share an interest in what Wallace Stevens has called the process
of "decreation," "making pass from the created to the uncreated," which

stands in contrast to destruction, which "is making pass from the created to nothingness." Decreation does not yield revelations of belief but the "precious portents of our own powers."[11] While Pound doubted the ability of his powers to make his poem cohere, the decreation of his poet-speaker, his culture, and his literary tradition, provided the basis for a new imaginary language that the poem makes possible even while it remains unheard.

NOTES

1 Pound quoted this phrase in the following: "The Approach to Paris, VII," *The New Age* 13.25 (October 16, 1913) (*EPCP*, I: 192); "Affirmations, IV. As for Imagisme," *The New Age* 16.13 (January 28, 1915) (*EPCP*, II: 9); "The Prose Tradition in Verse" (*LE*, 376); "Vers Libre and Arnold Dolmetsch" (*LE*, 437); and *ABCR*, 31.

2 See Jerome McGann, *Dante Gabriel Rossetti and the Game That Must Be Lost* (New Haven: Yale University Press, 2000), 66–83.

3 Dante Gabriel Rossetti, *Collected Poetry and Prose*, ed. Jerome McGann (New Haven: Yale University Press, 2003), 293.

4 My discussion of poetic ethos here is indebted to Charles Altieri's idea of constructivist abstraction, presented in his *Painterly Abstraction in Modern Poetry* (Cambridge: Cambridge University Press, 1989).

5 Peter Nicholls, "The Poetics of Modernism," in *The Cambridge Companion to Modernist Poetry*, ed. Alex Davis and Lee M. Jenkins (Cambridge: Cambridge University Press, 2007), 54.

6 Dante, *La Vita Nuova*, trans. Barbara Reynolds (Harmondsworth: Penguin, 1969), chapter 13.

7 I use a "w" to indicate a weak or unstressed syllable and an "s" to indicate a strong or stressed syllable.

8 Ronald Bush, *The Genesis of Ezra Pound's Cantos* (Princeton: Princeton University Press, 1976), 175.

9 George Kearns, *Guide to Ezra Pound's Selected Cantos* (New Brunswick, NJ: Rutgers University Press, 1980), 9.

10 Charles Bernstein, "Pounding Fascism", in *A Poetics* (Cambridge, MA: Harvard University Press, 1992) 125.

11 Wallace Stevens, "The Relations between Poetry and Painting," in *The Necessary Angel: Essays on Reality and the Imagination* (New York: Vintage, 1951), 175–6.

CHAPTER 3

Translation

Steven G. Yao

No less than he did for poetry, Ezra Pound successfully redefined both the conceptual and procedural terms for translation as a mode of literary production during the modernist period and after. Over practically his entire long career, Pound engaged in a sustained and enormously varied effort as both a practitioner and theorist of translation. Stretching at least from the early *Sonnets and Ballate of Guido Cavlacanti* (1912) all the way to the late collection of *Love Poems of Ancient Egypt* (1962), Pound published renderings of numerous different works from a wide range of languages, including Greek, Latin, Provençal, and classical Chinese, in addition to medieval Italian and Egyptian. Over and above the sheer volume of these efforts at rendering particular texts, he repeatedly, if never systematically, engaged in critical reflection about the practice, discussing both the larger cultural significance of translation and its proper methods. Taken together, his achievements in the arena of translation comprise a substantial and fundamentally important part of his overall accomplishment as a writer.

Pound's commitment to translation as a distinctive (and distinctively important) mode of literary production arose from a steadily deepening conviction about its generative role in the broader formation of a vital literary culture. As early as 1916, Pound hypothesized that "A great age of literature is perhaps always a great age of translations; or follows it" (*LE*, 232). Thirteen years later, any lingering doubts he might have harbored about the generative importance of translation in the rise of English literature had completely disappeared. Thus in "How to Read" (1929), his first attempt at a primer for modernism, he summarily declares that, after the period of purely indigenous Anglo-Saxon works such as "The Seafarer" and *Beowulf,* "English literature lives on translation, it is fed by translation; every new exuberance, every new heave is stimulated by translation, every allegedly great age is an age of translations" (*LE*, 34–5). In promulgating these views, Pound yet again demonstrates that he is something of a radical, being arguably the first broadly influential writer since at least the seventeenth century to bestow upon translation, over and above so-called original composition, an explicitly primary and generative, rather than a derivative or supplementary, role in the process of literary culture formation.

Previously within the history of literature in English, translation as a mode of literary production had always occupied a position of distinctly ancillary significance. Dante Gabriel Rossetti summarized the predominant attitude in English up to Pound concerning the significance of translation as a literary mode when in 1861 he called it, "the tributary art."[1] Even John Dryden, undoubtedly the most important figure in the history of translation into English before Pound, did not consider translation a driving force either in the development of a distinct national literature or the growth of a language; and his approach to the practice reflects such a theoretical bias. So, in the preface to his translations from Virgil, issued in 1697, Dryden explains of his rendering, "I have endeavored to make Virgil speak such English as he would himself have spoken, if he had been in England, and in this present age."[2] Far from letting Virgil's Latin change the idiom of the day, Dryden proceeds from the conviction that he should domesticate the foreign language to a contemporary vernacular, to smooth over any "heaves" caused by the contact between English and another language.[3] Such an approach casts translation as a formally derivative mode of literary production, one that merely domesticates or assimilates foreign texts to established conventions and norms of stylistic expression in English.

Accordingly, then, Pound's typically bold and sweeping assertion that "every new exuberance, every new heave [in English literature] is stimulated by translation" marks a definitive conceptual break from the established views about translation held since at least the Enlightenment. Such a claim also thereby underscores the crucial importance of translation as a literary mode within Pound's own critical framework and the trajectory of his individual career, as well as, indeed, that of the "allegedly great age" of modernism as a whole.[4] For in attributing to translation such momentous cultural significance, Pound epitomizes a general rethinking of (especially poetic) translation that took place among several major British and American writers during the early twentieth century. Solidly canonical figures such as W.B. Yeats, James Joyce, William Carlos Williams, T.S. Eliot, H.D., Virginia Woolf, Ford Maddox Ford, and Langston Hughes, among others, each contributed in some way to this dimension of Anglo-American modernist achievement.

Beginning at least as early as the summer of 1901 with Joyce's youthful renderings of two plays by Gerhart Hauptmann, *Before Sunrise* and *Michael*

Kramer, and continuing all the way through to the publication in 1956 of Pound's deeply personal and idiosyncratic version of Sophocles' *Women of Trachis*, feats of translation not only accompanied and helped to give rise to, but in certain instances even themselves constituted, some of the most significant modernist literary achievements in English. Working on them between 1926 and 1927, William Butler Yeats concluded his investigation into Greek tragedy as a model for the formation of a national, Irish dramatic culture by translating and producing on the stage both *King Oedipus* (1928) and *Oedipus at Colonus* (1934). Similarly, H.D. devoted considerable time and energy throughout her career to translating Greek poetry and drama, culminating in her 1938 translation of another classical Greek play, Euripides' *Ion*, and this lifelong practice profoundly affected her development as a poet. H.D.'s husband, Richard Aldington, produced four volumes of poems by various Greek and Latin poets in *The Poets' Translation Series* published by the Egoist Press. As its very title suggests, this series bespeaks the fundamental interconnection between translation and other modes of literary production within the writing practices of the modernists.

Comparably, William Carlos Williams translated poems by numerous French and Spanish writers, including Nicanor Parra, Silvina Ocampo, Pablo Neruda, Octavio Paz, Miguel Hernandez, Rafael Beltran Logroños, Mariano del Alcazar, Nicholas Calas, and even one poem, "The Cassia Tree," by the Chinese poet Li Bai.[5] And in addition to rendering numerous critical articles from French for publication in *The Criterion*, T.S. Eliot produced an English translation of St. John Perse's poem *Anabase* (1930), which he considered "a piece of writing of the same importance as the later work of Mr. James Joyce, as valuable as *Anna Livia Plurabelle*."[6]

Of course, it is Pound, himself, who stands out as the premier champion (or villain) in the showground of modernist translation. Both the sheer amount and the enormous scope of his efforts underscore the depth of his engagement with translation as at once a sustained and, more importantly, a generative writing practice. By the time he declared the importance of translation to the evolution of English literature in "How to Read," Pound had contributed to the development of modernist verse through two major works of translation: namely, the exquisitely rendered set of medieval Chinese lyrics based on the notes of Ernest Fenollosa in *Cathay* (1915) and the highly unconventional, and so critically reviled, treatment of the odes of Sextus Propertius in *Homage to Sextus Propertius* (1919).[7] In the words of George Steiner, Pound's translations of Chinese poetry in *Cathay* "altered the feel of the language [English] and set the pattern of cadence for modern verse."[8] While in the *Homage*, Pound freely rearranged the order of the Latin poet's odes and departed at various strategic points from his strict semantic meaning, thereby paving the way for translation to become a technique of independent textual construction during the modernist period. Over and above these major achievements, Pound produced a version of the *Dialogues of Fontenelle* (1917), as well as translating two works by Rémy de Gourmont: *The Natural Philosophy of Love* (1922) and *Dust for Sparrows* (1922). In addition, he produced a rendering through an intermediary French source of the Confucian governmental classic, the *Ta Hio* (1928), or, as he later came to call it when he translated it again in 1945, *The Great Digest*.[9]

The sheer abundance of translations produced by Pound and others during the period gives concrete, textual expression to the interest on the part of modernist writers, both in England and the United States, in foreign cultures and, most especially, languages as sources of both instruction and inspiration for renewing their own culture and expanding the possibilities of expression in English. This interest also manifests itself in the explicitly multi-linguistic dimensions of so many major modernist texts. For beyond simply producing a great many renderings of documents from various cultures and traditions, modernist writers also engaged in translation as a technique in the composition of their own "original" works.

Fragments and even extended passages from a vast array of texts in a wide range of languages comprise constitutive elements in a number of modernist poems and novels, which themselves oftentimes take the process of translation as one of their subjects. Here again, Pound serves as the prime example. *The Cantos* famously opens with a translation of a Renaissance Latin version of the Nekuia episode in Homer's *Odyssey*. And as Hugh Kenner has noted, Canto 1 "is not simply, as was Divus' Homer or Chapman's Homer or Pope's, a passing through the knot of a newer rope. It is *about* the fact that self-interfering patterns persist while new ways of shaping breath flow through them. It illustrates that fact, and its subject is in part that fact" (emphasis in the original; *PE*, 149). Indeed, translation figures so largely as both technique and subject in the remainder of Pound's poem, most notably in the "Malatesta" and "Chinese History" Cantos, that another critic has gone so far as to call *The Cantos* an "epic of translation."[10] Within the context of these general concerns, then, translation represented for Pound and the modernists an integral part of their collective program for cultural renewal, a crucially important mode of writing distinct from, yet fundamentally interconnected with, the more traditionally esteemed modes of poetry and prose fiction.

Together with legitimizing its cultural pedigree as a mode of writing (something which, on the whole, the modernists were only partially successful at), Pound played the biggest role in also reconfiguring the parameters for the very practice of translation itself, cleanly decoupling its linguistic from its more expressly literary dimensions. By doing so, he in turn helped make possible such subsequent achievements as the radical versions of the odes of Catullus by Louis and Celia Zukofsky, as well as the diverse efforts of contemporary poetic translators like Stephen Mitchell, W.S. Merwin, Kenneth Rexroth, and Robert Hass. During the course of modernism, translation as a literary mode rose to a level within the generic hierarchy fundamentally different from that which it had occupied during earlier periods of English literary history. This difference manifests itself in both the scope and the methods of the modernists in their efforts as translators.

Before Pound (and modernism more generally), literary translation functioned primarily as a means for renewing and strategically deploying the authority of the classics. Hence, the most renowned translators in English of previous eras – Golding and Chapman in the Elizabethan, Dryden and Pope in the Enlightenment, and Browning, Rossetti, and Swinburne in the Victorian – all derive their reputations specifically as translators from their renderings of various Latin and Greek writers and other figures explicitly connected with the classical tradition.[11]

While the modernists certainly coveted the monumental authority of classical writers, especially Homer, they also explored alternative sources for such enabling models, employing translation as a strategy by which to underwrite their own cultural ambitions and advance their own aesthetic and ideological ends. In doing so, they expanded the geographical and temporal domain of literary translation to include works outside the Western tradition entirely, as well as more recent figures by no means assured of their place in the canon. Thus, long before he gave a conceptual rendering of Homer in *Ulysses*, Joyce sought to promote in Ireland his taste for nineteenth-century Continental drama when he translated Gerhart Hauptmann, a relative contemporary, in his youthful version of *Vor Sonnenaufgang*. If Yeats and H.D. directed their efforts as translators exclusively to classical Greek drama and poetry, William Carlos Williams translated exactly contemporary poets writing in Spanish and French. Pound translated not only Sextus Propertius, but also Li Bai; and while *The Cantos* opens with a rendering of the Nekuia episode in *The Odyssey*, the poem also includes long passages culled from a Qing dynasty historical treatise. Indeed, some of Pound's most important translations include his deeply unorthodox, yet fascinating treatments of books from the Confucian tradition of political and social thought: *The Great Learning, The Unwobbling Pivot* (1947), and *The Analects* (1951).

Undoubtedly, however, the most dramatic change wrought by Pound and the modernists in the dimensions of translation as a literary mode lies in the extent to which formal knowledge of the source language no longer constituted a requirement for its practice. Before modernism, translators in English simply proceeded under the assumption that full comprehension of the source language represented a necessary condition for translation.[12] Indeed, theorists of translation before the modernist period made such knowledge a formal requirement for the practice itself. Thus, in 1711, Dryden asserts that "The Qualification of a Translator worth Reading must be Mastery of the Language he Translates out of, and that he Translates into," though he concedes that "if a deficience be to be allow'd in either, it is in the Original, since if he be but Master enough of the Tongue of his Author, as to be Master of his Sense, it is possible for him to express that Sense, with Eloquence, in his own, if he have a thorough Command of that."[13]

Exactly 150 years later, Matthew Arnold, the most influential theorist of translation during the Victorian period, took this requirement one step further, asserting that proper translation must include scholarship as a major component. In his famous essay "On Translating Homer," which began as a series of lectures at Oxford University in 1860, he argues:

> [The translator] is to try to satisfy *scholars*, because scholars alone have the means of really judging him. A scholar may be a pedant, it is true, and then his judgment will be worthless; but a scholar may also have poetical feeling, and then he can judge him truly; whereas all the poetical feeling in the world will not enable a man who is not a scholar to judge him truly. For the translator is to reproduce Homer, and the scholar alone has the means of knowing what Homer is to be reproduced. He knows him but imperfectly, for he is separated from him by time, race, and language; but he alone knows him at all.[14]

Ideally, for Arnold, translation unites the sensitivity and skills of a poet with the knowledge and learning of a literary scholar.

By contrast, modernist writers repeatedly engaged in translation, and sometimes achieved remarkable results, with partial, imprecise, faulty, and sometimes even no formal understanding of the languages in which the texts they translated were originally written. Moreover, as the case of Pound most clearly illustrates, modernist translators' knowledge of the source language had little to do either with their willingness to translate a given text or, indeed, the success of their translations. Indeed, Joyce had at best a tenuous grasp of German when he undertook *Vor Sonnenaufgang*. Yeats knew absolutely no Greek when he translated *Oedipus Rex* and *Oedipus at Colonus* in 1928, piecing together his versions from a number of preexisting renderings. H.D.'s knowledge of Greek remains a subject of considerable scholarly debate. And while Pound's formal training as a graduate student in comparative literature, as well as his gift for individual languages, underlie his translations of Cavalcanti, Arnaut Daniel, and other Romance poets, he repeatedly rendered texts from languages such as Chinese and Egyptian of which he had no formal understanding.

Among Pound's major feats of translation, *Cathay* consecrated the most fundamental change in the practical dimensions of literary translation in English wrought by the modernist period, a change virtually without precedent in the history of translation as a literary mode in English. Radically reconfiguring the operative parameters of translation as a mode of literary production, Pound's achievement obviated intimate knowledge of the source language as a precondition for translation by demonstrating in an irrefutable way that successful (that is, both aesthetically pleasing and culturally influential) results could be attained without thorough (or indeed, as in this case, even any) understanding of the original language of the text one translated. For when he began working from the notebooks of Ernest Fenollosa to produce his versions of the (mostly) medieval Chinese lyrics presented in *Cathay*, Pound had absolutely no knowledge of the Chinese language. At that time he had yet to assimilate Fenollosa's deeply problematic theory of the Chinese written character, so he did not even have the benefit of an *incorrect* understanding of Chinese.

Indeed, as he continued over the course of his career to translate works from the Confucian tradition, Pound came to believe that his lack of knowledge, far from being a hindrance, actually represented a decided advantage in his attempt to reproduce even the mode of signification encoded within the very characters of the texts themselves. His adherence to the evocative but vastly oversimplified theories of Ernest Fenollosa about the nature of the Chinese language merely allowed him to justify his own ignorance and, indeed, see it as a positive trait, one that made it possible for him to penetrate the layers of scholarship that had accumulated over time to arrive at a genuine, poetic understanding of Confucian political wisdom. Likewise, H.D. and Yeats explicitly rejected classical training as a barrier to authentic translation. And even though many of the translators themselves knew the languages from which they made their renderings, the editors of *The Poets' Translation Series* expressed the pervasive modernist distrust of scholarship when they described their intentions in the following terms:

The object of the editors of this series is to present a number of translations of Greek and Latin poetry and prose, especially of those authors who are less frequently given in English.

This literature has too long been the property of pedagogues, philologists, and professors. Its human qualities have been obscured by the wranglings of grammarians, who love it principally because to them it is so safe and so dead . . . The translators will take no concern with glosses, notes, or any of the apparatus with which learning smothers beauty . . . The first six pamphlets, when bound together, will form a small collection of unhackneyed poetry, too long buried under the dust of pedantic scholarship.[15]

Understandably, perhaps, such unorthodox beliefs and practices continue to provoke objections, either as expressions of an imperialist arrogance or, at best, as convenient rationalizations that serve to mitigate personal failings. Nevertheless, this valorization of modernist translators' own ignorance and the consequent willingness (and even insistence) to undertake renderings of texts for which they lacked command of the source language, together fundamentally differentiate the modernist practice of translation from that of previous eras in Anglo-American literary history. Thus, during the modernist period, translation occupied a manifold conceptual space: it constituted an autonomous literary activity that inspired sustained and varied critical reflection; it functioned as a specific technique in the construction of texts in a variety of different modes, ranging from "original" works to so-called adaptations to "translations" proper, as that term has been traditionally understood; and it embodied a comprehensive textual strategy for negotiating between the demands of transmission and transformation, between the authority of tradition and the demands of innovation, between the endowments of the past and the imperatives of the present.

Through the efforts of Pound in particular, translation came into its own during the modernist period, serving as an expressly generative and literary mode of writing, rather than a principally linguistic operation limited in scope simply to reproducing the "meaning" of a foreign text. No longer governed by traditional conceptions of semantic fidelity and the constraints of linguistic knowledge, it functioned, and should be viewed, as a mode of literary production fundamentally comparable to and, indeed, deeply constitutive of, the other major modernist forms of poetry and prose fiction.

NOTES

1 Rossetti made this statement in the Preface to his volume of translations, *The Early Italian Poets*, first published in 1861. See Dante Gabriel Rossetti, *The Early Italian Poets*, ed. Sally Purcell (London: Anvil Press, 1981).

2 As cited in George Steiner, *After Babel: Aspects of Language and Translation* (Oxford: Oxford University Press, 1975), 256.

3 Dryden's method as a translator, as well as his ongoing canonization within the domain of English literature, together reflect the dominance of "fluency" that Lawrence Venuti has described as the prevailing ideology for translation in Anglo-American culture. See Venuti, *The Translator's Invisibility: A History of Translation* (London: Routledge, 1995), especially chapter 2, 43–98.

4 For a more extended discussion of this issue, see my *Translation and the Languages of Modernism: Gender, Politics, Language* (New York: Palgrave Macmillan, 2002).

5 This is the same poet known through Pound's famous renderings as Li Po. Here, I employ the now standard Pinyin transcription of the name 李白 (Li Bai) to refer to the historical Chinese poet.

6 From the Preface to Eliot's translation, *Anabasis* (New York: Harcourt, Brace and Company, 1938), 10.

7 I refer here to the notorious tradition of attacks on the *Homage* that began almost immediately upon its initial, partial publication in the March 1919 edition of *Poetry* magazine. In the very next issue, the classicist William Gardner Hale famously derided Pound's abilities as a translator, enumerating various grammatical errors and other supposed linguistic "howlers." For the full, dyspeptic review, see William Gardner Hale, *Poetry* 26 (April 1919): 62.

8 Steiner, *After Babel*, 358.

9 In addition to these volumes specifically dedicated to his work as a translator, other significant translations Pound produced before 1929 include versions of some twenty poems by the troubadour poet Arnaut Daniel published in *Umbra* (1920) and a rendering of the Anglo-Saxon poem "The Seafarer," first published in *Ripostes* (1912). After 1929, the list becomes even more impressive in its diversity, both of languages and subjects. Such feats range from complete and fascinatingly incorrect versions of two more books in the Confucian canon of political and social thought, *The Unwobbling Pivot* (1947) and *The Analects* (1951), together with the *Shi Jing* (詩經), to which he gave the rather verbose title, *The Classic Anthology Defined by Confucius* (1954), to a collection of *Love Poems of Ancient Egypt* (1962), as well as his rendering of Sophocles' *Women of Trachis* (1956). The list could go on considerably.

10 See Richard Reid, *Discontinuous Gods: Ezra Pound and the Epic of Translation*. PhD Dissertation, Princeton University, 1986.

11 A major exception to this general trend is Fitzgerald, whose version of the *Rubaiyat* exerted a profound influence over both his contemporaries and such modernists as Pound. In the *ABC of Reading*, Pound offers the following as a critical exercise: "Try to find out why the Fitzgerald Rubaiyat has gone into so many editions after having lain unnoticed until Rossetti found a pile of remaindered copies on a second-hand bookstall" (*ABCR* 79–80).

12 Even such unorthodox translators as Abraham Cowley (1618–67) and Francis Newman (1805–97), brother to the famous Cardinal, both knew well the Greek from which they made their renderings of Pindar and Homer respectively. For

more on Newman and his debate with Arnold, see Venuti, *The Translator's Invisibility*, 118–47.

13 Dryden "The Life of Lucian," *Works of John Dryden*, vol. XX, ed. Alan Roper, Vinton Dearing, and George R. Guffey (Berkeley: University of California Press, 1989), 226.

14 Matthew Arnold, "On Translating Homer," in *Poetry and Criticism of Matthew Arnold*, ed. A. Dwight Culler (Cambridge: The Riverside Press, 1961), 218. Emphasis in the original.

15 Introductory Note to *The Poets' Translation Series* (London: The Egoist Press, 1915), 7–8.

CHAPTER 4

Romance languages

David Ten Eyck

In "Medievalism," his 1928 essay on Guido Cavalcanti, Ezra Pound described the uniqueness of medieval Italian poetry. The poets of this time, he writes "brought into poetry something which had not been in any so marked and developed degree in the poetry of the troubadours. It is still more important for any one wishing to have well-balanced critical appreciation of poetry in general to understand that this quality, or this assertion of value, has not been in poetry *since*" (*LE*, 150). This quality, he claimed, had its origin in the troubadours' shift from the classical aesthetic of "[p]lastic plus immediate satisfaction," to the "dogma that there is some proportion between the fine thing held in the mind and the inferior thing ready for instant consumption" (*LE*, 151). For Pound, the aesthetic shift initiated by the troubadours achieved its fullest expression in the Tuscan poetry of the *trecento* which "demand[ed] harmony in something more than the plastic" (*LE*, 151) and gave central importance to the interaction between the intellect and the senses. This poetic sensibility, he came to believe, found its most perfect expression in Cavalcanti's canzone "Donna mi prega," a poem for which he gained increasing admiration over the course of almost three decades of study.

Pound's first serious encounter with Cavalcanti's poetry likely came when he was a student at Hamilton College, between 1903 and 1905. In 1910 Cavalcanti appeared as part of his description of Tuscan poetry in *The Spirit of Romance*, and in 1912 Pound published translations of some fifty of his poems under the title *Sonnets and Ballate of Guido Cavalcanti*. Then, a decade and a half later, he began to take particular interest in "Donna mi prega," publishing critical essays on the poem and translating it twice. The second of these translations appeared as part of Canto XXXVI, where it stands as what Hugh Kenner called "a model of focused intellection and passion" (*PE*, 424).[1] Through this extended engagement with Cavalcanti, Pound sought to discover qualities not present in English verse, while at the same time formulating a transnational understanding of the European literary tradition. In both of these things, his study of Cavalcanti was exemplary of the way Pound had used Romance languages and literature since his student days.

As an undergraduate at the University of Pennsylvania and Hamilton College, between 1901 and 1905, Pound's study of Romance languages was often a way for him to resist the academic conventions of his time. In later life he recalled doing battle against the faculty and curriculum at the University of Pennsylvania in order to obtain the education he wanted. He told one correspondent that

[I] [e]ntered U.P. Penn at 15 with intention of studying comparative values in literature (poetry) and began doing so unbeknown to the faculty . . . In this search I learned more or less nine foreign languages, I read Oriental stuff in translations, I fought every University regulation and every professor who tried to make me learn anything except this, or who bothered me with "requirements for degrees."[2]

This sort of comparative approach was new at the time and was not accommodated by the degree programs in place at the University of Pennsylvania.[3] Pound consequently found himself obliged to study "across the grain of American University conventions" (Moody, 15) and following his sophomore year, having received below average grades and been frustrated by the rigidity of the university's requirements, he left Pennsylvania in order to continue his studies at Hamilton College. This choice was made in part because Hamilton's curriculum offered him greater freedom to pursue his education on his own terms. As Humphrey Carpenter points out: "[r]egulations at Penn laid down that he could only study for credit those languages (Latin and German) which he had offered at enrolment; at Hamilton he would be allowed to add Italian and Spanish" (ASC, 46). Pound enrolled in classes in French, Italian, and Spanish at Hamilton.[4] It was here, under the guidance of Professor William P. Shepard, that Romance languages and literature became his principal field of study, and Shepard's interest in troubadour poetry was a determining factor in encouraging Pound's own investigations of the subject.[5] In addition to his regular classes, Pound received courses in Provençal with Shepard outside the normal curriculum. He would later recall initiating these after Shepard had lent him "a book of french translations of [O]ld F[rench] & Provencal" (ASC, 56). Both Shepard's emphasis on poetry in his classes and his way of viewing the cultural history of medieval Europe in transnational terms attracted Pound. A 1904 letter to his parents, for instance, captures his excitement at Shepard's use of Canto ix of Dante's *Paradiso* to comment upon "medieval philosophy": "Got more medieval philosophy in one canto of Dante's Paradise than I ever expect to get again. Bill spent most of the time elucidating. He told me if I wanted any more I could go to Thomas Aquinas & the other medieval latin writers. I said 'No thanks this is enough' so we go on to Canto x" (Moody, 22). While attending Shepard's seminars, Pound also began to try his hand at translations and adaptations of Provençal verse. In the spring of 1905 he published a translation of a poem he described in a letter to his mother as "the Belengual Alba or Dawn song" and at about the same time he told his parents about the technical constraints imposed by a poem of Giraut de Bornelh which "contains sixty-eight lines and only five rhyme sounds and has been a stumbling block to several" (*ASC*, 57). Pound frankly and generously acknowledged Shepard's influence in the preface to *The Spirit of Romance*: "my thanks are due to Dr. Wm. P. Shepard of Hamilton College, whose refined and sympathetic scholarship first led me to some knowledge of French, Italian, Spanish and Provençal" (*SR*, 7).

In the fall of 1905, after two years at Hamilton, Pound returned to the University of Pennsylvania to pursue a Masters degree in Romance languages. The Professor of the subject at Pennsylvania was Hugo Rennert, a specialist in Spanish literature, and Pound enrolled in as many of his classes as possible. In the fall semester of 1906, for example, he took six classes with Rennert: "Old Provençal, Old French, Early Italian Poets, Dante, Old Spanish, and Spanish Drama" (Moody, 29). Under Rennert's supervision he began to write a dissertation on the plays of Lope de Vega, and on the basis of his work in Rennert's classes he earned a fellowship of $500 for a research trip to Spain during the summer of 1906.

Pound's choice of subject for his doctoral research perhaps reflects Rennert's influence more than his own primary interests. His initial choice had been to study Renaissance Latin authors,[6] and the records we have of his reading at the time show that he remained preoccupied with the poetry of Tuscany and the troubadours even as he began doing research for his thesis (Moody, 30–1). Yet whatever his motivations, there is no evidence that he did not take his dissertation seriously, and he made use of his time in Spain to study the works of Lope de Vega in the Royal Library in Madrid. In his second year as a graduate student, however, Pound's relationship with the University of Pennsylvania soured. He began to take courses with professors other than Rennert and did poorly, clashing with both

Felix Schelling, the head of the English Department, and Josiah Penniman, the Dean of the Faculty in the process. His fellowship was not renewed at the end of the academic year and he stopped work on his thesis soon after, thus ending his formal education.

ROMANCE PHILOLOGY AND EZRA POUND'S LINGUISTIC COMPETENCE

Pound's difficulties were due, in large part, to his refusal to accept the model of scholarship imposed by his teachers. Even while still in graduate school, he denigrated what he called "philology," a term he used to target the sterile rigor of scholars who spent their time "pondering over some utterly unanswerable question of textual criticism" (*EPCP*, 1: 5), while failing to appreciate the essential qualities of great literary works. This quarrel with academia spills over into the preface of *The Spirit of Romance*, where Pound attacks what he calls the "slough of philology." He informs his reader that *The Spirit of Romance* "is not a philological work," and announces his intention to study "certain forces, elements or qualities which were potent in the mediæval literature of the Latin tongues, and are, I believe, still potent in our own" (*SR*, 5).

The notion of literary scholarship that shaped Pound's study of Romance languages was no less demanding than the one preached by his teachers. But it involved approaching languages by way of literature, rather than the reverse, and as such it aroused the suspicion of men like Felix Schelling, who told Pound bluntly that he was either a humbug or a genius, leaving little doubt as to his personal opinion on the matter (Moody, 14). The most concise statement of Pound's attitude appears in a fragmentary observation, appended to his notes for one of the 1909 lectures on which *The Spirit of Romance* was based: "read all the lit before you learn the lang."[7] In his own study Pound followed this advice. Consequently, despite his lifelong interest in Romance literature, his mastery of Romance languages remained imperfect, at best, when judged by conventional standards.

Pound attained by far the greatest degree of proficiency in Italian, which came to be a second language to him. He lived in Italy from 1925 until 1945, then again from 1959 until the end of his life. Over the course of the 1930s, and particularly following the outbreak of World War II, he published essays, translations, and original poetry in Italian, including two wartime Cantos (LXXII and LXXIII). Yet even Pound's Italian cannot be termed native, being subject to occasional grammatical and lexical lapses and containing constructions that would appear unusual to a native speaker.

His daughter, Mary de Rachewiltz, who prepared the Italian translation of *The Cantos*,[8] summarizes the matter most concisely when she says of Pound's Italian that "the connections that resonate for him would occur only to someone who does not think in Italian."[9] Pound's knowledge of Spanish and French was much sketchier. He never lived in Spain, and following his work on Lope de Vega he made little further engagement with Spanish literature. Even in *The Spirit of Romance* the chapters on El Cid and de Vega read like something of an aside in a narrative primarily concerned with a literary tradition that flows from the Latin writers of medieval Italy to Provence and Tuscany, then northward through France to Elizabethan England. Pound's engagement with French was more longstanding. He lived in Paris between 1921 and 1925, and his translations, critical essays, and correspondence record the lasting influence of writers such as François Villon, Rémy de Gourmont, and French Symbolist poets like Jules Laforgue and Arthur Rimbaud. Yet the milieu in which Pound moved during his time in Paris was a cosmopolitan one and his mastery of the French language remained imperfect. The small body of correspondence he carried out in French contains numerous grammatical and lexical errors, as well as literal translations from English which would not make sense to a native speaker. His knowledge of Provençal was essentially limited to what he gained from the close study of individual poems or manuscripts.[10]

Pound's linguistic limitations were neatly summarized by Dudley Fitts, a translator and teacher of languages at Philips Academy, who reviewed the typescript of *The Pisan Cantos* in 1946 as a favor for James Laughlin. Knowing that Pound had composed the sequence during his incarceration by the US Army in 1945, without any recourse to his books, Laughlin asked Fitts to review his use of foreign languages in the text prior to its publication. He was told that

IF THIS TEXT COMES OUT AS IS – the hoss-laff that will go up from the people who we most want to engage – the literates – will be of no help to you, as a publisher, or to EzPo as a poet. It must be said that there is no indication here that Ez has ever been anything but a phoney, so far as his linguistic pretensions are concerned. True, one must make allowances for the circs. and his lack of books; mais quand-même: he has been doing it all his life and this is only an aggravated instance. His italian is mis-spelled, mis-accented. So is his spanish. I know no old Provençal, but I'd bet Debby's [Fitts's wife's] virtue on the proposition that it's no better. His french is all right, barring a few accents.[11]

Fitts's judgement of Pound's Italian is unduly harsh and his judgement of his French is overly indulgent, but there can be little argument with his overall assessment. Even at this stage of his career, however, it is unlikely that Pound would have been very concerned about the reaction of readers Fitts termed "the literates." He used foreign languages in *The Pisan Cantos*, as he had since his student days, as doorways onto knowledge accessible only outside of English, not as fields of study to be mastered.

ROMANCE LANGUAGES AS VEHICLES OF DISCOVERY

This attitude meant that Pound was temperamentally ill-suited for the type of scholarship required for a doctoral thesis. Yet in spite of being forced to abandon his dissertation, it is clear that his 1906 trip to Spain was a crucial formative experience. This was Pound's first independent trip to Europe, and he spent two months traveling from Gibraltar to Cordova, then on to Madrid, then north to Paris via Burgos. The records that survive from this time are marked by a sense of discovery that is both literary and personal. Pound's most complete account of the trip was written in the form of an extended letter to family friend Carlos Tracy Chester. This letter gives an indication of the attentiveness of the young poet's eye and is remarkable for the way it modulates between literary commentary and personal observations:

Of the colors of Spain no man knows anything until he has seen the fields of the south provinces in the maytime. Nor does one understand the richness of the old Spanish verse until he has seen the blazing scarlet of the poppies and stretches of yellow and purple and chalk white as jewels set in the reddish browns of the soil and unnumbered greens of the grasses, nor Lope's dawn marble footed treading the flowers of April.

> "A penas Leonora
> la blanca Aurora
> puso su pie de marfil
> sobre las flores de abril"

which is different from Shakespeare's dawn clad in russet and walking upon the hill dew.[12]

This letter was never published, but a shorter piece entitled "Burgos, A Dream City of Old Castile" appeared in the October 1906 issue of *Book News Monthly*. Here, Pound described a process of discovery whereby the knowledge of Spanish literature (called "Spain's old song-glory") allows a "dream Spain" to emerge from the impenetrable confusion of the "Spain of today". This process was especially explicit in an early draft of the article, entitled simply "Extracts from a Letter on Burgos":

After a period of unsatisfactory search and wandering through that inexplicable mixture of hell and paradise which no outlander can understand, but which we may call for convenience "Spain of today," it is a pleasant thing to find that there is a dream Spain, just as real as Spain's old song-glory and no more tainted with the appearance of modernity than the parchment psalter-leaf that Raymondo Altes has used to bind his mss. observations on how poems should be written.[13]

Pound's concern here is to merge his own experience of contemporary Spain with the country's "old song-glory" so as to give a definite form to essential realities which art has the unique power to seize and preserve. In 1912 he would undertake a walking tour of the south of France in much the same spirit, seeking to better understand the poetry of the troubadours through personal experience. Richard Sieburth, who reconstituted Pound's journal of these travels in *A Walking Tour in Southern France*, describes him "proceeding on the belief that the referential ground of troubadour song might be recovered through the simple exercise of 'inspective energy'" (*WTSF*, xv).

THE SPIRIT OF ROMANCE

This understanding of Romance literature as an imaginative space he could learn to inhabit through personal experience is recurrent in Pound's early writing, and it helps explain why he was so vehement in his refusal of "philology." The unique thrust of his interest inspired him to propose an alternative critical reading of the subject, first in a series of lectures that he delivered in London in 1909,[14] then in *The Spirit of Romance*, which was published a year later. Here, Pound proposed a technical and stylistic study, using the major works of Romance literature to demonstrate poetic possibilities hitherto undeveloped in English. At the same time he mapped out a transnational literary tradition, wherein medieval Romance literature stands as a cultural thread that connects modern Europe to antiquity. He insists upon the "pagan" lineage of Provençal song: "Provençe was less disturbed than the rest of Europe by invasion from the North in the darker ages; if paganism survived anywhere it would have been, unofficially, in the Langue d'Oc" (*SR*, 90). Then he evokes a gradual movement toward the more philosophical attitude he admired in Guido Cavalcanti and other Tuscan poets of the *trecento*:

Provence had had much paganism, unacknowledged, some heresy openly proclaimed, and a good deal of conventional piety.

Unquestioning they had worshipped Amor and the more orthodox divinities, God, Christ, and the Virgin. From Amor or his self-constituted deputies they had received a code of laws. To God and his saints they had prayed incuriously.

The Tuscan bookworms suddenly find themselves in the groves of philosophy, God becomes interesting, and speculation, with open eyes and a rather didactic voice, is boon companion to the bard.

Thought, which in Provence had confined itself to the manner, now makes conquest of the matter of verse. (*SR*, 104)

With this background in place, Pound asserts a connection between this tradition and the English lyric: "[a]fter the Trecento we get Humanism, and as the art is carried northward we have Chaucer and Shakespeare" (*SR*, 93).

A set of rough notes for one of his 1909 lectures concisely summarizes this use of Romance languages to propose a transnational European literary tradition. It notably makes a distinction between "symptomatic" authors who reflect the dominant spirit of their time and "donative" authors, who transmit an essential "*virtù*" across cultural and formal boundaries.[15] To illustrate the work of these "donative authors" Pound drew up a rough chart of European literary history which progresses from the medieval Latin writers of Italy through Elizabethan England:

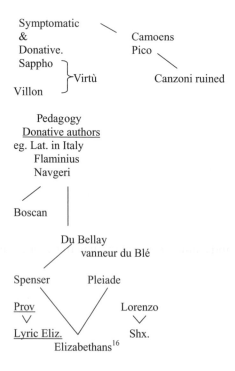

ROMANCE LANGUAGES AND EZRA POUND'S POETIC
DEVELOPMENT

Together with this historical overview, Pound's notes describe his intention
to study technical advances by medieval Romance writers in six areas:

1. rhythms
2. rime
3. diction
4. economy
5. observation of nature
   ? visionary interpretation . . .
6. music[17]

In his own early work he drew on such investigation of the technical
resources of Romance poetry to widen the possibilities available to him
in English verse. In poems such as "Na Audiart," "Dompna Pois de me
No'us Cal" or "Langue d'Oc," he sought to reproduce the musicality of
Provençal verse, which, he claimed in *The Spirit of Romance*, "melt[ed]
the common tongue and fashion[ed] it into new harmonies depending
not upon the alternation of quantities but upon rhyme and accent" (*SR*,
22). In so doing, he began to take a critical attitude toward conventional
English rhythm, adopting a stance that he would later formulate in terms
of the imagist doctrine that the poet should "compose in the sequence of
the musical phrase, not in sequence of a metronome" (*LE*, 3).

In his early volumes of poetry, Pound repeatedly used precedents from
Romance literature as models for his own writing. His first collection, *A
Lume Spento* (1908), included poems on French, Italian, and Provençal
themes. This continued in later volumes as he experimented with increasingly sophisticated literary personae and adaptations of poetic forms from
Romance literature. *Personae* (1909) contained repeated returns to medieval
Provence and Italy, including "Alba Belingalis," a new attempt at translating
the poem he had first encountered while studying with Shepard at Hamilton. The bulk of *Canzoni* (1911) was preoccupied with adaptations of the
canzone, ballata, and sonnet forms of the Italian trecento, and later collections like *Ripostes* (1912) and *Lustra* (1916) included renewed engagements
with the poetry of Provence, medieval France, and Italy.

The danger in such use of medieval Romance literature was that of
falling into a sterile aestheticism that withdrew from the contemporary
world in order to celebrate past beauty. It was a risk Pound occasionally
acknowledged, for example in "Revolt – Against the Crepuscular Spirit

in Modern Poetry," where he declared his intention to "shake off the lethargy of this our time" (*CEP*, 96). For Pound, however, any such revolt necessitated a vital engagement with the poetic tradition. So, over the first decade of his career, he experimented with ways of inhabiting the imaginative spaces opened by the poetry of medieval Provence, Italy, and France while striving at the same time to achieve a resolutely modern perspective in his own writing. By the time he came to write a poem like "Near Perigord" in 1915, his treatment of subject matter based on his study of troubadour verse was coupled with a sophisticated exploration of the formal repertoire he would employ in *The Cantos*, including temporal juxtapositions which work to establish a synchronic rather than diachronic presentation of time.[18] In the same way, his prolonged engagement with the poetry of Guido Cavalcanti helped Pound attain the formal clarity that typifies his epic poem. In part because of his tireless study of the Romance tradition, Pound's own finest writing in *The Cantos* achieves the quality he so admired in Cavalcanti's "Donna mi prega," and that he sought to celebrate with his translation of the poem in Canto xxxvi: "the suavity of a song . . . the neatness of a scalpel-cut" (*LE*, 159).

NOTES

1 For a succinct description of how Pound's appreciation of Cavalcanti's work evolved from his early Pre-Raphaelitism to the more sophisticated vision of Canto xxxvi, see Reed Way Dasenbrock, "Guido Cavalcanti Rime," in *The Ezra Pound Encyclopedia*, ed. Demetres P. Tryphonopoulos and Stephen J. Adams (Westport, CT: Greenwood Press, 2005), 141–3.

2 Ezra Pound, *EP to LU: Nine Letters Written to Louis Untermeyer by Ezra Pound*, ed. J.A. Robbins (Bloomington: Indiana University Press, 1963), 15.

3 For a summary of the state of comparative literature in American academia at the time see K.K. Ruthven, *Ezra Pound as Literary Critic* (London: Routledge, 1990), 6.

4 See J.J. Wilhelm, *The American Roots of Ezra Pound* (New York: Garland Publishing, 1985), 123–40, for the most complete account of Pound's studies at Hamilton College.

5 See Walter Pilkington, "Introduction," in *Letters to Ibbotson, 1935–1952*, ed. Vittoria I. Mondolfo and Margaret Hurley (Orono: University of Maine Press, 1979), 3.

6 See Wilhelm, *The American Roots of Ezra Pound*, 144. This subject was rejected by the Latin Professor, W.B. McDaniel, who objected that the faculty "shd. have to do so much work ourselves to verify your results" (*GK*, 215).

7 Yale University, Beinecke Library, YCAL MSS43, Box 137, folder 5947. Ezra, Pound, The Ezra Pound Papers. Beinecke Rare Book and Manuscript Library, Yale University. All quotations from these papers are from previously

unpublished material © 2010 by Mary de Rachewiltz and Omar S. Pound. Used by permission of New Directions Publishing Corporation.

8 Ezra Pound, *I Cantos*, trans. Mary de Rachewiltz (Milan: Mondadori, 1985).

9 Mary de Rachewiltz, "Afterword: *Ubi Cantos Ibi America*," in *A Poem Containing History: Textual Studies in The Cantos*, ed. Lawrence S. Rainey (Ann Arbor: University of Michigan Press, 1997), 268.

10 See Peter Makin, *Provence and Pound* (Berkeley: University of California Press, 1978), 3: "[Pound's] technical incompetence in Provençal was considerable . . . He was not incapable; in his final dealings with Arnaut Daniel, for example, he showed that armed with a crib in one foreign language he was quite capable of resolving the very intricate difficulties in another. But he was unwilling."

11 Harvard University, Houghton Library, bMS Am 2077 (576), folder 7.

12 Yale University, Beinecke Library, YCAL MS43, Box 8, folder 385. Pound's comparison between Lope's and Shakespeare's dawn reappears, in a truncated form, in *The Spirit of Romance* (*SR*, 209).

13 Yale University, Beinecke Library, YCAL MSS43, Box 69, folder 3083. p. 1.

14 For a discussion of these lectures see Moody, 116–17.

15 In "Medievalism" Pound offers the following explanation of the term "virtù": 'There is the residue of perception, perception which requires a human being to produce it. Which may even require a certain individual to produce it. This really complicates the aesthetic. You deal with an interactive force: the *virtù* in short' (*LE*, 151–2).

16 Yale University, Beinecke Library, YCAL MSS43, Box 137, folder 5947, pp. 1–2.

17 Yale University, Beinecke Library, YCAL MSS43, Box 137, folder 5947, p. 1.

18 For a discussion of Pound's poetic technique in "Near Perigord" see Terri Brint Joseph, *Ezra Pound's Epic Variations: The Cantos and Major Long Poems* (Orono, ME: National Poetry Foundation, 1995), 55–78.

CHAPTER 5

Letters

Demetres P. Tryphonopoulos

Pound was a persistent letter writer no matter where he was. From Wabash College in Indiana to the Disciplinary Training Center in Pisa or St. Elizabeths Hospital in Washington, he wrote to defend, cajole, instruct, and inspire. He wrote to writers, students, senators, publishers, newspapers, critics, friends, and enemies. His letters were guides, manifestoes, reports, and political statements. They agitated, praised, complained, and celebrated cultural follies, historical achievements, and individual works. They were never dull. Disciples and presidents, girlfriends and professors were his recipients. His first publication was a letter in the form of a poem to the Jenkintown, PA *Times Chronicle* in 1902. Nearly his last were letters written almost up to his death to William Cookson, editor of *Agenda*.

Many letters were literary in their focus. To Harriet Monroe, editor of *Poetry*, for example, he would often complain, criticize, and occasionally compliment her selections, while also demanding that she print new poets like Frost and Eliot. To William Carlos Williams, he praised his work, but urged him to get out of New Jersey and over to Europe. To Margaret Cravens, he wrote personal letters expressing his appreciation of her support. But his letters also became a platform for his more controversial and extreme views.

Though ignoring the often objectionable gradations of ideologies and beliefs held by Pound in the late 1920s and beyond is no longer tenable for critics and/or readers, it would be easier (though not defensible) to rationalize them or minimize their potency were one to be concerned only with the poetry or even only with the poetry and criticism. Attempts to defend or ignore Pound's transgressions become absurd in the face of certain of his letters, especially given the fact that in many of them he offers opinions and views that are more clearly expressed and more raw and frank, even if they are not different in import, from the same opinions as these are depicted in his essays and poetry.

It is widely acknowledged, then, that Pound's controversial (and objectionable) views are present in all of his writing, including his letters – letters that, moreover, are more often than not as cryptic and allusive as any of the later poetry; but even if we were willing to gloss over instances where such views are expressed in the poetry and some of the prose, we are unable to do so while faced with the naked truth of the letters in which Pound, speaking in the first-person singular, registers directly and unambiguously – if in a language that is idiosyncratic, aggressive, and exigent – what he thinks. Nevertheless, the most disturbing difference between the poetry and prose on the one hand and several of his letters on the other is surely the way Pound responds when he is invited by his correspondents, especially in letters exchanged during his St. Elizabeths years, to reconsider his views: his pig-headed refusal to entertain the possibility that he may be or have been wrong and offer some expression of apology, regret, or repentance is both a sign of his intransience but also represents, I believe, the strength of his convictions – however wrong-headed – and his frustration at his correspondents' unwillingness or failure to be persuaded to his way of thinking.

For every instance of something objectionable expressed or implied in the poetry and criticism, there are several examples of the same thing in the letters he wrote, especially those he wrote during his St. Elizabeths period (1945–58).[1] To date, thirty-one volumes of Poundian correspondence have been published; in his lifetime, Pound wrote a total of approximately a quarter of a million letters; and the Beinecke archive at Yale (the major depository archive of Poundiana) contains letters to hundreds of individuals and dozens to editors of journals. Academic and trade presses have been eager to publish Pound's correspondence in order to satisfy, it seems, the insatiable appetite of scholars and readers. Obviously, both literary critics and biographers have put to good use Pound's letters – the former (and older) of these critics, drawing mostly from the early D.D. Paige volume (now titled *Selected Letters*), have used them along with Pound's essays to provide information about his literary activities, his tradition of reading, the movements he initiated or participated in, his literary and artistic affinities, and especially his aesthetics; and the latter have used them to discover or confirm facts about his life, his discovery or championing of various writers, including for instance James Joyce and T.S. Eliot, but also for the proof they provide so copiously of his controversial opinions.

It is difficult to summarize or characterize Pound's vast output or the significance of the various kinds of letters he wrote during his lifetime. He did rely on several major subjects, however: literature and literary history;

politics; and economics. Persistent was a didactic tone that instructed the reader to act, to read, to discover. Three representative correspondences, the first two written over a longer period while the third covers Pound's St. Elizabeths period, illustrate these features. As limited as this approach might be, it is intrepidly designed to argue for the silliness of some of Pound's misguided ideas and make the case, first, for his famous obstinacy and, second, for his megalomaniacal, obsessive confidence in his ideas and reading of history, especially economic history. The three recipients are H.L. Mencken, Olivia Rossetti Agresti (or ORA as Pound calls her), and Archibald MacLeish.

Whether he is discussing literary history or art, aesthetics or economics, American history or anthropology, or scores of other topics, Pound always presents himself as the teacher. His "Ezuversity" (largely operating through his correspondence) is the place where many of his students, both those who were willing and those who did not wish to do so, had to attend. Though he did have his successes with several of his students (James Laughlin is one example), Mencken, Agresti, and MacLeish were reluctant and often antagonistic pupils. Especially interesting is the attempt and result of Pound's campaign to educate the elder statesman of American letters, H.L. Mencken, with whom he corresponded for four decades (1914–52).

The early letters between Pound and Mencken deal mostly with literary matters; but a few, beginning in the 1920s, wander off into topics such as Major Douglas' "Social Credit" theories and various political matters. It is not until the mid 1930s and again in 1937 and 1939, however, that animated and heated discussion of economics emerges, briefly, as a major motif. For instance, an outburst by Pound, whose exact cause remains elusive, kicks off an epistolary quarrel.

Writing on November 3, 1936, Pound accuses Mencken of being "as cowardly as Roosevelt's campaign speeches . . . Mencken is America's prize coward and evader" because he suffers from the inability or refusal "to express an honest opinion about anything." Here in part is Mencken's acerbic response (November 28, 1936) to what he calls Pound's "somewhat behind-hand . . . tirade":

You made your great mistake when you abandoned the poetry business, and set up shop as a wizard in general practice. You wrote, in your day, some very good verse, and I had the pleasure, along with other literary buzzards, of calling attention to it at the time. But when you fell into the hands of those London log-rollers, and began to wander through pink fogs with them, all your native common sense oozed out of you, and you set up a caterwauling for all sorts of brummagem Utopias, at first in the aesthetic region only but later in the regions of political and aesthetic baloney. Thus a competent poet was spoiled to make a tin-horn politician.

Your acquaintance with actual politics, and especially with American politics, seems to be pathetically meagre. You write as if you read nothing save the *New Masses*. Very little real news seems to penetrate to Rapallo . . . [2]

Reacting to Pound's charges about his lack of political backbone, Mencken is forced to explain to his correspondent his failure in misdirecting his energies and the plain fact that, choosing to live in virtual exile in Rapallo, Italy (where Pound had been residing since the mid 1920s), he has limited acquaintance with current political reality and is hardly entitled to an opinion. Following some back-peddling on both sides, this flare-up subsides and is not resumed until October 27, 1939, with Pound writing from Rapallo following his return from his 1939 trip to the United States. Here, Pound tries to enlighten Mencken about, among other things, the war. Moreover, this is the first letter in the correspondence containing some alarming allusions to a Jewish conspiracy ("It's a jew's War on europe. Any other race wd. admit it and perhaps be proud"), attacking those who are trying "to get american boys out to fight for the interest on britsch loans," pointing out that "god damn Frankie Roosenstein [is] our 32nd and damn near worst president," and concluding that "About 90% right and justice on the German side."

Given Mencken's well-known German leanings, one would have expected a more sympathetic response to at least some of Pound's speculations. Instead, Mencken seems rather cautious in his November 13, 1939 letter: he mentions his view of the US government's "imbecility," speculates that Roosevelt is "falling for every fraud of the British propaganda bureau" and shall lead his nation "into the war whenever he gets word from his English friends [which] . . . will come the moment Hitler begins to sweat them"; but he also confesses that he sees himself as "no prophet and no military critic" and, thus, has chosen to maintain "a discreet silence on the subject."

Pound's next letter (November 16, 1939) must have been written before he had seen Mencken's letter of November 13, 1939; it repeats many of the speculations contained in the one of October 27, 1939:

Someday you will have to pay MORE attention to things I have been boring people with for 20 years/ . . . and that Americans like ourselves KNEW something about up till 1863 when the U.S. was finally shat on by J. Sherman of Ohio working for the Rothschilds and N.Y. fahrts (Ikleheimer etc.) . . .

Social Credit (admitting that they are the worst organizers god ever let live) . . .

Also interview MacNair Wilson, a mild old episcopalian who has an eye on the gold exchange, and interworking of brit kike...
Imperial Chemicals, and Monds (Melchett) and Manshitster Guardian.
I haven't been able to get a line re/ who <u>sold</u> gas masks to 44 billyum brits. – Imp Chem or subsidiary?? THAT wd. or shd/ be news.
Fer garzacke show a little human curiosity...
You cd/ at least start the Sun correspondent on ENQUIRING econ if your Jewsfelt gang wont print anything detrimental or likely to keep America out of war.

This represents a cryptic but nonetheless unambiguous rehearsal of Pound's economic theories which were over twenty years in the making, including the implication (made more or less overtly) for the existence of a conspiratorial theory of history according to which American and foreign banks allegedly conspire and influence legislators and the public for their own profit.[3]

Pound must have been discouraged and baffled by Mencken's refusal to agree with him on monetary issues and his obstinacy in insisting in his letters on subjects such as the imminence of Roosevelt's decision to enter World War Two on the side of his British friends or the President's eagerness to run for another term.[4] Pound's palpable frustration is rooted in his failure to interest Mencken in "serious" discussion of economics and represents his general lack of success in tempting established literary, economic, and political thinkers to take seriously his monetary ideas.

The Agresti correspondence (1937–59) has the distinction of being the first one to be purchased by the Beinecke. It provides a cogent if distressing record of what Pound thought during his St. Elizabeth's years. Along with "Signora Agresti," who is mentioned in the opening lines of canto LXXVI, Pound believed that Mussolini's economic insights regarding the "Corporative State" could be neither suppressed nor destroyed – even after the breakdown of the fascist political system. Approval of Mussolini does not, however, necessarily entail a corresponding approval of Hitler – at least it is not so in ORA's case. Pound mentions Hitler in a number of his letters to ORA; clearly, he is attracted to some of the Fuehrer's ideas, including what he calls "H's monetary sanity" and his "intelligence about currency." The most interesting reference to Hitler is the one found in an October 31, 1953 letter:

Are you getting an italian edtn/ of Hitler's Table Talk ["Hitler's Secret Conversations"]?
Crazy as a coot, as Mus/ noted on first meeting him. BUT with extraordinary flashes of lucidity. He smelled the idiocy of judeo-xtianity, but had no basis either in Aristotle or Confucius...

Adolf had alzo a lucid moment re/ soja [soya]. plus some disordered profundities/ a quick or sharp mind rather than a powerful one.

ORA is clearly neither an anti-Semite nor a Hitler admirer; her response to Pound's inquiries about Hitler's *Table Talks* is direct and categorical:

I have not read Hitler's Table Talk and do not know whether an Italian translation is being published. But do not trouble to send it to me as I have much on hand now and should not have time to do more than glance at it . . . To my mind Hitler was a man of genius who was a monomaniac, and a dangerous one. Anybody who can deliberately not only plan but actually carry out the extermination of some six million people because they belong to a race which he regards as dangerous – the Jews – is to my mind a homicidal maniac, and his tragedy and that of the world was that he was accepted by a nation whom [to which] loyalty to a leader will lead to any excess.[5] (November 18, 1953)

ORA's refusal to engage in a dialogue about Hitler silences Pound. Pound's skirting of the holocaust – in 1953 – is the very point ORA takes exception to upon the mention of Hitler's name; uncharacteristically, Pound does not return to the subject of the *Table Talks* in the rest of this correspondence.[6]

Pound's views on Hitler also surface in the context of his correspondence with Archibald MacLeish. The two corresponded regularly in the twenties and thirties, but of particular interest are the letters they exchanged during the time, beginning in late 1955, when MacLeish was trying to engineer Pound's release from St. Elizabeths. Whatever MacLeish may have thought about Pound the poet and man, he had concluded that the reputation of the United States would suffer greatly were Pound to die in captivity. In the course of the delicate negotiations MacLeish conducted on Pound's behalf with Dr. Winfred Overholzer and the US government, he had to raise with the prisoner (and satisfy his own mind about) the degree of Pound's commitment in the mid 1950s to his earlier positions on Jews, economic conspiracies, fascism, and the like. In other words, Pound was offered an opportunity by MacLeish to revisit his positions of the late 1930s to the mid 1940s and to provide some evidence of what post-World War II experience (such as the Pisan experience and that of his St. Elizabeths incarceration) might have taught him.

Repeatedly, MacLeish makes an effort to elicit from Pound some recognition of the gravity of his situation, the enormity of some of his errors, and the wrong-headedness of some of his positions – with no perceptible success.[7] When in early June 1955 MacLeish tries, as he does on a number of other occasions, to pin Pound down by asking directly whether he would oppose his (MacLeish's) efforts given that they need take place within certain parameters, Pound responds (predictably and infuriatingly) with such evasive and inane pronouncements as "Obviously it is the kikes keeping me in here"; "Ez considers anti-Semitism unaristotelian and unscientific and that every man black yellow red or pink (as to cuticle) should be judged on his own merits"; and "As per Kuchur, dedicated to Basil [Bunting] and [Louis] Zuk[ofsky] – a Jew and a Quaker." Pound thus ignores MacLeish's opinions; in place of a "sign" of his understanding of his position he offers "luminous details" and, as he does in a letter quoted below, challenges MacLeish himself to use historical data to prove "when he thinks that I am nuttz" and "provide specific facts indicating where I go gooky."

Later on in the same year, MacLeish reports to Pound that it may be better that they wait until after the 1956 election for making a bid to free him; astoundingly but perhaps not unexpectedly (after all, by the early 1950s Pound seems to have become comfortable with his situation at St. Elizabeths, so much that it turned out to be one of his most productive "literary" periods), Pound is unperturbed about prolonging his "eleven year captivity" and continues – in his usual way – to deny, equivocate, and goad MacLeish, urging him to commit to the "Ezuversity" pedagogy and worldview:

To Archer 6 august
No, I don't ask you to spit on FDR, merely to admit that neither you nor he were or are absolootly infallible, that the low down cad and liar may have erred in some [of] his judgments.
I dunno whom you mean as the prospective Muss-Hitler, I didn't know you estimated some of the buzzards as highly as all that [that was McCarthy].
Very difficult after 30 years in Europe and eleven in captivity to estimate the allergy to civilization in some quarters.
Wars are made to make debt, and your old Fuhrer's war was bloody successful . . .

Later on in the same letter, he continues in a similar vein, championing certain of Hitler's ideas as he has done earlier in his October 31, 1953 letter to ORA from which I have quoted above:

I trust no Russian and damn few Jews.
Hitler had to be stopped/ no contest on that, but the man who first stopped him at the Austrian border was a wop
The enemy is iggurance/ and the Axis was made in London . . .
And brought Roosie's Muscovite friends into Europe instead of keeping them where they belonged East of Poland.
There was quite a good documentary on TV showing why Adolf had to be stopped, but giving no justification for going at it the wrong way.
The ballyhoo about Adolf was to keep your arboreal mind off FDR

And there were no gas ovens in Italy, a fact still concealed from the majority of the debauched yank-lectorate.

Pound repeats the phrase "there were no gas ovens in Italy" in a later letter to MacLeish. This, despite MacLeish's encouragement, is all he had to say about the subject of the Holocaust in this correspondence. Again, what he says might seem to imply an acknowledgement that there were gas ovens in Germany, but Pound refuses to say so directly.

MacLeish came to feel that the less Pound knew about the "elegant solution" he was trying to arrange, the better the chances for its success. Pound was sensitive to and cognizant of this and, on occasion, it infuriated him. But MacLeish stood his ground and often responded by challenging Pound as he does in the following letter of October 26, 1957, which, moreover, echoes the tone and substance of Mencken's November 28, 1936 letter from which I have quoted above:

I won't try to meet the left swings and right hooks in your last two letters. I can't discuss Harvard with you because you know nothing about it. I can't discuss the complicated matter of English common Law in American Courts because you don't use the precedents. (If you come across anything as nutty as that clipping about impeaching the Supreme Court in the acre of literature where you do know the vocabulary you wouldn't even bother to scrape it up). And I can't and won't discuss FDR with you because your information is all second hand and distorted. You saw nothing with your own eyes. And what you did see – Fascism and Nazism – you didn't understand: you thought Musso belonged in Jefferson's tradition and God knows where you thought Hitler belonged. I think your views of the history of our time are just about as wrong as they can be. But I won't sit by and see you held in confinement because of your views.[8]

As these and other letters demonstrate, Pound had no intention of reconsidering or compromising his views nor of cooperating with those wishing to secure his release; he continued to believe in the validity of his own opinions and actions and to suspect both the system and individuals who would not be persuaded (would not be educated) to accept what (forever) for him were self-evident facts and truths. MacLeish, nonetheless, went on to orchestrate Pound's release because, as he tells Pound, he was able to persuade himself and convince others that a man should not be locked for ever in a mental hospital for something he said without trial. This would not have happened had the question been whether Pound was still a fascist, or whether he was willing to deny the holocaust, or whether he had regrets over his Radio Rome broadcasts.

Ezra Pound remains one of the most controversial figures in literature, which his letters repeatedly confirm: the controversy is rooted in his politics, anti-Semitism, and championing of fascism. That Pound and his poetry have not been dismissed outright but remain, rather, the centre of much contentious debate is, arguably, a consequence of the scale of his aesthetic influence and the incomparability of his poetry – and it is also indubitably to the "Republic's" credit that Pound was set free in 1958, and at a time when the ovens of Auschwitz had hardly cooled off, he was awarded the Bollingen-Library of Congress award for poetry for the *Pisan Cantos* (1949). Finally, while Pound continues to be a controversial figure, his letters to three of his many correspondents discussed here offer us firm evidence for his racial, political, and economic inanities – something that is not readily available in other forms of his writing, with the exception, surely, of the Rome Radio speeches. But his letters as a whole, despite their stridency and insistence, provide an essential compass for understanding modernism; as he explained to Basil Bunting in 1936, "the poet's job is to *define* and yet again define till the detail of surface is in accord with the root injustice" (*SL*, 277).

NOTES

1 The major collections of Pound manuscript material (including his correspon-
dence) are the following: The Beinecke Rare Book and Manuscript Library,
Yale University; The Berg Collection, New York Public Library; The Butler
Library, Columbia University; The Lilly Library, Indiana University, Blooming-
ton, Indiana; The Manuscript Division, Library of Congress; The Humanities
Research Center, University of Texas at Austin; and The Special Collections,
Van Pelt Library, University of Pennsylvania.

2 Pound to H.L. Mencken; H.L. Mencken to Pound, Manuscript Collection,
New York Public Library, New York, New York. All subsequent quotations,
pp. 56–58, are from this collection. All are previously unpublished but will
all appear in the *H.L. Mencken and Ezra Pound Correspondence*, ed. Demetres
Tryphonopoulos (New York: Oxford University Press, forthcoming).

3 Pound corresponded with Willis A. Overholser for a few years (1938–40) and
with Robert McNair Wilson for twenty-five years (1934–59); the first is the
author of *A Short Review and Analysis of the History of Money in the United
States* (1936) while the latter wrote several books, including *Monarchy or Money
Power* (1933). Pound discovered in these books (and elsewhere) the "evidence"
for a conspiratorial history of money, including the assumption that bankers
conspire (with governmental complicity) against their customers to take control
of the economy.

4 This should explain the following feeble attempt to interest Mencken (March
24, 1940):

NO american journalist ever hears anything of interest. Look at "Time", all the marginalia. Never the roots./ I keep on hopin to interest you in how the wheeze works. Have you had read Overholzer's little booklet? 2. Are you beginning to think that 23 years work on my part aren't just an idle whim, and that I am still an economic crank AFTER I have compared all the rival systems and correlated as many facts as has been humanly possible. and have NOT been sold on any one sect, but dug out some horse sense that is common to the four best ones . . .

5 Pound in *"I Cease Not to Yowl": Ezra Pound's Letters to Olivia Rossetti Agresti*, ed. Demetres P. Tryphonopoulos and Leon Surrette (Urbana: University of Illinois Press, 1998), 126, 130.

6 The book's American title was *Hitler's Secret Conversations, 1941–1944* (1953; New York: Octagon, 1981). Considering Pound's apparent admiration for Hitler's *Table Talks*, which he read in early 1953, it is interesting to recall a story that circulated during the late 1940s, according to which sometime in late 1942 or early 1943 Pound visited Berlin and met with Hitler. An August 26, 1943 ORA letter makes it clear, however, that while such a trip was contemplated, it did not take place.

7 In one of his responses Pound wrote:

> No, ten thousand times No, it does not depend on view of Hitler/ I take it we are agreed that Adolf had to be stopped.
> Mus. had army on frontier and stopped Adolf's first attempt at Anschluss
> And later said, "nobody asked me and nobody thanked me for it."
> It was the damnable betrayal of Italy, starting with Versailles.
> Mus. first meeting with Adolf "That guy is completely nuts."
> France had flopped in 70 and 14, The sheer iggurnt idiocy of not maintaining balance of power in Europe
> I did not think I could educate, beyond a certain point and given time, Muss/ in the sense you take it/ I said that an intelligent wop considered that was the Job for those who knew something Mus.didn't . . . It was shitting on Mus. Italy preferring American to german alliance.
> As long as you think in blurs and refuse C. H. Douglas's definition of liberty : right to choose one thing at a time. And reject all Gourmont on dissociation of ideas etc. you will fall into traps. (January 17, 1956; Pound [Box 18] Archibald MacLeish Papers, Ms. Division, Library of Congress, Washington, D.C.)

All subsequent quotations, pp. 60–61, 62–63, are from this collection. Since Pound had not always insisted that "Hitler had to be stopped," it is curious that in this correspondence he sacrifices Hitler in order to rescue Mussolini. Moreover (in a letter dated January 19, 1956), Pound does not focus on what Mussolini may or may not have accomplished in Italy but chooses to talk about Mussolini in the context of European politics and his role as the right counterbalance to Germany (*ibid*).

8 Pound responded on October 29, 1957 as follows:

> My knowledge of FDR is direct as to his dirty voice tape recorded. As to the action of the Treasury in ten vols. And a few other details . . .

I did NOT think Muss was modeling himself on Jeff but that Mazzini should be made more use of and that the historic development can be traced

I never spoke about Germany precisely because I had not specific details and everything in my Jeff is firsthand

You absolutely 100% refuse to consider what position I did take, but for the nth time

No one but the German will bother to educaet the godamned Russian and keep the damned muji out of Europe

Nothing but a strong Italy could have made a balance to keep German power getting too big for its boots.

If you would look at a little history, damn it.

CHAPTER 6

Editor, anthologist

John G. Nichols

Ezra Pound's contributions to the formation of modernism are often recognized with regard to his constant experiments in poetic form, his literary criticism, and his mentoring (and occasional editing) of fellow modernists. His editorship of several poetry anthologies also point to his significance in the inception and coalescence of modernism as an aesthetic movement and academic field. Pound's four anthologies – *Des Imagistes* (1914), *Catholic Anthology* (1915), *Profile* (1932), *Active Anthology* (1933) – reveal his critical revision of the dominant forms of the anthology in order to produce readers as stewards of literary innovation.

Pound's anthologies bookend what Chris Baldick has termed a "great age of anthologies," when such literary compilations became a primary vehicle for circulating – and in the process defining – contemporary, modernist verse.[1] From the mid-teens through the early 1930s, an array of editors endeavored to fashion anthologies for a wider readership after World War I, when a general audience swelled to include student populations, largely made up of middle-class adolescents who enrolled in high school and university literature courses. Such editors included little magazine editors such as Harriet Monroe, literary reviewers such as Louis Untermeyer and Marguerite Wilkinson, and poets such as Conrad Aiken, Alfred Kreymborg, Amy Lowell, Edith Sitwell, and Ezra Pound.

Anthology editors' methods of selecting, and more significantly, introducing readers to the new poetry depended upon whether their anthologies targeted a "mainstream," general audience (which prior to 1930 included academic audiences) or select or "coterie" readerships. Louis Untermeyer and Harriet Monroe, editors of the era's more popular literary anthologies, provided editorial guidance for their general and academic readers by including ample prefaces and authorial biographies. For example, Untermeyer's *Modern American Poetry* (published in six editions from 1919 to 1950) and Monroe's *The New Poetry* (published in 1917 with revised editions in 1923 and 1932) focused primarily on literature from 1890 to the present and went through several editions that were marketed to both general and academic audiences. Both editors' anthologies featured lengthy explanatory prefaces, brief critical assessments, and biographies that attempted to define new literary movements and categorize emergent authors.

Most significantly, Untermeyer's and Monroe's anthology formats circulated an image of modernist verse as unequivocally established elements of a literary canon, for both organized poetry in ways that de-emphasized the literary and political conflicts inherent in anthology and canon formation, or what Marjorie Perloff has described as a "corporatization of information" in late twentieth-century anthologies. These texts typically arrange poets alphabetically or chronologically and provide benign biographies as well as favorable criticisms.[2] In a similar fashion, Untermeyer and Monroe invoked a narrative of accessibility that permeated their prefaces and introductions to the poets, emphasizing the new poetry's democratic style, by pointing to the use of "common" speech, dialect, and slang, or what Untermeyer described as the "language not of poetasters but of the people." Both advocated a return to poetic forms of the ballad and folk tale verse, and selected poets such as Whitman, Sandburg, Frost, Lindsay, Robinson, and Master as the dominant poets of the period. Consequently, they established a standard against which other poets were measured for their degree of appeal to "people who never before had read verse . . ."[3]

By contrast, anthologies with coterie associations (by such editors as Edith Sitwell and Alfred Kreymborg) eschewed connections with popular themes or common readers. Instead, they emphasized the new poetry's differences from prior and dominant literary traditions. In contrast to a generic title such as Untermeyer's *Modern American Poetry*, Kreymborg's anthology was entitled *The Others*; Sitwell's anthology bore the ambiguous title, *Wheels*. Coterie collections often printed only the most current poetry, unlike Monroe and Untermeyer's anthologies, which reprinted poets such as Dickinson and Lanier in order to trace new poetry's place within a continuous literary tradition. Coterie anthologies were typically only a fourth the size of mainstream anthologies, usually 100 pages or so compared to the 300 to 600 pages of Monroe's and Untermeyer's compilations. Even their length stressed an interest in presenting avant-garde manifestos rather than bibliographic surveys. While poetry by Sandburg, Frost, and Lindsay dominated more democratically defined anthologies, coterie anthologies displayed a diverse collection of poetry, by such authors as Mina Loy, novelist Evelyn Scott, essayist Nancy Cunard, and photographer Man Ray.

While mainstream anthologies made modernist writing seem established, organized, and accessible, coterie anthologies offered contemporary poetry culled from the latest little magazine. In addition to their titles, historical scope, length, and selections, coterie collections limited – if not abandoned – the kind of editorial apparatus Monroe and Untermeyer used to contextualize the poetry in their mainstream anthologies. Kreymborg's *The Others*, for example, subsumed a more traditional prose preface within a poetic dedication to "the others" that described new poets as "crusaders" who live outside of time (they "sneer" and "snarl" at the past, present, and future), eat "cocoanuts" [*sic*] and aim their poems "at your heads!"[4] No biographies or critical assessments of individual authors appeared. *The Others* concluded with neither indexes to poets or poems nor selected bibliographies. Rather, readers were asked to focus on the poems alone, without contextual, biographical, critical, or historical aid. While Untermeyer and Monroe's anthologies changed some poets and selections with subsequent editions, Kreymborg's and Sitwell's anthologies altered them each year, presenting an annual review of the very latest poetry rather than link poetry to past poetic traditions. Consequently, coterie anthologies represented modernist poetry as an evolving poetic project, and they required readers to constantly await the latest poetic innovations. Mainstream anthologies, even though they acknowledged the embryonic nature of the new poetry, portrayed it as within an ongoing literary tradition, and thus, placed readers in supervisory roles.

Pound's four anthologies explore the range of interactions between potential modernist readers and the new poetry, and thus embodied both coterie and mainstream anthological features. Always, however, Pound radically reimagined the anthology format, whether mainstream or coterie, to insert readers within the flux of literary tradition and selection. Pound argued for anthologies that "worked" or made bold statements in their selection of poets, ideally forcing students into literary debates, but still condemning any anthology that "does ALL their work for 'em" (*EPJL*, 269).

His four compilations reflect Pound's efforts in charting modernism's innovations; they display a greater length (from *Des Imagistes'* 63 pages to *Active Anthology's* 255 pages), varied content (works by such authors as T.S. Eliot, Wallace Stevens, Basil Bunting, and Louis Zukofsky), and, more significantly, radically different method of presenting modernist poetry to readers. Published at the onset of his career, Pound's first two anthologies, *Des Imagistes* (1914) and *Catholic Anthology* (1915), abjure explicit explanatory material such as prefaces and introductions. Instead, they favor implicit means of guiding readers through the thematic arrangement of poems, for example. *Imagistes* and *Catholic* are also some of the first modern coterie anthologies. Pound's later two anthologies, *Profile* (1932) and *Active*

Anthology (1933), contain more explicit introductory materials as Pound attempted to reassert his role as a prominent spokesperson for the modernist movement (later he was eclipsed by T.S. Eliot). These two anthologies retain a coterie emphasis on the latest and most experimental poetry, but they move closer to the mainstream anthology format that had dominated the literary market for the prior ten years.

Pound's anthologies, however, overtly engage questions about how to read modernist poetry, questions that other anthologies sidestepped. Unlike coterie anthologies, in which the architecture assumed that readers could handle reading challenges without overt guidance, and unlike mainstream anthologies, in which the format implied that readers could not read without heavy-handed prefaces and introductions, Pound's anthologies enact a complex and continually changing dialogue between readers and a developing contemporary verse. In order to maintain this discussion, Pound's anthologies continually pose the question of how to read a poetry that is defined by its breaking of linguistic codes and literary traditions. His first two anthologies, for instance, feature key poems that thematize reading as a subject, creating situations where readers encounter poems about the act of reading, initiating a metadiscourse on the experience of interpreting modernist writing. They also organize the poetry by style and theme, which invites a comparative reading practice wherein readers range across various poems, rather than organize their interpretation via chronology or by alphabetical listings. Even as Pound's later anthologies incorporate what had by 1930 become standard introductory materials such as prefaces and biographies, they reproduce such formats in a fragmented and deconstructed fashion, consequently challenging the facile contextualization that Untermeyer's and Monroe's anthologies had placed upon modernist poetry. In addition, Pound's anthologies substitute personal harangues for objective prefaces, blur generic distinctions between prose and poetry, and leave foreign phrases untranslated – all attempts to destabilize readerly comfort by subverting what had emerged as typical anthology structures in both coterie and mainstream anthologies.

ANTHOLOGIES AT THE SEAM OF TRADITIONS

Pound's first two anthologies, *Des Imagistes* and *Catholic*, envision modernist poetry as a kind of explanatory apparatus to itself, consequently blurring the lines between an anthology's illustrative prefaces and its collected poetry. On its surface, Pound's first anthology, *Des Imagistes* (1914), seemingly presents its literary works without extended explanation, practically daring readers to engage the poetic experiment of imagism without aid. The poems in *Des Imagistes* are identified according to author, though the order of the authors is neither alphabetical nor chronological. Instead, the poems are arranged according to their thematic and stylistic qualities, such as poems imitating classical or Asian verse traditions. *Des Imagistes* initiates its argument for a new poetry with its first poem, Richard Aldington's "Choricus," which boldly announces a break with the past with the opening line, "The ancient songs / Pass deathward mournfully."[5] Subsequent poems by Aldington, H.D., F.S. Flint, Lowell, and Williams complicate the dismissal of a classical poetic tradition by taking Grecian topics as their themes. However, those themes are updated as they are rendered in free verse, suggesting that imagism's primary focus is reinventing the past for a modern audience. The alternation between ancient images and modern verse culminates in Pound's poems, which contain both classically themed as well as Asian-inspired poems. While Pound's first two poems ("Δώρτα" and "The Return") echo Grecian subjects, the final four titles ("After Ch-uYuan," "Liu Ch'e," "Fan-Piece for Her Imperial Lord," and "Ta'ai Chi'h") are imitations of Chinese poetry. The fragmentary nature of these brief translated poems, so unusual in relation to the other anthologized poems, further cement the perception that imagism was not simply a new poetic movement, but a re-visioning of poetic history.

In *Catholic Anthology* (1915) Pound continues to rely on the collected poems' placement and juxtaposition as a guide to new poetic styles and topics, although here, the interpretative advice stemming from the poetry is more overt. The anthology's interest in literary innovation is mirrored by its cover, designed by Dorothy Shakespear, which resembles the sharp lines of Wyndam Lewis' *Blast* cover for the 1915 war issue. Moreover, as in *Des Imagistes*, the opening poem serves as a preface to the collection. Though Aldington's "Choricus" highlights the emergence of new verse tradition, W.B. Yeats' "The Scholars" imagines a past poetic spirit that has been corrupted by needless meddling. Yeats' poem details the endless, misguided toil of scholars who, "Edit and annotate the lines / That youug [*sic*] men, tossing on their beds / Rhymed out in love's despair / To flatter beauty's ignorant ear."[6] Yeats' poem initiates a call for a rejuvenated approach to living, a directive that the *Catholic Anthology's* more famous poems, Eliot's "The Love Song of J. Alfred Prufrock" and Pound's "In a Station of the Metro" reinforce with their ridiculing of middle-class life and even, as in Pound's poem, the transforming of such a life into Japanese haiku. As in *Des Imagistes*, Pound thematized the conditions of reading and writing literature. After his famous, "In a Station of the Metro," for instance, Pound placed the poem entitled "Further Instructions," which describes a young poet awaiting the fate of his poems in the literary marketplace. In contrast to the several other modernists represented in the anthology – Edgar Lee Masters, Robert Frost, Harriet Monroe, and Alfred Kreymborg – Pound presents his poetry as reflecting upon the process of writing poems and their subsequent position within a literary tradition.

ANTHOLOGIES TOWARD THE MAINSTREAM

Pound's final two anthologies, *Profile* (1932) and *Active Anthology* (1933), change the textual tactics by which his first two anthologies attempted to enlist readers in the project of reading for modernist poetry's startling innovations. Instead of relying solely on implicit interpretative guidance provided by poems about poetry or thematic groupings of poems, Pound's final two anthologies experiment with the more explicit forms of interpretative advice that mainstream anthologies increasingly used by the 1930s, such as prefaces and explanatory footnotes. Pound's incorporation of more overt guidance into his anthologies responds strategically to the dominance of mainstream anthologies in characterizing modernist verse to a wide readership. By the 1930s, such anthologies had marginalized coterie collections and had become the primary means of representing contemporary verse to general audiences. As these anthologies focused more on an academic readership, they began to solidify their hold on both current and future readers by gaining institutional acceptance within college and university literature courses. By the beginning of the 1930s, moreover, Pound's poetic departures from imagism in "Hugh Selwyn Mauberley" and early drafts of *The Cantos* had become characterized as unreasonably challenging, especially by Untermeyer's and Monroe's mainstream anthologies. Consequently, Pound's reliance on explanatory prefaces and notes attest to his interest in aiding readers while countering Untermeyer's and Monroe's claims about his unnecessary elitism. Yet, Pound's anthologies also retain the sense of difficulty that modernist verse produced, something that mainstream anthologies occluded in order to highlight for readers modernism's drive for experimentation and change.

With *Profile* and *Active Anthology*, Pound guides readers by adopting a more visible editorial role by means of prefaces and selected explanatory notes. However, Pound eschews the kind of educative, guiding editorial voice of the sort projected by Untermeyer and Monroe, for he downplays his own editorial authority by urging readers to pass judgement on the anthologies' selections. Often, Pound draws attention to the editorial process, challenging the supposed critical objectivity associated with expert editors. *Profile*, for example, contains a short preface in which Pound asserts that, "I am making no claim to present the 'hundred best poems' but merely a set of poems that have ut supra remained in my memory." By claiming to select poems based on memory, Pound highlighted the deeply personal, subjective criterion that determined poetic value, or as he describes it, "one remembers different sorts of things at different stages of the decay or development of one's taste."[7] As if to suggest how idiosyncratic one's sense of "taste" could be, Pound supplanted the anthology form's reliance on supposedly neutral biographic information for brief editorial commentaries that were interspersed between poems. They range from observations of compared poetic techniques to personal recollections of the lines Ford Madox Ford once recited at a dinner party.

In addition, Pound erases notions of authorship by organizing the anthology according to the significance of the poetic "reform" visible in the writing, arguing that "a change in style does not necessarily imply an absolute progress."[8] While *Profile* invites readers to view change as part of a literary tradition, it does not impose a narrative of teleological improvement onto the selections for readers; rather Pound encourages readers to determine and characterize the kind of change they witness. *Profile* offers a particularly wide range of poetry through which to chart change, for it contains selections as diverse as the poetry of the 1890s, the imagists, and the poetry in the periodical, the *New Masses*.

In *Active Anthology* (1933), published with the help of T.S. Eliot, Pound re-imagined the anthology's construction further still. He sharpened his assertion that anthologies served as essential tools for understanding contemporary poetry in relation to the past, remarking that he and Eliot agreed that, "existing works form a complete order which is changed by the introduction of the 'really new' work."[9] Unlike Pound's other anthologies, *Active Anthology* contains a long preface, though seemingly at the behest of F.V. Morley of Faber and Faber. Pound announces at the beginning of that anthology that he has been asked by Morley to write a fifty-page preface to contemporary poetry, to which Pound replies, "I shall therefore write a preface mainly about something else" and begins a lengthy comparison of his poetics versus Eliot's.[10] The chief point of disagreement Pound wishes to make, interestingly enough, is between their visions of readers. Pound characterizes Eliot as having a "much greater contempt" for readers than he himself does, noting that Eliot sees the need to "correct" readers' tastes through "commentation and elucidation." Pound, however, posits himself as a more egalitarian editor who provides commentary only in order to "turn a searchlight on something or preferably some work or author lying in shadow."[11] Pound's infamous hierarchies of poets (those grouped as geniuses versus those grouped as the starters of fads) suggest that Pound had his poetic preferences just as much as Eliot did. Yet, Pound's remarks about Eliot's and his own views of readers suggest the ways Pound wished to rely upon questions of reading and interpretative guidance to define and delineate modernist authors, in addition to characterizations of debates on poetic style and theme.

Despite Pound's previously self-avowed dislike of any editorial apparatus, *Active Anthology* places footnotes and explanatory material around the work of only one poet – Pound himself. Pound did not edit himself, however. Instead, he permitted John Drummond to make selections from his *Cantos* and Louis Zukofsky to provide notes for them. Zukofsky's notes, in particular, extend beyond brief historical glosses. Zukofsky asserts that the *Cantos* are a "living museum of facts" and he proceeds to quote fragments from the first thirty cantos in order to show how the poems generate a gradual historical progression.[12]

Pound planned to produce three additional anthologies during the 1930s after *Active Anthology*, though for unknown reasons – a lack of a publisher and World War II present themselves as possibilities – he did not. One anthology was to update the modern verse of *Active Anthology*. In yet another anthology, Pound planned to print poems with his marginalia on one side of a poem and T.S. Eliot's notes on the other, as if recording a running commentary between "Rabbit" and "Possum" about the latest modernist poetry. Such a venture suggests Pound's continued interest in producing anthologies that invited readers into literary arguments and to take sides or positions, rather than to accept the neutral prefaces of mainstream anthologies.

While *Active Anthology* concluded Pound's singular efforts in anthologizing poetry during the interwar period, it did not end his attempts to guide readers to examine recent poems for their new contribution to a literary tradition. Pound's later writings resonate with his vision of anthologies as vehicles for educating readers. In *ABC of Reading*, published a year after *Active Anthology*, Pound most succinctly outlined his advice on reading, offering up those famous dictums of "make it new" and "literature is news that STAYS news" and "dichten = condensare" (*ABCR* 29, 92) Frequently overlooked, however, is that *ABC of Reading* concludes with an anthology of readings or what he named "exhibits," by which, with the aid of Pound's notes, readers could read for innovation and change in language and literature. Characteristically, Pound prefaces this section by stating,

"The ideal way to present the next section of this booklet would be to give the quotations WITHOUT any comment whatever. I am afraid that would be too revolutionary. By long and wearing experience I learned that in the present imperfect state of the world, one MUST tell the reader" (*ABCR*, 95). However, as his previous anthologies suggest, Pound encourages readers to take on greater responsibility for interpretation. He continues in the preface that,

> In the present case I shall not tell the student everything. The most intelligent students, those who most want to LEARN, will however encompass that end, and endear themselves to the struggling author if they will read the EXHIBITS, and not look at my footnotes until they have at least tried to find out WHAT THE EXHIBIT IS, and to guess why I have printed it. (*ABCR*, 95)

As if to test the reader's resolve, four of the first five exhibits are in untranslated Italian, French, and Anglo-Saxon, with no footnotes. Though later sections would offer footnotes to translate certain key foreign words, the notes that Pound provides encourage the comparative analysis of style, verse, and rhythm that his prior anthologies had promoted through their scattered notes and introductions. In effect, *ABC of Reading* marks the culmination of Pound's experiment with the anthology form. Pound shifts the anthology's purpose as a compilation of literature to the background, instead foregrounding questions of how to read as a central component to a reader's encounter with literary culture.

Pound's poetic anthologies aimed for an interactive experience with readers that asked them to compare poems so as to repeatedly readjust their reading expectations, conditioning them to accommodate the latest poetic innovation and encouraging them to participate in his vision of a poetic history, what Kathryne Lindberg describes as "a series of revolutions and new inventions."[13] In comparison to mainstream and coterie anthologies from which he alternately borrowed and rebelled, Pound's intervention into the reader's experience can be considered violent, intrusive, and highly directive, even if his direction appears elliptical, fragmented, and obtuse. Such attacks upon readers' interpretative processes were justified, in Pound's eyes, by the dominance of mainstream anthologies by the 1930s. Readers had become "Untermeyered," Pound complained in his letters, such that they "NEVER HEER'D" of those poets he valued, such as Villon or Catullus (*EPJL*, 35). Only through the radical disruption of readers' expectations could Pound introduce readers to the poetic tradition he valued – one based on the flux of innovation. Such an explosive tradition required an anthology form that trained readers to question – as much as accept –

the order and rankings of the poems presented to them, or as Pound argued in a late anthology co-edited with Marcella Spann, *Confucius to Cummings* (1964), "Why is the poem included in the anthology?" should be the primary question put to any reader of an anthology.[14]

NOTES

1 Chris Baldick, *The Modern Movement: 1910–1940* (Oxford: Oxford University Press, 2004), 109.
2 Marjorie Perloff, "Anthologies: Bad Texts or 'Palaces of Wisdom'"? *Chronicle of Higher Education* (April 16, 1999), B6.
3 Louis Untermeyer, ed., *Modern American Poetry: A Critical Anthology* (New York: Harcourt Brace and Company, 1919), 15, 14.
4 Alfred Kreymborg, *Others for 1919: An Anthology of the New Verse* (New York: Nicholas Brown, 1920), v.
5 Pound, ed., *Des Imagistes: An Anthology* (New York: Albert and Charles Boni, 1914), 7.
6 Pound, ed., *Catholic Anthology 1914–1915* (London: Elkin Mathews 1915), 1.
7 Pound, "Preface," in *Profile*, ed. E. Pound (Milan: Giovanni Scheiwiller, 1932), 10, 14.
8 *Ibid.*, 9.
9 Pound, "Praefatio," in *Active Anthology* (London: Faber and Faber 1933), 9.
10 *Ibid.*
11 *Ibid.*, 10.
12 *Ibid.*, 247.
13 Katherine Lindberg, *Reading Pound Reading* (New York: Oxford University Press, 1987), 98.
14 *Confucius to Cummings: An Anthology of Poetry*, ed. Ezra Pound and Marcella Spann (New York: New Directions, 1964), 335.

CHAPTER 7

Education

Matthew Hofer

And if your kids don't study, that's your fault.
Tell 'em. Don't kid yourself, and don't lie.
(XCIX/725)

"*Il nemico è l'ignoranza*": Ezra Pound's daughter Mary de Rachewiltz once identified this terse proposition as her father's "slogan" in the years prior to World War II.[1] It can no less reasonably be understood as a lifelong maxim, an ideal instance of the "gists and piths" (*ABCR*, 92) that motivated and moved the poet, and did so long before he formulated that memorable phrase. Pound's unwobbling belief that "not knowing" is the real enemy gestures with appropriate force and emphasis to the twin functions of "to educate," from a verb suggesting both "to bring up" (*educare*) and "to lead out" (*educere*). That is to say, it invests education with an urgency that applies equally to the family and the polity, one which may be extended without distortion to an ethical responsibility for all serious artists (*aliter*: "the damned and despised *litterati*") (*LE*, 21). During the 1920s Pound concluded that "[t]he aim of state education has been (historically) to prevent people from discovering that the classics are worth reading" (*SPR*, 213). In response, as he became increasingly remote from the centers of culture and higher learning, his pedagogical rhetoric became increasingly concerned with the idea that "the mental life of a nation is no man's private property. The function of the teaching profession is to maintain the HEALTH OF THE NATIONAL MIND" (*LE*, 58).

For Pound, the process of education renders its objects fresh, precise, and vigorous. Even before he encountered the Confucian stone-books that influenced him so deeply, he implicitly shared the Confucian conviction that "[i]f a man keep alive what is old and recognize novelty, he can, eventually, teach."[2] An abiding desire to learn and to teach is a crucial unifying thread among his poems, translations, and critical prose. This desire led Pound to concepts that aim to span ways of knowing. It also led him to many of the stylistic innovations that characterize his body of work and many of the major personae who populate it. Indeed, the tropes most frequently employed to understand the *Cantos* – including the luminous detail, the ideogram, the periplum, the paideuma, and the requirement to "make it new" – each reveal a trace of the Poundian pedagogy that takes ignorance, in any of its forms, as the enemy. Whenever ignorance is the diagnosis, revelation is Pound's cure.

Pound spent much of his mature life battling against what he found decrepit, corrupt, or simply too restrictive in Western education. He began to develop his critique at the University of Pennsylvania (1901–3) while studying for an undergraduate degree he ultimately took in the form of a PhB certificate from Hamilton College in upstate New York (1905). He then gathered data as a graduate student at Penn, where he was effectively dismissed from the PhD program but earned the MA degree in Romance Languages (1907). Further confirmation of the obstructionist tendencies of US higher education followed from his attempts in 1910, 1920, and 1931 to submit other published texts to Penn to fulfill the requirements for the PhD. Unsurprisingly, all of these attempts failed, though he was finally awarded an honorary doctorate by Hamilton in 1939.

Pound summarizes the lessons of his student experience in *Guide to Kulchur* (1938), a book he claimed to have written "for men who have not been able to afford an university education or for young men, whether or not threatened with universities, who want to know more at the age of fifty than I know today, and whom I might conceivably aid to that object" (*GK*, 6). He testifies that his proposal to focus his study on texts "OUTSIDE the list of classic authors included in the curriculum," which he had supported with "the fact that Fellowships are given for research and that a thesis for Doctorate is supposed to contain original *research*," was rejected on the grounds that the faculty would "have to do so much work ourselves to verify your results" (*GK*, 216). An academic obstacle prompted his departure from Penn, when he ran up against a program that restricted upperclassmen from beginning study of a language they had not studied as underclassmen. Both strictures frustrated the young poet's innovative and comparatist commitment to literature, which preceded the sanction of an official academic "field" by decades. A misfit and nonconformist as a student, Pound's academic performance tended to be inversely proportionate to his interest in a subject, as he was unwilling to be conventional in his approach to subjects he cared about (Moody, 15). Moreover, he cultivated few undergraduate friendships and willfully alienated most professors. Yet he did develop close relationships with two, H.D. and William Carlos

Williams, who would become important modernists, and exhibited an easy informality with his few mentors, who genuinely seemed to respect him. During these years, Pound preferred to keep his relationships distant and valued quality over quantity in friends.[3]

As a junior professor, Pound was, once again, anything but an unqualified success. His controversial stint as professor and ostensible chairman of the department of Romance languages at Wabash College in Crawfordsville, Indiana, ended abruptly after just five months in the fall of 1907. With the exception of brief extension lectureships at the London Polytechnic in 1909–10, Pound had to wait more than three decades for another opportunity to teach in an institutional setting. In May 1938, he declined an unsolicited offer, which was won for him by Ford Madox Ford, to return to the United States and join the faculty of Olivet College in Michigan. Despite his by then thoroughly entrenched mistrust of academia, this was not an easy decision. One attraction of Olivet, in addition to a comfortable salary, was that it operated its own press – a requirement according to Pound for a proper modern university. But the poet was convinced he could do more to reform education outside the system than within it, and he was in any event unable to leave a difficult family situation, complicated by an ailing parent, in Rapallo. As a result, after his debacle at Wabash (over which he crowed to Williams that he hoped he had "taught 'em how to run a college"), Pound never again held a regular teaching position in a college or university.[4]

The problem with education, as Pound informed one of his favorite professors of English literature and Hebrew, Rev. Joseph "Bib" Ibbotson, is that "[p]edagogy has often fussed about how to get ideas to the student, long before it had anything substantial or useful to transmit."[5] Sensitive from the outset to a dual standard of substance and utility, Pound habitually imagined alternatives to what he viewed as the inanities of institutional education, a system that prized an ideal of "scholarship" rather than one of "humanity" (*SPR*, 191). He contended that conventional instruction in the liberal arts – as opposed to technical or practical instruction – erected "a barrier, a *chevaux de frise* of books and of mutual misunderstanding" between the degreed and the undegreed (*SPR*, 21). To foster a mode of education that would "give more points of contact with other men," Pound made plans to found a cosmopolitan College of the Arts, close to museums and libraries, for traveling American students and interested others (*SPR*, 122). This initial alternative to conventional education – prior to what James Laughlin has termed the "Network" of his "academy by mail"[6] as well as his legendary "Ezuversity" in Rapallo – may appear by contemporary standards of study-abroad and low-residency programs fairly conventional. In its emphasis on interdisciplinarity through the interaction of the arts, it was, in its time, decidedly radical. Given that all instruction at the College was meant to be offered by practicing artists, Pound arranged for a faculty that spanned the visual and plastic arts as well as literature and music. He even devised a prospectus for the College in June 1913, and optimistically advertised it in *The Egoist* of November 1914 (*SL*, 41–3).[7] But the London-based school he envisioned, which still stands as an idealized projection of his drive to reform education, never materialized to enroll a student.

As a poet and critic, Pound's early pedagogical focus is less concerned with the past-ness of the past than with how the past can be understood in the present. His preferred type of cultural or artistic study found frequent analogy with scientific study and invited the consideration of methods, particularly those that determine the production of knowledge. The 1911 essay "I Gather the Limbs of Osiris," for example, assumes the task of founding a "New Method in Scholarship" predicated on the "Luminous Detail." As a propaedeutic that sets the stage for the ideogrammic method and the collage form of Pound's later work, the modernist method of the luminous detail is "vigorously hostile to the prevailing mode of today – that is, the method of multitudinous detail, and to the method of yesterday, the method of sentiment and generalisation" (*SPR*, 21). It foregrounds the importance of interpretation by way of a series of discrete details that, when presented together without commentary, functions as "a permanent basis of psychology and metaphysics" (*SPR*, 23). These luminous details "govern knowledge as the switchboard governs an electric circuit"; they are, Pound accedes, "hard to find," but "swift and easy of transmission," and "a few dozen facts of this nature give us intelligence of a period" (*SPR*, 23).

The method of the luminous detail anticipates the ideogrammic method, illustrating how a set of accumulated details can promote profound and immediate comprehension of complex epistemological or ontological concerns. However, an ideogram differs from a collection of luminous details in that it depends upon the articulation of "relations" that are "more real and more important than the things they relate."[8] By shifting focus from facts *as facts* to how they are articulated, Pound is able not only to claim that "poetry agrees with science rather than logic" but also to calibrate poetic thinking to "the concrete of nature" in a way that respects the structure of time as it discloses the workings of the world. Through juxtaposition, the ideogrammic method makes available a "bridge whereby to cross from the minor truth of the seen to the major truth of the unseen."[9] This concept both informs the collage method of the *Cantos* and indicates how those poems are designed to instruct as well as delight.

The same concept of the ideogram that governs Pound's poetry also informs the role of teachers in the stewardship of their students. This is not a trivial point. Upon being asked in "The Teacher's Mission" "What ought to be done?," Pound calls sensibly if obviously for reflection, virtue, facticity, and a campaign against "human deadwood" (*LE*, 61). His only revolutionary charge entails the "[d]ispassionate examination of the ideogrammic method (the examination and juxtaposition of particular specimens – e.g., particular works, passages of literature) as an implement for acquisition and transmission of knowledge" (*LE*, 61). The nonintuitive, if not counterintuitive, aspect of the ideogrammic method for use by practicing teachers requires that the poet employ the adjective "dispassionate" for the "examination" he would mandate. It suggests that he expects resistance. Yet the ideogrammic method, as a paradigm for poetic thinking, was by no means meant to be restricted to poetry alone; to the contrary, Pound argued passionately and consistently for its broader educational value.

The "Exhibits" section of *ABC of Reading* addresses the limits of an idealized collage pedagogy that requires the student to look at passages or fragments of text rather than notes that promise to explicate them. In writing of prosodic criticism and literary instruction, Pound says that "The ideal way to present the next section . . . would be to give the quotations WITHOUT any comment whatever. I am afraid that would be too revolutionary. By long and wearing experience I have learned that in the present imperfect state of the world, one MUST tell the reader" (*ABCR*, 95). That is, as a critic, Pound laments that the ideogrammic method of juxtaposition is an inefficient way to present expository prose when he says "one MUST tell," not (only) show. He implies, intriguingly, that this might be different in a perfected world, and a decade later in the essay "Gold and Work" he characterizes "[e]ducation for these people" of Utopia (*SPR*, 337). Yet even in the imperfect present he archly refuses to "tell the student everything," since he expects that those students "who most want to learn" will find the examination of his juxtaposed textual specimens at least "as good a game as Torquemada's [Edward Powys Mathers] cross-word abominations" compiled for the newspaper the *Observer*. This statement points to a deep belief long held by Pound, not only in the potential of education to improve individuals, but also, and concomitantly, in the innate desire of individuals to be properly educated. Here, education is a "game," as learning in Utopia is "almost a joy" (*SPR*, 337).

A faith in the power of and desire for revelation animates *The Cantos*, as it must all ideogrammic production. In the spring of 1922, after the project of writing cantos had stalled for nearly two years, Pound renewed his commitment to revelation in the formal innovation of the Hell Cantos (xIV–xV), his first contemporary additions to his "poem containing history" (*LE*, 86). This response to Eliot's *The Waste Land* conspicuously refuses closure by offering a carefully maintained series of ellipses for the actual names of the damned the poet had consigned to hell. The retention of the final letter, or letters, of each atrophied name was designed to establish a presence-in-absence that provides sufficient purchase on each corrupt figure (and his sin) to allow generations of readers to think actively about which names might plausibly fit in the given blanks.

Whether or not the Hell Cantos are successful as poems, Pound's goal in writing them was to keep people thinking, to keep them vigilant, and maybe even to entertain them. It is an expressly pedagogical objective. The Malatesta Cantos (vIII–xI), composed directly after the Hell Cantos, change the game as they develop the revelatory tactics of the ideogram into a mature form of documentary collage. In these poems Pound suppresses all expository commentary as well as all conventional syntax, presenting instead concrete and still-relevant fragments rescued from the mailbag of a fifteenth-century Italian *condottiere*, the first "major persona" of his long poem. The point, for poetry as for prose, is that "[e]ducation that does not bear on L I F E and on the most immediate and vital problems of the day is not education but merely suffocation and sabotage" (*LE*, 62).

The significance of Pound's educational theory in terms of his practical pedagogy can be traced through his education of his daughter, Mary. In her memoir, the young Mary Rudge recalls learning from the man she called "Babbo" that "[e]ducation is worth nothing unless one has these two habits. Keep quiet, no useless chatter, don't talk to people you do not know. Or say interesting things, generally interesting, not personal." As he taught his daughter to value precision and eschew ambiguity, Pound also encouraged her to read aloud key passages from an "anthology of American literature edited by W. R. Benét and N. H. Pearson" on the principle that the "best way" to learn American history "was through the early American writers." *The Cantos*, of course, teach the same lessons, and do so in much the same manner, "in action, work, in streams and in flashes." When Mary grew older and more skilled, Pound invited her to do translations of English literature into Italian – she was eventually promoted to translating his *Cantos* into Italian – and she recalls feeling "flattered and challenged at being admitted into his workshop," since the "work, learning, was worthwhile, exciting."[10] The equivalence drawn among work, learning, and pleasure is telling, but not more so than the prevailing sense of the pupil as apostle, or the essentially ideogrammic nature of the poet's education of his daughter. All this points to what Pound envisioned for educational reform more broadly – and to how seriously he took it.

During the 1930s, while he was teaching his daughter in Rapallo, Pound also educated all comers in what is most commonly referred to as the "Ezuversity." James Laughlin, who later founded New Directions and became Pound's primary American publisher, offers firsthand insight into the nature of this education in the classics. He says that in Pound's lectures over the lunch table, that the poet "always spoke in the colloquial," "was a superb mimic and had total recall," and made every session "a performance by an actor with many personae" whose "hamming was part of his pedagogy." Laughlin also emphasizes that "[p]arody was part of his pedagogical arsenal," making special mention of Pound's "application of colorful slang to serious topics" (*tapinosis*) as he gave his pupils "Villon and the troubadours, or even Dante, in his vernacular." These same voice-based strategies were often employed in Pound's network of correspondence, which Laughlin figures as an enormous "tutorial of letters," complete with "reading assignments," that "reached hundreds of students, voluntary or involuntary." In reminiscing about Pound and education, the star pupil at the Ezuversity ultimately wonders most about the "lack of interest in Pound's wit," speculating that this oversight can only be explained by the fact that most critics "never had the opportunity to learn from his conversation how central humor was to him as a writer and as a critic."[11]

In education, evaluation mattered to Pound as much as analysis, though he did not believe that "taste" could be either taught or imposed, at least not in the same way as T. S. Eliot. Indeed, he considered this difference to be fundamental, since Eliot's "contempt for his readers has always been much greater than mine, by which I would indicate that I quite often write as if I expected my reader to use his intelligence, and count on its being fairly strong." This approaches something crucial in Pound's idea of education – its ends. That is, as a pedagogue, Pound's definitive goal can be summarized by a particularly resonant refusal: "Damn your taste, I would like if possible to sharpen your perceptions, after which your taste can take care of itself."[12] But even if a teacher cannot teach taste, Pound does assert that taste, like anything else, can be improved. He believes strongly that "[y]ou *can* quite distinctly teach a man to distinguish between one kind of book and another" (*ABCR*, 87). This is not as modest a goal as it might initially appear to be. In fact, this desire to distinguish justifies the project of literary criticism, as well as the allegedly impossible attempt to "teach" literature. It leads, as Pound observes, to the realization that

A great deal of critical rancour has been wasted through a failure to distinguish between two totally different kinds of writing.
A. Books that a man reads to develop his capacities: in order to know more and perceive more, and more quickly, than he did before he read them.
and
B. Books that are intended and serve as REPOSE, dope, opiates, mental beds.

(*ABCR*, 88)

While Pound does not advocate the elimination of category B – he, too, sometimes read purely for pleasure – when speaking as a teacher, he is unembarrassed about giving priority to category A. As "How To Read" makes perfectly apparent, Pound felt that the books that populate the first category define literature, and literature is what matters most. The books that develop readers' capacities not only inform individual thought but also animate communal action. They exist, Pound says, as a sustaining "medium," without which "the whole machinery of social and of individual thought and order goes to pot" (*LE*, 21).

At the end of his life, after he returned to Italy from incarceration in St. Elizabeths, a silence descended on Pound, and his teaching effectively ended. However, in St. Elizabeths, as an aging celebrity with relaxed social privileges, he attracted, and was willing to entertain, a large cohort including a set of politically suspicious epigoni. While it is perhaps unsurprising that a born teacher embittered by a sense of persecution would prefer the company of eager listeners to solitude, Pound's relation to this group – ostensibly the last he instructed in person – is relevant to his history with regard to education. It may very well be impossible to understand this situation with any real critical precision. Yet a pair of anecdotes about the squirrels that populated the asylum grounds where Pound held court suggests two distinct interpretative possibilities. In the more commonly accepted version, Pound, "[s]eated on the hospital lawn, discoursing and feeding the squirrels, was Abelard to a small group of disciples, mostly cranks and youthful acolytes."[13] But in a more ironic and critically self-conscious version of the same basic narrative, after Pound carried "his bathchair out onto the lawn, there to be surrounded by visitors and disciples," "[h]e loved to tease the squirrels. He would tie a peanut to a thread and toss it out to them. When the squirrel took it, he would jerk it away."[14] The question – here framed as metaphor – is whether the aged poet preferred to sustain these particular squirrels or to tease them. To this, no answer will be perfectly clear or entirely satisfying. Issues of postwar repentance versus recalcitrance hang in the balance.

Despite his long history of writing about education that began while he was still a student himself – and it is difficult to find an essay that does not address these questions – Pound's most misunderstood pronouncements about education are probably also his most famous. In *ABC of Reading*, he insists that "[r]eal education must ultimately be limited to men who INSIST on knowing, the rest is mere sheep-herding" (*ABCR*, 84). This statement, turning on the word "limited," is sometimes construed as evidence of a fundamental elitism. However, the assertion made here is not that anyone is innately unteachable, but, rather, that being teachable at the highest levels must invariably presuppose a powerful desire to learn.

A related claim from *Guide to Kulchur*, frequently cited without noting the elaboration that follows it, helps to clarify this distinction. Here, Pound first stipulates that "[t]he dull can neither penetrate the secretum nor divulge it to others," then explains that the "layman" "can only attain the secretum by greater labor [than that needed to discover the secrets of science], by an attrition of follies, carried on until perception is habit" (*GK*, 145). If dullness indicates the lack of an insistence to know (the settled ignorance that is the enemy), laity is merely an inevitable phase of development. Being identified as a "layman" is not properly understood as an assessment of quality or ability: the outsider or non-expert is tested for desire and tenacity, not for genius.

In an important footnote to Ernest Fenollosa's *The Chinese Written Character as a Medium for Poetry*, Pound testifies that the genius of modernist sculptor and artist Gaudier-Brzeska enabled him to read ideograms intuitively – but this was hardly meant to subvert education, or to discourage others from learning and profiting by the ideogrammic method.[15] To the contrary, this is encouragement, bearing witness to what is possible. Pound sometimes espoused something close to an "apostolic" model of apprenticeship, and he did say that "fools can only profane" the mysteries, but he also recognized that folly is always susceptible to attrition. For Pound, as for Confucius, this *is* education, and the argument of *The Unwobbling Pivot* proceeds from it: "What heaven has disposed and sealed is called the inborn nature. The realization of this nature is called the process. The clarification of this process is called education."[16]

NOTES

1 Mary de Rachewiltz, *Ezra Pound, Father and Teacher: Discretions*. Intro. Richard Sieburth (New York: New Directions, 2005), 135.

2 *Confucius*, ed. and trans. Ezra Pound (New York: New Directions, 1969), 199.

3 Gail McDonald, *Learning to Be Modern: Pound, Eliot, and the American University* (New York: Oxford University Press, 1993), 12–16. My sense not only of Pound's education but of his views on educational reform is deeply indebted to this remarkable study.

4 *Ibid.*, 48.

5 Ezra Pound, *Letters to Ibbotson, 1935–1952*, ed. Vittoria I. Mondolfo and Margaret Hurley (Orono, ME: National Poetry Foundation, 1979), 93.

6 James Langhlin, *Pound as Wuz: Essays and Lectures on Ezra Pound* (St. Paul, MN: Graywolf Press, 1987), 42.

7 McDonald, *Learning to Be Modern*, 50–1.

8 Ernest Fenollosa, *The Chinese Written Character as a Medium for Poetry*. ed. Ezra Pound (San Francisco: City Lights Books, 1983), 22.

9 *Ibid.*, 28, 23, 22–3.

10 de Rachewiltz, *Ezra Pound, Father and Teacher*, pp. 110, 112, 149.

11 Laughlin, *Pound as Wuz*, 5, 48, 50, 167.

12 "Prefatio Aut Cimicium Tumulus," Introduction to *Active Anthology*, ed. Ezra Pound, rpt. in *Polite Essays* (New York: New Directions, 1940), 135.

13 McDonald, *Learning to Be Modern*, 203.

14 Laughlin, *Pound as Wuz*, 24.

15 Fenollosa, *The Chinese Written Character*, 30–1.

16 *Confucius*, 99.

CHAPTER 8

Journalism

Eric Bulson

> Men of the future will not give a fahrt for the so-called poets unless they (the poets) combat the blackout of significant historical facts and the falsification of current news.
>
> Ezra Pound[1]

Ezra Pound was a poet first, a journalist second. Throughout his long life, he wrote thousands of literary essays, letters, editorials, and manifestoes for British, Japanese, American, French, and Italian newspapers so that his ideas could be transmitted in a timely fashion. To this day, however, Pound is not really remembered for his journalism, in part, because there is no comprehensive, annotated edition of his articles complete with translations.[2] Anyone trying to read through Pound's journalism is forced to track down a copy of the oversized, twelve-volume collection *Ezra Pound's Poetry and Prose Contributions to Periodicals* (without notes or context), which is hard to come by, or turn to the *Literary Essays* and the *Selected Prose, 1909–65*, both of them organized as a "greatest hits" series that emphasizes Pound's more "literary" side.

Pound's journalism, though occasional, is absolutely critical for anyone with an interest in his life and work. In fact, it was in the columns of the newspapers that he engaged most directly with the public, doing everything he could to get his ideas in circulation. He published "How to Read," for instance, in the book section of the *New York Herald* (1929) and had it reprinted in a Genovese newspaper, *L'Indice* (March 20, 1930) and the Tokyo-based *Japan Times Weekly* (February 20, and March 20, 1930). This mode of communicating with an international public through newspapers was Pound's way of keeping in touch with the world. In the 1910s and 1920s, he was mostly concerned with literary matters, and by the 1930s and 1940s, he shifted his attention to politics, economics, and history. And even if his subjects changed over the decades, his determination to educate the masses remained fixed.

From an early age, Pound realized how important the press was to the formation of public taste and opinion. He started off writing book reviews for *Munsey's Magazine*, *Book News Monthly*, and Ford Maddox Ford's *The English Review*. By 1911, he picked up a regular column in A.R. Orage's *The New Age*, a lively British periodical devoted to art, literature, culture, and socialist politics. It was here that he serialized two of his most influential literary essays, "I Gather the Limbs of Osiris" and "Patria Mia." With the arrival of the "little magazines" in the 1910s, he found a reliable outlet for his book reviews, editorials, commentaries, translations, and manifestoes, working as the "foreign correspondent" for Anglo-American magazines like *The Little Review*, *The Dial*, *Poetry*, and *The Egoist*. In this short period of time, he generated a significant body of critical prose that is required reading for anyone interested in literary modernism.

It was also at the height of the little magazines' heyday, however, that Pound began to have second thoughts about his role as journalist.[3] He was writing 10,000 words a week and began feeling as if his energy was being wasted. Writing articles and reviews in support of one's friends (and one's self) was time-consuming, and considering the meager payments, Pound wasn't always convinced it was worth the effort. "I have been pouring out journalism to pay the rent," he wrote to Margaret Anderson, editor of *The Little Review*. "But I can't get no poetries written. I simply *can't* run the triple ring circus forever" (*EPLR*, 212). But even if it was distracting, Pound could never tear himself away from this kind of editorializing. He had a compulsion to write in order to feel connected with the rest of the world, and for all of his complaints, one thing is certain: journalism acted as an antidote to the isolation that he often felt as the expatriate living in cities around Europe.

But Pound was not your run-of-the-mill journalist. He identified with the famous politicians, writers, and historians who preceded him. "Dickens was a journalist," he wrote in 1937, "Clemenceau was a journalist, Mussolini was and is the greatest of living journalists. America's most vivid historian was, and I suppose still is, a journalist. Henry Adams might have been a journalist if he had had the requisite energy."[4] Théophile Gautier, the nineteenth-century French critic, novelist, dramatist, was another one of Pound's ideal models. He admired Gautier for his staunch refusal to relinquish his critical autonomy amidst the intense pressures of the commercial art world. "I cling to the rock of Gautier," he wrote to Joyce in 1920, "deluding myself perhaps with the idea that he did journalism for years without becoming an absolute shit" (*P/J*, 174). Because of his strong opinions there are those who would certainly agree that he was deluding himself, but Pound was never writing articles to make friends. In fact, he was more intent on finding enemies to disagree with so that he could stir up conversation in the public sphere.

Pound lived abroad for most of his adult life, but he kept in contact with America, in part, by following the newspapers, which he usually picked up in foreign editions published in Paris and distributed across Europe. In the 1930s especially, he was an active respondent and wrote hundreds of letters to the editors of the *New York Herald* and the *Chicago Tribune*, ranting and raving about what he was reading. His responses can be acerbic, boisterous, nitpicky, and, at times, outlandish, but they are always entertaining, which might explain why the editors always found a place to print them. Reading them together, you get the sense that Pound was having a lot of fun in the process. Both in his letters and in his longer articles, he acted like a self-appointed court jester, someone present in the conversation to expose the lies and inaccuracies. When he found someone to disagree with, he was never afraid to unload. "With the progress of television," he wrote to the editor of the *Chicago Tribune* in 1930, "it is regrettable that no bright inventor has yet invented the telekick."[5]

Though Pound the poet was experimenting formally to make "it" new, as the journalist he was always coming up with ways to make news. His involvement with the *Japan Times Weekly* (an English language newspaper) in 1940, one arranged by Katsue Kitasono, is particularly instructive in this regard. When writing for Western newspapers, he was very much in control of his material: he knew his audience intimately and was never worried about offending them. Writing for a non-Western audience, however, Pound had to come up with ways to engage readers without alienating them. His articles are significantly toned down and he acts more like a patient instructor than an exasperated pundit. After publishing a few articles, he made his discomfort explicit: "I feel a little lost writing for an unknown public which must, in some sense, be a 'newspaper public.' Most of my criticism has been written for a nucleus of writers and I have to a considerable extent known their beliefs or known when I was infuriating them by attacking particular literary imbecilities."[6] In the two dozen or so articles Pound published there, he never raised his voice, but he did offer a lot of advice about contemporary Western literature, American history, the causes of the Second World War, the need for importing and exporting books, and the importance of Confucius and Mencius to the cultural rejuvenation of Europe. The regularity of his "Letter from Rapallo" column is evidence enough that Pound did manage to attract supporters, though we'll never know for sure what they made of his ideas.

When Pound first moved from Paris to Rapallo, Italy in 1924, he was hoping to finish the Cantos. At the time, he was following the vortex, as he called it, that fulcrum of cultural energy responsible for keeping literature and the arts modern. "Mi domandano perchè sto in Italia," he wrote in 1931, "Credono che vi stia solo per il mio interessamento agli archivi e ai monumenti architettonici (che non esistono qui dove vivo). Io invece trovo un senso di contemporaneità più (ametto) nelle idee, nella Anschaung sociale, che nella letteratura." (They ask me why I'm in Italy. They believe it's only because of my continued interest in archives and architectural monuments [that don't exist here where I live]. Instead I find a sense of contemporaneity more [I admit] in ideas, in the social *Anschaung*, than in the literature.)[7] Living in Rapallo between the world wars, Pound got involved with dozens of local, regional, and national Italian newspapers. His reputation as the distinguished American poet helped him gain access to the press, but it was his witty, irreverent, bombastic style and immense erudition, which he always wore lightly, that helped him to stay there.

When Pound first arrived in Italy, his reputation as the iconoclastic American poet preceded him. But by the time he was extradited back to the United States to stand trial for treason, he was known to a wider Italian audience, Mussolini included, as "il giornalista," the one who had written hundreds of newspaper articles between 1930 and 1945 for publications like *L'Indice*, *Il Mare*, *Il Meridiano di Roma*, and *Il Popolo di Alessandria*.[8] In these years, Pound was convinced that by writing journalism, he was simply playing the role of a public intellectual, who needed to speak truth to power.

These Italian articles make up the bulk of Pound's journalism, and they document his complicated transformation from the cosmopolitan, expat poet to the isolated Italian fascist broadcasting from Rapallo and Rome. Because these articles have not been translated, a number of myths and misunderstandings have grown up around them. So it is worth making a few general remarks. In the early 1930s, when Pound was first getting to know his Italian public, his articles were exclusively literary. He was as interested in looking back on Anglo-American modernist experiments in the 1910s as he was in trying to jumpstart contemporary Italian literature in the 1930s. He gives advice about translation, how to write and read poetry, what to read, and, perhaps most importantly, how to internationalize Italian literature and lead it toward another renaissance.

By the end of the 1930s, Pound enlists himself as a propagandist for Italian fascism and writes hundreds of articles on everything from Social Credit to Confucius. In Pound's mind, this turn to politics was not incommensurate with his role as a poet. In fact, he was using the medium of journalism in the late 1930s to champion a political program that would, he hoped, result in the rejuvenation of Italian culture under Mussolini's government. In Pound's mind, he was doing for Italian fascism what he had done already for modern literature in the 1910s: mobilizing forces, distributing accurate information, and centralizing supporters around a clearly articulated ideological program.

Reading through these articles, it's sometimes jarring to discover how familiar they sound. That's because they are. Many of the theories, rules, and principles he was using to define modern literature, language, and movements were being tweaked to accommodate his fascist beliefs. In fact, he had even tried to convince his readers that his friends Joyce, Eliot, Pound, Williams, and Cummings made up a *fascio* before Mussolini's party was even in power. No one understands, he wrote in "Arretrati e Snobisti," "che la nostra letteratura più viva, a Londra, trenta anni fa, fu una ribellione intelletuale contro il sistema che non veniva combattuto politicamente, sino all'inizio dell'Era fascista."[9] (Our most lively literature, in London, thirty years ago, was an intellectual rebellion against the system nobody was fighting against politically, until the beginning of the fascist era.) Remarks like these abound in Pound's fascist articles, and they are just one place in which we can observe how he understood his own role as a mediator, a cultural barometer of sorts, who used any available medium to consolidate movements, literary and political alike.

Pound's first stint as an Italian journalist began in 1930 when Gino Saviotti, editor of *L'Indice*, asked him to write a piece about Joyce. Pound was quick to oblige, and he provided a lengthy article in Italian (September 1930) that was adapted and translated from an earlier essay he had written for the *Mercure de France* in 1922. In the next year and a half, Pound wrote twenty-six articles for *L'Indice*, and with the exception of "Storicamente Joyce (e censura)," they were collected under the heading, *appunti*, or notes, a section specially created for this new "foreign correspondent." His involvement with *L'Indice* sounds very playful at times, but he was still interested in using it to promote a serious program. He wanted to help transform Italy into an international center for literature and the arts, and was convinced, in fact, that he could direct the modernization process if readers, local and regional, would follow his lead. His directions were explicit and direct: Italy needed to import more foreign books, overcome its francophilia, translate modern literature from other countries, and create a critical conversation about contemporary Italian literature.

In "Nunc Dimittis," Pound's collaboration is announced in a series of epistolary exchanges between him and Saviotti, who concedes that they will never agree on literary matters (Pound, for instance, prefers Cavalcanti to Dante), but nevertheless agrees to give his American confrère a column of the newspaper ("una rubrica speciale") to publish whatever he wants. Pound jumps right in and invites translators and writers from around the world to send him news about what is happening on the world literary stage. From then on, Pound uses his position as the foreign correspondent to generate a lively discussion about literary matters.

All of his articles circle back to the same idea: if Italy wants to Europeanize, and in the process become a cultural capital, then it needs to open itself up to foreign literature. Translation is critical to the success or failure of such an endeavor, and Pound provides advice based on his own experience in London and Paris twenty years earlier. In articles like "Lettera al Traduttore" (October 1930), "Traduzioni" (June 10, 1931), "Sperimentale" (June 5, 1931), and "Supplemento al mio Trattato D'Armonia" (October 10, 1931), Pound explains that translation does not involve exact word-forword transcription from one language to another. The translator has to find ways to condense the information that is being conveyed; the translation, in the process, will be shorter than the original but capable of capturing something at the core of the original meaning.

Pound received special treatment as the outsider. He was able to hurl insults, bash Italian critics, and ridicule writers without his status. Readers responded to his provocations, and during this time he inserted more than a dozen translations of foreign writers including Wyndham Lewis, Henry Adams, Robert McAlmon, Ford Maddox Ford, Henry James, Jean Cocteau, Leo Froebenius, René Taupin. It was also during this period that Pound began to revise his opinion of F.T. Marinetti. It seems that his own role as the cultural provocateur based in Italy made Pound realize that he had more in common with Futurism than he had been willing to acknowledge. "Ogni giorno che resto in Italia vengo più vicino alla posizione di Marinetti" (Every day that I remain in Italy I come closer to sharing Marinetti's position), he wrote in an article on Futurism. His sympathy with Marinetti's cause was so intense, in fact, that he was willing to make another pledge: "credo che se fossi vissuto in Italia fra il 1912 e il 1924 avrei fatto causa commune coi futuristi, non perchè stessi d'accordo con loro sui principii estetici, ma perchè non c'era ove andare altrove, sopratutto in questione della necessità della contemporaneità nelle percezioni che precedono l'opera d'arte." (I believe that if I lived in Italy between 1912 and 1924, I would have made common cause with the futurists, not because I agree with their aesthetic principals, but because there was nowhere else to go, especially when it came to questions regarding the necessity of the contemporaneity in the perceptions that precede the work of art.)[10]

When *L'Indice* downsized at the end of 1931, Pound's column was cut, but Saviotti helped his friend secure a position writing for *Il Mare*, Rapallo's literary supplement, which was published as a fortnightly. The audience was smaller, but Pound's energy did not abate. He continued to follow through with his program to engage (and enrage) Italian critics and writers while educating the public. In his first brief note, he justifies the need for what he calls *localismo*. Big cities, he explains, are not the only place where literature and the arts can thrive. It is also possible to nurture a lively local culture so long as it does not slip into the protection of a "stupidità locale."

Pound followed through with his promise to make *Il Mare* international, at least temporarily. Between 1932 and 1933, he contributed short pieces that were meant to trigger debate. If in *L'Indice* he was keen to educate translators about how and what books to import from abroad, he was now eager to take on Italian critics, who, he believed, contributed to the stagnation of contemporary letters. "Cari ragazzi e colleghi," he wrote, "il 93% della *carta stampata* in Italia è assolutamente illegibile perchè tutta scritta nella cadenza morta, ma MORRRRTAAAA, morta nella tradizione." (Dear students and colleagues, 93 percent of the paper printed in Italy is absolutely illegible because it is all written in that dead tone, but really deeeeeeeaaaaaaad, dead by the tradition.)[11] The inability of Italian critics to focus on contemporary literature and their refusal to circulate intelligent books from abroad made them nothing more than "parassitismo, chiacchiere d'eunuchi invidiosi di Don Giovanni" (parasites, chatty jealous eunuchs envious of Don Giovanni.)[12] Italian journalists did not get off much easier. "Agli occhi d'un Americano il giornalismo italiano è (impossibile negarlo) debolissimo." (To the eyes of an American Italian journalism is (it is impossible to deny) the weakest.)

In a postscript, he provides some practical advice that Italian journalists should heed if they want to sharpen their reporting. There should be suspense, surprises, something to excite the reader into caring about what's on the page. News, he writes, "è l'idea del giornalista circa la quantità di vero che il pubblico può tollerare senza un'indigestione mentale" (is the idea of the journalist around the quantity of truth that the public can tolerate without mental indigestion.)[13] When the literary supplement of *Il Mare* was dropped in July of 1933, Pound's experiment with Italian critics and writers came to an end. He continued nevertheless to write about music for the main paper of *Il Mare* until 1939, many articles occasioned by the concerts that he helped to organize in and around Rapallo. They were small, intimate events held at the Town Hall with an audience that rarely exceeded eighty, a majority of them connoisseurs of classical music. Over the years, the programs included Mozart's violin sonatas, Antonio Vivaldi's concertos, and Béla Bartók's string quartets along with the contemporary, experimental work of Igor Stravinsky, Claude Debussy, Erik Satie, and George Antheil.

When Pound signed on as a regular contributor to the Roman newspaper, *Il Meridiano di Roma*, in 1938 he turned his attention primarily to economic and political issues, but they were often woven together with what he had to say about American colonial history, Confucius and the ideogram, the internationalization of literature, and the creation of a fascist library. Throughout the early to mid 1930s he had kept in contact with British, American, and French newspapers, but as political alliances shifted, and his fascist sympathies became more pronounced, he was increasingly isolated. Pound wrote ninety articles for *Il Meridiano di Roma*, and in 1944 he even put together a separate edition under the title, *Orientamenti*. It was printed by the Venetian publisher Edizioni Popolari but pulled from the shelves and pulped when, some have suspected, the Salò regime intervened.

There is a reason, I suspect, that the *Meridiano* articles, in particular, have never been translated into English and collected in a single volume. They belong to Pound's fascist period and are regularly interspersed with his attacks against the British and American banking system, Frederick Delano Roosevelt, and a global network of secret Jewish organizations, whom he blames for the Second World War, the inequities of a global economy, usury, and the arms trade. Many of these articles make for uncomfortable reading. His attacks can be offensive, incendiary, and belong to that part of the poet that most of us would like to forget. As with Wyndham Lewis, Pound was one more high modernist figure who came under the sway of a reactionary political ideology, and he believed that liberal democratic governments in the West were being run behind the scenes by capitalist czars and Jewish secret societies, all of them intent on world domination. During these years, he was convinced that his journalism was a way to combat the misinformation that was being spread about Italy by the Western allies. Writing for fascist-run Italian newspapers also freed him, he believed, from the Jewish organizations who controlled the British and American press.[14]

Throughout the 1930s, Pound argued vigorously for an international press that would allow for the free exchange of ideas. Individuals needed more than one national news source if they were really going to get an unbiased presentation of what was happening around the world. He emphatically reiterated this idea in every newspaper he was involved with during this decade. His own contributions, he believed, were a way to reveal the truth about American and British economic corruption and counteract the misinformation that was being spread abroad about Mussolini and his government. "I am," he wrote in the *British–Italian Bulletin* (a fascist periodical) in 1936, "writing European propaganda for the sake of a decent Europe wherein the best people will not be murdered for the monetary profit of the lowest and rottenest, and wherein the divergent national components might collaborate for a sane, unstarved civilization."[15]

The Italian armistice of September 8, 1943 put an end to Pound's collaboration with the *Meridiano*, but for the next two years, he continued to write articles for other fascist newspapers that were willing to give him a column or two.[16] *Il Popolo di Alessandria*, a bi-weekly newspaper with limited circulation, was one of his more regular stints, though he ended up repeating a lot of what he had already said. He was still intent on the promotion of fascist culture, but he was becoming increasingly embittered by the fact that the Italians had switched sides, forcing Mussolini to form a puppet government overseen by the Germans. In the brief articles that appeared in *Il Popolo*, his anti-Semitic rants reached fever pitch, and he continued to lash out against a barrage of capitalists, usurers, and creditors, whom, he imagined were in cahoots with Churchill and Roosevelt.

Pound's engagement as the expatriate journalist ended abruptly when he was forced to stand trial for treason in 1945. From that moment forward, he was making news, but not in the way he ever imagined. Newspapers across the United States excoriated Pound for his unpatriotic behavior, and the attacks only got worse as excerpts from his radio broadcasts began to circulate. During his thirteen years in St. Elizabeth's Hospital, he contributed brief articles to publications like *The New Times* and *Edge*, both of them based in Australia, but they appeared unsigned or under a pseudonym. Writing in anonymity gave Pound an outlet for his ideas, but it was punishment of a different sort. He had spent his entire life using newspapers, little magazines, and other forms of print media to generate discussion about literature, economics, politics, and history, but at this point an audience was even harder to come by and he couldn't even acknowledge himself in public.

The rehabilitation of Pound in the 1950s and 1960s was made possible by figures like James Laughlin and T.S. Eliot, both of them keen to advertise the poetic, decidedly less political persona that could be found in the early poetry and letters. Pound would occasionally interrupt his solitude to give an interview to a European or American newspaper, but in these postwar decades, up until his death, he turned away from the newspaper and back to the *Cantos* he intended to finish when first arriving in Rapallo way back in 1924.

In the second preface to *Jefferson and/or Mussolini*, Pound writes: "I have never quarreled with people when their deductions have been based on fact, I have quarreled when they were based on ignorance, and my only arguments for 25 years have been the dragging up of facts, either of literature or of history. Journalism as I see it is history of to-day, and literature is journalism that *stays* news" (*JM*, xi). Though it may be customary to distinguish between the two Pounds, one a journalist, the other a poet, he never did so himself. For Pound, there was a time and place in his life for both. His poetry has certainly managed to "*stay* news," while the bulk of his journalism has been left behind in oversized volumes and archives that even his devotees ignore. That's the way it is with history sometimes, and Pound would have understood, perhaps better than anybody, that the "history of to-day" doesn't always make it past tomorrow.

NOTES

1 "Servizio di Comunicazioni," *Ana Eccetera* 2 (October 30, 1959). Reprinted in *EPCP*, VIII: 272.

2 The exception here is the music criticism that Pound wrote for *Il Mare* between 1932 and 1939, which has been translated and published in *EPM*. For an excellent overview of Pound's involvement with Fascism and his Italian journalism, see Tim Redman, *Ezra Pound and Italian Fascism* (Cambridge: Cambridge University Press, 1991) and Niccolò Zapponi, *L'Italia di Ezra Pound* (Rome: Bulzoni Editore, 1976).

3 Though I will be concentrating primarily on Pound's newspaper articles, I am using journalism here to refer to his essays and editorials for "little magazines" (as Pound himself did).

4 "Vortex," *Delphian Quarterly* (April 2, 1937): 16–18, 24.

5 "Questions for Mr. X," *Chicago Tribune* (Paris) (August 3, 1930): 4.

6 "Letter from Rapallo," *Japan Times Weekly*, April 18, 1940. *EPCP*, VIII: 31.

7 "Non Parlo d'Esportazione," *L'Indice* (February 10, 1931). *EPCP*, V: 276–77. All translations from the Italian articles are my own. Here and throughout I've retained Pound's grammatical mistakes in Italian.

8 See Zapponi, *L'Italia di Ezra Pound*, 57.

9 "Arretrati e Snobisti," *L'Indice* (March 7, 1943). *EPCP*, VIII: 204. For an overview of Pound's involvement with *L'Indice*, see Wayne Pound, "A Dash Of Barbarism: Ezra Pound and Gino Saviotti in the *Indice*, 1930–31" at www.cl.aoyama.ac.jp/~wayne/pound/A%20Dash%20of%20Barb.htm.

10 "Scultura (Lettera a Ernesto Thayaht)," *L'Indice* (April 10, 1931). *EPCP*, v: 283–4.

11 "Ecrevisse?," *Il Mare* (March 18, 1933): 4. *EPCP*, vi: 23–4.

12 "Critici e Idioti," *Il Mare* (September 17, 1932): 4. *EPCP*, v: 369.

13 "News," *Il Mare* (December 10, 1932). Unsigned, but Pound refers to himself in the article. *EPCP*, v, 384.

14 See, for instance, "Anglo-Israele," *IL Meridiano.* (January 12, 1941); *EPCP*, viii: 99–100; and "Gli Ebrei e Questa Guerra" (March 24, 1940). *EPCP*, viii: 19–21.

15 "For a Decent Europe," *British–Italian Bulletin* 2. 11 (March 14, 1936): 3. *EPCP*, vii: 33.

16 And it was one the editors seemed eager to forget. When a collected edition of *Meridiano* articles came out after the war, none of Pound's articles were included. His ideas, Niccolò Zapponi suspects, were too outlandish for the newspaper in the first place, and though they may have gained in prestige from his involvement during the war, the postwar Pound was more of a liability, someone brought back to his native country to stand trial. See Zapponì, *L'Italia di Ezra Pound*, 115–16.

CHAPTER 9

Politics

Alec Marsh

Ezra Pound's politics are a unique alloy of Jeffersonian populism, Chinese Confucianism, and his heterodox interpretation of fascism. Pound saw himself as a "left-wing fascist" because he was an economic determinist, but as a firm believer in the Jewish–Bolshevik conspiracy, Pound was also to the right of most Italian fascists, closer to their Nazi cousins.[1] During his incarceration at St. Elizabeths, 1945–58, Pound reappeared as an American-style right-wing extremist. Convinced that the Supreme Court justices were communists, Pound worked through surrogates to attempt to prevent the integration of American schools and roll back the liberal judicial activism that threatened his strict constructionist and thoroughly Jeffersonian view of the US Constitution. Pound believed that a corrupt economic system meant a corrupt politics; inevitably, war, famines, and general devastation must follow; therefore economic change must precede political change.

Pound's politics evolved because his imagination was syncretic; he found meeting points between poetical, political, and economic programs that others found completely incompatible. The ideogrammic method of heaping like things together that became Pound's main poetic tactic in *The Cantos* is syncretic. *The Cantos* "rhyme" ancient Greece with ancient China, John Adams with Chinese history, Mussolini with Confucius. He thought analogically: "Mencius has gone into [Confucian] detail as . . . Van Buren has gone into detail from a Jeffersonian basis" (*SPR*, 96). His distinctive "Volitionist" economics was a marriage of Social Credit thinking with the stamp scrip mechanism of Sylvio Gesell – never mind that neither Major Douglas nor Pound's Gesellite correspondents could see any point of agreement. The title of his main political treatise, *Jefferson and/or Mussolini*, captures concisely Pound's ability to find concord where others saw only difference.

Confucius provided a "totalitarian" ethics for an integrated culture (*SPR*, 99). "Totalitarian," Mary Cheadle reminds us, "is a word Pound used unapologetically"; he means by it much what Mussolini meant, rendered in

96

a Confucian idiom; "an intelligent integrity that begins with the individual and extends to the whole social or political body."² The opening of the *Ta Hio* tells us to look into our hearts and ascertain the correct definition of words, then through self-discipline we can put our own houses in order. The men of old, Pound translated, "having order in their own homes, [then] brought good government to their own states; and when the states were well governed the empire was brought into equilibrium" (*TAH*, 33). On this "unwobbling pivot" of equity and justice, all political differences could be reconciled. To speak in crude Hegelian allegory, if Jefferson is Pound's primal thesis, and Mussolini is Jefferson's anti-thesis, then Confucius is their synthesis.

Pound's politics are rooted in the "Fathers of the Republic" (*SP*, 143), especially Thomas Jefferson (1746–1826), who wrote the Declaration of Independence and The Bill of Rights, and in John Adams (1735–1826), Ambassador, drafter of the US Constitution, second President, scion of a long line of public men and profound historians. Pound would devote a long sequence of Cantos to Adams (LXII-LXXI), comparing him implicitly to the good emperors of China. Though most historians and their contemporaries saw them at odds, Pound regarded their ultimate reconciliation, recorded in the Jefferson – Adams correspondence, as "a shrine and a monument" to American civilization at its highest; moreover their letters constituted "a still workable dynamo" that could re-energize America in decay (*SPR*, 117).

Jefferson's political legacy is as complex and contradictory as the man. Monticello, Jefferson's plantation near Charlottesville, Virginia, was a utopian microcosm provided with the latest technology (some devised by Jefferson himself) while remaining a slave state. The ambiguous Jeffersonian tradition is synonymous with the republican ideals and racial tragedy of the United States and Pound himself. Like lesser Presidents since, Jefferson became impatient with the Constitutional restraints he himself had invented. He attempted to stifle freedom of the press; yet, overriding Congressional objections and Constitutional entanglements, he engineered the "Louisiana Purchase," which made the USA a continental power.

It was Jefferson the man of action Pound praised in *Jefferson and/or Mussolini* (*JM*, 11). Mussolini *and* Jefferson? Pound asks that we imagine what "Mussolini [would] have done in the American wilderness in 1770 to 1826" and "What would Thomas Jefferson do or say," in Italy *c.* 1933 (*JM*, 25). How would each act?

In all its idioms, American, Italian, and Chinese, Pound's politics is agrarian, even physiocratic, in positing "the abundance of nature" as the basis of all value. To the physiocrats, all wealth came from the earth; it was the "net product" and limited to "agricultural produce." Farmers were the lone productive class; others merely shifted and divided the net product in myriad ways that were dogmatically "non-productive." Physiocratic ideology is evident in Jefferson's most characteristic statements, "the proportion which the aggregation of the other classes of citizens bears in any state to that of its husbandmen is the proportion of its unsound to its healthy parts, and is a good enough barometer whereby to measure its degree of corruption."[3]

Famously, Pound's corruption barometer was measured in usury. Like Jefferson, he assumed that any society was corruptible by "the arts of commerce." In "Immediate Need for Confucius" (1937) Pound claimed that "any Western work of art" was datable "by reference to the ethical estimate of usury prevalent at the time of that work's composition; the greater the component of tolerance for usury the more blobby and messy the work of art." "The kind of thought that distinguishes good from evil, down to the details of commerce," he explained, "rises into the quality of line in paintings and into the clear definition of the word written" (*SPR*, 90). Usury, Pound adds, is a specifically "Western disease" that arises from a want of proportion – troublingly, a Semitic trait (*SPR*, 100, 104) – as opposed to the republican probity of the Founding Fathers, the tidy sages of China, and the clean hard aesthetic of modernism. This would be a constant theme in Pound's criticism. When proportion is attained, then value arrives as what the physiocrats called "*jouissance*," echoes of which remain in Jefferson's "pursuit of happiness" in the Declaration of Independence. Pound would rephrase this as "The Production is the beloved" (CIV/762).

Pound shared Jefferson's understanding that the decisive social conflict was between debtors and creditors. In the 1890s Jefferson's analysis expressed itself in the mass movement of Populism, rooted in the agricultural South and West, where farmers found themselves chronically threatened with foreclosure by North Eastern creditors – "Wall Street." The Populists demanded a greater supply of money through the free coinage of the abundant silver found in the West and the revocation of the Gold Standard, instituted in the so-called "Crime of '73," which centralized power in the hands of big banks and a few creditors. "The Money Question," which would obsess Pound and determine his mature politics, was *the* political issue during the poet's childhood. His later politics, especially the "money pamphlets" and brief histories written in Italy during the Second World

War, like *An Introduction to the Economic Nature of the United States*, are squarely in the populist tradition that derives from Jefferson, runs through Andrew Jackson's "Bank War" against the First US Bank, and through the money question of Pound's childhood.

Like Jefferson's, Pound's conflicted politics are dedicated at once to individual freedom and economic justice and to a suspicion of finance capitalism; he wants local autonomy, but also a firm hand protecting the state against rapacious financiers. Politics and economics being twins, Pound's politics evolved along with his economic thinking, which after the near collapse of capitalism in the Great Depression took up much of his time. That the ideal reader of *Jefferson and/or Mussolini* was FDR (to whom it is dedicated) expresses Pound's belief that Jeffersonian reforms steered by a genius at the top could save the world from financial and political disaster; that is, from a bankers' war against civilization. Pound believed that wars are made to create debt because under the perverse values of economic liberalism debt is equivalent to wealth. To prevent the global war demanded by the liberal economy, Pound wanted to install "a sane economic system" as a check on the big lie that liberal capitalism and political liberty were compatible (*EPEC*, 177). Pound's attraction to fascism, ironically, was Pound's steadfast antiwar politics.

As fascism had no special economics, Pound thought the pragmatic Mussolini might be persuaded of his economic vision. Pound met with Mussolini on January 30, 1933 to talk about it. The master politician praised noncommittally the gift copy of *Draft of* xxx *Cantos* ("e divertente") and patiently considered Pound's economic questions. These were later reduced to eight queries, which Pound circulated as his "Volitionist Questionnaire." Although Mussolini did little more than grunt evasively in response to agree/disagree questions like "It is an outrage that the state should run into debt to individuals by the act an in the act of creating real wealth," Pound left convinced Mussolini saw his points (*EPEC*, 255).

Ignored by FDR, Pound soon gave up on the "New Deal." By autumn 1934 he was pessimistic that the "new Economics" could find a hearing, writing to Hugo Fack that "Roosevelt is still sniveling to hold onto profit system" (*EPEC*, 115, 125). It was roughly then, Leon Surette believes, that Pound caught the anti-Semitic bug.[4] As a joke, the Jewish and communist poet Louis Zukofsky sent him *Liberation*, the organ of the American Christian Party run by "Colonel" William Augustus Pelley, a Hitler-crazed populist, whose "Silvershirts" were a visible, if ineffective, expression of American fascism. Incredibly, Pound was enchanted by *Liberation*, which rehearsed well-worn American right-wing and anti-Semitic themes that were as new to him as they were old hat to the American extreme right. Pound's adherence to a number of dubious documents dates from this period.

His Jeffersonian populist outlook attuned Pound to the anti-Roosevelt right in the United States. He listened carefully to Father Coughlin's rousing speeches on the radio, subscribed to his publications and wrote him with political and economic advice. He corresponded with the Silvershirts, and with Huey Long, offering to become his "Sekkertary of Treasury" should Long become President in 1936.[5]

In Italy, after the League of Nations embargo prompted by the invasion of Abyssinia, Pound became an outspoken advocate of the theory of Jewish conspiracy. In 1938 he read the Italian translation of *Mein Kampf.* In 1940 he told Odon Por that *The Protocols of the Elders of Zion*, while rumored to be fake and "DAMN dull, hideously written," were the "absolute condensation of history of the U.S.A. for the past 50 years" (*EPEC*, 247). Once the war started, Pound fully endorsed the German view that a local European war had been blown into a world-wide conflict by England and the Jews. He feared, correctly, that FDR was prepared to enter the war in Europe in order to maintain the liberal economic system at all costs. Writing Congressman Voorhis after the war's outbreak in September 1939, he stated "The whole of the neutral nations of Europe are unanimous in believing that NO extension of the war beyond Poland is the least necessary at this time. Only England and the yidds are driving for any such extension. It is in great measure an anglo-judaic war against Europe" (*EPEC*, 226). Pound never revised this view and spent considerable energy in the 1950s trying to prove it.

In April 1939, Pound traveled to the United States at his own expense to try to prevent the war. Por gave Pound some parting advice: "try to adapt your ideas to reality – Otherwise one remains a looney."[6] Politically, the trip was a fiasco: on landing Pound gave a press conference that resulted in embarrassing newsphotos. Pound failed to meet with FDR and, flamboyantly dressed, lounged in congressional offices, treated as a diverting crank (*EPWB*, 80–1). Practically his sole success was to plant in a tiny newspaper the declaration: ["]War against Germany in our time would be war against an honest concept of money."[7]

Pound had already talked hopefully on Rome Radio of "the economic triumph of fascism"[8] and began broadcasting twice a week, starting in January 1941. After Italy declared war, Pound paused, but by January 1942 he was back on the air. His broadcasts continued steadily after Italy's surrender in 1943 until 1945. Taken together, they constituted the most personally damaging political act of Pound's life. Never published in their entirety, some are anti-Semitic rantings; some are lectures on *The Protocols* and *Mein Kampf*; others, harmless yatter. Pound always maintained that the broadcasts were a concerned American patriot's free speech. He did not realize that what was personal expression in peacetime might be seditious in wartime. Had Pound remained in the United States in 1939, opinions like those spoken over Rome Radio could have led to a trial for sedition, as they did for a number of Roosevelt's more vociferous critics.

Pound was never tried after his arrest, detention, and flight to Washington. Ruled unfit, he was remanded to federal custody until he could understand the charges against him. He remained at St. Elizabeths Hospital, a federal facility for the insane, in legal limbo until 1958. In 1949 the Bolligen Prize for *The Pisan Cantos* embroiled the poet in a damaging public controversy that haunts his legacy. Anti-Pound partisans were quick to equate Pound's unapologetic anti-Semitism with treason. Few read the poems, but Pound's visibility prevented early dismissal of the charges against him.

Under the circumstances overt political action was impossible, so Pound politicked clandestinely, through anonymous articles in Poundian newssheets published by friends, by encouraging dissident scholarship like Eustace Mullins' exposé of the Federal Reserve Bank (1954) and his biography of Pound, *That Difficult Individual* (1960), through his own Confucian translations (1950, 1954), and through commenting on current events via highly coded cantos: "the Cantos are a political implement," he told a correspondent in 1957.[9]

In 1951, Pound was visited by John Kasper. A product of Columbia University from an extreme evangelical Christian right-wing milieu, he would become Pound's most energetic and radical emissary to the world outside St. Elizabeths.[10] Kasper was instantly appointed his representative in New York and introduced to David Horton, and the Square $ Press was born.

In 1954, Kasper opened "The Make It New Bookshop," dedicated to Pound's curriculum in Greenwich Village, stocked with an impressive variety of right-wing literature, Joe McCarthy's speeches, and good poetry. Ironically, in light of later events, the bookstore attracted many African-Americans, including the most (politically) Poundian of American poets, the young Leroi Jones.

What turned Kasper into one of the most fearsome racists of the 1950s was editing the *Gists of Agassiz* at Pound's request. Despite the fact that Agassiz was Swiss, Pound wanted to promote him as a great American writer; he may not have realized that he was also the father of scientific racism. The last respected scientist to deny evolution, Agassiz believed in the separate creation of the human races, arguing for "intelligent design," a significant neo-Platonic theme in *The Cantos*. Agassiz's racism had a deplorable effect on both Pound and Kasper. Both absorbed Agassiz's racial science and became convinced that people of African descent were predestined to be farmers, not legislators, and that blacks' racial *paideuma* made them subservient to the master races, the Greeks and the Chinese.

Evolution must have bothered Pound, for it proves there is no "clear demarcation" between species. A species is only an ideal type, a variable within limits, and thus (given time) in danger of drifting into something else; so racial purity is a fiction. Pound could use the segregationist term "mongrelization"; "Nothing," he wrote Kasper in April 1956, "is more damnably harmful to everyone, white AND black than miscegenation, bastardization and mongrelization of EVERYTHING,"[11] an idea authorized by Agassiz, who believed racial mixing sapped cultural vitality.

Kasper preached this doctrine throughout the south in the 1950s; it infects the late *Cantos* as well. Opaque as these poems are, they present a universe fixed according to a hierarchical plan mirrored on earth by Confucian order. In the late cantos, Pound warns us he is writing in "Aesopian language" (c/733). In code, he attacks the Warren Court, and upholds segregation ("Maintain antisepsis/ Let the light pour"[xciv/655]).

To be near Pound, Kasper opened a new bookshop, called "The Cadmus," in Georgetown. On June 4, 1956 Kasper called a press conference to announce the formation of the Seaboard White Citizens' Council (SWCC) headquartered at the Cadmus. Atypically, Kasper's WCC banned Jews. Its motto, "Honor-Pride-Fight: Save the White," would later be transferred to the National States' Rights Party (NSRP), which Kasper helped found. Registration forms for the SWCC are in Pound's papers; there is no evidence that he joined.

Photos of charred crosses burned on the lawns of Chief Justice Warren, and others, days after the Supreme Court ruled that the Charlottesville Public Schools would desegregate, were published in the SWCC pamphlet, *Virginians on Guard*, that Kasper took south on his campaign to save the white race a few weeks later. The thirty-two-page work was designed to influence a Special Legislative Session in Richmond called to codify Virginia's "massive resistance" to school integration (August 27–September 23). Pound disliked the cover, a scurrilous rant that reminded him of *BLAST* ("DAMN ALL race-mixers / the stink: Roose, Harry & Ike / GOD BLESS JEFF / JAX/ & John Adams") – it demanded that the NAACP should all be jailed, and the "9 SUPREME COURT SWINE" hanged.[12] He had little objection to the contents, however, because he had vetted the document carefully and contributed two of the articles himself.[13] Altogether, *Virginians on Guard* may be read as "making new" the Constitution of Virginia (penned by Jefferson himself) to current emergency conditions. Writing to Noel Stock, (then a rabid Poundian) about it, he thought "[a] few / 2 points at least quotable" . . . "the rest VERY local."[14]

"Very local" meant the emphasis on "race mongrelism," and the inflammatory doctored pictures of black men with white women inside. But in the fifty-two increasingly strident proposed laws some of Pound's core political ideas are evident (1) in the plan to issue Gesellite money, (2) Pound's definition of usury.[15] The cover also quoted Canto LII on the subject of the Jews: "better keep out the jews / or yr / grandchildren will curse you" (LII/257). The overall thrust is Poundian politics focused on a "Very local" problem: how to resist completely, unequivocally, and absolutely racial integration. It is hard to judge completely Pound's investment in Kasper's campaign because the hundreds of letters Pound wrote Kasper have not surfaced. But he paid attention to his actions.

Such activities hurt Pound's case for release from St. Elizabeths. On trial for conspiracy, Kasper invariably brought up Pound: how was it that America's foremost poet and patriot sat incarcerated, while communist agitators ran free? Why was a patriot like himself before the bar, when decisions like *Slowchower* protected communist teachers from corrupting America's youth? At the end of January 1957, *The New York Herald Tribune* ran a front-page exposé on the Kasper/ Pound connection, "SEGREGA-TIONIST KASPER IS EZRA POUND DISCIPLE." Kasper was shown in his bookshop with a racially integrated group of employees and friends. The story had serious repercussions for both men. For Pound, it undoubtedly delayed his release. Kasper's comrades in the KKK, on the other hand, thought he might be an *agent provocateur*.

Pound reassured many he was not a racist: "NO, naturally I do not dislike africans [*sic*]. or afro-americans," citing Langston Hughes and Roland Hayes as proof; "neither to the best of my knowledge does Kasper," he added. "Kasper," Pound said, "believed the Lute of gassir [*sic*] superior to a Liberian imitation of Hart Crane commended by Allen Tate." He refers to Melvin Tolson's anthem, "Liberia," meaning that indigenous African culture as described by Frobenius is "pure" whereas mongrelized African-Americans only imitate.[16]

On August 1, 1957, Kasper announced the formation of the segregationist "Wheat In Bread Party" (WHIB), named by Pound. It recalled his chant against usury, Canto XLV: "With usura, sin against nature / is thy bread ever more of stale rags / is thy bread dry as paper / with no mountain wheat, no strong flour" (XLV/229). The thought is revived in *Thrones*, "The strength of men is in grain" (CVI/772). The tiny WHIB party actually ran candidates for local office in Tennessee, where Kasper would be based for the next several years when not in jail. WHIB may be considered the direct forerunner to the NSRP, which ran Kasper for President in 1964.

Pound, in Italy since May of 1958, refused offers by Peter Russell and Lawrence Ferlinghetti to print clarifications of his relationship with Kasper. "Katz is Katz" was all he would say. In 1959 Pound wrote to David Horton from the Brunnenburg his final political manifesto:

PROGRAM
in search of a party
(i.e. a party capable of studying history before rushing into party politics.)

I.
Every man has the right to have his ideas examined one at a time.

II.
Not to falsify history, either ancient or contemporary. (And to recognize enemies of humanity the individuals, with name and address, who do just that, pouring out millions to make an ass of the people.

III.
To keep out of debt (public and private).

Two days later he added notes insisting on the "quality of food . . . the history of agriculture . . . the value of rye as against wheat," and that "attention be paid to curricula in educational effort." He also demanded "Representation by trades and professions, and in labour organizations," as in the *corporazione* of fascism and affirmed "the principles of division of powers, and ballot."[17]

Pound's final "Program" is a meld we can call "Jeffersonian fascism." An agrarian program, its emphasis on debt condenses Jefferson's famous letter to Madison, where he writes that "the earth belongs to the living."[18] The program represents a politics unadulterated by usury, while reminding us to read *The Cantos* for content, as an educational effort, no matter how disturbing.

NOTES

1 Tim Redman, *Ezra Pound and Italian Fascism* (Cambridge: Cambridge University Press, 1991), 156–7.

2 Mary Cheadle, *Ezra Pound's Confucian Translations* (Ann Arbor: University of Michigan Press, 1997), 58.

3 Alec Marsh, *Money and Modernity: Pound, Williams and the Spirit of Jefferson* (Tuscaloosa: University of Alabama Press, 1998), 35–41, 15.

4 Leon Surette, *Pound in Purgatory: From Economic Radicalism to Anti-Semitism* (Urbana: University of Illinois Press, 1999), 239–49.

5 Redman, *Ezra Pound and Italian Fascism*, 161.

6 Pound, Correspondence with Odon Por, Yale University, Beinecke Library, YCAL MSS Box 41, folder 1758.

7 Pound, Correspondence with David Horton, Yale University, Beinecke Library, YCAL MSS 43, Box 22, folder 990.

8 Redman, *Ezra Pound and Italian Fascism*, 158.

9 *Ezra Pound/ Letters/ John Theobald*, ed. Donald Pearce and Herbert Scheidau (Redding Ridge, CA: Black Swan, 1984), 44.

10 Pound, Correspondence with John Kasper, Yale University, Beinecke Library, YCAL MSS, Box 26, folder 1126.

11 *Ibid.*, folder 1130.

12 Jacket copy, John Kasper, *Virginians on Guard* (Washington, DC: Seaboard White Citizens' Councils, 1956).

13 Pound, "Academia Bulletin Zweck," Yale University, Beinecke Library, YCAL MSS, Box 66, folder 2838.

14 Pound quoted in Michael J. Alleman, "'A Pound of Flesh': Ezra Pound at St. Elizabeths," Dissertation (University of Texas, Dallas, 2007) 60.

15 Kasper, *Virginians on Guard*, 10–11.

16 Pound, Correspondence with Kasper, folder 2105.

17 Pound, Correspondence with David Horton, Box 19, folder 854.

18 Thomas Jefferson to James Madison, September 6, 1789, in *The Writings of Thomas Jefferson*, ed. Paul Leicester Ford (New York: G. P. Putnam, 1899), v: 116.

CHAPTER 10

Economics

Leon Surette

Ezra Pound's economic views first manifest themselves in the late years of World War I, when Pound was in his early thirties. There is no controversy about what led Pound to consider himself an apostle of economic reform. It was the arrival in 1917 of Clifford Hugh Douglas at the offices of *The New Age*. *The New Age* was a journal of arts and opinion edited by A. R. Orage, a Nietzschean, former Theosophist, and later Gurdjieffian apostle in New York city. Pound had been a regular contributor and a frequent denizen of its editorial offices since 1912. Orage allowed him to write on pretty much whatever interested him. *The New Age* was an important source of income for Pound, as well as a platform from which he could pronounce his views on art, politics, and religion.

Orage and his friend Holbrook Jackson had taken over *The New Age* in 1907 with financial assistance from wealthy Fabians – among them George Bernard Shaw. However, the journal was never an organ of Fabian opinion, aspiring to be open to all stripes of political and cultural opinion, specializing in "alternative" views on religion, politics, and economics. Although definitely a "little magazine," it was not obscure. Frequent contributors included G. B. Shaw, H. G. Wells, Arnold Bennet, G. K. Chesterton, Hilaire Belloc, T. E. Hulme, Herbert Read, Katherine Mansfield, and Edwin Muir, as well as Pound.

Douglas was an industrial engineer, quite innocent of any training in economics. But while reorganizing the Royal Aircraft Works at Farnborough during the First World War, he made a startling discovery: the wages, salaries, dividends, and retained profit of the factory added up to a smaller sum than the aggregate price of the goods it produced – the aircraft. This is known as the A + B theorem. From this observation he drew the conclusion that it would be impossible for the workers, managers, *and* owners of any factory to purchase the product of that factory with their collective incomes. If this were true for one factory, it would be true for all.[1] The consequence would be a chronic, structural shortfall of purchasing power in the economies of industrial nations. He believed that industrial economies compensated for this inadequacy in two principal ways – exports and war. The former disposed of otherwise unsaleable goods by selling them to foreigners, the latter by destroying them. The fact that World War I was followed by economic depression in Europe seemed to confirm his analysis. The anomaly of American postwar prosperity was removed after 1929.

Douglas' discovery gave birth to the economic doctrine known as "Social Credit" and a fringe political movement of the same name. ("Fringe" except for Canada, where it became mainstream, and even formed long-standing provincial governments in Alberta and British Columbia.) Social Credit offered a simple solution to the well-recognized ills of industrial economies, which were: (1) the apparent inability of domestic economies to absorb an industrial nation's output – necessitating exports to maintain employment;[2] (2) the need to keep wages low in order to maintain those exports; (3) the business cycle – recurring economic downturns causing unemployment and business failures. Those ills of industrial capitalism had long since been identified by such critics of capitalism as John Ruskin, Karl Marx, J. S. Hobson, P. J. Proudhon, and Silvio Gesell. In the early twentieth century they were being addressed (often in the pages of *The New Age*) by S. G. Hobson (unrelated to J. S.), G. K. Chesterton, Hilaire Belloc, G. D. H. Cole, and the Fabians.[3] Accordingly, Douglas received a warm welcome from Orage.

Social Credit belongs to a class of economic theories known as "under-consumptionism," because they hold that it is possible for an economy to produce more goods than it can consume at prevailing prices. The capacity of an economy to consume the goods it produces is governed by the relationship between prices on the one hand, and wages, salaries, and dividends on the other. The dominant view among economists – called equilibrium theory – held that prices and wages automatically adjust to clear the markets. For example, if more goods and services were on offer than the quantity of existing wages, salaries and dividends could purchase at prevailing prices, those prices would fall. Conversely if wages, etc. exceeded the supply of goods and services, prices would rise.

The equation that underpins this counterintuitive doctrine is known as "Say's Law," because it was first articulated in Jean Baptiste Say's 1803 *Treatise on Political Economy*. Galbraith explains Say's Law as holding "that, from the proceeds of every sale of goods, there was paid out to someone somewhere in wages, salaries, interest, rent or profit... the wherewithal to buy that item. As with one item, so with all. This being so, there could not be a shortage of purchasing power in the economy."[4] Clearly, this is precisely the inverse of Douglas' A + B theorem, which holds that the total of the wages, dividends, and profits disbursed in the production of a good is always *less* than the price of the good. Both cannot be true.

Say's Law was challenged by Malthus in 1820 and by Karl Marx in *Das Kapital* (1867). However, David Ricardo's quick response to Malthus ruled the day within "orthodox" economics until the publication of J. M. Keynes' *The General Theory of Employment, Interest and Money* in 1936 "brought it to an end."[5] As any reader of the daily press will know, Keynesian economics has since been consigned to the dustbin of economic ideas – at least by the media. The slayer of Keynesian economics was the late Milton Friedman, who revived Say's law in the simplified form: "supply creates its own demand." This new orthodoxy is not called Friedmanism, but more descriptively, "supply side economics." It is important to be aware that there is, in fact, no longer an orthodoxy. Keynesians and Friedmanites continue to battle it out, not to mention Marxist and "welfare" economists. Nonetheless, the discipline is dominated by the supply siders. Pound ought to have welcomed Keynesian economics, as many Social Creditors did, but he did not.

The point to be taken from this brief – and inadequate – history of economic thought is that the issue in question – the possibility of insufficient purchasing power in an economy – has been controversial within economics for at least 200 years, and continues to be so to this day. We should also have in mind that at the time Douglas was writing, there was no controversy amongst professional economists. As John Kenneth Galbraith put it: "Until late in the '30s no candidate for a Ph. D. at a major American university who spoke seriously of a shortage of purchasing power as a cause of depression could be passed."[6] Since Social Credit doctrine breached Say's Law, it was rejected by all and sundry as moonshine. Literary-critical commentary on Pound's enthusiasm for Social Credit – if negative – is grounded on Say's Law; or – if positive – on an acceptance of underconsumptionist arguments – whether Marxist or Douglasite.

I shall not adjudicate the merits of either position. My point is simply that since professional economists have been unable to settle the issue during the last two centuries, Pound's acceptance of Social Credit economics cannot count as evidence of his stupidity, venality, or malignity. Indeed, it may reasonably count as evidence of his public-spirited wish for general prosperity. However, we will see that his principal motivation was a desire to place the arts on a sound economic footing. Lord Desai, in his recent assessment of Pound's economics, *The Route of All Evil: The Political Economy of Ezra Pound*, admits as much, concluding that "Pound thinks like a moralist not an economist."[7] Apparently Desai regards the two modes as mutually exclusive – something with which Pound would be inclined to agree.

What accounts for Pound's susceptibility to the promise of a technical solution to poverty that would leave society otherwise undisturbed? To begin, we should place him in the context of literary utopian dreamers, beginning with Coleridge's and Southey's plan to find wives and emigrate to America where they would create an utopian society on the banks of the Susquehanna. That plan came to nothing – except for Coleridge's disastrous marriage. But other utopian schemes were actualized, the most celebrated being George Ripley's Brook Farm (1841–6), inspired by the French utopian, Charles Fourier. Upton Sinclair's experiment at Helicon Hall in 1907 lasted only months. Both schemes were halted by disastrous fires, but they were already coming to grief through internal dissension.

Pound was never involved in such a scheme, but he did propose an utopian community in "Revolt of Intelligence v": "There are several score of men in Europe who, given two dozen chosen companions and funds equivalent to the often-mentioned 'cost of the late war for one day,' could . . . set up a centre of civilisation preferable to any this era provides. I should not suggest a desert for the site, nor too remote a locality, like Tahiti; but let us say Antwerp, or Leyden, or Pavia."[8] The closest he ever came to such a community were his "Ezuversity" at Rapallo and later – more unhappily – his "audiences" on the lawn of St. Elizabeths.

Long before he came into contact with Douglas, Pound – like many others in the first decade of the twentieth century – was already thinking in terms of an epochal change in Atlantic culture. If we are to understand Douglas' appeal to Pound, we need to consider the historical circumstances toward the end of World War I when Douglas and Orage worked out Social Credit theories. A crucial component of those circumstances was the widespread belief of Americans that the war marked the end of an era, and offered the hope, in President Wilson's words, of "a new world order."

However, Europeans were not so attracted by the competing models for that new order – capitalist America and Bolshevik Russia. Although ordinary men and women were traumatized by the obscene slaughter of the War, the leaders of Britain and France hoped for a return to the prewar state of affairs – at least for themselves. They saw the dismantling of the Hapsburg and Ottoman Empires not as an opportunity for "self-determination" as President Wilson did, but rather as an opportunity to extend and buttress their own empires. Wilson's dream of a new world order did indeed change the map of Europe, but it did not stop the victors from dividing up the spoils of the collapsed Ottoman Empire. And the American people were uninterested in reforming the world order. Congress refused to ratify the League of Nations treaty in November, 1919, and – in a gesture of moral superiority – enacted Prohibition two months later. Both acts symbolized America's withdrawal into its prewar isolationist mode. Thus both Europe and America failed to return to the dynamism and optimism that had marked the prewar period. In Europe ordinary men and women desired nothing better than to return to the *status quo ante*, forgetting how unsatisfactory that had been. For their part, the Americans reveled in the "Roaring Twenties," marked by an explosion of closet civil disobedience and criminality fueled by bootleg liquor.

These postwar developments were completely at odds with Pound's utopian tendencies. Before the war he had been an enthusiastic proponent of a modern "Renaissance." The thesis of his 1912 *New Age* series, "Patria Mia," was "that America has a chance for Renaissance" (*PM*, 11). Pound believed that an American renaissance would be instigated by the discovery of forgotten, ignored, or rejected ideas and practices, as the Renaissance had been by the fall of Byzantium, bringing Greek art and philosophy to Italy. Pound's Greece was China; London was the new Byzantium, and New York, the new Florence. Pound himself was perhaps Ficino and Petrarch rolled into one.

Pound was first introduced to Chinese culture by Allan Upward, telling his mother in a letter of October, 13, 1913, "You'll find Giles 'Hist. of Chinese Literature' a very interesting book. Upward has sort of started me off in that direction. I have also embarked on a French translation of Confucius and Mencius." His enthusiasm for China remained a constant in his work for the rest of his career. Even though his Sinophilia was scarcely compatible with his economic radicalism, Pound found ways to accommodate the two – just as he later strove to accommodate fascism to both earlier enthusiasms. The American sinologist Ernest Fenollosa supplanted Upward as his guide to China, his next Byzantium:

"Ernest Fenollosa's finds in China and Japan, [and] his intimate personal knowledge, are no less potent than Crisolora's manuscripts. China is no less stimulating than Greece, even if Fenollosa had not had insight . . . these new masses of unexplored arts and facts are pouring into the vortex of London. They cannot help bringing about changes as great as the Renaissance changes, even if we set ourselves blindly against it" ("Affirmations VI," 410–11, in *GB*, 116–17.)[9]

He added, anticipating his postwar dissatisfaction with London: "The complete man must have more interest in things which are in seed and dynamic than in things which are dead, dying, static."[10] So when C. H. ("Major") Douglas showed up in the *New Age* offices on Cursitor Street in 1917 with a scheme that would distribute the wealth created by industrial capitalism equitably, Pound was primed to accept it as a component of his renaissance.

The New Age was the crossroads for the two dominant – and mutually hostile – radical ideological postures of prewar Britain. On the left were the Fabians, democratic socialists whose political arm reached into the Labour Party. They drew their inspiration primarily from the utilitarians, but joined the collectivist propensities of socialist thinkers such as Proudhon and Marx to that resolutely individualistic doctrine. On the right was a less cohesive group whose intellectual leaders were G. K. Chesterton and Hilaire Belloc. They drew their inspiration from Thomas Carlyle and John Ruskin, and were accordingly "reactionary" in social and political thinking, looking to the Middle Ages for their social and economic models. Belloc and Chesterton were vigorous Catholic converts. The Fabians were, on the whole, militant atheists.

Prior to Douglas' arrival on the scene, Orage was promoting something called "Guild Socialism." Its leading theorists were S. G. Hobson and G. D. H. Cole.[11] They attempted to create a set of political and economic policies that drew on Ruskinian medievalism, Proudhonian socialism, and Georges Sorel's syndicalist movement. Its principal goal was to achieve an egalitarian economic regime while preserving private property, individual rights, and religious belief – all three of which were discarded by Marxists, but only the last by Fabians. Pound was not attracted to Guild Socialism – largely because of its Christian piety; "Chester–Belloc" was a favorite target in the interminable articles Pound published in *The New Age* during and immediately after World War I.

Between June, 1919 and January, 1920, Pound published two long series in *The New Age* – "Pastiche. The Regional" and "The Revolt of Intelligence" – which represent his effort to work out a political posture for postwar conditions. He is primarily concerned to resist the egalitarian tendencies of all varieties of socialism, arguing that "it is for the health of civilisation" that "unjust concentrations of power" and wealth "should occur." He has in mind the Renaissance model of wealthy patrons supporting the arts. His protest that he is not "running counter to the policy of this paper or sanctioning the 'capitalist system,'" reveals that he had not adopted Guild Socialism, nor was he yet committed to Social Credit, which *did* sanction the capitalist system.[12]

Social Credit was first articulated in a nine-part series by Douglas running in *The New Age* – concurrently with Pound's articles – from February
5 to April 1, 1920, and published as *Economic Democracy* later in 1920. An
indication of Douglas' influence on Pound is that he added the crime of
"usury" to his list of grievances, implausibly catalogued in a Spring 1920
review of W. H. Hudson's *The Naturalist in La Plata*: "A bloated usury, a
cowardly and snivelling politics, a disgusting financial system, the sadistic
curse of Christianity work together . . . that an hundred species of wild fowl
and beast shall give way before the advance of industry." And he is still
pressing his elitist defense of the extraordinary individual through the analogy of endangered species: "that the plains be covered with uniform and
verminous sheep, bleating in perfect social monotony; but in our alleged
'society' the same tendencies and the same urge that the bright plumed and
the fine voiced species of the genus anthropos, the favoured of the gods,
the only part of humanity worth saving, is attacked."[13]

From about this time, Social Credit's condemnation of banks of discount
as usurious exploiters of humanity became a fixed component of the socio-
cultural theory that animated *The Cantos* – along with Fenollosa's theory of
the ideogram and Confucian political theory. But it was not until the advent
of the world-wide depression following the New York Stock Market crash
of 1929 that Pound began to write obsessively about economic matters.
By 1931 he was in correspondence with followers of Silvio Gesell, and was
attempting unsuccessfully to sell Gesell's idea of *Schwundgeld* or "Shrinking
money" to the Douglasites, who would have no part of it.

With the publication of Keynes' *The General Theory of Employment,
Interest and Money* in 1936, orthodox economics moved toward the underconsumptionist posture of Social Credit – though not all the way. However,
Pound continued to count Keynes as an antagonist. For a while he flirted
with the equally eminent American economist, Irving Fisher, who endorsed
Gesellite monetary theories. But in the end Pound went his own way, vainly
attempting to accommodate Gesellite policy prescriptions with Douglasite
ones. As a result, he found himself at odds with both camps. His Gesellite
flirtation unfortunately put him in touch with the Briton, Arthur Kitson,
and the German-American, Hugo Fack, both of whom were anti-Semitic.

Many commentators have seized on Pound's quarrel with both the Douglasites and the Gesellites as evidence that he outgrew Douglas in the forties.
While it is true that he tried to reconcile Gesell with Douglas, and invoked
Mussolini's policies as (imperfect) exemplifications of either or both in
such works as *Gold and Work* and *An Introduction to the Economic Nature
of the United States* (both published in the penultimate year of the war),

he never abandoned either Douglas' policy prescription of a national dividend, nor Douglas' hostility to banks. Moreover, Pound came to adopt the anti-Semitism that befouled the work of Douglas, Kitson, and Fack, in addition to the American conspiracy theorist, Willis A. Overholser and the radio priest, Father Coughlin. All of these men attributed the economic travails of the West to the evil machinations of Jewish bankers, who blocked rational economic reforms so as to preserve their wealth and power.

However, the crucial event determining Pound's political identity was not his association with these men, but his interview with the Italian dictator, Benito Mussolini in January 1933. From that point on he was an admirer, and imagined that he had the ear of the great man. Shortly afterward, he was approached by the Hungarian journalist, Odon Por, then resident in Italy and director of the grandly titled Istituto per gli Studi di Politica Internazionale. Por was a long-time economic radical, and, like Pound, an alumnus of *The New Age* – though they had not met in London – and a fascist (but not an anti-Semite). Together they fondly imagined that they could persuade the fascist regime to accept their economic advice. As events spiraled toward another disastrous European war, and Pound came under the influence of the men listed above, he became increasingly hostile to the democracies, and increasingly shrill in his polemic, culminating in the broadcasts that earned him an indictment for treason.

What Keynes said of Major Douglas in *The General Theory of Employment, Interest and Money* could equally well be said of Pound:

The strength of Major Douglas's advocacy has, of course, largely depended on orthodoxy having no valid reply to much of his destructive criticism... Major Douglas is entitled to claim, as against some of his orthodox adversaries, that he at least has not been wholly oblivious of the outstanding problem of our economic system. Yet he has scarcely established an equal claim to rank – a private, perhaps, but not a major in the brave army of heretics – with Mandeville, Malthus, Gesell and Hobson, who, following their intuitions, have preferred to see the truth obscurely and imperfectly rather than to maintain error, reached indeed with clearness and consistency and by easy logic but on hypotheses inappropriate to the facts.[14]

Unhappily, the workings of the world economy are understood by very few – if by anyone – and those who understand them best all too often exploit their understanding for their own profit. Eighty years minus one after the onset of the Great Depression, the media is once again full of reports of financial chicanery, regulatory incompetence or dereliction, and widespread economic distress suffered by ordinary citizens around the world. And, as in Pound's day, we are told by some experts that the "laws" of economics must be allowed to work out our destiny without interference. Pound was convinced that such nostrums were lies – as indeed they often are. But it does not follow that the liars actually control events – as Pound believed. Nevertheless, he confronted them on the economic battlefield throughout his life.

NOTES

1 Pound incorporated the A + B theorem in Canto xxxviii/190, first published in Orage's new journal, *The New English Weekly*, in September 1933.

2 See, John Maynard Keynes, *The General Theory of Employment, Interest and Money* (London: Macmillan, 1964), 382–3.

3 For an account of these economic "heretics" as Keynes called them, see Chapter 23 of Keynes' *General Theory*: "Notes on Mercantilism, the Usury Laws, Stamped Money and Theories of Under-consumption."

4 John Kenneth Galbraith, *Money: Whence it Came, Where it Went* (London: Andre Deutsch, 1975), 218.

5 *Ibid.*, 219.

6 *Ibid.*

7 Meghnad Desai, *The Route of All Evil: The Political Economy of Ezra Pound* (London: Faber and Faber, 2006), 111.

8 *The New Age* (January 8, 1920): 153.

9 "Affirmations VI," *The New Age* (February 11, 1915): 410–11.

10 *Ibid.*

11 In his "introduction" to Georges Renard's *Guild's in the Middle Ages* (London: G. Bell and Sons, 1919), G. D. H. Cole identified the medieval provenance of Guild Socialism, and alluded to the role of *The New Age* in launching it:

> Moreover, in our own times, an even more determined attempt is being made to apply the lessons of the Middle Ages to modern industrial problems. Mr. A. J. Penty's *The Restoration of the Guild System*, published in 1907, began this movement, which was then taken up and transformed into the constructive theory of National Guilds, first by Mr. A. R. Orage and Mr. S. G. Hobson in *The New Age*, and later by the writers and speakers of the National Guilds League. (6–7)

12 "Pastiche. The Regional. ix," *The New Age* (September 11, 1919): 336.

13 *The Little Review* 7 (May/June 1920): 13–17.

14 Keynes, *General Theory*, 370.

CHAPTER II

Radio broadcasts

Benjamin Friedlander

In November 1939, only a few months after Germany invaded Poland, Ezra Pound set forth a propaganda plan for America, sharing it first with Cornelio di Marzio, editor of *Meridiano di Roma* (a fascist newspaper already publishing Pound's articles), and then with various representatives of the Italian government. The plan concerned a wide-ranging series of publications, but in pressing forward – Pound was politely rebuffed in December, then again more firmly in April – he shifted his emphasis from print to radio. This was not a surprising turn. The disruption of shipping made print an unreliable medium for reaching the USA, and Pound had come to believe (as he told an Italian functionary) that "the absolute predominance of Jews in the North American press . . . obstructs in an absolute fashion the possibility of making [Italy's] voice heard in the United States."[1]

Though no great lover of the radio (Pound thought it a "God damn destructive and dispersive devil of an invention" [*SL*, 342]), he had gained some small experience of the technology in preparing his operas for the BBC, and had developed an appreciation for the medium's political reach in considering the career of Father Coughlin.[2] In 1936, offering *The Listener* a series of essays on what he would do as "minister of Kulchur in Utopia," Pound was told by the editor, "If you want to be a Minister . . . you will have to broadcast" (quoted in *EPRO*, 196). By May of 1940, he had come to the same conclusion, working out "a lucid rhetorical scheme" for radio propaganda for the United States with numbered points grouped under the headings "scope" and "methods."[3] Eventually, Pound's perseverance paid off. In November – five months after Italy entered the war and a year after his initial overtures – the Ministry of Popular Culture invited him to submit scripts. His security clearance was still being processed when Pound made his initial broadcast in January 1941; a scattering of US newspapers reported the event.

Pound's employment by the Ministry of Popular Culture signaled no radical break from his earlier commitments, but the moment was hardly propitious for a deeper entanglement with Mussolini's regime. A resident of Italy since 1924, Pound had been a public advocate for the fascist cause since meeting "Il Duce" in 1933, supporting the invasion of Ethiopia and contributing articles to the *British–Italian Bulletin*, a journal run by the Italian embassy in London. In one of those articles, he frankly acknowledged his propagandistic aims, but took pains to disclaim a nationalist agenda: "I am not writing Italian propaganda, any more than I am writing British propaganda. I am, if you like, writing European propaganda for the sake of a decent Europe wherein the best people will not be murdered for the monetary profit of the lowest and rottenest" (*EPCP*, VII: 33). Such a disclaimer would prove unconvincing once war had broken out in Europe. America was still officially neutral when Pound first went on the air, but a survey published in 1938 showed Americans turning against the fascist countries by a margin of twenty to one, creating what the *New York Times* called a "sympathy bloc" with England and France.[4] The onset of war did nothing to change this. As a consequence, in making his initial broadcasts from Rome, Pound was not simply continuing his earlier efforts in a new medium; he was also choosing sides in a widening conflict, aligning himself with a nation that the majority of his listeners already viewed as an enemy.

Not that Pound shared in this judgement. From his perspective, Mussolini was, if anything, more American than Roosevelt, a fulfillment of the political aspirations of the founding fathers. As he wrote in 1935, "The heritage of Jefferson, Quincy Adams, Jackson, Van Buren is HERE, NOW *in the Italian peninsula* . . . not in Massachusetts or Delaware" (*JM*, 12). From this position it followed that a loyal US citizen should adhere to the fascist program, even if it meant denouncing his own leaders. "Am I American?" he asked a correspondent in 1939, answering his own question, "Yes, and bugger the present state of the country, the utter betrayal of the American Constitution" (*SL*, 322). Pound, it bears remembering, was not alone in this view of Roosevelt's administration. His favorite congressman, the isolationist George Tinkham, employed a similar rhetoric on the floor of the House, denouncing what he took to be a secret agreement with England as "disloyal to the United States and traitorous."[5] But Pound's antiwar stance was only superficially isolationist; his opposition to US intervention served a broader political agenda, one that tied Italy's example – and Italy's fate – to radical change at home on the model of Mussolini's autarchy.

Countering the notion that America could save democracy by intervening in Europe, Pound began one early broadcast, "Democracy is saved, or saves itself, when men of absolute honesty get to the center and take control . . . I don't think you'll save democracy by stopping Italy's internal reforms."[6] In another he declared: "The war is not a war between nations. It is not even a war between races. It is a war of a small and very dirty clique of money lenders against the whole of humanity" – a war in which the American government was, in Pound's view, "in sympathy with the wrong side."[7] The right side, of course, was in sympathy with Italy and Germany, and did have a racial agenda, but Pound was generally sly about divulging these beliefs in his first year of broadcasting. Only occasionally did he make his allegiances clear, targeting his enemies with a vulgarity that would become the norm in 1942 and after. Much of this vulgarity took the form of race-baiting. Referring to England as "Anglo-Judaea," he pronounced Churchill's "gang, whether kike, gentile, or hybrid," as "not fit to govern," and he gave Roosevelt a series of Jewish names ("Jewsfelt," "Roosenstein," "Rosefield"), denouncing F.D.R.'s spokespeople as "[t]hese chicken-headed fat mammies [who] have never given a glance at our history" (*EPS*, 4, 7, 17, 387–8). Ultimately, however, the bare fact that Pound was transmitting from Rome was more damning to his audience than anything he said. Even before Pearl Harbor, his reputation suffered considerably. A 1941 essay by William Carlos Williams called Pound "a pitiable spectacle," and the syndicated columnists Pearson and Allen equated him, as Williams had done, with the British propagandist "Lord Haw Haw" (William Joyce), who broadcast from Berlin during the bombing of London and was executed after the war for treason.[8]

Pound's decision to spend the war in Italy was not an easy or inevitable one. At the very moment when he had, at last, made headway with the Ministry, he was still attempting to book passage to the USA, making arrangements to store his art and library with the family of Ubaldo degli Uberti (a retired admiral who would publish Pound's most overtly fascist cantos near the end of the war). Even after he began broadcasting, Pound went to the trouble to renew his passport; the US State Department – aware of his activities and hoping to spur his departure – took the unusual step of granting a mere six months' extension. Pound's passport was just reaching its expiration date when Japan attacked Pearl Harbor. But the question of Pound's wartime residence would not have posed a serious problem, legally speaking, had he only stayed away from the microphone. Clearly, he had an inkling of this, since initially Pound did retire from broadcasting, preparing a statement that *Time* magazine cited with relief in January – the issue was still on the newsstands when Pound returned to the air.⁹ The last sentence of that return broadcast has often been cited as a prophecy of Pound's own fate: "Whom God would destroy, he first sends to the bug house" (*EPS*, 27). The line echoes Pound's characterization of Roosevelt in the same talk "as a President whose mental condition was NOT . . . all that could or should be desired of a man in so responsible a position or office" (*EPS*, 23).

Given his acknowledgement that the USA was now legally at war, Pound's justification for resuming his broadcasts is surprisingly vague. Citing Mencius ("the true sage seeks not repose" [*EPS*., 24]), he affirms the necessity of maintaining communication across the Atlantic, whatever trouble it might cause. "The United States," he declares, "has been MISinformed. The United States has been led down the garden path, and may be down under the daisies. All thru shuttin' out news" (*EPS*, 24). Pound's task, then, as he understood it, was largely pedagogical. The content of that pedagogy, as it unfolds in his other broadcasts, encompasses three general aims: (1) to inform his listeners about the root causes of war; (2) to expose the conspiracy of profiteers whose interests were served by war; and (3) to advocate for the solutions proposed by fascism, including the eugenic solution to the racial character of the conspiracy.

Although Pound's propaganda work was initially motivated by ideology, not self-interest, money probably played a role in the degree of his involvement, and may have served as an incentive for continuing after Pearl Harbor. Pound was fifty-six years old in 1942, with two families to support, and his parents were also living in Italy, but because of the disruption of mail his father's pension checks and Dorothy Pound's annuity from her trust fund were not arriving. Further, Pound was unable to earn money from his publishing contacts in England and America, and he was no longer receiving royalty payments. He did continue to write articles for the Italian press (most of it still uncollected in English), but the Ministry provided him with a dependable income as well as a chance to address the English-speaking world. "During the last war I communicated to the US in the Little Review," he reminisced in one broadcast, praising the Italian government for having offered him an alternative: "You tie me down by one foot in Rapallo, and block every other opening, and for the sake of God's light, they open me up this air. Who does? ROME does!"¹⁰

Pound, for his part, adopted a professional attitude in his broadcasts, overseeing such details as the music that would follow his talks, and seeking advice from William Joyce, with whom he initiated a correspondence in the summer of 1941 (When Joyce told Pound that he would not "presume to criticize," Pound replied, "You needn't worry about the word 'criticize' / call it guidance if you like ... New technique for Unkle Ez. A poem has to be good in 200 years / or it is bad. Quite different technique for talk that has to take effect NOW or never." Pound's pay was commensurate with his commitment. According to the statement given his Allied captors, he was paid 350 lire for every broadcast of a talk he himself delivered (about $18), and 300 lire for broadcasts of scripts that others read.[11] This was not a negligible sum. A single script would have supported a working-class family in central or south Italy for several weeks. Middle-class families, of course, earned substantially more, especially in the north, but since Pound composed multiple scripts for each week, each broadcast two or three times, his monthly income was certainly comfortable, at least until General Badoglio's surrender in September 1943, when Pound curtailed his on-air role and the Italian economy went into free-fall.

A 1945 accounting of payments from the Ministry of Popular Culture, signed and dated by Pound on Ministry stationery, shows him receiving 49,432 lire in 1941 (about $2,500, more than a US civil servant), followed by payments of 58,391 lire in 1942 and 43,187 lire in 1943. Nor is this accounting complete. Only three checks are listed for 1944, totaling 2,050 lire, and none for 1945, although Pound continued to be involved with Italian radio until the end of the war, admitting to his interrogators that he received monthly stipends right up until his arrest. In all likelihood, the full extent of Pound's radio work will never be known. We are especially unclear about his on-air activities after the Justice Department filed its indictment for treason in July 1943, the Federal Communications Commission having suspended its monitoring of Pound's broadcasts at that time.[12] We do know that Pound subsequently wrote for a program called "Jerry's Front Calling." Unfortunately, only a few traces of his late collaboration with Germany survive, among them a script in German that begins, "No, I do not speak against my fatherland. I fight in this century-long war between ... usury and anyone who does his honest day's labor with brain or fist."[13]

Pound's broadcasts occasionally make reference to government announcements, but they are not commentaries on the day-to-day progress of the war. This is largely due to their manner of preparation: Pound wrote out his talks in advance, then recorded them in batches for subsequent transmission. Yet the paucity of topical reference served his purpose well, as Pound's principal theme was not the war itself, but war's underlying cause. "You do not, not officially, YET know what the war is about," he begins one broadcast (*EPS*, 338). The problem, in Pound's view, was not simply ignorance, but "the crawling slime of a secret rule . . . that . . . eats like a cancer into the heart and soul of all nations" (*EPS*, 73). Responding to that secret rule, Pound's pedagogical project became a form of counter-insurgency. "If I go on poundin' from day to day," he declares, "I will finally teach you kids why you got drug into this war (if you survive it), and when you know that you will . . . fight like hell and fight somethin' nearer home than the Philippines" (*EPS*, 162–4). The two principal lines of argument in this "poundin'" are first, economic, second, racial. By and large, the economic argument takes precedence, as one would expect given Pound's longstanding advocacy of monetary reform.

For Pound, "[t]here is no understanding of history without some under-standing of finance," of currency manipulation and usury (*EPS*, 262). These financial "wangles" are used to create debt, which in turn places the entire population under the control of a few (*EPS*, 265). "They call it international kapital," he declares. "It is not international . . . It is subnational. A quick-sand UNDER the nations . . . destroying all law and government, destroying the nations" (*EPS*, 55). But notwithstanding his emphasis on debt as the root cause of war, Pound's economic analysis is overshadowed, finally, by his denunciation of the parties responsible. Generally, this denunciation is how his racial argument gets raised. For example: "The Talmud . . . is the dirtiest teaching that any race ever codified," "the one and only begetter of the Bolshevik system" (*EPS*, 117). Or elsewhere: "The Jews have worked out a system, very neat system, for the ruin of the rest of mankind, one nation after another" (*EPS*, 256).

Indeed, since the Jews are responsible for this ruinous "system," eco-nomics alone is insufficient for appreciating its full nature or for counter-acting its effects. "[I]t becomes increasingly difficult to discuss American affairs EXCEPT on a racial basis," Pound asserts; "the alien race wormed into the system. Kills off not only a government system but the race itself" (*EPS*, 113, 199). The crudeness of Pound's language is often shocking when he touches on this theme. He speaks of "[t]he Freudian Jew, paralyzing the nucleus of will in his goyim victim," of "[t]he unFreudian chewess eating like a boll weevil into the creative will of her victim" (*EPS*, 297). He derides "[t]he Anglo-Saxon race" for having let itself be "ruled by Jews" (*EPS*, 339), and he lets loose a steady stream of variations on the word "kike" (kikery, kikocracy, kikette, kikeria, kikosophy). It is only in the context of such uninhibited rhetoric that Pound can imagine himself restrained when he advises, as he does in a broadcast from 1943, "I think it might be a good thing to hang Roosevelt and a few hundred yidds IF you can do it by due legal process, NOT otherwise" (*EPS*, 289). Presumably, Italy's racial laws and Germany's more aggressive use of the courts provided him with his model.

Here and there, Pound allows that not all Jews are usurers, and not all usurers Jews, but these disavowals of a racial agenda are only superficial. Persistently, he identifies his targets in racial terms, and when his invective is not explicitly racial, it is implicitly so, animalizing or pathologizing his enemies in a manner that gains coherence within the overall context of his eugenic discourse. A few key broadcasts elaborate this discourse, notably "With Phantoms" (1942), a talk in which Pound sets forth approvingly "the THREE planks of the Hitler program" as outlined in *Mein Kampf.* These consist of "health" (eugenics), personal responsibility, and the "STUDY of history" (*EPS*, 139–40).

Pound's endorsement of *Mein Kampf* indicates how far his attraction to fascism had moved in the 1940s beyond Mussolini's economic reforms. In his radio broadcasts, race law ("health"), autarchy ("responsibility"), and the uncovering of hidden plots ("history") also prove immensely attractive. "TWO basic texts," he informs his audience, "were enounced in EUROPE . . . Mussolini's . . . 'Discipline the economic forces,' " and Hitler's "on the problem of human breeding" (*EPS*, 154). Inattention to these two teachings had, for Pound, led to the degradation of everyday life in the Allied nations; fascism, as he saw it, was the only solution. Without equivocation he asserts, "EVERY social reform that has gone into effect in Germany and Italy should be defended" (*EPS*, 319).

There are indications that Pound conceived of his radio talks as forming a book, but they were written first and foremost for oral delivery, and some acquaintance with the surviving recordings is essential for appreciating their character and impact as propaganda. The National Archives at College Park, Maryland, preserves the recordings made by the US government.[14] The sound quality is often poor, but even the poorer recordings are useful for reminding a listener that the talks were not simply discrete works within Pound's oeuvre, but part of a broader propaganda project on the part of the Italian government.[15] News programs preceded them, musical programs followed; on at least one tape, Pound is heard participating in a stiff, on-air conversation with other broadcasters. But setting aside Pound's assimilation into Italy's programming, the recordings are valuable for turning our attention to the question of delivery.

Regarding performance, Pound had, apparently, quite determinate thoughts, writing to William Joyce in 1941, "I think I have got my voice right at last," fol. 1117), and appending a script from 1943 with the reminder, "to be read with the slow nasty drawl, which is evidently the only speech of which the sheenies are capable."[16] Yet notwithstanding this precision, opinions have varied greatly on the final result. *Poetry* magazine, in an editorial that severed ties with Pound, spoke of "his voice scolding like a disgruntled squirrel," and a wartime book on radio propaganda emphasized his "domineering tones."[17] Julien Cornell, Pound's lawyer, recalled him as "speaking in the folksy drawl of a plainsman from the Western United States," and others have heard more elaborate acts of impersonation.[18]

According to Charles Norman, "Pound gave many of his talks in stage-American sectional accents – if Yankee, more nasal . . . if western, more 'folksey' and drawling."[19] Hearing less coherence, C. David Heymann describes a broader range of voicings, not all of them matters of accent: "The palaver poured forth in a variety of tongues – flat, pedantic, scolding tones intermingled with exaggerated Southern drawls, Western plainsman lulls, Cockney growls. He switched from one to another without warn-ing, breaking at times into a torrid rage, slurring his words, ranting at a low-pitched roar."[20] Heymann's description makes especially vexed the problem of ascertaining Pound's intentions. Indeed, his description raises the possibility that Pound was losing control of his intentions. An elabo-rate masquerade such as Norman describes was certainly within Pound's power. The correspondence is replete with examples of Pound's mimicry, much of it performed as comedy – ethnic comedy on occasion, as in the Irish-accented set pieces performed for James Joyce (*PJ*, 241, 259) – and the radio talks do not stint on such forms of burlesque, some of it focused on regional accent, some of it class-based, some of it ethnic. As any student of blackface minstrelsy knows, however, burlesque can veer wildly from appropriated pleasure to exaggerated disdain, and it may be that the ten-sion with which that veering was held in check (for instance, the tension with which Pound balanced his affection for America with disgust for its government) can explain the disfiguring vehemence with which his imper-sonations were offered. But setting aside their character as performance, the voicings add two significant dimensions absent from Pound's printed text: a sense of the gravity of his actions, and a sense of the intensity with which those actions were carried out. The scripts are abstract, disembodied; the recordings corporeal, concrete.

Pound's career as a propagandist is the strongest evidence we have of his unyielding commitment to political change, and the profound price he paid for that career – thirteen years' imprisonment – makes the radio broadcasts one of the central facts of his life. Yet the surviving scripts and recordings are rarely treated as central documents; they have an aberrational status among Pound scholars, who for many decades received them with embarrassment and apologetics, segregating them from Pound's other prose and from his poetry. Indeed, one of the ironies of Pound's posthumous reception is that *The Pisan Cantos* should stand at the very center of his reputation, while the wartime writings that led directly to that poem are entirely marginal. There are good reasons for this marginality, most notably the unpleasantness of the content, but lack of attention has led to distortions, and permitted mischaracterizations to stand uncorrected. Clearly, there can be no coherent account of Pound's thought as a whole (especially with regard to such key issues as history, economics, race, violence, and the body) so long as the radio talks remain compartmentalized. Needed now, then, is a more complete and more reliable edition of the existing texts, supplemented by a compilation of the surviving recordings, and a more sustained scrutiny and contextualizing of the texts already in print.

NOTES

For their assistance in preparing this chapter, the author thanks Carla Billitteri, Giovanni Miraglia, and Demetres Tryphonopoulos.

1 Pound did not direct his political writing in the 1930s nor his subsequent radio speeches to the United States alone. He expended a sizable amount of energy in addressing Britain (with many of his broadcasts framed specifically for a British audience). Because of his American citizenship, however, Pound's broadcasts to the United States acquired a special status, both legally and with regard to his sense of himself as a patriot. My focus here is on the propaganda directed at the United States. Niccolò Zapponi, *L'Italia di Ezra Pound*, passage trans. Carla Billitteri (Rome: Bulzoni Editore, 1976), 61.

2 In 1935, in the *New English Weekly*, Pound held out hope that "Coughlin's nine million adherents can turn from passive listening to active enquiry" (*EPCP*, VI: 332). On Coughlin's influence on the content of Pound's radio broadcasts more generally, see Leon Surette, *Pound in Purgatory: From Economic Radicalism to Anti-Semitism* (Urbana: University of Illinois Press, 1999), 261–70.

3 Timothy Redman, *Ezra Pound and Italian Fascism* (Cambridge: Cambridge University Press, 1991), 208n.14.

4 George Gallup, "U.S. Survey Shows Enmity to Fascism," *New York Times* (July 27, 1938), 7. Note in this regard Pound's 1943 comment, "the Republican chiefs . . . thought Mr. Gallup's Jew-aided poll was an indication of popular feeling" (*EPS*, 248).

5 "Assail Hull Denial of Naval Intelligence," *New York Times* (March 15, 1938), 1.

6 Ezra Pound, "Transcript," February 28, 1941, Princeton Listening Center Records, Box 16, "ROME Feb 16–Feb 28, 1941," Seeley G. Mudd Manuscript Library, Princeton University.

7 Ezra Pound, "Transcript," March 17, 1941, Princeton Listening Center Records, Box 16, "ROME March 17–March 31, 1941," Seeley G. Mudd Manuscript Library, Princeton University.

8 William Carlos Williams, "Ezra Pound: Lord Ga-Ga!," *Decision* 2.3 (September 1941): 16–24; and Drew Pearson and Robert S. Allen, "The Daily Washington Merry-Go-Round," *Galveston Daily News* (November 14, 1941), 16.

9 "Retirement," *Time*, 39.4 (January 26, 1942): 53–4. Pound's first talk after Pearl Harbor was broadcast January 29, 1942.

10 Ezra Pound, *"If This Be Treason..."* (Venice: privately published, 1948), 3.

11 Yale University, Beinecke Library, folder 1117. Information on Pound's earnings is drawn from Document 6, "Sworn Statement by Ezra Pound," *LC*, 58–67; the financial records in Yale University, Beinecke Library, folder 5301; William D. Grampp, "The Italian Lira, 1938–45," *Journal of Political Economy* 54. 4 (August 1946): 309–33; and Scott Derks, *The Value of a Dollar: Prices and Incomes in the United States 1860–2004* (Millerton, NY: Grey House Publishing, 2004).

12 The fullest account of Pound's late propaganda work, in print as well as radio, is given by Redman in *Ezra Pound and Italian Fascism*.

13 Yale University, Beinecke Library, folder 5291, my translation.

14 The surviving recordings (housed with the Records of the Foreign Broadcast Intelligence Service, Record Group 262.5) cover all or part of 170 broadcasts made between October 2, 1941 and July 25, 1943; some of these are repeat transmissions, but the collection also includes numerous unpublished talks, most notably forty-two broadcasts delivered between July 1942 and February 1943, a gap of time not documented in *EPS* and often cited as a period of mysterious quiescence on Pound's part. It is likely that those recordings were long misplaced and only recently came to light.

15 See on this point Bruno Foa, "The Structure of Rome Short-Wave Broadcasts to North America" in *Propaganda by Short Wave*, ed. Harwood L. Childs and John B. Whitton (Princeton: Princeton University Press, 1942), 151–80. Although based on a study of broadcasts from before Pearl Harbor, Foa's essay cites Pound as "the trump card of Radio Rome" (155n.) and folds the content of Pound's talks into his survey of basic themes (167).

16 Yale University, Beinecke Library, folders 1117, 5273.

17 Eunice Tietjens, "The End of Ezra Pound," *Poetry* 60. 1 (April 1942): 39; E. Tangye Lean, *Voices in the Darkness: The Story of the European Radio War* (London: Secker and Warburg, 1943), 92.

18 Julien Cornell, *The Trial of Ezra Pound: A Documented Account of the Treason Case by the Defendant's Lawyer* (New York: John Day, 1966), 1.

19 Charles Norman, *Ezra Pound* (New York: The Macmillan Company, 1960), 387.

20 C. David Heymann, *Ezra Pound: The Last Rower: A Political Profile* (New York: Viking Press, 1976), 105.

CHAPTER 12

Law

Robert Spoo

In 1956, BBC producer D.G. Bridson visited St. Elizabeths Hospital to record Ezra Pound reading from his poems. Pound began one of the taping sessions with a monologue in which he described the "four steps" that had led to his incarceration. The first step had been his quarrel with an American passport official in Paris who had tried to interfere with his return to London in 1919. The second was being told that an American judge had declared: "In this country there ain't nobody has got any goddamned rights whatsoever." The third was the boast of a prosecuting attorney: "All that I'm interested in is . . . seeing what you can put over." The fourth and final step was learning from Senator Burton Wheeler in 1939 of President Roosevelt's effort to "pack" the Supreme Court. That was where Pound "took off from." "When the Senator is unable to prevent breaches of the Constitution . . . the duty, as I see it, falls back onto the individual citizen. And that is why . . . when I got hold of a microphone in Rome, I used it" (*ASC*, 823–5).

The "four steps," with their fairy-tale causality, are a distilled chronicle of Pound's disenchantment with America and liberal democracies. Like his encapsulation of economic wisdom in the slim broadside he called *Introductory Textbook (in Four Chapters)*, Pound's "four steps" seek to elucidate a world of complexity with the simplicity of a village explainer. Each of the "steps" purports to document a perversion of law by a tainted official: a desk jockey in the passport office for whom red tape was a religion; a judge whose sense of legal realism had declined into cynicism; a district attorney who flaunted prosecutorial indiscretion; a ruthlessly pragmatic chief executive keen to abuse his power of judicial appointment. In contrast to this rogues' gallery, Pound paints himself as a reluctant hero who was compelled to take up vigilante justice after legal officialdom had abdicated its responsibilities. One can almost hear the music of the Declaration of Independence swelling in the background: "[W]henever any Form of Government becomes destructive of [inalienable rights], it

is the Right of the People to alter or to abolish it, and to institute new
Government." The difference is that Pound describes his seizing the reins
of justice as not merely a right but a "duty." In doing so, he sketches a
defense to the treason charges he never had a chance to combat in the
courtroom: he had been forced (the law calls this a defense of "necessity")
to pour his righteous rage into a Roman microphone in order to prevent a
greater harm from being inflicted by lawless leaders.

Pound was essentially a moralist crying in the wilderness of the modern
metropolis. His indictments of grasping financiers, corrupt politicians,
and pandering publishers were rarely grounded in a specific idea of legal
culpability. His classification of villains was more Dantesque than juristic.
His famous definition of usury – a "charge for the use of purchasing
power, levied without regard to production; often without regard to the
possibilities of production" (XLV/230) – offers broad moral generalization
but no precise legal framework for determining impermissible exactions of
interest (in the manner, say, of usury statutes). Pound's rage was usually
too capacious to be bothered with the sort of detail that engrosses lawyers,
judges, and legislators.

Law as historical theme or morality tale emerges often in Pound's writings, particularly *The Cantos*. From the decrees of the Chinese emperors (LII–LXI), to the lawyerly and constitutional preoccupations of John
Adams (LXII–LXXI), to the meditations on the common law set down by
the sixteenth-century jurist Sir Edward Coke (CVII–CIX), law plays a role in
adumbrating Pound's typological vision of moral heroism in history. Yet it
was in his engagement with contemporary laws and legal problems, often
as letter-writer or journalist, that he recorded some of his most revealing
attitudes toward art and society. Here, Pound did grapple tangibly with the
details of law's coercive force. In this chapter I discuss the most significant
and enduring of his practical legal preoccupations: passport regulations,
book tariffs, copyright statutes, and obscenity laws.

Between 1915 and 1935, Pound repeatedly inveighed against laws – mostly
operative in the United States – that he regarded as meddlesome interferences with the ability of writers and their works to gain free passage across
national borders and exposure to new audiences. For Pound, an indispensable condition of creativity was the artist's ability to move freely in
time and space – to have access to unfamiliar ideas and *moeurs*. Writing
to the English poet F.S. Flint in 1912, he defended his preoccupation with
medieval poetry by explaining that "I have not been penned up within the
borders of one country and I am not minded to be penned into any set
period of years." Just as he had "escaped the limitations of place" through

a restless expatriate wanderlust, so he resisted "the limitations of time" by making the works of long-dead poets – Dante, Guido Cavalcanti, the twelfth-century troubadours – central to his métier.[1]

But travel in time and space can occur only to the extent permitted by law. In Pound's view, laws that mandated passport controls, literary purity, book tariffs, and discriminatory copyright protections were essentially restraints upon the body and mind of the individual.[2] Writing in *Poetry* in 1917, he denounced the barriers to international understanding that had been erected by America's book tariff and copyright laws, declaring that "Transportation is civilization." Laws that hinder "the free circulation of thought," he added, "*must* be done away with" (*EPCP*, II: 190). Abolishing such obstructive regulations would serve the same purpose as learning a foreign language or publishing works in translation: a broadening of the mind through international and transhistorical travel.

PASSPORTS

Pound's hatred of passport restrictions was indelibly fixed in Paris in 1919 when a petty official emerged from behind a partition in an American passport office and tried to prevent him from returning to England. "Damn the partition!" Pound exclaims in Canto VII. "Paper, dark brown and stretched, / Flimsy and damned partition" (VII/25). So upset had he been over this incident (from his first visit to Paris since the war) that he included the flimsy, Dilbert-like partition among the signs of postwar decay chronicled in this Canto.[3]

Passports and visas became requirements for international travel during the Great War. In December 1915, President Woodrow Wilson issued Executive Order No. 2285, which required American citizens traveling abroad to obtain passports. "These documents are rendered necessary," the Order explained, "because the regulations of all European countries and of several other foreign countries require passports or other documents of identification of all persons who enter their boundaries." For much of US history, passports had been optional, but the outbreak of war in 1914 had sealed their importance in controlling the movements of "hostile aliens, suspicious neutrals, potential spies, and displaced populations."[4] A federal law enacted in May 1918 provided that, upon Presidential wartime proclamation, "it shall . . . be unlawful for any citizen of the United States to depart from or enter or attempt to depart from or enter the United States unless he bears a valid passport."[5] The statute imposed heavy fines and imprisonment for violations. The Passport Act of 1926 further enlarged the power of the Secretary of State to issue passports to American citizens in foreign countries, subject to rules prescribed by the President.[6]

Pound never tired of attacking what he viewed as Wilson's attempt to use passports "to tie all serfs to the soil" (EP/JQ, 181). He raged at "Woodie Wilsi's rough necks," the petty bureaucrats who were permitted by law to tyrannize over travelers.[7] For Pound, the fact that hired officials could enforce a "closed frontier" meant that "free lines of communication between one country and another"[8] depended on the whim of a "pie faced Y.M.C.A. clerk" (*EP/JQ*, 180). The "flimsy and damned partition" that Pound encountered in 1919 became for him a symbol of thwarted international communication – an evil he felt he had been given the means to overcome when the Italian Ministry of Popular Culture made the airwaves available to him in 1940.

BOOK TARIFFS

What passports were to the body in transit, book tariffs were to the mind migrating in textual form. From 1864 to 1913, federal law imposed a 25 percent tariff on books entering the United States. In 1913, the tariff was reduced to 15 percent, still an obstacle for ordinary book purchasers. By then, the import duty was levied only on books published in English; foreign-language works were on the free list. Even English texts came in duty-free to public libraries and educational institutions, as long as orders were limited to two copies.[9] It was widely recognized that this "tax on knowledge" protected the interests of American printers and bookbinders. American Bible manufacturers, for example, protested that if the tariff on imported Bibles were reduced, the US Bible-making industry would be destroyed. One commentator retorted, "The price of Bibles to a hundred million people is to be maintained in the interest of a few hundred people engaged in their manufacture!"[10] By 1914, the United States and Russia were the only major powers that still levied a tariff on books published abroad.

Pound described the book tariff as "a hindrance to international communication." In *The New Age*, he noted that books have "an immaterial as well as a material component, and because of this immaterial component they should circulate free from needless impediment." It was a category error, he insisted, to treat literature "as a commerce or as manufacturing." The real harm fell on American writers, who as a result of the high cost of imported books came to innovations in foreign literature too late. The tariff thus contributed to "a provincial tone in American literature to its

invalidation" (*EPCP*, III: 227). American publishing was also stultified.
Instead of expanding their lists of classical reprints, for example, publishing houses could compete cheaply with foreign publishers by selling the
same titles at sub-tariff prices. In the absence of a tariff, American firms
would have an incentive, Pound thought, to issue different works in genuine competition with foreign publishers. If that were to happen, Pound
would have "two chances of getting a cheap issue of Golding's *Ovid*, or
Gavin Douglas' *Virgil*, which now I can not get save by sheer luck in finding a 1719 issue of one and a three dollar reprint of the other" (*EPCP*, III:
228).

Pound believed that all books should be exempt from tariffs, but especially those by "living authors, and of those the non-commercial books,
scholarship and belles lettres most certainly" (*EP/JQ*, 22). One reason for the
growing number of American expatriates, Pound suspected, was the high
cost of books imported into the United States. He admired the lawyer and
art collector John Quinn who in 1913 had worked tirelessly on an amendment of the US Tariff Act that removed the duty on imported paintings
and sculpture less than twenty years old. Representing the Association of
American Painters and Sculptors, Quinn helped forge a bill that conferred
duty-free status on all imported art, new and old.[11] Because only original
artwork could come in free under the revised law, the amendment had
the added virtue, Quinn boasted, of turning back many fake old masters,
which were taxed at the usual rate as "copies."[12]

Pound urged a comparable amendment of the book tariff: "AT LEAST
the first 3000 copies of ANY book of which there is no American edition
should go in free. After that there may be some question of favoring the
printer at the expense of the public" (*EPCP*, II: 228). Such a compromise
would allow the most deserving readers – students, scholars, budding
authors – to obtain new foreign works at competitive prices.

COPYRIGHT LAWS

Like passport regulations, copyright laws had the capacity to inhibit international communication. Backed by law, a rights-holder could permit
distribution of a copyrighted work in some countries and deny it in others.
And, as with book tariffs, the supra-competitive pricing that copyrights
allowed often discouraged importation of new works. Throughout much
of the twentieth century, protectionist features of US law empowered
customs officials to seize books that had not been printed on American
soil in accordance with "manufacturing" requirements inscribed into the

copyright act.[13] If not complied with, these requirements withheld American copyright protection from foreign-origin works, encouraging a form of legalized piracy within the United States. What was banned at the docks could thus reappear, sometimes in distorted forms, as knockoff copies issued from the shops of "bookleggers." These items could then compete cheaply with more expensive, copyrighted works by American authors.

Pound was profoundly dissatisfied with American copyright law as it stood in the first decades of the twentieth century. One of his chief purposes in demanding a new copyright law was to make it "easier for an author to retain the rights to the work of his brain than for some scoundrel to steal them" (*EPCP*, III: 208). Legalized American piracy of foreign works was a theme he returned to again and again in the 1920s and 1930s. Various authors of his acquaintance – James Joyce most notably – fell victim to American bookleggers.

When Congress finally granted rights to foreign authors in the Chace International Copyright Act of 1891,[14] protection came at the price of large concessions to American book manufacturers. Chief among these was the requirement (known as the "manufacturing clause") that a foreign work in any language could acquire copyright protection in the United States only if it was printed from type set within the country and if two copies were deposited in the Copyright Office on or before the date of first publication anywhere else. Although resourceful or well-connected foreign authors might be able to satisfy this tricky requirement of first or simultaneous publication in the United States, others could not.

The 1909 US Copyright Act – the law in force when Pound was waging his journalistic battles – modified the manufacturing clause but did not abolish it. First, the Act granted automatic protection to foreign-language works of foreign origin by exempting them from the manufacturing requirements.[15] Second, although foreign-origin works in English still had to be printed in the United States to acquire an American copyright, the 1909 Act relaxed this requirement by providing a thirty-day "*ad interim*" copyright if a copy of the foreign edition was deposited in the US Copyright Office within thirty days of its publication abroad. Once a copy was deposited, the work then had to be reprinted on US soil within the thirty-day *ad interim* window. Failure to do so – and thus to give American book artisans their due – would result in loss of American copyright after *ad interim* protection had expired.

Thus, when Pound assailed the US copyright law as "originally designed to favour the printing trade at the expense of the mental life of the country" (*EPCP*, V: 229), he had in mind a history of codified protectionism

for the domestic book trade that rendered the United States an outcast
from the international copyright community. The manufacturing clause,
together with other copyright formalities, prevented the United States from
joining the Berne Convention for the Protection of Literary and Artistic
Works for more than 100 years after other major nations had signed it.
The manufacturing clause and the book tariff combined to give a dubious windfall to the American book trade: while the tariff raised barriers
to legitimate literary competition from abroad, the copyright law encouraged inexpensive piracies of foreign works. Both laws lined the pockets of
domestic publishers and book manufacturers, and both treated books as if
they were mere articles of commerce – all to the detriment of international
communication.

Convinced that something must be done, Pound used the pages of *The
New Age* in 1918 to "set down a sketch of what the copyright law ought to be,
and what dangers should be guarded against." Pound began his "sketch,"
entitled "Copyright and Tariff," by declaring that "[t]he copyright of any
book printed anywhere should be and remain automatically the author's,"
and "[c]opyright from present date should be perpetual" (*EPCP*, III: 208).
Under his proposal, copyright in a work published anywhere in the world
would vest automatically and exclusively in the author – tacitly repealing
the manufacturing clause and bringing US law closer to the principles
of the Berne Convention, which protected the rights of authors as long
as their works were first published in any member country.[16] Curiously,
Pound's scheme would have legislated a "perpetual" copyright, even though
this would have been unconstitutional in the United States, where the
Constitution empowers Congress to grant copyrights for "limited Times"
only.[17]

No sooner had Pound announced his perpetual copyright, however,
than he dramatically qualified it: "BUT the heirs of an author should be
powerless to prevent the publication of his works or to extract any excessive
royalties." He went on: "If the heirs neglect to keep a man's work in print
and at a price not greater than the price of his books during his life,
then unauthorised publishers should be at liberty to reprint said works,
paying to heirs a royalty not more than 20 per cent. and not less than
10 per cent" (*EPCP*, III: 209). This provision – effectively creating what
the law calls a "compulsory license" – would have stripped noncompliant
heirs of the power to prevent reprinting of authors' works or to raise book
prices above those that existed during the authors' lifetimes. In effect, heirs
would become stewards of their ancestors' works. If they were not diligent
in keeping those works in print, their exclusive property right would vanish

and their only remedy for unauthorized uses would be a right to damages in the form of royalties withheld by the state-licensed publisher.

Pound's daring proposal did not end there. Declaring that "the protection of an author should not enable him to play dog in the manger," he added a second, even more aggressive compulsory license (*EPCP*, III: 209). Under this exception, a foreign author would retain exclusive rights to control reproduction, distribution, and translation of a work in the United States unless the author failed to have it printed in or imported into the country, or did not grant translation rights for an American edition. If the author slumbered on these rights or refused to exercise them, an American publisher or translator could step forward and apply for permission to make use of the work. If the author did not reply within a reasonable time, the publisher or translator could proceed with the proposed use, with the sole duty of paying a royalty of between 10 percent and 20 percent. Pound had fashioned yet another penalty for the copyright owner's failure to make works available to the public.

Pound's copyright scheme manifested a tension between authors' rights and the public's interest in accessible works. Beginning with a grant of perpetual monopoly, he ended by carving out extremely broad exceptions that would permit any qualifying person to issue reprints or translations of works that authors or their heirs had failed or refused to keep in circulation. Pound's proposal was thus radically free-trade and deeply committed to promoting international understanding and a borderless culture. Moreover, his scheme was consistent with his later theories of money, which were likewise grounded on principles of utility and free circulation. Pound was ultimately more interested in supplying the market with affordable books than in increasing protections for authors.

OBSCENITY LAWS

Pound detested laws that regulated literature by turning it into an article of commerce and subjecting it to the discretion of petty officials. Book tariffs and copyright laws were offenders in this regard, but they could not compare to the abuses made possible by federal and state obscenity laws. Pound never tired of assailing Section 211 of the US Criminal Code, which subjected to seizure "[e]very obscene, lewd, or lascivious, and every filthy, book, pamphlet, picture, paper, letter, writing, print, or other publication of an indecent character, and every article or thing designed, adapted, or intended for preventing conception or producing abortion, or for any indecent or immoral use." Pound remarked in 1917 that "the statute which lumps literature and instruments for abortion into one clause is so fine a piece of propaganda for the Germans that it would be disloyal to publish it [in England] till after the war" (*EP/JQ*, 132).

It was under Section 211 that the October 1917 issue of *The Little Review* was seized for containing "Cantleman's Spring Mate," Wyndham Lewis' tale of a British soldier who seduces and abandons a young woman. In 1919–20, the same law permitted seizure and burning of three issues of *The Little Review* containing installments of Joyce's *Ulysses*, as well as criminal charges against the magazine's editors for publishing the portion of Joyce's "Nausicaa" episode in which Leopold Bloom masturbates while admiring Gerty MacDowell at the beach. Pound was disturbed to learn that federal judge Augustus Hand had rejected Margaret Anderson's challenge to the seizure of the October 1917 *Little Review*. Judge Hand – cousin of the more famous Learned Hand – had ruled that portions of Lewis' story exhibited "a tendency to excite lust" that justified seizure by the Postmaster General.[18]

Pound was equally outraged by Judge Hand's observation in the same opinion that "numerous really great writings . . . doubtless at times escape [Section 11] only because they come within the term 'classics,' [and] have the sanction of age and fame, and usually appeal to a comparatively limited number of readers."[19] Pound assailed this rationale in essay after essay, as well as in his poem "Cantico del Sole" (*P*, 1926, 182). Yet it was Judge Hand who in 1934 wrote the opinion for the Second Circuit Court of Appeals that affirmed Judge John M. Woolsey's decision to allow a copy of *Ulysses* to enter the United States. Although Judge Woolsey's ruling – that *Ulysses* was not obscene under the Tariff Act – is justly celebrated as a blow to censorship, Judge Hand's affirmance actually carried more legal weight, as the decision of a higher court.

After the seizure of the *Little Review* number containing "Nausicaa," Pound and John Quinn agreed that the "only justification of the parts of Ulysses is the whole of Ulysses" (*EP/JQ*, 199). This argument would not have succeeded in most courts in 1920, but by 1933–4 Judges Woolsey and Hand were ready to entertain it, and they made it the chief basis for ruling that *Ulysses* was not obscene. Pound thought that works like *Ulysses* and "Cantleman's Spring Mate" should go free for another reason as well. Writing to Quinn in 1920, he suggested that Section 211 was "unconstitutional, from the Jeffersonian angle" (*EP/JQ*, 199). This idea – that laws banning works of serious literary or artistic value violated the freedoms of speech and press – was even more ahead of its time than the notion that judges should treat works as organic wholes. It was not until much later in the century that the First Amendment would become a centerpiece for litigating the lawfulness of allegedly obscene literature, art, and film.

Pound could not have known in 1920 that twenty-five years later he would again be driven to invoke free speech as a defense to a criminal charge. Had his treason trial gone forward, he would undoubtedly have wanted to argue that "free speech without free radio speech is as zero" (LXXIV/440) – though his lawyer would have urged an insanity defense. Pound's Rome Radio broadcasts were in a sense the culmination of a career devoted to overcoming obstacles to international communication. Pound's "four steps" might have been convenient notation in 1956 for the causes that had led to his radio speeches, but in 1940–5 his desire to reach war-bound listeners in other countries had been paramount. Freedom of movement, freedom to import books and ideas – these were always uppermost in Pound's thinking about the law. In taking the microphone in Rome, he was seeking, however misguidedly, to bypass the "flimsy and damned partition" that had been created by bad laws and good wars.

NOTES

1 Pound, unpublished draft letter to F.S. Flint (*c.* May 1912), in the Ezra Pound Collection at Yale University's Beinecke Library (YCAL MSS 43, Box 17, folder 743).
2 For discussions of Pound's views on censorship, copyright, passports, and Prohibition, see *Ezra Pound and Senator Bronson Cutting: A Political Correspondence, 1930–1935*, ed. E.P. Walkiewicz and Hugh Witemeyer (Albuquerque: University of New Mexico Press, 1995), 24–33.
3 For Pound's use of the Paris passport incident in Canto VII, see David Farley, "'Damn the Partition!' Ezra Pound and the Passport Nuisance," *Paideuma* 30.3 (2001), 79–90.
4 *Pound and Cutting*, 29.
5 Act of May 2, 1918, ch. 81, §§ 1–2, 40 Stat. 559.
6 22 U.S.C. § 211a.
7 *Pound and Cutting*, 50.
8 Letter to Gratia Sharp, November 30, 1927, in *Pound, Thayer, Watson, and The Dial: A Story in Letters*, ed. Walter Sutton (Gainesville: University Press of Florida, 1994), 329.
9 These facts are set forth in "The Tax on Ideas," an address by the President of the American Library Association, printed in *Bulletin of the American Library Association* 8 (January–November 1914), 73–7.
10 *Ibid.*, 75.
11 "Praises Underwood for Free Art Fight: Removal of Tariff on Modern Works Largely Due to His Efforts, Says John Quinn," *New York Times* (September 26, 1913), 10.

12 B.L. Reid, *The Man From New York: John Quinn and His Friends* (New York: Oxford University Press, 1968), 159.

13 See Act of March 4, 1909, ch. 320, §§ 31–3, 25 Stat. 1075.

14 Act of March 3, 1891, ch. 565, 26 Stat. 1106.

15 Act of March 4, 1909, ch. 320, § 15, 35 Stat. 1075.

16 See Berne Convention, art. 2, § 1 (1886).

17 US Constitution, art. I, § 8, cl. 8.

18 *Anderson v. Patten*, 247 F. 382 (S.D.N.Y. 1917).

19 *Ibid.*, 384.

CHAPTER 13

Textual criticism

Mark Byron

INTRODUCTION

For the past half-century, Pound's prolific and varied work has presented itself both as a rich landscape and as a perilous terrain for scholarly editors of his writing. There is a pressing need to establish correct and authoritative texts of Pound's poetry, translations, critical prose, musical compositions, reviews, letters, sound recordings, and assortments of archival material. Much of this material presents serious challenges to conventional notions of textual stability and authority, and in some cases confounds all attempts to harness it into published, readable forms. Despite such complexities, the general picture of Pound's influences, contacts, and working materials has come into sharper focus, allowing scholars of Pound's work to base their critical judgements upon increasingly more reliable texts.

But this is not uniformly the case across Pound's writing. Texts in different genres present their own editorial problems and requirements, and questions of textual status and stability will range in urgency and extent across genres. At base, however, the editor's prime tasks remain: to present texts in optimally stable forms, or to account for why stability is not achievable; and to make plain the rationale and methods of the editing process, including (and perhaps especially) situations wherein no obvious alteration or correction has been made to a document beyond its presentation in publishable form.

The Cantos presents the most notorious and illuminating collection of textual problems and editorial challenges in the Pound archive: from the identification and attribution of words, ideograms and other textual elements, to the establishment of authority for their inclusion (or otherwise), to the merits of competing or parallel witnesses. *The Cantos* is epic in its aspirations, its materials, its composition, and in its protracted, serial, imbricated publication history. The latter part of this chapter will be devoted to a brief summary of past and present editorial work on *The*

Cantos, including a report on the rapidly evolving digital variorum edition initiated by Richard Taylor some years ago and co-edited by Taylor and Byron more recently. First, however, mention needs to be made of the status of Pound's texts more generally.

POUND'S TEXTS

Pound's prodigious output is wide-ranging both in genre and subject matter. His literary legacy has benefited from devoted and astute critical elucidation and awareness of the state and condition of the materials. Editorial expertise is evident in the publication of volumes of letters, various genres of prose and reviews, and some of Pound's own incomplete editorial projects. This editorial terrain is uneven: some vitally important volumes of source material require fresh editorial treatment, and the burgeoning stream of republication of Pound's texts (especially in Italy) signals the desirability of an integrated, articulated editorial approach. The establishment of reliable texts is arguably the most basic and profound task of textual criticism, and is the foundation for all significant critical analysis. Classical philology saw textual criticism and hermeneutics as twin disciplines for good reason.

The range and number of editions of Pound's writing forbid enumeration, but a typology of publications can clarify which texts require further (or perhaps initial) editorial treatment. It should be noted that Donald C. Gallup's division of Pound's work in his *Ezra Pound: A Bibliography* (and Archie Henderson's significant subsequent additions) serves to enumerate all known texts by Pound and those to which he contributed. It is a masterwork of descriptive bibliography, itself a cornerstone of textual criticism. Motivating the following divisions, however, are degrees of authorial direction and textual stability, and the possibility and desirability of scholarly editorial intervention.

Texts published in periodicals and trade editions during Pound's lifetime

This important category of primary documents includes: individual poems appearing in dozens of journals and books of poetry from *A Lume Spento* (1908) to the collected *Cantos* (1948 and subsequently); reviews and essays in journals; "textbooks" such as *How to Read* (1931) and *ABC of Reading* (1934); such monographs as *The Spirit of Romance* (1910), *Gaudier-Brzeska* (1916), *Guide to Kulchur* (1938), and *Confucius* (1947); and other texts published with Pound's imprimatur. Faber and Faber in the United Kingdom and New Directions in the United States published most of these texts in parallel. Pound's direct involvement in the fact of publication (including his intermittent dissatisfactions with the finished published work) governs questions of textual reliability, additionally influenced by conformity to the house style of commercial publishers. Few of these texts have received scholarly editorial treatment in English (Ira B. Nadel's edition of Pound's *Early Writings* is one exception): there is a clear need for a multi-volume critical edition of Pound's collected works.

Numerous individual poems and fragments of pre-*Cantos* material have been edited and published in journals and as appendices to larger editions. C. G. Petter's "Pound's *Personae*: from Manuscript to Print"[1] is one example among several in which critical editorial attention is paid to Pound's drafts, corrections, and annotations in the transmission from manuscript to print. The journal *Paideuma* functioned for many years as a primary critical site for discussion of the status of Pound's shorter poetic texts and as a forum in which to untangle textual ambiguities.

Michael King's edition of the *Collected Early Poems* (1982) is a preliminary step in the scholarly treatment of Pound's published poetic texts. The original title pages of Pound's six earliest volumes are included in facsimile reproduction, and King gathers poems excluded by Pound in his *Personae* (1926). But the texts of the poems appear without significant editorial apparatus and are accompanied by a cursory bibliographical essay signaling the desirability of a critical variorum edition of Pound's early poetry. The Library of America *Poems and Translations*[2] also reproduces Pound's poetic texts (as well as a representation of his prose) without significant editorial intervention. However, the mere fact of this volume's existence indicates renewed cultural respect for Pound.

Similarly, Mary de Rachewiltz's edition of Pound's *Opere Scelte* (Selected Works) collects translations of Pound's early poetry by many of Italy's great modern and contemporary poets, along with selections of his prose translated from English or, in some instances, in the original Italian; although the texts are given a light editorial touch, the volume appears in Mondadori's Meridiani series and thus positions Pound's writing in a context of significant cultural prestige. Massimo Bacigalupo gives two poetic texts particularly sensitive editorial treatment in his Italian editions of *Hugh Selwyn Mauberley* and *Homage to Sextus Propertius*.[3] These contain parallel English and Italian texts and lists of variants, demonstrating an acute awareness of issues of textual stability, and an adept hand in reconciling such issues with a clear reading text.

Editions, translations, and anthologies edited by Pound

This group includes such texts as *Sonnets and Ballate of Guido Cavalcanti* (1912), *Certain Noble Plays of Japan* (1916), Remy de Gourmont's *Natural Philosophy of Love* (1922), *Ta Hio* (1928), and *Love Poems of Ancient Egypt* (1962) among many others. These, too, can be considered primary documents in Pound's corpus, containing works by others, edited by Pound, but they are yet to receive editorial treatment beyond pre-publication copy-editing. Several of these texts offer direct insights into Pound's own conception of appropriate bibliographic and editorial activity. The notes and page proofs of the *Sonnets and Ballate* and the subsequent *Guido Cavalcanti Rime* (1932) provide a clear picture of Pound's philological methods and his intentions for his translations. The Cavalcanti notebooks housed in the Beinecke Rare Book and Manuscript Library at Yale University demonstrate that Pound took his editorial task very seriously, recording variants in all manuscript copies of Cavalcanti's poetry. Such philological sensibilities indicate Pound's technical as well as aesthetic interest in textual forms.

Archival resources

Pound scholarship is blessed with access to extensive archival resources, principally the Ezra Pound Collection and the Olga Rudge Collection at the Beinecke Library, the Harry Ransom Humanities Research Center at the University of Texas at Austin, and the Lilly Library at the University of Indiana. Columbia University and other institutions also hold significant documents. Scholars have produced innovative editions of manuscript material, anticipating the kind of publication Pound might have intended from manuscript evidence.

Richard Sieburth's edition of Pound's 1912 notebooks, *A Walking Tour in Southern France: Ezra Pound Among the Troubadours*,[4] is a case in point: Pound had abandoned a projected volume titled *Gironde* in late 1912, the typescript soon misplaced, while the surviving manuscript notebooks bore a cryptic and piecemeal surface structure. Sieburth employed an ingenious editorial method: he undertook Pound's walking tour and found that many textual cruxes resolved themselves in the landscape and architecture of southern France. This method of practical editing achieves enviable clarity.

The notebooks themselves are transcribed and annotated (but only lightly edited) and accompanied by postcard photographs. Introductory notes and annotations to each notebook section provide sufficient supporting material, and offer the reader subtly mediated access to some of Pound's primary materials and methods of composition.

David Anderson's edition of Pound's notes, translations, and essays on Cavalcanti[5] duly annotates the poetic texts and records variants between *Sonnets and Ballate of Guido Cavalcanti* (1912) and *Guido Cavalcanti Rime* (1932), although Pound's own lists of variants in the latter are not reproduced. The texts reliably reflect Pound's desired translations of the poems, but neither the manuscript facsimiles for which Pound had paid, nor his own rich (if not always precise) notebook materials are included in whole or in part. Further, Pound's obscure essay on Cavalcanti's *Donna mi prega* is presented without any critical analysis. A new edition, including facsimiles and notebooks, would be of great scholarly benefit: a digital edition would allow for the inclusion of relevant material that would otherwise sit silently in the archive.

Several other publications, not intended as critical editions, have sought to bring varied archival material to light. Maria Luiza Ardizzone's edition of *Machine Art and Other Writings*[6] presents essays written by Pound between 1927 and 1943, now housed in the Beinecke Library. Another vivid example is Maria Costanza Ferrero De Luca's exquisite edition of *Ezra Pound e il Canto dei Sette Laghi*.[7] De Luca presents Canto XLIX, the so-called "Seven Lakes" Canto, alongside a facsimile reproduction of the *tekagami* (the seventeenth-century Japanese album) that inspired the poem – in effect curating the object owned by Pound and relating his own text (and substantial critical exegesis) to it.

Pound's intense interest in various media is reflected in his archive: the presence of musical scores, literary manuscripts, draft novels, sketches, concert promotional material, and other items present singular challenges and opportunities to scholars who wish to employ these resources in discussions of the state of Pound's texts. In Margaret Fisher's *Ezra Pound's Radio Operas* (2002) archival research establishes the important working relationship between Pound and Edward Harding, his producer at the BBC. In addition to letters, the radio script, and producer's notes to the 1931 production of *The Testament of François Villon*, Fisher frames the radio operas with regard to studio layouts, radio techniques, and other practical dimensions of the radio medium, bringing together primary materials and critical resources to provide the reader with essential information regarding the status of Pound's "text."

Letters

Following from D. D. Paige's edition of the *Selected Letters of Ezra Pound* (1950) dozens of volumes of Pound's letters have appeared. Many of these volumes focus upon a single correspondent – James Joyce, Wyndham Lewis, Dorothy Shakespear – while others present Pound's epistolary activities within a larger framework, such as Zhaoming Qian's *Ezra Pound's Chinese Friends: Stories in Letters.*

Textual criticism takes a central place in editions of Pound's letters but faces two crucial challenges. Firstly, editorial discretion must be exercised to present Pound's correspondence without unduly altering its meaning. A balance must be struck between cleaning up obvious errors and incoherencies, on the one hand, and preserving Pound's unique and at least partially phonetic orthography, on the other. Most editors of Pound's letters have chosen (wisely) to present his words as diplomatically as possible, since "[t]o tidy up such deviations would destroy the original flavour."[8] Editorial emendations, in square brackets, are kept distinct from authorial insertions in pointed brackets. Most editors also regularize Pound's erratic spacing and paragraph breaks, producing a more coherent reading text but at some semantic cost. Occasional photographic reproductions of particular letters provide readers with a visual sense of Pound's epistolary practices.[9]

Secondly, his letters often give critical information or interpretative insight into his poetic texts. Pound wrote often and expansively to his editors and friends about matters of stylistics, bibliography, and the printing and publication of his texts. He was acutely concerned with the semantic import and bibliographic presentation of his work, and was well informed in matters spanning the creation, transmission and publication of his texts. These epistolary documents are crucial artefacts of the creative process in their own right, therefore their own materiality is of primary consequence.

THE *CANTOS*

An overview of textual criticism and The Cantos

The text of *The Cantos* provides a radical challenge to theories of text and methods of scholarly editing. The dispersed and accretive nature of the textual record presents an immediate logistical challenge to assembling a system of published variants or witness files: cantos were published singularly or in small groups in journals, then gathered into "decads" to be published in book form, and eventually absorbed into collected works. The collected *Cantos* developed as quite different texts in the United Kingdom and the United States until 1975, when Faber abandoned its printing plates and adopted those used by New Directions. Matters of continuous pagination, regularized style, and even the numerical scripts used to identify cantos were not adequately met for decades following the first collected edition of 1948.

The Cantos has received substantial textual critical attention. Several monograph studies[10] have considered the state of the text or specific sections of it, and numerous essays explores issues of authority, emendation, and text stability from a variety of perspectives.[11] Both Jerome J. McGann and Jean-Michel Rabaté have described the text of *The Cantos* as an instance of a poem that doubles as its own critical edition, bearing the trappings of its archive on the text's surface.[12]

There is not sufficient space to rehearse all of the issues arising in the attentive textual criticism given to *The Cantos*. However, one might characterize much of this scholarly work as diagnostic: pressing problems of authority and attribution (of composition and of emendation) are investigated; the stemmatic history of the text is presented from the smallest particle to the published "decads" and the collected editions;[13] and foundational theoretical and practical notions of text, authorship, correction, commentary, and the figure of the author – the *ego scriptor* – are revised and transformed in light of *The Cantos* and its passage through history.

Practical attempts to edit the poem – by Pound himself and in collaboration with his editors and leading scholars – reached various points of impasse. The magnitude of the problem is such that one critic asserts that a "critical edition of *The Cantos* is not very likely for the present or the immediate future, and for some time beyond as well."[14] But there are sound reasons for a more optimistic view of the textual future of *The Cantos*, beginning with reconsiderations of what a critical edition of the text might look like, and consequent ways in which governing textual problems might be remedied and explained.

The Cantos: *a challenge to textual criticism and editorial theory and practice*

A viable critical edition of *The Cantos* must resolve a number of issues that go to the heart of modern editorial theory and practice. To start, how can a large number of variant readings be reconciled into a readable critical edition? And how does one determine the relative authority of variant readings, where it is often not possible to determine the degree to which a particular person is responsible for specific word choices and arrangements?

Pound was acutely aware of the implications of textual variants and took very seriously the scholarly task of correcting the text of *The Cantos*. Events in his personal history impeded direct influence over the appearance of his poem, particularly his detention in the Pisan Disciplinary Training Center in 1945 and subsequently at St. Elizabeths in Washington, DC. Despite the arduous efforts of the scholars Hugh Kenner and Eva Hesse, and James Laughlin of New Directions, Pound's enthusiasm to correct his text flagged after his return to Italy in 1958. Kenner and Hesse each suggested hundreds of (often different) emendations. Were Pound to agree to these changes, a degree of authority from *ego scriptor* would have come into force, allaying, at least in practical terms, problems of attribution and agency.

Yet, the history of the poem's composition and transmission into print is instructive in itself. While imprisoned in Pisa, Pound relied upon Dorothy Pound, Olga Rudge, and Mary de Rachewiltz to prepare typescripts for T. S. Eliot at Faber and Laughlin at New Directions. Pound relied upon Dudley Fitts to correct Greek passages in *The Pisan Cantos*, but was unable to oversee fully the results of this collaboration. The Chinese characters introduced profound problems of authority and authorship. Who authored each of the variants arising in these documents? Should they remain a part of the text's biography, and if so, in what form? Eventually, Pound became resigned to the state of his text, embracing "published readings as having been sanctioned by time and the printer."[15] The composition and transmission of *The Cantos* into print offer abundant information crucial to critical analysis of the text, and a most illuminating window into material practices of writing and publishing throughout the twentieth century.[16]

Jerome McGann has shown how material aspects of the text's production leave a record of socialization in published instances of *The Cantos*, transforming such evidence from vexatious sources of corruption to valuable particulars that can legitimately inform critical analysis. This model also takes into account the various reading publics for which the text was intended, and, inasfar as relevant data can be obtained, the actual reading publics at different instances of the text's published life. An accretive view of *The Cantos* might be expressed in the potent method of genetic editing, adopted from German textual theory and the French tradition of *critique génétique*. Such a method accounts for the development of the published documents from pre-publication material, and seeks to recount as fully as possible the conditions of this process. A genetic edition of *The Cantos* would be an imposing thing, but well within conceptual range.

Work on parts of *The Cantos* is well underway. Ronald Bush and David Ten Eyck are completing a comprehensive study of the composition of *The Pisan Cantos*, which aims to provide a full history of the text's evolution and post-publication career, integrating full textual apparatus and contextual material into their print edition of the text. Explicit concern for sound editorial methods does not solve all textual cruxes or render obsolete controversies over text composition, but rather provides valuable evidence for scholarship.

The digital variorum edition of Pound's Cantos

The extensive variety of modes in which *The Cantos* has been published – in full and in various installments – recommends an accretive editorial method. Scholars should be presented with all available textual (and contextual) information regarding the evolution of the text and its current published state. Richard Taylor's compilation of variant files and associated annals material toward a variorum edition fulfils such requirements. His *Variorum Edition of "Three Cantos"* (1991) exhibits both the magnitude of appropriate textual apparatus, and the obvious logistical problems of compiling such a monument of scholarship in print form. Three factors motivated the decision to move the variorum edition to the digital medium:[17] (1) the obvious benefits to scholarship in making explicit the socialized nature of the published text's career; (2) the inhibiting constraints of producing a coherent reading text in print that includes stemmae, every published variant (in English) of every canto, and integrated annals material (not to mention such multimedia as audio and video recordings); and (3) the emergence of software able to perform complex collations as well as sophisticated mark-up of witness files that best represents the bibliographic codes inherent in the material.

The scholarly principles of a variorum edition of *The Cantos*, regardless of its medium of presentation, are to collect, collate, and annotate every known published witness of the text. The digital variorum edition maintains these principles for every canto – the edition is confined to English language witnesses in the first instance, but of course there is no logical impediment to the inclusion, in future, of published texts in translation. The aim is to produce the fullest record of the published text, including selected digital reproductions of the deluxe editions of 1925 and 1928 and other strategically chosen editions (such as 1930, 1948, and 1970). Space permits only a brief description of the architecture of the digital variorum, with a focus on its specific scholarly functions and virtues compared to codex presentation.

The Juxta collation function of the variorum edition is perhaps the most critical scholarly tool because it provides the basis for a new and comprehensive understanding of the publication history of *The Cantos*.[18] Immensely useful, it allows readers to choose any combination of base text and witness files for comparison although its current version is limited in two ways. Juxta does not represent spatial variants of text on the page – an element of especial hermeneutic significance in the case of *The Cantos*. Nor does it distinguish between capitals and lower case, but simply variations in spelling. Juxta is one component of the variorum edition: every witness file marked-up for inclusion in the collation also exists as a marked-up XML file, adopting the fifth version of the Text Encoding Initiative's protocols (TEI P5), a standard designed specifically for digital mark-up in the humanities.[19] These files are tagged with relevant links to annals material, digital reproductions of selected printed texts (with the potential to be expanded to include every available published instance of a particular canto), scholarly annotation, and sound recordings, with the potential for links to related visual and audiovisual materials. An integrated web environment is under construction using Adobe Dreamweaver software and Flash plug-ins for multimedia components.

The virtues of a digital variorum edition of Pound's *Cantos* are readily apparent: a large range of source material in various media can be brought together in one location; critical editorial tasks such as collation can be carried out by custom software quickly, precisely, and in visually and logically coherent fashion; a potentially enormous amount of annals material can be tagged to the poetic texts and reconfigured, depending on the specific needs of the reader; and the range of critical, historical, and other contextual material is only limited by the labor of mark-up and potential issues of permissions. Of course, any digital edition must be held to the same scholarly standards as its codex counterpart, and every editorial choice must be justified locally and in a general editorial rationale. Yet the advantages of comprehensiveness and coherence make plain that a well-structured digital edition provides scholars with powerful tools, perhaps ushering in a new phase of analytic and hermeneutic insight into Pound's texts.

CONCLUSION

Pound's prolific output in a variety of genres has provided textual scholars and editors ample material to shape within the critical record and many leading textual scholars have found themselves drawn to Pound's texts. This dialectic is most fortunate for Pound studies, yet limits to the adequate representation of Pound's orthography and his use of compositional space are particularly acute problems for textual scholarship. Advances in the still-emergent field of digital textual editing offer the most compelling solutions to these problems of critical representation and will stake out new areas of critical and hermeneutic inquiry. New scholarly digital skills will be capable of establishing, at last, a comprehensive set of Pound's texts.

NOTES

1 C. G. Petter, "Pound's *Personae*: from Manuscript to Print," *Studies in Bibliography* 35 (1982): 111–32.

2 Ezra Pound, *Poems and Translations*, ed. Richard Sieburth (New York: Library of America, 2003).

3 Mary de Rachewiltz, ed., *Opere Scelte* (1970; Milano: Mondadori, 1981); Massimo Bacigalupo, ed., *Hugh Selwyn Mauberley* (Milan: Il Saggiatore, 1982), and *Ommagio a Sesto Properzio* (Genoa: S. Marco dei Giustiniani, 1984).

4 Pound, *A Walking Tour in Southern France: Ezra Pound Among the Troubadours*, ed. Richard Sieburth (New York: New Directions, 1992).

5 David Anderson, *Pound's Cavalcanti* (Princeton: Princeton University Press, 1983).

6 Maria Luiza Ardizzone, ed., *Machine Art and Other Writings: The Lost Thought of the Italian Years* (Durham, NC and London: Duke University Press, 1996).

7 Maria Costanza Ferrero De Luca, ed., *Ezra Pound e il Canto dei Sette Laghi* (Reggio Emilia: Diabasis, 2004).

8 Zhaoming Qian, ed., *Ezra Pound's Chinese Friends: Stories in Letters* (Oxford: Oxford University Press, 2008), xxiii.

9 Two such examples are Louis Dudek ed., *DK: Some Letters by Ezra Pound* (Montreal: DC Books, 1974) and Vittoria I. Mandolfo and Margaret Hurley, eds., *Ezra Pound: Letters to Ibbotson, 1935–1952* (Orono, ME: National Poetry Foundation, 1979).

10 Ronald Bush, *The Genesis of the "Cantos"* (Princeton: Princeton University Press, 1979); Christine Froula, *To Write Paradise: Style and Error in Pound's* Cantos (New Haven: Yale University Press, 1985); and Peter Stoicheff, *The Hall of Mirrors: Drafts & Fragments and the End of Ezra Pound's* Cantos (Ann Arbor: University of Michigan Press, 1995).

11 *A Poem Containing History: Textual Studies in The Cantos* is a collection of essays edited by Lawrence Rainey (Ann Arbor: University of Michigan Press, 1997), entirely devoted to textual criticism and *The Cantos*.

12 Jerome J. McGann, *The Textual Condition* (Princeton: Princeton University Press, 1991), 129; Jean-Michel Rabaté, "Pound, Joyce and Eco: Modernism and the 'Ideal Genetic Reader,'" *Romanic Review* 86.3 (1995): 485.

13 The best description of the texts of *The Cantos* is found in Richard Taylor, "The Texts of *The Cantos*," in *CCEP*, 161–87.

14 Rainey, Introduction to *A Poem Containing History*, 8.

15 Richard Taylor, "Towards a Textual Biography of *The Cantos*," in *Modernist Writers and the Marketplace*, ed. Ian Willison, Warwick Gould, and Warren Chernaik (Houndmills: Macmillan; New York: St. Martin's, 1996), 223–57.

16 For further exploration of this theme, see Mark Byron, "Ezra Pound's *Cantos*: A Compact History of Twentieth-Century Authorship, Publishing and Editing," in *Modern Book History*, ed. Kate Longworth, special edition of *Literature Compass* 4.4 (July 2007): 1158–68.

17 Ned Bates' "Kybernekyia: A Hypervortext of Ezra Pound's Canto LXXXI," whilst modest in its aims, shows the referential powers of hyperlinks and the ways complex ancillary material can be arranged intuitively. See www.uncg.edu/eng/pound/canto.htm.

18 Juxta was developed by the Applied Research in "Patacriticism" Group at the Institute for Advanced Technology in the Humanities at the University of Virginia, and first released in May 2006. The latest version 1.3 was made available on 21 July 2008 and can be downloaded at www.juxtasoftware.org/download.html.

19 The protocols and their guidelines can be viewed and downloaded from www.tei-c.org/Guidelines/P5/.

CHAPTER 14

Archives

Caterina Ricciardi

On March 1, 1944, upon receiving the Accademia Chigiana Quaderni dedicated to Vivaldi, Olga Rudge wrote to Count Chigi Saracini: "[Pound] looked envyingly at those elegant volumes! – his notes on the Malatesta manuscripts, and the Siena Cavalcanti, and the famous 'Monte' are always on his mind, but now it seems that his 'Studi Sienesi' will be published in . . . Venice!"[1] Unfortunately, that plan was never realized, but Olga's letter gives us an idea of the high regard Pound had for the material that the Sienese sources provided for three separate projects.

Pound's systematic use of archival documentation had begun in 1911 when his reading of the troubadours shifted from secondary to primary sources. His belief in the "resurrection" (*SL*, 131) of lost details (for instance, Arnaut's melodies), together with his increasing need to test the accuracy of a printed text would in the long run shape his twofold personal philological *techné*, consisting of "paleography," as with the 1932 *Cavalcanti*, for which he required reproductions of manuscripts "so as to show what we really do know and can know . . . How the stuff was first written down" (*EPS*, 373); and then of recovering "the facts, original documents, etc.," in order to prove "how loosely some history is written" (*EPS*, 180). Consequently, the " 'aesthetic' pleasure" he derived from the " 'unmediated' experience with the documents produced by a culture that fascinated him"[2] would never be entirely separate from the intellectual pleasure that the transmission of cultural data was capable of providing.

But it was not until he discovered the Tempio Malatestiano in 1922 that this activity became one of his main concerns. His two-month Italian library tour (from February to April 1923), undertaken after a perusal of secondary works on Malatesta at the Bibliothèque Nationale in Paris, would decidedly accelerate the development of his still inchoate Cantos. With Sigismondo and the politics of his time, in which he was enmeshed, the whole architecture of the Renaissance cycle would emerge before him. In the next few years his crosschecking of data in the archives of the great families of Florence, Mantua, Bologna, Milan, Modena, and Venice would serve for the Florence/Medici, Ferrara/Este, and Venice Cantos, revealing at the same time a fundamental historiographical problem. As Pound argued in 1942, recalling his "job on Sig. Malatesta": "IF documents DISAPPEAR with remarkable coincidence, say reports on an event in February 1424, there was something someone was trying to KEEP from the public. 'Specially if the dispatches for a particular day disappear from six archives simultaneous [*sic*], and *so weiter*'" (*EPS*, 138).

By the early forties this kind of archival lacuna had developed into a basic tenet of Pound's polemical view of the methods and politics of cultural transmission, and may also have informed his poetics of quotation, and driven him to pursue his quest for documents. It is no wonder then that in the late twenties, shortly after the completion of the Renaissance Cantos, he entered the Archivio di Stato and the Biblioteca Comunale in Siena, which he continued to explore (for various purposes) until 1937, when the anti-usury *Fifth Decad of Cantos* was published. In hindsight, these Cantos stand out as the last fruit of Pound's archival labors, which he seemingly undertook for the sake of both a proper understanding of "civilization" and an enriched ability to contribute to it culturally.

Pound enjoyed working in the then rather unevenly organized Italian libraries, which were at the same time museums and, often, architectural masterpieces, suffused at once with an aura of cultural solemnity, Italian pride, and decadence, and promising, in their established albeit often dilapidated "antiquity," any and every kind of random or unexpected discovery. In the Vatican, for instance, he was so impressed by the "civility, in the high fine sense of the word" of the place that in the long run, he declared, he would "have to join the Monsignori against Babbitt" (*GK*, 155). This was, of course, a pleasantry, but it is true that the "Monsignori" he met were the last representatives of a vanishing race: the ecclesiastical literati who for centuries (ever since "Pope Nicolo" [CIV/759], a former librarian) had overseen the preservation of knowledge.

In fact, in the twenties and thirties the immense heritage of books and manuscripts in Italy was still undergoing a process of "secularization" which had led to a bureaucratic redistribution of separate collections to regionally centralized structures: national and local state libraries, where private and confiscated monastic holdings were assembled, and the so-called Archivi di Stato, which housed documents related to the history of the former city-states. A few ecclesiastical institutions (notably the Ambrosiana and the Capitolare), spared by the revolutionary governmental reshuffling, were left with their original identity. In that process, however, little was done to conform to the by now higher standards of library organization, with appropriate spaces, new archival theories, thorough cataloguing and subject classification of the multifarious once dispersed holdings, and, where necessary, the replacement of the old ecclesiastical staff.

Not until 1907 had new regulations been introduced promoting reorganization of the collections and opening the way to a decidedly postunitarian generation of "librarians" (e.g. the excellent Dazzi at Cesena and the less appealing Massera at Rimini), in place of the now eliminated figure of the priestly "prefect." Yet thorough modernization was never really achieved. During the fascist era there was much preaching about the "dignity of [library] service" but the traditional view of the library as a mere container of precious material for a reading élite was still widespread,[3] and the signs of centuries of ecclesiastical curatorship had not vanished.

ARNAUT, FAIDIT, AND THE AMBROSIANA: AURAL PATTERNS ("LUMINOUS DETAILS")

No wonder that in Pisa Pound would recall: "I knew but one Achilles in my time / and he ended up in the Vatican" (LXXX/522). Clearly, Pound had not forgotten the prefect Monsignor Ratti who, on July 27, 1911, had received him at the Ambrosiana Library in Milan, where the only two extant melodies for Arnaut's poems were preserved.[4] Their meeting was a fortunate occurrence since soon after, in 1912, Ratti would move to Rome as Vice-Prefect (becoming Prefect in 1914) of the Vatican Library. A scholar and palaeographer himself, Ratti had, starting in 1907, undertaken a program of reclassification and retranscription of the incunabula and manuscripts at the Ambrosiana, together with a reorganization of the art gallery, with its unique collection of portraits by Luini and Ambrogio de' Predis (see *Mauberley* and Canto XLV).

When Ratti was elected Pope (Pius XI) in 1922, the "Sound slender" passage *à la* Arnaut that opens Canto XX/89 had not yet been written. With a closer reading of that intricate musical patterning one may also detect a belated homage to the above-mentioned "Achilles," who politely led the way among old shelves to that "jewel box," the *chansonnier* manuscript, filed as "R. 71 sup." The Monsignore may also have pointed out some of the other Ambrosiana treasures, such as several codices of Propertius and Ovid: "Qui son [Here are] Properzio ed Ovidio" (XX/89), the last words of the "Sound slender" passage, seem to be spoken by the librarian himself, even as the Canto moves toward "settant'uno R. superiore (Ambrosiana)" (XX/89), where "Arnaut's" scores of "Chansson do'ill mot son plan e prim" and "Lo

ferm voler q'el cor m'intra" were to be found. The "musical notation,"
Pound told his parents, "accords exactly with my theories of how his music
should be written" (Stock, 146). Subsequently his translations in "Arnaut
Daniel" (1920) would take a different turn, incorporating, in a sense, the
music. He could now distinguish between "the music of *Chansson doil
mots*" and "the movement [not the "music"] of *Can cai la fueilla*," and the
new form would show "part of that which I mean" (*LE*, 112): the unity of
mots et son.

 "R. 71 sup." appears to have been an invaluable source for Pound.
It contained eighty-one melodies for poems by thirty-two celebrated
troubadours, some of which (by Bernart de Ventadour, Pons de Capdoill,
Gaucelm Faidit) he transcribed, rewrote in modern notation, and had
published or premièred.[5] The remaining 183 extant original scores were
assembled in four folders at the Bibliothèque Nationale in Paris, where
Pound worked in the spring of 1912. But the greatest number of airs he
photostated were in Milan. Announcing a troubadour concert in London
in 1918, he wrote to John Quinn: "Fortunately, I've the reprods. of the Milan
mss. and some copies we made of various mss. in Paris, so we'll be able to
go ahead despite the Biblioteque [*sic*] Nationale's being closed" (*SL*, 131).
By then he had ceased collecting medieval music. He was moving forward,
toward Malatesta and the Renaissance, and yet on December 11, 1923 he
had his own arrangement for solo violin of Faidit's song "Fort chant oiaz"
(i.e., "Plainte pour la Mort du roi Richard Coeur de Lion") played in Paris
by Olga Rudge. On the printed program one reads: "Air dèchiffré [*sic*] du
Manuscrit R. 71 superiore Ambrosiana, par M. Ezra Pound" (*EPM*, 249). It
was Olga's and Ezra's first joint venture. Their collaboration was to reach its
highest pitch in the late thirties with the catalogue of Vivaldi's manuscripts
in Turin, the unpublished Chilesotti 'baroque' collection (*EPM*, 328)
and the Janequin score (LXXV/470–1) obtained from Paris through the
Princesse de Polignac (*SL*, 254). Years later the "Siena Cavalcanti" would
follow.

CAVALCANTI (PALAEOGRAPHIC PHILOLOGY)

The Genoa/Marsano *Guido Cavalcanti Rime. Edizione rappezzata fra le
rovine*, published in January 1932 in amputated form, sprang from Pound's
passionate desire for the unattainable beauty of the pristine text. This is
why, in an unpublished "defense," he upheld the genuine merits of what
might appear to be mere textual labor, and fragmentary at that. Certain
"features" of *Rime* were worth all the trouble involved, "especially," he

wrote, "in the typographic disposition, relation of text to gloze, the tables, the photostat reproductions (Manuldruck [*sic*]) of the complete text taken from 32 different MSS. in such a way as to give a fairly clear idea of the paleographic history without waste of the student's time, substituting the photos for description."[6]

His investigation of the surviving textual records of Cavalcanti's poems had started in 1927, when he realized that Francesco Zanzotto's edition in *Parnaso Italiano* (1846), which he had used for *The Sonnets and Ballate of Guido Cavalcanti* (1912), was based on a long tradition of printed texts. Consequently, he began retracing Cavalcanti's "paleographic history" back to the 1527 Di Giunta edition, and even earlier, when, around 1929, he heard of an Aldine printing of "Donna mi prega" in the 1514 Oxford Petrarch codex, a text which he soon had photostated by Adrian Stokes (*LE*, 190). By then, standard editions apart, he had examined eighty-odd manuscripts (including the "Escorial" obtained thanks to Padre Elizondo [*GK*, 158]), and was able to select the thirty-two on which he would base his own philological reading. *Rime* and the essay "Cavalcanti" testify to his intense research in no fewer than ten Italian libraries. Only forty pages of photographic reproductions of the best manuscripts (instead of the originally planned forty-eight), appeared in *Rime*, due to Pound's shortage of funds.

In the end he relied on the Di Giunta Laurenziano–Rediano codex ("Ld"), which he collated with a number of variants, e.g. "*The MSS. Ce, Mm, Rh, Lh, Lb and La*" (*LE*, 175) (indicating Chigiano, Marciano, Riccardiano, and various Laurenziano subsections) for the "Donna mi prega" text alone. "Wherever I do not follow the Giuntine to the letter," he wrote in the "Ad Lectorem E. P." foreword to *Rime*,

I do not wish to oppose it, nor that of Cicciaporci. I simply give other variants that seem interesting to me. I am, generally speaking, "against" the succeeding editors, but I understand, alas, the temptation to print an innovation. The text was already established for the most part. There was little need for a new editor. But before putting out a bilingual edition I had a just curiosity. I had to know and not just suppose that the text of Cicciaporci was correct ["era giusto"].[7]

The years overlapping two quite different decades in Pound's career were indeed dedicated in part to an untiring quest for the authentic *lectio* of Cavalcanti's poems, differing from the *vulgata*, and from the most recent – and, for him, not always trustworthy – editions (Arnone, 1881; Ercole, 1885; Rivalta, 1902). He searched for melodies of the period, but found only one item in the Sienese Archivio di Stato, which "is not a fragment of melody, but two lines of police record: [the composer Pietro] Casella judged for being out after curfew" (*LE*, 171). But in Siena he also found the Biblioteca Comunale codex, which contained three poems questionably attributed to Cavalcanti. Pound decided with regret to jettison the codex. One of the three songs was in fact the canzone to Fortune whose first stanza (the only one he believed to be by Cavalcanti) he had quoted in *The Spirit of Romance* and would later use again in Canto LXXXVI/586: "La donna che volgo / Man under Fortune." By 1928, however, he was "inclined to sustain" that there was "an approximate certainty of his [Cavalcanti's] having written the canzone to Fortune" (*LE*, 171), and in a 1934 (and 1954) footnote to "Cavalcanti" he argued:

Whole question of authenticity of the other canzoni thrown wide open again by examination of manuscript I. ix. 18 in Comunale di Siena. (*LE*, 171)

Thus, with Olga Rudge's publication on his behalf of the *Tre Canzoni* in the 1949 "Quaderno," thereby filling that debatable gap, his contribution to Cavalcanti scholarship came finally to a halt.

Librarians/prefects, sacristans, and photographers were not minor actors in this undertaking. In "Ad Lectorem E. P." Pound thanked some of them for "courtesy and assistance received in various libraries." Thus, it is no surprise that *Rime* was dedicated to a librarian (and dear friend), Manlio Torquato Dazzi, for his help in preparing the Italian text. Dazzi was in Verona in 1929 when, for the second or third time, Pound examined codex DCCCII (Capitolare II), which contained sonnet VII: "Chi è questa che vien, ch'ogni uom la mira, / Che fa di clarità l'aer tremare!"[8] Afterwards they had lunch at the Trattoria dei Dodici Apostoli. Quite strikingly, the events of the day are thrice recalled in the *Cantos* (LXXIV/468, LXXVIII/501, XCI/634), as if they had come, with time, to signify Pound's quest for textual accuracy.

The *lectio* "l'aer tremare" ("and the air, the air, / Shaking ["l'aer / tremare"], air alight with the goddess" [IV/14]) was a philological stumbling-block Pound had been tackling since the 1910/1912 "Introduction" to *The Sonnets and Ballate*, where he called Carducci and Arnone "blasphemous" for accepting the reading "*E fa di claritate tremar l'aere*" (which would hardly rhyme with "parlare") instead of "following those mss.," as Ciccia-porci did, which read "*E fa di clarità l'aer tremare.*"[9] Overtly, as early as 1911 he had based his research on more than one (Zanzotto) of the published editions of Cavalcanti's poetry rather than, as in *Rime*, on his personal scrutiny of the manuscripts, in order to "know" whether "the text of Cicciaporci was correct." Cicciaporci's "l'aer tremare," he wrote in 1929, "is not a 'fantasist' reading"; he "found it in manuscript and did not form it out of conjecture. The other reading is bad, it is indeed very bad."[10]

Nonetheless, Pound wished to dispel all uncertainties, so, with his *Rime* on the point of being printed by L'Aquila Press, he went to Verona, where he finally determined (on the basis of a now apparently missing manuscript, i.e. Capitolare II) that Cicciaporci was "correct." Whatever the identity of the "affable put[t]ana" ("bitch") "wanting to adjust the spelling of Guido / as it is *not* in the 'Capitolare'" (XCI/501), it could be supposed that she worked under the then prefect Monsignor Turrini, himself an excellent student of early music and a restorer of manuscripts (the Adige flood of 1882 had damaged many of them). His complaint arose from the memory of his own preservation of one Capitolare *lectio*, which, together with his response to the debatable Sienese manuscript, was to be his last addition to the textual puzzle presented by Cavalcanti.

EARLY AND SIENESE CANTOS ("FACTS, ORIGINAL DOCUMENTS")

If *Cavalcanti* was conceived as a philological edition with a great (and costly) display of sources (a four-page list of codices [*Rime*, XIII–XVI]), which was meant to substantiate what Pound had ultimately decided was the definitive Cavalcanti text (although later, in *The Cantos*, he reconsidered the "memoria" [*LE*, 164] or "memora" *lectio* [LXIII/353, LXXVI/472]), in *The Cantos* his sources, whether primary or secondary, constitute an implicit groundwork, even when individual voices can be heard (Varchi, Broglio, Andrea Benzi, Pisanello, Tician). The few exceptions to this "vow of silence" are therefore to be considered curiosities rather than evidence of respect for philological convention.

We know, for instance, that Pound consulted two editions of Pius II's *Commentarii* at the Vatican Library,[11] and yet a key execration from the Pope's invective against Sigismondo is retrieved, strangely enough, from a footnote in Yriarte ("*Yriarte, p. 288*" [X/44]), and capitalized for emphasis. Likewise, Pound reproduces a passage from Filippo Strozzi's letter about Sigismondo leaving Sienese territory in 1454 without his "post bag" (the *Carte Malatestiane* in the Siena Archive, reproduced by Yriarte), as taken from an article (published in 1879 by the Sienese prefect Luciano Banchi) which he found quoted in a footnote by Yriarte.[12] Together with some echoes from Broglio's unpublished "Cronaca" in the Gambalunga Library at Rimini ("*bestialmente*"), Yriarte on Pius II and the *Archivio Storico* "Review" are among the few sources referred to in the disparately assembled Malatesta Cantos: thus footnotes from a scholarly commentary are promoted to a part in the main narrative!

Essentially, Pound based his Renaissance and Monte dei Paschi Cantos on published works: C. E. Yriarte (1882) for Malatesta, Antonio Frizzi (1791–1809) and Giambattista Pigna (1570) for Ferrara, and Giambattista Lorenzi (1868) just for the Venice Canto xxv. These sources served for translation with scant philological care or, contrastingly, underwent verification through close scrutiny of original documents. The latter is the case with Malatesta's 1449 letter to Giovanni de' Medici about the "*Maestro di pentore*" in Canto viii. Pound found a transcription of that letter in Yriarte who, thrown off, perhaps, by the "Magnifice vir" of the incipit ("Magnifice vir, *tanquam frater, et compater carissime*"), identifies the recipient as "Laurent le Magnifique."[13] Lorenzo was born in 1449, while Giovanni, the youngest son of Cosimo, was then twenty-eight.

This may explain Pound's visit to the Florentine Archivio di Stato in March 1923, where he cleared up the error by deciphering the partly illegible "tergo" ("back") of the document. Omitting the "Magnifice vir," he carefully transcribed from the original: "*Fratem tamquam / Et compater carissime: tergo / . . . hanni de / . . . dicis / . . . entia*," then filled in the blanks and thus corrected Yriarte with his "Equivalent to: / Giohanni of the Medici, / Florence" (viii/28). The word "tergo" (in parentheses in the *Criterion* version, and in Mary de Rachewiltz's Italian translation) is his sign that – as with "chucked away / (*buttato via*)" (viii/28), instead of Yriarte's mistranscribed "gettata via"[14] he has personally scrutinized the document, thus rejecting Yriarte twice, although "gettata via" is trivial compared with the "Laurent le Magnifique" blunder. In Florence Pound must also have consulted other documents, such as the "Register of the Ten of the Baily": "(*gente di cavallo e da pie*) etc. / Aug. 5 1452, *register of the Ten of the Baily*" (viii/30), for details which helped elucidate the role Florence played in Sigismondo's political career.

Local sources can show how intertwined the web of *quattrocento* documents is, with papers relating to a single event spread out among the archives of the former city-states. Any reconstruction of the facts, or filling in of gaps, would thus require extensive archival counterchecking (which is what Pound often did). The Venetian Canto xxvi, meanwhile, is a good example of how material kept in Venice was deemed capable of shedding new light on, for example, Sigismondo, Cosimo, Nicolò d'Este, the Gonzagas, Carlo Malatesta, or the Greek Emperor. In the foreground is the poet himself, reclining, as in his youth, "under the crocodile," by the "column," just in front of the Doge's Palace, and not, this time, resurrecting the gods of old afloat in the air (Canto III), but patching together an assemblage of scraps of "secret" insets ("secretissime"), with a myriad of dots, about what appears to be a coda to the Malatesta Cantos.

Here, a series of quotations about previously unreported episodes, seems, in the end, to suggest a single source. They tell of Matteo de Pasti suspected in 1461 of plotting against Venice; the Venetian ambassador Segundino soothing the angry Pope in 1462; the neutrality of Venice in the 1462 war against Sigismondo; and finally, "Senato Secreto, 28th of October, / Came Messire Hanibal from Cesena: / 'Cd. they hoist the flag of St. Mark" (XXVI/121–2). In fact, all these fragments must come from the "Registers" containing the Venetian Senate papers known as "Deliberazioni" and "Secreti," formerly kept in the Doge's Palace and later removed to the Venetian Archivio di Stato. Mary de Rachewiltz's Italian translation frequently offers us the key to distinguishing unpublished material (which she renders in current Italian) from printed sources (Yriarte or Frizzi).

The Venetian light is distinctly fading by the time we reach seventeenth century Siena. As the first lines somewhat breathlessly state ("as in register / Nov. 1624" [XLII/209]), Cantos XLII and XLIII, based on the nine volumes of Narciso Mengozzi's *Il Monte dei Paschi di Siena e le Aziende in Esso Riunite* (1891–1925), do revolve around a single occurrence: the foundational act of the Monte dei Paschi. Textual evidence (the "weed sprout over the cornice" [XLII/210], echoes from the *palio* underway outside) indicates that the poet is reading in the rooms of Palazzo Piccolomini, where both the Archivio di Stato and the Monte are located, and jotting down random notes on facts that occurred in 1622–24. The first Canto closes with a pictograph of the Monte accompanied by the names of the alleged signers of the act of foundation (XLII/214). Thus, rather suddenly the mountain looms. Yet Canto XLIII resumes the poet's search, repeating the process of hasty annotation of sifted data, till the Register itself is cryptically introduced: "1251 of the Protocols marked also / X, I, I, F, and four arabic / OB PECUNIAE SCARSITATEM" (XLIII/216).

It could be that Pound, disturbed by the uproar from the *palio*, stalked about the library in search of the "unmediated" master document: the notary Livio Pasquini's "Register of Protocols," which, in the Canto, he identifies by its call number, and from which he then appropriated, in upper case, the most poignant information (not, indeed, the names of the signers). In the Register he must also have examined the naive sketch of a small mountain with a tree on its summit, and read the hardly decipherable names of the signers: "Marcello di [or "de"] illmi domini Hypoliti domini Austinis."[15] But neither "Chigi" nor "Soffici" appears in the original document. While, apparently, as in both Cantos, "partly giving the impression of reading a crabbed legal document,"[16] here he keeps playing with names.[17] The "Chigi" and "Soffici" of the previous Canto are in fact patent interpolations (see "1251 of the Protocols"). While "Soffici" remains obscure, it could be that, with the spurious "Chigi," Pound is paying ironic homage to the "Roman" Chigis (the influential Sienese bankers established in Rome), or perhaps to the patron of music Count Guido Chigi Saracini, the founder of the Sienese Accademia Chigiana. Hence it is worth noticing that at the end of Canto XLII, before his encounter with the original document and near his foundational act interpolation, Pound draws the Chigi coat of arms (six mountains) rather than the logo of the Monte dei Paschi (three mountains).

Be the "Chigi" insertion homage or mere playfulness, the Monte dei Paschi Cantos, as a whole, with their jumble of inaccurately transcribed names, do show, ironically, "how loosely," sometimes, "some history is written."

NOTES

1 The letter, dated March 1, can be found at the Archivio dell'Accademia Chigiana, Siena (B, XII, 250 [original in Italian]). The Venetian publisher was probably Edizioni Popolari.

2 Lawrence S. Rainey, *Ezra Pound and the Monument of Culture. Text, History, and the Malatesta Cantos* (Chicago: University of Chicago Press, 1991) 185.

3 Cf. Paolo Traniello, *Storia delle biblioteche in Italia. Dall'Unità a oggi* (Bologna: Il Mulino, 2002), 11–22, 131–9, 170–86.

4 See Stock, 139. R. Murray Schafer argues that Pound found Arnaut's melodies at the Ambrosiana in 1906, when he was a "Fellow in Romantics" from the University of Pennsylvania (*EPM*, 28).

5 In collaboration with Walter Rummel (*Neuf chansons de Troubadours*) in 1912, and with Agnes Bedford (*Five Troubadour Songs*) in 1920.

6 David Anderson, *Pound's Cavalcanti. An Edition of the Translations, Notes, and Essays* (Princeton: Princeton University Press, 1983), xxvii. Anderson does not specify whether this undated manuscript at the Beinecke was written before or after the book was published, and thus whether the "defense" was meant as an apology for the patchwork Pound, as editor, had been forced to make on the original material ("rappezzata fra le rovine") or rather as a reply to the reviewers, notably the abrasive Mario Praz in Italy, and the mild Etienne Gilson in *The Criterion* 12. 46 (October 1932): 106–11. For the original edition in Italian, see *Guido Cavalcanti Rime. Edizione rappezzata fra le rovine* (Genoa: Marsano, 1932).

7 Anderson, *Pound's Cavalcanti*, 8; *Guido Cavalcanti Rime*, 8.

8 On Pound at the Capitolare see G. M. Cambié. "Otto foglietti di appunti di Ezra Pound alla Capitolare." *Civiltà veronese* (new series). 4. 2. (June–September 1989): 23–34; and S. M. Casella. " 'To adjust the spelling of Guido'," in *Ezra Pound 1972/1992*, ed. L. Gallesi (Milan: Greco & Greco, 1992), 155–98.

9 *Guido Cavalcanti Rime*, 44.

10 Anderson, *Pound's Cavalcanti*, 255.

11 Rainey, *Pound and the Monument of Culture*, 128.

12 Charles Yriarte, *Un condottiere au XVe siècle* (Paris: J. Rothschild Editeur, 1882), 282.

13 "Sigismond, arrêté devant Crémone par les travaux du siège, écrit à Laurent le Magnifique et lui demande un peintre pour les chapelles du temple de Rimini" (Yriarte, *Un condottiere*, 380–1).

14 Rainey, *Pound and the Monument of Culture*, 68–72.

15 On Pound and the *Registro dei Protocolli*, and photostatic reproductions of the call number and the passage involved, see Valerio Fusi. "Appendice," and "Pound e l'Archivio di Stato di Siena. Note sulla storia del Monte dei Paschi." in Ezra Pound, *La Quinta decade dei Cantos*, trans. Mary de Rachewiltz (Rimini: Raffaelli, 2006), 119–32.

16 Carroll F. Terrell, *A Companion to the Cantos of Ezra Pound*, 2 vols. (Berkeley: University of California Press, 1980), I: 172.

17 For a correct transcription of the names in Cantos XLII and XLIII see Mary de Rachewiltz and Maria Luisa Ardizzone's "Commento" in *I Cantos*, ed. Mary de Rachewiltz (Milan: Mondadori, 1985), 1532–3.

CHAPTER 15

The Lives of Pound

Ira B. Nadel

Lives of Ezra Pound are never dull. Inescapably contextual, they are also polemical and political. His life has repeatedly, and perhaps too conveniently, been placed into one of those three slots, anticipating his frequent presentation as an agitator, editor, poet, economist, critic, and even crank.

Early portraits of Pound, often by contemporaries, emphasized his unusual personality and radical approach to poetry. In London between 1908 and 1920, articles spoke of his curious American manner, described as brash, flamboyant, and very much in the image of the radical poet. A parody in *Punch* (June 23, 1909) describes a "Mr. Ezekiel Ton" eager "to impress his personality on English editors" as "the newest poet going." His original poetry blends "the imagery of the unfettered West, the vocabulary of Wardour Street, and the sinister abandon of Borgiac Italy." A month later the *Bookman* (London) outlined his American pedigree, emphasizing his ancestors who "went out to the New World in the seventeenth century." He is a distant relation of Longfellow and has supposedly written and burned two novels and 300 sonnets, a sign of his singular self criticism and productivity. And he is only twenty-three.[1]

Pound himself contributed to the myth. In 1913 he published "How I Began" and by 1915 began to appear in *Who's Who* with his own self-inscribed entry. It begins with "POUND, EZRA, M.A.; vorticist," and continues to stress his education and travel, and that he is "informally literary executor for the late Ernest Fenollosa." He then lists his publications and ends with "*Recreations*: fencing, tennis, searching The Times for evidence of almost incredible stupidity." The entry stood until 1919, when he identifies himself as "poet; London Editor of The Little Review." He also adds, after his remark about Fenollosa and work on Noh drama, that he is "a follower of Confucius and Ovid." He also alters his *Recreations* to read "the public taste and that of Sir Owen Seaman." Seaman was a parodist and editor of *Punch* from 1906 to 1932. In 1920 Pound changed his entry again to read "poet and constructive critic," maintaining the reference to Seaman. By

1925, he shifted his entry to identify himself as "poet and hack writer." All other details remain, although the reference to Sir Owen Seaman has gone. By 1929, he changed his "occupation" to "poet and composer."[2] Each of these alterations mark an adjustment in his biography and self-image.

Pound worked hard to uphold his compelling narrative. He came out of the West and from an America grappling with its own cultural identity. He followed Whistler, James, and Stein to Europe. To assert himself, he assumed a role, performing for audiences in England, France, Italy, and later America. Often in a sombrero and flamboyant cape, he affected the image of the "cosmopolitan Yankee Muse" crossed with a bohemian. He would sometimes wear a green shirt with the collar half open and a loosely knitted tie; in a photo of a visit to Wilfred Scawen Blunt in January 1914, Pound stands at ease in his flowing, open collar, unlike the formally dressed Yeats, Aldington, and F.S. Flint.[3] On other occasions, he would wear spats and a black velvet jacket offset by vermillion socks and a grey overcoat with buttons replaced by squares of lapis lazuli. No one could forget him.

Phyllis Bottome, British novelist and short story writer, first met Pound at a literary tea party given by May Sinclair in prewar London. She remembered that he "made the impression on me of an electric eel flung into a mass of flaccid substances." He had the face of "a scholarly satyr" and was an "intensely uncomfortable young man, even to himself." "Every word he said," she added, "had a meaning; and a meaning that very often had not occurred to anyone but himself." He also took every risk necessary to proclaim the truth but often did not take "sufficient time to make sure of his truth before he proclaimed it."[4] Later accounts of his life buried such personal insights, replacing them with social detail, literary fact, and political documents. Academic biographers especially hesitated to be so candid, although many did have personal contact with him.[5]

Early accounts accepted the image of the Wild West Pound, overlooking the clue in the title of his early work, *Personae* (1909). Early biographical squibs, either for his books or the press, always presented Pound as the American taking London and then Paris by storm with his energy and American ways. He was the unorthodox and uncouth American who first became bohemian, later drifting to the *noir* style of a gangster. A photograph illustrating the first is Pound in his dressing gown in his Paris studio in 1923. He stands in a state of *déshabillé* in his bohemian *atelier*, entirely nonconformist in pose and dress. The image, reproduced in C. David Heymann's *Ezra Pound: The Last Rower*, unites art and craft.[6]

Highlighting the *noir* style is a portrait of Pound taken by Bill Brandt in Vienna in 1928. Here, with fedora pulled down almost over his eyes and with the collar of his top coat turned up, he glares at the viewer, daring him or her to challenge his politics or poetics. He is defiant. Photos of him taken at Rapallo in 1938 by James Angleton (later to be a high ranking CIA officer) show Pound scowling in a leather jacket and furthering his sinister image now within a neo-fascist context.[7]

Published biographies soon began to appear, alternating between Pound's efforts as the instigator of Anglo-American modernism and his extreme politics. The former, originally limited to memoirs and brief accounts of Pound in passages by Yeats, D.H. Lawrence, or William Carlos Williams, stressed his overturning the poetry of the Decadents and Georgians with such radical notions as imagism, vorticism and an epic for the times, *The Cantos*. Hugh Kenner's *The Poetry of Ezra Pound* (1951), while primarily a critical study of the poetry, contains various biographical details that reinforce Pound's work as a modernist. The biographies, appearing mostly after his trial and incarceration at St. Elizabeths from 1945 to 1958, emphasize his political beliefs and were often written by acolytes who did not find issue with the extremism of his radio broadcasts, the intensity of his anti-Semitism, or the controversy over the Bollingen Prize of 1949.

Charles Norman's *Ezra Pound* (1960) and then Eustace Mullins' *This Difficult Individual, Ezra Pound* (1961), illustrate the swings of interpretation from poet to polemicist. Norman begins by arguing that Pound is accessible and that he is a teacher as well as a poet and early modernist. Norman also acknowledges the help of many front-line participants, from the former Mary Moore of Trenton to Conrad Aiken, Alvin Langdon Coburn, H.D., Richard Aldington, Dorothy Pound, and Mary de Rachewiltz. The result is impressionistic rather than rigorous with often puzzling statements and unbalanced diction: "Pound's mind was operating on several levels, not all of them of equal perspicuity" Norman writes about Pound's social and political ideas as expressed in Rapallo in 1935.[8] Quotations and excerpts take up a large number of pages, while Norman writes with Poundian exaggeration. Of *The Cantos*, for example, he claims it is "the most autobiographical poem in the English language." He then shifts to a Poundian preference for colloquialism, explaining that Pound's poetry sags "from an overfreightage of materials," but when he stops quoting from other sources, Pound becomes "a magician of metric" – so much so that one falls "in love again with the English tongue."[9] This anecdotal account of Pound celebrates his "nobility" and, despite its evident shortcomings, must be credited for being one of the earliest biographical narratives.

Mullins is more partisan. Working at the Institute of Contemporary Arts in Washington, he met Pound in 1949 through Dorothy and became a

regular visitor and later informal secretary. Highly critical of the government and the treatment of psychiatric patients at St. Elizabeths, Mullins
mixes up facts in what becomes a prejudiced and often melodramatic
account of Pound. Descriptions of horrific hospital life vie with admiration for Pound. At one point, following a Tuesday afternoon with him,
Mullins declares, "I was suddenly committed to him and to his ideals . . . I
would be involved in his struggle." Highly charged language in support of
Pound and his cause, opposing his imprisonment as a "political prisoner,"
fashions the remainder of the swiftly moving narrative, which Mullins
terms "the case *for* Ezra Pound." Pound, he argues, was not pro-fascist: he
actually "shielded a number of Jews from the Nazi exterminators," including a rabbi from Budapest. He also claims a communist guerilla named
Sbarbero hunted Pound in northern Italy.[10] Mullins' defense of Pound is
excessive in its partisanship. Photos taken during Pound's St. Elizabeths
period, however, add visual authenticity to the account.

Patricia Hutchins countered the politics and excess by returning to
Pound's London years in *Ezra Pound's Kensington* (1965), while Julien
Cornell, his lawyer, attempted a dispassionate account of Pound's trial in
The Trial of Ezra Pound (1966). He was quickly superseded, however, by
Harry Meacham's *The Caged Panther. Ezra Pound at St. Elizabeths* (1967).
This account, by one who developed a friendship with Pound, Dorothy,
and Archibald MacLeish during the Washington years, strenuously worked
to revise the negativism of Pound's radio broadcasts and the reasons for
his incarceration at St. Elizabeths. Uneven and partisan, it does, however,
contain material from various meetings with Pound and includes letters
relating to Pound at St. Elizabeths to and from MacLeish, Hemingway, and
Frost. The book essentially tries to defend Pound from the charges brought
against him, while revising the story of Frost's involvement to show that
he was less active than reported.

Efforts to remove the political and return to the literary in Pound
biography began to emerge in the seventies, but with a growing sense
of Pound as arrogant and careless, especially in his supposed knowledge
of economics and foreign languages such as Chinese. Biographies became
alternately more objective but unsympathetic.

Noel Stock's *Life of Ezra Pound* (1970), originating partly from time
spent with Pound at Brunnenburg, was sober, factual and, to some, dull.
This was in contrast with Pound's active role in fashioning the biography,
which Stock partly described in his "Preface," although he does not reveal
that the work was subject to approval by Dorothy Pound. This meant,
of course, that it could not be entirely frank. Stock had published Pound

in Australia and was rewarded by Pound's personal involvement in aiding Stock's research. Stock also had the advantage of interviewing Dorothy Pound, as well as Olga and Mary de Rachewiltz. He actually moved into Brunnenburg and identifies the castle as the site from which he completes the book.

Compensating for his contact with Pound and any subjective response was a determination to be objective, leading the critic D.J. Enright to open his review of the biography with this sentence: "Noel Stock's *Life of Ezra Pound* belongs to the class of . . . studiously researched biography which before long will be written by computers."[11] It is not a critical biography and the only sense of conveying a living figure comes from Pound's words himself, Enright adds. The literary criticism itself is thin, although Stock is sound on Pound's eccentricities or "ignorances" but excessive on certain details: for example, that Pound drank eight lemonades on a day in June 1898. By 1970 it was also a given that Pound was the "number-one turbine" of modernism and the point did not have to be restated, according to Enright. Appearing the following year, Kenner's *The Pound Era* offered an intellectual biography, avoiding personal details, while reinforcing what we already knew: that Pound was *the* instrumental modernist. After Kenner it seemed unnecessary to repeat this, but later biographers could not resist retelling the story of Pound's role in getting Joyce published, Frost noticed, or *The Waste Land* edited.

The emergence of the journal *Paideuma* in 1972 initiated a prolonged academic interest in Pound, with several early volumes containing a "Department" entitled "The Biographer." In volume 1, number 1, the editors make clear that they wanted facts to destroy the false myths about Pound by gathering "a sufficient phalanx / of particulars" (LXXIV/461). But "cold biographical fact must be supplemented by . . . his human qualities" they add.[12] One of the first to contribute was the novelist Richard Stern, who offered "A Memory or Two of Mr. Pound." Stern had published *Stitch*, his novel about Pound, in 1965, and recalled several Venetian encounters with the poet in 1962–3 when Stern lived in Venice while working on the novel and again in 1965. He befriended Pound and the two intermittently spoke. He also provides specific details about Pound's death, several (but not all) of them incorporated by Humphrey Carpenter in his 1988 biography (*A Serious Character*).

The biographies of the seventies, however, were unable to keep to the "cold facts" *Paideuma* wanted. Instead, they stressed a Pound who was unrepentantly political, purposeful, and partisan. In 1976, C. David Heymann, author of the first biography to appear after Pound's death on November 1,

1972, emphasized the political Pound (*Ezra Pound: The Last Rower*), while E. Fuller Torrey in 1984 underscored the anti-Semitic and psychotic Pound who was not, he argued, insane, although he might have harbored seditious ideas (*The Roots of Treason: Ezra Pound and the Secret of St. Elizabeths*). Heymann, in his somewhat reductive and sensationalist account, had the advantage of reviewing the newly released FBI file on Pound. Torrey drew from his direct experiences as a member of the psychiatric staff at St. Elizabeths and access to Pound's psychiatric records. He, perhaps more than any earlier biographer, recognized that Pound "was easy to hate yet difficult to dislike" and understood that his task was to prove Pound was not insane, despite the conclusion of four psychiatrists plus Dr. Overholser, Director of St. Elizabeths (who pressured one of the four to revise his opinion) that he was "unfit to stand trial."[13] To do so, Torrey offers a full account of Pound's life, emphasizing the war years and St. Elizabeths.

In the midst of these biographies, Hilda Doolittle offered her tempered narrative memoir of early Pound, more as lover and poet than proselytizer. *End to Torment* appeared in 1979. In 1980, an attempt to popularize Pound took the form of Peter Ackroyd's illustrated life of the poet, *Ezra Pound and His World*. Seven years later, John Tytell offered a semi-neutral life, a restatement hopeful that Pound, the bohemian who initiates the march toward modernism, would supplant any political prejudice against him (*Ezra Pound: The Solitary Volcano*). He also sought to offset Torrey's psychiatric focus. Interspersed with these efforts were James Wilhelm's factual volumes focusing on Pound's American roots and then on his years in London and Paris, followed by a volume on the so-called "tragic years" (*The American Roots of Ezra Pound*; *Ezra Pound in London and Paris 1908–1925*; *Ezra Pound, The Tragic Years, 1925–1972*).

And then in 1988, Humphrey Carpenter's 1005 page biography landed, offering the fullest and largest narrative to date. This was the first since Stock to attempt a complete life, this time unchallenged by Dorothy Pound. But it is a work that reads the poetry indifferently (if at all), while marshaling fact and event from a panoply of sources. His focus is on a multiple Pound, uncritically mixing the sinologist with the economist, the foreign affairs "expert" with the poet. Pound's use of personae dominates Carpenter's approach, emphasizing that Pound was fundamentally an actor, citing Charles Olson's comment that Pound "does not seem . . . to have inhabited his own experience." Carpenter identifies Pound as an "agile and slippery . . . creature," admitting that sorting out the history of Pound is almost impossible from start to finish (*ASC*, xii, 1). Heading each of the five parts of the biography is a different name used by Pound, from the youthful "Ra" to "Grampaw," and finally "Personae" to highlight his shifting identity.

Carpenter, like Torrey, believes that Pound was sane, despite his legal defense that he was unfit to stand trial. He furthermore believes that he was kept at St. Elizabeths longer than necessary partly because he was well-known, implying that the director was jealous that another hospital might claim him if released or transferred. The sheer volume of material gathered by Carpenter has made his biography the standard account for more than two decades. Supplementing it is Anne Conover's dual biography (*Olga Rudge & Ezra Pound*, 2001), the only joint biography of the two figures. A biography of Mary de Rachewiltz by Carol Shloss is now nearing completion.

Some nineteen years after Carpenter, and thirty-five years after Pound's death, the first of a two-volume biography of the poet appeared, *Ezra Pound: Poet, A Portrait of the Man and His Work. I The Young Genius 1885–1920*. Written by A. David Moody, the 2007 work excels in narrating Pound's publishing self, using his publications to tell the story of his life – not dramatically but accurately and bibliographically. In the line of Richard Ellmann or Leon Edel, Moody lets Pound's work tell the story. Unlike recent literary biography which has diverged from this path, preferring to separate texts from the life to concentrate more on personal rather than literary details, Moody links the two. He also manages to balance the simultaneous careers of Pound as critic with that of foreign editor and literary instigator. But it is clear that above all, Pound is for Moody a poet.

Moody not only traces in detail the evolution of key poetic texts but shows how Pound became active as an editor for *The Dial*, *Poetry*, *The Little Review*, and other little magazines. It was Yeats and John Quinn, for example, who were responsible for promoting Pound to Scofield Thayer as a literary agent picking the best new writers to forward. However, it was also made clear to Pound that his own unconventional work would only occasionally find its way into print. Consequently, Thayer printed "The Fourth Canto" but rejected Cantos v, vi and vii (Moody, 390–1). But as Pound began to invite Joyce, T.E. Lawrence, and others to contribute to *The Dial*, he was, in turn, asked to re-submit his avant-garde writing – to appear in a special section of the journal labeled "Modern Forms."

Moody stresses the energy of Pound, beginning with his fierce attacks on the moribund and outdated. And rather than try to reconcile the conflicting elements of Pound's life and ideas, Moody sets as his goal the recovery of a sense of complexity, while engaging with the "challenging originality of his poetry and the disruptive, regenerative force of his genius" (Moody, xii).

His sources are the many archives and works published and unpublished of Pound, as he details the story in volume I up to 1920, when Pound publishes *Instigations* then *Hugh Selwyn Mauberley*, becomes foreign agent for *The Dial*, has his first meeting with Joyce, and decides to leave London for Paris. Volume II, anticipated in 2012, will continue the narrative.

Not to be overlooked are the fictional lives of Pound or rather Pound in fiction. These presentations reveal other dimensions of his life and reflect the appeal of his character in ways that balance or expand scholarly narratives. Richard Aldington, to become H.D.'s husband, could not resist satirizing Pound in his novel *Death of A Hero* (1929) as Frank Upjohn, a painter but modeled on Pound, a figure who invents a new school of painting every season, as Pound seemed to do with poetry. In his short story "Nobody's Baby" (1932), Aldington satirizes Pound as the musician Charlemagne Cox, exaggerating his manner, especially his American dialect and bohemian dress. H.D. herself presented Pound as the poet George in HERmione (1927; published 1981), the writer who mysteriously returns to Philadelphia having lost his college position.

Richard Stern presents Pound in *Stitch* (1965), a story about an American writer in Venice. *Famous Last Words* (1981), by the Canadian Timothy Findley, presents Hugh Selwyn Mauberley as an American who has gone to Europe in 1919 to find Pound, who would become his mentor. The discovery of Mauberley's frozen body in the bombed-out Hotel Elysium at the end of the war allows a Lt. Quinn to read and decipher the poem of Mauberley's life etched on the walls of two hotel rooms with a silver pencil. Findley continued his interest in Pound in *The Trials of Ezra Pound*, a drama published in 1994. Three recent fictional portraits of Pound occur in the experimental *Poundemonium* (1986) by Julián Ríos, *Pronto* (1993), a mystery set in Italy by Elmore Leonard, and *Villa Vittoria* (1997) by C.K. Stead. This last focuses on an Olga-like character and a late attempt to photograph her, a picture that would have unexpected revelations.

Whether in fact or fiction, the life of Pound is not over. Newly emerging materials demand incorporation. The letters of Pound and Dorothy during the Pisan period, published as *Letters in Captivity* (1999), and Homer L. Pound's memoir, *Small Boy, The Wisconsin Childhood of Homer L. Pound* (2003), are two such examples. New textual details on, for example, the composition of *The Pisan Cantos*, illustrate the continued importance of poetic materials in reinterpreting the life. The Marcella Spann Booth archive at the Ransom Center at the University of Texas at Austin, received only in 2009, is another new resource: it contains over 700 letters plus photographs, as well as a scrapbook of Pound's release from St. Elizabeths and return to Italy. Such original documents necessitate fresh retellings of Pound's Odyssean life.

NOTES

1 "Publisher's Announcements. Mr. Welkin Mark's New Poet," *Punch* (June 23, 1909): 449, rpt. in *EPCH*, 6; "A new poet makes his debut," *Bookman* (July 1909), *ibid.*, 60.

2 "Ezra Pound," *Who's Who* (London: A.C. Black, 1915), 1741; *Who's Who* (1919), 1998; *Who's Who* (1920), n.p.; *Who's Who* (1925), 2313; *Who's Who* (1929), n.p.

3 Douglas Goldring, *South Lodge* 48; for photo see *ASC*, 370 ff; Moody illustration 28, 304 ff.

4 Phyllis Bottome, *From the Life* (London: Faber and Faber, 1944), 71, 72, 73.

5 Those that did – Charles Norman, Eustace Mullins, Harry Meachem, Noel Stock – veered away from offering personal assessments but not descriptions, often including the color of his beard or, in his late life, his silence.

6 C. David Heymann, *Ezra Pound: The Last Rower* (New York: Viking, 1976), 44–5.

7 For a discussion of Pound's American image see Ira B. Nadel, "The American Image of Ezra Pound," *Paideuma* 34 (2005): 121–48.

8 Charles Norman, *Ezra Pound* (New York: Macmillan, 1960), 331.

9 *Ibid.*, 335.

10 Eustace Mullins, *This Difficult Individual, Ezra Pound* (New York: Fleet Publishing, 1961) 26, 28, 246–7.

11 D.J. Enright, "Dialect and Analect, A Life of Ezra Pound," in *Man is an Onion, Reviews and Essays* (London: Chatto and Windus, 1972), 123.

12 Carroll F. Terrell, "Wanted: A Phalanx of Particulars," *Paideuma* I.1 (Spring/Summer 1972): 103.

13 In E. Fuller Torrey, *The Roots of Treason: Ezra Pound and the Secret of St. Elizabeths* (New York: McGraw-Hill Book Company, 1984), xix, 191–2.

PART II

Historical and cultural context

CHAPTER 16

The classics

Peter Liebregts

Ezra Pound was twelve when in 1897 he enrolled in the Cheltenham
Military Academy near Wyncote, where he was given a solid grounding
in English, Latin, Greek, history, and mathematics.[1] We find a reference
to the classical curriculum in a letter to his parents in June 1898, when he
writes about his forthcoming holiday: "no more Latin, no more Greek /
no more smoking on the sneak"[2] – the conventional outburst of joy of
the schoolboy who is (temporarily) freed of the tedium of many hours
spent in learning grammar. At the Academy, both Greek and Latin were
taught by Frederick James Doolittle, known among the cadets as "Cassius"
because of his lean and hungry appearance. Pound later recalled in *Guide
to Kulchur* that a man called Spenser recited a long passage from the *Iliad*
to him, which "was worth more than grammar when one was 13 years old"
(*GK*, 145), while in Canto LXXX/532 we read that "old Spencer (,H.) . . . first
declaimed me the Odyssey." However, J. J. Wilhelm has shown that no
existing bulletins of the school mention him, while his name does not
appear in the census rolls of Wyncote and vicinity.[3]

When Pound looked back on his school years in "Early Translators of
Homer" (1918), he observed that he probably was not "the sole creature
who has been well taught his Latin and very ill-taught his Greek" (*LE*, 249).
The subsequent critical assumption that Pound was reasonably competent
in Latin, but that his mastery of Greek was far from flawless, may have
been strengthened by his own occasional overstated observations on the
learning of the classics: "Really one DON'T need to know a language. One
NEEDS, damn well needs, to know the few hundred words in the few really
good poems that any language has in it. It is better to know [Sappho's]
POIKILOTHRON by heart than to be able to read Thucydides without
trouble" (*SL*, 93). Such a statement would explain why Pound stated in
1935 that he was "Too god damn iggurunt of *Greek*" to translate the *Odyssey*

(*SL*, 274). Indeed, Michael Reck, one of Pound's close friends in his later years, observed that the poet's Greek was not large, and was mainly read with the help of the Loeb Classical Library translations.[4] However, James Laughlin, Pound's American publisher, claims that Pound did have a fair knowledge of Greek, but that only the accents posed a problem; they would send passages containing Greek to the poet and translator Dudley Fitts "to clean up."[5]

Paradoxically, both accounts by Pound's friends are probably true. Anyone who has ever tried to master Ancient Greek is familiar with the frustrating experience that this takes far more effort than learning Latin, and that despite the more intense labor, one tends to forget Greek more easily after a short period than Latin after a very long while. Whatever Pound's range of knowledge of Greek may have been, whenever he tried to brush up his rusty Greek (as he tried to do in the 1950s), he apparently never experienced the liberating swiftness of ease and comprehension which helped him to enjoy his study of Latin texts.

Still, the occurrence of Greek in Pound's writings sometimes demonstrates a meticulous precision. He used, for example, the word "phaloi" in the poem "Coitus": "The gilded phaloi of the crocuses / are thrusting at the spring air" (*P*, 1990, 113). When the word was printed as "phalloi," Pound wrote to the publisher Elkin Mathews that the printer apparently was "not a hellenist, he seems to confuse the Greek PHALOS, plu. PHALOI (meaning the point of the helmet spike) with the latin Phallus" (*P/J*, 286). As the title of the poem and the image were obviously meant to evoke an erotic context, Mathews thought Pound's spelling had been rightly emended, [6] yet Pound had been particular in producing the exact image he wanted.[7]

We know that for his use of Latin Pound consulted the famous dictionary of Lewis and Short (1879), while for his Greek he relied on the great Greek–English Lexicon of Liddell and Scott (first published in 1843). (Pound even made his attempt to translate a poem by Stesichorus with the aid of Liddell–Scott an integrated part of Canto XXIII.) In the case of Greek, more often than with Latin, Pound had to resort to bilingual editions, such as the already mentioned Loeb Classical Library, and the French bilingual Budé-series. In his readings of Greek literature in the original Pound also would use a Latin crib, because, as he stated with a certain panache in "Notes on Elizabethan Classicists," Latin is "the only language into which any great amount of Greek can be in a lively fashion set over." He also added the typical sentiment that it was "much better that a man should use a crib, and know the content of his authors than that he should be able to recite all the rules in Allen and Greenough's *Grammar*" (*LE*, 239).

In 1901, Pound was admitted to the University of Pennsylvania on account of his good Latin. As a regular student who worked on a Bachelor of Science track which exempted him from Greek, he continued to study Latin, among other things, and in his first academic year he read Livy and other basic authors, as well as Horace's *Odes*. In 1902 Pound began to concentrate on Latin with five courses that included the poetry of Catullus, Tibullus, Propertius, Horace, Lucretius, Virgil, and Ovid. In that same academic year, Pound played the part of one of the fifteen maidens in the chorus of an undergraduate production of Euripides' *Iphigenia Among the Taurians*, presented in translation by the Department of Greek. William Carlos Williams later recalled that Pound, wearing a blond wig, "waved his arms about and heaved his massive breasts in ecstasies of extreme emotion."[8] This may have been the most remarkable event of Pound's sophomore year at Penn, as his academic work was not exceptional, having earned him not a single distinction.

In 1903, Hamilton College in Clinton, New York, admitted Pound as a candidate for the Bachelor of Philosophy degree, something which again exempted him from Greek. But although Pound was already concentrating on Latin, Anglo-Saxon, the Romance languages, and medieval history, he devoted some of his spare time "plugging away" at Greek.[9] He also shared a great interest in the Provençal troubadours with William Pierce Shepard, Professor of Romance Languages and Literatures, under whose influence he came to treat them as forerunners of the Italian poets inspired by Neoplatonism. Thus in an indirect way, his studies were still related to the examination of Greek culture.

POUND, THE CLASSICS AND COMPARATIVE LITERATURE

Pound had entered university with the intention, as he later stated on several occasions, of studying comparative values in literature. Comparative literature was still a radically new type of literary knowledge at the turn of the century. The first Chair of Comparative Literature was established at Harvard University in 1890, followed by a Department in 1904, five years after the first Department of Comparative Literature had been inaugurated at Columbia University. The first *Journal of Comparative Literature* did not survive its first year in 1903.[10] During his days as a student Pound was thus still confronted with the study of literature as philology, mainly concentrating on textual cruces and grammatical difficulties, a practice derived from the German scholarly approach to classical texts.

This became a problem when in 1905 Pound returned to the University of Pennsylvania to work on his Master's degree in Romanics. He studied *inter alios* Catullus and Martial with Walton Brooks McDaniel, Assistant Professor of Latin. Although Pound later claimed that "his search for clarity and hardness in verse had its roots in his early reading" of these Roman poets,[11] the negative sides of his university education overshadowed the positive gains. Pound later blamed McDaniel, in *Guide to Kulchur*, for being a part of a system that encouraged laziness and lack of originality. When he wanted to do a thesis on authors outside the curriculum, McDaniel advised him to confine himself to the accepted authors. They would at least guarantee definite results, whereas unknown authors could prove to be a waste of academic time.

McDaniel was most likely opposed to the study of those Renaissance authors writing in Latin about whom Pound wrote in the essay "Raphaelite Latin" (1906). According to Pound, they were neglected, because the

scholars of classic Latin, bound to the Germanic ideal of scholarship, are no longer able as of old to fill themselves with the beauty of the classics, and by the very force of that beauty inspire their students to read Latin widely and for pleasure; nor are they able to make students see clearly whereof classic beauty consists. The scholar is compelled to spend most of his time learning what his author wore and ate, and in endless pondering over some utterly unanswerable question of textual criticism.[12]

Pound's stance towards education would remain anti-philological throughout his life. Philology was not, according to him, the means to instil a sense of beauty in the student or reveal the "spirit" of the literary work. In "Provincialism the Enemy" (1917), he denounced the academic "ideal of scholarship" which "says in effect: you are to acquire knowledge in order that knowledge may be acquired" (*SPR*, 161). Among Pound's criticisms of the educational system, we find him objecting to the way Latin and Greek were taught as objects in themselves, rather than as keys to worlds whose discoveries and philosophies about the human condition were still valid for an understanding of the modern world. His ultimate aim in reading and learning was not to live the scholar's life of texts, but to search for life in texts.

This is already clear from his seminal *The Spirit of Romance*, which contains an enormous amount of quotations without much explication. This method of direct presentation of the "luminous detail," worked out more fully in "I Gather the Limbs of Osiris" (1911–12), should, according to Pound, enable the reader to see how the work of a particular author, or a single poem, or even just one line, is "an invention, a definite contribution to the art of verbal expression" (*LE*, 17). This method in Pound's creative work takes the form of quotations, allusions, personae, translations, and imitations. Pound translated (parts of) those works which he regarded of importance because of their techniques and historical value, serving him at the same time as exercises in literary craftsmanship and/or as masks.

POUND AND GREEK POETRY

There may be three reasons why Pound valued ancient Greek poetry. First of all, he regarded it as a prime example of *melopoeia*, a perfect aesthetic marriage between sound and sense, which was enhanced by the wide range of complicated metrical patterns, a second reason for Pound's interest, as he believed the study of Greek prosody could expand the possibilities of English verse. Thus his poem "The Return," with its variations on the units of the choriamb and the adonic, is an attempt to transpose Greek quantitative metre into English free verse. And thirdly, the mythopoeic quality of the Greek classics was an expression of an attitude toward the universe and its forces in a highly imaginative and non-doctrinal manner.

With regard to the Greek classics, Pound's canon consisted of the poets Homer, Sophocles, Sappho, Ibycus, and Theocritus, and Bion's poem *Death of Adonis*. Of these, Homer is unquestionably the champion in Pound's books of poetry and prose, and it is significant that in its "final" version *The Cantos* opens, as a sort of homage, with a rendering (in an imitation of Anglo-Saxon poetry) of a Renaissance Latin translation of a passage of Book 11 of the *Odyssey*, which was to be one of the great models for Pound's *magnum opus*. Two lyrical poets stand out in Pound's view: next to Ibycus (sixth century BC), regarded as a proto-imagist (and honored with a version of "The Spring" in *Lustra*), there is Sappho (seventh century BC) because of her "Ode to Aphrodite" (the "Poikilothron") and Fragment 31, from which Pound often quoted or referred to. He did pay tribute to Sappho's art in "Apparuit," his only attempt to write a poem in English with the use of the Sapphic stanza, while his poems "Papyrus" and "Ἰμέρρω" are good examples of an evocation in English of the fragmented heritage of Sappho's craft.

A similar experiment in transposition is Poem IV of *Hugh Selwyn Mauberley*, as its use of alliteration, assonance, anaphora, and rhythmic syncopation is adapted from *Death of Adonis* by Bion (*c.* 100 BC), a poem which according to Pound was essential study for anyone interested in metrics. Theocritus was Pound's favorite poet of the Hellenistic period

(323–30 BC), as a representative of the highly learned, self-conscious, and metrically innovative poetry of this time, all elements to be found in Pound's work as well. His "An Idyl for Glaucus," using Ovid as an intertext, may be seen as Pound's tribute to a poet he regarded as one of the models of the Browningesque dramatic monologue.[13] With regard to Sophocles, it must be said that in *How to Read* Pound was still rather negative about the Greek dramatists as he saw in them a decline from Homer, upon whom they were very much dependent for their effects. Later in his career, how-ever, Pound came to recognize the importance of Sophocles, and during his stay at St. Elizabeths he produced his versions of *Elektra* (1949) and the *Trachiniae* (*Women of Trachis*, 1954), also because he felt affinities with the predicaments of the protagonists.

POUND AND ROMAN POETRY

Pound's Latin canon is also one of poetry, and includes Catullus, Propertius, Ovid, and Martial. In the context of his time, this is rather notable, as these poets were generally regarded as inferior to Horace and Virgil, perhaps not coincidentally the two poets most associated with (the establishment of) Rome as an empire. In this respect, the enormous re-evaluation of Catullus, Propertius, and Ovid in the course of the twentieth century as poets who in many ways are now regarded as closer to our (post)modern(ist) age, is partly due to Pound's championship. Though Pound did not really dislike Horace (and translated some of his Odes), he regarded him as "the perfect example of a man who acquired all that is acquirable, without having the root" (*LE*, 28). He, therefore, is not of any use "save to the Latin scholar" (*SL*, 87). Despite Pound's interest in epic poetry, he denounced Virgil as "a second-rater, a Tennysonianized version of Homer" (*SL*, 87), and claimed that the *Aeneid* "has no story worth telling, no sense of personality" (*LE*, 215).[14]

The spirit of Martial, who called certain of his epigrams "Xenia," a title also used several times by Pound, is most evident in the volume *Lustra* with its pithy poems and satiric mocking of society and its conventions. This collection may be said to have inaugurated the period of Pound's most intense involvement with Roman poetry (culminating in *Homage to Sextus Propertius*), as it also contains poems in the Catullan spirit, such as "Ladies." Among Pound's translations, we may find versions of several of Catullus' poems, including the well-known "Odi et amo" (LXXXV), and a reworking of poem IV in "Phasellus ille" (*Ripostes*). Throughout his entire work, and especially in *The Cantos*, we find references to Catullus' Sirmio as one of Pound's "holy places."

One of Pound's most (in)famous translations is *Homage to Sextus Propertius*, which has aroused a long debate over its merits as a translation, and even the application of this term has been the subject of many discussions. Yet it is clear that in this "anti-philological" text, Pound's supposed mistakes, denounced by champions of literal translations as howlers, are often (but not always) deliberate mistranslations to evoke the melopoeic quality of the original or to create puns and associative wordplays. Moreover, in his rendering of several of Propertius' poems, Pound blurs the distinction between translation, imitation, and original composition to create a persona which questions notions of epic poetry, of politics and imperialism, of gender and eroticism, a persona which K. K. Ruthven has aptly called "Propoundius." At the same time, Pound's version may be seen as a creative commentary on Propertius' elegies. Without doubt, *Propertius* has become a key text in any discussion about the translation and transmission of classical texts.[15]

Where Homer was Pound's favorite Greek poet, Ovid served as his Latin counterpart, although Pound never seemed to have much interest in the whole of the Roman poet's output. Thus the *Amores* and *Ars Amatoria* are absent in Pound, as are the *Heroides*, although he did note their importance as models for the dramatic monologue: "Ovid, before Browning, raises the dead and dissects their mental processes" (*SR*, 16). Yet for Pound, Ovid meant the *Metamorphoses* (already behind the early poem "The Tree" in *Hilda's Book*). In *The Spirit of Romance*, Pound praised Ovid for having stated:

"Convenit esse deos et ergo esse credemus."

"It is convenient to have Gods, and therefore we believe they exist"; and with all pretence of scientific accuracy [Ovid] ushers in his gods, demigods, monsters and transformations. His mind, trained to the system of empire, demands the definite. The sceptical age hungers after the definite, after something it can pretend to believe. The marvellous thing is made plausible . . . (*SR*, 15)

Pound even claimed in a 1922 letter that "the Writings of Confucius, and Ovid's *Metamorphoses* [are] the only safe guides in religion" (*SL*, 183). Apart from its presentation of the vital forces of the universe and man's encounters with the divine in particular forms, the structural principle of Ovid's *Metamorphoses* supplied Pound's *Cantos* with a model in several ways, the most important being, of course, the principle of metamorphosis. Despite the variety of the various transformations in Ovid's poem, they are variations on basic patterns, just as *The Cantos* presents us with a metamorphic recurrence of archetypal events and persons. Ovid may even be called a proto-ideogrammatist as he has arranged his stories in such a way that one may establish links between the various tales in terms of similarity or contrast. The *Metamorphoses* thus helped Pound in various ways to present his view of the universe as consisting of "the permanent, the recurrent, the casual" (*SL*, 239).

CLASSICAL PROSE AND TRANSLATIONS

Pound hardly recommended classical prose writers because he regarded almost all of the prose before 1750 as not of "the least use to a man trying to learn the art of 'changing language'" (*LE*, 30). But even here he offers some exceptions: he wrote admiringly of Apuleius' *Golden Ass* in *The Spirit of Romance*, and praised Longus (? second century AD) for his "delicate nouvelle" *Daphnis and Chloe* (*LE*, 30). He also admitted that Herodotus "wrote history that is literature" (*ibid.*) – but dismissed Thucydides as the "first journalist... we have thrust upon us," "Fleet Street muck that he is" (*SL*, 93). Pound, however, was not as faithful to his prose writers as he was to his poets: he later rejected Herodotus' *Histories* in *The Great Digest* (1928) as "a mere collection of anecdotes."[16] The exceptions to the rule were the Greek philosophers, particularly Aristotle and Plotinus, both of whom were quoted increasingly in his poetry and prose from the 1930s onward. Especially in *Guide to Kulchur* we find Pound's admiration for Aristotle's *Nicomachean Ethics*, while Plotinus and Neoplatonism can be found throughout Pound's work, but most extensively and explicitly in *Rock-Drill* and *Thrones*.[17]

Pound's canon of the classics also included translations, because, as he stated in *How to Read* (1929), "some of the best books in English are translations" and are "in themselves better reading than the 'original verse' of their periods" (*LE*, 34–5). Pound even called the translation of the *Aeneid* by Gavin Douglas (1474–1522) "better than the original, as Douglas had heard the sea" (*LE*, 35), unlike Virgil, that "highly cultured but non-seafaring author" (*ABCR*, 118). He also valued Marlowe's translation of Ovid's *Amores* (1597), and praised the translation of the *Metamorphoses* (1567) by Arthur Golding (1536–1605) as "the most beautiful book in the language" (*ibid.*, 127). Although Pound did appreciate certain parts of Chapman's *Odyssey* or Pope's *Iliad*, he did not include translations from the Greek in his canon for the very simple reason that there was "no satisfactory translation of any Greek author" (*LE*, 35). In a letter to Iris Barry, he advised her, if she could not read Greek poetry in the original, to use Latin translations, as most English translations are "hopeless" (*SL*, 87). Pound very much disliked the work of one of the most popular translators of Greek poetry of the twentieth century, Gilbert Murray, Regius Professor of Greek at Oxford from 1908 to 1936. With great approval he quoted in a 1934 letter T.S. Eliot's words in "Euripides and Professor Murray" (1920) that he had "erected between Euripides and the reader a barrier more impassable than the Greek language" (*SL*, 263)[18] – a barrier he himself tried so hard to level. Whatever one may think of Pound's linguistic abilities, one cannot deny that with his many renderings of foreign verse, including the classics, he has had an enormous impact on the theory and practice of translation. Through his work, he taught readers to look at the classical tradition in a new light, and "made it new."

NOTES

1 For a detailed description of Pound's education, see Noel Stock, *The Life of Ezra Pound* (London: Penguin, 1974) 12–45; J.J. Wilhelm, *The American Roots of Ezra Pound* (New York: Garland, 1985), 77–9 and 96–115; Gail McDonald, *Learning to Be Modern: Pound, Eliot and the American University* (Oxford: Clarendon Press, 1993), 8–25; Moody, 8–33.

2 Quoted in Wilhelm, *American Roots*, 79.

3 *Ibid.*, 78.

4 Michael Reck, *Ezra Pound: A Close-Up* (New York: McGraw-Hill, 1968), 118, 120.

5 James Laughlin, *Pound as Wuz: Recollections and Interpretations* (London: Peter Owen, 1989), 8.

6 See *EPCH*, 124.

7 This sort of precision, however, is not always appreciated by Poundians; K.K. Ruthven, *A Guide to Ezra Pound's Personae (1926)* (Berkeley: University of California Press, 1969), 52, also translates "phaloi" simply as "phalluses."

8 W.C. Williams, *The Autobiography of William Carlos Williams* (New York: New Directions, 1951), 57.

9 Quoted in *ASC*, 55.

10 See K.K. Ruthven, *Ezra Pound as Literary Critic* (New York: Routledge, 1990), 6–7.

11 See Stock, *Life*, p. 28.

12 Pound, "Raphaelite Latin," *Book News Monthly* 25.1 (September 1906): 31.

13 See my "Ezra Pound's 'An Idyl for Glaucus,'" *Journal of Modern Literature* 19.1 (Summer 1994): 171–8.

14 Pound's work does contain some Virgilian echoes; see Donald Davie, *Studies in Ezra Pound* (Manchester: Carcanet Press, 1991), 270–84. On Pound and Roman poetry, see Ron Thomas, *The Latin Masks of Ezra Pound* (Ann Arbor, MI: UMI Press, 1983); Daniel M. Hooley, *The Classics in Paraphrase* (Selingsgrove, PA:

Susquehanna University Press, 1988); Peter Davidson, *Ezra Pound and Roman Poetry* (Amsterdam: Rodopi, 1995).

15 See J.P. Sullivan, *Ezra Pound and Sextus Propertius: A Study in Creative Translation* (Austin: University of Texas Press, 1964); Nial Rudd, *The Classical Tradition in Operation* (Toronto: University of Toronto Press, 1994), 117–58.

16 Ezra Pound, *Confucius* (New York: New Directions, 1969), 19.

17 On this aspect, see my *Ezra Pound and Neoplatonism* (Madison, NJ: Fairleigh Dickenson University Press, 2004).

18 T.S. Eliot, *Selected Essays* (London: Faber and Faber, 1951), 62.

CHAPTER 17

Provençal and the troubadours

William D. Paden

> Pound, in the teens and 1920s, understood the literary logic of mod-
> ernism, with its poetics of difficulty and allusiveness, more clearly
> than any of his contemporaries. He pushed his insights further, into
> an extreme, enormous, all-but-unreadable book – the "Cantos" . . . .[1]

By the age of fifteen Ezra Pound "already knew, apparently, pretty much
what he wanted to do – that by the time he was 30 he 'would know more
about poetry than any man living' " (Moody, 13). He first read Browning's
Sordello in 1904. "I began to get it on about the 6th reading," he would
write to his father, and he thought he might be able to model his own long
poem on Browning's difficult epic about the Italian adventurer who became
a troubadour.[2] Within a year he found a way to study Provençal.[3] In spring
term of 1905, the last trimester of his senior year at Hamilton College, he
was introduced to the language by Professor William P. Shepard, cementing
a relationship that would last as long as Shepard lived.[4] Pound and Bill,
as Pound called him, read H. J. Chaytor's *Troubadours of Dante*, which
included poems by Sordello as well as Bertran de Born, Arnaut Daniel,
and others whom Pound would continue to read for years.[5] In May the
Hamilton Literary Magazine published his version of a text in Latin and
archaic Provençal that he called the "Belangal Alba."[6]

After graduating from Hamilton, Pound returned to the University of
Pennsylvania (where he had spent his freshman and sophomore years),
near his family's home in the Philadelphia suburb of Wyncote. In 1905–6,
as a student in the Master's program in Romanic Languages, he studied
almost exclusively with the Hispanist Hugo Rennert, working on Spanish
(Old Spanish, Spanish Drama, Spanish Literature), Old French, Italian
(Petrarch), and more Provençal.[7] He bought a copy of Carl Appel's *Provenzalische Chrestomathie* (Provençal Anthology) in the second edition (1902)
and dated it 1905, presumably in the fall when he began his work with
Rennert.[8] He received the Master's degree in 1906 and was awarded a

fellowship to begin the doctoral program, but soon found that he was losing his taste for academic work. After two more terms of Provençal with Rennert, as well as courses on the Sicilian poets, Dante, the Poem of Fernán González (a Spanish epic history), more Spanish drama, and the *Chanson de Roland*, he began to accumulate incomplete work, and in spring term he finished not one course.[9] His fellowship was not renewed, nor was he offered an instructorship. In 1907 he left the university.

His four terms of Provençal study would bear fruit in poems that occupied him from 1908 to 1919; the most famous of these is "Near Périgord," which Hugh Kenner has called "the Ur-Canto." In 1910 he published *Provença*, collecting material that he had published elsewhere, much of it inspired by the troubadours. In *The Spirit of Romance* (*SR*, 1910) and elsewhere he published prose pieces on the troubadours.[10] In 1911 he visited the lexicographer Emil Levy in Freiburg and discussed a textual crux in Arnaut Daniel.[11] He planned a book of translations from Arnaut that he submitted to several publishers, but bad luck dogged the venture, and the book was never published. Pound worked on Arnaut from 1911 to 1920, eventually finding other outlets.[12] As part of his project he procured from the libraries of Milan and Paris reproductions of Arnaut manuscripts that he planned to include in the book.[13] In 1912 and 1919 he traveled to the South of France.[14] His copy of Appel's *Provenzalische Chrestomathie* bears evidence that he continued to consult it until 1961.[15] He referred to the troubadours, including citations in Provençal, from Canto II to the incomplete Canto CXVII, published in 1969.

In the years when Pound studied Old Provençal it was a topic of intense cultivation in Europe and America; now that the focus of contemporary interests has shifted, it can be difficult for readers to imagine how compelling the troubadours were in his time.[16] Appel's *Provenzalische Chrestomathie* would go on to six editions, followed by two reprints, to satisfy the burgeoning demand. The second edition, which Pound owned, and Chaytor's *Troubadours of Dante*, were newly published when he used them. In 1904, the year before Pound took up Provençal, the leading poet of the modern language, Frédéric Mistral, shared a Nobel Prize for his accomplishments as a poet and philologist – exactly the combination of arts that Pound would bring to his study of the troubadours.

The Provençal poets had enjoyed renown since the twelfth and thirteenth centuries, when their songs echoed and were imitated in Northern France, Spain, Portugal, Italy, Germany, and possibly England.[17] They were remembered and revered wherever Dante and Petrarch were read: they help to populate the *Divine Comedy* in all its three otherworldly regions, from

Inferno (Bertran de Born) to Purgatorio (Arnaut Daniel and Sordello) to Paradiso (Folquet de Marselha), and Petrarch acknowledged them among the sources of his inspiration. In addition to these poetic intermediaries, two strands of thought show more direct awareness of the troubadours over the centuries. One, the more widespread, is biographical; it focuses on the *vidas* and *razos*, the prose "lives" of the troubadours and the "reasons" why they wrote individual songs; the other, more scholarly, turns to the lyric texts themselves, and is concerned with editions, dictionaries, and the Provençal language. Both these strands would affect Pound, and both had sustained long and vigorous histories when he became interested in them.

The biographical strand began in the thirteenth century with the composition of the first *vidas*, which sought to weave the poems into an account of the poet's life. The *vidas* and *razos* were retold, at first uncritically but with increasing awareness of their unreliability as history, in the sixteenth century by Jean de Nostredame and in the eighteenth by Jean-Baptiste de La Curne de Sainte-Palaye, his popularizer the Abbé Claude Millot (who confessed that he did not read Provençal himself), and their English translator Susanna Dobson. By the nineteenth century the lives of the troubadours were enshrined in the *Biographie universelle*.[18] Pound knew Ida Farnell's translation of the Provençal prose texts, as well as books on the troubadours by Francis Hueffer and Justin Smith that take a biographical approach.[19] The *vidas* and *razos* are represented in both Chaytor's *Troubadours of Dante* and Appel's *Chrestomathie*. The skepticism regarding their veracity that was memorably expressed by Gaston Paris in 1893 – a skepticism that is widely shared today – seems not to have influenced Pound, who preferred to "see a mythic grandeur in the poets' lives."[20]

The more critical tradition began in the early nineteenth century with the first major printed collection of troubadour texts, the *Choix des poésies originales des troubadours*, by François-Just-Marie Raynouard (1816–21). In an interview in 1818 Goethe, the poet and sage, recommended this anthology to Friedrich Diez, a young scholar in search of a project; taking the suggestion to heart, Diez went on to initiate the scholarly study of the troubadours and to found the discipline of Romance philology. Raynouard himself launched serious study of the Provençal language with a six-volume dictionary, published in 1844, that was supplemented (but not replaced) by the lexicographer Emil Levy in eight magisterial volumes that appeared from 1894 to 1924.[21] A compendium of Romance philology, the *Grundriss der romanischen Philologie*, began to appear in 1888 and went into a second edition before the first one was complete. The *Grundriss* encompassed eight Romance languages in the first volume and attempted to include all their literatures, especially the early ones, in the second, with supplementary chapters on history, history of science, and history of art; a preliminary program called for history of music. Despite Pound's protest that his *Spirit of Romance* "is not a philological work," one may see in it a program fundamentally similar to that of the *Grundriss*: "I have attempted to examine certain forces, elements or qualities which were potent in the medieval literatures of the Latin tongues, and are, I believe, still potent in our own" (*SR*, 5). Some philologists claimed that their domain was coextensive with the humanities.[22]

Nineteenth-century poets and writers were well aware of the troubadours, the word "troubadour" having entered the English vocabulary in the century preceding.[23] Among the German Romantics, Uhland and Heine both wrote short poems depicting Bertran de Born as a magician with words, and retelling the death of Jaufre Rudel. Keats, in the "Ode to a Nightingale," expressed yearning for "Provençal song, and sunburnt mirth." In London, *The Troubadour* was the title of a short-lived literary magazine that was published for six months in 1822. In the same year Eleanor Anne Porden published a poem in sixteen books, *Coeur de Lion*, imagining that Bertran de Born accompanied Richard Lionheart on the third crusade, and that he shared a tragic love with Richard's sister.[24] In *Sordello* (1840), which has been called "the key poem of the Victorian age," Browning uses the Italian troubadour as an *alter ego*. He does so again with Jaufre Rudel in "Rudel to the Lady of Tripoli"; like the troubadour of legend, Browning "would later fall in love with Elizabeth Barrett without having met her."[25] Swinburne, too, must have been moved by the story of Jaufre, which he represented twice, in "The Death of Rudel" and "The Triumph of Time"; he imitated one of Guiraut Riquier's pastourelles in "An Interlude," as Pound knew, and modeled "In the Orchard" on an *alba*, a poem of lovers' parting at dawn. Victor Pierre Laurens represented Bertran de Born as *Le Tyrtée du Moyen Age* (1863), likening him to Tyrtaeus, the ancient Greek poet who urged the Spartans to make war. In his large compilation of European poetry Longfellow reprinted translations from eighteen troubadours, including two women.[26] Toward the end of the century Wilde, in his sonnet "Amor Intellectualis" (1881), recalled Browning on "Sordello's passion."[27] Tennyson, in his verse play *Becket* (1884), represented Eleanor of Aquitaine declaring herself a troubadour. Giosue Carducci wrote on "Jaufré Rudel" (1888), as did Edmond Rostand in his verse drama, *La princesse lointaine* (1895). In 1900 Maurice Hewlett, whom Pound would later know well, represented Bertran de Born in a novel, *The Life and Death of Richard Yea-and-Nay.*

So the troubadours were in the air in Philadelphia as well as in London and Paris, and Pound, as an aspiring poet, could scarcely have avoided breathing them in. They were borne along in the wake of Romantic medievalism and by association with colorful figures such as Richard Lionheart and his mother, Eleanor of Aquitaine. They were known primarily from the mythic narratives of the *vidas* and *razos*, which account directly or indirectly for the knowledge of them shown by Uhland and Heine. The *vida* of Jaufre Rudel provided all that was necessary for Browning and Swinburne to write their poems about him, although Carducci quotes Jaufre's own poetry directly. As for Sordello, Browning may have learned all he knew of him from his father's copy of the *Biographie universelle.*[28]

When Pound took it up, Provençal was a well-established element in the American college curriculum. The troubadours had first been taught, to my knowledge, in 1869, when Ferdinand Bôcher lectured at Harvard on early French and Provençal literature; by 1872 Bôcher was teaching a course on "Philology of the Romance Languages" that included consideration of Provençal, Italian, French, and Spanish. Later in that decade Provençal was taught at Johns Hopkins by A. Marshall Elliott, who would found the Modern Language Association in 1883. By 1904, when Pound entered Hamilton, Provençal was being taught regularly at Harvard, Yale, Princeton, Columbia, Johns Hopkins, and Chicago. It was typically taught in a larger context, along with French philology or as a central component of Romance philology in general. Paradoxically, despite its central position, it was more often taught than studied in a scholarly way.[29] Some professors who taught Provençal never published on it, as was true of Bôcher and Elliott, although they published in other areas. Charles Hall Grandgent, the Dantist and eventual president of the Modern Language Association, taught Provençal at Harvard as a second-semester, half-year course, every year or every other year from 1886 to 1931, but he published on it just once, though memorably: his concise *Outline of the Phonology and Morphology of Old Provençal* remains useful to specialists to this day.[30] Henry Roseman Lang, who taught Provençal at Yale from 1893 to 1921, was primarily a scholar in Portuguese but wrote a valuable, brief study of "The Relations of the Earliest Portuguese Lyric School with the Troubadours and the Trouvères."[31] Henry Alfred Todd taught Provençal from 1885 to 1925, first at Johns Hopkins and then at Columbia, using Appel's *Chrestomathie* and Chaytor's *Troubadours of Dante* as Pound would do at Hamilton, but he published only occasional reviews in the field; he was co-founder, with Elliott, of the Modern Language Association, and another eventual president. The community of these scholars and others like them who taught Provençal on the graduate or undergraduate level, many using the same textbooks, and many among the leaders in their profession, asserted the importance of the troubadours for understanding the past – and by implication the present as they understood it.

The two men who taught Pound Provençal, William Shepard and Hugo Rennert, provide further understanding of his context. Both were born near the institution where they were educated and where, after going to Germany for the doctorate, they returned to teach. With PhDs in hand, both Pound's eventual mentors were promptly appointed to positions in their home institutions. Shepard spent four years as Associate Professor and was promoted to Professor in 1900 without publishing beyond his dissertation. He continued to teach at Hamilton until he retired in 1940; he died in 1948. Rennert, having already served as an instructor, was appointed Professor in the year of his doctorate, and continued until ill health forced him to take a leave of absence in 1925; he died, without retiring, in 1927. Pound mentioned Rennert in Canto XX, published a year later, and Shepard in Canto LXXXX, in the year of his death. Perhaps he knew when both his former teachers passed away.

When Pound studied with Shepard during his junior and senior years, Shepard was the only teacher of Romance languages on the faculty. Hamilton was a very small school, admitting about forty freshmen each year. A student in the class of 1924 remembered Shepard as "a tall, cadaverous man, quite dapper and neatly attired, [who] stepped down the front stairs of the language building and into his chauffeur-driven car."[32] When Pound took Provençal, Shepard gave him a grade of B; the same quarter he made A's in Old English and French, a B in Spanish, and a D in German. His curriculum in his last undergraduate quarter consisted of courses in five languages. At this time Shepard had not yet begun to publish on Provençal; his first publications after the dissertation appeared in 1906, including a substantial article on Provençal syntax in *PMLA* and a verse translation of three songs by Bertran de Born in Kiplingesque style. After that his production accelerated gradually, leading to what was described as "the first critical edition made by an American of a Provençal text of any consequence,"[33] and then editions of a troubadour manuscript and a fourteenth-century Passion. His last book, an edition of the troubadour Aimeric de Péguilhan, was completed after his death by a younger colleague. Philology for these men was a life's work that could, if necessary, be relayed to a new generation.

Rennert had completed his doctorate four years before Shepard, and was ten years older. When he taught Pound he had already reached mid-career.

In 1904 he published his monumental *Life of Lope de Vega*; in 1905, on the basis of his edition of a Galician troubadour, he was named to the Royal Galician Academy. His study of *The Spanish Stage in the Time of Lope de Vega* would appear in 1909, the year when he joined the Royal Spanish Academy in Madrid; the expanded Spanish version of his life of Lope, in collaboration with Américo Castro, came in 1919.

After Pound's ignominious departure from the graduate program, Penn refused to grant him a doctorate that could have been awarded on the basis of his independent publications, as his father suggested in 1920, no doubt at Pound's prompting. Pound wrote to his father in a fury, calling Rennert "a poor thing without backbone" and "a natural worm."[34] In his anger the poet, the man of imagination, distanced himself from the textual and factual orientation of literary scholarship. He was not wrong to do so. Rennert's assistant J. P. Wickersham Crawford, who poured out his admiration for his master in two obituaries, stressed that Rennert was averse to anything beyond a reliable text and factual biography; in his massive life of Lope de Vega he avoided the subject of Lope's plays.[35] Rennert was receptive to recent theories of textual criticism, according to Crawford (although this is not apparent in his work); Shepard was more skeptical, as he explained in a carefully reflected statement.[36] Neither Shepard nor Rennert ever published literary criticism, much less work in "comparative values in literature (poetry)," which was what Pound intended to study when he went to college (Moody, 14). The most we can say is that as a young man, at about the time when he taught Pound, Shepard had done verse translations.[37]

In sharp contrast to his rejection by Penn, Pound was awarded an honorary doctorate by Hamilton in 1939. One may assume that Shepard was involved in some way as one of Pound's teachers, although he seems not to have attended the ceremony, perhaps because of his wife's poor health. Pound discussed the degree with Joseph Ibbotson, who had taught him English and Anglo-Saxon; it was offered and conferred by William H. Cowley, who became President of Hamilton in 1938. The citation read in part:

Your feet have trodden paths . . . where the great reading public could give you few followers – into Provençal and Italian poetry, into Anglo-Saxon and Chinese . . . Your Alma Mater . . . is an old lady who has not always understood where you have been going, but she has watched you with interest and pride if not always with understanding . . . Whether or not your theories of society survive, your name is permanently linked with the development of English poetry in the twentieth century . . .[38]

This language makes clear that the President and faculty of Hamilton meant to keep their distance from Pound's social views, which were approaching their virulent phase. At a ceremonial luncheon following the degree ceremony, he engaged in embarrassing polemic with the anti-fascist speaker.

As a poet, Pound followed many others who had cultivated an interest in the Provençal troubadours; as a young scholar he followed those who read them according to their understanding of the canons of Romance philology. But Pound integrated the troubadours into the logic of modernism in a revolutionary way. In his "poetics of difficulty and allusiveness," he attempted to merge the troubadours into the imaginative reality of his poem and his time, to make them instrumental in what he called his paideuma, "the gristly roots of ideas that are in action" (*GK*, 58). As David Moody has written, "He wanted to make the *virtu* of the past a force in the present . . . to refashion the mentality of his world" (Moody, 195, 407). Pound would have had the troubadours, real poets who had sung once, sing again and be heard, truly heard, in their own medieval tongue – along with others who wrote in French or Italian or Spanish, in Latin, Greek, or Chinese. He failed, of course, as he acknowledged more generally in Canto CXVI: "I cannot make it cohere." Like Whitman, Pound strove to contain multitudes; unlike his fellow American poet, he strove to contain many languages, wide swaths of history, and much of the globe. Despite his manifest flaws, his was a glorious failure.

NOTES

1 A. O. Scott, "The Best Mind of His Generation" [on David Foster Wallace], *The New York Times* (September 21, 2008), Week in Review, 3.

2 Michaela Giesenkirchen, " 'But Sordello, and My Sordello?' Pound and Browning's Epic," *Modernism/Modernity* 8.4 (2001): 640n4.

3 In this chapter I shall call the language Provençal as Pound and his contemporaries did, although scholars now call it Occitan to avoid the misleading limitation to Provence, east of the Rhône, which is only one part of the region where the language was spoken; see William D. Paden, *An Introduction to Old Occitan* (New York: Modern Language Association of America, 1998). I shall use the word "troubadour" to refer to a poet who wrote or sang in Provençal.

4 "A letter in March of 1905 to Isabel said that he was engaging in 'extra work with Bill [Shepard] next term in Provençal, "The Troubadours of Dante"'": J. J. Wilhelm, *The American Roots of Ezra Pound* (New York: Garland, 1985), 133. "Bill shep gave me the Provençal. There was no provençal course, and I cd.n't have paid him. I mean GAVE": Charles Norman, *Ezra Pound*, rev. edn. (New York: Funk and Wagnalls, 1969), 356.

5 H. J. Chaytor, *The Troubadours of Dante* (Oxford: Clarendon Press, 1902).

6 Ezra Pound, *Poems and Translations*, ed. Richard Sieburth (New York: Library of America, 2003), 94, 1260. Pound called his version "Alba Belingalis" in *P*, 1909. This was not Pound's first published poem: Donald Gallup, *Ezra Pound, A Bibliography* (Charlottesville: University Press of Virginia, 1983), 225.

7 Wilhelm, *The American Roots*, 144.

8 Carl Appel, *Provenzalische Chrestomathie: mit Abriss der Formenlehre und Glossar*, 2nd edn. (Leipzig: O.R. Reisland, 1902). Pound's personal copy was loaned to me in 1979 by Professor R. Murray Schafer of Simon Fraser University; see William D. Paden, "Pound's Use of Troubadour Manuscripts," *Comparative Literature* 32 (1980): 411–12.

9 Wilhelm, *The American Roots*, 151–2.

10 "Il Miglior Fabbro," on Arnaut Daniel; "Proença," on troubadours in general, using Chaytor, Appel, and other sources; "Geste and Romance," on narratives in Provençal (the romance of *Flamenca*), Spanish, and French; "Psychology and Troubadours," on "chivalric love"; all in *SR*. "Troubadours – Their Sorts and Conditions" and "Arnaut Daniel" in *LE*.

11 Canto xx/89–90. J. J. Wilhelm, *Ezra Pound in London and Paris 1908–1925* (University Park: Pennsylvania State University Press, 1990), 72–3. Paden, "Pound's Use," 409–10.

12 Line Henriksen, "*Arnaut Daniel* [unpublished]," in *The Ezra Pound Encyclopedia*, ed. Demetres P. Tryphonopoulous and Stephen J. Adams (Westport, CT: Greenwood Press, 2005), 18.

13 Paden, "Pound's Use," 412.

14 On 1912 see *WTSF* and Moody, 182–195. On 1919, Wilhelm, *Ezra Pound in London and Paris*, 228–36.

15 Paden, "Pound's Use," 411–12.

16 "For many decades Ezra Pound's interest in that literature has seemed a youthful freak, like the green shirt with glass buttons he wore to Giessen when he was 25": Kenner, *PE*, 78. "If it is easy now to think of Pound as upsetting the staid English scene by means of a revolutionary poetics, it is less easy to explain why he was so fascinated in the beginning with the medieval French troubadours. Yet there is no doubt that in his mind the troubadours came first, not the Imagists": William Pratt, "Pound as a Modern Troubadour," in *Ezra Pound and the Troubadours: Selected Papers from the Ezra Pound Conference, Brantôme, France 1995*, ed. Philip Grover (Gardonne, France: Editions Fédérop, 2000), 32.

17 On the troubadours' influence abroad see *A Handbook of the Troubadours*, ed. F.R.P. Akehurst and Judith M. Davis (Berkeley: University of California Press, 1995). Their influence in England is now largely discounted, but see H. J. Chaytor, *The Troubadours and England* (Cambridge: Cambridge University Press, 1923), and Jean Audiau, *Les troubadours et l'Angleterre* (Paris: J. Vrin, 1927).

18 *Biographie universelle, ancienne et moderne* with *Supplément*, 85 vols. (Paris: Michaud frères, 1811–62).

19 Ida Farnell, *The Lives of the Troubadours* (London: D. Nutt, 1896), mentioned by Pound in *SR*, 62. Francis Hueffer, *The Troubadours: A History of Provençal Life and Literature in the Middle Ages* (London: Chatto & Windus, 1878; rpt. New York: AMS Press, 1977). Justin Harvey Smith, *The Troubadours at Home: Their Lives and Personalities, Their Songs and Their World* (New York and London: G. P. Putnam's Sons, 1899). For evidence that Pound used Hueffer and Smith see K. K. Ruthven, *A Guide to Ezra Pound's Personae (1926)* (Berkeley: University of California Press, 1969), 180, 196.

20 James J. Wilhelm, "The Troubadours as Guides to Poetry and Paradise," *The Later Cantos of Ezra Pound* (New York: Walker, 1977), 38. Gaston Paris, "Jaufre Rudel," *Revue historique* 53 (1893): 225–60; rpt. in Paris, *Mélanges de littérature française du moyen âge* (Paris: Champion, 1912), 498–538.

21 François-Just-Marie Raynouard, *Lexique roman* (Paris: Silvestre, 1844); Emil Levy, *Provenzalisches Supplement-Wörterbuch* (Leipzig: O.R. Reisland, 1894–1924). A compact one-volume version is Emil Levy, *Petit dictionnaire provençal-français* (Heidelberg: C. Winter, 1909).

22 Henry Alfred Todd, "Present Problems of Romance Philology," *Congress of Arts and Science: Universal Exposition, St. Louis, 1904*, 8 vols. (Boston: Houghton, Mifflin, 1905–7) III: 256.

23 For more see Helen May Dennis, *A New Approach to the Poetry of Ezra Pound through the Medieval Provençal Aspect* (Lewiston, PA: Mellen, 1996), 1–55.

24 Eleanor Anne Porden [Franklin], *Coeur de Lion; or, the Third Crusade* (London: Whittaker, 1822).

25 Britta Martens, "'Knight, Bard, Gallant': The Troubadour as a Critique of Romanticism in Browning's Sordello," in *Beyond Arthurian Romances: The Reach of Victorian Medievalism*, ed. Lorretta M. Holloway and Jennifer A. Palmgren (New York: Palgrave Macmillan, 2005), 44.

26 *The Poets and Poetry of Europe: with Introductions and Biographical Notices*, ed. Henry Wadsworth Longfellow and Cornelius Conway Felton (Cambridge, MA: Metcalf, 1845; rev. edn. Boston: Houghton, Mifflin, 1888). The translation of a poem attributed to Richard Lionheart is anonymous, and may be by Longfellow himself.

27 Oscar Wilde, "Amor Intellectualis," in *Poems by Oscar Wilde with the Ballad of Reading Gaol*, 17th edn. (London: Methuen, 1927), 145.

28 "Sordello," *Biographie universelle*, XLIII: 131–5. This is the view taken by Stewart W. Holmes, "The Sources of Browning's *Sordello*," *Studies in Philology* 34 (1937): 483; by William Clyde DeVane, *A Browning Handbook* (New York: Appleton-Century-Crofts, 1955), 75; and by John Pettigrew and Thomas J. Collins, eds., *The Poems* (New Haven: Yale University Press, 1981), I: 1040. Browning's more recent editors argue loyally that he probably read Provençal, may have consulted Sordello manuscripts, and almost certainly consulted other authorities including Dobson's translation of Sainte Palaye and Millot: John Woolford and Daniel Karlin, eds., *The Poems of Browning* (London: Longman, 2007), I: 368–369.

29 From 1881 to 1917, sixty-six dissertations and seven MA theses in the Romance languages were accepted at Johns Hopkins; none refers to Provençal in its title. See John L. Gerig, "Advanced Degrees and Doctoral Dissertations in the Romance Languages at the Johns Hopkins University: a Survey and Bibliography," *Romanic Review* 8 (1917): 328–40.

30 Charles H. Grandgent, *Outline of the Phonology and Morphology of Old Provençal* (Boston: Heath, 1905; rev. edn. 1909, rpt. 1973).

31 *Modern Language Notes* 10 (1895): 104–16. John L. Gerig, "In Memoriam: Henry Roseman Lang," *Romanic Review* 25 (1934): 266–7.

32 Reuben C. Cholakian, "Portrait of a Professor: William P. Shepard, 1870–1948," *Hamilton Alumni Review* 33.1 (Fall 1967): 4–9, quoting Professor George L. Nesbitt.

33 *Les poésies de Jausbert de Puycibot, troubadour du* XIIIe *siècle*, ed. William P. Shepard, Classiques Français du Moyen Age 46 (Paris: Champion, 1924). H. Carrington Lancaster, "American Bibliography for 1925," *PMLA* 41 (1926): 31.

34 Wilhelm, *The American Roots*, 154–5.

35 "Regret was expressed here and there that Rennert had paid so little attention to Lope's plays . . . Rennert preferred to write a biography rather than a critical study because he was more interested in the collecting and assembling of facts than in literary criticism": Crawford, *Revue Hispanique* 74 (1928): 270.

36 Rennert's edition of "Der spanische Cancionero des Brit. Museum (Ms. add. 10431)," *Romanische Forschungen* 10 (1895): 1–176, was declared to be "the first edition . . . of any fifteenth-century collection of Spanish verse that followed the newer methods of textual criticism" by Crawford, *Revue Hispanique*, 264. Shepard, "Recent Theories of Textual Criticism," *Modern Philology* 28 (1930): 129–41.

37 In a letter dated January 6, 1932, Shepard agreed with something Pound had written: "As to gents who 'combine scholarly rudiments with traces of perception of literary values', they aren't numerous in the USA, as you well know" (Yale University, Beinecke Library).

38 Norman, *Ezra Pound*, 369.

CHAPTER 18

Dante and early Italian poetry

Tim Redman

Pound first read Dante in 1904 as an undergraduate at Hamilton College in upstate New York. His Dante instructor, Professor William Shepard, "Shep," admired Pound's seriousness as a student of languages. Pound's study of Dante continued for another sixty-eight years, until his death in 1972.

He continued to study Dante in 1904, following Shepard's lectures in medieval poetry, with a great deal of excitement. Pound's principal literary correspondent during that time was his mother, and whatever parental conflict he experienced as a teenager was with her. The United States had manifested considerable anti-Catholic sentiment from before its founding, and that prejudice was reinforced by the waves of Italian Catholic immigrants who were arriving on its shores, many of them living in tenements in South Philadelphia. Pound's parents, Homer and Isabel, who lived in a Philadelphia suburb, volunteered as missionaries in those slums, trying to convert the Italians to their Presbyterian version of Christianity.

Of course there was an American Dante movement in New England centered on Boston. Longfellow was the first instructor of Dante at Harvard, starting in 1836, and there was a kind of Dante club or cult in Boston in the latter part of the nineteenth century. America needed an epic and perhaps Dante might do. He had denounced the corruption of the Catholic Church and clergy. When Isabel Pound expressed her approval that Ezra was reading Emerson, he exploded:

Also madam you needn't begin to crow just because I happen to hear a little Emerson. He and all that bunch of moralists. What have they done? . . .

He [Dante] fought in battles where he probably encountered much more personal danger than Mr. Roosevelt in Cuba. He also held chief office in his city and that for clean politics and good government . . . some centuries before Luther he dared put a pope in hell & a pagan without its gates & prophesy the fall of the temporal and evil powers of Rome . . .

O yes Emerson to make one think (merely to detect his limitations).

But find me a phenomenon of any importance in the lives of men and nations that you can not measure with the rod of Dante's Allegory.[1]

Pound's passion for Dante is evident, but he is also describing a Dante made palatable for Americans, Dante as the first Protestant.

Pound's love and deep study of the troubadours of Provence, especially, following Dante's lead, of Arnaut Daniel, is treated elsewhere in this volume. The Albigensian Crusade (1209–29) destroyed that luminous culture, but not Provençal influence on European poetry. It migrated to the brilliant court of Frederick II of Sicily (1194–1250), known as "Stupor Mundi" (the Wonder of the Earth), who supported an Italian version of Provençal poetry known as the "scuola siciliana" (the Sicilian School). Giacomo da Lentini (fl. 1233–40) was a member of Frederick's court who brought troubadour poetry into Italian; he is also credited with inventing the sonnet form. Pier della Vigna (1180–1249) was another Sicilian poet. Both are in Dante's *Divine Comedy*.

Pound continued his study of Romance philology as a graduate student at the University of Pennsylvania in 1905–6. He states that his first prose book, *The Spirit of Romance* (1910), was a summary of his notes from taking Dr. Hugo Rennert's seminar. Around that time also Pound read Dante Gabriele Rossetti's volume of English translations of early Italian poets. Rossetti's poetry and his translations had an enormous impact on the development of Pound's early poetic style, and they provide most of the translations Pound employs in *Spirit of Romance*. As Basil Bunting remarked in an interview much later, "When Pound arrived in London [in 1908], Rossetti was his mother and his father."[2]

Pound had studied carefully Dante's book of literary criticism, given the title by posterity *De Vulgari Eloquentia* (On the Common Speech). The unfortunately incomplete book is a careful defense, in Latin, of the need for poetry in Italian, a revolutionary argument that no one had ever attempted. Dante's poetics would greatly influence Pound's, not just his *The Spirit of Romance* but later, more mature works, such as *The ABC of Reading* (1934). Reed Way Dasenbrock has cautioned us to stop regarding both Pound and Dante as two-book poets only, Dante as the author of the *Vita Nuova* and the *Commedia*, Pound as the author of *Personae* and *The Cantos*. Dasenbrock shows that "many of the themes of Pound's politics . . . can be made explicable by reference to the ideas of *De Monarchia*."[3]

Both Dante and Pound were also critics of the first rank, theorists, and political writers, heavily engaged in the social and cultural issues of their day. Both were extremely learned poets, in the tradition of Callimachus, Catullus, and Ovid that extended past Dante to Milton, Leopardi, Eliot, and Pound. Of course, both Dante and Pound started as lyric poets in their first important collections and then made the transition to epic poets in their second important work. That fact is primary. But they wrote other works that also parallel each other, Dante's *De Vulgari* and Pound's *ABC of Reading*, Dante's *Monarchia* and Pound's *Jefferson and/or Mussolini*, and perhaps even Dante's *Convito* and Pound's *Guide to Kulchur*. In many senses, Pound's project takes up where Dante's left off.

GUINIZELLI AND CAVALCANTI

Dante begins his treatise, *De Vulgari*, by considering three language groups, Germanic, Slavic, and Romance, and then, within the latter, the three separate groups named for the word for yes: *oc*, *oïl*, and *sì*. He gives precedence to the latter, which is the Italian group. His first Italian example is from "Dominus" (Lord/Master) Guido Guinizelli's great canzone "Al cor gentil rempaira sempre amore" (Love finds dwelling always in the gentle heart). He admits the excellence of the refined Sicilian school poets such as Giacomo da Lentini, but believes that the Sicilian dialect is too coarse to support an elegant vernacular poetry. Dante settles on Tuscan poets, Guido Cavalcanti, Lapo Gianni, and Cino da Pistoia, as well as himself, as the group (which he dubs "il dolce stil nuovo" [the sweet new style] in the *Commedia*, the only contemporary use of that phrase), as most worthy to bring about the flourishing vernacular poetry that he advocates. Of this group, I will focus on Cavalcanti and Dante, and I will also focus on Guinizelli, as the poets most relevant to Pound.

Dante believed (and Pound agreed) that the canzone (song) was the highest form of poetry, and Guinizelli (in Pound's spelling Guinicelli), Cavalcanti, and Dante were all masters of that difficult form. In *De Vulgari* Dante gives most examples from his own work, as is understandable. He cites the work of Guinizelli, whom he also calls "Maximus" (Great), five times (two of them of the same canzone), and Cavalcanti three times. Dante also frequently cites Cino da Pistoia, but Pound, although following Dante in paying lip service to Cino's importance, does not seem much interested in him. Following Dante, Pound's emphasis in *Spirit of Romance* is predominantly on Guinizelli. That emphasis would change drastically over the next few years.

Pound acknowledges Guinizelli's "famed and beautiful canzone" (*SR*, 104), quoting the first four lines of its first two stanzas in Rossetti's translation. Pound recognizes that the Italian canzoni make considerable use of the philosophy developing at universities such as Bologna: "The Provençal canzone can be understood when sung. Tuscan canzoni often require close study in print before they will yield their meaning. But after one knows the meaning, their exquisite sound, spoken, or sung, is most enjoyable" (*SR*, 113). He also quotes, though he does not identify, contemporary criticism that showed "the dangers of the philosophical love song," Bonagiunta da Lucca's sonnet "To Guinizelli": 'You that have changed the manner and the pleasing songs of love, both form and substance, to surpass every other troubadour . . . you surpass every man in subtlety; but so obscure is your speech, that there is none found to explain it' (*SR*, 108). Pound at first agreed with that criticism. In "Troubadours – Their Sorts and Conditions," he wrote that "the second, and to us the dullest of the schools, set to explaining the nature of love and its effects . . . This peculiar variety of flame was carried to the altars of Bologna, whence Guinicelli [*sic*] sang: '*Al cor gentil ripara sempre amore*' . . . And Cavalcanti wrote 'A lady asks me' [Donna me prega]" (*LE*, 103).

Pound, still the aesthete caught up in the worship of Beauty, the ideals of chivalric love, and the mastery of his craft, misses, however, the central importance of Guinizelli's canzone for Italian society of his time. The difficulties of its Aristotelian science, with its metaphors of potency and act aside, "Al cor gentil" is not only the founding document of the "dolce stil nuovo," but also a declaration of independence of the emerging Italian middle class. The fourth stanza contains the new doctrine of a relaxed new style:

> The sun strikes the mud all day:
> The mud stays vile, nor does sun lose its heat;
> the haughty man says: "I am noble by descent":
> I compare him to mud, true nobility to the sun.
> For no man may believe
> there is nobility outside the heart,
> in the condition of being an heir,
> if his heart is not bent toward virtue –
> just as water reflects the beams,
> and heaven holds the stars and all their splendor.[4]

In Guinizelli, the central figure of courtly love, that of the "donna angelica," the angelic lady whose power spiritually uplifts the lover and can be the source of his salvation, is freed from the confines of the court and the nobility, and made applicable to the worthy members of the middle class. These were often merchants and they were gaining both political power and wealth in the city-states of Italy of Dante's time. Such ideas, about exaltation through love, filtered through Rossetti and the pre-Raphaelites, exercised a powerful attraction for the young Pound, who wrote in his early poems and acted in his early life not so much as a man in love, but as a man in love with the idea of Love.

This Guinizzellian idea of the spiritual benefit of a love for an idealized lady had a powerful effect on Dante as well, both in his *Vita Nuova*, which describes his early love for Beatrice, but also in his *Commedia*, which Charles Singleton in an eponymous book has described as a journey to Beatrice. But equally powerful in the *Vita Nuova* is the Cavalcantian idea of love, as it is presented in Cavalcanti's great canzone "Donna me prega." The poem is a response to a sonnet addressed to him by Guido Orlandi. The sonnet is given in full in *Spirit of Romance* but it is not in Rossetti so I presume it is Pound's own translation. It begins: "Whence moveth love and whence hath he his birth, / What is his proper stead, wherein he dwelleth, / And is he substance, accident or memory, / A chance of eyes, or a desire of heart?" (*SR*, 112). Cavalcanti's response, "Donna me prega," is the most difficult poem in any of the languages I know; it is also the most formally constrained of any poem I know. It consists of five stanzas and a coda. Each stanza has fourteen lines in *endecasillaba*, meaning that each stanza contains 154 syllables. Slightly more than one third of the syllables in each stanza are rhymed, and the same rhyme scheme with the rhyming syllables in exactly the same place repeats in each of the stanzas. David Anderson tells us that Rossetti had dismissed the canzone "as a dull, scholastic analysis of love, lacking emotion," and he did not translate it.[5]

In his canzone, Cavalcanti outlines a precise phenomenology of love using the Aristotelian science of his time. Cavalcanti's overall view of love strikes us as considerably more modern than that of his predecessors and contemporaries. He presents love as a disease, a kind of a disaster. He is the other great influence on Dante's *Vita Nuova*, which describes the young Dante's love for Beatrice as rendering him faint, speechless, pale, barely able to stand, and awestruck in her company, but miserable without it. After emphasizing Guinizelli in *Spirit of Romance*, Pound would publish a book of translations of Cavalcanti, *The Sonnets and Ballate of Guido Cavalcanti*, in 1912. Pound's opinion of Cavalcanti and "Donna me prega" would shift radically, and he would continue his work on Cavalcanti for twenty-five years, culminating in a remarkable edition, *Guido Cavalcanti Rime* (1932), and another translation of "Donna me prega" which appears as Canto XXXVI in *Eleven New Cantos* XXXI–XLI (1934), at the exact center of that group and, not I believe coincidentally, at the exact center of the first seventy-one Cantos, at which point Pound intended to move on to what he believed would be his *Paradiso* section.

Maria Luisa Ardizzone explains: "For Pound, Cavalcanti and Dante are two sides of the same coin in that they articulate complementary aspects of the culture of the Middle Ages: philosophy and science in Cavalcanti, theology in Dante."[6] Pound originally wrote in *Spirit of Romance* that Cavalcanti was "less subtle" than Dante, but in a note to the 1929 edition he states "I retract this expression" (*SR*, 110). And one should note that Pound wrote an opera, *Cavalcanti*.

The Divine Comedy *and* The Cantos

The vexed question of the influence of Dante on Pound's *Cantos* must be considered next. The very title of the work, *The Cantos*, records Pound's debt. And on a number of occasions Pound himself stated that his work was specifically modeled on Dante's *Commedia*. After coming to the end of his first seventy-one Cantos and preparing to write his *Paradiso*, he arranged to meet with George Santayana, the former Harvard philosophy professor living in Venice. He wrote to Santayana on December 8, 1939: "having dealt with 'money in history'" he now had to tackle "philosophy or my paradise" (*SL*, 331). Donald Hall's revealing interview with Pound from 1962 gives further insight into the influence of Dante on *The Cantos*:

I began the *Cantos* about 1904... The problem was to get a form... Obviously you haven't got a nice little road map such as the middle ages possessed of Heaven... the first thing was this: you had six centuries that hadn't been packaged. It was a question of dealing with material that wasn't in the *Divina Commedia*... taking the modern mind to be the medieval mind with wash after wash of classical culture poured over it since the Renaissance.[7]

Pound, however, downplayed any influences, telling Hubert Creekmore in February 1939: "As to the *form* of *The Cantos*: all I can say or pray is: *wait* till it's there. I mean wait until I get 'em written, and then if it don't show, I will start exegesis. I haven't an Aquinas map. Aquinas *not* valid now" (*SL*, 323).

As Pound was preparing to write his *Paradiso*, World War II began. Pound worked on his *Cantos* during the war, but only published two, LXXII and LXXIII, in Italian, during the war. They did not appear in the standard edition until 1991: they are very pro-fascist, although not particularly scandalous for wartime propaganda. Not surprisingly, as I have stated elsewhere,

they pay homage to Dante and Cavalcanti, and might be considered two
more Hell Cantos. Instead of trying to find structural correspondences,
critics have taken clues from the first of *The Pisan Cantos*, Canto LXXIV, to
develop ideas of links between Dante and Pound. The first such hint is:

> Le Paradis n'est pas artificiel
> but spezzato apparently
> it exists only in fragments unexpected excellent sausage,
> the smell of mint, for example,
> Ladro the night cat . . .   (LXXIV/458)

Pound's view, that Paradise is not artificial but fragmented, experienced in
broken moments such as the taste of sausage or the smell of mint or the
appearance of Thief, the night cat, has caused a reexamination of all of *The
Cantos* as containing experiences of hell, at times; of purgatory, at times;
and of heaven, at times: not as locations in the text, but as states of mind.

Earlier lines in the same Canto offer another important clarification: 'I
don't know how humanity stands it / with a painted paradise at the end
of it / without a painted paradise at the end of it' (LXXIV/456), with the
repeated adjective giving a clear indication of Pound's own belief in pagan
immanence rather than Christian transcendence. Pound states his view in
two places. The first is in a letter to his future wife Dorothy Shakespear:
"I dare say we've the whole divina commedia going on inside of us" (April
21, 1913; *EPDS*, 206). The second is in an article that was published in
the Paris edition of the *Chicago Tribune*, entitled "Who's Who Abroad,"
with a photo of the life mask of Pound by Nancy Cox McCormack, which
describes his ongoing *Cantos* as a "Pagana [Pagan] Commedia" (June 28,
1926). *The Cantos* is an isomorph of the *Commedia* in both the biological
and chemical senses of that term.[8] This, I would suggest, can best be
observed by looking at the ethical dimensions of both works.

Both works are, in James Wilhelm's excellent formulation, epics of
judgment.[9] And despite Pound's ultimate rejection of Christianity, both are
anchored in the deadly sin of avarice. Pound's condemnation of usury stems
from its origin, as he wrote early and late, in avarice. And although Dante
treats all of the deadly sins, his political philosophy, the two suns, the need
to separate the Pope's spiritual powers from the Holy Roman Emperor's
temporal powers, the cause of his exile and condemnation, derive largely
from his condemnation of the avarice of the medieval church.

Pound's definition of epic – a poem containing history – takes form
from Dante's own use of history in the *Commedia*. Pound's focus on
usury is an isomorph of Dante, taking Marx's economic reading of history

as his model. Usury for Pound has nothing to do with the taking of interest, as it did in Dante's time. Instead, it is caused by the crisis of referentiality characteristic of Pound's time and seen first, not in linguistic philosophy but in currency manipulation, the condition of either having insufficient currency in circulation to fully utilize the productive capacity of a nation (seen in the bimetallic debate of the nineteenth century) or having so much artificial currency in circulation as to lose all contact with the real economic issues involved (mortgage derivatives come to mind). Both problems involve manipulation, or fraud, represented first in Dante and then in Pound by the figure of Geryon.

Pound's own flawed version of hell, Cantos (XIV and XV), makes explicit the connections between war profiteers, financiers, politicians, and the press lords who had inflicted the First World War upon the millions who died and the tens of millions who suffered:

> Profiteers drinking blood sweetened with sh-t,
> And behind them [Zaharof]f and the financiers
>   lashing them with steel wires.
> And the betrayers of language
>   . . . . . . n and the press gang
> And those who had lied for hire . . .   (XIV/61)

Politicians such as Lloyd George, Woodrow Wilson, and Winston Churchill are also placed in Pound's hell. Its use of scatological language is a condensation of the language found in Dante's hell. It conveys Pound's outrage, but excessively; Dante's nuanced gradations of evil are much more effective. But then, Dante had an Aquinas map. Usurers and usura, Pound's Geryon, make their first appearance in these Cantos.

Canto XVI starts with a description of Pound's Purgatory, but he quickly changes to anecdotes about the First World War. But in a real sense, most of Pound's *Cantos* are a kind of Purgatory, an attempt to examine human error as it occurs throughout history, especially history after Dante. Perhaps the most profound overall similarity between Pound and Dante is that both poets are educators. Dante's *Purgatorio* is extremely didactic; each of the terraces displays an explicit moral lesson for those whose sins are being expiated. Dante is attempting to educate all of humanity but his principal targets are spiritual and temporal rulers. Pound's principal audiences are what he hopes will be a newly awakened citizenry but also those in power. He sent a copy of his first thirty Cantos to Mussolini, who was reading it when Pound arrived for his audience in 1933. Both poets moved in high political circles for a time but without effect.

Pound refers several times to his attempt to write a Paradise, and the section that appeared in 1959, "Thrones de los Cantares XCVI–CIX," refers specifically to a section of Dante's *Paradiso*, named for the order of angels (thrones) who watch over it. In Canto XXI of *Paradiso*, Beatrice and Dante ascend to the sphere ruled by Thrones, the sphere of Saturn, the god who ruled during the Golden Age. Beatrice repeats the same metaphor: "Let your eyes be mirrors for the figure that will appear to you within this mirror."[10]

Pound's conversation with Donald Hall about this section gives us the best explanation we have of how he was modeling his efforts on Dante and how they diverged from Dante. Hall asks about "Thrones" and what Pound intends to do with the remaining *Cantos*. He responds:

It is difficult to write a paradise when all the superficial indications are that you ought to write an apocalypse. It is obviously much easier to find inhabitants for an inferno or even a purgatorio. I am trying to collect the record of the top flights of the mind ...

An epic is a poem containing history. The modern mind contains heteroclite elements. The past epos has succeeded when all or a great many of the answers were assumed, at least between author and audience, or a great mass of audience. The attempt in an experimental age is therefore rash ...

The thrones in Dante's *Paradiso* are for the spirits of the people who have been responsible for good government. The thrones in the *Cantos* are an attempt to move out from egoism and to establish some definition of an order possible or at any rate conceivable on earth. One is held up by the low percentage of reason which seems to operate in human affairs. *Thrones* concerns the states of mind of people responsible for something more than their personal conduct.[11]

Pound, the greatest epic poet since Dante, used him as his model throughout his own lifetime project. Towards the end of his life, at age eighty-five, in a 1970 film by Howard Mantell, *Ezra Pound, the Poet's Poet*, Pound said of his influences: "I learned from Browning, and I'm still learning from Dante."

NOTES

1 Pound in Tim Redman, "Pound's Debt to Dante," in *Dante e Pound*, ed. Maria Luisa Ardizzone (Ravenna: Longo Editore, 1998), 161.
2 Basil Bunting interview for *Ezra Pound: Voices and Visions*, Series Program 10; sixty minutes. Annenberg/ CPB Collection, 1988.
3 Reed Way Dasenbrock, *Imitating the Italians: Wyatt, Spenser, Synge, Pound, Joyce* (Baltimore: Johns Hopkins University Press, 1991), 173.

4 Guido Guinizelli, in *German and Italian Lyrics of the Middle Ages*, ed. and trans. Frederick Goldin (Garden City, NY: Anchor Books, 1973), 289.

5 David Anderson, "Introduction," *CAV*, xixn.

6 Maria Luisa Ardizzone, *Guido Cavalcanti: The Other Middle Ages* (Toronto: University of Toronto Press, 2002), 10.

7 Pound in Donald Hall, *Poets at Work: The Paris Review Interviews*, ed. George Plimpton (New York: Viking Penguin, 1989), 138.

8 'The Cantos is isomorphic with respect to the *Commedia* in the biological sense of an organism different in ancestry [Browning, for example] but having the same form or appearance... *The Cantos* are also isomorphous with regard to the *Commedia* in the chemical sense of a compound capable of crystallizing in a form similar to another compound' (Redman in *Dante e Pound*, ed. Ardizzone, 159).

9 James Wilhelm, *Dante and Pound, The Epic of Judgment* (Orono: University of Maine Press, 1974), throughout.

10 Dante Alighieri, "Paradiso," *The Divine Comedy*, Canto XXI, trans. Allen Mandelbaum (London: Everyman, 1995), 477.

11 Pound in Hall, *Poets at Work*, 155–7.

CHAPTER 19

America

Emily Mitchell Wallace

"The most *American* thing that ever lived," said Dorothy Shakespear Pound about her husband.[1] Pound cherished his citizenship as an immutable fact, even when accused of treason. Among Americans he greatly admired, Henry James and T. S. Eliot became British subjects, and James Abbott McNeill Whistler disavowed his birthplace of Lowell, Massachusetts, claiming instead St. Petersburg, Russia. But Pound never considered denying his nationality in any way. And his native land was always in his thoughts all of his long life. He wrote to William Carlos Williams in January 1935: "A man's physical presence is infinitely less than his imaginative presence . . . I am much more present in Rutherford at this moment than in Chiavari or in the next valley" (*EP/WCW*, 157). In his quaint sliver of an autobiography, "*Indiscretions; or, Une Revue de Deux Mondes*" (1923), Pound boasts and apologizes in the same sentence: "It's one thing to feel that one could write the whole social history of the United States from one's family annals, and vastly another to embark on any such Balzacian and voluminous endeavor" (IND, 6).

Pound's American roots and character, and his virtues and flaws, achievements and failures, as well as those of his country, require a canvas as large and grand as the continent itself, but here are some fragments on a miniature scale. Figuratively speaking, the tense interplay between the poet and American institutions can be dubbed bipolar, that is, highly emotional and sometimes irrationally manic or depressive behavior on both sides. At times the poet was a complete Yankee Doodle Dandy, in the best sense, though the feather in his hat was not macaroni but macaronic (a mixture of languages). In 1912 he stated his belief in the inevitability of "our American Risorgimento," which "will make the Italian Renaissance look like a tempest in a teapot" (*SL*, 10) and he worked selflessly toward that goal as long as possible. At the other extreme, he said of Mauberley, "he had been born / In a half savage country, out of date" (*P*, 1990, 185). Pound also expressed his fear that he could not support his family in the United States nor himself survive as a poet nor even, physically, much less emotionally, stay warm in an inhospitably cold milieu. Yet these statements arose out of severe homesickness.

The response of his compatriots toward his poetry ranged from the belief of his friend Bill Williams that Pound was America's "greatest and rightest poet"[2] to the contempt of Professor Felix Schelling at the University of Pennsylvania, who contradictorily dismissed young Pound's poems as "notorious" and the poet himself as a transient weed in a giant forest.[3] After Pound's Rome broadcasts every American felt qualified to express an opinion, and one part of the American government awarded him the Bollingen Prize for Poetry at the same time another branch kept him confined for legally attested psychiatric infirmity that made him unfit to be tried for alleged treason. The treatment of Pound remains unique in American literature, as he is unique, and places him in the company of Ovid, exiled from Rome for some unrecorded offense to the emperor, or Dante, exiled from his native Florence under a sentence of death if he returned, or Blake, considered insane, and charged with high treason (and acquitted).

AMERICAN FRONTIER: BIRTH IN HAILEY, IDAHO

During his childhood in Philadelphia and New York, Ezra heard many stories from his family about the frontier boom town in the Big Wood River Valley of Idaho at the foot of the Sawtooth range, "the Switzerland of America," where he was born October 30, 1885. His father, Homer Loomis Pound (born in Wisconsin), had been appointed by President Chester A. Arthur as the government land recorder in Hailey. Ezra Weston Loomis Pound may have been the first baby christened in the brand new Emmanuel Episcopal Church, the most handsome structure in Hailey – red brick, stained glass, hardware like William Morris designed, and hitching posts behind the church. The hitching post became a cherished metaphor for Pound of home, the place one works from.[4]

Because Hailey had five newspapers, we know a lot about the Land Office and the Emmanuel Church and the social and political activities of Homer Pound and his extended family.[5] Homer's father, the Honorable Thaddeus Coleman Pound (Lt. Governor and Acting Governor of Wisconsin, and three-term Congressman), who made and lost several fortunes in railroads, lumber, mining, and other American enterprises, bequeathed grandson Ezra a conflicted but thoroughly American combination of passionate patriotism and suspicion of political shenanigans.[6] *Indiscretions*, Pound's sketch of the Wild West in the styles of Dante and Henry James, records strange stories as moral parables that cast an uncanny light on later events, for instance, the sad fate of Sampson the elephant, who, just before Ezra's birth, broke loose in Hailey from the traveling circus, and the cowboys shot at him with their six shooters, and the maddened elephant got wedged between two box cars (IND, 39).[7] Pound wanted to be buried in Hailey with a copy of Gaudier-Brzeska's bust of him (made by Isamu Noguchi) on his grave. Both grave and copy of Gaudier bust are now in Venice, the first on San Michele, with a stone simply incised "EZRA POUND" (designed by American sculptor Joan FitzGerald), the second on the island of San Giorgio.[8]

CRADLE OF AMERICAN LIBERTY: BOYHOOD IN PHILADELPHIA

In 1887 Isabella Weston Pound with her infant son traveled east from Hailey during a blizzard behind a Baldwin locomotive made in Philadelphia and fitted with the first rotary snow plow. In 1889 President Benjamin Harrison appointed Homer Pound Assistant Assayer at the Mint in Philadelphia, so Ezra grew up where William Penn began his Holy Experiment in freedom of religion and Brotherly Love, where the Declaration of Independence and the US Constitution were drafted and signed, where the capitol of the new nation was established for George Washington's two terms as President, where new ideas and inventions, including many civic firsts by Benjamin Franklin, were born.[9]

In the nineteenth century, although Philadelphia had become the premier industrial city, it was called "the Athens of America" because of its Greek architecture and the intellectual vitality of its citizens. Homer Pound worked in the Greek temple of the second US Mint, which was next to the new City Hall. Pound's study of languages and his reverence for Greek, his global embrace of people and of literature, his ebullient optimism about the possibilities of American culture, his pragmatism and inventiveness, his pacifist yearnings, his extraordinary generosity, his obsession with the Constitution and economics, grew out of his formative years in Philadelphia. In his Cantos about John Adams, Pound calls his hometown "the happy, the peaceful, the elegant / Philadelphy" (LXV/364).[10]

Young Ezra's maternal grandmother, Mary Weston, a descendant of a Wadsworth who arrived in Boston in 1632 on the *Lion*, often visited him in Wyncote, a suburb of Philadelphia. Grandmother Weston read Dickens, Scott, Kipling to Ra (Ezra's childhood nickname), and long poems by his great-granduncle Henry Wadsworth Longfellow, the most celebrated poet in America at that time, and told him about Captain Joseph Wadsworth, who in 1687 saved the Connecticut Charter (a constitution written by the people) by hiding it in an oak. Ra also frequently saw Grandmother Weston in New York when he visited the uncle after whom he was named, the lovable, rich Ezra Brown Weston of Manhattan and Washington, who married Frances Amelia Wessells Freer, known as "Aunt Frank."[11] After her husband's death in 1894, Aunt Frank in 1898 took twelve-year-old Ra and his mother to Europe for three months, and again in 1902, with both parents, the summer before his sophomore year at the University of Pennsylvania.

Forty years later, on May 13, 1942, it was a Wadsworth who would not allow Ezra Pound to board the last Diplomatic Train leaving Italy for Portugal,[12] even though there was room for him and the rest of his family.[13] Protracted diplomatic negotiations among the warring nations had arranged that from Lisbon the Swedish ship *Drottingholm* would take American citizens to the United States. The American official who rejected Pound, George Wadsworth, was the chargé d'affaires in Rome, who had permitted Pound's passport file to hold a note labeling him a "pseudo-American."[14] After the war, US judges ruled that stripping American citizens living abroad of their citizenship is unconstitutional,[15] and the State Department changed its procedures, but that was too late to help our Yankee Doodle Dandy find a safe hitching post during the war.

GENIUS REJECTED BY THE UNIVERSITY OF PENNSYLVANIA

As a scholar at the University of Pennsylvania, Ezra Pound aspired "to a career with honor / To step in the tracks of his elders" (xxix/144). He was rudely rejected, not for wrongdoing on his part but exactly the opposite, by two professors who held positions of power at the university from Pound's matriculation in 1901 until 1939. A member of the class of 1905 at the University of Pennsylvania, Pound spent his junior and senior years at Hamilton College, returning to Penn as a graduate student, earning an MA in 1906 and winning a Harrison Fellowship for research on his doctoral dissertation. Unexpectedly, in his second year of intense graduate study, 1906–7, Josiah Penniman, Dean of the Faculty, flunked Pound in English literary criticism. The "failure" is suspect because (1) Pound's class notes in the Beinecke archive at Yale show that he understood the course, (2) Pound had already published his first three essays, which are still read today, and nothing by Penniman is, and (3) Penniman taught his subject (Rymer, Dennis, Collier, etc.) like a "drill manual"[16] and did not tolerate disagreement. An immediate consequence of failing Penniman's course was that Pound's graduate fellowship was not renewed and he had to find a job, which he did, in the Midwest, with the help of a professor at Hamilton. Penniman became Provost (equivalent then to President) and remained head of the university until 1939.[17]

The opposition of the other Penn professor, Felix Emmanuel Schelling, head of the English department for forty-five years, was even more lethal because of his immense influence in the academic world at large. Professor Schelling, Penniman's fraternity brother, a handsome man of charm and wit, a much published poet and scholar, (1) lied about Pound's academic record and embellished his own by encouraging his students to address him as Dr., though his PhD was an honorary one from a college he had never attended and which had no graduate program,[18] (2) spread nasty rumors about Pound and told him to his face that he was "either a humbug or a genius,"[19] (3) made it impossible for Pound to get a job on the east coast, even in the preparatory schools, and (4) blackballed, during the next three decades (in 1910, 1920, 1932), the PhD Pound had earned and the honorary degree(s) he deserved (Schelling had two honorary degrees from the University of Pennsylvania).[20]

For whatever combination of envy, arrogance, and fear of genius, Penniman and Schelling ridiculed their young student when he was most vulnerable and impressionable, and never invited him back to the campus, even for an hour's reading, though Pound had by 1920 at the age of thirty-five become an international celebrity praised for his prose as well as his poems, and had published more than all the University of Pennsylvania literature and languages faculty together. Schelling's eccentric opinions are epitomized in his reason for refusing to grant Pound the same academic rights accorded other students. He wrote Pound in 1917 that the university is not here for "the extraordinary man": "College, after all, is for mediocrity; and as we are overweighted with mediocrity in the world, there is justification for it." In 1938, still hostile to Pound's achievements as a poet and scholar and patron to other artists, and blind to his need for a job in America as Europe descended into war, Schelling published his 1917 statement that "College . . . is for mediocrity" and frivolously wondered if his defense of mediocrity was "wholly wise."[21]

INVOLUNTARY EXILE AND CREATING AN AMERICAN RENAISSANCE IN LONDON AND PARIS

Pound's closest friends at the University of Pennsylvania, William Carlos Williams and Hilda Doolittle, confirm the injustice of the way Pound was

treated. "I watched Ezra – by direct effect – suffering the thrusts of his professors," Williams wrote, and "he was not exactly a voluntary exile."[22] H.D.
in her autobiographical novel HERmione calls the Pound character "the high
water mark of the intelligentsia of the period," and has another character agree with Schelling, "West Philadelphia sustains our mediocrities."[23]
Concerning the so-called "scandal" in Crawfordsville, Indiana,[24] of Pound's
helping a stranded "Victor/Victoria" ("Seraphitus/Seraphita"[25]) actress in a
blizzard, Billy and Hilda believed Ez had behaved charitably, but gossip in
Philadelphia gleefully transferred the female/male impersonator's professional identity to the Good Samaritan, labeling him "bisexual."[26] Shunned
by Philadelphia, Pound in 1908 went to Venice and published his first book
of poems, which he took to London to give to W. B. Yeats, and was by
1909 at the center of literary and artistic life in England.

The most remarkable aspect of Pound's youthful triumph was his effec-
tiveness in helping other writers, sculptors, painters, photographers, musicians. There is no poet who has been more generous to other artists. James
Joyce, Yeats, T. S. Eliot, and Ernest Hemingway (the last three Nobelists in
Literature) acknowledged with gratitude Pound's indispensable help,[27] as
did H.D., Williams, Marianne Moore, Robert Frost, Louis Zukofsky, e.e.
cummings, Robert Lowell, and many others – as W. H. Auden said, almost
all twentieth-century poets are in Pound's debt,[28] and as Hemingway said,
Pound was a "saint" who "would help anyone" who needed help.[29]

As the inaugural foreign editor of America's influential *Poetry*, *The Little
Review*, and *The Dial*, as contributor and advisor to dozens of other little
magazines world-wide, and as a translator, Pound bridged centuries and
continents and oceans. His output under his own name was prodigious,
but to pay the bills he also wrote under pen names: William Atheling as a
music critic, B.H. Dias as an art critic, Marius David Adkins as a drama
critic for one periodical, T.J.V. for another, John Higgins for still another,
altogether more names than Actaeon's dogs in Ovid.

Despite discouragement Pound held to his dream of an American renaissance. In 1912 he published eleven articles in the London *New Age* intended
for a book, *Patria Mia* (My Country). Pound's American publisher lost the
typescript, which was not found until 1950. *Patria Mia* sets forth Pound's
youthful plea for an American "super college" modeled after the American Academy in Rome, but larger, at which a hundred or so serious artists
would "work at painting, sculpture, architecture, musical composition, and
all branches of literature, and any other art one might think of." He said
it is "important that young artists should mix with young artists working
in other media. The personal acquaintance with older artists who have

been discoverers is a thing beyond all price" (*PM*, 70–1). No formal faculty would be needed, only the opportunity for artists to interact.

The Great War interrupted Pound's search for a patron to fund his "super-college." And his optimistic declaration that "I have beaten out my exile" (*P*, 1990, 94) proved not only premature, but also incapable of fulfillment, with disastrous effects on his mental health. Nevertheless, with the gifts he possessed, high intelligence, pragmatic optimism, generosity, curiosity, Pound created an international network of artists. In *Patria Mia* he says: "It is the patriotism of the artist, and it is almost the only civic duty allowed him, that he achieve such work as shall not bring his nation into world's eyes ridiculous" (*PM*, 23).

In the realm of literature Pound achieved his civic duty to America early on. Without money or position he behaved like Lorenzo il Magnifico, encouraging individual artists, and creating conditions for the sharing of ideas and techniques through discussion, translation, argument, appreciation. Guy Davenport said that one of his friends, on a dare, telephoned Pound in St. Elizabeths, and an attendant said he would ask Mr. Pound to come to the phone. "After a while, she heard the voice of Ezra Pound. 'Start a renaissance,' it said, and hung up."[30] When Pound died in 1972, Davenport ended his beautiful tribute to Pound with four words: "He was a renaissance."[31]

UNEASY EXILE OF *IL POETA AMERICANO*: *JEFFERSON AND/OR MUSSOLINI* AND JOHN ADAMS

In 1927 and 1928 Pound created *Exile*, a literary journal of four issues that encompassed Yeats' "Sailing to Byzantium," Williams' "The Descent of Winter," and "A Chapter from Joe Gould's Oral History." Pound's *Exile* editorials seemed slightly off-key, mentioning "unemployment" and "forces that work toward war," and disclosing a tense uneasiness about impending disasters. Wall Street crashed in October 1929, and the 1930s became a nightmare of unemployment world-wide and, in Europe, forces working toward war. Pound was not premature in his anxiety, nor at this point paranoid, but he lacked an American hitching post. Hemingway disparaged Mussolini to Pound by emphasizing how dangerous it would be to criticize Mussolini while the Pounds were guests of Italy.[32] But Pound's customary optimism deserted him when he tried to figure out how to survive economically in the United States with his parents, his wife Dorothy, and Olga Rudge and their daughter Mary.

Pound corresponded voluminously with American senators and congressmen, historians and economists, in addition to literary friends, including line-by-line critiquing of Laurence Binyon's translation of Dante and W.H.D. Rouse's Homer. Aware that his PhD might help him find work in America, he wrote in late 1931 to "The Professor of Romance Languages" at the University of Pennsylvania asking whether some original research he had just completed could be considered as his "thesis for doctorate." The acting chairman warmly responded that Pound should send his "dissertation" and that the "six units" missing on Pound's graduate record (probably only four units, if that) and the "seven-year rule" could be "waived by the Executive Committee on the recommendation of the department."[33] The "thesis," already in press as a book, was Pound's costly, scholarly edition of *Guido Cavalcanti Rime*, which he graciously inscribed and mailed to his alma mater on January 21, 1932, with a letter mentioning "T.S. Eliot's appointment to Harvard" and suggesting that "my editing of Guido" be compared with Eliot's "brochure on Dante."[34]

Harvard's response to Eliot's pamphlet had been an invitation to give the Norton Lectures in Poetry. The University of Pennsylvania's response to Pound's sumptuous book was a bureaucratic statement from Edwin Williams (now chairman), apologizing for the "considerable time" taken "to consult the proper University authorities" – Penniman and Schelling were still in full power – and explaining that Pound must re-enroll: "I have had a catalogue sent you which I hope will make clear just what the requirements are . . . and I shall be glad to endeavor to elucidate any points."[35] This disingenuousness would seem comic were the consequences not so tragic.

Pound repressed the insults of his university,[36] and outwardly continued to overwhelm reviewers with the high quality and quantity of his publications. He edited two anthologies, *Profile*, 1932, and *Active*, 1933, and contributed to many others. He wrote two textbooks, *ABC of Economics*, 1933, and *ABC of Reading*, 1934, and other books and pamphlets on economics and reading. He translated *Confucius, Digest of the Analects*, 1937, and wrote *Guide to Kulchur*, 1938, for those "who have not been able to afford a university education" (*GK*, 6). *A Draft of* xxx *Cantos* appeared in 1930, and by 1940 three installments (1934, 1937, 1940) of forty-one more cantos were published, a stupendous achievement of deeply researched exhibits of good government and just economics with emphasis on China, Thomas Jefferson, and John Adams.

Reviewers in the United States did not comprehend Pound's yearning that the United States live up to the vision of Jefferson and Adams. Banks should be for the people, Pound presciently declared, quoting Adams: "I / never approved I abhorred ever our whole banking system / . . . / taxing the public for private individuals' gain" (LXXI/416).[37] Pound's brilliant study of Adams[38] praises what Adams represented for him: "pater patriae / the man who at certain points / made us / at certain points / saved us / by fairness, honesty and straight moving" (LXII/350).

What stands out in Pound's dilemma of divided loyalties is *Jefferson and/or Mussolini*, written in February 1933, a year after the final rejection from the University of Pennsylvania, but not published until 1935. Both William Carlos Williams and Marianne Moore praised parts of this tendentious book, but we can now see that his well-intentioned attempt to serve two masters was doomed. His adoptive country was kinder to him than the land of his birth,[39] and he wanted to reciprocate, but he remained an American, and Italians accepted him as *il poeta americano*. Labeling Pound a fascist is profoundly misleading because his emotional sympathy for Jefferson and Adams is obviously much greater. There are, as Pound warns in a Pisan canto, "distinctions in clarity... John Adams... there is our norm of spirit" (LXXXIV/559–60). Throughout the 1930s Pound sought Adams' "fairness, honesty and straight moving" (LXII/350) and not finding that "norm of spirit" (LXXXIV/560) in significant places like his university, he was thrown off balance.

ECONOMIC DURESS. BITTERSWEET REPATRIATION.
AMERICAN JUSTICE. "NO CHIH³."

From April to June 1939 Pound visited the United States in an effort to prevent his country from entering the European war.[40] His grandiose and delusional effort hid confusion and fear about a situation far beyond his control. The political part of his visit was a failure and the literary part only a mild success. Pound desperately needed help, of every kind, but returned to his family and the chaos in Europe without a practical plan for repatriation. His friends did not perceive that he needed a sponsor, a job, a residence in America, a hitching post. Selfless and effective in helping others, Pound was constitutionally unable to beg for help for himself. As war approached, bank accounts were frozen,[41] his correspondence interrupted, and the American consuls in Italy increasingly rude.

Money saved for passage to America could not be touched while there was still a chance to return, so while the Pounds waited for that chance, the pittance paid for the radio broadcasts became essential for survival.[42] Pound did not say so, insisting instead that he was an American patriot trying to inform his compatriots about the causes of war and economic injustice, but Reynolds and Eleanor Packard told the FBI that "the American Embassy's attitude forced him into broadcasting from Italy."[43] Economic duress left Pound little choice but to continue the Rome broadcasts and in addition, as aid for his five dependents, to apply to the Italian government for authorization to draw a small sum monthly from his own account in an Italian bank, which was granted. Pound refused to make excuses for himself, other than "there is no *chih*,[44] and no root" (CX/801), no hitching post and no root in his native soil, like Bill Williams.[45]

Many ironies and paradoxes emerge from examining how Pound was treated by his own government. The FBI investigation intended to prove him guilty of treason instead decisively documents his persistent efforts to return home, and the uncertainties of the consuls about whether he had "lost" his citizenship by living abroad.[46] Astonishingly, as late as 1948, three years after the war ended, Pound's Jenkintown bank account remained blocked by the Alien Property Custodian under a law directed at nationals of Italy. When Julien Cornell, Pound's lawyer, explained the bizarre reason for the continuing restriction on his American bank account, Pound indignantly and lucidly replied: "IF I were italian, how the hell do they charge me [for treason] as an American? Really LUNACY is abroad worse than in S. Liz."[47] This highlights several problems embarrassing to his government. The US Treasury Department and State Department considered Pound not American enough to be accorded the rights of his citizenship, as demonstrated by their lack of protection both before and after the war, but his Justice Department judged him absolutely American enough to be indicted for alleged treason in 1943 and re-indicted in 1945 despite uncertainty, according to the FBI files, about his citizenship. The most poignant paradox is that from Pound's perspective, his indictment for treason and imprisonment were the best assurances he had that his government did consider him to be an American citizen, a bittersweet and terrifying way to be repatriated! When he turned himself in at Genoa, he said, "I rely on the American sense of justice."[48] To his lawyer in Washington, nine months later, he wrote, "constitution a religion."[49]

A distinguished English critic suggests that Pound's "America *patria* to which he vowed himself" may seem "imaginary," but it is "the American republic that existed – so Pound thought, and I'm not sure he was wrong – as a dream in the minds of its founders."[50]

NOTES

1 Dorothy Pound in Marion Mitchell Stancioff, "How I Remember Ezra Pound," *America* (March 17, 1973): 240–1.
2 William Carlos Williams, *Collected Poems* I, ed. A. Walton Litz and Christopher J. MacGowan (New York: New Directions, 1986), 276; first published in "A Folded Skyscraper," *American Caravan* (1927): 219.

3 Schelling, "The Egotist," in *Summer Ghosts and Winter Topics* (Philadelphia
  and London: Lippincott, 1924), 43: notorious for his poetry. "Contemporary Poetry," *Schoolmen's Week*, Proceedings of the University of Pennsylvania,
  (1922) 283: "Miss Amy Lowell . . . the eccentric Mr. Ezra Pound . . . Carl Sandburg . . . I do not feel that such are to be studied to the exclusion of even the
  Victorians, that grove of giant growth to stand memorable when these little
  straggling, flowery, thorny herbs and weeds will have gone their predestined way
  into the herbariums of the historian of the curiosities of literature." Schelling
  excluded Browning from the giant Victorians, predicting in an address before
  the Browning Society of Philadelphia that "The poetry of the future will not
  consist of psycho-poetics." In "Robert Browning and the Poetry of the Future,"
  Two Essays on Robert Browning (privately printed, 1890), 22.

4 Pound translates chih³ in *Confucius, Analects*, Book IX.20: "Alas I see him
  advance, I never see him stop (take a position)." Pound's commentary on
  this passage: "There is no more important technical term in the Confucian
  philosophy than this *chih³*, the hitching post, position one is in, and works
  from." Pound, *Confucius, The Great Digest, The Unwobbling Pivot, The Analects*.
  (New York: New Directions, 1969), 232.

5 The best source of the information in the Wood Valley newspapers is Waller
  B. Wigginton, "The Pounds at Hailey," *Rendezvous*, Idaho State University, 4
  (1969): 31–68. The Hailey newspapers reported the activities of Homer's wife,
  Isabel Weston Pound, his mother, Susan Angevin Loomis Pound, his sister,
  Florence Leonia, married to David Foote, who all moved east with Homer
  and followed him to Philadelphia, his father, Thaddeus Coleman Pound, who
  was estranged from his wife and visited her and their children irregularly, and
  Homer's mother-in-law, Mary Parker Weston, who came to Hailey when Ezra
  was born. They all had stories to tell. Other sources include: George A. McLeod,
  History of Alturas and Blaine Counties, Idaho (The Hailey Times Publisher,
  1950); "*What Thou Lovest Well Remains*"–*100 Years of Ezra Pound*, ed. Richard
  Ardinger (Boise, ID: Limberlost Press, 1986); *Hailey Emmanuel Church: The
  Early Years, 1881-1901*, ed. Rev. Jim and Marilyn Watkinson (printed in Twin
  Falls, ID, 1991); *Blaine County Centennial, 1995* (Hailey: Wood River Journal,
  1995); Homer Loomis Pound, *Small Boy: The Wisconsin Boyhood of Homer
  L. Pound*, ed. Alec C. Marsh (Hailey, ID: Ezra Pound Association, 2003);
  Paideuma, Orono, ME, *Ezra Pound and American Identity*, ed. Hugh Wite-
  meyer (Fall and Winter, 2005).

6 Wendy Stallard Flory profiles Thaddeus Pound in picaresque detail, contrasting
  him with Mary Weston, in "An American Childhood," *The American Ezra
  Pound* (New Haven and London: Yale University Press, 1989), 13–41.

7 Hailey now has several lifesized statues of elephants but not one of Pound.
  Nearby Ketchum has a bust of Ernest Hemingway, Pound's devoted friend.

8 Scott Preston reports that in the mid-seventies, "Princess [Mary] de Rachewiltz
  offered to ship a copy of a bust of her father that stands in a garden somewhere
  in Italy, and the Hailey City Council had an awful time trying to decide what
  to do with such a gift. The Council finally agreed that placement in the city

park might be risky due to probable vandalism, so they settled, with some lingering controversy, on the yard at the County Courthouse." In "And This Is the House Where Ez Was Born," *"What Thou Lovest Well,"* ed. Ardinger, 74.

9 For several decades in the eighteenth century Philadelphia was the most fascinating city on earth, says David McCullough. It was the largest city after London in the English-speaking world, its port the primary entry point for immigrants to all the colonies, its neighborhoods developed to protect and retain native languages and ethnic traditions. The Quaker City became an international banking center, and still preserves the Greek Revival buildings of the First Bank of the United States, the Second Bank, and the Mercantile Exchange. McCullough offers vivid descriptions of Philadelphia in *John Adams* (New York, London: Simon & Schuster, 2001). Other sources include: Nathaniel Burt, *The Perennial Philadelphians* (Boston and Toronto: Little, Brown, 1963); *Philadelphia, A 300-Year History*, ed. Russell F. Weigley (New York and London: Norton, 1982); *Designing Penn's Greene Country Town*, essays by Thomas G. Beischer, Michael J. Lewis, Elizabeth Milroy, *Pennsylvania Magazine of History and Biography* (July 2006): 257–329; *Images of America: Center City Philadelphia in the 19th Century*, ed. Jenny Ambrose, Charlene Peacock, Erika Piola, Sarah Weatherwax, Linda Wisniewski of the Print and Photograph Department of the Library Company of Philadelphia (Chicago, San Francisco: Arcadia Publishing, 2006); Gary B. Nash, *First City: Philadelphia and the Forging of Historical Memory* (Philadelphia: University of Pennsylvania Press, 2006).

10 Pound echoes John Adams, who wrote, "happy, peaceful, the elegant, the hospitable, and polite city," quoted by McCullough, *John Adams*, 87.

11 J. J. Wilhelm vividly describes the New York environment of Uncle Ezra and Aunt Frank in "The Warm Little World of Uncle Ezra," 29–47, and of "Ma Weston and the Children's Hour: The Wadsworths and All That," 49–65, in his *The American Roots of Ezra Pound* (New York: Garland, 1985).

12 *The Evening Bulletin–Philadelphia* (Friday, June 5, 1942): 2:

EZRA POUND'S PLEA DENIED

Woman says U.S. Refused to take American Poet from Italy

New York, June 5–(AP)–Nancy Horton, American Woman who returned Monday from Italy on the Swedish liner Drottingholm, says Ezra Pound, American poet who has been broadcasting Italian propaganda, was refused permission to leave Italy aboard a diplomatic train carrying other Americans.

Miss Horton said Pound told her that George Wadsworth, U. S. Charge d'Affaires in Rome, had informed him he could not return to the United States.

13 Last Diplomatic Train: According to Reynolds and Eleanor Packard, correspondents for United Press (and bridge-playing friends of George and Norma Wadsworth), as of December 1941, "The Italians had 127 notables to Wadsworth's 21" (*Balcony Empire*, [Oxford: Oxford University Press, 1942], 339). That is six times more Italians than Americans. "Notables" were civilians outside the main categories of consular officials and news correspondents. The

difference may have been that the Italians recognized poets, musicians, painters, sculptors as "notables," and George Wadsworth did not. The Packards describe how the American Embassy forced many Americans to leave who did not want to leave. So Pound was right to persist because there was room for him on that last Diplomatic Train.

14 On October 11, 1941, J. Wesley Jones, Department of State, Washington, sent an internal memorandum to Ray Atherton, Department of State, which begins: "You may desire to add to your list of pseudo-Americans living in Italy the name of Ezra Pound." Declassified document [PO99], Department of State, Division of European Affairs.

15 Significant Supreme Court decisions about United States citizenship and nationality after WWII include:

(1) *Trop v. Dulles*, 356 US 86, 92–93 (1958): plurality opinion by Chief Justice Warren (with three Justices concurring and one Justice concurring in result) held unconstitutional the statutory loss of nationality upon conviction for desertion from the armed forces of the United States during time of war on foreign soil. The deserter did not involve himself in any way with the foreign state. The plurality concluded that this was a penal statute that imposed cruel and unusual punishment since it left the expatriated citizen stateless.

Two sentences by the Chief Justice of the United States in his opinion deserve emphasis here:

"Citizenship is not a license that expires upon misbehavior."

"Deprivation of citizenship is not a weapon that the government may use to express its displeasure at a citizen's conduct, however reprehensible that conduct may be."

(2) *Schneider v. Rusk*, 377 US 163 (1964): A section of the new 1952 Nationality Act was held unconstitutional; it provided that a naturalized citizen would lose citizenship by continuous residence for three years in the country of origin. A majority of the Justices concluded that the section was discriminatory and therefore violated due process since no restriction against the length of foreign residence applies to native-born citizens in the 1952 Nationality Act.

(Some persons in the State Department and the Federal Bureau of Investigation questioned whether Pound had expatriated himself by living abroad for so many years.)

(3) *Afoyim v. Rusk*, 387 US 253 (1967): A section of the Nationality Act of 1940 that a United States citizen would "lose" his citizenship if he votes in a foreign political election was held unconstitutional because "Congress has no power under the Constitution to divest a person of his United States citizenship absent his voluntary renunciation thereof."

Some decisions that rely on the holding in *Afoyim v. Rusk* include:

(a) *US v. Matheson*, 532 F.2d 809 (2d Circuit 1976): there must be proof of specific intent to relinquish United States citizenship before an act of foreign naturalization or oath of loyalty to another sovereign can result in expatriation of an American citizen.

(b) *Vance v. Terrazas*, 444 US 252 (1980): The Fourteenth Amendment requires that the government prove that an expatriating act was accompanied by an intent to relinquish United States citizenship; on remand *Terrazas v. Muskie*, 494 (Northern District of Illinois) F. Supp. 1017, affirmed sub nom. *Terrazas v. Haig*, 653 F2d 285 (7th Circuit 1980): an act of expatriation is not in and of itself sufficient to destroy one's citizenship, and the government must establish a specific intent to relinquish citizenship.

16 Pound, "How to Read," *The New York Herald Tribune Books* (January 13, 1929): 6: "One was asked to remember what some critic (deceased) had said, scarcely to consider whether his views were still valid, or ever had been very intelligent." This stimulating, therefore controversial, essay subtitled "Largely Autobiographical . . . ," is most easily found in *LE*, edited by T.S. Eliot, where a footnote on the first page changes "institutions of learning" to "Institutions for the obstruction of learning."

17 Photographs of Penniman and Schelling are in E.M. Wallace, "Youthful Days and Costly Hours," in *Ezra Pound & William Carlos Williams: The University of Pennsylvania Conference Papers*, ed. Daniel Hoffman (Philadelphia: University of Pennsylvania Press, 1983), 14–58.

18 No graduate program: letter from the Corresponding Secretary of Franklin and Marshall College, Lancaster, Pennsylvania, June 11, 1898, to "Prof. Felix E. Schelling, PhD": "I am directed to give you official notice that the Board of Trustees . . . in consideration of meritorious work in English Literature, unanimously conferred upon you the degree of Doctor of Philosophy." In Schelling file, archives, University of Pennsylvania.

19 Schelling, March 30, 1920, to Wharton Barker, a trustee of the University of Pennsylvania, in Schelling Papers, carbon copy, Van Pelt Library, University of Pennsylvania: "I remember him as a remarkably idle student, absolutely evading all work to such an extent that I recall saying to him, 'Mr. Pound, you are either a humbug or a genius.' . . . I am sure the Faculty would not recommend that Mr. Pound be granted the degree of Ph.D. for the simple reason that he has done none of the work demanded of such a student. The question of an honorary degree for Mr. Pound upon the basis of his eccentric and often very clever verse is quite another matter and one which I hardly feel that I am competent to raise." Pound wrote a long letter from London, August 26, 1920, to Wharton Barker refuting Schelling's statement that Pound had done none of the work, carbon copy, YCAL. Barker replied September 22, 1920, with carbon copy to Homer Pound, YCAL, that "so long as Dr. Penniman and Dr. Schelling are in opposition," nothing can be done, and added, "I regret very much that I am unable to serve you and your father." Barker was not a friend of Schelling, but as a candidate for President of the United States (in 1900 on the Populist Party ticket), he became a friend of "Governor Pound" and his son Homer and grandson Ezra.

20 The University of Pennsylvania awarded Schelling a Litt.D. in 1903 a LL.D. in 1909.

21 Schelling, "A Word About Fellowships," *The General Magazine and Historical Chronicle* 40.2 (January 1938): 171–6. Pound had written to Schelling, November 17, 1916, suggesting that the university offer a fellowship to Carl Sandburg,

that is, an invitation to be what we now call a poet-in-residence (*SL*, 98–100). Schelling had replied on January 8, 1917, and the carbon copy of his letter to Pound is in the Schelling Papers, Van Pelt Library, University of Pennsylvania, with the paragraph about mediocrity cut out to paste into "A Word about Fellowships," written more than two decades later. Schelling may have intended the 1938 essay as a sort of apology to Pound. W. B. Yeats more penetratingly summarized the situation in his poem "The Scholars" (written and published in 1919): "Lord, what would they say / Should their Catullus walk that way?" Also quoted in Wallace, "Youthful Days" (note 17).

22 Williams, "A Tentative Statement," *The Little Review* (May 1929): 96: "suffering the thrusts of his professors"; 97: "driven out like Ezra Pound."
   Williams, "Ezra Pound: His Exile as Another Poet Sees It," *New York Evening Post Literary Review* (February 19, 1927): 10: "not exactly a voluntary exile." Reprinted in EPCH, 224–7.

23 H.D., *HERmione* (New York: New Directions, 1981), 71, 150.

24 H.D., *End*, 43: "scandal, if a scandal at all."

25 "Seraphitus/Seraphita": Pound's innocence is also attested by H.D.'s comment in *End*, 11: "*Séraphita*. A story by Balzac. The Being, he-her, disappears or dies in the snow. Séraphitus. Ezra brought me the story." The endnote by Norman Holmes Pearson and Michael King, 63, also confirms Pound's intention to help the actress. Years later the actress saw Pound in London and thanked him for saving her life.

26 H.D., *End*, 14–15.

27 E.M. Wallace, "Some Friends of Ezra Pound: A Photographic Essay," with thirty-five photographs, *The Yale Review* (Spring 1986): 331–57.

28 W.H. Auden: "There are very few living poets, even if they are not conscious of having been influenced by Pound, who could say, 'My work would be exactly the same if Mr. Pound had never lived.'" "A Tribute to Ezra Pound," broadcast over WYBC, the Yale Broadcasting Co., 1955. Mimeographed transcript copy in Yale University, Beinecke Library, Yale Catalogue. Published in *Ezra Pound at Seventy* (New York: New Directions, 1955). And see Marjorie Perloff, "The Contemporary of Our Grandchildren: Pound's Influence," in *Ezra Pound among the Poets*, ed. George Bornstein (Chicago and London: University of Chicago Press, 1985), 195–229.

29 Hemingway, *A Moveable Feast* (New York: Scribner's, 1964), 108, 110.

30 Guy Davenport, "Civilization and Its Opposite in the 1940s," in *The Hunter Gracchus* (Washington, DC: Counterpoint, 1996), 97: "an outrageously brave thing: to call St. Elizabeths (this is *res gestae*, forties) one evening and ask to speak to Ezra Pound," who is "the most influential, perhaps the greatest American poet of the twentieth century" (95).

31 Davenport, "Ezra Pound 1885–1972," in *The Geography of the Imagination* (San Francisco: North Point, 1981), 176.

32 Ernest Hemingway to "Respectabillissimo," (November 21, 1926), Yale Catalogue: "If you actually and honest to God . . . admire and respect the gentleman [Mussolini] and his works all I can say is SHIT . . . . I will take practical steps

by denouncing you here in Paris as a dangerous anti-fascist and we can amuse one another by counting the hours before you get beaten up in spite of your probity – which in such a fine country as it must be would undoubtedly save you." In reply, November 22, [1926], Hemingway Papers, Kennedy Library, Boston, Pound remarked on his young friend's "atrabilious nature !!!!!!" as "all to the good if you can focus it on production." In a letter of July 22, 1933, Yale Catalogue, Hemingway called Pound "a natural patriot. It is a good thing to be and listed as a virtue."

33 Letter from Edwin B. Williams, Acting Chairman, Department of Romance Languages, University of Pennsylvania, to Ezra Pound, December 8, 1931, Yale Catalogue. Waiving a few details of the requirements was a fairly routine procedure, and it would have been entirely appropriate in Pound's case.

34 Letter from Pound to Edwin B. Williams, January 21, 1934, Van Pelt Library, University of Pennsylvania.

35 Letter from Edwin B. Williams, Chairman, Department of Romance Languages, University of Pennsylvania, to Ezra Pound, March 19, 1932, Yale Catalogue.

36 James Joyce found Pound so off-balance a year later that he asked Hemingway to join him for dinner with Pound in Paris. By 1934 Pound had recovered sufficiently to accept Harvard student James Laughlin at the "Ezuversity" in Rapallo. In 1936 another Harvard undergraduate, Robert Lowell, pleaded to be admitted. Also at Harvard Lincoln Kirstein and Varian Frye published Pound in *Hound & Horn*, and at Yale undergraduates James Jesus Angleton and Reed Whittemore featured Pound in *Furioso*. A UPenn graduate, D. D. Paige, edited the first book of Pound's letters. And so on. As Harriet Monroe wrote in *A Poet's Life* (New York: Macmillan, 1938), 268: "Ezra Pound was born to be a great teacher . . . . American universities . . . failed . . . missed a dynamic influence which would have been felt wherever English writing is taught." Pound publicly refuted UPenn's repeated and illogical rejections (e.g. see note 16), but the insults sank deep into his unconscious, eventually to erupt, while the second great war approached, as paranoia, with the most terrible symptom being a twisted projection of his repressed humiliations and fears onto the Jews, intelligent, rejected, defenseless people caught like himself in a similar plight. Because it was too painful for him to acknowledge that his exile from academe and an honorable repatriation might be permanent, he instead accused rich and powerful Jews and non-Jews alike of usury in an illogical and incoherent manner. This was the most prominent and uncontrollable symptom of his paranoia, emerging disastrously at the time of the most catastrophic tragedy of the century. This was the stigmatized mental illness of his middle years, roughly 1935–1960, an illness recognizable by illogical, delusional anti-Semitic statements, particularly when they are compared with his statements about Jews in his first fifty years and his last twelve years, which are remarkably unprejudiced, when compared with his contemporaries, and often totally philoSemitic.

37 Adams continues: "and if I say this in my will / the American people would pronounce I died crazy" (LXXI/416).

38 A. David Moody in "Composition in the Adams Cantos," *Ezra Pound and America*, ed. Jacqueline Kaye (New York: St. Martin's, 1992), 79–92, examines the beginning of LXVI, written in early 1939, and concludes that it is "formidably controlled writing": "Pound must have been in an intensely energized state to have been able to compose something so structured at such speed and with such economy."

39 For example, Venice, Rapallo, and Sant' Ambrogio have placed commendatory plaques on or near the buildings where Pound lived, but Philadelphia, where the young poet-scholar spent his formative years, has no sign anywhere to mark his residence there.

40 James Laughlin told the FBI that the Italian government sponsored the trip, but there is no documentary evidence for this. Olivia Shakespear died in 1938, leaving "substantial means" to her only child Dorothy Pound (*ASC*, 556). The Italian liner *Rex* was partially empty, and Pound was given a suite in First Class. On this voyage he became friends with Count Vittorio Cini, who lived in Venice in a palazzo near the bakery above which Pound had rented a room when he arrived in Venice in 1908. In 1972 Count Cini arranged for Pound's funeral service in the Palladian splendor of San Giorgio Maggiore. Noguchi's copy of the Gaudier bust of Pound is in a garden cared for by Cini Foundation (see note 8 above).

41 As war approached, Dorothy Pound's English bank account was frozen in late 1939 pursuant to Britain's Trading with the Enemy Act (though she was an American citizen), so her attempt in June 1940 to transfer money from her London bank to Pound's Philadelphia bank failed. Dorothy's Chase Manhattan account also became inaccessible, as did Homer Pound's government pension. And in June 1941 Mussolini suddenly froze all American bank accounts in Italy.

42 In addition to the payment for broadcasts (which was equivalent to $10 and $17 each), Pound's Press Card entitled him to a 70 percent discount on railway travel throughout Italy and free lodging in Rome while he was recording the broadcasts. After World War II the lower Federal courts in the United States held that the Defense of Duress can be established by showing threats of economic deprivation if the ability to secure the necessities of life is adversely affected thereby: *Stirpa v. Dulles*, 233 F.2d 551 (3d Circuit 1956): economic duress precluded expatriation resulting from foreign government employment; in this case Stirpa worked for an Italian auxiliary police force.

43 FBI, Freedom of Information Act Release of Documents Concerning Ezra Pound 100–34099, Section 9, "Summary of Case," 33257: "They recalled POUND said that the American Embassy's attitude forced him into broadcasting from Italy to the United States for the Italians." Details in *Balcony Empire* (Note 13) confirm that "They" is Reynolds and Eleanor Packard.

44 The Chinese ideogram for *chih³* looks like a hitching post.

45 Letter from Pound to William Carlos Williams, January 31 [1946]:

> "The pure products of America
>   go Cr a z y"
>   all right old bull-pup !
>   who said it   ??
>   però
>   mañana
>   Jara
>   otro
>   dìa
>   31   EzP
>   Jan

Pound transformed the Spanish proverb "but tomorrow will be another day"
by using Italian accents on the first and last Spanish words and changing the
verb, "will be," from Spanish "sera," to another word, not Italian "sarà" with
its accent, but "Jara" with a capital "J" and no accent. "Jara" translates into
botanical Latin as cistus and into English as rock rose, a plant native to the
Mediterranean that does not transplant easily: *But tomorrow, rock rose, another
day*. In a 1935 letter to Williams Pound observed, "Yr/ parents moved out,
and planted the infunt Willum [*sic*] in alien field." In a 1960 note to Florence
Williams, Pound lamented, "East West, Home's best. Still I don't know how I
could have rooted in." Thus the expatriate accused of treason commends the
success of his rock rose peer, who is flourishing in America in the "alien field"
to which his parents transplanted him, and contrasts that success with the
failure of Ezra Pound, pure product of America (New England ancestry from
the beginning, frontier birth, Philadelphia childhood), to root in and not "go
Cr a z y."

The 1946 letter is a pitch-perfect, poetic performance seeking to reassure,
explain, and express affection. In creating a high compliment and a hopeful
declaration for the future out of an obvious banality simply by changing the
verb to the name of a flower, Pound demonstrated that the part of his brain
that created poems was not "Cr a z y." (The quotation at the beginning of
the letter comes from a poem, "To Elsie," by Williams.). A person can be
paranoid in one part of his mind and function beautifully in other ways. A
definition of paranoia in *Black's Law Dictionary*: "A form of mental distress
known as delusionary insanity, and a person afflicted with it has delusions
which dominate, but do not destroy, the mental capacity, and, though sane as
to other subjects, as to the delusion and its direct consequences the person is
insane." This helps to explain the ongoing controversy about whether Pound
was sane or insane. Like all of us, he was neither totally sane nor totally insane,
or as T. S. Eliot precisely put it, "neither sane, nor insane."

Pound's January 31 [1946] letter was first published in E. M. Wallace,
"Lettres d'Exiles: La Correspondance entre William Carlos Williams et Ezra
Pound," translated into French by Jacques Darras, *in'hu*, Paris (Winter 1981):

46. In *Selected Letters of Ezra Pound and William Carlos Williams*, ed. Hugh Witemeyer (New York: New Directions, 1996) 287, with "Jara" transcribed as "sara," and "[sic]" at the end of the proverb. The 1935 letter is in *ibid.*, 157. The 1960 note to Florence Williams has not been previously published and is in YCAL.

46 The FBI devoted considerable effort to trying to determine whether or not Pound had expatriated himself, and concluded: "Through [blackout] it was ascertained by Special Agent [blackout] that no State Department official can testify that the subject is or is not an American citizen. A State Department official can testify that from the information appearing in the State Department files a passport would be issued to the subject for return to the United States only." Freedom of Information Act Release of Documents Concerning Ezra Pound 100–34099, Section 9, "Summary of Case," 33247. A lawyer for Pound could have shown how Pound was deprived of the protections due an American citizen *before* the United States entered the war. The defense could also have emphasized how fully Pound had cooperated with the FBI. Impressed by Pound's helpfulness and openness, J. Edgar Hoover, Director of the FBI, repeatedly told Frank Amprim, the Special Agent interrogating Pound, to prompt Pound to try to remember an occasion when two Italians *at the same time* saw him give a broadcast. The Constitution requires two witnesses to the same overt act of alleged treason, a requirement the FBI did not succeed in meeting in Pound's case. It is sad to reflect that the amount of taxpayer money spent by the FBI and other parts of the government to build a case against Pound could have started Pound's "Super College" with a handsome endowment.

47 Pound's letter about not being a national of Italy [January 1948] begins: "Dear JC are YOU stark raving. ??" In Julien Cornell, *The Trial of Ezra Pound: A Documented Account of the Treason Case by the Defendant's Lawyer* (New York: John Day, 1966), 105.

48 Pound's statement, "I rely on the American sense of justice," is at the end of an interview by Edd Johnson, Genoa, May 8, 1945, published in the *Philadelphia Record* and the *Chicago Sun*. Quoted in *ASC* 651.

49 The letter, January [26], 1945, saying "constitution a religion," was written from the prison ward of St. Elizabeths Hospital to Julien Cornell, *The Trial of Ezra Pound*, 75.

50 Donald Davie, "For the Opening of the Ezra Pound Exhibition in Rapallo, June 1, 1985," *Ezra Pound, un poeta a Rapallo*, ed. Massimo Bacigalupo (Genova: Edizioni San Marco dei Giustiniani, 1985), 94.

CHAPTER 20

Venice

John Gery

From his youth until his death, Ezra Pound found in Venice not only a hospitable environment for writing and living, but a paradigm for the design of *The Cantos*. Merely to cross its bridges, admire its legion of palazzi, or navigate its lagoons is to engage in Venice's brilliant light, eerie shadows, merger of water and architecture, intricate history, and unique blend of vibrancy and decay. As the center of a 1200-year long maritime power, with its unusual republican style of government and international commerce, *La Serenissima*, of course, has had its share of writers from Marco Polo (1256–1324) and Paolo Sarpi (1552–1623) to Carlo Goldoni (1707–93) and Gabriele D'Annunzio (1863–1938), figures who have distinguished it as among the world's most intriguing cities. And the number of visiting writers it has fascinated is great and ever-growing, from Petrarch (1304–74) to Joseph Brodsky (1940–96). Even with this rich legacy, to consider Venice as Pound did, especially in his poetry, is not only to rediscover it through the imagination of an exiled American modernist, but to appreciate how Pound's own art, despite its difficulties, is immediate and vital.

Pound's first visit to Venice occurred at age twelve with his Aunt Frank in 1898. He intended "to return" (*PDD*, 6). And return he did, at least six more times before he was thirty-five (*PDD*, 6): in 1902, with Aunt Frank and his parents; in 1908, after his dismissal from Wabash College, when he published there *A Lume Spento*, his first volume of poems, and composed his "*Venetian sketch-book – 'San Trovaso' –*" (*CEP*, 55); in March 1910, meeting with Olivia and Dorothy Shakespear; in 1911; in spring 1913, when he met with H.D., her parents, and her husband Richard Aldington (*SL*, 19–20); and in 1920, when he began writing "Indiscretions or, *Une Revue De Deux Mondes*," a rare foray for Pound into memoir.[1]

With the birth of Mary, his daughter by Olga Rudge (1895–1996), in 1925, until the 1940s, Pound regularly traveled to Venice, especially after 1928, when Rudge purchased a small house (three rooms, one on top of the other) on Calle Querini in the city's Dorsoduro district, south of the

Grand Canal across from Saint Mark's Square. Because Pound and Rudge were not married, he steadfastly maintained lodgings elsewhere during each visit, but he spent considerable time at Calle Querini. In those years, he found Venice conducive not only to his work but also to raising Mary, who would visit from the Italian Tyrol, where she lived on a farm under the care of a Tyrolean couple her parents had contracted after her birth.[2] During World War II, Rudge lost possession of her Dorsoduro house and had to take sanctuary in Rapallo on Italy's west coast.

In November 1945, she regained access to Calle Querini a few days before Pound was flown from the Disciplinary Training Center in Pisa to Washington to stand trial for treason. But of course, Pound could not return to Venice himself until after his release from St. Elizabeths Hospital in 1958. After that, especially during his last decade, he divided his time between Venice, Rapallo, and Brunnenburg in the Tyrol, where Mary then lived with her family. It was from the house on Calle Querini on October 31, 1972 that the deathly ill Pound walked to the small canal at the end of the block, there boarding a boat for Venice's S.S. Giovanni e Paolo hospital, where he died that night. Today he is buried in the Protestant section of San Michele cemetery, an island just north of the main island. Rudge, who died in 1996, is next to him.

Besides working in Venice and spending time with his family and many friends – from painter Italico Brass and pianist Katherine Heyman in 1908 to scholars Carlo Izzo and Manlio Dazzi in the 1930s to sculptor Joan Fitzgerald and poet Peter Russell in the 1960s – Pound embraced the city itself. From the first, it struck him as a fountainhead of art, an historical epitome of good (and corrupt) rule, and a context where human design mingles gracefully with natural beauty. In time, Venice came to represent for him nothing less than the *paradiso terrestre*, or earthly paradise, he would depict in *The Cantos'* most sacrosanct passages. Yet while Pound's Venice certainly corresponds to the Venice well known for its Gothic and Renaissance architecture, grand Piazza San Marco, desolate island of Torcello, and remarkable artists from Bellini to Canaletto, it remains distinctive. Because, as a poet, Pound brings to Venice his American modernist vision, one that dwells on images, sounds, texts, and textures, his is a Venice he shapes as much as describes.

To be sure, the city's beauty influenced Pound as a young, impressionable, ambitious poet, but over the seventy-four-year span he visited and resided there, exercising an imagination as fluid as the tides in the lagoon, he continued to find in Venice his own poetics. In fact, from the "San Trovaso" sketchbook through *Drafts & Fragments of Cantos* cx–cxvii, Venice emerges as Pound's most sustained setting, together with Rapallo. It is also the only major city that figures prominently throughout *The Cantos*, appearing first in Canto II, and consistently reappearing until Canto CXVI, where the image of the "gold thread in the pattern" (LXVI/817) of the mosaics in the Byzantine church on Torcello invokes the "splendour" Pound's epic has strived to achieve from the first. To trace Venice through *The Cantos* is to discover nothing less than Pound's evolving epic vision itself.

THE SAN TROVASO SKETCHBOOK

In "Indiscretions," Pound praises Venice as an ideal place to write because, he says, it can "give one again and once more either the old kick to the sense or any new perception" (*PDD*, 3). But among those "new" perceptions about Venice *not* worth recording, perceptions which Pound self-consciously lists in a sentence two pages long, is the Venice of postcards, "or the possible 'picturesque' of roof-tiles, sky-tones, mud-green tidal influx, cats perched like miniature stone lions on balconies, etc." (*PDD*, 4). Since "that has been 'done'" about Venice, "der alte Venezia" for Pound "demands a different approach" (*PDD*, 5). Having immersed himself in many books on the subject – including, in English, John Ruskin's *The Stones of Venice* (1853), William Carew Hazlitt's *The Venetian Republic: Its Rise, Its Growth, and Its Fall, A.D. 409–1797* (1860), William Dean Howells' *Venetian Life* (1866), Henry James' *The Wings of the Dove* (1903) – Pound had less interest in "very general observations" about the "Queen of the Adriatic" (*PDD*, 5) than in particular canals, vistas, artworks, and Venetians he encountered. Indeed, considered as any accumulation of images and details, Pound's depiction of Venice resembles an ordinary visitor's unsystematic approach to the city more than a critic's (such as Ruskin's) more methodical one.[3]

Indeed, some of Pound's earliest poems about Venice read like journal entries: "High-dwelling 'bove the people here" begins "Prelude: Over the Ognisanti" (*CEP*, 59), which opens *A Quinzaine for This Yule: Being selected from a Venetian sketch-book – "San Trovaso."* Looking onto a gondola repair yard across San Trovaso canal from his second-story window, in lodgings where by a stroke of luck Pound lived for free from June until August 1908, the poem's speaker refutes his own loneliness, given not only "mine own great thoughts for paladins / Against all gloom," but more importantly, "the swallows and the sunset" and "life below me, / In the garden, on the waters" (*CEP*, 59). Another poem, "Night Litany," considered "Pound's first sustained invocation of Venice in poetry"[4] and the only San Trovaso poem he retained in *Personae* (1926), beckons the "God of waters" to "make clean our hearts within us / And to our lips show forth thy praise, / For I have seen the / shadow of this thy Venice / floating upon the waters" (*CEP*, 60–1). Overall, these early poems capture the twenty-two-year-old poet lingering by canals or at San Marco, "sketching" his American impressions of Venice much as James Whistler had on his earlier visits. Although fifty-six years later Pound came to denigrate these poems as "a collection of stale creampuffs" demonstrating "the depth of ignorance, or rather the superficiality of non-perception" of their maker (*CEP*, 314), they demonstrate the young poet's keen awareness of his setting and, beyond that, the imagistic qualities soon to emerge in his work.

Two fragments in the San Trovaso sketchbook suggest the two sides of Pound's earliest impressions of Venice. In one, using diction stylized even for its time, the poet gazing at the stars wonders whether " 'twere better, forge of thine own soul / Thy hand-wrought image in the things of earth" in original poems, or "in a gentler fashion" to "[weigh] man's song" as a scholar (*CEP*, 248). Pound, of course, went on to pursue both these passions, but these lines display him self-consciously indulging his solitude in Venice to reflect on his future. By contrast, an isolated line preceding this poem reveals a predominant motif of Venice for Pound, when, in a haiku-like phrase, he imagines the city's ubiquitous marble columns as trees, rather than as architecture: "Marble smooth by flowing waters grown" (*CEP*, 248). Such sharp contrasts in diction can be found throughout the sketchbook, some lines expressing Pound's unfettered visionary sweep, others revealing his uncanny penchant for the telling image.

VENICE AND *THE CANTOS*

A few poems Pound wrote after departing Venice in 1908 concern the Veneto, including "Silet," "'Blandula, Tenulla, Vagula','," and his adaptions from Catullus, the Veronese poet. But once he turned to *The Cantos*, the city began to figure prominently again. Through the first thirty Cantos, Venice appears not as a haven of regret, delight, or decadence – as it has been for Goethe, Byron, Mann, Hemingway, and others – but as a shimmering matrix "taking light in the darkness" (xxvi/121), a *paradiso terrestre* whose images burst into being, discovering their own form. Later, when Venice appears in Cantos xxxi–lxxii, not surprisingly given Pound's evolving concerns in the 1930s, he focuses on its economic and geopolitical history. Then in *The Pisan Cantos*, having lost access to the city during his detention in Pisa and incarceration in Washington, he begins to catalogue churches, campos, restaurants, streets, acquaintances, and artworks in Venice by name, according to his particular memories of each, across time. Finally, in the late Cantos, Venice, while not figuring quite so prominently as earlier, nonetheless joins in a cavalcade of the beautiful and (arguably) the true. But despite this varied presentation, throughout *The Cantos* Venice remains indefatigably Pound's Venice.

In his major formulation of Venice through the first thirty Cantos, Pound shapes three distinct aspects of the city: (1) Venice as a setting for the epic poet himself (Pound's "dark wood"), (2) Venice as a *paradiso terrestre*, especially through its light, stones, sounds, and ubiquitous water, a blend of nature and artifice, creating "a sort of heaven of cut and squared masonry,"[5] not as an idealized place, but one "which grew into its natural setting . . . without making the setting conform to it,"[6] and (3) Venice as a precursor for modernist culture, especially evident in its art, governance, and autonomy. The first dimension, Pound's "subjective" Venice, opens Canto III:

> I sat on the Dogana's steps
> For the gondolas cost too much, that year,
> And there were not "those girls," there was one face,
> And the Buccentoro twenty yards off, howling "Stretti"
>
> (III/11)

In the first Ur-Canto from which this passage derives, the poet recalls how in Venice in 1908 he struggled with the overpowering voice of Robert Browning's *Sordello*, in attempting to discover an epic voice to match his predecessor's. The "stone seat" of the "Dogana's curb" contrasting Browning's "palace step" (*P*, 1990, 231), in the earlier version, Pound here consolidates into "the Dogana's steps," referring to the stone promontory on the east tip of Dorsoduro overlooking the Venetian lagoon, so that what emerge are both the poet's sense of impoverishment ("the gondolas cost too much, that year") and his awe of his context ("Gods float in the azure air," III/11).

Pound reprises "Stretti" in Cantos XXVI–XXVII in illuminating fashion. In XXVI, he again remembers how in 1908 "at night they sang in the gondolas / And in the barche with lanthorns" (XXVI/121). But the more revealing passage occurs in XXVII, where, thinking back in 1927, he forgets whether he first heard "Stretti" in "1908, 1909, 1910" yet does recall hearing it a second time, sung by a washerwoman in Venice in 1920, as well as again "this year, '27" in Milan. By now, though, he no longer associates the song with only "one face," but with "those faces" of "two young ladies" (like the ones Browning had in mind?) with "lakelike and foxlike eyes" (xxvii/129–30). Though only one word, "Stretti" proliferates in meaning, as through its recurrence, the poet's personal experience assumes greater significance, conveying how he has clearly outgrown Browning's influence. The opening of xxvi further provides a subject rhyme for these lines in iii, as well as it anticipates the Pisan Canto lxxvi, as we shall see.

In iii, after the poet's introduction in Venice, the imagery quickly dissolves into a paradisal moment with "Gods," from which iv, xvii, and others expand. The opening of iv, "Palace in smoky light, / Troy but a heap of smouldering boundary stones" (iv/13), ostensibly concerns the destroyed ancient city of the *Iliad*. But later, when xxi describes the Palazzo Ducale by the Venetian lagoon as "baseless . . . there in the dawn / With low mist over the tide-mark" and floating "nel tramonto [at sunset] / With gold mist over the tide-mark" (xxi/98), or again in xxv as "in the dawn, the mist, / in that dimness" (xxv/117), it is difficult not to re-envision Troy's palace enshrouded in "smoky light" as that other palace in Venice glimmering at dawn or sunset. Pound compounds Venice into something much more than a place of personal reverie. As with his early image of marble "grown" smooth by "flowing waters," here he starts to capture not only social experience, but the experience "of beauty incarnate," as he later defines it in *Guide to Kulchur* (*GK*, 107).

This imagery of stone, water, and light co-mingling returns throughout *The Cantos*, including in xvii, directly after the Hell Cantos of World War I, therein constituting the epic's first major rise. Though still echoing that same San Trovaso fragment, the epic now erupts, becoming extra-Venetian:

> Flat water before me,
>   And the trees growing in water,
> Marble trunks out of stillness,
> On past the palazzo,
>   in the stillness,
> The light now, not of the sun. (xvii/76)

Hugh Kenner observes how Pound's Venetian imagery is "concentrated in a Luminous Detail guidebooks ignore" (*PE*, 346). Throughout the Cantos, he argues, the Venetian light " 'not of the sun,' and its stone forests not of the order of nature," make the city "the most complexly ambiguous of all the sacred places, the most wholly an assertion of sheer will" (*PE*, 348). The scenery invokes W.B. Yeats' "artifice of eternity" in "Sailing for Byzantium,"[7] yet unlike Yeats, the poet here expresses no wish to abandon nature. As Tony Tanner argues, from Pound "we receive glimpses and intimations of the organic and the inorganic, of nature and art, working, moving, surging together"; indeed, "Venice at the height of its glory – is, and should be seen as, a *triumph* of nature."[8]

The third early aspect of Pound's Venice, found most prominently in Cantos XXV–XXVII, is less intimate than the first and considerably less sublime than the second. Instead, the clustered passages cited from Venetian law and letters in these Cantos parallel the Malatesta Cantos before and the Nuevo Mundo, Chinese, and Adams Cantos afterwards, as Pound includes Venice in his tour of essential history. XXV, for example, with its opening three pages iterating the construction of the Palazzo Ducale between 1255 and 1415, punctuated by the image of it suspended "in the dawn, the mist" (XXV/117), is, despite sudden shifts, more straightforward than may appear. However, rather than satirize the early Republic, these and other fragments work "imagistically" to expose its mores. While Pound may be examining "the territory of what is more real than the ordinary," he "does not offer a formula for doing so."[9] Rather, as a modernist concerned with accuracy more than judgement, he does not exhort the Republic so much as explore its cultural foundations. Though not as enchanting as IV and XVII, these Cantos keep Pound's Venice from becoming "the possible 'picturesque'" he derogates in "Indiscretions" (*PDD*, 4).

This third aspect of Pound's Venice joins the other two (Pound's individual engagement with the city and his evocation of its beauty) to comprise a cross-section of *The Cantos*' myriad of voices overall. In later Cantos, he echoes yet reconfigures these concerns. When Venice appears in XXXI–XLI, which it does less often, it is generally as "*luogo di contratto*," a place of contracts, or "may we / say the place where the deal is made" (XXXV/175).[10] Although through the *Fifth Decad of Cantos* and the Chinese and Adams Cantos, Venice recedes as a significant locus, giving way to Siena, Rapallo, China, and America, it remains pertinent to Pound's thought. When it returns in *The Pisan Cantos*, it is transformed, as the earlier aspects merge, allowing Pound's voice to sound with its greatest poignance, yet remaining as precise as before. Though Pound's Venice here loses its imagistic edge, his candor is more compelling than ever. Indeed, his specificity risks being obscure, becoming a "private" poetry counter to the personae that dominate his shorter poems. But instead, Venice now provides an opportunity for metonymy, shaped by his characteristic economy and fidelity of expression. Pound's quoting a phrase overheard on the Lido, praising the skulls in a painting by Carpaccio, or invoking the canals in Dorsoduro works like an epic trope – indeed, not unlike the tropes he lifts from *The Odyssey* and *The Divine Comedy* elsewhere – as he creates a voice thereafter double-edged, a voice intimate yet elevated.

Though found throughout *The Pisan Cantos*, Pound's Venetian tropes surface most prominently in LXXVI. Divided into discrete strophes that document the poet's shifting mind, the Canto catalogues various spirits, people, and "bricabrac" (LXXVI/473) that press the poet's memory. A third of the way into it, he recalls how James Joyce's ability to retain "the conversation / (or 'go on') of idiots," while remarkable, was not as impressive as that of "Miss [Sara] Norton" (LXXVI/476), daughter of the eminent Charles Eliot Norton. Significantly, she was also one of the two women Pound met in Venice in June 1908 who, because they were departing earlier than anticipated, offered him use of their room above the San Trovaso canal across from the gondola repair yard, allowing him to remain in Venice two more months rent-free. Remembering Miss Norton precipitates a remarkable string of Venetian memories that punctuate the rest of the Canto, from an exchange at Florian's restaurant that same summer about D'Annunzio's play *La Figlia di Jorio* (LXXVI/476) to an encounter at the Lido in the 1930s (LXXVI/481), as Pound juxtaposes images of Venice to those of Rapallo and the Disciplinary Training Center.

The Canto reaches its major turning point in lines echoing the Cavalcanti Canto, XXXVI, lines which Olga Rudge believed express "the most important thing in *The Cantos*":[11] "nothing matters but the quality / of the affection – / in the end – that has carved the trace in the mind / dove sta memoria" (LXXVI/477). Although only fifty-five lines, the Canto's closing passage of Venetian details, loaded "ply over ply" (IV/15),[12] redirects the epic. At one point, the incarcerated poet draws a parallel between his idle days in Pisa and those in Venice in 1908, as he recalls the moment thirty-seven years earlier when, contemplating his future, he almost "chuck[ed]" the proofs ("le bozze") of *A Lume Spento* into San Vio canal (LXXVI/480).

Within this nexus of memories, however, rather than dwell on his past, Pound reprises his sacred and historical views of Venice, looking outward at everything from the recently rebuilt Accademia bridge (a civic improvement he attributes to the fascists) to the grand palazzi on the Grand Canal, to the single artwork in Venice he praises more than any other, the intricately carved marble "sirenes" on the balustrade in Santa Maria dei Miracoli church, "the jewel box" (LXXVI/480). Carved by Tullio Lombardo (c. 1455–1532), these delicate, austere figures captivated Pound from the first and came to embody the epitome of human achievement. Despite their specificity, or *because* of it, the Venetian details in *The Pisan Cantos* convey more than paradisal beauty or Venetian culture. When later Pound catalogues the artworks Olga Rudge had to abandon in fleeing her Venice house, or when in LXXXIII he asks, "Will I ever see the Giudecca again? /

or the lights against it, Ca' Foscari, Ca' Giustinian / or the Ca', as they say, of Desdemona" (LXXXIII/552), his details take on a significance beyond memory, a significance informed by his sustained method. As much as the city shapes the epic's contours, the epic comes to shape the city's contours in kind.

In the late Cantos, especially *Drafts & Fragments*, Venice once again changes character, as Pound's glimpses of it become even more cryptic or elusive than in the Pisans. Most prominently, he invokes Torcello, the oldest settlement in the Venetian lagoon, now mostly depopulated, with its bell tower, or "quiet house" where "[t]he crozier's curve runs in the wall" (CX/797), where can be found "the gold thread in the pattern" (CXVI/817) in the church's stunning Byzantine mosaics. Torcello serves as the capstone of Pound's paradisal Venice, implicit with the power of nature and artifice central to his life's project. Yet an earlier passage from *Thrones* suggests a further importance of the city to him: "But in Venice more affirmations / of individual men / From Selvo to Franchetti, than any elsewhere" (CIV/763). For Pound, not only is Venice the paradigm of "beauty incarnate," but it provides refuge for those individuals who might otherwise be suppressed or forgotten. "[T]here is something intelligent in the cherry-stone / Canals, bridges, and house walls / orange in sunlight" (CXIII/808), he remarks in *Drafts & Fragments*. For one who spent most of his life in exile, to have found a home as uniquely beautiful as Venice and then to be buried there surely constitute a privilege conferred on only the most fortunate of poets.

NOTES

1 See also H.D. (Hilda Doolittle), *End to Torment: A Memoir of Ezra Pound by H.D.*, ed. Norman Holmes Pearson and Michael King (New York: New Directions, 1958), 5–6.

2 Mary de Rachewiltz, *Ezra Pound, Father and Teacher* (New York: New Directions, 1975), 10–11.

3 As A. Walton Litz observes, Pound "was the most occasional and particular of poets: hence his apparently odd admiration for Thomas Hardy, whose poems . . . are almost always based on particular memories" ("Ezra Pound in Venice, 1913," in *Ezra Pound a Venezia*, ed. Rosella Mamoli Zorzi [Florence: Leo S. Olschki Editore, 1985], 34).

4 Tony Tanner, *Venice Desired* (Cambridge, MA: Harvard University Press, 1992), 279.

5 Donald Davie, *Ezra Pound: Poet as Sculptor* (New York: Oxford University Press, 1964), 129.

6 James J. Wilhelm, *The Later Cantos of Ezra Pound* (New York: Walker and Company, 1977), 188.

7 W.B. Yeats, *The Collected Poems of W.B. Yeats* (New York: Macmillan, 1956), 192.

8 Tanner, *Venice Desired*, 308.

9 Peter Makin, *Pound's Cantos* (Baltimore: Johns Hopkins University Press, 1985), 163–4.

10 Canto XL uses the Latin phrase, "De banchis cambi tenendi" (XL/197), dated 1361, to characterize the Fondaco dei Tedeschi, the mercantile exchange by the Rialto bridge, founded in the thirteenth century. See also *Jefferson and/or Mussolini* (New York: Liveright, 1970), 32.

11 Anne Conover, *Olga Rudge & Ezra Pound: "What Thou Lov'st Well . . ."* (New Haven, CT: Yale University Press, 2001), 271.

12 Carroll F. Terrell, *A Companion to The Cantos of Ezra Pound*, 2 vols. (Berkeley: University of California Press, 1980), 1: 8, 1: 13. The phrase, used to describe the mask in a suit of armor, derives from *Sordello* v, lines 161–6.

CHAPTER 21

London

Peter Brooker

Hugh Selwyn Mauberley (1920) is Pound's most sustained London poem, in his own words "distinctly a farewell" to the city he had come to in 1908 with such high hopes, but now departed in a mood of some bitterness and regret.[1] The poem was also, Pound wrote to John Quinn, a portrait of "today", the culmination at this point of his attempt to write modern verse with a modern content (*EP/JQ*, 195). As commentators have regularly reported, the poem chronicles moments in artistic history from the Pre-Raphaelites and the nineties, and their legacy in the Edwardian period, directly naming or alluding to a number of writers and artists, including Flaubert, Rossetti, Swinburne, Victor Plarr, Ernest Dowson, Lionel Johnson, Selwyn Image, Max Beerbohm, Arnold Bennett, and Ford Madox Ford. In addition, it refers indirectly to the First World War poets and to the vorticist sculptor Henri Gaudier-Brzeska, killed in action in June 1915.

But none of this, it has to be said, is of "today" if we understand this to designate the moment of composition in 1919–20. The poem includes nothing of Pound's "Contacts and Life," in the words of the poem's preferred subtitle, associated with imagism or – aside from the possible reference to Gaudier-Brzeska – the vorticist movement; nothing to evoke Wyndham Lewis, T.S. Eliot or Joyce, and no reference to Pound's involvement in a series of "little magazines" in the period 1913–20 or to the important figures who influenced his thinking such as Allen Upward, A.R. Orage, Ernest Fenollosa and Major C. H. Douglas. The most "contemporary" aspect of the poem, in the sense that this was what occupied Pound in the late 1910s, is its interest in music or of verse to be sung, especially in the twin poems "Envoi" (dated 1919), modeled on Edmund Waller's "Go Lovely Rose!" and "Medallion," the last poem in the second sequence, titled and dated "Mauberley (1920)."

Both poems, it is said, refer indirectly to the singing of Raymonde Collignon, whose rendition of Provençal songs, including Pound's own versions, had much impressed him. He reviewed her singing in 1918 and 1920 and at the end of this second year was himself to publish *Five Troubadour Songs*, adapted with the pianist Agnes Bedford from the original Provençal. But we would be hard pressed to call this verse-music itself "modern" (compared with his later Opera *Villon* and the "Vorticist" compositions of George Antheil Pound was to encounter in the 1920s) and an interest in the Provençal poets and the relation of verse, speech, and music was well established on Pound's arrival in the city and then consistently pursued throughout his London years and beyond.

Hugh Selwyn Mauberley is governed of course by the figure of Mauberley himself, a failed poet or generic artist figure "out of key with his time" and "wrong from the start" (*CSP*, 205) who has drifted further into a febrile aestheticism.[2] If we wish, as commentators invariably have, to read Mauberley as a persona expressing a tendency Pound recognized in himself but had rejected, then we are likely to read the poem as a retrospect on Pound's early years in London, before the advent of imagism and up to around 1912: "a bad year," wrote Pound, when poets "ran about like puppies with the tin cans of Swinburnian rhyming, of Browningisms."[3] If Pound was surveying his own London career in Mauberley from the "today" of 1919–20, then much of the personal biography and cultural experience of the immediate prewar and the postwar years was omitted.

At the same time, an alternative view of London, set very much in the here and now of Pound's present view of England and the capital appeared in the 'Hell Cantos' (later Cantos XIV and XV), drafted in late 1919.[4] To Wyndham Lewis, Pound wrote that they were "a portrait of contemporary England or at least Eng. as she wuz when I left her" and later to John Drummond that they represented "specifically LONDON. The state of the English mind in 1919 and 1920" (*SL*, 191, 239). Here the subject is less that of the displaced poet than a corrupt and obstructive establishment, a set of foul practices Pound gathered under the sin of usury.

Pound's mode here – more vicious satire than bittersweet elegy – and thus his view of London, would seem to operate at a quite different register than *Mauberley*. Nevertheless, in some ways this distinction is less stark than it appears. A hell does after all appear in *Mauberley*: of those fated combatants who "walked eye deep in hell / believing in old men's lies, then unbelieving" (*CSP*, 208). Also, Pound spoke in the 1930s of Mauberley as "ANY non-producer in the stink of London 1919" (Moody, 377), thus tossing him, along with politicians, clergy, bankers, and press men into the cloacal slime of the postwar cesspit. Mauberley's failure to bring a "reforming sense / To his perception / of the social inconsequence" or to consider the "relation of the state to the individual" (*CSP*, 218–19) also brings him within the range of Pound's contempt at the end of the decade.

Can it be that Mauberley as a type of the "modern aesthete" as David Moody describes him (Moody, 382) belonged not simply to the early years of Pound's London but persisted into the later 1910s? And persisted in close proximity to Pound himself: a figure who shared Pound's abiding interest in the relation of music and verse but lacked the energy of his reforming zeal in the world of letters and increasingly in economic and political affairs – and indeed only added to Pound's frustration in the hell of London. Eliot had said Pound's hell was a hell for other people not oneself[5] but we might instead detect another distinction, closer to home, between Pound's "serious artist", the modern poet, satirist, and castigator of a world gone wrong, and his sometime twin and "semblable," the modern aesthete. Both were inhabitants of London, both indeed its products, one its passive symptom, the other its scourge and alienated rebel. But both too, whether or not they "buried" each other, as Pound wanted to suggest Mauberley buried E.P.,[6] were done for by the culture of London.

Pound's method had led him from the beginning to inhabit a series of masks or personae. In some, such as the figure Bertran de Born, the troubadour and warrior had combined as one. The composite Pound of the *Five Troubadour Songs* and the "Hell Cantos" looks like a version of this hybrid type, but the later poems and experience of London would seem to reveal an uneasy face-off between the singer as effete poetaster and the firebrand campaigner. The tensions become more evident and self-conscious, and it is the latter, the fiery judge and jury rather than the sweet jongleur, who steps forward, the simple solution ousting the complex melody. At the same time, we can view these years as witness to the increasingly aggravated modulations of a set of broader social tensions: namely those marking the divided figure of the modernist immigrant artist shifting between cultures.[7] *Mauberley*, said Pound, was "an attempt to condense the James novel" (*SL*, 180), and in a sense this whole period played out Henry James' "international theme" of an encounter between American innocence and brash vulgarity and European civilization and corruption: a tale in which the young Pound seeks his way in the cultural capital of Europe (as he believes), is at first enthralled and an object of curiosity, only to be disillusioned and rejected, in a common refrain of Pound's closing essays, by a moribund establishment and incorrigibly provincial cultural mentality.

However, a good deal of the artistic activity, excitement and innovation of Pound's London years, roughly between 1913 and 1919, is at best abbreviated in this account. This was the period of Pound's involvement in imagist and vortex London and the world of "little magazines," and of the publication, notably, of his *Ripostes, Lustra, Cathay*, and *Homage to Sextus Propertius*. It included, too, the drafts of Cantos I to III, as they were first published in 1917 and then heavily revised *before* the writing of *Mauberley* and the "Hell Cantos." In the composition of *The Cantos* especially, from Pound's early thoughts on an American epic and the mention of work on a long poem in 1915 to the drafts at the end of the decade, London was host to a different and longer narrative than *Mauberley* allows, and one which plainly reaches beyond this period.[8]

I want to view this story, nonetheless, with the Jamesian *Mauberley* in mind, primarily as that of the American émigré modernist seeking renown and influence in the European capital. The early Pound's London was a literary and bookish city, or, in his words, "the place for poesy" (*SL*, 7). He appeared to have little interest in the ways modernization was shaping the capital and everyday life through changes in population, occupation, transport, and communications, or of the position of women and the suffrage cause or of London as the seat of empire and world finance. He came to London to meet Yeats, as he said, to get in the swing of its literary scene – and principally to succeed. His letters home (not unlike Eliot's) tell how he was meeting people and getting on. He made his way consequently through contacts with the one-time members of the Rhymers Club, Selwyn Image and Victor Plarr; with the poet-scholars, including notably Laurence Binyon, associated with the British Museum which served as his own first base; or with others, including Maurice Hewlitt, through the publisher Elkin Mathews and his Bookshop on Vigo Street, just off the Café Royal. He met Ford Madox Hueffer through May Sinclair, Ernest Rhys and Lawrence through Hueffer, and through Fredric Manning met Olivia and Dorothy Shakespear and was thus in time introduced to Yeats.

The English, including the British Museum crowd and Hueffer and Wyndham Lewis, tended to view Pound, whether charitably or dismissively, as an American interloper – the "cowboy songster . . . in a tengallon hat" as Lewis remembered.[9] Nevertheless, Pound became noticed and networked, making his way in the London society of such as Lady Low and Mrs. Eva Fowler, who invited young poets to take tea or to give lectures in their drawing rooms or salons. Olivia Shakespear and Dorothy were the most important examples of this class, the first because of the introduction to Yeats, with whom she had had an affair, and the second because she brought him the admiration and high-minded innocent love of a young middle-class English girl. Dorothy was entirely respectable and for five years their relationship was pursued – if this is the word – in a desultory and ethereal fashion, governed by social convention regarding a young woman's conduct, and, until the Shakespears relented, by the parents' frustration at Pound's "American ways" and, principally, his lack of sufficient income to marry their daughter (*EPDS*, 154).

Donald Davie has agued that in marrying Dorothy, Pound "had *married* England."[10] If so, there was no urgency about the match on his part, for he was out of London and away from England for fifteen months after the first shoots of a romantic attachment had appeared. The couple first met in January 1909 and apparently came that year to a private understanding during the period Dorothy attended his lectures on "The Development of Literature in Southern Europe" at the Regent Street Polytechnic. But after a brief holiday in Europe in March 1910, when he was joined by Dorothy and her mother at Lake Garda on Sermione and in Venice, Pound left London in June for the USA and did not return until August the following year. He visited his parents in Pennsylvania, met William Carlos Williams and his father in New Jersey, and after a stay in New York, sailed to London, almost immediately to travel to Paris and thence to Sermione, once more, and on to Giessen, Germany to see Hueffer. Dorothy, London, and England were not so compelling as it seemed.

Instead, Pound kept to his own priorities, combining a bardic sense of poetry's grand mission with a dedication to the craft of prosody. His visit to the USA was particularly important in both respects before his return in what was essentially a second arrival in London – effectively, after another four months in Europe in mid 1912, with the subsequent launch of imagism. His London reputation up to 1910 had been of an esoteric inheritor of the nineties and devotee of early European literary culture (he was "really a great authority on the troubadours," said Yeats[11]), but who was in his very "American" professionalism something new and unsettling in a world of cultivated amateurism.[12]

While in the USA, Pound continued his apprenticeship, practicing the complex forms employed by Arnaut Daniel and Guido Cavalcanti. Dorothy had researched verse forms in the British Museum and the result was his translations and imitations, and the poems of *Canzoni* (1911), dedicated both to Dorothy and, as etiquette would have required, to her mother. His second unspoken dedicatee, however, was America. As the early "What I feel about Walt Whitman" (written February 1909) and admiration of James McNeill Whistler suggests, Pound felt that for all their differences, he shared a lineage, a message and a mission with both. In "Patria Mia," the record of his American sojourn, serialized in the *New Age* (1912), he expounded his thesis that, despite all appearances, "America has a chance for Renaissance" (*PM*, 11). The series "America: Chances and Remedies" followed in *The New Age* in May–June, 1913 and this vision arguably never left him.

Poetry, thought Pound, would educate the emotions and intellect and thus administer to a cultural renaissance. To this end, he planned in 1912 to present America with the fruits of his work. In a drafted "Epilogue" he presented himself and five books, *The Spirit of Romance, Canzoni, Ripostes*, and the translations of Arnaut Daniel and Cavalcanti as "the spoils, my nation" of one returned from exile "with gifts." "America," as David Moody comments, "was unmoved" (Moody, 149). Pound's cultural mission, so conceived, was stillborn. A second related event, his meeting with Ford at Giessen, has become legendary. Presented with Pound's *Canzoni*, Ford reportedly rolled on the floor in disbelief at Pound's archaic mannerisms. Ford's histrionic roll "saved me two years, perhaps more" said Pound, "and sent me back to my proper effort, namely toward using the living tongue" (*SPR*, 431–2). The story is Pound's own, not Ford's, and stands, as intended perhaps, as a punctual moment in Pound's transformation, on his second arrival back in London, into a more modern poet.

What followed were poems such as "Portrait d'une Femme" and the "new stuff" of "Contemporania" written as he told his parents "in an utterly modern manner." As a purposefully modern poet Pound was now to pursue his task in London, seeking out and promoting the signs of new work in fellow authors. Accordingly, he set himself "a course in modern literature" and read James, Turgenev, Flaubert, and "the Russians" and acquainted himself directly in a visit to Paris in April 1913 with younger French poets. Whereas earlier, at the point of preparing *Canzoni* for publication, Pound had thought the French "a gutless lot,"[13] by 1913 his mind was changed, prompting the series of essays "The Approach to Paris" where he recommended the invention and intelligence of Jules Romaines, Charles Vildrac, George Duhamel, and their associated Parisian "vortex" (*SPR*, 386).

He married Dorothy in April 1914 but, arguably, was already beyond the England she represented and the world of English letters he had wanted at first to join. By this time he was established as the impresario of the new, the "demon pantechnicon driver" of Lewis' description,[14] hauling the past into the present, accelerating through literary and artistic movements, delivering advice and diktats as pedagogue and editor. Much of Pound's London career and beyond could be charted in terms of these latter roles. His first meaningful employment in London was as a lecturer at Regent Street Polytechnic. His "A Few Don'ts," (like the later

"How to Read" and other guides) and the prospectus for a College of Arts in November 1914, along with his admonitory letters (such as to the young Iris Barry), were inspired by the need for curricular reform for poets and students of art and literature. If he came to London to see Yeats, he came to serve more as the editor who helped modernize Yeats' verse. Others, including Harriet Monroe, H.D., John Cournos, Iris Barry, and, of course, Eliot, were similarly beneficiaries, usually in their own estimation, of Pound's blue pencil. His professional editorial role, rarely a comfortable or long-lasting one, between 1913 and 1920 on *Poetry* (Chicago), *The Little Review*, and the *Athenaeum*, and as reviewer on *The New Age*, *The Egoist*, and elsewhere, were part of the pedagogic mission. His lesson was that the axioms of precision and hardness should be understood simultaneously as technical desiderata and an assurance of clear thinking and cultural health – something he entrusted increasingly to a select "Party of Intelligence."

Around 1914–15, Pound was operating on all fronts; this was "The Ezra Pound Period" in Iris Barry's words, its centre of gravity more Belotti's in Soho and the nearby Restaurant de la Tour Eiffel, at this time a centre of vorticist activity, than Kensington. It was in this period too that an explicitly broader agenda began to appear, its range stretching in the *New Age* series "Affirmations" across imagism and vorticism to an "Analysis of the Decade." But the "Vortex of London" came to include not only the busy traffic of artistic and intellectual stimuli, as in this essay, but also the physical experience of the city. Pound's comments on its street architecture were included in a group of reports included in the series of "Art Notes" written for the *New Age* between 1917 and 1920 under the name of B. H. Dias.

Walking the city brought out less the ambivalent *flâneur* than Pound the cultural critic, who read the tenor of social taste and the quality of civic life in the beauty of a door frame in Dean Street, the ill-proportioned setting of a window in Kensington, or who saw "the horror of London" in the "grey-yellow brick" common in Islington and south of the Thames.[15] Pound's complaint everywhere was against machine-made ornament, but he was equally alert to the "great beauty" of domestic architecture and to the inequalities of class expressed in its material fabric as well as to the incompetence of the authorities and hack designers. "[E]very man walks in the streets," said Pound, each has a dwelling, and for the appearance of the city to improve "there must be a great popular rebellion" in favor of a simplicity of form that would come, in Pound's eyes, from a meeting of architecture and sculpture.[16]

Postwar London prompted this new broader civic agenda in Pound as it did in Edward Wadsworth and Lewis, notably in the latter's *The Caliph's Design. Architects! Where is Your Vortex?* Pound and Lewis were alike avid reformers but were equally frustrated in their ambitions. In particular, in his own immediate sphere, in championing the best new work, Pound became aware of obstacles to its publication and distribution and thus to the renaissance it would otherwise inaugurate. Hence his impatience with the timidity of editors such as Harriet Monroe who had been slow to appreciate Eliot, and with the printers and publishers who obstructed the publication of Dreiser, Joyce, and Lawrence. The pressing issue was censorship and, allied to this, the economics of production and distribution of information, and therefore of wealth and power. In 1918 Pound met Major C.H. Douglas, author of *Economic Democracy* (1920). The poet who had learned clarity from Ford and Fenollosa found a teacher with a simple answer to the waste and ills of society and a proponent of a system of social credit to bring about economic justice. And this he adopted as his own message.

Pound himself came up against a pusillanimous morality over the publication of the full text of *Lustra*, and in the shape of George Prothero, editor of the prestigious *Quarterly Review*. Prothero refused a piece by Pound because of his involvement in *Blast*: "it stamps a man too disadvantageously," said Prothero (*LE*, 358). Other editors, if for different reasons, followed suit. Pound lost reviewing posts on the *Athenaeum* and *Outlook*. Simultaneously, A.R. Orage excised his column of "Art Notes." It is hardly surprising that Pound turned to a guru with a straightforward answer to the problem of economic well-being. But this was not all. Academics who had found fault with his "creative translations" of the "Seafarer" and Chinese poetry attacked the free renderings of his Latin source in *Homage to Sextus Propertius*. And if F.S. Flint is to be believed, Pound had also alienated some earlier companions: "you spoiled everything by some native incapacity for walking square with your fellows," Flint told him. "You have not been a good comrade, voilà!."[17] Imagism had given way to the more dynamic vorticism and although Pound insisted, perhaps rightly, that vorticism was alive and well – as in the technique of the *Cantos* – the London Vortex had no more been sustained than its principal organ *Blast*.

The comparison in so much, finally, of Pound's London years was with T. S. Eliot. In a number of ways Eliot was Pound's shadow, accomplice, and contrary. But as an American in Europe, Eliot was, very like Pound, keen to be recognized in London, since London imposed its opinion "on all the English speaking world," though this was, he added pointedly, "like breaking open a safe – for an American." To his mother in 1919 he claimed he had "far more *influence* on English letters than any other American has ever had, unless it be Henry James."[18] He had defended Pound against his detractors in 1917 though he later remembered his early poetry as "rather fancy old fashioned stuff".[19] His was, in sum, a calculated success. Pound's calculations went askew: in the event, neither London, Paris, nor New York, the metropolitan axis of his wished-for renaissance, was to provide a supporting artistic culture. The London years, plangently recalled in *The Pisan Cantos*, had nonetheless brought him to the point where he was ready to embark on the life of self-exile devoted to the world epic of *The Cantos*. This was hardly to be predicted in 1908, but Pound's metamorphosizing personality and London trajectory came to comprise what we recognize now as one of the major narratives of international modernism.

NOTES

1 Note on the title page of the first American edition of *Mauberley* in *P*, 1926.
2 We might think this description refers to the "E.P." of this poem's title, "E.P. Ode Pour L'Election De Son Sepulchre" but the distinction between Mauberley and Pound is far from straightforward.
3 *The Egoist* (January, 1 1915): 12.
4 Noel Stock, *The Life of Ezra Pound* (London, Penguin, 1974), p. 286.
5 T. S. Eliot, *After Strange Gods* (London: Faber and Faber), 1934, 47.
6 "Mauberley buries E.P. in the opening poem," said Pound; Thomas E. Connolly, "Further Notes on Mauberley," *Accent* 16 (Winter 1956): 59.
7 On the figure of the modernist as immigrant, see Raymond Williams, *The Politics of Modernism* (London: Verso, 1989), 44–6, and Colm Tóibín, "The Art of Being Found Out," *London Review of Books* (March 20, 2008), 24–7.
8 Pound suggested he had "various schemes" in mind for the poem as early as 1904 or 1905; see Donald Hall, "Ezra Pound," *Writers at Work. The Paris Review Interviews*, 2nd series (New York: Penguin, 1977a), 36; Moody, 23–4, 306.
9 Wyndham Lewis, *Blasting and Bombadiering. An Autobiography (1914–1926)* (London: John Calder, 1982), 274.
10 Donald Davie, *Studies in Ezra Pound* (Cheadle: Carcanet, 1991), 223.
11 W.B. Yeats, *Letters of William Butler Yeats*, ed. Allan Wade (London: Hart-Davis, 1954), 543.
12 Lewis, *Blasting*, 275–6.
13 Cited in Robert Schultz, R. "A Detailed Chronology of Ezra Pound's London Years, 1908–1920, Part One: 1908–1914," *Paideuma* 11 (1982): 464, 463, 461.
14 *Blast 2* (1914), ed. Wyndham Lewis (Santa Rosa, CA: Black Sparrow Press, 1981), 82.
15 Pound, "Art Notes. *Buildings – 1*," *The New Age* (August 29, 1918): 287–8, in *EPVA*, 75, 83, 74.

16 Pound, "Art Notes. *Parallelograms,*" *The New Age* (October 17, 1918): 400–1, and see "Art Notes. *Super-fronts,*" *New Age* (October 24, 1918): 414, in *EPVA*, 82, 85.

17 F. S. Flint, letter to Pound, July 3, 1915, in *The Imagist Revolution 1908–1918*. A Keepsake, Harry Ransom Humanities Research Center (Austin: Texas, 1992), unpaginated.

18 *The Letters of T. S. Eliot, Vol.1, 1898–1922* (London: Faber and Faber, 1988), 102, 392, 280.

19 Donald Hall, "T.S.Eliot," *Writers at Work. The Paris Review Interviews*, 2nd series (New York: Penguin, 1977b), 95.

CHAPTER 22

Paris

Patricia Cockram

WHY PARIS?

Along a margin in Francis Picabia's July 10, 1921 issue of the Dadaist journal *391* rambles Ezra Pound's joking epigram: "Paris quoi? Paris contre le monde?? Quoi? Et je suis ici depuis trois mois sans trouver une maîtresse convenable."[1] Pound and his wife Dorothy settled in Paris in April of 1921 and stayed until late 1924, when they moved to Italy, a sojourn that would prove more fruitful than its brevity might suggest. During this short time, Pound met and worked with many of the artists he already admired; composed an opera; published a book on music; arranged housing for James Joyce and his family and introduced Joyce to Sylvia Beach, who would publish *Ulysses;* met the violinist Olga Rudge, who remained his lover and helpmate to the end of his life; continued to contribute essays, poems, translations, and criticism to periodicals; and most important, wrote several new cantos for his long poem and substantially revised the seven Cantos he had begun in London, altering his approach to the entire work. By the time Pound left Paris, exhausted, over-stimulated, distracted, and unwell, he had prepared sixteen cantos for publication in a luxury edition by William Bird's small publishing house, Three Mountains Press. This edition, *A Draft of XVI Cantos*, which did not appear until 1925, was the first publication of *The Cantos* in book form.

It was in Paris that Pound made the most radical innovations in *The Cantos*, a work still in its infancy when he left London. The importance of these changes cannot be overstated, and may in large measure be attributed to his encounter with the French avant-garde Dadaists, especially Picabia and Cocteau. Pound tended to become attached to movements that were defiantly – and sometimes dangerously – new: in London he quickly moved from imagism, a movement he had devised, to vorticism, then in Paris to Dada, and finally, through economics and politics, to Italian fascism. Poetically, the formal rebellion that reached its high point in London with *Blast* found an even more important and far-reaching new expression during Pound's brief but important engagement with the Dadaists in Paris. While the Paris Dadaists were different from Pound, the movement's blithe rejection of artistic, poetic, syntactic, and typographic conventions, and its inclusion of elements from the visual arts, music, and politics affected Pound in ways that have yet to be appreciated.

Pound's choice of Paris was hardly surprising: French art and literature had long provided him with subjects for study and inspiration for reviving English poetry, beginning with his translations and imitations of the troubadour poets of medieval Provence: in his 1910 book *The Spirit of Romance*, he praised them for the development of vernacular poetry in Europe and for their unadorned verse and formal innovation, elements which would help him break away from the clichés of late nineteenth-century English poetry in his own work.

Pound published his first translation from Provençal poetry in 1905, several months before graduating from Hamilton College at age nineteen with the second prize in French. By the age of twenty-one, he had completed a master's degree at the University of Pennsylvania and was teaching Romance languages at Wabash College in Indiana. Like many young American poets who considered themselves modern, Pound was strongly influenced in his early work by English Pre-Raphaelite poets like Dante Gabriel Rossetti, who also translated the troubadours. When Pound moved to London to modernize his own style, to create a new, clearer, harder-edged poetry in English, French poetry and ideas would be an important factor in his search, beginning with the medieval French poets he was then teaching and re-translating.

Although Pound's interaction with W. B. Yeats, T. S. Eliot, and Ford Madox Ford were significant during his London years, his interest in French poetry and thought continued to grow. From T. E. Hulme he learned about Henri Bergson, and from his friend the French sculptor Henri Gaudier-Brzeska he adopted his theory of the primacy of form over content. His focus eventually turned from the medieval troubadours to the modern French poets, particularly for their musicality and metrical experimentation, and during his frequent travels in France, Pound delved into the work of contemporary French writers who had been Symbolists and free-verse poets or were their heirs. Remy de Gourmont, Jules Remain, Charles Vildrac, Francis Jammes, Henri de Régnier, Tristan Corbière, Laurent de Tailhade, Henri-Martin Barzun, Paul Fort, Jules Laforgue, Arthur Rimbaud, and Guillaume Apollinaire were among the poets Pound discussed in a series of articles he wrote beginning in 1912 for *New Age* called "The

Approach to Paris." In these, and articles and reviews in *Poetry, The Little Review*, and *The Dial*, for whom he became the Paris correspondent,
Pound published frequent translations of their work with commentary, urging young American and British writers to read the contemporary French
poets.

As early as 1913, explaining in *The New Age* why he lived in England,
Pound already mentioned Paris as an alternative, in case "the rotten shell of
a crumbling empire" did not turn out well.[2] In his reviews of contemporary
French poets for *Poetry* and in "The Approach to Paris," he claimed that
poetry in France was at least twenty years ahead of anything being written
in England. Rémy de Gourmont, whose poetry and criticism Pound began
translating in 1913, was an especially important influence through his poetry
and fiction but especially his criticism. Before leaving London, Pound
translated de Gourmont's *Physique de l'amour* as *The Natural Philosophy
of Love*, an eccentric work of personal philosophy that accorded with and
intensified Pound's thinking about the connection between sexual and
intellectual potency. His two-part obituary of de Gourmont in *Fortnightly
Review* and *Poetry* praised the older writer's "force" and ideas.[3] In his
assertion that de Gourmont's greatness was in his intelligence and his
ability to communicate his ideas, there is a hint of what Pound would later
praise in Picabia.

As Pound became disenchanted with England, particularly after World
War I, Paris seemed a logical alternative, a city full of creative ferment
and the kind of cross-genre pollination that he was already seeking in his
own work. Always prone to intense early enthusiasms, he soon advised
Joyce to move to Paris too, partly because it would be an inexpensive place
to live, a perpetual concern for Joyce, and also because he felt sure that
Ulysses could be published there. As he had done in London, Pound quickly
managed to meet everyone of interest in Paris. Only Natalie Barney could
be said to have known more people. These encounters were not merely
social; Pound was a master at absorbing ideas from those around him,
and the vast numbers of artists, musicians, and writers, both French and
exiles, provided not only entertainment and opportunities to be useful, but
important ideas for his own work.

Among the many artists and writers Pound met in Paris, including
Picasso, Stein, Hemingway, Cocteau, and Picabia, were the avant-garde
American composer George Antheil, who would inspire Pound to write
his *Antheil and the Treatise on Harmony*, as well as some sonatas of his
own; the sculptor Constantin Brancusi, whose work Pound saw as the
culmination of what Gaudier-Brzeska might have achieved had he lived;

Sylvia Beach, who would, with Pound's encouragement, bravely undertake the publication of *Ulysses;* William Bird, whose Three Mountains Press would bring out *A Draft of XVI Cantos*; and finally, the Dadaists, who were the most outrageously avant-garde artists working at the time, and whose syncretic work achieved some of the effects Pound was reaching for.

Tristan Tzara's belief that war had changed the world – that now nothing counted, that all assumptions, all beliefs, were to be discarded – formed the genesis of the later French version of his Dadaist Manifesto. Dada called for a world made new. That Pound was ready for such a change is evident in the Mauberley sequence, though not in the Cantos written before he moved to Paris. Pound's outraged negation of Horace's heroic phrase, "non dulce, non et decor," his condemnation of "liars in public places," and the assertion that "We see *to kalon* / decreed in the market place" (*P*, 1990, 187) show us not only a Pound who would identify with the anti-war stance of the Dadaists, but also one whose satiric view of aestheticism – a view developed in London through his collaborations with A. R. Orage, Wyndham Lewis, and Henri Gaudier-Brzeska, among others – accorded, at least in theory, with Dada's anti-art position.

The modernists – and especially the Futurists and the Dadaists – were part of an earlier trend towards what Michael Levenson calls the "ascendancy of novelty." In Levenson's view, the dominant intellectual culture in the early years of the twentieth century was not a contest between novelty and tradition but rather a contest of novelties, within which a turn back to primitivism as in *Ubu Roi* – and in Pound's incorporation of historical and mythological fragments from ancient or primitive cultures – was a radical break with the earlier concept of an historical trajectory that was moving always in one direction.[4]

For Pound, Paris soon became not only the antidote to the complacency and non-novelty of London; it was the locus of a new group which, in its turning away from the recent past, sublimated their generation's anger into a form of nihilism suffused with a sense of fun. While many of the characteristics of Dada were not necessarily new in themselves, and although Dadaist journals bear some resemblance to *Blast* and other early avant-garde documents, including those of Futurism, the combination of so many of these elements with Dada's determined randomness made it an important rupture nonetheless. And whether Pound was a true Dadaist or not, Dada gave him new ideas and techniques that we see as early as the first revised Cantos. If, as the early Dadaists claimed, nothing had meaning, including Dada, then anything could have meaning, anything could be art.

Although Pound was temperamentally at odds with such a random and apparently carefree approach to art, Dada appealed to his ongoing obsession with the new and his eagerness to affront conventional notions of art and propriety. Furthermore, his increasing concern with the political implications of modernity, with economics, and with the artist's place in public life, disposed him to approve of Dada's rejection of all concessions to the marketplace. Dadaism avoided the self-importance of vorticism, and its open and irreverent approach to all the arts contributed to a further turn away from the aestheticism that Pound had been struggling to leave behind. Pound discovered in Dada a set of new ideas and attitudes that would enable important changes in his own work.

As John Alexander, Richard Sieburth, and others have pointed out, what Pound appreciated especially in the work of Picabia, Léger, and other Dadaists was the concept behind the work, the thought of the work's creator, beyond or even despite the work itself. He had criticized Picabia's work in early reviews, but after his exposure to Dada, Pound began to praise Picabia as in a 1921 review he wrote for the *New York Evening Post:* "In his beautiful and clear pictures . . . there is perhaps not a sign of visual sensitivity, or at least of that kind of visual *receptivity* which underlies the nervous outlines of a Picasso, but there is a very clear exteriorization of Picabia's mental activity."[5] These insights – especially the recognition that Dada's value lay in its *conceptual* aspect – would significantly change Pound's approach to his own long poem.

Three samples of Pound's writing appeared in *Le Pilhaou-Thibaou*, the July 1921 edition of *391:* "Moeurs Contemporaines," translated by "Christian" (Georges Herbiet); the epigram quoted at the beginning of this chapter; and "Kongo Roux" in French. It is "Kongo Roux" that can be considered the most credible as a Dadaist work. It contains, in apparently random order, fragments of statements by Pound or quoted from others, erratic typography, insertions, diagonal lines, and graphic elements. The poem proposes a "denationalist city," and an insertion at the far edge of the page asserts, "We will call it Kongo or Venusberg or new Athens, depending" (*EPCP*, IV: 165). The inclusion of references to credit, usury, and the papacy put the poem's Dadaist credibility somewhat in doubt, but its breezy tone and disdain for the market do not.

Pound's work appeared in several other Dadaist journals, including Theo van Doesburg's *Mécano* (yellow) 1, where "Yeux Glauques" would appear in English on the yellow side, with an abstract drawing titled "Hommage à Ruskin" by van Doesburg placed at a right angle to the poem. The surrounding pages included drawings, poems, and aphorisms by van

Doesburg, Jean Crotti, Tristan Tzara, Piet Mondrian, Paul Eluard, F. T. Marinetti, Umberto Boccioni, and Francis Picabia. Despite the conventional shape of Pound's poem, which had appeared first in "Hugh Selwyn Mauberley" in 1920, its inclusion in the quirkily designed avant-garde *Mécano* signaled his continued interest in Dadaism.

Shortly after his participation in *391* and *Mécano*, Pound reworked the Cantos he had composed up to this time, making extensive changes, moving or eliminating earlier work. This is where we can begin to see the importance of Paris, and especially Dada. George Bornstein has argued persuasively in *Material Modernism* that, especially for writers like W.B. Yeats, Marianne Moore, and Ezra Pound, the bibliographic code is "an important constituent of meanings." To lose or ignore these records, Bornstein argues, is to "give a mistaken notion of permanence and completeness by [freezing and disseminating them] in only one of their multiple forms."[6]

Bornstein's is a particularly suggestive argument when one looks at the earliest cantos, and the context of their revisions. What Bornstein has called the "huge variation [in] the linguistic code" between the early versions of the first Cantos and the later versions is more than linguistic, however; it signals a change in perception and poetic method.[7] It allows for a discontinuity the earlier versions do not have; it expands the geographic, cultural, and historic landscape of the poem; it embraces influence – and extends it beyond the English and European traditions. Richard Sieburth has pointed out many of these changes, but a close look at the first three revised Cantos will show additional influences, of Paris and the Parisian avant-garde, on *The Cantos*.

Canto I, more or less as we know it today, was at the end of the original Canto III (*EPCP*, II: 243). Unlike other revisions from this period, this section was not significantly changed, beyond some tightening of a line here and there, but the move makes a difference. Standing alone as a Canto – as the opening of the entire poem, in fact – the Homer/Divus material appears less like the continuation of an inventory of cultural forebears and more like a ready-made. Furthermore, the appearance of "And" at the beginning of the poem and "so that:" at the end leaves the Canto open now. This and the "found objects" quoted throughout the later Cantos suggest the influence of the Dadaists.

Canto II shows more noticeable changes, and it is here that we see the cultural opening mentioned above. What we know as Canto II had been Canto I with the almost identical "Hang it all, there can be but one *Sordello*!" (*EPCP*, II:216). From there, however, the early version is addressed entirely to Browning, and its references either point to the background of

Browning's *Sordello* and the Western tradition,[8] especially to the material Pound treated in *The Spirit of Romance*, or catalogue Pound's own search for new influences. This version could be considered consistent with what Michael Levenson identifies as the nineteenth-century view of the present as part of an historical continuum, whereas the revised Canto signals the shift Levenson describes toward a view of the present as always already new.[9]

The new version, now Canto II, discards much of the poem. The continuum is broken. Gone is the trajectory of the earlier version, which moved backward from Browning to Sordello to other Provençal poets, to Dante to Catullus, then to the question of how Pound would find his own Sordello, and finally to brief allusions to Picasso, Lewis, and Confucius, all names that would have been in Pound's consciousness at the time. The new Canto II shifts rapidly from Browning to Li Po's criticism of So-Shu to the daughter of a Celtic sea god to a visual image from Picasso that now actually adds, like a collage – or an ideogram – to our picture of the "Sleek head, daughter of Lir" from line 7 (II/6). An expanded heteroglossia gives the poem both its form and its content. It is a poem containing history, but in collage-like leaps, fragmented syntax, and many new cultural allusions. Not only are there now more such non-Western, non-Anglo-American references; they are meaningful. They are not mere cultural markers to point the way to a new poetics; they *are* the poetics. The tale of the tribe has expanded. Paris was a far more cosmopolitan city in the early twentieth century than London and was enlivened by the presence of Russians, Eastern Europeans, Italians, Africans, and Asians, as well as expatriate Americans black and white. Pound had not yet discovered Frobenius, but he had already translated Chinese poetry and Confucian thought and written about the "ideogramic method." It was in Paris, however, that he found the means of incorporating new voices meaningfully in *The Cantos*.

Historical synchronicity and the expansion of references having been established in Canto II, Pound continues in a similar vein. Although the addition of graphic and musical elements occurs much later in *The Cantos*, we see the inclusion of visual allusions entering the poem beginning with the second Canto. Visual references and multiple voices continue in Canto III, which begins with a line adapted from one that occurred about halfway through the original Canto I. The new version begins in a similar vein, but the only remaining reference to Browning is "those girls":

> I sat on the Dogana's steps
> For the gondolas cost too much, that year,
> And there were not "those girls," there was one face
>
> (III/11)

Separated from the Browning material now, these lines take us into another collage-like Canto in which cultural layers and found phrases proliferate, including not only images from Venice past and present, but a fragment of a Neapolitan song ("Stretti"), a reference to Persephone, and a quoted fragment from D'Annunzio, just in the first few lines, before we move back to Greek mythology and forward again to the Renaissance with a detour by way of Confucius.

The allusions in these revised Cantos, and those that follow, are distinguished by two important characteristics that signal a change from the earlier versions: they are historically and culturally discontinuous, but even more important, the relations to each other and to the work as a whole are no longer ones of influence; their relations are now conceptual. They are often conflated with other figures to suggest a value or a theme: thus, in Canto III, Kore, Ignez da Castro, and Isabella d'Este, all figures from different cultural traditions and eras, are related as mythic female figures, and Mio Cid recalls other strong masculine figures that were iconic for Pound: Odysseus and Malatesta. The layering of allusions and memories, both personal and mythic, which constitutes a kind of conceptual rhyming, continues from this time on in *The Cantos*. It is in Paris that the "ideogramic method" really begins.

By 1924 Ford Madox Ford was settled in Paris and got his *transatlantic review* under way, providing yet another venue for Pound and Joyce, as well as Stein, Hemingway, e.e. cummings, and many others, but Pound decided that he had to leave Paris. The surrealists who succeeded Pound's friends the Dadaists were becoming socialists and communists, and Pound felt that art could not survive in a society run by "committee." He continued to submit articles to journals, but most of his income now came from translations, many of them anonymous and presumably not of his choosing. He was also dismayed that Paris had become a popular tourist destination, and Dorothy had never liked France. Most important, however, he began to find it hard to work. There were too many distractions, many of them pleasant, and he needed a quiet place to write. In the fall of 1924, he and Dorothy left for Italy and settled in Rapallo. Olga soon followed and took a house nearby. Pound still had publishing interests in France: William Bird was about to bring out his *Draft of* XVI *Cantos*, and Nancy Cunard, who took over Bird's small publishing house, renaming it Hours Press, would publish another luxury edition, *A Draft of* XXX *Cantos* with initial letters drawn by Dorothy. Pound stayed in touch with his many Paris friends by letter and visited often. Dorothy's son Omar would be born there, and the Pounds would attend the Paris performance of his opera *Testament de*

Villon. Exciting and productive as his sojourn had been, however, Paris had never needed Pound, and Pound no longer needed Paris.

NOTES

1 *391: Pilhaou-Thibaou* 15 (July 10, 1921): 12. The quote runs down the right margin of the page and is signed "EZRA."

2 "Through Alien Eyes," I, *The New Age* 12 (January 16, 1913): 252.

3 "Remy de Gourmont" I, *Fortnightly Review* 98 (n.s.): 588 (December 1, 1915): [1159]–1166 and "Remy de Gourmont," II, *Poetry* 7 (January 1916): 197–202.

4 Michael Levenson, London Modernism seminar, Birkbeck College, London, June 2, 2007. Forthcoming in his volume *Modernism* (Yale University Press, 2010).

5 Quoted in Rebecca Beasley, *Pound and the Visual Culture of Modernism* (Cambridge: Cambridge University Press, 2007), 172.

6 George Bornstein, *Material Modernism* (Cambridge: Cambridge University Press, 2001), 2.

7 *Ibid.*, 37.

8 Among those mentioned are Catullus, Dante, Arnaut Daniel, Peire Cardinal, Altaforte Mohammed's windows (only in that they looked on a similar garden), Wordsworth, Botticelli, etc.

9 Levenson, *Modernism*.

CHAPTER 23

Rapallo and Rome

Massimo Bacigalupo

RAPALLO AND THE OCCASIONS OF *THE CANTOS*

Pound lived mostly in and near Rapallo, just south of Genoa, from 1924 to his death, and this place and its landscape permeated his mature poetry. In Cantos XVII–XXX we find many Mediterranean settings in which Odysseus and his avatars rest from their voyages, and the theme is repeated in the "fertility Cantos" of the 1930s, especially XXXIX, XLVII, and XLIX, where Pound creates his own rituals out of old Rapallo customs (the "sepulchres," i.e., floral church decorations, of Maundy Thursday, the lights floated in the bay on summer nights).[1] Pound wanted to evoke a true religion of the people, beyond (or before) Judaism and Christianity, and used the material at hand, for example, Christian ceremonies, that looked as if they may well have derived from pagan customs.

In the 1920s Rapallo provided the model for an aesthetic pleasance, in the 1930s the backdrop for a more strenuous "totalitarian" vision, a religion of sexuality, abundance, and fertility. In the 1940s it became the lost paradise of *The Pisan Cantos*, that shuttle throughout between the beautiful Pisan landscape and memories of the Tigullio (as the Bay of Rapallo is called), where Pound had passed the greater part of his maturity. There he had toiled at his poetry, criticism, and economics, and had loved his wife and the mother of his daughter, and had delighted in the goings-on of village life: the pharmacist who lent him the *Gazzetta di Genova* for 1815 (*CP*, 140), the wise farmers who expressed simply and unforgettably his own religious feelings:

> Baccin said: I planted that
> > tree, and *that* tree (ulivi)   (LXXXVII/593)
> Luigi, *gobbo*, makes his communion with wheat grain
> > in the hill paths
> > > at sunrise   (XCVII/699)

These are thumbnail sketches from the cantos written in St. Elizabeths Hospital, which are more didactic and relentless than the Pisan sequence. Pound is using his Rapallo experiences to drive home his view of a natural religion, and places Baccin and hunchback (*gobbo*) Luigi next to Kang Hsi and Leo the Wise, and the other enlightened rulers celebrated in his broken "paradiso." When Pound returned to Rapallo in 1959 after his American exile, he was still looking for traces to record in his "palimpsest." He found there inspiration for the closing passage of the last finished Canto, CXVI: "But to affirm the gold thread in the pattern / (Torcello) / al Vicolo d'oro / (Tigullio)" (CXVI/817).

Vico dell'oro ("Alley of Gold") is a dingy street in old Rapallo. The name reminded Pound of the mosaics in Torcello, another sacred place, and of the goddess Venus, always associated with gold. Here she was again, beckoning him at journey's end, "to lead back to splendour" (CXVI/817).

Pound is still "The Englishman in Italy," an heir of Browning and Shelley (and Byron, whom he much admired), and thus he remained for his Italian acquaintances: an eccentric member of the foreign colony that thrived in Rapallo as in other Italian resorts. Rapallo was so popular that in 1905 an extensive guidebook in English was called for, *Rapallo – Walks and Environs*, describing the same monuments and local customs that were to figure in *The Cantos*. Just as Byron wrote *Childe Harold's Pilgrimage*, so Pound recorded in his long poem his own Italian travels, chiefly to Venice (also celebrated by Byron) and Verona, to Sigismondo Malatesta's Romagna, and to his very own Liguria.

D. H. Lawrence had lived down the coast in Fiascherino ten years before Pound discovered Rapallo, and Lawrence described memorably in his letters his delight with the climate, the olive trees, the good-humoured (and sometimes good-looking) natives. Pound belonged to Lawrence's generation, and like Lawrence sought to be a liberator from sexual and mental taboos, idealizing the South and its people. Like Lawrence and other Protestants, he believed that popular Catholicism was less oppressive than Protestantism in matters of personal behavior and sexuality, that it was really paganism in a new dress. And like Lawrence, Pound was a Protestant prophet inveighing against obscurantism and all kinds of "obfuscation," never doubting that he had seen the light and could be a trailblazer.

THE EXILE: CAVALCANTI AND YEATS

In his early Rapallo years, the late 1920s, Pound was relatively isolated from the life of the town, editing two issues of his little magazine *The Exile*, doing archival research for Cantos XVII–XXX, setting up in Paris performances of his opera *Villon*, and immersing himself in Dante's contemporary Guido Cavalcanti, of whom he planned a de luxe critical edition just as Cantos I–XVI and XVII–XXVII were published in sumptuous neo-gothic limited editions. When the Cavalcanti project ran aground, he took it to a Genoa printer and issued the edition at his own expense, with an Italian frontispiece, and no indication of the editor's name: only his initials on the back cover and at the top of the Italian foreword: "AD LECTOREM E.P." This shows how Pound could never really distinguish public from private. Were readers to take this edition as "printed for the author" and available only from him? On the other hand Pound's colossal ego goes hand in hand with his modesty. His imprint is everywhere in this strange and ill-fated book, yet his name appears nowhere. This is the concept he was to express memorably in Canto LXXXI: "To have, with decency, knocked . . . To have gathered from the air a live tradition" (LXXXI/542). It's not the individual talent but the tradition that matters. The love goddess speaks to and through the poet.

Pound's Rapallo *Cavalcanti* found its way into the hands of Mario Praz, the future dean of English studies in Italy, who wrote a witty and wicked review of Pound's foolhardy venture.[2] It was easy to point out that a man who barely spoke Italian could hardly attempt a critical edition of a thirteenth-century poet – as if an Italian poet-scholar with a sketchy knowledge of England and English were to attempt a scholarly edition of Donne! But Pound's *Guido Cavalcanti Rime* is to be read as the work of a poet copying for his own use the text of another poet. Since Pound believed he had some authority as a medievalist, he couched his transcription in the trappings of textual study, and wrote a prefatory essay, the often-quoted "Mediaevalism" (*LE*, 148–55), which is full of wild statements and generalizations about "Mediterranean" sanity – as if this had anything to do with Cavalcanti. It had much more to do with Pound on the tennis courts in Rapallo, discovering his new neighborhood, visiting Portovenere and the so-called Byron Grotto, entertaining Yeats with puzzling explanations of the form of *The Cantos* and with stories about the Rapallo cats.[3]

Yeats and his wife were in Rapallo on and off from 1928 to 1930: for Yeats a most productive period, in which he found time to compose (among other things) *A Packet for Ezra Pound* with its stately description of the village, and drafted "Byzantium." Yeats was even spurred on by Pound to write a response to his friend's Cavalcanti studies, an essay that Yeats never finished. But with characteristic genius, he had gotten to the root of the matter: "I would delight to comment upon it in this strain," he wrote Pound on September 23, 1928: "'Whether this is Cavalcanti or not I neither know nor care – it is Ezra & that is enough for me.' I would then go on, all out of my own head & without compromising you in any way, & say that it was your religion, your philosophy, your creed, your collect, your nightly & morning prayers...."[4] This is the attitude we must take to Pound's multifarious undertakings if we are to make anything of them: "it is Ezra & that is enough for me."

Pound celebrated his arrival in Rapallo by writing in "Mediaevalism" of the "Tuscan" aesthetic: "The senses...seem to project for a few yards beyond the body. Effect of a decent climate where a man leaves his nerve-set open, or allows it to tune in to its ambience, rather than struggling, as a northern race has to for self-preservation, to guard the body from assaults of weather" (*LE*, 152). This is Pound the sun-worshiper, the priest of sex, *à la* D.H. Lawrence. But he also wants to allow for energies and perceptions of a visionary kind, yet distinct from Christian tradition, and he characteristically looks for historical precedent, in Provence and Tuscany as later in China. He is always in the act of teaching his version of history:

> Builders had kept the proportion,
>   did Jacques de Molay
>   know these proportions?
> and was Erigena ours?   (xc/625)

That is, were these mystics and thinkers adept in the "mysteries of light" – were they members of a secret tradition? The question is partly rhetorical. This is Pound's tradition, and he has little doubt that he belongs to a line of elect. Pound never forgets the role of instructor. Even in the middle of the Chaucerian and Biblical pastiche of his most quoted Canto, LXXXI, he finds time to tell us that between Chaucer and Shakespeare, so far as words set to music go, "for 180 years almost nothing" happened. The notion of forms and ideas resurfacing after going underground for long stretches is often suggested, and *The Cantos* actually intends a mapping of periods and people in which the sacred flame burned again.

    In Rapallo Pound believed he had found a place where he could work quietly, enjoy the climate, reach Paris in fourteen hours, Rome in six, Venice in eight, and thus get the best of town life and of the European capitals whenever he needed them. In a piece written in the 1930s, he compared the quiet he enjoyed in Brancusi's Paris studio to having his mind "sluiced clean . . . in the Gulf of Tigullio on a June day on a bathing raft with the sun on the lateen sails" (*EPVA*, 307). His friend Father Desmond Chute, a British resident of Rapallo, remembered being introduced to *The Cantos* when Yeats showed him the opening lines of the large-format *Cantos XVII–XXVII*: "So that the vines burst from my fingers . . ."[5] Pound is seeking to retrieve in his poetry the "Tuscan" mood, the sensual yet clear vision which he attributes to Guido, Dante, and company.

Later, he would also stress among the reasons for his move to Italy his interest in fascism, which had come to power in 1922 and was well established by early 1927, when Hemingway and his friend Guy Hickock visited him in Rapallo, and Hemingway gave his scathing account of the "new" Italy in the story "Che Ti Dice La Patria?" (comprising three episodes set in Liguria). In the Rapallo-edited *Exile*, Pound did in fact quote with approval both Lenin and Mussolini: his imagination responded to men of action who seemed to have simple answers to big problems and who had a flair for resounding phrases. Mussolini was originally a socialist journalist who eventually had his sayings inscribed on the walls of every Italian town to indoctrinate his countrymen.

The Cantos is similarly a collection of quotations that Pound believes to be impressive: like Mussolini, Pound is under the illusion that words can clinch the matter, do the trick. Concurrently, he insists that words are to be "precise." Thus, on the opening page of *The Pisan Cantos* he mourns and celebrates the "dead bullock" Mussolini (thus alluding to sexual prowess) and then goes on to list other purveyors of words that are action: "but a precise definition / transmitted thus Sigismundo / thus Duccio, thus Zuan Bellin, or trastevere with La Sposa / Sponsa Christi in mosaic till our time / deification of emperors" (LXXIV/445). Art and power go together: Mussolini and Sigismondo Malatesta, as exponents of the "precise definition" and presumably of "secret knowledge," appear together with the painters Duccio and "Zuan Bellin" (Giovanni Bellini in Venetian spelling as in Canto XLV) and with the anonymous mosaic-makers of Santa Maria in Trastevere, a Rome cathedral, on the apsis of which is portrayed Mary's mystical wedding to Christ (the theme of spousal, *sposa*, is never too far).[6]

THE EZUVERSITY

From 1930 Pound began to write more frequently in Italian, contributing items to *L'Indice*, a Genoa literary journal edited by Gino Saviotti

(1892–1980) and published by the same house that issued the salvaged *Guido Cavalcanti Rime*. After *L'Indice* folded, Saviotti and Pound launched the *Supplemento Letterario* of the Rapallo weekly *Il Mare*. Pound contributed his notes ("Appunti"), brief articles, an interview with Ford Madox Ford (in the first issue, August 20, 1932), and arranged for the reprint of earlier essays in Italian translation ("Vorticism", "French Poets"). With time he became fluent in written Italian, and his pieces were probably printed with minor editorial revisions (especially of such arcane matters as the Italian use of apostrophes that Pound never mastered).[7] Also, his Italian foreword to *Guido Cavalcanti Rime* is clearly his original work. This long rapport with the Italian language would eventually lead to the composition during 1944–5 of the two brilliant Italian Cantos LXXII–LXXIII, and of numerous Italian drafts for subsequent Cantos that were never completed but that Pound was to make use of (from memory) in writing *The Pisan Cantos*.[8] Italian had become Pound's second tongue, and in his use of it he proved his genius for language. His wartime Italian pamphlets, *Carta da visita*, *Oro e lavoro*, *Confucio: Studio integrale*, etc., some of them printed in Rapallo, all show an effective use of the language.

In his editorial work for the *Supplemento Letteraria*, Pound secured the collaboration of several associates, among them Basil Bunting, also living in Rapallo at the time, and the Spaniard Juan Ramon Masoliver and the German Eugen Haas, who were language instructors at the University of Genoa. Masoliver went on to have a significant career as writer and critic. Thus, in Rapallo by the early 1930s Pound had a circle of friends and collaborators, and the *Supplemento* still makes interesting if uneven reading.[9] Filippo Tommaso Marinetti, the founder and impresario of futurism, also contributed some items. It was at this time that Pound buried the hatchet and began commending Marinetti and his companions. (In the days of vorticism he had attacked them, but that was partly because vorticism was so obviously an offspring of futurism that it had to denounce its parent to make room for itself.)

The *Supplemento Letteraria*, however, remained a provincial organ, though involved in literary sparring with the more powerful figures of the period. Saviotti, Pound's co-editor, shared his contempt for the more fashionable French writers like Proust and Valéry, and for their Italian imitators, but had little to offer as an alternative. Pound printed a story (in Italian translation) by Robert McAlmon, whom he praised as a first-rate writer, and he often wrote that there was nothing in contemporary Italian literature that interested him, or that was "modern" enough. But during the war he discovered Enrico Pea's *Moscardino*, a graphic short novel

about country life in Tuscany, and produced an effective English translation (marred by many misunderstandings to be sure). For once his critical
acumen stood him in good stead, for Pea's poetic prose is still praised by
the cognoscenti. (He remains, nonetheless, a minor writer.)

Another important department of Pound's Rapallo life was his work as a
composer (he drafted a second opera on *Cavalcanti*), concert organizer, and
promoter of musical research. Here, his chief associates were Olga Rudge
and Gerhart Münch. Pound would introduce their concerts in the City
Hall with short talks, and brought distinguished musicians to Rapallo. He
celebrated this in *The Pisan Cantos* by reproducing the violin score of his
beloved "Song of the Birds" by Jannequin-Da Milano-Münch, an example
of the intermittences of beauty, and by lovingly instructing himself and his
readers: "Lawes and Jenkyns guard thy rest / Dolmetsch ever by thy guest"
(LXXXI/539).

Remembering the months spent in Rapallo in the mid 1930s, James
Laughlin called Pound's generous and heady instruction to the young
like himself "The Ezuversity." This was not solely a metaphor. In spring
1936, when Italy was overrun by enthusiasm for Mussolini's apparently
successful invasion of Ethiopia, Pound and his associates advocated the
creation in Rapallo of an "International Cultural Center," run by the *Mare*
group and catering to "students of outstanding capacity," while also serving
the more humble function of "welcoming and preparing serious tourists
and travelling scholars" of little means for their Italian travels.[10] Though
nothing came of this, *Guide to Kulchur*, composed in 1937, can be read as
the syllabus of the ideal Ezuversity (inclusive of a compact and magisterial
travel guide to France and Italy).

In this way Pound found in Rapallo a home for all his interests – literature, music, economics, history, education, even anthropology – and a
group of sympathetic collaborators. He also found there vigorous earthy
roots for his poetry. It is significant that when in Canto LXXX he recapitu-
lated his life as three acts of departure, he wrote:

> so that leaving America I brought with me $80
> and England a letter of Thomas Hardy's
> and Italy one eucalyptus pip
> from the salita [path] that goes up from Rapallo
> (if I go)
> (LXXX/520)

From America he brings the indispensable dollar, from England the Lesson
of the Master (Hardy, Yeats, Blunt in Canto LXXXI), from Italy the secret

of the seed, of nature, and a social dream, a utopia, in which culture and nature are one. If this was not to be in historical fact, it could always be imagined in the poem.

JOURNEYS TO ROME

Though Pound visited Rome early on, and described with irony the funeral of a Roman patrician in Canto XXVIII, he usually associated the city with its sumptuous baroque monuments, which were alien to his purist tastes. The Sack of Rome in 1527 was to him the symbolic date in which the dissociation of sensibility set in. One of the collaborators of the *Mare Literary Supplement*, Francesco Monotti, served as a secretary to Mussolini and may have arranged the meeting between Pound and the Duce of January 30, 1933, recounted in Canto XLI. Pound recorded with approval Mussolini's comment that *The Cantos* was "divertente," and elsewhere (XCIII/646) his question "Why do you want to put your ideas in order?", to which he answered "For my poem." Though there have been claims to the contrary, Mussolini remained unaware for the remainder of his life of Pound's existence.[11] Italy was full of poetasters pestering him with praise. He was only interested in Pound as a journalist. Monotti also took an interest in the aborted Cavalcanti edition, and tried to publish it under the auspices of a fascist institution – to no avail (possibly because it was not difficult for an Italian to call the bluff of Pound's Cavalcanti scholarship).

In 1939 Pound became a regular writer for *Meridiano di Roma*, a national literary weekly, and in 1941–3 was often in Rome to record his broadcasts for Rome Radio. By now he was familiar with the city and had identified monuments to his liking, like the Santa Maria Trastevere mosaic of Canto LXXIV. For Christmas 1938 he brought his daughter Mary to Rome, introduced her to his friend Archbishop Annibale Pisani of the Vatican Library, and hurried her from St. Peter's oppressive nineteenth-century decorations to the medieval churches he admired: "this [i.e., the meeting with Pisani] was before St. Peter's, / in move toward a carrozza [horse-carriage] / from the internal horrors (mosaic) / en route to Santa Sabina / & San Domenico / where the spirit is clear in the stone" (XCIII/643). He was to refer again to the contrast between baroque St. Peter's and his beloved medieval churches in the upbeat catalogue at the end of *Thrones* (CIX/794).

In Rome Pound was pleased that some fascist officials showed willingness to act promptly on his requests, and to fight for their ideals when the time came: "[Delcroix] grabbed his phone and called un ministro. / Bottai [minister of education] also phoned Torino / instanter, to dig up Vivaldi, /

And ministri went to the fighting line / as did old Marinetti" (xcii/641). But as often as not he met with indifference when trying to find outlets for his pamphleteering. Even *Jefferson and/or Mussolini* found no publisher in Italy until 1944, when Pound produced his own Italian adaptation of the original. When his Venetian friend Carlo Izzo, an anti-fascist at that, translated *Social Credit – An Impact*, and the editor who had expressed interest backed out, Pound wrote Izzo: "Don't tyke it to 'eart, son. If that's how they are, that is that. At any rate I am not responsible. 99% of all effort is wasted . . . hence the need of making 100 . . . Do you expect Italian editors to ANSWER letters inside of 20 days?"[12] In the lines about Bottai and Delcroix (from 1954) Pound was intent on eulogizing the fascist regime by selective examples. The reality, even for him, was different. And in 1935, at age fifty, he could separate more clearly the wish from the fact.

There are not many Rome-related epiphanies in Pound's work. One is the visit with his daughter in Canto xciii. In his effervescent *Visiting Card*, written in Italian and published in Rome in 1942, he famously claimed that "To replace the marble goddess on her pedestal at Terracina is worth more than any metaphysical argument" (*SPR*, 290). Terracina is south of Rome by the Circeo promontory. This fantasy of the return of the gods is at the center of an Italian wartime draft, in which Pound remembers getting drunk in a Rome hotel and somehow predicting the coming of the gods.[13] This may be the episode referred to in the lines "and from under the Rupe Tarpeia / drunk with wine of the Castelli / 'in the name of its god'" (lxxiv/463). The Tarpeian Cliff is an ancient Roman landmark, also the name of a restaurant. The Castelli wine is typical Roman fare, a light claret from the Frascati region.

Also, among the more obscure Pisan recollections is the "boredom of that roman on Olivia's stairs / in her vision / that stone angle all of his scenery / with the balustrade" (lxxviii/503). Even Leopold Bloom's musings could hardly beat this for obscurity, and the reason is obvious: Bloom is a created character, whereas these are Pound's "real" recollections, to some of which the key has been lost, in this case with the death of Olivia Rossetti Agresti (see above). This particular Roman was an eccentric vagabond who would beg from Olivia. Pound also wrote up his escape from Rome after the armistice of September 8, 1943, when the regular Italian army collapsed. He took to the road and mythologized his journey in *Gold and Work* ("On the 10th of September last, I walked down the Via Salaria and into the Republic of Utopia" – [*SPR*, 306]) and in Canto lxxviii/498: "the man out of Naxos past Fara Sabina." Naxos is associated with Dionysus, and Pound moves from myth (the god of frenzy) to myth (Fara Sabina is a name with ancient connotations).

Pound was to return to Rome, despondently, in 1960–1, when he spent time as a guest of a fascist diehard and gave Donald Hall his meandering *Paris Review* interview. He was quickly losing his health and his mental resilience, and Desmond O'Grady remembers him turning up at his apartment in Rome looking for a place to spend the night, still "the man out of Naxos," restless to the end.[14]

The crucial biographical fact of Pound's last phase was his estrangement from Olga Rudge between 1955 and 1962.[15] It was only when his condition became critical in early 1962 that she came again on the scene in order to rescue him – and this time to remain with him until his death. Pound's final decade in Rapallo and Venice was silent but contented, protected as he was by his wary and energetic collaborator in art and life.

NOTES

1 For details see M. Bacigalupo, "Ezra Pound's Tigullio," *Paideuma* 14.2–3 (1985): 179–209; "Ezra Pound's 'European Paideuma,'" *Paideuma* 30.1–2 (2001): 225–45; "Tigullio Itineraries: Ezra Pound and Friends," in *Ezra Pound, Language and Persona*, ed. M. Bacigalupo and W. Pratt (Genoa: University of Genoa, 2008), 373–447.

2 M. Praz, "Ezra Pound," *La Stampa* (August 13, 1932), rpt. in *Cronache letterarie anglosassoni* (Rome: Edizioni di Storia e Letteratura, 1950), I: 176–8.

3 See *CP*, 92, and W.B. Yeats, *A Vision* (London: Macmillan, 1959), 1–6.

4 Yeats in R. F. Foster, *W. B. Yeats: A Life*, II, *The Arch-Poet 1915–1939* (Oxford: Oxford University Press, 2003), 381.

5 XVII/76. See D. Chute, "Poets in Paradise," *The Listener* 55.1401 (January 5, 1956): 14.

6 "Duccio" could be the sculptor Agostino di Duccio (1418–81) who worked for Sigismondo Malatesta in Rimini, mentioned in Canto XX, but the earlier appearance of a "Duccio" in the usury Canto XLV, part of the Siena sequence, would suggest the Sienese master Duccio di Buoninsegna (1255–1318). In any case, Pound clearly approves of both artists. The Sienese Duccio would seem to be particularly pertinent because of his public function as spokesman for the Siena community. Furthermore, by the 1930s Pound knew that in Italy and elsewhere "Duccio" was always understood to refer to the Siena master, and he would have written otherwise had he wanted to remind the reader of his lesser known namesake.

7 For example, Pound always writes "Io son' la luna" (LXXVI/473, LXXX/520) for "Io son la luna", and "cantar'" (LXXII/425); "crepitar'" (LXXII/427); "son'", "veder'" (LXXII/441). In all these cases the final apostrophe is supererogatory. This may be a matter of taste, since Pound favored inconsistent and old-fashioned spelling.

However, new evidence I have seen shows that his published texts were always heavily revised by *Il Mare*'s editor.

8 See *CP*, 169–93, and M. Bacigalupo, "Ezra Pound's Cantos 72–73: An Annotated Translation," *Paideuma* 20.1–2 (1991): 9–41.

9 It has been reprinted in its entirety: *Il Mare: Supplemento letterario 1932–1933* (Rapallo: Comune, 1999).

10 E. Pound, "Rapallo centro di cultura," *Il Mare* 29.1416 (May 2, 1936): 1. See also E. Dodsworth, "Rapallo centro internazionale di cultura Fascista?", *Il Mare* 29.1408 (March 7, 1936): 1; Stock, 430.

11 Yvon de Begnac in *Taccuini mussoliniani* (Bologna: Il Mulino, 1990) claimed that Mussolini during his final years referred in de Begnac's presence to "my friend Ezra Pound," but these revelations were published only in 1990 and are (according to specialists) obvious *ex post facto* fabrications.

12 Quoted in M. Bacigalupo, "Pound/Izzo," in *Ambassadors: American Studies in a Changing World*, ed. M. Bacigalupo and G. Dowling (Genoa: University of Genoa, 2006), 72.

13 *CP*, 171–3 and M. Bacigalupo, "Cantos 72 and 73," 28–9.

14 D. O'Grady, "Ezra Pound: A Personal Memoir," *Agenda* 17.3–4 and 18.1 (1979–80): 288.

15 See M. Bacigalupo, "Sant'Ambrogio in the Half-light: Growing up near Olga Rudge and Ezra Pound," *Paideuma* 26.1 (1997): 30–1.

CHAPTER 24

Pisa

Ronald Bush

The Pisan Cantos, composed while Pound was incarcerated in the US Army Disciplinary Training Center (DTC) near Pisa in the summer of 1945, trail a long prehistory. In the late twenties and thirties Pound started preparing for the philosophical Paradiso with which he intended to conclude *The Cantos*. After 1939, though, while he was still assembling his materials, the war changed everything. Especially after the heavy Allied bombardment of Northern Italy during the last two years of World War II, Pound's focus turned from philosophy toward history. Lamenting the ruin of Italy's cultural patrimony, he composed a suite of poems in Italian beginning with what are now Cantos LXXII and LXXIII and including still unpublished texts that echo through the poem we know.

Throughout the complex evolution of Pound's Italian and English compositions, his preoccupation with memory persists. Pound's philosophical preparations concern the way memory can reunite us with our divine beginnings. The wartime Italian writings stress the power of monuments to consolidate what is sometimes called collective or cultural memory. And in *The Pisan Cantos* themselves, Pound joins both to an urgent struggle to retain his deepest self, producing a suite whose lineaments his wife Dorothy recognized immediately upon receiving it in the post. These Cantos, she wrote him back, are "your self, the memories that make up yr. person" (*LC*, 131).

PARADISO

Pound's extensive philosophical preparation for the "cielo sereno e filosofico" (serene philosophical heaven) that he told his daughter Mary in 1945 was to form the last third of *The Cantos* (*IC*, 1566) grew out of his own struggle to edit and interpret Cavalcanti's thirteenth-century canzone

"Donna mi prega." Pound had become fascinated by Cavalcanti's account of how love illuminates, rendering the mysterious way we apprehend the intellectual form of love and how that form transforms our psyche, causing us to remember our connection to divine intelligence. His speculations, first formulated in essays published in 1928 and 1929 and later collected in *Literary Essays* under the title "Cavalcanti," underpin the substantially different translations he undertook in "Cavancanti" and in Canto XXXVI.[1] Pound's prose postulates a medieval synthesis of two apparently disparate classical systems – Aristotle's rigorous definitions of substance, matter, and form, and the Neoplatonists' understanding of the emanation and return of divine intelligence, or *nous*.[2] Drawing on the all but forgotten Del Garbo commentary on Cavalcanti's poem and immersing himself in Ernst Renan's *Averroès et l'averroïsme*, Pound attempts to recapitulate the impulse that first assimilated Plotinus (d.270) to Aristotle in late classical texts such as the so-called "Theology" of Aristotle and then, in the ninth and tenth centuries, inspired Erigena (d.877) and Avicenna (d.1037). The ultimate implication of this philosophy, Pound believed, was that the soul transformed by the form of Love lifts itself into or "remembers" the realm of the active intellect – the *nous poietikos or intelligentia agens* that Aristotle postulated in *De Anima* III.v and that Avicenna and Averroes, to the consternation of St. Thomas Aquinas, insisted was both eternal and separable from the individual mind.[3]

Pound read a Latin digest of Avicenna's metaphysics in the twenties and studied Aristotle's *De Anima* in the thirties, but delayed beginning his new poems until he could properly study Erigena's Latin in Volume 122 of Migne's *Patralogia Latina*.[4] He got hold of the text in Venice in December 1939 (his readings show him using Cavalcanti's language as a gunsight), where he also spoke at length with the philosopher George Santayana. What Pound took from those encounters helped shape the rest of *The Cantos*,[5] beginning with the emotional climax of *The Pisan Cantos* as the speaker of Canto LXXXI experiences the intellectual form of Love and in transport exclaims, "What thou lovest well remains, / the rest is dross" (LXXXI / 540–1).

THE WAR

As Pound began drafting his "cielo sereno e filosofico," though, the relentless stresses of living in enemy territory with foreign income blocked, foreign post halted, food scarce, and American bombers overhead inevitably took their toll. As he lamented in July 1943, he greatly desired to sort out

whether Western thought had progressed or declined since the Middle
Ages and to ask questions such as, "Have we got better at thinkin'? Do we
think with greater clarity? Or has the so-called program of science merely
got us all cluttered up mentally and pitched us into greater confusion?,"
but he was prevented from doing so because of "this tiresome war" (*EPS*,
373–4).

At that point, Pound's thoughts turned toward a function of memory
not entirely divorced from *nous*, but heavily inflected by Italian suffering
and Italian politics.[6] During the winter of 1943 and again in the summer
and fall of 1944, Allied bombing aimed at anti-aircraft installations on the
Ligurian coast and at the port city of Genoa damaged buildings around
Rapallo, including churches. After Florence fell in September 1944, the
raids only increased. To the east on the so-called Gothic Line, Rimini and
Forlì continued to see heavy fighting, and the fate of Bologna hung in the
balance. At the end of 1944, the Allies, exhausted by this effort, dug in
for the winter. Though they managed to take Ravenna on December 5,
Bologna remained in Axis hands until the following spring.[7] Meanwhile, in
Europe above the Alps the Battle of the Bulge raged on, allowing Mussolini
a last hope that the invasion of Europe might be turned back.

In response to the bombs that day by day decimated the architecture of
Italy, Mussolini's government, now based in northern Italy, launched a propaganda campaign to depict the bombing as cultural terrorism – the kind
of thing that Robert Bevan has recently called a deliberate attempt to erase
"the memories, history and identity attached to architecture and place."[8]
Hoping to win back ordinary Italians to fascism, Mussolini's Ministry of
Popular Culture urged the press to emphasize how much of Italy's cultural
patrimony had been damaged beyond repair. And headed by fascist sympa-
thizers, the press complied.[9] Genoa's *Il Secolo*'s *XIX*, for example, carried as
a regular feature, "I monumenti che il nemico ci distrugge" (Monuments
the enemy has destroyed). The installment that appeared on Sunday June
4, 1944 told of the collapse during late 1943 and early 1944 of the Tempio
Malatestiano in Rimini. This account shook Pound to the bone, recounting
as it did the destruction of his personal paradigm for Renaissance culture.[10]

The damage in Rimini, though, proved to be only one of many shocks the
press administered that season, not only in *Il Secolo* but in other newspapers
Pound read, including the anti-Semite Farinacci's *Regime Fascista* and the
Corriere della Sera of Milan, the most important newspaper still under
fascist sway.[11] In 1944 the *Corriere* copied *Il Secolo* in its own series, "L'Italia
Artistica Mutilata," and on September 4 announced the destruction of
another of Pound's cherished monuments, this time the brilliant mosaic

chamber outside Ravenna commonly known as the mausoleum of the
Empress Aelia Galla Placidia. According to the *Corriere*, Ravenna had
suffered multiple attacks, and almost all the great public buildings of the
city that had once been the capital of the Byzantine Exarchate had been
badly damaged.

Another running series featured in the *Corriere* was called "Sangue Italiano" (Italian blood). These pieces systematically lauded the attempts of
Italy's citizen heroes and Mussolini's new Black Shirt brigades to assist
Germany's defense of La Patria. On October 1, under the headline "Sangue
Italiano: L'eroina di Rimini" (the heroine of Rimini), the paper told the
stirring but apparently fabricated story of an "anonymous, radiant heroine
from Rimini," who, having been "raped by two Australians," deliberately
led a group of Canadian soldiers into a minefield and, dying, announced,
"Ho vendicato il mio onore" – I have vindicated my honor.[12] And on
Monday November 20, 1944, the subject concerned another patriotic sacrifice amid battles around Forlì, not far from Rimini in the direction of
Bologna. Below headlines that triumphed Mussolini's "fede nella riscossa
della Patria" (faith in the resurgence of the Fatherland) and trumpeted the
promise of one of Mussolini's officials that "ritorneremo" – we Italians shall
return – the paper told the story of "Sangue Romagnolo" ("Blood of the
Romagna") in the form of a story (possibly also fabricated) of anonymous
women who, becoming "voluntarie della morte" (volunteers for death) in
Mussolini's cause, risked their lives at Forlì's gate by shielding fascist snipers
and obstructing the entrance of Allied troops.

In Rapallo, Pound responded viscerally to the pro-Axis animus of these
pieces and was moved to begin new Cantos – as a gesture of loyalty, in
Italian. The most important single spur to his composition was a long summary of wartime damage in the Sunday *Corriere* of December 3, 1944, which
was immediately followed by a patriotic obituary for Filippo-Tommaso
Marinetti. After a subhead that railed against "La calata degli iconoclasti"
(the descent of the iconoclasts), the summary proffered horrifying pictures
of the bomb-damaged Basilica of Sant'Ambrogio in Milan and the Tempio
Malatestiano in Rimini and related ruin all over Northern Italy. The cities
of Forlì and Ravenna, it observed, "have not had peace for months," and
the great churches of Ravenna had been reduced to ruins. But the *Corriere*'s
core message emerged in its lead: "From sacred and profane monuments to
masterpieces of painting, sculpture and the decorative arts, the catalogue
of destruction is endless: *once more the barbarian storm has descended on
soil that tends the traces and the spirit of the highest civilisations*" (emphasis
mine). The very fire of civilisation itself ("il fuoco delle più nobili civiltà"),

readers were told, rooted as it was in Italian soil (*terra*), hung in the balance in a conflict between culture and barbarism.

The true barbarism of the American bombers, the *Corriere* explained, consisted of a destructive "iconoclasm" – a revulsion from artistic form – shared by Italy's more insidious cosmopolitan noncombatants. The ruin of Italian culture owed as much to international (read: Jewish) finance as to Allied bombing. Therefore, even if Italy's remaining treasures were to escape the chaos of battle, "in the wake of the invasion a crowd of special interests ("una folla di interessi") has targeted our artistic heritage." Financial speculation and inflation had put in place an art market that would spirit away what had not been destroyed, unless Italians responded with "the duty to resist . . . the allurements of plundering finance" ("allettamenti della moneta rapinatrice"). As the *Corriere* consoled its readers, however, because of the efforts of fascist Italy the cause of European civilisation had not yet been lost. Some monuments had survived, and Ravenna and Bologna continued to resist. Crucially, the article emphasized the nation-building work of Dante, who fostered "the resurrection of the nation" ("la resurrezione della Patria") and whose tomb continued to protect the still untaken Ravennese "fragrant pine wood" ("la dolce pineta") immortalized in *Purgatorio* XXVIII:20.

Two weeks later, at 11 o'clock on December 16, 1944, Pound listened to the radio as Mussolini, making what was to be his last major public speech from the Teatro Lirico in Milan, called on Italians to take heart from the Allied difficulties in the Marches and farther north in Belgium and to mount a counter-offensive ("riscossa") to take back their native land.[13] The following day the *Corriere* provided a full text of the speech under the headline "Da Milano E' Squillata La Diana della Riscossa" ("the reveille for a counterattack has been sounded in Milan").

ITALIAN DRAFTS

The *Corriere* stories of November and December 1944 propelled Pound into four months of almost continuous composition in Italian, beginning on or soon after December 3 and continuing until April 1945. The Italian propaganda campaign amplified the shame Pound felt as a countryman of the Allied bombardiers and reinforced his conviction (later incorporated into *The Pisan Cantos* themselves) that the war was a contest between a civilized culture of religion and art and a barbaric culture of iconoclasm. In both phases of his work, Pound honors the *Corriere*'s admonition to preserve the memory of what had been so recently lost. And, especially in the Italian verses, Pound focuses on a dialogue with ghosts – a series of great souls whose courage is meant to inspire resistance to the random destruction of the Italian culturescape and whose expression recalled the reigning spirit of Latin civilization.[14]

Within a month of reading "La calata degli iconoclasti" and two weeks after Mussolini's call for a *riscossa*, Pound had completed two poems echoing Mussolini's call to action. These would eventually take their place as Cantos LXXII and LXXIII of the published *Cantos*.[15] In them, the recently deceased Marinetti himself cries out for action. Rather than quoting Mussolini directly, however, the Cantos allow two historical analogues to voice fascist defiance in Mussolini's provincial home, the Romagna. In Canto LXXII, which records "Rimini arsa e Forlì distrutta" (LXXII / 428: "Rimini is burned, Forlì is in ruins") and suggests the ruin of Ravenna in the disturbed sleep of Galla Placidia, the primary spokesman is Ezzelino da Romano, for thirty-four years the Ghibelline Lord of the March of Treviso and a figure in *Inferno* XII. At Canto LXXII/427 it is Ezzolino who repeats the government's pledge, "torneremo" – we will return. In Canto LXXIII on the other hand, the Florentine aristocratic poet Guido Cavalcanti announces Mussolini's "diana / della riscossa" (LXXIII/438) and retells with admiration the *Corriere*'s story of the heroines of Rimini.[16]

Buoyant with his progress, Pound extended his composition in Italian to an expansive suite that, like the "Sangue Italiano" articles in the *Corriere*, aimed to raise Italian morale by providing avatars of courage. Like Cantos LXXII and LXXIII, these unpublished Italian poems dramatize the defiance exhibited by the citizen heroes of Rimini and Forlì. The new poems, however, also affirm art's power to preserve the remembered monuments that on December 3 the *Corriere*, had called "segni della nostra secolare supremazia civile [che] saranno ricordate, sempre, come prove della barbarie altrui" – "the traces of our secular civic supremacy [that] will be remembered, always, along with the barbarism of others." Pound touches on this central theme in a quiet moment of Canto LXXII, where the spirit of Galla Placidia recalls the music of the past. Fragments written immediately after Cantos LXXII and LXXIII echo Placidia's melancholy in the voice of a young girl – a *sfollata* (homeless refugee) of the kind Pound himself had become after he was displaced from his flat in Rapallo. Envisioned on the hillpath (*salita*) above Rapallo, the waif speaks of herself as a wandering Madonna, displaced like "'l'Assunta" (the Virgin of the Assumption) from one of Liguria's bombed churches.

From the internal coherence of the surviving texts and from provisional schemas Pound left among the papers, we can piece together the structure of Pound's never completed Italian sequence, which extends to dozens of pages of rough typescript drafts and produced semi-finished typescripts of two poems labeled Canto LXXIV and LXXV.[17] The most authoritative schema runs as follows:

> Salita
> Cunizza.
> =
> [shift
>   basinio
> courage
>   <Sidg.
>   *La Rocca*
>   Cat Sf.
>   uscita
>   A[s]sunta
>   Erigena
>   ⎰Eliseo
>   ⎱Imp.

Pound's outline begins with his own visionary encounters on the *salita* of Rapallo – first with *la sfollata* and then with the Renaissance poet Basinio of Parma, whom Pound encounters on the ancient Via Aurelia in the company of his patron Sigismondo Malatesta on the way to finalize a treaty. Basinio recounts to Pound a fading vision of the great thirteenth-century beauty, Ezzelino da Romano's sister, "Cunizza." The sequence then shifts to two great outbursts of defiance – Sigismondo Malatesta's blast against the corruptions of the modern world (modeled after Sordello's rage in *Purgatorio* VI) and Caterina Sforza's ringing statement of contempt for her captors on the walls of her fortress ("La Rocca") in Forlì. Malatesta, lord of Rimini, a legendary patron of the arts and a fierce scourge of papal Rome, gives historical resonance to the Axis defenders of his home city. And Caterina Sforza, the great Renaissance virago and ruler of Forlì, epitomizes the spirit of her heroic descendants at Forlì's gates. According to Guicciardini, Caterina, addressing the rebels who thought they could safely allow her temporarily to leave the city because they were holding her children for ransom, once safely on the walls of a nearby fort "lifted her skirt and exclaimed defiantly, 'Don't you think, you fools, that I have the stuff to make others?'"[18] (On another occasion, rather than surrender to Cesare Borgia, she attempted to blow the powder magazine under her own castle aerie – "il Paradiso.")

Pound's outline then rises out of its wartime inferno. After a Landoresque imaginary dialogue between Scotus "Erigena" and Dante, the suite ends with an ambiguous Lotus-like "Eliseo" (Elysium) and an equally ambiguous limbo populated by all-too human "Imperatori" (Emperors) – especially Hadrian – and by (a figure identified in other versions of the schema) Lorenzo de' Medici.[19] Its real climax, though, occurs before "Erigena" in "l'Assunta." Strongly anticipating Canto LXXIV/466 of the published *Pisan Cantos*, which testifies to the resurgent power of "ΕΙΚΟΝΣ" ("certain images" "formed in the mind"), Pound presents "Assunta" as an icon, both in the sense of a sacred object and as an Aristotelian aid to memory.[20]

IN THE CAMP

At Easter 1945, Pound informed his daughter Mary that he had drafted new Cantos but had not gone on with them (*IC*, 1569). Pondering their future, Pound himself was hurtled into another life. By May 1945 the Americans took Rapallo and on May 2 he tried to surrender to the US Army. After much confusion, a near execution by Italian *partigiani*, and weeks of interrogation in Genoa by the FBI, he was transferred on May 24 to an open-air cage in the US Army Disciplinary Training Center (DTC) near Pisa, to be held there until the US government saw fit to proceed with a trial for treason.[21] The Center harboured some soldiers turned real criminals, among them rapists and murderers. But the camp was also a rehabilitation center for soldiers convicted of lesser crimes, who later were returned to combat.[22] Pound remained there, just short of sixty years old and forbidden to speak to a soul, for about three weeks, under a relentless sun alternating with the pelting rain and evening dampness of an Italian summer. He then collapsed, complaining of strained eyesight and suffering symptoms that included "violent and hysterical terror," "claustrophobia," "confusion," and a temporary but "complete loss of memory" – signs that the camp doctors feared might be "premonitory" of a mental breakdown.[23] (Later he told a psychiatrist that he felt "as though the upper third of [his] brain were missing" and that "[my] mainspring [had been] busted."[24])

Pound was removed from the open cage a day or two before June 13 and on June 18 assigned an officer's tent in the camp's medical compound, still technically forbidden to speak to fellow inmates. At that point, his Italian drafts still in his head but his identity wavering, he began once more to compose, this time in English. By day he wrote his verse longhand, using pencil and small writing pads. In the evenings, permitted the use of an army typewriter, he recopied and revised, cursing his mistakes. (When he neglected to make corrections before pulling the pages, he was forced laboriously to reinsert his top copy and two carbons. He therefore sometimes corrected the individual leaves by hand, separately and inconsistently, and soon was working with hopelessly mixed sets.) Starting around the beginning of July, by July 14 he had completed sixty mansuscript pages of Canto LXXIV, only then to radically revise them, opening up material for the rest of the suite. He finished Canto LXXIV by July 26, Canto LXXVI by August 2, Canto LXXVIII by August 7, Canto LXXX by September 1, Canto LXXXII by September 8, and Canto LXXXIII on September 14.[25] At that point, Pound thought he had finished his work. On October 2 he wrote his wife Dorothy that "I have done a Decad 74 / 83 . . . which dont seem any worse than the first 70" (*LC*, 101). But when she mentioned the death of J.P. Angold, a correspondent and promising poet, and he learned that several fascist collaborators were facing death, Pound decided to compose a coda to the completed sequence. The new Canto (LXXXIV) began with a cry of grief, and before he knew it had turned into a bitter farewell to 'il Capo [Mussolini], / Pierre [Laval], [and] Vidkun [Quisling]" (LXXXIV/559). In effect, this unforeseen conclusion reinforced the sequence's political tenor, and Pound finished the job by moving ten angry and as yet unplaced lines, beginning "The enormous tragedy of the dream in the peasant's bent shoulders" to the opening of Canto LXXIV.

A less political account of *The Pisan Cantos* was anticipated by Dorothy Pound, when she, before she had even received a letter from Ezra, reminded him of a project they had spoken about previously: "I only hope captivity is not proving bad for your health, & that you are able to work at some writing or other. The moment perhaps for those 'memories'?" (*LC*, 91). In Peter Makin's words, "the *Pisan Cantos* is, first, a simply cry of pain and, second, a naming-over of what has been known, sorrowing over the lost, and trying to find, in what is left, some hope-worthy meaning and reason to go on.'[26] At the end of Canto LXXIV, Pound alludes to the philosophical account of memory embodied by "Donna mi prega" ("nec accidens est but an element / in the mind's make-up," LXXIV/469) and to the Italian drafts' admonition to remember Italy's destroyed patrimony ("stone after stone of beauty cast down / and authenticities disputed by parasites," LXXIV/468). But the Canto goes beyond both, urgently improvising a twentieth-century poetic idiom nervous and flexible enough to articulate the most fleeting nuance of a man on the verge of drowning who saves himself by the elemental exercise of his mnemonic power:

> How soft the wind under Taishan
> > where the sea is remembered
> out of hell, the pit
> out of the dust and glare evil
> > > (LXXIV/469)

Perhaps the most attractive feature of *The Pisan Cantos*, though, is that in his request for self-redemption Pound ultimately transcends himself. Haunted by the work of François Villon, another "poet and gaol-bird" (*SR*, 167) placed among common criminals and charged with a capital crime, Pound discovered his poem's definitive form as he responded to the rhetorical stance of Villon's "Testament." Not only did he tune his ear to the complex mixture of tough talk and compassionate lyricism that drives Villon's reminiscences in, for example, "Le Testament"'s stanza XXIX (which Pound translated in *The Spirit of Romance* as "Where are the gracious gallants / That I beheld in times gone by. / Singing so well, so well speaking, / So pleasant in act and in word. / Some are dead and stiffened, / Of them there is nothing more now. / May they have rest, but in Paradise, / And God save the rest of them," *SR*, 171); but he imitated Villon's ongoing dialogue with the rough crew of criminals around him. The result inflected *The Pisan Cantos* toward a poetic dialogue with other voices and other perspectives. And Villon's precedent did more than encourage Pound to import into the poem the real words of his fellow inmates and his guards. It also propelled the suite toward genuine sympathy. In a prominent example, we are shown a black guard providing the table on which Pound composes, speaking a negro dialect that might have inspired derision but instead is perceived as true grace:

> thank Benin for this table ex packing box
> "doan yu tell no one I made it"
>   from a mask fine as any in Frankfurt
> "It'll get you offn th' ground"
>   (LXXXI/538–9)

It is this kind of prison dialogue that moves *The Pisan Cantos* into Villon's universal compassion, which Pound had observed in *The Spirit of Romance* and entertained in *Le Testament* (his 1923 opera based on Villon's texts), but did not truly enter before Pisa.[27] More than anything else in the poem, such dialogues effect Pound's movement beyond broken pride toward forgiveness, restoring his power to feel. So in Canto LXXX, an echo of Villon's plea in "Rondeau," "repos donnez a cils"[28] (grant him rest), elicits an echo in Pound's own French that both sounds the keynote of an enlarged humanity and marks the apex of the poem's achievement: "Les larmes que j'ai creées m'indondent / Tard, très tard je t'ai connue, La Tristesse, / I have been hard as youth sixty years" (LXXX/533).

NOTES

1 The full set of Pound's writings on Cavalcanti can be found in *CAV*. For the broad outlines of Pound's interpretation, see Peter Makin, *Pound's Cantos* (London: Allen and Unwin, 1985), 186–95.

2 Pound's irresistible pull toward Plotinus' idea of man's participation in the sea of pure intelligence was a persistent theme in his career. (See Peter Liebreghts, *Ezra Pound and Neoplatonism* [Madison, NJ: Farleigh Dickinson University Press, 2004].) Starting in 1928, he was delighted to discover that the great Arab philosophers, transmitted via Ernest Renan, burnished its lustre with Aristotelian authority. In Renan's *Averroès et l'averroïsme* (Paris: Michel Lévy Frères, 1861), 134–5, 142ff., the mind is imagined as interfacing with the pure and objective receptivity of the agent intellect, which, in a phrase Pound never forgot, is said to be a "transparent crystal."

3 On the continuing controversy among Western and Arabic commentators about Aristotle's notion of the active intellect, see Herbert A. Davidson, *Alfarabi, Avicenna, and Averroes on Intellect: Their Cosmologies, Theories of the Active Intellect, and Theories of the Human Intellect* (Oxford: Oxford University Press, 1992).

4 Maria Luisa Ardizzone, in *Ezra Pound e la scienza: Scritti inediti o rari* (Milan: Scheiwiller, 1987) 31, 47 [n66], identifies the edition of *De Anima* that Pound consulted: the Italian condensation, *Aristotele, Dell'Anima. Passi Scelti e comentati da Vito Fazio-Allmayer* (Bari: Laterza, 1924).

5 For a serious if sometimes misleading treatment of this material, see Maria Luisa Ardizzone, "Pound's Language in *Rock-Drill*: Two Theses for a Genealogy," *Paideuma* 21 (1993): 121–48; "The Genesis and Structure of Pound's Paradise: Looking at the Vocabulary," *Paideuma* 22 (1993): 13–37; and "Pound as Reader of Aristotle and His Medieval Commentators and Dante's *Commedia*," in: *Dante e Pound*, ed. Maria Luisa Ardizzone (Ravenna: Lungo Editore, 1998), 205–28.

6 A more complete account of the impact of these conditions on *The Pisan Cantos* can be found in Ronald Bush, "'The Descent of the Barbarians': *The Pisan Cantos* and Cultural Memory," *Modernism/Modernity* 14 (2007): 71–95.

7 The most detailed account of these battles that I know is contained in Amadeo Montemaggi, *Linea Gotica 1944* (Rimini: Quaraldi, 2004).

8 Robert Bevan, *The Destruction of Memory: Architecture at War* (London: Reaktion Books, 2006), 8. Bevan adds, "These buildings are attacked not because they are in the path of a military objective: to their destroyers, they *are* the objective."

9 See Lawrence Rainey, *Ezra Pound and the Monument of Culture* (Chicago: University of Chicago Press, 1991), 212.

10 *Ibid.*, 212–13.

11 Tim Redman, *Ezra Pound and Italian Fascism* (Cambridge: Cambridge University Press, 1991) 197–8. Redman (240), notes that the *Corriere*'s pliant position in regard to Fascism can be adduced from the cordial relations between its

editor, Ermanno Amicucci, and Fernando Mezzasoma, the RSI's Minister of Popular Culture and a correspondent of Pound's.

12 Rainey, *Monument of Culture*, 244–5.

13 Pound recorded the time and the day he heard the speech on p. 7 of the notebook in which he drafted Cantos LXXII and LXXIII. Manuscript in Yale University, Beinecke Library, YCAL MSS 53, Box 29, folder 624. All previously unpublished material by Ezra Pound, Copyright © 2010 by the Trustees of the Ezra Pound Literary Property Trust; used by permission of New Directions Publishing Corp., agents for the Trustees. All published material by Ezra Pound used by permission of New Directions Publishing Corp.

14 Charles Olson, in his account of conversations that took place immediately after Pound's forced return from Pisa to Washington DC, notes that Pound was "himself excited at having rediscovered a Dante method. He especially mentioned the use of a ghost to speak." See Catherine Seelye, ed., *Charles Olson & Ezra Pound: An Encounter at St. Elizabeth's* (New York: Viking, 1975), 69.

15 For commentary on Cantos LXXII and LXXIII, see Rainey, *Ezra Pound and the Monument of Culture*; Eva Hesse, *Ezra Pound: Die Ausgefallenen Cantos LXXII Und LXXIII* (Zurich: Arche, 1991); and Robert Casillo, "Fascists of the Final Hour: Pound's Italian Cantos," in *Fascism, Aesthetics, and Culture* ed. Richard J. Golson (Hanover: University Press of New England, 1992), 98–127. Annotated English translations of Cantos LXXII and LXXIII have now been published (followed by annotated English translations of the typescripts of the Italian Cantos LXXIV and LXXV) by Massimo Bacigalupo. See "Ezra Pound's Cantos 72 and 73: An Annotated Translation," *Paideuma* 20 (1991): 11–41. Cantos LXXII and LXXIII now appear in the *Cantos* on pages 423–41.

16 For readings of Cantos LXXII and LXXIII that note some of these contemporary resonances, see Casillo, "Fascists of the Final Hour," and Rainey, *Ezra Pound and the Monument of Culture*.

17 See Ronald Bush, "Towards Pisa: More From the Archives about Pound's Italian Cantos," *Agenda* 34 (1996/7): 89–124. The provenance of all of Pound's typescripts referred to below unless otherwise indicated is Yale University, Beinecke Library, YCAL MSS 53, Box 29, folder 627. For an annotated reading of the provisional Cantos LXXIV and LXXV, see Bacigalupo, "An Annotated Translation," and Ronald Bush, "'Quiet, Not Scornful'?: The Composition of the *Pisan Cantos*," in *A Poem Containing History: The Cantos of Ezra Pound*, ed. Lawrence Rainey (Ann Arbor: University of Michigan Press, 1997), 169–212.

18 See Ernst Breisach, *Caterina Sforza: A Renaissance Virago* (Chicago: University of Chicago Press, 1967). Breisach (103) alludes not only to Guicciardini but to contemporary sources for the story (including Machiavelli's letters to the rulers of Florence, which reported that she said something much ruder). For a reading of Pound's unpublished draft, see Ronald Bush, "The Expatriate in Extremis: Caterina Sforza, Fascism, and Ezra Pound's *Pisan Cantos*," *Revista di Letteratura d'America* 25 (2005): 27–43.

19 For more complete accounts of the "Salita," "Cunizza," "Erigena," "Imperatori," and "Eliseo" drafts, see Ronald Bush, "Towards Pisa: More From the Archives"; "Towards Pisa: Ezra Pound's Roman 'Emperors'," *Revista di Letteratura d'America* 23 (2003): 135–59; and "'The Descent of the Barbarians'."

20 For commentary, see Ronald Bush, "Ezra Pound's Fascist 'Europa': Toward the *Pisan Cantos*," in *Europa! Europa? The Avant-Garde, Modernism and the Fate of a Continent*, ed. Suscha Bru *et al.* (Berlin: De Gruyter, 2009).

21 For the facts of Pound's experience in the camp, see especially *LC* and its principal sources: Julien Cornell, *The Trial of Ezra Pound* (New York: John Day, 1966) and William Van O'Connor and Edward Stone, eds., *A Casebook on Ezra Pound* (New York: Thomas Y. Crowell, 1959).

22 See for example Stanley I. Kutler, "'This Notorious Patient'," *Helix* 13/14 (1983): 133.

23 See *ibid.*, 133–4 and Cornell, *The Trial of Ezra Pound*, 21, 14.

24 Robert D. Gillman, MD, "Ezra Pound's Rorschach Diagnosis," *Bulletin of the Menninger Clinic* 58 (1994): 317–18. Gillman quotes Pound's files at St. Elizabeths.

25 For more on the chronology of Pound's composition of *The Pisan Cantos* and his revision of Canto LXXIV, see Ronald Bush, "Remaking Canto 74," *Paideuma* 32 (2003): 157–86.

26 Makin, *Pound's Cantos*, 239.

27 For a more extended discussion of *The Pisan Cantos*, Villon, and prison poetry, see Ronald Bush, "Poetic Metamorphosis: Ezra Pound's *Pisan Cantos* and Prison Poetry," *Revista di Letteratura d'America* (forthcoming).

28 See Anthony Bonner, *The Complete Works of François Villon* (New York: Bantam, 1960), 122.

CHAPTER 25

Imagism

Ethan Lewis

What did imagism do for Pound and what, in turn, did Pound do for imagism? The answers yield "a language to think in" (*LE*, 194) regarding Pound's emphasis on precision as a means of carving distinctions between terms. That process, an ethical end-in-itself, also delineates components of a Poundian model culture.

Imagism originated in the tea room of the British Museum. Or so its narrative would have it. In the fall of 1912, Pound read H.D.'s poem, "Hermes of the Ways," there in the company of H.D. and Richard Aldington. After making changes, Pound rapidly wrote "H.D. Imagiste" at the bottom of the typed sheet now slashed with his pencil marks, according to H.D. in her memoir, *End to Torment*. Of course, imagism was not a whimsical inspiration. Pound had been led to this concept through his study of Arnaut Daniel, Cavalcanti, and Dante, writers of precision and detail. He had actually formulated the term "imagist" when reworking the proofs of *Ripostes* in the spring of 1912. By 1914, his anthology *Des Imagistes* appeared, soon challenged by Amy Lowell's fuller and competitive anthology, *Some Imagist Poets* (1915). The politics of the movement soon overtook the quality of the poetry and Pound turned elsewhere.

But precisely because Pound transcended imagism, it plots horizon points for marking Pound's development. A poet wed to imagism necessarily focuses on "small things," risking confinement to "a poetic of stasis."[1] Yet by presenting at one moment multiple matters arranged in interactive "complexes"; by creating illusions of "freedom from time and space limits" (*LE*, 4); this small static aesthetic set the course for the modernist long poem. The operative strategy in "Pagani's, November 8"—

> Suddenly discovering in the eyes of the very beautiful
> Normande cocotte
> The eyes of the very learned British Museum assistant.
>
> (*P*, 1990, 157)

– resembles that of Canto XCI:

> Miss Tudor moved them with galleons
> from deep eye, versus armada
> from the green deep
> > he saw it,
> in the green deep of an eye:
> Crystal waves weaving together toward the gt/
> > healing
> > > (XCI/631)

The Canto lines are freighted with more significance – and but constitute a node relating with ideas in surrounding passages. Yet discernment of the seascape "in the green deep of an eye" mirrors discovering one set of eyes in another's.

Moreover, the substance of poetic materials, differing in import, is of like consistency. In neither poem nor passage does the second sighting constitute a metaphoric vehicle; "Pagani's" does not present one set of eyes in the terms of another – at least no more than sea momentarily replaces, and thereby enhances, the royal eye. The correlated members reflexively deepen comprehension of their counterpart – each "acts as some sort of predication about" the other.[2] Pound calls this interaction of actually perceived objects "absolute metaphor." "In . . . poem[s] of this sort, one is trying to record the precise instant when a thing outward and objective transforms itself into a thing inward and subjective" (*GB*, 85, 89).

As with tintype, an early form of photography using an underexposed image on iron that preceded film, so in opus magnus. Imagism "made possible" *The Cantos*, and "opened the way," additionally, to *Paterson*, *Maximus*, *The Bridge*, *A*, *The Waste Land*, and *Four Quartets*.[3] Hence, the why for studying all of Pound under the imagist rubric.

The focus, first, is on the hygienic dictates of imagism, posited by Pound in a now famous treatise, premising clarity without forfeit of complexity. These principles require more concrete definitions, which Pound himself provides. "Direct treatment of the thing, whether subjective or objective," he translates into "objectivity," or "the statement that portrays, and presents, instead of making a comment." "Concentration," "precision," "laconic speech" gloss the second "Imagiste" tenet, to "use absolutely no word that does not contribute to the presentation."[4]

The third imperative, "regarding rhythm, to compose in the sequence of the musical phrase, not in the sequence of the metronome," Pound elsewhere idealizes as "'absolute rhythm' . . . correspond[ing] exactly to the emotion or shade of emotion to be expressed" (*LE*, 9).[5]

Yet the image is, additionally, a process, "that which presents an intellectual or emotional complex in an instant of time." Not the "complex" itself,
rather the language of presentation. In it is often displayed an approxi-
mation – on the poem's own terms, in "the resolution of difficulties to its
own comprehensive organization"[6] – of the qualities of the complex. This
mimetic penchant fundamentally derives from the emphasis on clarity.
Language ought, in Fenollosa/Pound's phrase, be "brought close to *things*."
"[I]n a healthy state," opines Eliot, "Language . . . presents the object, is so
close to the object that the two are identified."[7]

Modernist authors of recondite works paradoxically laud clarity. "Poetry
must be *as well written as prose*. Its language must be a fine language, departing in no way from speech save by a heightened intensity (i.e. simplicity)"
(*SL*, 48). "Good writers," Pound declares, "keep the language efficient . . . .
keep it accurate, keep it clear . . . Language is the main means of communication" (*ABCR*, 32). Throughout, Pound accentuates the clarity and
simplicity of the language, not necessarily of what the language expresses.
And the importance Pound ascribes to "meaning" somewhat surprisingly
reinforces this distinction. "Great literature is language charged with meaning to the utmost possible degree" (*ABCR*, 28; *LE*, 23) – "charged," it might
be glossed, in inverse proportion to the "degree" to which the language may
be explicated. For as many have observed,[8] "meaning" for Pound and his
contemporaries was by nature intuitive, communicated in words pared of
discursive language ("rhetoric" is Pound's term) that only obstructs meaning. "Meaning" and "talk about the matter" (*LE*, 29) are at odds, like the
"intensive" and "extensive manifolds" of intuition and analysis in Hulme's
adaptation of Bergson.

Among the best examples of modern clarity without forfeit of complexity
is this statement: "The 'one image' poem is a form of super-position, that
is to say, it is one idea set on top of another" (*GB*, 89). Twenty-one simple
words surround one abstract term (compound parts of which are simple in
themselves) in a syntactically precise arrangement – mirrored, practically,
by a similarly clear little poem:

> The apparition of these faces in the crowd:
> Petals on a wet, black bough.   (*GB*, 89)

No obscurity here – yet how does the piece work? What does the statement
mean?

Regarding his imagist years, Pound is his own best critic, for, again, the
principal devices in his method elucidate more obscure remarks about the

image. Interpretative metaphor lends imagery within the Image an extra concreteness, the "hard light" and "clear edges" Pound required (*SL*, 38). Super-position, which integrates this metaphor into an image-structure, manifests the image as "speech" and as "word beyond formulated language" (*GB*, 88). Super-position presents two literal "things" ("ideas"), rather than one literal and one figurative; and Pound's image is not these things presented, but the presentation of their interaction. In activity and essentials (including not only the "ideas," but the structure of the poem also), the Pound image paradoxically segregates the objects that it joins. Thus, it embodies the emphasis on clarity with which Pound's work, and age, were imbued.

REALITY OF FIGURE

The most cohesive explication of the image comes in "Vorticism,"[9] with its crux the passage cited above, p. 272. The image, "itself the speech" and "the word beyond formulated language," inheres in a special type of metaphor, where the figure owns an added dimension of concreteness.

All poetic language is the language of exploration. Since the beginning of bad writing, writers have used images as ornaments. The point of Imagism is that it does not use images *as ornaments* . . . I once saw a small child go to an electric light and say, "Mamma, can I *open* the light?" She was using the age-old language of exploration, the language of art. It was a sort of metaphor, but she was not using it as ornamentation. (*GB*, 88)

Pound interprets "ornament" conventionally, as "adornment": something that may favorably gild the object but is accessory to it. Hence, "the great gulf" between Petrarch's "fustian" and Cavalcanti's "precise interpretative metaphor." "In Guido the 'figure,' the strong metamorphic or 'picturesque' expression is there with purpose to convey or to interpret a definite meaning. In Petrarch it is ornament, the prettiest ornament he could find, but not . . . irreplaceable" (*LE*, 153–4). Thus, one deduces, an "interpretative" figure proves essential to the presentation of its tenor: as actually perceivable as that for which it is the trope; "*there* with purpose," "permanent," "absolute" (*GB*, 84–5). To apply Hulme, it could not be interpreted as a "counter" with which "to pass to conclusions without thinking."[10]

Though abhorring allegory (*LE*, 9), Pound posits a parable for composing "great literature," i.e., "language charged with meaning to the utmost possible degree" (*ABCR*, 28; *LE*, 23). The child submits a literal report of her thought. Ideally, the artist does the same, differing only in his awareness that he employs metaphor. Hence, "the language of exploration" (vis-à-vis "ornamentation") is the language of imagism.

This reality of figure Pound seeks in his incessant emphasis on interpretative rather than descriptive language. To interpret means to re-conceive with added perspective; or re-construct in other terms. Reality of figure, further, elucidates Pound's demand for concrete imagery. *Pace* an image's "ideas" set one atop another as if perceptible; each must be presented as a distinct entity, for they are not to coalesce into a unified impression. The image, he writes, is "the word beyond formulated language" (*GB*, 88).

To speak of figurative reality denominates the subjective as real as its objective correlate. This concept could scarce be set apart enough from a notion Pound abominated, namely that reality is by nature subjective. Pound's faith in intuition, in the existence of facts accessible to all via "accurate," "clear" reporting, denotes a world outside the self to which separate selves have access. Subjective impressions number among realities to be objectively recorded, thence shared. The imagist poem – demanding "direct treatment of the thing whether subjective or objective" – is the register: "In a poem of this sort one is trying to record the precise instant when a thing outward and objective transforms itself, or darts into a thing inward and subjective" (*GB*, 89). The syntax, foregrounding "thing," elucidates: interpretative metaphor presents a thing as real in its "inward and subjective" state as in its "outward and objective."

IN THE IMAGE OF "METRO"

At times, this reality can be tested:

> The apparition of these faces in the crowd:
> Petals on a wet, black bough.

The absence of a connective creates "a sense of fusion, or even confusion, between the ideas, which leads Pound to speak of the 'one image poem.'"[11] One cannot tell simply from reading the poem, that the second line is a figure for the first. We must be provided an anecdote: "Three years ago in Paris I got out of a "metro" train at La Concorde, and saw suddenly a beautiful face, and then another and another, . . . and I tried all that day to find words for what this had meant to me" (*GB*, 86–7). Omit this, and there's no knowing whether "The apparition of these faces in the crowd" is compared to a figure of "Petals on a wet, black bough," or whether the poem presents the converse.

But in fact, "The apparition . . . resembles petals" would inaccurately gloss "Metro"'s effect, even if we know the context:

The relation between the parts of Pound's poem appears to be an ambiguous relation between the figure and the ground, so that one may choose to consider the faces in terms of the petals, or vice versa. Although evidently a poem about "faces," the use of the colon, in place of the words "are like," makes the ambiguity possible and gives the poem a richness it would not have were it a simile.[12]

We have come to the matter's core, "the radiant gist" in Pound's lexicon.[13] The poem may be about "faces," but is not an image of them, conveyed via metaphor. The ambiguity fostered by punctuation forces us to experience each image as an actuality, as a potential tenor for which the apposite term serves as vehicle. The image is of the "faces" and the "petals" jointly. It is, really, neither one construed "in terms of" the other, nor the "fusion" of the two into a unified whole. Thus, one preferably labels this effect a simultaneity of terms – cognizant of the relative imprecision of this phrase inasmuch as presentation in language permits at best an illusion of simultaneity.[14]

Yet remembering Pound's insistence on "that which presents" to "record the precise instant," we must further qualify our definition. An image is evidently *of* its images only when it posits an interaction between them. Pound fastidiously indexes "complex" to its "technical" meaning "employed by the newer psychologists" (*LE*, 4). His usage, therefore, denotes a "system of 'emotionally toned' ideas."[15] The image is then *of* a system or process of images. "It does not appease itself by reproducing what is seen, but by setting some other seen thing in relation."[16] Scanning the lines, the mind mimes this interaction: "darting" from one line to the next, back to the initial line, to the second again in attempting to fathom their relation. "Vorticism" synopsizes: "The 'one image poem' is a form of super-position . . . one idea set on top of another" (*GB*, 89).[17]

Earlier, I remarked that Pound's dictum on "the 'one image poem'" clarified his rather cryptic explanation of the image as "itself the speech and the word beyond formulated language." We can see now that it is "speech" by being, literally, "formulated language": i.e., the "form" of "one idea" –

The apparition of these faces in the crowd:

– "set on top of another":

Petals on a wet, black bough.

But the image is *of* these "ideas," we noted, only by recording their inter-action: "the precise instant when a thing outward and objective transforms itself, or darts into a thing inward and subjective." And this interplay is "beyond formulated language," since words cannot compass it as words can "ideas." And yet the commerce may itself be thought of as a "word," insofar as it exists within the image grammar (i.e., the functions and relations of components in the image).

This interpretation predicates another sense of image, by implying that the work reflects Pound's theories in its structure. And indeed, save for a few cautionary exempla (the deliberately perverted "L'Art, 1910" [*P*, 1990, 118]; more significantly, lines marring separation in the "Usura" Canto [XLV][18]), a consistent analogy pertains between image and poetic form. There is a correlation of an "idea" to a line (or in certain poems, to a group of lines or a stanza), so that "one idea set on top of another" is structurally replicated by one line (or a group of lines or a stanza) set upon another. Thus we can see (actually, not see) "the precise" interactive "instant" "beyond formulated language" in the space between juxtaposed lines. In *Gaudier-Brzeska*, Pound comments that the "beauty" of the image results from "'planes in relation'" (*GB*, 121). One might read "In a Station of the Metro" *geometrically*:

> The apparition of these faces in the crowd: = []
> Petals on a wet, black bough   []

Of course, structural super-position by itself cannot produce the image. Unless analogous to "one idea set on top of another," the arrangement of lines is meaningless (evident once one considers that every multi-stanza poem – not to mention every pair of lines – instances structural super-position).

Hence, the analogue functions interpretatively. Like a Chinese ideo-graph, it presents "shorthand pictures" of the actions it relates. Fenollosa puns aptly as unwittingly, remarking a "compounding," where "two things added together do not produce a third thing but suggest some fundamental relation between the two."[19]

In miming interpretative metaphor, the lines illumine its operation. Juxtaposed, they connect "ideas" conveyed – as a metaphor joins things by their likeness. Yet because the lines do not enjamb, they keep the "ideas" distinct – as an interpretative metaphor, affirming respective actualities of tenor and vehicle, distinguishes – hence, separates – the same "ideas" it joins.

Why did this paradoxical process so appeal to Pound? The answer inheres in his version of the modernist emphasis on clarity. Imagism may be perceived as part of a larger reaction to the language the new age inherited from the Victorian – an idiom "slushy and inexact," its "application of word to thing go[ne] rotten" (*LE*, 21). Imagism, aimed at "bring[ing] language close to *things*" (*CWC*, 367), would reverse this degeneration.[20] But of what does verbal hygiene precisely consist? How does language itself (as distinguished from the abstruse message it relates) convey clarity?

In Pound's work, by carving distinctions. Pound once described his personal revolt from his Victorian legacy in terms of learning to make "a language to think in" (*LE*, 194). Such discourse is definitively interpretative. Directly treating things warranting discrete delineation, it must also exhibit the active mind working upon things. (Pound actually distinguished imagism from impressionism by just this quality of "*conceiving* instead of merely reflecting and observing" [*GB*, 89].)

Carving distinctions keystones Pound's poetics. "No science save the arts will give us the requisite data for learning in what ways men differ" (*LE*, 47). "The whole of great art is a struggle for communication... And this communication is not a leveling; it is not an elimination of differences. It is a recognition of differences" (*LE*, 298). Precision proves essential to the task. One "can [even] be wholly precise in representing a vagueness" (*LE*, 44). "In a Station of the Metro" poses a case in point, wherein "vagueness" derives from distinctly rendering each "idea" so as to interact with the "idea" apposed to it.

Yet the "one image poem," the most concentrated expression of Pound's concern with distinction, when first construed in these small works, is better comprehended in his opus magnus. Absent superfluity, the image carves distinctions via separating the very terms it joins. The paradox is a function of interpretative metaphor, integrated with the poetic structure through super-position. Varied forms of these devices, and some further implications, merit remark.

(1) We note first that implicit super-position – the tacit juncture and separation of what is conveyed and the state of mind for which it is the object – underlies any image, which transcribes "an equation for a mood."[21] Thus, apparent one-dimensional presentations such as "Ts'ai Chi'h" and "The Jewel Stairs' Grievance" (the last more suggestively symbolic; also foregrounding "hard light, clear edges," qualities Pound prized) still yield parallel realities.

(2) Super-position may prove manifest in ways that don't involve the colon – via manipulation of syntax ("Alba," "Pagani's, November 8"); or by

rendering a single "idea" ambiguous to effect an aporia: complementary, or even mutually exclusive images. (Instanced in several Pound images, most keenly in "Dance Figure.")

(3) He who eschewed "the conventional taste of four or five centuries and one continent" (*GB*, 90), would no more limit his own technique to sense perception and poetic structure. Pound often constructs an image from super-positions of times ("The Return," "Spring"); places ("Fish and the Shadow," "Pagani's"); phenomena (stasis/action, "Gentildonna"); amplification/development ("The Coming of War"); viewpoints (subjective/objective, certainly; but even the perceptions of disparate viewers; even report apposed to opinion ["Liu Ch'e," "A Girl," "Fan-Piece: for Her Imperial Lord"]).

(4) Spatio-temporal super-posings, especially, propel *The Cantos*, which makes no pretense to "consist . . . in one image, enforced by movement and music" (*GB*, 94). Pound intended, rather, an "epic," "a poem including history" (*LE*, 86) – which must thus compass heroes and events, models and cautionary tales from all recorded times anywhere. The operative principle in *The Cantos* evolves from the *parva opera*, much as "the forces which produce the branch-angles of an oak lay potent in the acorn."[22] Pound perceived he might ply the same poetic on larger game. Hence, he never reneged on his theory of the image; retaining it actually keyed his development.

NOTES

1 Reed Way Dasenbrock, *The Literary Vorticism of Ezra Pound and Wyndham Lewis* (Baltimore: Johns Hopkins University Press, 1985), 93; Kenner, *PE*, 159.

2 Herbert N. Schneidau, *Ezra Pound: The Image and the Real* (Baton Rouge: Louisiana State University Press), 64.

3 Cf. Kenner, *PE*, 186, where he calls *The Cantos*, *Paterson*, and "the work of T.S. Eliot . . . the Symbolist heritage in English." As my inclusion of Olson and Zukofsky denotes, this "heritage" also engendered objectivism.

4 "A Retrospect" [1918] (*LE*, 3–14). The material therein garnered dates from 1911–17, with the kernel doctrine, "A Few Dont's," first appearing in *Poetry* [1913].

5 See also *ABCR*, *LE* and *GB* throughout.

6 William Carlos Williams, remarking "the purpose of art" (*Selected Essays*, [New York: Random House, 1954] 120). Williams' distinct modernist imagism is recounted in Ethan Lewis, "The Liberation of Words: Williams' Verbal Imagism," *South Dakota Review* 31.3 (fall 1993): 18–42.

7 Ernest Fenollosa, *The Chinese Written Character as a Medium for Poetry*, ed. Ezra Pound (1936; San Francisco: City Lights Books, 1968), 13; T.S. Eliot, *Selected Essays* (New York: Harcourt Brace and World), 285.

8 John Gage, *In The Arresting Eye: The Rhetoric of Imagism* (Baton Rouge: Louisiana State University Press, 1981); Schneidau, *The Image and the Real*; Sir Frank Kermode (*Romantic Image* [London: Routledge and Kegan Paul, 1957]); Michael Levenson (*A Genealogy of Modernism* [Cambridge: Cambridge University Press, 1984]), and Sanford Schwartz (*The Matrix of Modernism* [Princeton: Princeton University Press, 1985]) all discuss the intuitive theory of knowledge underlying imagist poetics.

9 Premiering in *Fortnightly Review*, September 1914, and reprinted in *GB* (81–94). By 1914, Pound had subsumed imagism, as he conceived it, under vorticism, "roughly speaking, expressionism, neo-cubism, and imagism gathered together in one camp" (*GB*, 90). His allegiance to the vorticist movement could in fact be seen as his attempt to save imagism from the dilutions of Amy Lowell and her clan, anthologized in *Some Imagist Poets* (1915–17). The details of the Pound–Lowell disagreement (no schism, for they were never allied) are related in various forms. Some retellings have Pound leaving the imagists behind him; others report the movement taken out from under him. In either case, it warrants underscoring, Pound took his "imagism" with him when he disassociated from the Lowell group.

10 T[homas] E[rnest] Hulme, *Further Speculations*, ed. Sam Hynes (Minneapolis: University of Minnesota Press, 1955), 79.

11 Robert Kern, "Frost and Modernism," *American Literature* 60. 1 (March 1988) 10.

12 Gage, *In the Arresting Eye*, 62.

13 William Carlos Williams, *Paterson* (New York: New Directions 1963), 186.

14 Gage's deconstruction of the illusion of simultaneity compels; See *In the Arresting Eye*, 60–2. See also Ethan Lewis, "'This Hulme Business Revisited' or Of Sequence and Simultaneity," *Paideuma* 22, 1.2 (Spring and fall 1993): 255–65.

15 Schneidau, *The Image and the Real*, 33, citing Bernard Hart, *The Psychology of Insanity* (1912).

16 Kenner, *PE*, 186, 185, linking "that which presents . . ." to the mysterious "Doctrine of the Image," which Pound referred to with his basic principles, but never expressly articulated. Pound's reference came in an anonymous interview given F.S. Flint as part of their effort to launch the movement.

17 For detailed treatment of why versions featuring the semicolon don't fundamentally alter reader response, see Ethan Lewis, "Super-Position: Interpretive Metaphor" *Paideuma* 23, 2.3 (fall and winter 1994): 203–4.

18 See Ethan Lewis, "Grammaria Usurae: Representational Stratagems in Canto xlv," *Paideuma* 28, 2.3 (fall and winter 1999): 223–8.

19 Fenollosa/Pound, *The Chinese Written Character*, 8–9, 10.

20 Schneidau believes the initial impetus behind imagism *wholly* hygienic. Though overstating the case, that stress is justified.

21 "Great works of art...cause form to come into being. By the 'image' I mean...an equation...not something about *a, b*, and *c*, having something to do with form, but about *sea, cliffs, night*, having something to do with mood" (*GB*, 91–2).

22 Fenollosa/Pound, *The Chinese Written Character*, 10.

CHAPTER 26

Vorticism

Miranda Hickman

Writing from Rapallo in 1924, Ezra Pound waxed nostalgic to his comrade the painter and writer Wyndham Lewis, reminiscing about a moment a decade earlier when he and Lewis had converged in London's *avant-guerre* artistic milieu. In 1914, Pound and Lewis had both been members of the newly emergent avant-garde movement of vorticism, known chiefly for its paintings – which featured a bold, angular, dynamic version of the geometric abstract idiom prevalent in the visual arts of the early twentieth century – but also involving sculpture, literature, and photography. Lewis had spearheaded the movement; Pound had joined it in mid 1914.

In his retrospective letter, Pound recalled *Blast*, the short-lived periodical (1914–15) that had served as vorticism's official organ and housed its manifestoes. A foot in height, with a bright puce cover stamped with aggressive black sans-serif lettering, *Blast* sported an outlandish visual code that signaled avant-garde defiance and mischief – and, as Paige Reynolds notes, that resonated with the visual signatures of advertising of the climate.[1] Lewis would later fondly remember *Blast* as "that hugest and pinkest of magazines."[2] The magazine's contents – including hyperbolic manifestoes "blasting" Victorianism in gigantic type; geometric paintings; a phantasmagoric avant-garde play by Wyndham Lewis entitled *Enemy of the Stars*, ventured as an example of literary vorticism – sustained the audacity signaled by the magazine's bibliographic code.

In his letter, Pound would flag *Blast*'s size and colour: "I have just, ten years an a bit after its appearance, and in this far distant locus, taken out a copy of the great MAGENTA cover'd opusculus. We were hefty guys in them days; an of what has come after us, we seem to have survived without a great mass of successors" (*PL*, 138). Here, Pound uses "appearance" to refer to the magazine's publication, but the word also highlights the magazine's visual cues, and the jocular "opusculus" (in Latin, "small book") emphasizes through irony the magazine's formidable size. Pound's own majuscules both recall the lettering of *Blast* itself (which used enormous letters to suggest avant-garde ferocity) and indicate the importance Pound accorded the magazine in memory.

Through its "great" assertive physicality, *Blast* came to serve as a metonym for Pound for the stature he remembered his and Lewis' enjoying at that juncture ("We were hefty guys in them days"). In the 1924 letter, Pound initially distances himself from this remembered heyday both geographically ("in this far distant locus") and temporally ("in them days"), suggesting a halcyon era gone by. Later in the letter, however, Pound wonders if he and Lewis might "kick up" any "more or any new devilment": along with his mention of "successors," these remarks indicate Pound's desire to revive vorticism in a new cultural milieu (*PL*, 138). Later, I will address how Pound's work of the 1920s and 1930s came to be importantly informed by his desire to resurrect vorticism in a "locus" far distant from the London context out of which it began. This chapter focuses on what initially brought Pound to vorticism; how the movement developed; the significance he attached to it; what the movement provided him; and how vorticism guided his later work and thought.

At a 2008 exhibition of Wyndham Lewis' portraits at London's National Portrait Gallery, curated by Paul Edwards with Richard Humphreys, although the exhibition showcased Lewis' work of the 1920s and 1930s, the gift shop featured *Blast*-themed items: tote bags, coffee mugs, lapel buttons, T-shirts, earrings. The trivialization that attends commercialism aside, this witnesses the way that, although *Blast* lasted only two issues until the Great War eroded the conditions that made it possible, its own bellicose "blast" overcome by the aggression of the actual war (the second issue of *Blast*, a "War Number" that commented on the war, was the last); and although in 1914, vorticism was received with at best lukewarm reviews as a derivative of Italian futurism and merely yet another movement in an avant-garde context teeming with such movements,[3] *Blast* has nonetheless subsequently assumed "hefty" stature in art-historical and literary-historical chronicles of the early modernist period.

Reprints of *Blast* published in the 1990s through Black Sparrow Press, later available through Gingko Press, have assured that the magazine's two issues have remained before the eyes of readers interested in modernism's history. *Blast*'s commanding dimensions and brash bibliographic code render it eminently appropriable as a symbol of vibrant avant-garde activity of this moment. Much as it came to stand for early avant-garde triumph and the beginnings of modernism for Pound, it has come to play a similar role in accounts of Anglo-American modernism – in part because Pound's own perspective became so pivotal to later understandings of modernism's development. Despite *Blast*'s inauspicious beginnings, then, and despite the small part vorticism continues to play in narratives of art history of the early twentieth century, both *Blast*, and by extension vorticism, have achieved prominence in literary modernism's own narratives of origin.[4]

Initially a movement of painters, led by Lewis and emerging also from the work of painters Frederick Etchells, Helen Saunders, Jessica Dismorr, Cuthbert Hamilton, and William Roberts, as vorticism took shape in 1914, it also came to involve sculptors (Henri Gaudier-Brzeska and Jacob Epstein), writers (Pound and Lewis), and a photographer (Alvin Coburn). Vorticism's multidisciplinarity prompted Pound to theorize the movement in the first issue of *Blast* as committed to what he termed the "primary pigment": for him, this meant that the skilled vorticist artist would choose as occasion for an artwork a "concept" or "emotion" for which her or his artistic medium was best suited, and thus would express it with maximum intensity.[5]

Pound's reading of the central impetus of vorticism, however, differed notably from Lewis', which had dominated the movement during the months of its inception and continued to lead as the movement developed. Just before the publication of the first issue of *Blast* in June of 1914, Pound supplied the movement's name with his use of "vortex" as a shorthand for a locus of whirling, dynamic energy (Pound had invoked "vortex" in this sense in a December 1913 letter to William Carlos Williams, where he used it to refer to cultural centers such as London) (*PW*, 23). But the movement had been coalescing for some months preceding this name-giving, without Pound's membership. As late as April 1914, a letter from Pound to James Joyce, characterizing vorticism as Lewis' movement, indicates that Pound was not yet directly involved (*PJ*, 26).

Before Pound joined the vorticists, the movement had evolved from an effort by Lewis and a group of fellow painters to distinguish themselves from others in their milieu on both aesthetic and personal grounds. In so doing, they were engaging in the process of "incremental self-differentiation" that Janet Lyon reads as pivotal to avant-garde identity formation – one so characteristic of the London avant-guerre milieu from which vorticism emerged that it was often difficult to tell where artistic disagreements left off and the need to assert difference began.[6] Lewis and his cohorts initially distinguished themselves by staging a ruckus whose bombast and invective would become hallmarks of vorticism's socio-political work: their much publicized break with the Omega Workshops.

The Omega, a Bloomsbury-based London atelier founded by artist and critic Roger Fry, inspired by William Morris-inspired Arts and Crafts ideals, sought to introduce into domestic environments the innovative designs of early twentieth-century Post-Impressionist art. In 1913, Lewis and his group of proto-vorticists were contributing to the Workshops. At London's Courtauld Gallery, the room featuring Omega artifacts displays work by central Omega artists such as Vanessa Bell, Duncan Grant, and Winifred Gill side by side with a plate thought to be designed by Wyndham Lewis and a small painting by Frederick Etchells.

By the fall of 1913, however, a quarrel had arisen between Lewis' group and the Omega about a commission that Fry, they claimed, had unjustly appropriated from them. Lewis announced their ire in a public "Round-Robin" letter, distributed to the press, that highlighted their dispute as well as aesthetic and philosophic differences.[7] The letter suggested not only a desire to vent indignation but also an effort to announce their own coming-of-age as abstract artists developing their own convictions and idiom.

In December of 1913, following the fracas, Lewis and a group of the painters who would by the next year be associated with vorticism exhibited together in the "Cubist Room" at a show in Brighton[8] (participants included core vorticists such as Frederick Etchells, Cuthbert Hamilton, William Roberts, and Edward Wadsworth, as well as figures more peripheral to the movement such as Christopher Nevinson, Jacob Epstein, and David Bomberg),[9] at that point demonstrating a distinctive approach – one that Lewis described in the exhibition catalogue as "underlin[ing] the geometric bases and structure of life."[10] The rupture with Fry and the Omega solidified the distinct identity of this band, as did their later insistence on their difference from other avant-garde groups such as the Italian Futurists and Cubists, with which, in style and mission, they were in important ways aligned.

In *Blast*'s manifestoes and essays, Lewis presented the vorticists as having steered a middle course between the Scylla and Charybdis of unfocused Futurist bombast and Cubist stasis.[11] This reveals a pattern typical of the vorticists' position-taking as led by Lewis' maneuvers: they emphasized their differences from groups to which they were significantly similar, placing themselves in the field of artistic production by the coordinates of these kindred groups, then refining their location by disavowals of congruence. Usually, the vorticists proceeded by critiquing one characteristic in particular of a group of this kind – a quality that, in a Bloomian swerve, the vorticists would seek to "CORRECT."[12]

As of 1913, the abstract visual language of the Omega Workshops was significantly akin to that of the nascent vorticists. As "Post-Impressionists" in the sense theorized by Roger Fry, Omega artists specialized in an abstract idiom guided by the principle of "significant form" – the axiom that, as Clive Bell noted in *Art*, shapes, lines, and colors could themselves carry significance, apart from any representational work they performed.[13] The proto-vorticists likewise worked from this premise (in *Blast 1*, Lewis would publish Kandinsky's *On the Spiritual in Art* [1912] to establish this position), and like the Omega artists, they developed a highly geometric idiom. Whereas Omega geometricity, however, tended to be gently curving, sloping, and biomorphic, vorticist geometric canvases generally featured sharp angles, jagged shapes, and severe diagonals, creating an effect of instability and consequent dynamism. As Reed Dasenbrock notes, the diagonals of vorticism generate a "sense of motion,"[14] handled according to the assumption articulated by the Futurist architect Antonio Sant'Elia: that "oblique and elliptic lines are dynamic."[15] Through diagonals, angular and edgy shapes, compositions suggesting imbalance and elements on the verge of falling down or apart, and stark swaths of bold color, the vorticists created the effect of what Dasenbrock calls "dynamic formism."[16]

Through their energized geometric canvasses, the Vorticists also thereby conjured an attitudinal climate of aggression and driving force. This signature vorticist coding of their abstract geometric language to signify aggressive dynamism also suggests an investment, and a campaign, central to vorticist work. While vorticist geometrics certainly expressed the stark contours and aggressive modernity of the first machine age, I would suggest that they issued from an ambivalence central to the formation of vorticism – a generative ambivalence with respect to *fin-de-siècle* Aestheticism. On the one hand, Lewis and other Vorticists responded favorably to the characteristic *fin-de-siècle* celebration of artifice: as the manifestoes of *Blast* attest, the Vorticists championed the ability of the artist's mind to, as Wilde's Vivian in "The Decay of Lying" puts it, "teach Nature her proper place."[17]

In the manifestoes of *Blast 1*, Lewis declares, "Bless the Hairdresser. He attacks Mother Nature for a small fee."[18] The typical Vorticist treatment of the human body (with which vorticists often engaged, as in famous pieces such as Epstein's *Rock-Drill* and Gaudier-Brzeska's *Red Stone Dancer*), which often involves representing the body as geometric so as to imply that which is mechanical and robotic, suggests this Aestheticist valorization of powerful artifice over weak nature: like the Aesthetes of the *fin de siècle*, vorticists stage an imaginative conquest of the merely organic body, here transposed into the key of the machine age.

On the other hand, Lewis, whose thought dominated vorticist theory, also exhibited an anxiety with respect to the effeminacy with which, by the early twentieth century, the climate of the *fin de siècle* had come to be closely associated. In the mid 1890s, the trials of Oscar Wilde had, as Lewis puts it, "electrified" the art world,[19] displaying before the public an image of the homosexual male read as "effeminate." The trials, along with late nineteenth-century developments in sexology, contributed to what Foucault notes as the era's increasing construction of the male homosexual as a legible effeminate "species"[20] – and given Wilde's linkage in the public mind with Aestheticism, also contributed to the cultural reading of *fin-de-siècle* art as participating in a destabilization of hegemonic masculinity. These developments, and the cultural climate to which they helped to give rise, played an important role in generating what I have read as vorticism's defining campaign against effeminacy.[21]

As a result, the semiotic work of vorticism was devoted to articulating a form of dynamism that would counter characteristics that Lewis and the vorticists associated with effeminacy: by way of their geometric idiom, they played out a form of masculinity, though one distinct from forms that Lewis deplored as displaying emotionalism he read as effeminate, whether Hemingway schoolboy heroics or Futurist machismo.[22] In the London prewar context, the cultural work of vorticist art was recognized as rejecting Aestheticist effeminacy: the vorticists even stressed in their initial salvoes in their "Round Robin" letter to the Omega that they were repudiating a group of "Dissenting Aesthetes" "whose Idol is . . . prettiness, with its mid-Victorian languish of the neck, and its skin 'greenery-yallery' "[23] – the last expression a satirical shorthand for effeminate Aestheticism drawn from Gilbert and Sullivan's comic opera *Patience* (1881). Central to vorticism's project, then, was the establishment of an attitude that conveyed a form of masculinity that, in Lewis' view, could oppose what Lewis phobically rejected as unwelcome effeminacy associated with male homosexuality.

Pound, meanwhile, responded to the masculine ethos of vorticism as providing an avenue out of the imagist movement, which he read as going feminine in an unfortunate way. After launching imagism in 1912–13, by 1914, Pound was increasingly troubled by the presence in the movement of Amy Lowell, whom he saw as attempting to displace him as the movement's leader and whose approach of the "democratized committee" (which, for Pound, read as feminine) he regarded as diluting Imagism's aesthetic and critical standards (*SL*, 38). Out of this disillusionment, he turned toward vorticism. Writing in 1913 during the months of imagism's beginnings, Pound had defined the "image" as "an intellectual and emotional complex in an instant of time" (*LE*, 4), suggesting a poetic that gave rise to poems such as his "In a Station of the Metro," whose image of the "wet, black bough" captured a conceptual and emotional response to "the apparition of these faces in the crowd." After joining the vorticists in 1914, Pound markedly revised his definition of the "image": now it was a "vortex . . . from which, through which, and into which, ideas are constantly rushing" (*GB*, 92). This definitional revision suggests Pound's desire not only for an escape from the power dynamics of the imagist movement (which, he said, were robbing him of his "machinery" to promote good new work; *SL*, 38) but also for an aesthetic that connoted more motion than imagism had initially displayed. In *Blast 1*, significantly, Pound featured as an exemplar of vorticist work H. D.'s imagist poem "Oread." The former association between H. D.'s poem and imagism, together with the conspicuous dynamism the poem conveys, suggests Pound's desire to rewrite imagism as vorticism: as he read it, vorticism could renew imagism – usher it into a more dynamic phase.

Pound had long shown a commitment to such dynamism. The early years of his career had been significantly guided by his fascination with the medieval troubadours of southwest medieval France such as Arnaut Daniel and Bertran de Born. Initially, Pound was compelled by the troubadours not only because of their virtuosic verse, but also because of their ability to evoke, through both their biographies and the personae of their poetry, figures who joined extraordinary aesthetic skill with dynamic warrior prowess. Pound features the warrior figure he inferred from the troubadours, and from the work of Bertran de Born in particular, in such early poems as "Sestina: Altaforte." Pound's attraction to this hybrid of artistry and martial ability would recur in his career – through, for instance, his engagement with the figure of Sigismondo Malatesta, Renaissance freelance soldier (*condottiere*), also poet and patron of the arts, on whom he modeled his hero for his Cantos VIII–XI; and then once again, this time with dire political consequences, through his longstanding fascination with the strongman Mussolini. Throughout the decades, Pound consistently idealized the heroic male who could embody both the man of action and the man of sensibility – and Pound wanted this man to display driving force.

As Lawrence Rainey notes, however, when Pound was delivering lectures on the troubadours in London of 1912, he felt increasingly eclipsed, read as quaint spokesman for faded antique glamor. This was especially true as he was upstaged by another lecturer displaying modern vigor and vitality at other venues in London at the same time – F. T. Marinetti, leader of the Italian Futurists, who was regaling packed houses with diatribes against the dusty past.[24] Although Pound would express skepticism about Marinetti's antics and ideas, I would argue that Marinetti's sweeping bombast and spectacle clearly rhymed for Pound with the whirling energy he admired in such troubadours as Bertran de Born, and they evoked the swashbuckling energy driving the kind of avant-garde activity he preferred.[25]

For Pound, then, the attraction of vorticism derived partly from its ability to generate, through the affect of its statements and work, the kind of masculine force, dynamism, and wattage that he both admired and read as savvy: Marinetti's style of avant-garde activity was playing well across London when Pound's own lectures were drawing scant audiences. Thus for a constellation of reasons, Pound was well positioned to join Lewis and the other vorticists during the summer of 1914 with enthusiasm.

Pound's literary contributions to *Blast* per se, however, were largely unsuccessful – a few pugnacious poems that, along with Rainey and Dasenbrock, I would dismiss as failures. But in the manifesto he contributed to *Blast* 1 ("Vortex, Pound"), Pound began to theorize vorticism in a way that differed significantly from the way Lewis had, and that indicated other reasons for Pound's interest in the movement: in his reading, vorticism was more than just a rejection of Futurism and Cubism through precise geometry that suggested dynamic energy. For Pound, vorticism was also a richly multidisciplinary movement whose practitioners sought the "primary pigment," developing in their work ideas best expressed in the media they chose. As he noted of what he read as vorticism's guiding principle, "We go to a particular art for something which we cannot get in any other art" (*EPCP*, II: 4).

For Pound, however, what would constitute vorticism's more significant achievement and legacy was the intelligence its practitioners displayed about how to handle aesthetic form for maximum impact, and how to make a work of art succeed chiefly by virtue of its form. In 1915, Pound was crediting the vorticists with having awakened him to the forms of his environment: the perspective he associated with vorticism, he noted, sensitized him to new "ways of seeing the shape of the sky as it juts down between the houses. The tangle of telegraph wires is conceivable not merely as a repetition of lines; one sees the shapes defined by the different branches of the wire" (*EPCP*, II: 5). Pound would later term this inspirational vorticist viewpoint the "form sense" (*GK*, 134).

In later years, the vorticist example would continue to represent for Pound a high-water mark of astute work with form and of art whose power derived primarily not from its subject matter or representational capacity, but rather from its use of form. In 1930, he was noting that, "[F]ew . . . plastic artists have been strong enough to depend on form alone, dispensing with the stimulus or support of a literary content . . . In England the courage" to develop work relying chiefly on formal design "reached its known maximum in the period 1911 to 1914 as shown in the work of Wyndham Lewis, Gaudier, and in a few works of Epstein" (*EPCP*, v: 217).

But by the early 1930s, Pound was pointing back to a movement widely understood to belong to the past. Even in 1924, as Pound wrote to Lewis, he was acknowledging that the movement was "distant": vorticism had declined after the Great War, many of its practitioners having enlisted, some having been killed (such as Gaudier-Brzeska); others, like Lewis himself, having returned from war carnage sobered and soured both on the antic bellicosity for which he had been known and on the geometric idiom, which came to remind Lewis of skeletal bodies subjected to violence.[26] As Lewis notes,

The "vorticists" enjoyed a life of a year or two, no more. They were snuffed out by the Great War . . .

The War came a few months after the publication of *Blast* No. 1. I, who had been the principal exponent of "vorticism," attempted to keep the vorticist flag flying for a short while, then became a soldier: Gaudier Brzeska was killed in action within six months of the outbreak of war . . . Hulme, the philosopher journalist of "abstraction" in 1914, was killed in action in 1917 . . . We all went over into the War, and lost our "Vortex" in it.[27]

As a result *Blast* ended, and although as of late 1919 Lewis considered bringing out a third issue of *Blast* (likely spurred by Pound), this never coalesced.[28] In 1920, there was an attempt to rekindle some of the vorticist group in an exhibition of work from a band of artists calling itself "Group X," but this never caught fire.[29]

However, in a piece of 1919, Pound showed marked reluctance to accept the "death of vorticism." "Gaudier-Brzeska's life work" had been "stopped by a german bullet," he noted, but in his view, vorticism had "not yet had its funeral" (*EPCP*, III: 279). Beginning work on his Malatesta Cantos in the early 1920s, Pound unfolded these Cantos through whirling images in motion that suggest vorticist dynamic forms. Moreover, as his 1924 letter to Lewis suggests, he began seeking opportunities to reawaken the movement outside of England. David N. Wright argues that Pound's involvement with First-Wave avant-garde cinema in Paris 1921–24 was fueled by his reading of the experimental films of Abel Gance ("La Roue") and Ferdinand Léger ("Ballet Mécanique") as "vorticist"; in the work of these filmmakers, Pound discovered evidence that the formal intelligence and dynamic energy – the dynamic form – of vorticism was continuing in the new medium of film, and this attracted him to the milieu. Involved in "Ballet Mécanique" in 1924, Pound noted to his father that he was "at work" on a "Vorticist film."[30] In 1928, he would continue to call the man with whom he worked on "Ballet Mécanique," Dudley Murphy, a *"vortecin"* (*EPCP*, V: 61).

As I have argued in *The Geometry of Modernism*, Pound's desire expressed in 1924 to revive vorticism in a "far distant locus" began to play out even more forcefully in the 1930s.[31] At that juncture, living in Italy, Pound came to believe that such a revival was already underway. Pound's increasing investment in Mussolini's fascist Italy in the 1930s was importantly informed and strengthened by his belief that in the visual culture of Italy around him, he discerned signs of a resurrection of the vorticist project. The visual forms Pound witnessed, for example, at the massive 1932 exhibit, the *Esposizione del Decennio*, organized by Mussolini's Italy to commemorate the regime's first decade and persuade spectators of fascist Italy's might, bore significant resemblance to those in which he had been immersed through vorticism: the bold, sans-serif, enormous lettering of "DUCE" on the exhibition's walls, the whirling, dynamic, masculine heroic action suggested by its collage and montage effects, and the multimedia extravaganza the exhibition displayed, provided Pound with ample evidence that the vorticist ideal was being realized in a new form – now in the context of an entire culture rather than just a movement in the arts. Accordingly, for Pound, Italy read as the site of a new manifestation of vorticism. I would also argue that Mussolini came to read to him as a type of vorticist hero, akin to the hero he had constructed for his Cantos based on Sigismondo Malatesta, whom Peter D'Epiro calls a "vorticist condottiere."[32]

While Pound's comments in 1924, then, chiefly indicate nostalgia for a youthful zenith, the place that vorticism later came to occupy in his imagination, as having set the gold standard in the arts both through its dynamism and intelligence about form, created a powerful forcefield in Pound's thought: one that drove his formal commitments in *The Cantos*; shaped his cultural hermeneutic; and in the 1930s, significantly guided his responses to Mussolini's Italy. His discovery in Italy of visual forms he read as vorticist deepened his faith in the fascist regime as hosting an environment in which the arts and the artist could flourish. Ultimately, Pound's discerning in Mussolini and his rising nation the combination of artistic brilliance and warrior prowess he had admired from early days onward – admiration which drew him to the vorticist movement and which was significantly reinforced through his engagement with vorticism – played a significant role in the continuation and strengthening of his loyalty to Mussolini's regime. In Italy, especially as he saw artists being courted to contribute to exhibitions such as the *Esposizione del Decennio*, Pound perceived opportunity to once again assume the status of a "hefty guy," this time in the context of a new nation led by another such hefty guy, "Il Duce."

NOTES

1 P. Reynolds, "Chaos Invading Concept: *Blast* as a Native Theory of Promotional Culture," *Twentieth Century Literature* 46.2 (2000): 238–68.

2 W. Lewis, *Rude Assignment* (London: Hutchison and Co., 1950), 135.

3 See L. Rainey, "The Creation of the Avant-Garde: F. T. Marinetti and Ezra Pound," *Modernism/ Modernity* 1.3 (1994): 210.

4 That *Blast* is now also featured in the Modernist Journals Project, http://dl.lib.brown.edu:8081/exist/mjp/index.xml, which digitizes periodicals central to Modernism's development, has helped to maintain the central place of *Blast* in accounts of Modernism's genesis.

5 *Blast 1*, ed. W. Lewis (Santa Rosa, CA: Black Sparrow Press, 1992), 154.

6 J. Lyon, *Manifestoes: Provocations of the Modern* (Ithaca, NY: Cornell University Press, 1999), 99.

7 *The Letters of Wyndham Lewis*, ed. W. K. Rose (London: Methuen and Co, 1963), 46. For a sustained account of this dispute, see J. Rothenstein, *Modern English Painters: Lewis to Moore* (New York: St. Martin's Press, 1956), 26–7.

8 W. Wees, *Vorticism and the English Avant-Garde* (Toronto: University of Toronto Press, 1972), 34.

9 Accounts of vorticism from Wees (*ibid.*), Reed Way Dasenbrock (*Literary Vorticism*, [Baltimore: Johns Hopkins University Press, 1985]), and Richard Cork (*Vorticism and its Allies* [London: Arts Council of Great Britain, 1974]) indicate that the artists often mentioned in connection with vorticism had relationships to the movement of varying kinds and degrees of involvement. Dasenbrock, for instance, notes that whereas Bomberg and Epstein had many connections with the vorticists, they refused official affiliation with the movement (*Literary Vorticism*, 56); Wees also characterizes them as "peripheral" (*Vorticism and the English Avant-Garde*, 151). Nevinson, meanwhile, while supportive of Lewis' group's break with Fry and involved in the planning of *Blast*, identified as an English Futurist, and after a quarrel between the vorticists and Futurists in June of 1914, remained outside the vorticist group (Wees, *Vorticism and the English Avant-Garde*, 151).

10 Wyndham Lewis, "The Cubist Room," *The Egoist* 1 (January 1, 1914): 8–9.

11 See, for instance, Wyndham Lewis, "A Review of Contemporary Art," *Blast 2*, (Santa Rosa, CA: Black Sparrow Press, 1993), 38–47.

12 For Lewis' statement about what the vorticists would seek to "correct," *ibid.*, 41.

13 As Bell put it, "lines and colours combined in a certain way, certain forms and relations of forms, stir our aesthetic emotions." See *Art* (New York: Stokes, 1913), 8.

14 Dasenbrock, *Literary Vorticism*, 41.

15 A. Sant' Elia, "Manifesto of Futurist Architecture," in *Futurist Manifestoes*, ed. U. Apollonio (Boston: MFA Publications, 1970), 171.

16 Dasenbrock, *Literary Vorticism*, 41. Artists whose work is traditionally associated with vorticism include not only the vorticist nucleus of Lewis, Edward Wadsworth, Cuthbert Hamilton, Frederick Etchells, Jessica Dismorr, and Helen Saunders, but also painter Christopher Nevinson (who became a Futurist), sculptor Gaudier-Brzeska, and figures with slighter links to the movement but associated with its idiom, such as sculptor Jacob Epstein and painter David Bomberg. For me, it is the dynamic form produced out of an effect of instability, and the consequent inability of the viewer's eye to come to rest easily in a composition bristling with tumbling lines and diagonals that themselves do not come to a restful balance, that provides the sine qua non of vorticist work. As a result, there are many pieces by artists associated with vorticism that do not read to me as vorticist. The work of Dismorr, Saunders, and Bomberg, for instance, generally does not display the aggressive dynamic diagonals featured here.

17 Oscar Wilde, *The Complete Works* (New York: Harper and Row, 1989), 970.

18 *Blast 1*, 25.

19 Lewis, "The Skeleton in the Cupboard Speaks," in *Wyndham Lewis on Art*, ed. W. Michel and C. J. Fox (New York: Funk and Wagnalls, 1969), 335.

20 M. Foucault, *The History of Sexuality: An Introduction*, vol. 1 (New York: Vintage, 1989).

21 M. Hickman, *Geometry of Modernism* (Austin: University of Texas Press, 2006). See esp. chapter 1, "Wyndham Lewis, Vorticism, and the Campaign Against Wildean Effeminacy," 27–88.

22 Lewis would later note in "The Skeleton in the Cupboard Speaks" that the "attitude" characteristic of vorticism was not that of the "tough guy": "There were no schoolboy heroics, of the emotional Hemingway order about it." Instead, vorticism involved "the sternness and severity of mind that is appropriate to the man who does the stuff (in contrast to the amateur who stands rapt in front of it once it is done . . .)." This attitude, he concludes, was *"professional."* *Wyndham Lewis on Art*, 342.

23 Lewis, *Letters of Wyndham Lewis*, 49.

24 See L. Rainey, *Institutions of Modernism* (New Haven: Yale University Press, 1998), chapter 1, 10–41.

25 For the avant-garde footprint in which Pound was invested, see his *Contemporania* sequence from 1913, *Poetry* 2.1 (April 1913), 1–12.

26 Lewis, *Rude Assignment*, 128.

27 Lewis, "Skeleton in the Cupboard," 335.

28 Wees, *Vorticism and the English Avant-Garde*, 210.

29 The "Group X" exhibition took place at Heal's Mansard Gallery in March 1920, including work by Lewis himself as well as the original vorticists Jessica Dismorr, Frederick Etchells, Edward Wadsworth. "Group X," *Wyndham Lewis on Art*, 184.

30 Pound, Letter to Homer Pound, January 1924, quoted in D. Wright, "Subversive Technologies," PhD Dissertation, McGill University, 2007: 141.

31 Hickman, *Geometry of Modernism*, ch. 2.

32 P. D'Epiro, *A Touch of Rhetoric: Ezra Pound's Malatesta Cantos* (Ann Arbor, MI: UMI Research Press, 1983), 1.

CHAPTER 27

Music

Margaret Fisher

A & C Black's 1929 *Who's Who* carried Ezra Pound's entry as "Poet and composer." The music consisted of *Le Testament* (in three versions) – an opera on François Villon's poem of the same name, and ten violin pieces, including a setting of "Sestina Altaforte." A first essay on the relationship of poetry to music ("I Gather the Limbs of Osiris") eventually led to a weekly column as music critic for *The New Age*. Pound's sustained training of his ear gradually brought him to composing from this foundation in criticism. The sequence was, of course, backwards: composition came last.

Pound fought a hidden war against the "tyranny of words" and his own musical ignorance. Though he played elementary piano, his background hardly prepared him for the outré reaches of music theory and notation he undertook. Trained as a medievalist, Pound taught himself to read troubadour music, transpose *cantus firmus*, and transcribe the medieval *neums* into Western notation. In a modern idiom he studied overtones in harmonization, customized "melodic" minor scales to his needs, and developed composer's shorthand for polyrhythms and ostinati. We shouldn't be distracted by reports of a crude singing voice or tone-deafness. Neither presented an obstacle to composition or theory.

Music, in short, presented rough terrain. Ironically, Pound's ur-text for composition was a seminal work of literary criticism: Dante's *De vulgarii eloquentia*. Dante advocated *armonia* in the words and spelled out, with examples, the methods to achieve it. Returning to this work for a refresher on the arrangement of syllables, the application of dissonance, the delight in experiment, we gain entrée to Pound's music.

Music and words in the Middle Ages inspired some of the most far-reaching principles in Western criticism – Guido D'Arezzo's *symphoniam grammaticae admireris* (harmony of language, the *Micrologus*), and Dante's *armonia* (the measure of true or divine proportion, *Convivio* I.V.13). Medieval criticism, a branch of philosophical inquiry, proceeded by formal methods of division to expose the structural properties of a work and reveal its treatment. Through division one would know the construction of the whole work of art.[1] Pound approached music in exactly this manner, as a philosophy of art that examined the division of sound into vertical and horizontal units. He later identified the setting of words to music as a form of criticism, but not "literary criticism."[2] Composition independent of the poet's voice, for purely aesthetic or structural purpose, was secondary.

Had Pound relied solely on medieval philosophy, he could hardly have hoped to make a convincing or relevant case for music. He also grounded himself in twentieth-century musicology, philology, and the emerging fields of acoustics, ethnomusicology, and recording technologies.

MOTZ EL SON

Professional musicians befriended Pound all his life, each bringing him closer to the overarching goal – restoring poetry to the state of *motz el son* (the troubadour's symbiotic art of words conjoined to music), in modern voice, in English, with primacy given to melody: "The condition of music was invoked to argue for *vers libre*, the liberation of poetry from metrical imprisonment to find its natural cadence" (*EPM*, 469). American concert pianist and composer Katherine Ruth Heyman, author of *The Relation of Ultramodern to Archaic Music* (1921), helped Pound argue against the dominance of tonality and the fixed matrix of Western harmonic laws. Her book introduces "aural spacing," Noh's "space between tones," and rhythmic properties inherent in the musical interval.[3] "Space between tones" would be central to Pound's theory of harmony.

PARIS

Pound's medievalism – archaic in America and marginalized in London – still had cachet in Paris, where his musicological interests took root in 1910. The city's medieval revival (1871–1905) lingered on in art and scholarship. When Paris succumbed to "institutionalization of medievalism," François Villon and Pablo Picasso kept Montmartre bohemian. Old French could be heard in the gothic, stained-glass church décors of the cabarets.[4] Occitan thrived in the print culture of preeminent troubadour scholar Alfred Jeanroy. Culture wars over the troubadours' use of rhythmic modes flourished under the press of Pierre Aubry, fiery young musicologist. His *Cent motets du xiiie siècle* (1908) used a new photographic process to publish music manuscripts in facsimile, surely catching Pound's attention (he borrowed a thirteenth-century *alba* from Aubry for *Testament*). This was all grist for Pound's mill. Discovering two Arnaut Daniel music manuscripts in Milan's Biblioteca Ambrosiana (1911) Pound, too, took up the practice of assembling photographic collections of early manuscripts. He turned his wheel against the rhythmic modes, away from Jeanroy and toward Emil Lévy, author of *Petit dictionnaire provençal-francais*, legendized in Canto xx. If music was rough terrain, Pound would stake his territory.

Paris was also Petri dish for a thriving occultism fueled by the revival of medieval rituals. Séances to reawaken spirits of the dead (especially following World War I) and theories of reincarnation were ubiquitous. Pound would use song to resuscitate the poets on his short list of the Western canon: Sappho, Catullus, Cavalcanti, and Villon. Theosophy and Rosicrucianism attracted Claude Debussy and Eric Satie, the quintessential medieval modernist of Montmartre, and Walter Morse Rummel (d.1953), pianist-composer, troubadour enthusiast, interpreter of Debussy, and Pound's close friend.

Sharing a passion for the poetry of *motz el sons*, Pound and Rummel searched the Bibliothèque Nationale for overlooked troubadour songs. When Rummel arranged nine troubadour songs for publication, Pound contributed rhythmic transcriptions for the two Arnaut Daniel melodies, and English lyrics for all.[5] Pound's first musicological endeavors had found a venue, even in an avowedly non-scholastic edition.

LE MOT JUSTE

Searching for the appropriate terminology, Pound in his early prose forecast the need to set words to music: "Poetry is a sort of inspired mathematics, which gives us equations . . . for the human emotions" (*SR*, 14). A credo emerged: "I believe in an ultimate and absolute rhythm," one that could carry and convey the perception of emotion in the cadence of the words.[6] "I Gather the Limbs of Osiris" speaks of the "inner form of the line . . . which must be preserved in music" (*EPM*, 31–2). Imagism moved the terms from theory into practice: "As regarding rhythm: to compose in the sequence of the musical phrase, not in sequence of a metronome" (*LE*, 3). Visiting Pierre-Jean Rousselot's phonological laboratory in Paris (1913), Pound recorded "The Return." The precise durations of the vowels appeared on "lampblacked paper," making tangible the "feel of sapphics."[7] The principle and terminology continued to evolve. A theory of "great bass" encompassing rhythm *and* harmony emerged, after which the metronome became de rigueur.

DOLMETSCH, FRANCO OF COLOGNE, CAMPION

Music temporarily yielded to Yeats, the Fenollosa editions, and marriage, among other activities, but introduction to Arnold Dolmetsch in the fall of 1914, unlocked the way forward. A colorful character, publicly mistrusted by England's early music academics, Dolmetsch (d.1940) was a thoroughly trained early music specialist. He built instruments, documented early performance techniques, and performed on original instruments with original tunings.[8] He sold Pound a clavichord, which, unlike a piano, has almost no sustain – an attractive feature to a musician interested in distinguishing words rather than blending them.

The acquaintance extended Pound's musical training into the baroque period, when vocal music waned. Perhaps the abstraction of instrumental music provided the necessary dissociation for Pound to recognize Dante in the baroque. His essay "Vers Libre and Arnold Dolmetsch" opens, "Poetry is a composition of words set to music" (*LE*, 437). If Dante was ur-text to Pound's musical endeavors, Dolmetsch provided the necessary and brilliant interdisciplinary gloss in *The Interpretation of the Music of the* XVII *and* XVIII *Centuries* (1915), with its "direct bearing on poetry." Dolmetsch's account of baroque performance practice dovetails seamlessly with Dante's exposition of the art of arranging syllables and words. Each work recommends ornamentation to achieve unexpected, rich harmonization between sounds. Dante wrote that simple ornamentation of the words involved the inevitable, necessary use of monosyllables. In music, this fell to the grace notes. Deeper ornamentation of words was catalogued in Dante's famously "shaggy" words (long, aspirated, or accented words; words with double consonants); in music, the compound grace notes, longer mordents, and trills. The two texts lynch-pinned Pound's music and poetry.[9]

Pound saw potential for techniques that might revolutionize rhythmic structure to shore up the *libre* side of *vers libre*. Dolmetsch's citations of Mace, J. J. Rousseau, and Couperin on musical rhythm might hereforth apply to poetry. Grace notes find analogue in anapestic motion ("*But* say I want to," "*Say that* I"); the mordent in choriambic filler ("Needs *such a* ragbag," "Not *in the* least"); trills, their correlative in shaggy English triplets ("*quirks and tweeks*", "*flapping and slipping*") where the interest revolves around the discord of adjacent or similar surfaces, where three words fit the space of two beats. These examples from "Ur-Canto" 1, eventually discarded, proved too obvious and facile. Other experiments would follow.

Dolmetsch was the *force majeur* behind Pound's auto-didacticism in music. Once immersed in early music notation and theory, Pound gravitated to the discourse on rhythm. Compositionally, Pound took his bearings from the implied word rhythms driving plain-chant. To notate those rhythms, he was indebted to Franco of Cologne, whose *Ars cantus mensurabilis* (thirteenth century) had the result of detaching music from rhythmic modes and classical poetic constructs. Franco's codification of the note shapes added mensural dimension to each note, rendering the *neums* of plain-song notation obsolete.[10] This revolutionary advance held the potential to liberate each note from the tyranny of its position in the line. One can appreciate the implications for syllables in a line of poetry. Pound would mine the depth of Franco's invention: rhythm underlies all musical structure, but until rhythm was systematized, there could be no logical relationship between the time interval and harmony. Pound's treatise on harmony would spell out the logic of that relationship: time interval and pitch, like words and music, must be considered as interdependent elements to achieve the best effects.

The idea of such a relationship was thoroughly modern, and still is. Pound's music theorizing fits within the kind of avant-garde synthesis that fueled American radicalism and European modernism in music. Invention cultivated primitivism, folk culture, and jazz; was anchored in the physics of sound – ratios, tunings, and the psychology of reception. Hermann Helmholtz's *On the Sensations of Tones* (1863) profoundly influenced American composers Cowell, Antheil, Partch, and, probably, Pound. Like Cowell, Pound considered all musical pitch a matter of frequency.[11] At a certain threshold, frequency becomes audible to the ear as pulse (percussion) or pitch. Pound understood that the harmonics arising from the inherent predictable division of sound waves of the inaudible slower frequencies will subliminally interact with the sounds that fall within hearing range. Pound's interest in tapping this perceptual ability to adjust for harmonics outside of hearing range had earlier been explored by the English composer Thomas Campion (d.1620), whose music lay neglected in the British Library.

Dolmetsch undoubtedly was one portal to Campion. Another may have been Ernest Rhys, founding member of the Rhymers Club.[12] Dedicating his 1929 translation of Guido Cavalcanti's poem "Donna mi prega" to "Campion, his ghost," Pound made oblique reference to Cavalcanti's and Campion's shared practice of developing poetic turns of logic through musical phrasing.

Campion's mastery of the epigrammatic form – the short swell of logic destined for undertow – with all the surprise and naughtiness that comes naturally and pleasurably to Campion – shapes his music and poetry this way: the desired feeling of the entire poem or song is established in the rhythm of the first line. The poet-musician dissociates thought from feeling on intimate as well as grand terms, and in two idioms. The challenge loomed large. Pound's "absolute rhythm" had accounted for the inner form of the line, not the whole shape of a poem.

LE TESTAMENT AND CAVALCANTI IN LIGHT OF CAMPION

We see the distance traveled when we compare Pound's first opera *Le Testament* (1923, to Villon's poem of the same name) to the second, *Cavalcanti* (1931–3, settings of Cavalcanti's poetry). Emphasizing Villon's irregular speech rhythms in *Le Testament*, the composer's parsing of the syllables and words begets ineluctable cadences in irrational mixed meters. Hugh Kenner's chapter "Motz el son" in *The Pound Era* aids our listening. Pointillism in the instruments enhances the distinct properties of the words. It prevents the diverse timbres from blending, a strategy seen in *The Cantos* where Chinese, Provençal, and Greek reinforce the English words to achieve a striking lack of "melodious blending" (Kenner's term, *PE*). Pound wrote, "The primary interest is a musical interest in the strength and firmness of the melodic line . . . The interest held by the single melody, then by that melody sustained or 'forced onto' a ground tone, then successively against another melody, against another scale system; one rhythm forced against another."[13]

Generally, one feels no underlying pulse or imminent destination in *Testament*'s melodies. An elusive, unpredictable downbeat emphasizes the "subtle joints of [Villon's] craft," (*SR*, 88), bringing forward into music the insights of "Psychology and Troubadours." Pound's model was the long Provençal rhythm pattern, with its delayed repetition (attributed by Pound to Arabic influence). One listens to the opera syllable by syllable and still appreciates the opera's "great aesthetic arch" that begins with simpler accompaniment at the unison or octave, rises to increasing complexity and dissonance, peaks with the orgiastic choral number, and succumbs to a "final septet . . . a rich monophonic texture which gradually reduces itself . . . to a simple poignant unison chant."[14]

It is *Cavalcanti* that benefits from the interest in Campion: the first line of each number contains the emotion of the entire song-poem. Here, because the word rhythms have their basis in lyricism rather than colloquial speech, tempo rather than local rhythms become critical. Tempo and melodic outline set the emotional tenor and anticipate the shape of each song.

Pound had to master the traditional tripartite interaction of rhythm – local durations, divisions of meters into bars, and tempo. *Cavalcanti* is filled with modular melodic and rhythmic cells that help avoid repetition

Figure 1: Three examples of first lines of selected arias, *Cavalcanti*

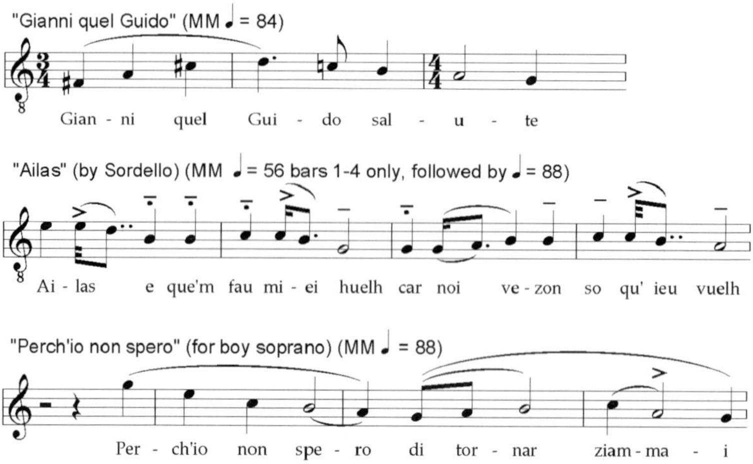

of the larger pattern units.[15] The ear recognizes structure in the interplay of these cells and their relationship to the poem's first line. The effect is of an extended melodic line. Line construction in *The Cantos* exhibits similarities: " 'long lines' of thought, argument, and design cross each other in every canto."[16]

Pound managed to extract persona from the octave and tritone: sonic markers that flag concepts important to *Cavalcanti's* philosophy. Pound's music intervals impart a rhythmic dynamic and therefore a specific feeling. His use of the first and second overtones (e.g. the singer's ranges in "Perch'io non spero") distinguish degrees of innocence and experience to enhance the drama. The tuneful setting of [most] first lines stays in the ear and plays against all that follows – a notable achievement given that Pound through-composed his melodies.

Pound's music can be better evaluated when one knows its function and structural foundations. The overriding question concerns the preservation of Villon's and Cavalcanti's original word sounds, rhythms, and seams, usually lost in translation, to demonstrate how the elements join to make larger units.

MELOPOEIA

Campion illuminates Pound in significant ways. His theorization of the bass line in music, *A New Way of Making Fowre Parts in Counter-point* (*c.* 1613), provides historical context to Pound's "great bass" theory. Campion's summary of MELOPOEIA *sive Melodiae condendae ratio* (1592) by Seth Calvisius, musician, mathematician, and astronomer of Leipzig, suggests a source for Pound's term *melopoeia*. Calvisius, and Campion after him, established rules for triadic harmony that stayed true to the tonal center of a song. Campion's innovation was to develop harmonic relations from the bass part rather than the tenor, the *cantus firmus*. His rules for a formal bass – the horizontal succession of bass notes and the chords rising above them – respected the naturally occurring ratios determined by the bass fundamental and the overtone series, and considered the psychoacoustic ability of the ear to account for overtones. "Great bass" would extend and simplify Campion's premise by identifying these ratios as the *only* measure of proportion, in pitch as well as in tempo.

Pound directed *melopoeia* to his own purpose, defining it as poetry in which "the interest and intent . . . largely centres in the sound," in which the poet uses "words as a melodic stimulus" and relies almost entirely on sound for "conveyance of emotion." Such poetry is dependent on "the actual beat, rhythm, and timbre of [the] words for the emotional effect of [the] work." *Melopoeia cantabile* were lyric poems made to be "delivered with varying pitch." Pound set to music only poems of this type, explaining that, even if such poetry were built upon complex ideas, *melopoeia cantabile* made its major contribution through sonic values alone.[17] The terms "absolute rhythm," inner form of the line, etc. were discontinued. *Melopoeia*, like *armonia*, had staying power.

Pound's "Melopoeia" (1930) notes a critical difference in values between Greek verse and its renaissance in the poetry of Provençe, "Roughly speaking the emphasis shifts from the sound to the meaning, and from the strophe to the individual line."[18] Pound embeds this shift of emphasis within his operas (backwards) from *Testament*'s individuation within the line, to *Cavalcanti*'s extended line and its influence, to an unfinished third opera *Collis O Heliconii* (1933), which conceived rules for the strophe as the primary musical unit (the aforementioned invention with "melodic" minor scales).

WILLIAM ATHELING, AGNES BEDFORD, GEORGE ANTHEIL,
AND OLGA RUDGE

Under the pen name William Atheling, Pound reviewed chamber and vocal concerts for *The New Age*, December 1917 to January 1921. The complete published reviews edited by R.M. Schafer provide essential background to "Atheling's" milieu, scope, preferences, and lacunae. The review of a November 1919 concert led to a lifelong friendship with Agnes Bedford (d.1969), English pianist and vocal coach. She took "the whole Villon work down from Ezra's singing and performances on the piano," and gave advice regarding *Cavalcanti*.[19] The letters between Pound and Agnes Bedford document Pound's completion of *Testament* on his own in Paris (1921), the BBC broadcasts (1931), the composition of *Cavalcanti* in Rapallo, Italy (1931–3), and Pound's changing ideas about composition; e.g., his struggle to master metronomic time once he grasped the potential of tempo *and* percussion to participate in the harmony.

When the Pounds moved to Paris in 1921, modernism had broken with medievalism; artists moved fluidly between science and industry, nonsense and dissonance. Dada and Surrealism filled the cafés and theaters; jazz, the cabarets. Picasso and Stravinsky mined a neo-classical vein. Satie was alive but Debussy had died. Pound's wheel turned against them both. Paris would tease from Pound's Villon score the extremes – archaic hexatonic scales and a fifteen-foot alpenhorn, liberated by modernist discontinuities of meter, style, and dissonance.

Paris friendships with Americans Olga Rudge (d.1996), a concert violinist specializing in contemporary music, and George Antheil (d.1959), avant-garde composer and sensational, scandal-loving pianist, propelled Pound into the world of twentieth-century musical experimentation. In fall, 1923, Pound began composing his first solo violin works in a modern idiom expressly for Rudge, exhibiting a composer's interest beyond the setting of words. He engaged Antheil to re-score *Testament* on a new rhythmic basis. Antheil, a superb "stenographer" of music, duly noted the precise duration of each syllable from Pound's recitation.[20] The resulting irrational meters and micro-rhythms had no parallel in music. Much of the score, now considered the opera's ur-text, was unperformable in its time. Of note were the dissonances and polyrhythms calculated from ratios, tritones, and instrumental timbres, anticipating Henry Cowell's harmonic experiments with rhythm.[21] Rudge never accepted the 1923 Pound/Antheil score, arguing it was unnecessarily complicated and therefore impractical. Her letter of October 20, 1924 reassured Pound that the seasoned musician could feel the "steady pulse under the bar" and would not accent the beat. But the difficult metrics were, instead, about poetic construction, directed to the ear of the literati. *Testament*'s "Dame du ciel" clearly presents Pound's intention to do away entirely with a steady pulse; it fits an entire line of poetry to one or two irrational measures, accents the downbeat *and* proceeds with micro-rhythms that cancel any sense of underlying beat.[22]

The centerpiece of Pound's output in 1924 is the slim volume *Antheil and The Treatise on Harmony*, overbearing on its surface, yet not without insight and one revolutionary proposal.[23] The argument is singular: music composition must defer to the composer's ear and instinct, over rules. The 1923 Pound/Antheil score forecast many of the ideas presented in *Treatise*. The friendship with Antheil yielded influence both ways for about a year before it tapered off,[24] and Pound's wheel turned toward Stravinsky.

In *Treatise*, Pound isolates the time interval between one sound and another as the crux of harmonic construction. This was a radical approach to harmonic technique that eschewed the Western tradition of vertical or triadic harmony to rely solely on time constraints: "A SOUND OF ANY PITCH, OR ANY COMBINATION OF SUCH SOUNDS, MAY BE FOLLOWED BY A SOUND OF ANY OTHER PITCH, OR ANY COMBINATION OF SUCH SOUNDS, providing the time interval between them is properly gauged; and this is true for ANY SERIES OF SOUNDS, CHORDS OR ARPEGGIOS."[25]

Pound's subjectivist principle conceptually outpaced Schoenberg's twelve-tone objectivist model. Antheil's system of TIME–SPACE organization, a replacement for organization by pitch, was inherently biased for complex, asymmetric, and fast tempi, a short-lived Modernism, like Futurism, that thrived on innovation and surprise, and aspired to "new melodic aesthetic."[26] Pound, allowing for any sequence of pitches, created an open system that could accommodate any aesthetic. The time interval – a matter of local rhythms and overall tempo – determines the auditor's perception of relativity and continuing influence between and among tones: "Music is a composition of frequencies." The *Treatise* conjoined music and words under one rule: control of the time duration was the underlying form of the work of art.

Pound's philosophy of art pushed beyond *Testament*. The Murphy/Léger film *Ballet Mécanique*, intended for Antheil's music, also holds time duration as its underlying form. Pound, a friend of Murphy's, assisted in the editing lab. A diagram of the film's mathematical divisions according to "arithmatical" laws, "from slow motion to extreme speed," has been attributed to Léger, but the captions are in Pound's hand. The concept involved the frequency and duration of images. A graph of seven "vertical . . . clearly defined temporal units" interrupted by "horizontal penetrations" shows Pound thinking about film in terms of music's vertical and horizontal constructions.[27] We can guess the rest: the film would test the eye/brain capacity to process information at varying frequencies: the number of repetitions and frames per image contrasts with the ear/brain capacity to recognize varying frequencies as pitch or pulse.

With Pound's relocation to Rapallo, Italy in 1924 the application of "great bass" across disciplines moved toward a theory of genius based on a person's "sense of time-division and/or duration."[28]

"*Supplemento Al Mio Trattato d'Armonia*" (1931) expounded on "great bass" relationships as the proper source for tempo. Having defined music as nothing more than "a composition of frequencies, microphonic and macrophonic,"[29] Pound proposed "great bass" to relate the parts: "[the] main base in all musical structure" resides in the ratio between the slower frequencies or vibrations that are the percussion of the rhythm and tempo (the "bottom note of the harmony") and the notes written for the instruments (*GK*, 233). R. Murray Schafer summarizes Pound's explorations this way, "*Absolute rhythm* governed the [local] proportions of the elements of masterpieces; *Great Bass* [ratio] links the elements [microphonic and macrophonic] into an indivisible whole" (*EPM*, 479). These concepts bypassed harmonic development conceived as chordal construction.

A 1926 Paris salon concert at Salle Pleyel previewed excerpts from *Le Testament* and tested the new "great bass" theory with an overture played entirely on its overtones, for *cornet de dessus*, an instrument with a fundamental tone of D_2 (five ledger lines below bass clef).[30]

THE COMPLETE OEUVRE

Pound ceased composing in 1934. The complete music oeuvre consists of five versions of the one-act opera in Old French, *Le Testament* (1920, 1923, 1926, 1931, 1933–4), the three-act *Cavalcanti* in Italian (1931–3, first performed in 1983), an incomplete third opera *Collis O Heliconii* on poems of Catullus and Sappho (1933, first performed in 2002), two mature violin works – "Sonate 'Ghuidonis'" and "Al poco giorno" (the latter to rhythms of Dante's sestina) – and a handful of miscellaneous violin works.[31] The output is a musical exposition of diverse poetic or recitation forms from ancient times through the Middle Ages: plain-chant, plainte, roundel, sestina, frottola, canzone, ballata, lay, chanson, and motet. Pound's music emerges not as guardian of a particular style or aesthetic, but as a unique, if idiosyncratic and somewhat uneven, vehicle that breaks with metrical convention and analytical prose to consider and critique poetic form.

Experiments coetaneous with Pound's oeuvre, some treating the same poets and/or poems, are: Eric Satie's *Socrate*, Kurt Weill's "Jenny's Song" (*Three-Penny Opera*), Debussy's "Dame du ciel," Carl Orff's "Collis O Heliconii" for chorus (*Catulli Carmina*), and Orff's settings of identical excerpts from Sappho and Catullus (*Trionfo di Afrodite*). Pound's use of collage to interpolate popular music hints at the more complicated collage structures of Charles Ives. Both composers mined texts and diverse music to create an art of counterstatement; of melodies, ply over ply.

RAPALLO CONCERTS AND *THE PISAN CANTOS*

Devoting long hours to composition, Pound began evidencing a composer's interest in music beyond his initial interest in the *armonia* of words. He produced a Rapallo concert series (1933–9), anchored by Rudge and the German pianist-composer Gerhard Münch, and noted for its recovery of Vivaldi. World War II effectively silenced further activity related to music until the writing of *The Pisan Cantos*.

From LXXII forward, birds punctuate *The Cantos* with melody and coun-terpoint. LXXXII reshaped the swallows of Canto IV ("'Tis. 'Tis. Ytis!" – a grace note on the latter), into "Terreus" as notes on the staff

f   f
   d
    g

LXXV continues the philosophical inquiry concerning words and music. It reprints a music line by Münch that reaches back to Janequin's choral work *Chant des Oiseaux*. The marvel was that "the birds [plural] were still there" since Münch worked from Francesco da Milano's arrangement of *Oiseaux* for lute. Münch's preservation of Janequin's original vocal intervals in the violin line was the point of insertion into the poem: "I think Janequin inherited from the troubadours the fine clear cut representation of natural sound, the exactitude of birds and flowers," earlier classified by Pound as "music of representative outline" (as contrasted to structure; e.g., Bach).[32] While LXXV continues the interest in artistic lineage, it did not require "genius" to keep the birds in the music. The salient point was recognition of the birds, an affirmation of intelligence and "forma" in nature. Songbirds became the "absolute symbol or metaphor" for *motz el son*. They "cut a shape in time";[33] they resist melodious blending. We hear their melodic and rhythmic patterns distinctly, even in counterpoint; they help us appreciate the music of words in any language. The polyrhythms in "Père Noé," and more generally the instrumental hocketing in *Testament* had attempted this kind of distinction.

Performed frequently in Rapallo, Münch's *Oiseaux* always delighted the audience. Such pleasure cut through centuries of theory and across disciplines. Terrell identifies LXXV as the pivot that turns the poem to the paradisal section of *The Cantos*.[34]

One can bird-watch throughout the Pisans, where the words, when whistled, enact the "singing quality" of *The Cantos*.

> three solemn half notes
> > their white downy chests black-rimmed
> on the middle wire
> > periplum   (LXXXII/547)

NOTES

1 J. Allen, *The Ethical Poetic of the Later Middle Ages: A Decorum of convenient Distinction* (Toronto: University of Toronto Press, 1982), 126.

2 "Dateline," *Make it New* (1934) in *LE*, 74. "The history of literary criticism is largely the history of a vain struggle to find a terminology which will define something" (*SR*, 13).

3 K.R. Heymann, *The Relation of Ultramodern to Archaic Music* (Boston: Small, Maynard & Co., 1921), 54.

4 E. Emery and L. Morowitz, *Consuming the Past, The Medieval Revival in fin-de-siècle France* (Farnham, UK: Ashgate Publishing, 2003), 3; S.M. Whiting, *Satie the Bohemian: From Cabaret to Concert Hall* (Oxford: Clarendon Press, 1999), 418.

5 W. M. Rummel, *Neuf Chansons de Troubadours des XIIième et XIIIième Siècles* (London: Augener, 1913).

6 "Introduction" to *Sonnets and Ballate* (November 1910), in *CAV*, 18.

7 R. Sieburth, http://writing.upenn.edu/pennsound/x/text/Sieburth-Richard_Pound.html (August 7, 2008).

8 Pound, "Arnold Dolmetsch," *New Age* (January 7, 1915): 246–7, in *LE*, 431; M. Campbell, *Dolmetsch: The Man and His Work* (Seattle: University of Washington Press, 1975), 194; R. Merritt, *Early Music and the Aesthetics of Ezra Pound* (Lewiston, NY: The Edwin Mellen Press, 1993), 43.

9 Dante, *De vulgari eloquentia* II.7.6, trans. Robert Haller, in *Literary Criticism of Dante Alighieri* (Lincoln: University of Nebraska Press, 1973), 47–8; Arnold Dolmetsch, *The Interpretation of Music of the XVII and XVIII Centuries* (1916; London: Novello and Co., 1946), 98–9.

10 We continue to use Franco's notational system today. J. Stevens, *Words and Music in the Middle Ages* (Cambridge: Cambridge University Press, 1986), 451n44. Also see, Dolmetsch, 439 *Interpretation*.

11 See R. Hughes, *Cavalcanti: A Perspective on the Music of Ezra Pound* (Emeryville, CA: Second Evening Art, 2003), 129–38. Pound and Antheil attended Cowell's

Paris debut at the Salle Erard on November 17, 1923, but Pound never met Cowell.

12 E. Rhys, ed., *The Lyric Poems of Thomas Campion* (London: J.M. Dent & Co., 1896). Rhys refers to Campion's treatise in this edition. Also see *SR*, Post-postscript.

13 On Pound's affinity with Cubism, see G. Antheil, *Bad Boy of Music* (Garden City, NY: Doubleday, Doran, 1945), 120. Pound, "Le Testament" (n.d., Yale University, Beinecke Library, YCALMSS 43, Box 138, folder 6013).

14 R. Hughes, *Ezra Pound's Opera: Le Testament de Villon*, LP liner notes (Berkeley: Fantasy 12031, 1972).

15 I am grateful to R. Murray Schafer for letting me read his unpublished study of *Cavalcanti*, where he discusses Pound's use of melodic and rhythmic cells. Schafer suggests a resemblance to fourteenth-century *Ars nova* techniques.

16 J. Winn, *Unsuspected Eloquence* (New Haven: Yale University Press, 1981) 336.

17 Pound, "Song" (n.d.), in *EPRO*, 156–7. The earliest use of *melopoeia* that I could find by Pound is in a review of Jean Cocteau's *Poésies 1917–1920*, *Dial*, 70.1 (January 1921), in *EPCP*, IV: 133. Pound originally considered the foremost musical property to be the time interval but appears to have adjusted his ideas to include timbre and pitch.

18 "Melopoeia," in "How to Read," in Ezra Pound, *Machine Art and Other Writings*, ed. Maria Luisa Ardizzone (Durham, NC: Duke University Press, 1996), 95.

19 Letter, Agnes Bedford to Dorothy Pound, November 19, 1967 (Lilly Library, Indiana University, Bloomington).

20 Antheil, *Bad Boy of Music*, 124.

21 H. Cowell, *New Musical Resources* (written 1919, first published Knopf 1930), ed. David Nicholls (Cambridge: Cambridge University Press, 1996).

22 "Dame's" pronounced dissonance affords a valuable study of "great bass." Even when, at Rudge's insistence, Pound re-scored *Le Testament* into simpler meters, "Dame" retained her irrational meters; e.g., 23/16, 31/16, 17/8. See M. Fisher, "Great Bass: Undertones of Continuous Influence," *Performance Research* 8.1 (2003): 23–40.

23 Antheil reports Pound borrowed from his rebellious papers on music and worked them into a theory. However, Pound's reference to overtones did not draw from Antheil's written notes, perhaps too obvious to a musician to be written down (Antheil, *Bad Boy of Music*, 117–20). Pound names names to index his talking points. These must be researched to understand the whole of his arguments.

24 Antheil wrote Pound, "My four-hour opera is very much influenced by yours. Same technique" (May 1925, archives of the George Antheil Estate, El Cerrito, California, Charles Amirkhanian, executor).

25 Ezra Pound, *Antheil and the Treatise on Harmony* (Chicago: Pascal Covici, 1927), 10.

26 Antheil, *Bad Boy of Music*, 118.

27 The music was not paired to the film when it was first shown. S. D. Lawder, *The Cubist Cinema* (New York: New York University Press, 1975), 131–2. This explains why Lawder was unable to "align" the film's time structure in the diagram with Léger's written description of the film's organization.

28 *GK*, 73, 197. See also, Fisher, "Great Bass," throughout.

29 Yale University, Beinecke Library, (YCAL MSS43 Box 138, folder 6080); Pound, *Antheil and the Treatise on Harmony*, 30.

30 Information about the instrument custom-built by Toyoji Tomita to realize Pound's score is to be found in R. Hughes and M. Fisher, eds., *Le Testament* (Emeryville, CA: Second Evening Art, 2008), 2–3.

31 Hughes and Fisher, *Le Testament*; R. Hughes, ed., *Complete Violin Works of Ezra Pound* (Emeryville, CA: Second Evening Art, 2004); M. Fisher, *The Recovery of Ezra Pound's Third Opera, Collis O Heliconii* (Emeryville, CA: Second Evening Art, 2005). A full account of the BBC broadcast is in Fisher, *EPRO*.

32 *GK*, 151–52. See also Schafer's comments on "metempsychosis" in music, *EPM*, 328.

33 *ABCR*, 54; *EPM*, 379; *CAV*, 18; letter, Pound to Mary Barnard, December 2, 1933, in Mary Barnard, *Assault on Mount Helicon* (Berkeley: University of California Press, 1984), 55; also see *EPM*, 390–1.

34 C. Terrell, *A Companion to The Cantos of Ezra Pound* (Berkeley: University of California Press, 1993), II: 389.

CHAPTER 28

Visual arts

Rebecca Beasley

The visual arts played a major role in Ezra Pound's career. His poetry, especially *The Cantos*, testifies to a deep engagement with painting, sculpture, and architecture, and his essays reveal an aesthetics profoundly shaped by the visual arts. Conversely, as art critic, agent, and visual theorist, as well as poet, Pound directly contributed to early twentieth-century visual culture, and his writings, especially those on vorticism, have proved enduringly influential for subsequent generations of artists and critics. Pound's involvement with the visual arts was at its height from 1913 to 1924, the periods of early and high modernism, when he was living in London and Paris. But his education in the visual arts began not in early twentieth-century Europe, but in late nineteenth-century America.

PHILADELPHIA: 1885–1908

Pound was born at a moment when the United States was exhibiting an unprecedented fascination with European visual culture. During the last thirty years of the nineteenth century, the country experienced a rapid rise of interest in painting, sculpture, and the decorative arts as, following the Civil War, massive industrial growth fostered a prosperous leisure class seeking to invest in, and display, its cultural capital. The great private art collections, such as those of J.P. Morgan and Isabella Stewart Gardner, began to take shape, national art societies were formed, and the major art schools and museums were established: the Metropolitan Museum of New York and the Boston Museum of Fine Arts were founded in 1870, the Philadelphia Museum of Art in 1876, and the Art Institute of Chicago in 1879.[1] European art dominated these collections: initially, the fashion was for the art of the French Salon and paintings by Old Masters, and by the end of the century the United States had become the major market for French Impressionist painting. A modified Impressionism had also become the dominant note in American painting, both in the work of celebrated expatriates such as Mary Cassatt, John Singer Sargent, and James McNeill Whistler, and residents William Merritt Chase, Childe Hassam, John Twachtman, and J. Alden Weir.[2]

Intersecting with the rise of Impressionism, but expressed in the more popular decorative arts and in literature, as well as fine art, was the vogue for art for art's sake, or aestheticism. John Ruskin's writings had been published and anthologized in the United States since the 1850s, his ideas promoted for their moral and spiritual justifications of art by immensely influential critics and teachers such as Charles Eliot Norton, Harvard's first Professor of Fine Art. During the late 1870s and 1880s the aestheticist craze was at its height: Clarence Cook's *The House Beautiful* was published in 1879, Oscar Wilde arrived to begin his American lecture tour in 1882, James McNeill Whistler's *Arrangement in Yellow and White* exhibition toured the following year, and the American publication of *Marius the Epicurean* in 1885 launched a belated enthusiasm for Walter Pater.[3]

In 1889, at the age of three, Pound moved with his family to Philadelphia, which placed him in one of the nation's centers of visual art production, collection, and display. In 1876 the city had hosted the Centennial Exhibition, the major catalyst in the late nineteenth-century art industry, and from 1880 the Pennsylvania Academy of Fine Arts began its systematic acquisition of major works by living American artists. In its permanent collection Pound would have seen contemporary works by Cecilia Beaux, William Merritt Chase, Thomas Eakins, Childe Hassam, and Winslow Homer, and between 1900 and 1908, he could have attended special exhibitions including *Teijiro Hasekana: Watercolors, Exhibition of Photographs Arranged by the Photo-Secession, Modern European Works from the Collection of Peter Schemm, Robert Henri* and *Ernest Lawson: Paintings*.[4] As an undergraduate, Pound was engaged with the art world of Philadelphia through friends such as the painters Frank Reed Whiteside, who had studied at the Academy and in Paris, and William Brooke Smith, the dedicatee of Pound's first book of poetry, who was a student at the School of Industrial Art and knew the future precisionists Charles Sheeler and Morton Schamberg, then both studying at the Academy.[5]

Pound's writings from the period provide a strong indication of his early aesthetic tastes. "Art," an unpublished essay written during the winter of 1906–7, reviewed exhibitions at the Academy and two Philadelphia art clubs, drawing on an aestheticist vocabulary: it was explicitly modeled on the criticism published in *The Black Mirror*, a New York art journal that promoted American Impressionism. Another essay, written a month later, praised Whistler's *The Gentle Art of Making Enemies* as an antidote to Ruskin's *Modern Painters*.[6] His first published literary criticism and his earliest poetry also drew directly on this turn-of-the-century visual culture. In "Raphaelite Latin" (1906) and "M. Antonius Flaminius and John Keats" (1908) Pound styles himself as an aestheticist critic, championing a love of beauty over utilitarian scholarship, and invoking Whistler and J.W. Waterhouse to illustrate his points (*EPCP*, 1: 5, 17–18). His juvenilia includes ekphrastic verse ("Nel Biancheggiar," "For Italico Brass"), Browningesque poems about painters,[7] and, in the San Trovaso notebook (1907–8) and *A Quinzaine for this Yule* (1908), a series of programmatic poems that define art as the creation of beautiful form out of chaos (*CEP*, 72, 253–4, 231–58, 53–72).[8] At the very beginning of his career, therefore, we see Pound, like other aesthetes, turning to visual culture to explore questions of aesthetics and to establish his professional identity – that of the Whistlerian artist-critic.

LONDON: 1908–20

Pound arrived in London in 1908, the year one might argue marked the beginning of the modernist movement in art in Britain. In January and February the International Society's annual exhibition had included works by Cézanne, Denis, Gauguin, Matisse, and Signac; in July the new Allied Artists' Association had organised its first "London Salon," a British version of the Parisian Salon des Indépendants, which fostered a new generation of British artists and introduced contemporary European artists to a British audience. Between 1910 and 1914 a further series of exhibitions rapidly established the new orthodoxy of Post-Impressionism, Cubism, Expressionism, and Futurism in contemporary art, including Roger Fry's two survey exhibitions, *Manet and the Post-Impressionists* (1910) and *Second Post-Impressionist Exhibition* (1912–13).[9]

Fry's ambitious *Manet and the Post-Impressionists* was greeted by notoriously disparaging reviews in 1910. The works of Cézanne, Van Gogh, and Gauguin, represented in the exhibition as the most important of the Post-Impressionist painters, and of Matisse and Picasso, their contemporary successors, proved particularly divisive. But British critics had become better informed about modern art by the time the *Second Post-Impressionist Exhibition* opened just two years later: "the battle is over and won," wrote a previously unsympathetic critic, "Post-Impressionism has taken firm root among us."[10] Furthermore, the second exhibition demonstrated the extent to which British artists had absorbed the lessons of contemporary art abroad: Clive Bell curated the exhibition's English section which included work by Vanessa Bell, Frederick Etchells, Fry, Spencer Gore, Duncan Grant, Wyndham Lewis, and Edward Wadsworth. Although this group was marked by certain omissions – notably the Fauvist Rhythm Group – it is significant that in 1912, Bloomsbury artists, future vorticists, and members of the Camden Town Group exhibited together under the umbrella term of Post-Impressionism. Even though Lewis' work was identifiably influenced by Picasso's, where Bell and Grant were clearly more indebted to Matisse, it was not until the autumn of 1913 that distinctions between the British artists began to become recognizable, and the source of polemic.

In October, Lewis, Etchells, Cuthbert Hamilton, and Wadsworth split acrimoniously from the Omega Workshops, Roger Fry's applied arts company. The same month, Frank Rutter's *Post-Impressionist and Futurist Exhibition* opened, promoting an alternative genealogy for Post-Impressionism from Fry's: Camille Pissarro, rather than Cézanne, was situated at the point of origin, and (in contrast to the *Second Post-Impressionist Exhibition*) the Italian Futurists, German Expressionists, and a substantial number of British artists were shown. The Bloomsbury artists were not included. By November Lewis was cultivating an association with the Italian Futurists, whose first London exhibition in March had been a critical sensation and a financial success. In December, Lewis' secessionist group exhibited with the Camden Town Group in the *Exhibition of the Work of English Post Impressionists, Cubists and Others* at the Brighton Public Art Galleries, an association that was in the process of being formalized as the new London Group. In March 1914 Lewis founded the short-lived Rebel Art Centre to promote the English Cubo-Futurists, soon to be re-named vorticists, and in early July Lewis published the first of two numbers of their periodical, *Blast*.[11]

It was not until this polemical period of 1913 that Pound became actively engaged in contemporary art. He had been aware of developments in French painting since early 1911, when he read Marius de Zayas' "The New Art in Paris" in the New York magazine, *Forum*, and he was a regular visitor to T.E. Hulme's Tuesday night salon, which was also attended by the Camden Town painters and future vorticists. But when he visited Paris to see the exhibitions described by de Zayas, he was unimpressed: "Freaks there are in abundance," he remarked.[12] At this point Pound was more interested in the Tate Gallery's exhibition *Loan Collection of Works by James McNeill Whistler* (1912), described in his "Patria Mia" articles and his poem "To Whistler – American" (*EPVA*, 1–2, 217–18). A year later, however, Pound began to develop his knowledge of contemporary art:

in July he met the French sculptor Henri Gaudier-Brzeska at the Allied Artists' Association exhibition (*GB*, 44), and soon after purchased two of his works, *Samson and Delilah (The Embracers)* (1913) and *Boy with a Coney* (1914).[13] In November he attended Rutter's *Post-Impressionist and Futurist Exhibition*, singling out Jacob Epstein's sculpture for particular praise, and he also attended Epstein's solo exhibition at the Twenty-One Gallery (*EPVA*, 237).[14] Pound finally entered the debates in print in February 1914: his first piece of art criticism, "The New Sculpture," discussed Epstein's work via an idiosyncratic interpretation of T.E. Hulme's lecture "The New Art and Its Philosophy."[15] Over the next six months, Pound published three more articles, discussing Epstein and Gaudier, Wadsworth and Lewis, and his "Affirmations" series the following year set out an interdisciplinary aesthetic that combined painting, sculpture, music, and literature (*EPVA*, 179–93, 5–29). Pound's most substantial work of art criticism, *Gaudier-Brzeska: A Memoir*, was published in 1916, following Gaudier's death fighting in the Great War. Between 1917 and 1920 he wrote an "Art Notes" column for *New Age*, under the pseudonym "B.H. Dias" (*EPVA*, 30–145).

Pound's writing on contemporary art was significantly informed by his interest in East Asian art and literature.[16] Since 1909 he had been a close friend of Laurence Binyon, head of the Sub-Department of Oriental Prints and Drawings at the British Museum and author of the acclaimed *Painting in the Far East* (1908). Letters record that Pound attended Binyon's lectures in 1909, and that in 1913 he and his future wife, the painter, Dorothy Shakespear, were studying Japanese prints in the British Museum (*EPDS*, 177, 190).[17] Later the same year, Pound began editing the papers of the recently deceased American philosopher and orientalist Ernest Fenollosa who, like Binyon, promoted traditional East Asian art as a model for contemporary Western art. The writings of both Fenollosa and Binyon are important sources for the interdisciplinary vocabulary Pound developed in the "Affirmations" series, and in the second issue of *Blast*, he highlighted Binyon's relevance to vorticism by quoting from his 1914 book, *The Flight of the Dragon*.[18]

Although the timing of Pound's increased interest in the visual arts is suggestive of a connection with imagism, an idea fostered by Pound's inclusion of Whistler and Kandinsky in his imagist genealogies, there is little evidence of direct influence (*EPVA*, 152, 202–3). Pound's 1913 definition of the image as "that which presents an intellectual and emotional complex in an instant of time" is resolutely non-visual, and his 1914 conception of the "primary pigment" insists that "Every concept, every emotion presents itself in the vivid consciousness in some primary form. It belongs to the art of this form . . . the image, to poetry; form, to design; colour in position, to painting; form or design in three planes, to sculpture" (*LE*, 4; *EPVA*, 151). Occasional works of ekphrasis, or "notional ekphrasis,"[19] such as "Dogmatic Statement on the Game and Play of Chess: Theme for a Series of Pictures," testify to a leakiness in the concept of the primary pigment, but most aspects of imagist poetry that invite comparison with the visual arts (use of precise imagery, organisation by juxtaposition), can be traced to imagism's two main literary sources, French Symbolism and the Japanese haiku (*EPVA*, 153–4). A more compelling case can be made, however, for the influence of visual culture on *The Cantos*: early drafts refer to the work of Gaudier, Lewis, Picasso, Wadsworth, and the Italian Futurist, Giacomo Balla, as models, and the poem's organization, which Pound later named "the ideogrammic method" in allusion to Fenollosa's essay, "The Chinese Written Character as Medium for Poetry," draws on his admiration for the effect of what he called the "form-motifs" and "radicals in design" of vorticist painting.[20]

PARIS: 1920–4

Towards the end of 1920 Pound moved to Paris. During the war, Pound had become increasingly critical of what he saw as the provincialism and intellectual conservatism of British culture, and France appeared to have been able to maintain its prewar avant-garde culture. In Paris, the new wartime little magazines, Jean Cocteau's *Le Mot*, Amédée Ozenfant's *L'Elan*, Pierre Albert-Birot's *Sic*, continued to promote a modernist aesthetic, and Picasso and Matisse, both non-combatants, continued their experimental work. Yet, as the war drew on, avant-garde painting turned away from the prewar analyses of modes of perception and abstraction, in favor of a neo-classicist style which culminated in the Ingres revival of the immediate postwar period.[21] Wyndham Lewis, surveying the trends in Parisian painting in 1919 in a book Pound admired, deplored the "David-Ingres phase in which painters in Paris are at present indulging."[22] The classicism of French painting also came under attack from the Paris Dada movement, which took form in 1920, when Tristan Tzara, of the original Zürich Dada group, arrived in Paris at the invitation of Francis Picabia.[23]

By the time Pound settled in Paris, he had already aligned himself with the Dadaists by appearing in Tzara's *Dadaphone*, and writing a "Lettre anglaise" for the Dada-affiliated *Littérature* (*EPCP*, IV: 24, 82).[24] His "Paris Letters" for the New York-based *Dial* consistently present the group as the most interesting and intelligent of the Paris writers and artists, more important, even, than Picasso and Braque. This judgement is often cited as evidence of Pound's inconsistency of taste, but this is no mere caprice.[25] Pound's journalism of the 1920s argues that the political events and economic changes of the previous eight years require that the arts must now turn from formal experimentation to engagement with issues of immediate social and political concern, following the lead of the Zürich Dadaists: "The main interest is not in aesthetics; certain main questions are up for discussion, among them nationality and monotheism," he writes, "the present phase of the discussion began with the *heimatlos* in Switzerland, during the war" (*EPVA*, 170). Pound repeats this argument in his single venture into Dadaist form, "Kongo Roux," published in Picabia's periodical, *391* (*EPCP*, IV: 165).

Although Pound read Dada as part of a satiric tradition he traced back to French Symbolism, at this point in his career he maintained a hard distinction between satire and "permanent" works of art, and the characteristic Dadaist "squibs" as Pound called them, did not constitute art in this sense (*EPCP*, IV: 104, 204). Yet during this period Pound begins to revise his definition of art in such a way as to shift attention from the aesthetic qualities of the product to the intelligence of the producer. This enables him to significantly broaden his category of art: it will soon include speeches, economic treatises, and industrial machines as well as literary, visual, and musical artworks. Even the art works Pound encountered during this period that were least troubling to his earlier definitions of art, Picabia's drawings of machines, Fernand Léger's paintings, and, above all, Constantin Brancusi's sculptures, are appreciated as an "exteriorization of [. . .] mental activity."[26] Nevertheless, within this definition, Pound's Paris criticism exhibits a variety of response. In the Brancusi number he organized in 1921 for *The Little Review*, Pound describes Brancusi's sculpture as an "approach to the infinite *by form*, by precisely the highest possible degree of consciousness of formal perfection." For Pound, Brancusi represents not only the extension and perfection of vorticist formalist principles, but also a contemporary example of the Neoplatonic idealism he finds in Dante and Guido Cavalcanti. This would seem to be a reversal of the pro-Dada argument for an engaged art, but for Pound, the two co-exist: Brancusi's sculpture is the positive response to the Dadaists' satirical analysis. Brancusi's sculpture, Pound's essay concludes, provides intellectual refreshment and an educational model for young sculptors "in a world full of junkshops, a world full of more than idiotic ornamentations, a world where pictures are made for museums" (*EPVA*, 214).

MATURE AESTHETICS: 1924–72

By October 1924, when Pound left Paris for the Italian Riviera, the main structural elements of his aesthetics were in place, worked out in his many essays on contemporary art. The distinction Pound developed in his writing about the Dadaists and Brancusi, between art as analytical experiment and art as pure form, is central to *The Cantos*: its historical sections, structured around intelligent, disruptive "factive personalities," are its Dadaist pole; the visionary descriptions of paradise, its Brancusian. But in *The Cantos*, contemporary visual art, like contemporary literature, appears only in brief references; the visual art of earlier periods, however, is central to the poem. In place of Picabia's squibs and Duchamp's found objects, Pound presents the fifteenth-century Tempio Malatestiano, "a jumble and junk shop" that expresses the intelligence of *The Cantos*' first "factive personality," Sigismondo Malatesta (*GK*, 194, [ii]). In place of Brancusi's "temple of QUIET," Pound presents "the forest of marble" of quattrocento Venice (*EPVA*, 307, xvii/78).

During his early career, Pound's interest in Renaissance visual art was effectively a literary interest, shaped by the writings of Browning and Ruskin and his own esoteric theory that traced a Neoplatonic tradition through the songs of the Provençal troubadours, the poetry of Dante and Guido Cavalcanti, to *quattrocento* sculpture.[27] In the early 1920s, however, Pound began to comment on Renaissance art more frequently and with greater specificity. This was in part the result of his research on the Tempio Malatestiano, with its fresco by Piero della Francesca, its bas reliefs by Agostino di Duccio, and its façade designed by Leon Battista Alberti. But this research coincided with the hardening of Pound's conviction that twentieth-century European culture was fundamentally and strategically hostile to artists and creativity. From this point Pound begins to systematically compare the impact of the patronage culture of the early Renaissance with the commodity culture of the twentieth century, concluding that "there is no place for sculpture or painting in modern life . . . The stuff is vendible or non-vendible, it is scraps, knick-knacks, part of the disease that gives us museums instead of temples, curiosity shops, instead of such rooms as the hall of the Palazzo Pubblico in Siena or of the Sala di Notari in Perugia" (*EPVA*, 173). Even the best twentieth-century works of art, Pound implies, are inevitably "knick-knacks" because they exist within a debased economic system that has marginalized art and artists. In *The Cantos*, therefore, the *quattrocento* stands as Pound's example of a period in which art exists not in museums, but in or on public buildings that can be seen and used by the general populace. Unlike the optimistic 1915 series "The Renaissance," where the comparison between Renaissance and contemporary artists was deployed to present the vorticists as the leaders of a new renaissance, *The Cantos* presents no contemporary art as comparable with that of the *quattrocento*: the poem is concerned instead with the conditions under which a future renaissance might occur. From October 1922, Pound, disastrously, began to think those conditions were being created in Italy by a leader he considered a twentieth-century Sigismondo: "Mussolini is the first head of a state in our time to perceive and to proclaim *quality* as a dimension in national production. He is the first man in power to publish any such recognition since, since whom? – since Sigismond Malatesta" (*SPR*, 200).

As Pound became increasingly didactic in his politics and economics, he became less responsive to particular works of art. By the thirties, he saw works of art as just one type of a culture's "material forms" from which he believed the economic health of a society could be diagnosed (*J/M*, 83), an argument he made in Canto XLV, the "Usura Canto": "with usura/ hath no man a painted paradise on his church wall" (XLV/229).[28] From the mid 1920s, therefore, Pound's canon of great artists became relatively static: in a letter from 1932 he wrote that the "first rate artists and writers" were Brancusi, Picabia, Cocteau, Picasso, Lewis, Joyce, Eliot ("up to end of Waste Land") and himself, a list unchanged for a decade.[29] Although he occasionally noted the work of younger artists over the following years, Salvador Dali, Hilaire Hiler, Joan Miro and Heinz Henghes in the thirties, Sheri Martinelli and Buckminster Fuller in the fifties, they are presented only as new versions of his existing templates, whether vorticist, Brancusian or *quattrocento*. The visual arts cease, under these conditions, to be agents of transformation in Pound's poetry; they operate instead as its illustration.

NOTES

1 Nathaniel Burt, *Palaces for the People: A Social History of the American Art Museum* (Boston: Little, Brown and Company, 1977), 75–85, 177, 249–50, 296–302.

2 H. Wayne Morgan, *New Muses: Art in American Culture, 1865–1920* (Norman: University of Oklahoma Press, 1978), 118–38.

3 Jonathan Freedman, *Professions of Taste: Henry James, British Aestheticism and Commodity Culture* (Stanford, CA: Stanford University Press, 1990), 79–88, 102–14; Doreen Bolger Burke *et al.*, *In Pursuit of Beauty: Americans and the Aesthetic Movement* (New York: Metropolitan Museum of Art/Rizzoli, 1987), 22–50.

4 Frank H. Goodyear, Jr., "A History of the Pennsylvania Academy of the Fine Arts, 1805–1976," in *In This Academy: The Pennsylvania Academy of Fine Arts* (Philadelphia: Pennsylvania Academy of the Fine Arts, 1976), 12–49.

5 Noel Stock, *Ezra Pound's Pennsylvania* (Toledo, OH: Friends of the University of Toledo Libraries, 1976), 32–3, 56; James J. Wilhelm, "The Letters of William Brooke Smith to Ezra Pound," *Paideuma* 19 (1990): 163–8 and also Wilhelm's *The American Roots of Ezra Pound* (New York: Garland, 1985), 99–101.

6 Yale Catalogue, 86.3710. See Rebecca Beasley, *Ezra Pound and the Visual Culture of Modernism* (Cambridge: Cambridge University Press, 2007), 29–39.

7 Yale Catalogue, 86.3712.

8 George Bornstein, "Pound's Parleyings with Robert Browning," in *Ezra Pound Among the Poets*, ed. Bornstein (Chicago: University of Chicago Press, 1985), 106–27; Mary Ellis Gibson, *Epic Reinvented: Ezra Pound and the Victorians* (Ithaca, NY: Cornell University Press, 1995), 60–2, 35–8, 219–22.

9 J.B. Bullen, ed., *Post-Impressionists in England* (London: Routledge, 1988), 4–5; Frank Rutter, *Since I Was Twenty-Five* (London: Constable, 1927), 180–99; Anna Gruetzner Robins, *Modern Art in Britain, 1910–1914* (London: Merrell Holberton/Barbican, 1997), 7–12.

10 Bullen, *Post-Impressionists*, 248.

11 S. K. Tillyard, *The Impact of Modernism, 1900–1920: Early Modernism and the Arts and Crafts Movement in Edwardian England* (London: Routledge, 1988), 218–20; Robins, *Modern Art in Britain*, 116–37, 28; Wendy Baron, *Perfect Moderns: A History of the Camden Town Group* (Aldershot: Ashgate, 2000), 61–70; Paul Edwards, *Wyndham Lewis: Painter and Writer* (New Haven: Yale University Press, 2000), 95–100.

12 Yale Catalogue, 59.2666.

13 Evelyn Silber, *Gaudier-Brzeska: Life and Art* (London: Thames and Hudson, 1996), 128, 263, 269, *EP/JQ*, 22. Although in December 1913 Pound and Dorothy Shakespear intended to buy Gaudier's *Torso 3*, it seems to have been bought by Dorothy's mother, Olivia Shakespear (*EPDS*, 285–7, 289).

14 Yale Catalogue, 60.2672.

15 *The Collected Writings of T.E. Hulme*, ed. Karen Csengeri (Oxford: Clarendon Press, 1994), 268–85.

16 Zhaoming Qian, *The Modernist Response to Chinese Art* (Charlottesville: University of Virginia Press, 2003), and *Orientalism and Modernism: The Legacy of China in Pound and Williams* (Durham, NC: Duke University Press, 1995).

17 Yale Catalogue, 59.2659.

18 Ezra Pound, "Chronicles, III: Lawrence Binyon [*sic*]," *Blast* 2 (1915): 86.

19 John Hollander, "The Poetics of *Ekphrasis*," *Word and Image* 4 (1988): 209.

20 Yale Catalogue, 69.3101, 70.3103, 3105; *EPVA*, 9, 27; *ABCR*, 26, Ronald Bush, *The Genesis of Ezra Pound's* Cantos, rev. edn. (Princeton: Princeton University Press, 1989), 45; Reed Way Dasenbrock, *The Literary Vorticism of Ezra Pound and Wyndham Lewis* (Baltimore: Johns Hopkins University Press, 1983), 100; Christine Froula, *To Write Paradise: Style and Error in Pound's Cantos* (New Haven: Yale University Press, 1984), 6, 74–75.

21 Kenneth E. Silver, *Esprit de Corps: The Art of the Parisian Avant-Garde and the First World War, 1914–1925* (London: Thames and Hudson, 1989), 29–115, 245–63.

22 Wyndham Lewis, *The Caliph's Design: Architects! Where is your Vortex?*, ed. Paul Edwards (Santa Barbara, CA: Black Sparrow Press, 1986), 109.

23 Michel Sanouillet, *Dada à Paris* (Paris: CNRS, 2005), 119–48, 180–94, 210–20, 305.

24 John Alexander, "Parenthetical Paris, 1920–1925: Pound, Picabia, Brancusi and Léger," in *Pound's Artists: Ezra Pound and the Visual Arts in London, Paris and Italy* (London: Tate Gallery, 1985), 81–120; Richard Sieburth, "Dada Pound," *South Atlantic Quarterly* 83 (1984): 44–68; Andrew Clearfield, "Pound, Paris, and Dada," *Paideuma* 7 (1978): 113–40.

25 William Carlos Williams, "Ezra Pound: Lord Ga-Ga!," *Decision* 2.3 (1941): 21.

26 "Parisian Literature," *Literary Review, New York Evening Post* (August 13, 1921): 7.

27 Peter Robinson, "Ezra Pound and Italian Art," in *Pound's Artists*, 137–43; *LE*, 153.

28 Miranda B. Hickman, *The Geometry of Modernism: The Vorticist Idiom in Lewis, Pound, H.D., and Yeats* (Austin: University of Texas Press, 2005), 114.

29 Ezra Pound, Letter to Josef Bard, January 25, 1932, Ezra Pound Collection, Harry Ransom Humanities Research Center, The University of Texas at Austin, box 5, folder 6.

CHAPTER 29

Confucius

Feng Lan

If a man have not order within him
He can not spread order about him

(Canto XIII/59)

In the Western intellectual tradition, Ezra Pound stands as a unique Confucian disciple. After Christian missionaries to China first introduced the thought of Confucius to European readers in the seventeenth century, the Chinese sage consistently attracted admirers and adherents including such renowned Western thinkers and writers as Leibniz, Voltaire, and Emerson. But unlike his distinguished predecessors, whose interest in Confucianism stemmed primarily from the presumption that its rational philosophy could serve to legitimize their own Enlightenment ideal of a modern socio-political formation founded on reason, Pound was drawn to another element. Within Confucianism, he located the empowering means to resist the socio-political alienation of humanity engendered by the conditions of Western capitalist modernity.

With this profound agenda, Pound was able to surpass all his Western predecessors both in the depth of his grasp of Confucian ideas and in the extent of his commitment to transmitting these ideas – "the blossoms from the east" – to the West (XIII/60). But Pound was never content to act merely as a passive transmitter of Confucian ideas. Instead, he sought to establish Confucianism's contemporary relevance by reinventing a new Confucian humanist discourse – an ideological weapon that could help him to address effectively the "immediate need" of a Western world in crisis (*SPR*, 75). He effected this reinvention of Confucianism through his creative translations, poetic configurations, and theoretical formulations.

Pound's lifelong engagement with Confucianism evolved through three phases, which can be characterized successively as imitative, creative, and comprehensive. His early approach to Confucian ideas was imitative, largely enabled by his reading of previous Western translations of Confucian works. Pound may have read "a little Confucius as early as July 1907," but his serious relationship with Confucianism started in September 1913, when he came to digest Guillaume Pauthier's French translation of Confucian works, *Confucius et Mencius: Les quatre livres de philosophie morale et politique de la Chine* (Stock, 176; Moody, 238, 240–1). It was at this same time that Pound also developed an acute passion for classical Chinese poetry and art, and that passion may have "sparked" what would become his abiding interest in Confucian philosophy.[1]

Pound's study of Confucian works during this period was obviously fruitful: in 1914, he published his first article on Confucius. In this short piece he exhibited an impressive understanding of basic Confucian tenets, and made a strong case for a liberal Confucianism with its "core" value invested in the assertion of the self.[2] Then, from the mid 1910s to the late 1920s, Pound maintained such a vigorous enthusiasm for Confucianism that he made frequent references to Confucius and created extensive commentaries on Confucian ideas in his writing. His Confucian dedication during this first stage culminated in the 1928 *Ta Hio*, his first English translation of the Confucian work *Da xue*, or *The Great Learning*, faithfully rendered from Pauthier's French version.

The second, creative phase of Pound's relationship with Confucianism spanned from the early 1930s to the end of World War II. During this period, Pound's commitment to Confucianism became firmly established, as indicated by his 1934 declaration that "I believe the *Ta Hio*," namely the doctrines about the self, family, and social order advocated in the Confucian work *Da xue*.[3] Yet what really characterized Pound's dedication to Confucianism during this period of creative engagement was his increasing endeavor to reinterpret Confucian works to serve his own agenda. For this purpose, Pound began to learn Chinese in the mid 1930s so as to avail himself of the original texts of Confucian scriptures instead of exclusively relying on existing translations. In addition to his English translation of excerpts of *Lun yu*, or *The Analects* (1937), such efforts on Pound's part resulted in a retranslation of *Da xue* into Italian (1941, 1942), and a new Italian translation of another Confucian work, *Zhong yong*, or *The Doctrine of the Mean* (1945). The poetry Pound composed during this period, in particular the Chinese History Cantos (LII–LXI), was saturated with rich allusions to Confucian premises. Moreover, besides a number of articles in English and Italian focusing solely on Confucianism, Pound's prose writing in this phase – essays, correspondences, radio speeches – was replete with his reinterpretations of Confucian doctrines.

With the end of the Second World War, Pound's Confucian exploration entered yet another period, namely the comprehensive phase. His imprisonment after the war at Pisa and then St. Elizabeths seemed to create a new space in which he was able to contemplate Confucian teachings with the intuition of a poet and the energetic perceptiveness of a social critic. These replaced the utilitarian mentality of a self-styled political reformer. Unlike his poetry during the 1930s and early 1940s, which was often charged with explicit and monotonous political contentions, Pound's postwar Cantos were characterized by an arduous spiritual quest, sustained by, among other things, his extensive quotations from Confucian texts and his intensified inscription of a Confucian anthropocosmic vision.

In contrast to the incoherent and fragmentary reflections on Confucianism in his postwar poetry, his prose translation of Confucian works into English during this period was conducted in a rigorously systematic and comprehensive manner. During his custody at St. Elizabeths in Washington, Pound published his complete English translations of *Da xue* (entitled *The Great Digest*, 1947), *Zhong yong* (entitled *The Unwobbling Pivot*, 1947), and *Lun yu* (entitled *Confucian Analects*, 1951), the first three of the four quintessential Confucian books. As for the fourth book, *Mengzi*, or *The Works of Mencius*, Pound translated four chapters into English from its Book One and published them in 1947. In addition, he rendered *Shi jing*, or *The Book of Songs*, into English, although the poems in *Shi jing* do not necessarily advocate Confucian principles. Nonetheless, similar to many Confucian *literati* in Chinese history, Pound believed that since this poetic collection was allegedly edited by Confucius, familiarity with these ancient Chinese poems was indispensable for the all-around intellectual accomplishment of a Confucian; hence the title of his translation, *The Confucian Odes, The Classic Anthology Defined by Confucius* (1954).

Such an extraordinary and persistent dedication to promoting Confucian works attests to Pound's deep conviction in the power of Confucianism for redeeming the troubled Western world. What Pound found particularly useful in Confucianism was its essentially humanist vision, which in his eyes seemed to radiate from every page of Confucian scriptures. Pound's determination to reconstruct a valid Confucian humanism informed his way of negotiating with the Confucian tradition. On the one hand, he positioned himself as a direct heir of the pre-Qin classical Confucianism, "the true tradition" that he believed to be founded by Confucius, carried forward by Zengzi, and brought to the culmination of a unified and persuasive system by Mencius.[4] In contrast to his insistence on recuperating true Confucian values from this originary source, Pound rejected as irrelevant what he called the "later dilatations," or "dilutations," of Confucianism, including especially the Song-Ming neo-Confucianism represented by Zhu Xi.[5]

Pound's dismissal of neo-Confucianism was partly due to the influence of writings by some earlier Jesuit missionaries to China such as de Moyriac de Mailla; most of these missionaries to China, notwithstanding their generally friendly "accommodationist" attitude toward Confucianism, disliked the neo-Confucian school because they saw it as a product of theological adulteration by the heretical doctrines of Buddhism and Daoism. But the more crucial reason for Pound's aversion to neo-Confucianism was that in his view this later development of Confucianism had abandoned much of the classical founders' humanist commitment, and that inadequate desertion was disclosed, for example, in Zhu Xi's theory that espoused the authority of the Heavenly Reason at the cost of suppressing the earthly and private desires of the individual human being. On the other hand, however, in spite of his repeated call for returning to the original teachings of Confucius and Mencius, Pound never treated Confucianism as a set of static doctrines. Rather, he regarded it as a dynamic body of truth and wisdom, which needed to be constantly revised – or "made new" in his famous dictum – in the face of an ever-changing world. In other words, Pound was at once a fundamentalist and a revisionist Confucian.

To some extent, the seemingly dialectical position Pound demonstrated in this regard may shed light on his controversial reinterpretations of Confucianism. The most polemical of his practice of reinterpretation was his Confucian translations. A prevalent, and for that matter misleading, assumption has been that Pound mistranslated Confucian works because he hardly knew Chinese. Indeed, Pound never achieved a proficient mastery of Chinese, notwithstanding his efforts to learn this language from the mid 1930s, but his reading knowledge in classical Chinese with the assistance of dictionaries was stronger than has been recognized by contemporary scholars. Moreover, it is important to remember that Pound's translations were built on the basis of the Confucian translations by Pauthier and especially Legge, two of the most learned orientalists that Europe ever produced. Apparently, Pound never doubted his mentors' sinological scholarship; what he doubted was their ability, as well as intention, to render in their versions true Confucian ideas: that is why Pound claimed that *his* was "the first" Western translation of Confucius "by a Confucian."[6] In fact, Pound's English translations reveal an unmistakable trace of Legge's impact in the usage of diction and sentence patterns. Pound diverged from Legge mostly when dealing with Chinese ideogrammic characters in which, he believed, were hidden original and important Confucian concepts. In these instances, Pound would go directly to the Chinese texts and work out his own interpretations with the aid of dictionaries.

Pound primarily relied on two strategies to decipher Chinese characters in Confucian texts, both of which served his overriding agenda of reconstructing a Confucian humanist discourse. The first is etymographic interpretation. This strategy assumes that the pictorial nature of Chinese characters inscribes the authenticity and truthfulness of the ideogrammic sign system, in whose etymological visibility safely reside the original ideas of the antique writer. This strategy of etymographic archaeology allows the translator to remove irrelevant semantic deposits built on and around the character in the course of history in order to penetrate to the original meaning registered in the ideogram. Thus, etymographic interpretation must have appeared to Pound the ideal tool for fulfilling the twofold function with which he tasked the serious translator: to restore the lost, original perception and then to bring it back to bear on contemporary cultural reformation.

In practice, what the etymographic interpreter does is to decompose a character into a number of smallest meaningful units, and then reorganize their sememes to reproduce the supposedly primordial idea. Pound's rendering of the Confucian term *cheng yi* 誠意 (usually rendered as "make thought sincere") in *Da xue* provides an illuminating illustration. By subjecting both characters to a powerful etymographic reading, Pound ended up translating this concept as "sought precise verbal definitions of their inarticulate thoughts (the tones given off by the heart)."[7] Such a rendering, as we will see, immensely contributed to Pound's formulation of a new theory of poetic language.

The second strategy Pound utilized was subjecting what he regarded as key characters to a forcible univocal interpretation, even if that might mean a drastic departure from prevalent Confucian exegesis either in China or the West. This strategy allowed him to eliminate possible contextual and conceptual ambiguity or contradiction that a character in a Confucian term might give rise to. By so doing, Pound apparently hoped he could reinvent a unified Confucian discourse characterized not only by its internal ideological coherence, but also by its consistency with the larger pattern of values that Pound received from the Western traditions he privileged, especially the liberal tradition of humanism. Take for example the central Confucian tenet *ke ji fu li wei ren* 克己復禮為仁, which Pound translated as: "Support oneself and return to the rites, that makes a man."[8] Pound's translation diametrically differs from all major Western Confucian translations of the same passage, as represented by Legge's version: "To subdue one's self and return to the propriety, is perfect virtue."⁹

The disagreement between Pound's "support the self" and Legge's "subdue the self" lies not so much in their opposing understandings of the verb *ke* in this passage as in their different conceptions of the noun *ji* (self). Unlike most Confucian exegetes, Zhu Xi for one, who deemed the self an undesirable element of being and thus something that must be overcome and subdued, Pound embraced the self as a positive generative entity, the only source of nurturing forces for the cultivation of an individual person. More importantly, he identified the self as the only terrain on which rests the supreme virtue of *ren* 仁, the "*Humanitas . . .* the man and his full contents." Not surprisingly, in Pound's Confucian translations, "fulfilling himself" is consistently equated with the attainment of "full manhood."¹⁰

Pound's revisionary interpretation of Confucian works was instrumental to his undertaking to redefine and reframe the concerns of Confucianism in three major areas: the problem of language, the individual in relation to the state, and spiritual beliefs. The problem of language had engaged Pound from the beginning of his career. Then, as was typical of modernist writers, Pound the young poet felt that the English language was a corrupted medium in urgent need of remedy, because it could no longer truthfully articulate thought and objectively signify the thing it stood for. Such a concern drove him to participate in "the revolution of the word," namely the avant-garde literary movement, in his formative years before World War I (*PE*, 49). However, by the end of the 1910s, Pound began to question his mission of revitalizing language, for he feared that his practice in experimental poetry – his quest for a precise poetic idiom – lacked sufficient legitimacy as a vehicle for making cogent socio-political assertions, and thus appeared to be slipping into the entrapment of a futile aestheticist game. Such a pursuit, as suggested by Pound's poetic persona in "Hugh Selwyn Mauberley," would only further marginalize the modern poet and diminish the social and political value of poetry.

It was from Confucius' doctrine of *zheng ming* 正名 (rectify the name) that Pound soon obtained the needed justification. In Pound's interpretation, the doctrine reinforced his conviction that language must be redeemed whenever possible, for it played too crucial a role in social and cultural change. Language in this sense was not a mystified divine gift, but rather a human product that could be damaged by inappropriate use. To maintain the efficiency of language, therefore, remained a human responsibility, and failure in this undertaking would not only result in poor thinking and a weakening hold on reality but also lead to anti-social conduct and even social destruction. Here, it is noteworthy that in valorizing the *zheng ming* doctrine, Pound incorporated his own notion of precise language. As a result, what the revised *zheng ming* doctrine came to address was no longer the issue of political correctness in using feudal names, but, rather, what Pound deemed a universal concern with the precise use of language. Since, according to Pound, the poet was the only member of society dedicated to verbal precision from which derived the essential value and beauty of poetry, the *zheng ming* doctrine gave the modern poet a new legitimacy by assigning him the social task of keeping language efficient.

Pound also drew heavily from the above-mentioned Confucian doctrine of *cheng yi*. A pivotal concept in the system of Confucian thought, *cheng* or "sincerity" has at least two essential meanings. It first denotes a cognitive condition in which the individual succeeds in transforming the knowledge about the external world into a moral and intellectual force for self-cultivation. Its second meaning is ontological; here it refers to the primordial condition of being – or the absolute power of Being that furnishes all kinds of life with meaning – and thus stands for a higher mode of existence that the individual strives to attain. Pound integrated the rich philosophical implications of this concept with his contemplations on the nature and function of language by interpreting *cheng yi* in terms of a linguistic exertion of seeking precise verbal definition. Such a revision gave his theory of precise language a profound epistemological and ontological foundation, a theory that championed a redeemed language not only as the key to social problems, but also as the bridge for reconnecting the human world with the world of nature as well as with the world of transcendental eternity.

The influence of Confucianism on Pound's political orientation and praxis has been a controversial subject.[11] Central to Pound's political vision was his firm belief that the individual self constituted the sole source of light and energy for personal development and social reform; and that belief was tremendously reinforced by the Confucian doctrine of self-cultivation and order. In various stages of his career, Pound was able to readjust his political stance by incorporating different aspects of this Confucian doctrine into his radical individualism and cultural elitism. Contrary to a widely held opinion that he turned to Confucianism under the spell of its authoritarian ideology, in his early years Pound was initially attracted to Confucianism precisely because he found in it premises that empowered his fight for "the conservation of the individual rights."[12] Such rights – freedom of thought and expression, privacy, and self-development – received elaborate reconfigurations from a Confucian perspective in Pound's prose and poetry during this period, constituting a major theme of his liberal discourse then against the "coercive evils" of state institutions and social establishments.

For Pound, Confucianism not only upheld the autonomy of the sovereign individual, but also convincingly solved the tension between the private pursuits of the individual and his public responsibility. From the early 1930s onward, when confronted with a chaotic world, Pound appeared to pay increasingly close attention to the social consequences of self-cultivation as formulated in a number of Confucian doctrines. Under the scrutiny of Pound's forceful reinterpretation, these doctrines came to posit self-making not as a process toward self-confinement but rather as a form of self-liberation, through which the individual attains full actualization by applying self-knowledge to social practice – that is, by converting the knowledge of human nature obtained via self-introspection into a discourse of public virtues and using it to help organize social relations. In addition, Pound's rereading of Confucian works enabled him to reconceptualize the formation of the state as a new social order that grows out of the subjective order of the duty-bound individual and that functions by coordinating, instead of asserting, the rights of all individuals.

Notably, in this conception the duty-bound individual in Pound's configuration was no longer an ordinary person, but an elite and super individual who incarnated the collective will, or rather, the collective creative power of all in the ideal state, for an orderly operation of human civilization. Pound's elitist vision did not originate with Confucianism; it was an intrinsic tendency rooted in the liberal tradition of Western individualism with which Pound identified from the beginning of his career. Nevertheless, Confucian ideology indeed resonated with, and effectively reinforced, such a vision. After all, the individuals often celebrated in the Confucian canon are unexceptionally a few enlightened sage-kings from Chinese history, the same type of cultural heroes that Pound always admired in the history of the West. Such an elitism, enhanced by the conservative spirit of orthodox Confucianism, developed into Pound's autocratic volitionism, which placed the hope for a harmonious social order only in the will of the privileged cultural hero.

As for the inspiration of Confucian spirituality, in the early 1920s Pound already recognized Confucianism as one of the "only safe guides in religion."[13] His growing interest in Confucian religiosity resulted from his deepening disappointment with Christianity, which in his view had been contaminated by "historical diseases" such as usury. Meanwhile, even though he still cherished some useful spiritual values received from disparate Western traditions such as European pagan mythology, Neoplatonic mysticism, and Enlightenment philosophy, Western civilization as a whole had failed to provide him with a compelling system for organizing valid ethical and religious experiences. For Pound, what Confucianism offered was precisely a totalizing "system" (*GK*, 24), a unifying scheme whereby he was able to reorganize his previously fragmented beliefs and reinstate their intelligibility. More importantly, Confucianism supplied a host of empowering doctrines about human nature, the cosmos, and the transcendental, which enabled him to construct a coherent narrative of human existence by bringing together the human world, the natural world, and the divine world.

Of these doctrines, Mencius' postulate of the innate goodness of humanity and, in particular, his formulation of *si duan* (four beginnings), reaffirmed Pound's belief in the natural nobility of human nature in opposition to the Judeo-Christian doctrine of original sin. By grounding the inborn human nature in the four Heaven-endowed predispositions – benevolence, righteousness, propriety, and wisdom – Confucianism convinced Pound of the intrinsic potential in human nature for self-perfection. In addition, Pound was greatly enlightened by the Confucian doctrine about the partnership among the three primordial entities: humankind, earth, and heaven. The doctrine envisioned nature as a dynamic process of constant creation, a holistic universe inhabited by both spiritual and material beings, and a rational arrangement of cosmic relations bringing human beings the benefits of material abundance as well as the blessing of moral revelations. Sustained by such a Confucian perspective, Pound developed an eco-ethical view to demand a new relationship between humankind and nature, a view that served as a counterforce against the anthropocentrism he found pervasive in various post-Renaissance discourses of the West.

Furthermore, like many of his Western contemporaries in the post-Nietzschean world filled with a sense of doubt and fear after the "death" of God, Pound was deeply concerned with the disconnection between the ultimate destination of human life and the divine source of creation. In the Confucian imaginary of a benevolent and pantheistic Heaven, he found an unorthodox and yet useful theological paradigm. Integrated with the Neoplatonic notion of Light, the Confucian Heaven in Pound's revisionist elaboration appeared like a Supreme Intelligence, with its divine process or *Dao* manifested in the rational patterns of nature as well as in the creative power of the human intellect. Such a paradigm not only reassured Pound of the existence of an almighty transcendental entity, but also reinforced his resistance to the hegemony of Judeo-Christian monotheism.

Essential to Pound's theological formulation was Mencius' theory of *jin xin* (exert the heart/mind to the utmost). The theory of *jin xin* recognized the human capability for internal transcendence enabled by the innate human predisposition of *xin*, or heart/mind. According to this theory, as also reconfigured in Pound's poetry, one can achieve internal sagehood by exerting to the utmost degree the effort of the heart/mind in self-cultivation; and since sagehood is informed by the divine will of Heaven, the heart/mind becomes the legitimate entrance into the Heavenly kingdom. Thus, completely exerting the potential of the heart/mind will enable one to attain the ideal state of being wherein humanity and Heaven are united (LXXXVI/581; XCIX/722). Such a triumphant moment of the completely exerted heart/mind is captured in Pound's poetry, in which the sincere Confucian individual is seen to ascend to partake of the glory of the divine light (LXXIV/449).

Pound's program of Confucian humanism merits appropriate evaluation on at least three accounts. First, his approach greatly enriched his creative writing, lending his poetry a meaningful thematic line, a unifying structure, and a powerful hermeneutic continuity. Second, Pound's endeavor reinvigorated Western humanism by bringing into it fresh insights from the Confucian tradition. Third, Pound's exploration opened up new possibilities for the further development of Confucianism in the cross-cultural contexts of our modern times. By reinventing Confucianism to bear upon the challenging conditions of the West, Pound's revisionary project enlarged, as well as updated, the theoretical perspectives of Confucianism, and transformed it into a humanistic discourse with which to address the concerns of the modern world.

NOTES

1 For a convincing argument on this point, see Zhaoming Qian, *The Modernist Response to Chinese Art* (Charlottesville: University of Virginia Press, 2003), especially the section on "Pound and Pictures of Confucian Ideals," 47–63. Qian also cites several important Pound letters relating to Confucius. Also see Hugh Kenner, "Inventing Confucius," *PE*, 445–59.

2 Ezra Pound, "The Words of Ming Mao 'Least among the Disciples of Kung-Fu-Tse'," *The Egoist* 1.24 (December, 14, 1914): 456.

3 In the 1930 article "Credo," in reply to T.S. Eliot's question about his religious belief, Pound asked his "enquirer to read Confucius and Ovid" (*SPR*, 53). Then in "Date Line," published in 1934, Pound made an even clearer statement: "As to what I believe: I believe the *Ta Hio*" (*LE*, 86). In 1937 he published "Immediate Need of Confucius," *SPR*, 89–94.

4 Pound to Fengchi Yang, November 7, 1941 in *Ezra Pound's Chinese Friends: Stories in Letters*, ed. Zhaoming Qian (Oxford: Oxford University Press, 2008), 38. See also Feng Lan, *Ezra Pound and Confucianism: Remaking Humanism in the Face of Modernity* (Toronto: University of Toronto Press, 2005) 149.

5 Pound in Zhaoming Qian, *Ezra Pound's Chinese Friends*, 105.

6 Cited in David Gordon, "And Moore: Marianne on Ezra's Confucius," *Paideuma* 18. 3 (1989): 149.

7 Ezra Pound, *Confucius: The Great Digest, the Unwobbling Pivot, the Analects* (New York: New Directions, 1969), 29–31.

8 *Ibid.*, 243.

9 James Legge, *The Chinese Classics: Confucian Analects, the Great Learning, the Doctrine of Mean* (Hong Kong: Hong Kong University Press, 1960), 1: 250.

10 Pound, *Confucius*, 22, 179.

11 See for example Hong Sun, "Pound's Quest for Confucian Ideals: The Chinese History Cantos," in *Ezra Pound and China*, ed. Zhaoming Qian (Ann Arbor: University of Michigan Press, 2003), 96–119.

12 See Donald Hall, in "Interview with Ezra Pound," in *Writers at Work: The Paris Review Interviews*, ed. George Plimpton, second series (New York: Viking Press, 1963), 53–4.

13 Writing from Paris on July 16, 1922, Pound told Harriet Monroe: "I consider the Writings of Confucius, and Ovid's *Metamorphoses* the only safe guides in religion" (*SL*, 183).

CHAPTER 30

The Orient

Zhaoming Qian

EARLY CONTACT

For Pound the Orient primarily meant China and Japan and his initial exchange with the Far East was through visual media. Born in Hailey, Idaho and raised in Pennsylvania, Pound witnessed America's early vogue for Japonisme and Chinoiserie. His parents, like many who had admired Far Eastern artifacts at the Centennial International Exhibition (1876), had a Ming vase in their house in suburban Philadelphia. Pound entered the University of Pennsylvania in 1901, just in time for a rich collection of Chinese wood-carvings, ink paintings, and calligraphic objects mounted in the newly opened Free Museum of Science and Art, now the University of Pennsylvania Museum. On a visit to his beloved "Aunt Frank" in New York City in his last years in America, he was shown a screen-book with waterscape scenes alongside manuscript poems in Chinese and Japanese. This screen-book, a relic from Japan, was to become the main source of Canto XLIX.[1]

Pound's appreciation of the Orient was, nevertheless, awakened not in America but in England in 1909, and what first opened his eyes to the unique strength of oriental aesthetic were a series of lectures on "Art and Thought in East and West" by the British Museum Assistant Keeper of Oriental Art, Laurence Binyon (1869–1943). As a frequenter of the British Museum, Pound had the freedom to inspect for himself the rare artworks Binyon had described, and as one of Binyon's circle of friends haunting the Vienna Café, he had the privilege to discuss all aspects of oriental culture with the curious as well as the expert during lunch hours.

This opportunity, extending throughout the pre-World War I period, to learn from England's most eminent connoisseur of oriental art, and to study the British Museum collection of Chinese and Japanese art objects,

proved immensely favorable when Pound set out seriously to explore the
Orient in 1913–14.

In the fall of 1913 Pound had the good fortune to be introduced to Mary
McNeil Fenollosa, the widow of the American orientalist Ernest Fenollosa
(1853–1908). She understood that Pound was eager to know more about the
Orient and was sympathetic to her husband's scholarship. She gave him
Fenollosa's notes and unfinished manuscripts with the encouragement to
edit a book on Japanese Noh drama and an anthology of Chinese poetry.
Pound's road to the Orient was charted.

The promised Fenollosa papers began to arrive in London in late 1913.
Pound chose first to interpret and rewrite Fenollosa's rough translations of
Noh plays, frequently turning the former's prose into poetry. The Noh play
Nishikigi came out in print as early as May 1914 in *Poetry*, although *Certain
Noble Plays of Japan*, introduced by W. B. Yeats, and *"Noh" or Accomplish-
ment*, introduced by Pound himself, did not appear until September 1916
and January 1917, respectively. Whereas from the Japanese haiku Pound
learned the formula of "super-position," from the Noh plays he rooted
out the technique of "Unity of Image," which he occasionally used in *The
Cantos*, from "The pine at Takasago" in Canto IV/15 to the final *Drafts and
Fragments* (1969). When publishing *Women of Trachis* (1956), a work for
the stage, he again thought of the Noh, requesting it to be performed by
Noh players, who alone, he believed, were suitable for *"the highest peak of
Greek sensibility"* (*WT*, 3).

In the fall of 1914, Pound undertook to retranslate the poems of Li Bo
(701–62) and other masters he found in Fenollosa's Chinese poetry notes.
Without any knowledge of the Chinese language, his chance of success
seemed slim. Yet, reflecting on *Cathay*, the result of this enterprise, in
1935, he insisted that "Fenollosa's work was given to me in manuscript
when I was ready for it" (*MIN*, 8). Pound's claim is justified in view of
two facts. Shortly before *Cathay*, he had been initiated into the aesthetic
of the Orient via the British Museum. The Chinese and Japanese art
objects that had impressed his eye could serve as guides clarifying settings,
situations, and states of mind essential to a comprehension of classic Chinese poetry. Immediately before he received the Fenollosa papers, Pound
had studied H. A. Giles' *A History of Chinese Literature* (1901) and tried
his hand at Chinese poetry by adapting four of Giles' versions – "After

Ch'u Yuan," "Liu Ch'e," "Fan-piece, for Her Imperial Lord," and "Ts'ai Chi'h."

From the sinologist point of view, the poems of *Cathay* include numerous deviations. When one compares these poems with the Chinese originals and Fenollosa's notes, however, one becomes aware that many of the misrepresentations are attributable to Fenollosa's flawed notes. In his reworkings, Pound has, in fact, corrected some of Fenollosa's mistakes. Wai-lim Yip has used "Lament of the Frontier Guard" as illustration to show that "Pound has occasionally (by what he calls 'divine accident') penetrated below a faulty crib to the original and come out right."[2] T. S. Eliot is substantially correct in calling Pound "the inventor of Chinese poetry for our time" ("Introduction," *SP*, xvi). In *Cathay* Pound created a proper vehicle for getting Chinese poets across to twentieth-century English-speaking readers, disregarding their "rhymes" and "tones," while following their verbal constructions and methods of presentation. Succeeding translators of Chinese poetry from Arthur Waley to Gary Snyder all owe a debt to Pound for providing a sound model.

Pound's *Cathay* enterprise coincided with his move from imagism toward vorticism. *Cathay* poems such as "The River-merchant's Wife," "The Jewell Stairs' Grievance," and "The Exile's Letter" deserve to be viewed as imagist and vorticist masterpieces. It was not by accident that when *Cathay* came out in April 1915 almost all the major modernists – W. B. Yeats, Ford Madox Ford, William Carlos Williams, and T. S. Eliot – applauded its robustness. Ford, in particular, commented, "If these were original verses, then, Pound was the greatest poet of the day," which should indicate that the English critic had perceived affinities between modernist and Chinese sensitivities (quoted in Stock, 174). After all, *Cathay* paved the way for Pound's transition to high modernism. It was in *Cathay* that he completed his adaptation of a poetic idiom for *The Cantos*. Indeed, the *vers libre* in *Cathay* resurfaces not only in Pound's Chinese Cantos but in countless other parts throughout the modernist epic.

In the winter of 1914, Pound discovered with excitement Fenollosa's drafts of a lecture on "The Chinese Written Character as a Medium for Poetry." By February 1915 he was alluding to "the force of Chinese ideographs *without knowing it*" (*EPCP*, 11:19). Four months later, he hailed the essay as "a whole basis of aesthetic," adding caustically "the adamantine stupidity of all magazine editors delays its appearance" (*SL*, 61). "The Chinese Written Character," abridged and polished, came out in installments in the *Little Review*, September–December 1919. It was reprinted the following year in

Instigations. The essay is largely responsible for the "ideogrammic method," a poetic Pound developed for *The Cantos*.[3]

INQUIRY INTO CONFUCIANISM

Pound's work on the Fenollosa papers led to his inquiry into Confucianism. In Guillaume Pauthier's French version of the Confucian Four Books (*Les quatre livres*, 1910) he discovered a philosophy that he hoped would correct Western civilization. Consequently, Confucius recurs again and again in *The Cantos*. Canto XIII is a eulogy of Confucius' respect for the individual. Cantos LII–LXXI juxtapose early Republican America with China, from Confucius' ideal semi-legendary rulers Yao and Shun to Qing emperors Kangxi (1654–1722; r. 1662–1722) and Yongzheng (1678–1735; r. 1723–35) as a way to suggest the right forms of government. Cantos LXXXV and LXXXVI pay tribute to the Confucian tenets found in *Shu jing* or the Book of History, and Cantos XCVIII and XCIX to Kangxi's "Sacred Edict." In the 1940s and early 1950s, Pound translated into English three of the Confucian Four Books and all 305 odes of the Confucian Book of Odes.

GUIDES OCCIDENTAL AND ORIENTAL

In his early dealings with China and Japan, Pound depended very much on eighteenth- to nineteenth-century English, French, or Latin versions of Chinese texts. In September 1928, he confessed to his father that although he knew how the Chinese character worked, he could not read a Chinese poem: "For Cathay I had a crib [in English] made by Mori and Ariga."[4] Although he had owned a set of Robert Morrison's multivolume *Dictionary of the Chinese Language* since 1914, he did not start learning the Chinese language until around 1935. Hugh Kenner writes that Pound's forte in 1936 was "looking up characters one by one in Morrison."[5] As late as 1941, he could do little more than that. By 1951, nevertheless, he was able to read *Shu jing* in the original, "at least recogniz[ing] a few terms without having crib on next page."[6] *Shu jing* was one of many Chinese classics Harvard scholar Achilles Fang (1910–95) sent to him that year.

But it is wrong to assume that Pound's Far Eastern projects were exclusively guided by eighteenth to nineteenth-century orientalists. In 1914–15, precisely during his Fenollosa venture, Pound became friends with the

Chinese scholar-official F. T. Sung (1884–1941) and the Japanese dancer Michio Ito (*c.* 1892–1961). If he did not get much help from the two for his *Cathay* undertaking or Noh studies, he was to make a point of not letting a Chinese or Japanese intellectual go without procuring some assistance. The Japanese artist Tami Koume (1893–1923), whom he first met in 1916, ended up as his incontestable guide to the Noh. In a letter of 1936 to the Japanese avant-garde poet Katue Kitsono, Pound wrote, "[S]ince Tami Koume was killed in that [1923] earthquake, I have had no one to explain the obscure passages or fill up the enormous gaps of my ignorance" (*SL*, 282).

The Chinese missionary and college president Pao Swen Tseng (1893–1978), on a visit to Rapallo in 1928, came to Pound's rescue in his failed attempt to interpret the Chinese poems in his parents' (originally Aunt Frank's) screen-book. Her oral translation of the eight poems led to Canto XLIX. In the 1930s when there were no Chinese around to assist him in his Confucian studies, Pound turned to his Japanese correspondent Katue Kitsono, asking him to look for "a cheap edition" of the Confucian Odes and to find out what had "become of a group of neo-Confucians gathered round a chink named Tuan Szetsun."[7] Katue was not able to answer the question about neo-Confucians but he did send Pound a Chinese edition of the Confucian Odes in four volumes, an indispensible source of his *Classic Anthology Defined by Confucius* (1954).

Séraphin Couvreur's trilingual and James Legge's bilingual Book of History (*Shu jing*) have been identified as guides for Cantos LXXXV–LXXXVII; and Joseph Rock's monographs on China's Naxi (Na Khi) ethnic group as sources of the Naxi passages in the late Cantos. What is less known is the degree of Pound's Chinese friends' involvement in these projects. Just as Miss Tseng helped Pound with the screen-book's Chinese poems, so Achilles Fang prepared his use of *Shu jing* in Cantos LXXXV–LXXXVII. P. H. Fang, a PhD student at the Catholic University of America and a Naxi native, visited Pound at St. Elizabeths Hospital from 1953 to 1958. He, rather than Rock, first introduced Pound to the Naxi rites and pictograms used in *Thrones* (1959) and *Drafts & Fragments* (1969).

Among Pound's Confucian translations only *Ta Hio: The Great Learning of Confucius* (1928) and *Confucius: Digest of the Analects* (1937) were made without the aid of a Chinese associate or guide. In retranslating two of the Confucian Four Books into Italian, he obtained assistance from Fengchi Yang (1908–70) of the Italian Institute for the Middle and Far East. As to his late Confucian translations, Achilles Fang contributed more than a "Note on the Stone-Classics" to *The Great Digest & The Unwobbling Pivot* (1951) and an introduction to *The Classic Anthology Defined by Confucius* (1954). He oversaw the production of the two volumes from cover designs through corrections of romanized spellings and lining up Chinese characters with English translations.

ORIENTALISM AND THE ORIENT

Pound's career evolved through three periods: the early years (1908–20), defined by his imagism and vorticism; the middle years (1920–45), characterized by his "ideogrammic method" and enthusiasm for Mussolini's fascist economics; and the later years (1945–72), informed by his late Confucianism. To a remarkable degree, his transition from one stage to another parallels the shifts in his exchange with the Orient. His rise from imagism to vorticism, for example, coincided with his study of Chinese poetry and Japanese Noh drama via the Fenollosa papers. His adoption of the "ideogrammic method" for *The Cantos* is directly linked to his preoccupation with Fenollosa's essay "The Chinese Written Character as a Medium for Poetry."

Pound's most "fascist" period corresponds to his work both with J. A. M. de Mailla's *Historie générale de la Chine* and *Li ji* (*Book of Rites*) for the Chinese History Cantos and with his translations of two of the Confucian Four Books. And finally, to account for his later Cantos, one must grasp the importance of his post-World War II commitment to Confucius: his late Confucian translations and his engagement with the *Book of History* and the "Sacred Edict" for the *Rock-Drill* and *Thrones* sections of *The Cantos*.

Pound's career-long exchange with the Orient raises questions important to the current debate about Orientalism. Is Orientalism a monolithic and constant conception? Did every European and American believe in Western cultural superiority? Pound, for one, apparently did not. From his initial engagement with the Orient, he took a stance that was drastically different from his predecessors and peers. Whereas most other Westerners, as Edward Said has asserted, explored the Orient "for dominating, reconstructing, and having authority over [it]," Pound looked to China for an alternative to modernity.[8] This attitude would puzzle – even shock – his Chinese contemporaries in their attempt to replace Confucianism with a Western model.

Pound's friend F. T. Sung, for instance, shared an anti-Confucian stance with other Chinese modernists. During their meeting in London in early

1914, Sung handed over to Pound an article in English that attributes early Republican China's poverty to Confucian teachings. Despite his disapproval Pound arranged to have it published in the London *Egoist*. In an introductory note to the article (entitled "The Causes and Remedy of the Poverty of China"), he contradicts Sung's pessimistic view by referring to China as a nation that "has replaced Greece in the intellectual life of so many occidentals" (*EPCP*, I: 229). In "The Renaissance," a February 1915 essay, Pound restates that "this century may find a new Greece in China" (*LE*, 215). In "Laurence Binyon," another 1915 essay, he disassociates from his mentor in oriental culture, ridiculing his "mind constantly hark[ing] back to some folly of nineteenth-century Europe, constantly trying to justify Chinese intelligence by dragging it a little nearer to some Western precedent" (*EPCP*, III: 99). In "China," a 1918 review article, he criticizes Arthur Waley, the translator of *A Hundred and Seventy Chinese Poems* (1918), for his "touch of occidental patronage for the poor oriental" (*EPCP*, III: 126). In "Immediate Need of Confucius," a 1937 essay, Pound further argues that "Western contact with the Far East was made in an era of Western degradation" (*SPR*, 76). All in all, Pound's statements about the Orient from the mid-1910s onward identify him as anything but a hegemonic orientalist.

Another issue in our understanding of Pound's Orient is the tendency to overemphasize his exclusion of, and hostility to, non-Confucian Chinese traditions. Pound was radically biased against Taoism and Buddhism during the 1930s and 1940s. Starting from the early 1950s, however, he opened himself up to these religions. In November 1951, after reading Arthur Waley's version of Taoist founder Laozi, he asked Achilles Fang: "Does Lao contain ANYTHING useful that is NOT in the Four Books (and their preludes, the Shih [Odes] and the Shu)?" Seizing this opportunity, Fang brought up Laozi's most vocal proponent, Zhuang Zhou (Chuang-Tzu), as being "of great importance to sensible Confucians."[9]

Between 1953 and 1956, moreover, Pound talked with P. H. Fang about the mysterious rites of the Naxi tribe that fuse Confucian ancestral worship with Taoism and Buddhism. Their conversations, along with Rock's descriptions of the Naxi rites, inspired Pound's haunting poetry about the "wind sway" ceremony – "²Hăr-²la-¹llü ³k'ö / of the wind sway, / The nine fates and the seven / . . . " (cx/797). The passage focuses on the possibilities of life after death, a departure from Canto XIII, where Confucius is quoted as saying "nothing of the 'life after death'"(XIII/59). Going over all of this material makes it easy to understand why in the mid-1950s Pound would admit his oversight to William McNaughton: "There's no doubt

I missed something in Taoism and Buddhism. Clearly, there's something valid, meaningful, in those religions."[10]

To this day, many readers are still apt to associate Pound's Orient with an approach that dismisses phonetic elements in the Chinese language. This association has to do with Pound's promotion of Fenollosa's essay, "The Chinese Written Character as a Medium for Poetry." For George Kennedy this essay is "a mass of confusion" based on a "complete misunderstanding" of the Chinese language. For James Liu it is responsible for the fallacy "common among Western readers outside sinological circles, namely, all Chinese characters are pictograms or ideograms."[11] The aim of Fenollosa's essay is to push for concrete, natural thinking and writing as suggested by the primitive Chinese character. Nowhere in his essay does Fenollosa claim that "*all* Chinese characters are pictograms or ideograms." What he states is that "*a large number of the primitive* Chinese characters, even the so-called radicals, are shorthand pictures of actions or processes" (emphasis added). Fenollosa never denies the existence of sounds in the Chinese character. Instead, he stresses that the Chinese character "speaks at once with the vividness of painting, and with the mobility of sounds."[12] But yet, in the second half of the past century, the critical opinion of Kennedy and Liu was echoed and reechoed until Fenollosa's name, along with Pound's, became synonymous with the so-called pictographic approach, an approach that refuses to recognize phonetic elements in Chinese.

In an effort to defend himself, Pound wrote that Fenollosa "did not claim that the average Chinese journalist uses this instrument as a 'medium for poetry' but that it can and has been so used."[13] This argument, though valid, cannot clear away the condemnation of his disregard of Chinese sound in favor of its pictorial quality. We mustn't overlook the changes in Pound's understanding of the Chinese language. Going over the manuscripts again in 1935, Pound discovered Fenollosa's concern with sounds in Chinese poetry. On March 11, 1937, he told Katue Kitasono: "When I did *Cathay*, I had no inkling of the technique of sound, which I am now convinced *must* exist or have existed in Chinese poetry" (*SL*, 293). In the early 1950s, Pound made strenuous efforts to learn the pronunciation of Chinese characters. In a letter of February 1951 to Achilles Fang, Pound inquired, "What could save infinite time and labour fer pore mutts trying to learn a little chinese, esp/ SOUND." In another letter to Fang (February 1952), he expressed his regret for not having done so earlier: "For years I never made ANY attempt to hitch ANY sound to the ideograms, content with the meaning and the visual form."[14] Later that year, when visiting Chinese student Angela Jung (Palandri) reminded him that he had belittled the usefulness of Chinese sound, he protested that "one's opinions change; he should not be held responsible for what he said or wrote decades earlier."[15]

In the late Cantos Pound's use of Chinese becomes both pictographic and phonetic. Cantos LXXXV–LXXXIX and XCVI–XCVIII are replete with Chinese characters accompanied by their phonetic symbols. Canto XCIX experiments with English–Chinese mixed alliteration: "fei (four), waste time, flounder in business" (XCIX/716). Canto CX even offers a single-line poem in Chinese syllables: "yüeh$^{4-5}$ / ming^{2} / mo$^{4-5}$ / hsien^{1} / p'eng^{2}" (CX/798).

The Beinecke Rare Book and Manuscript Library of Yale University keeps a typescript of forty-five pages entitled "Preliminary Survey," which Pound sent to Achilles Fang for evaluation in January 1951. It testifies to Pound's tremendous effort at the detail of Chinese sound and sense that winter. As a poet he was looking for sound symbolism. Even with no access to archaic Chinese pronunciation, he speculated: "Despite exceptions a good many ch sounds can be read as indicative of place or of motion... YUAN in a number of cases has clearly to do with circling, enclosing." Fang did not think much of O. Z. Tsang's *Complete Chinese–English Dictionary*, upon which Pound based his abandoned survey. However, he admired Pound's interpretation of the Confucian word chih 止 as "the point of rest" and "the hitching post sign."[16]

NOTES

1 In a discarded fragment in *I Cantos*, Pound states "and my gt aunt's third husband / received in ms from a friend / the 49th canto –" *IC*, 1536.

2 W. Yip, *Ezra Pound's Cathay* (Princeton: Princeton University Press, 1969), 84.

3 The recently published *The Chinese Written Character as a Medium for Poetry: A Critical Edition*, ed. H. Saussy *et al.* (New York: Fordham University Press, 2008) includes both Pound's 1919/1936 text and Fenollosa's original manuscripts at Yale. The latter brings to light for the first time Fenollosa's concern with the sounds and rhythmic patterns of Chinese poetry, which Pound elected to drop.

4 *Ezra Pound's Chinese Friends: Stories in Letters*, ed. Z. Qian (Oxford: Oxford University Press, 2008), 17.

5 Hugh Kenner, "More on the Seven Lakes Canto," *Paideuma* 2.1 (Spring 1973): 43.

6 *Chinese Friends*, 53.

7 *Ezra Pound & Japan: Letters & Essays*, ed. Sanehide Kodama (Redding Ridge, CT: Black Swan Books, 1987), 39, 102.

8 Edward Said, *Orientalism* (New York: Random House, 1978), 3.

9 *Chinese Friends*, 122.

10 Quoted in W. McNaughton, "A Report on the 16th Biennial International Conference on Ezra Pound," Brantôme, France, 18–22 July 1995," *Paideuma* 27.1 (spring 1998): 130.

11 G. Kennedy, "Fenollosa, Pound and the Chinese Character," *Yale Literary Magazine* 126.5 (1958): 28; J. J. Y. Liu, *The Art of Chinese Poetry* (Chicago: University of Chicago Press, 1961), 3.

12 Fenollosa, *The Chinese Written Character*, 9.

13 Pound, "Note," *Catai*, trans. Mary de Rachewiltz (Milan: Strenna del Pesce d'Oro, 1960), 45.

14 *Chinese Friends*, 54, 77.

15 A.J. Palandri, "Homage to a Confucian Poet," *Paideuma* 3.3 (winter 1974): 307.

16 *Chinese Friends*, 208–28, 208, 227, 52.

CHAPTER 31

Little magazines

Craig Monk

With signature aplomb, Ezra Pound wrote in 1928, in the back of the fourth number of his magazine *The Exile*, about "the periodicals in which the struggle took place."[1] What we now call modernism had been articulated by this time, and Pound had secured an enviable reputation within the movement; F. R. Leavis later credited him with having helped affect "a new start" and "a decisive reordering of the tradition of English poetry."[2] By the end of the 1920s, the literary establishment was "ready to feed almost anyone who will write anodyne monographs about" the poetic upheaval in which he had participated, Pound noted, even though it "would never have fed" at the time "any of the men who did the work."[3]

Little magazines, launched without the prospect of commercial success, had provided necessary support, though the esteem in which he held *The Dial*, *The Egoist*, *The English Review*, *The Little Review*, *Poetry*, and *The Transatlantic Review* scarcely implied the scope of his own engagement with such publications. *Ezra Pound's Poetry and Prose*, a collection of his periodical work over a period of seventy years compiled by Lea Baechler, A. Walton Litz, and James Logenbach, fills eleven quarto volumes, and Donald Gallup's bibliography lists more than seven hundred contributions to magazines before Pound himself launched *The Exile*. Mark Morrisson points out that while modernist periodicals often "found only small readerships and led brief lives," writers used these publications to demonstrate to their readers "a lively, even exhilarating, awareness of opposition" to the literary establishment "and of the possibilities that the new century provided for an alternative art to become part of the public sphere."[4]

Yet it seems unusual that, owing to the undeniable efficacies of the little magazine for emerging artists, Pound did not seek his own periodical until 1927 or that, by that time, such a venue could still be important to him. "I don't think it's any of the artist's business to see whether or no he circulates," he wrote *Poetry* editor Harriet Monroe in August 1912, "but I was nevertheless tempted, on the verge of starting a quarterly, and it's a great relief to know that your paper may manage what I had, without financial strength, been about to attempt rather forlornly" (*SL*, 44). Instead of fronting money himself, Pound was content to broker relationships with a series of editors, embracing a form he described as "impractical publication" so that familiar methods of dissemination could be redeployed in service of an unfamiliar art. He later confessed that "the history of contemporary letters has, to a very manifest extent, been written in such magazines,"[5] but the reconciliation of a nascent modernism with the literary establishment was still the financial ruin of many of them. Pound thus took considerable risk to launch *The Exile* in order to continue a longstanding and increasingly perilous program that stretched beyond the ambitions of most modernists: to promote collaborators he believed overlooked, to air his views on a range of social issues, and by so doing to affect profound change in the United States.

Perhaps the most convincing indication that Pound was ready to launch a periodical came in a letter to his father on October 27, 1926. "Have spent past week having fool ideas about starting a magazine; WITHOUT interference for ONCE," he wrote Homer Pound. "Dont know that I shall get round to doing it. Have you any suggestions?"[6] He mentioned it again less than a month later. "Am rather thinking about starting a magazine," he repeated on November 15. "At present am looking for contributors . . . Several people seemed cheered at prospect of unfettered publication. That's about as far as it has got."[7] Indeed, he had a long history of getting his friends into print. "I want an 'official organ' (vile phrase)," he explained to Margaret Anderson in early 1917, as he began his collaboration with *The Little Review*.

I mean I want a place where I and T. S. Eliot can appear once a month (or once an 'issue') and where [James] Joyce can appear when he likes, and where Wyndham Lewis can appear if he comes back from the war. DEFINITELY a place for our regular appearance and where our friends and readers (what few of 'em there are), can look with assurance of finding us. (*SL*, 160–1)

While much had changed in the subsequent decade, the desire to logroll his friends had not, and in the weeks between letters to his father he canvassed them once more. He counseled the composer George Antheil to save up "any manifestos, or other verbal manifestation of yr. might. geelory an majesty" that might help fill "a seerious magazine."[8] He told e. e. cummings that he was thinking of starting "a infinitesimal review" as an "outlet," and he asked the poet to help him identify, specifically, worthy people who had been unable to break into print "at any price." While he would not "announce publication" until he found "at least three items of interest," he had already decided that he would not accept "slabs of 'work in progress' unless there is some vurry speshul reason for it" (*SL*, 275). Though he was in need of support, James Joyce was not invited to publish in *The Exile*, as Pound disapproved of the prose that would be published eventually as *Finnegans Wake*. He described his planned magazine to his old friend as a "periodical designed to deal with various matters not handled elsewhere," but Pound judged it unsuitable to anyone looking for serialization on a predictable schedule. "I don't see that it can be much direct and immediate use to you," he concluded, finally. "If I had an encyclopedicly large monthly, the kewestion wd. be different" (*SL*, 281). Eventually, Pound took great pride in having published parts of "Adolphe" by John Rodker "and a little work by [Robert] McAlmon, W. C. Williams, Louis Zukofsky." He also printed Richard Aldington, Morley Callaghan, Ralph Cheever Dunning, and W. B. Yeats. Although some of these collaborators had been struggling to place their recent work, Pound considered unknown poet Howard Weeks his only significant find. "I printed very little of Weeks because he seemed to me a man of great promise," he later observed. "I mean, one felt that his work was bound to be ever so much better in the course of the next few months. The few months were denied him."[9] Pound discovered that publishing his own magazine could be as unpredictable as relying solely upon the editorial judgements of others.

Supporting his friends was of undeniable importance to him, but Pound had also used little magazines to publish his early criticism. While he described A. R. Orage's *New Age* as a publication "not primarily concerned with letters," for example, it was enough of "an open forum" to print in 1911 and 1912 both "I Gather the Limbs of Osiris" and "Patria Mia."[10] If the former fell short of its aim "to recover and renew the vital principle of his civilization," in David Moody's recent rereading of this series of contributions, it provided Pound with an opportunity "to declare his genius."[11] In the latter, however, Pound declared "that America has a chance for Renaissance," but the country was lacking the kind of "enthusiasm and a propaganda" that his writings could provide. "I have no desire to flatter the country by pretending that we are at present enduring anything except the Dark Ages," he concluded (*SP*, 102, 111). Pound thought that creative works, themselves, could bring profound change to intellectual life in the United States. "He had an idea that the finest poetry would free the populace from the tyranny of mass emotions and received ideas," Moody argues further, "that by the 'melody of words' it would draw the minds and wills of its hearers into harmony with the true nature of things."[12]

Though Pound still maintained that "any scrap of creative work" was more valuable "than lengthy discussion of what might be but is not,"[13] a revived interest in prose was fueled by his conclusion that the United States had not developed the guiding sense, the discrimination it had then been lacking. Ira Nadel reminds us that "as a venue for his political and social views," *The Exile* followed a period of "almost two decades" during which Pound "expressed little concern for US domestic matters."[14] If he had been preoccupied with his *Cantos*, he confessed to his father that his focus was again shifting. "I seem to have a sort of head of steam up," he wrote, "for the editorial part of the show."[15] By the time the first number of the magazine appeared, he was asking Americans "whether there is *any* mental activity" beyond that of those countrymen who were proposing radical political alternatives. "At present, in that distressed country, it would seem that neither side ever answers the other; such ignoring, leading, in both cases, to ignorance," he concluded. "I should like a small open forum in which the virtues or faults of *either* side might be mentioned without excessive animus."[16]

From his perspective, American society had lost the ability to draw clear distinctions between public and private affairs, and he felt that he could play a role in helping to redefine terms. "The artist, the maker is always too far ahead of any revolution, or reaction, or counter-revolution or counter-re-action for his vote to have any immediate result," he later wrote, "and no party program ever contains enough of his program to give him the least satisfaction."[17] For this reason, he hoped his magazine would be a place where he could print occasional thoughts, as no other editor was likely to grant him "freehand for a series of articles."[18]

Though he never lacked confidence, Ezra Pound was by this time a middle-aged man; he had been abroad for nearly twenty years. In a letter to John Price, he wondered "as to what proportion of my own stuff the possible reader wd. stand."[19] He had asked his correspondent, previously, "By the way, supposing that I as an author should wish to publish something in an American periodical where would you suggest that I send it?"[20] The reply could not have been encouraging. "I had better say frankly that I have read little of your prose, and thought none of that good," Price confessed. "It appeared to be frantically dashed off."[21] Pound countered only that his essays were intended for "the sphere of action" and could not be judged as "art and letters."[22]

An obscure New York newspaperman, Price nevertheless played an important role in launching *The Exile*. He hoped to work as "an independent editor and publisher," he told Pound, "because I love reading so damned much that I want to do everything I can for the men who write what I like to read."[23] He had written Pound to complain about *Two Worlds*, the magazine in which Samuel Roth pirated the work of expatriate writers for readers in the United States. "I have already spent a certain amount of time and postage stamps trying to contradict the statement that I was contributing editor to ROTH or to anyone else," the poet grumped in reply. Price's letters touched further upon a number of sore spots, including the state of American copyright and obscenity laws. "Have you any connection with [some] organization trying to interfere with literature on grounds other than those of literary merit?" Pound quizzed. Any unwarranted suppression of art was "most destructive to the possibilities of civilization in any bearable form," and it represented "the most evil element in America."[24]

Price himself was interested in publishing a magazine that would pay to reprint expatriates' writings, but after Pound complained that agents and booksellers often swindled writers, Price changed his thinking. "I repeat," he soon concluded, "I would like to act as American agent for modernist individuals, groups, and firms abroad. I am willing to give all my spare time to it at present, and if it should ever develop into a big enough undertaking to support me, would devote full time to it."[25] With this newfound support, Pound committed to *The Exile* and announced in early 1927 that he would try "to run her for a year" to see if "the show" could find "its own feet."[26]

The two men planned to print 500 copies of each number, 200 of which Pound hoped to distribute in Europe. Price was concerned that there would be only 300 copies for the United States, but that number could grow once the magazine was printed in America, an enterprise that would also help secure copyright protection. When Pound discovered that this plan cost twice as much as he hoped to secure from copy sales, he suggested that Price "print the opening paragraphs of every story and the first five lines of each poem on a broad side (cheapest possible form)" and sell one copy to secure government protection for *The Exile*.[27] Unfortunately, the Assistant Registrar of Copyrights in Washington quickly set the men straight, assuring them that protection "could not be secured here without printing it entirely in the United States."[28] Pound raged about discrimination against quality authors whose works were apt to be pirated, and he fumed that American publishing costs were prohibitive. "The American printing price is out of the question," he wrote. "Excellent example of American laws framed

AGAINST the mind and in favour of material. Printer favoured above the author."[29] While magazines could be imported to the United States without duty, customs officials still charged Price for the copies of the first number Pound shipped him, judging the publication a book because the "Spring 1927" on its cover page was not a specific enough publication date and Pound neglected to state how frequently *The Exile* would appear. "Poison their lives," he advised Price, subsequently. "But of course in veiled and polite language. They cant do anything against formality."[30] As the delays mounted, however, he began to rail against "the sonzof bitches," himself, and the customs office came to represent the bureaucracy that strangled American life.[31] The heightened language of his letters foreshadowed the intemperate tone of the essays he had forthcoming.

When Pound began his association with *The Little Review* a decade before, he fretted that while he had "come to the end of making free contributions to anything," he might still be expected to do magazine work exclusively for "love." But he told Margaret Anderson, "One does not want to see the country slide back into the arms of Harpers and the Atlantic."[32] While his work with Price did little to calm his money fears, he found the opportunity to defend America against its genteel influences once more irresistible. He set out with the hope that the creative material he published might be provocative. "I think we may as well say, you need send nothing more for the present unless it strikes you as very ODD," he instructed Price about unsolicited manuscripts, "as wholly *unlike* the pork being used in American magazines."[33] Price imagined that Pound might save the "last 10 to 15 pages" in order to print "comment, onslaughts, theories, notes."[34] But Pound imagined, instead, a series of "jabs" delivered where the reader least expected them.[35]

This desire to confront his countrymen thus also colored the tone of his messages to them. "Anybody attempting to contribute to this periodical ought to know at least two languages," he announced. "If intending collaborators do not already know French, I suggest that they learn it first and submit manuscript after they have."[36] If prospective writers seemed to know little about life beyond the United States, Pound was disappointed that few submissions engaged thoughtfully conditions at home. "Twenty years ago most of the American writing talent was drawn off into writing about civic affairs," he observed. "The present crop of young writers, with perhaps no more talent, are too lazy to occupy themselves with civic affairs, even when these impinge on the writers' own."[37] Unfortunately, there was now no place to which these writers could go in order to sharpen their senses. "Twenty years ago one could go to London or Paris, and probably to

Munich and Vienna and finds things admirably done," he suggested. "Now there is absolutely nowhere that a young man can go with advantage unless he be protected with the most lively critical and comparative instinct."[38] In the absence of this critical acumen, young writers were interested only in their "own, often quite uninteresting interior,"[39] leaving them unsuited to take up the responsibility "to drive back the government into its proper place."[40]

Stinging from his experience with American customs authorities, Pound developed greater bluster in his published prose. Wendy Flory has pointed out that, if judged solely on his writings on literature, he appeared "lucid, reasonable, and in control of his emotions" well into the 1930s, a period in which "his state of mind . . . progressively declined." Insofar as his essays in *The Exile* foreshadowed an interest in economics that would come to dominate his thought, they demonstrate how easy it was for him to slip into seemingly "involuntary tirades" of hyperbole.[41] He was soon talking about "the loss of *all* distinctions between public and private" in the United States that made it possible for the government "to mess into other people's affairs," and he blamed "the ineffable rudderlessness" of the American people, their apparent inability to root their own actions and habits of thought in "any main principle whatsoever."[42] The representatives who worked on their behalf thus deserved no respect. "All bureaucrats ought to be drowned," he screamed from the pages of the magazine. Of elected officials, he said: "Damn, and again damn, and yet again damnblast the lot of 'em."[43] Pound reported with glee the response of a customs appraiser who surveyed the first number of *The Exile*. "Say, the fellow that wrote that stuff in your magazine must be a narcotic fiend!" the official judged. "Nobody has thoughts like those except under the influence of drugs!"[44] It was ironic that in the midst of his mounting anxiety, then, Pound turned to the American publishing industry for help.

When launching his review, he originally wanted nothing to do with houses in the United States. "So many people have gone bust trusting American publishers," he confided to Price.[45] "There is NOTHING in it for a publishing house. And I dont think the possible audience wd. ever be enough to make it so."[46] But, after the first number appeared, Pascal Covici expressed an interest in *The Exile*. "I am rather taken with the idea of bringing it out here in Chicago," he wrote the poet, "under your absolute editorship of course."[47] In addition to the magazine, Covici was willing to print two manuscripts on which Pound had been working. "Mind, I am not promising any fortunes," he continued, "but I believe I could do a great deal for you . . . as I am deeply interested in your work and will do everything possible for greater sales."[48] Pound wrote to his mother that "Mr Covici is on the square."[49] While Pound later suggested that Archibald MacLeish had "put up most of the printer's expenses for" the first number of *The Exile*,[50] John Price's careful records show that postage and advertising costs alone imperiled the whole enterprise. Indeed, there is evidence that Covici had his own concerns about assuming responsibility for a little magazine, hoping but to cover "the cost of printing and distribution."[51]

In fact, only three additional numbers appeared. "As you know, I undertook the publication of *The Exile* out of the high regard which I have for Ezra Pound as a Force," he confessed to the disappointed poet in September 1928. "That opinion has not changed in the least, but, unfortunately, my luxury budget has begun to falter, and as I think you will be able to see, *Exile* is a luxury for a publisher. It has become a luxury which I am afraid I can no longer afford."[52] Pound asked his father before Christmas, "Know anyone who wants to BUY the paper?"[53] No one did. Catherine Turner has considered the ways in which a burgeoning modernism had, by this time, grown more appealing to commercial houses, as publishers and authors convinced a skeptical public that reading modern writing was necessary in order to keep "abreast of the times." Promoted "as a new literature of quality," modernism would help "make sense of the various changes the twentieth century had brought."[54] It was to frame the achievement of modern art, however, that little magazines lived and died, and anything beyond this most practical function was blunted in Pound's case by the difficult, contrarian positions he took.

The trauma of publishing his own little magazine sent Pound into a brief period of retrenchment. He published in November 1930 a summary of "Small Magazines" to argue that no "few sheets in small and tawdry format" should ever be assumed to be "wholly devoid of merit," however. "There are plenty of people over forty who are willing to acknowledge that Mr. Joyce, Mr. Eliot, and the rest appeared (past tense) ten or fifteen years ago in small and allegedly eccentric magazines," he continued. These publications thus provided the "roots" of a genuinely "new thing." But no one seemed interested in what was happening at that time, ignoring "writers who will, in ten or fifteen years, hold analogous positions in the world of letters" on the strength of work appearing "in magazines as apparently tawdry and freakish" as the ones in which he had promoted his friends.[55]

As a venue for his own poetry, little magazines had been less important for some time. *Personae* (1926) had been printed by Boni and Liveright in New York, and T. S. Eliot had edited *Collected Poems* (1928) for Faber in London. Nancy Cunard's Hours Press had just issued *A Draft of xxx Cantos* (1930) in Paris. But if periodicals still appealed to Pound as an outlet for his critical prose, he would soon have greater success placing that work with publishers, too. *How to Read* (1931) was followed by *ABC of Economics* (1933), *ABC of Reading* (1934), and *Make it New* (1934). While there is no doubt that Pound made use of little magazines for the rest of his life, the sorts of magazines with which he was most commonly engaged in the 1930s demonstrate how he saw them, increasingly, as a venue divorced from the observations on literature that defined his earliest work. He contributed polemical writings to the *New English Weekly*, for example, a new Social Credit magazine A. R. Orage launched in London in 1932. His work with the fascist *British Union Quarterly* and *British–Italian Bulletin*, in which he defended Italy's invasion of Ethiopia, demonstrated the lengths to which Pound would go to apply his ideas on economics. "Pound's views are neither static nor perfectly consistent," Leon Surette observes. He describes the poet's thought through this period as "a snowball picking up bits of detritus and dropping other bits as it rolls along."[56] From his work in *The Exile*, Pound's rants began to gain an undeniable and tragic momentum. His enduring desire to influence American life would, soon, bring him into even greater conflict with the government of the United States.

NOTES

1 Ezra Pound, "Data," *The Exile* 4 (autumn 1928): 104.
2 F. R. Leavis, "Epilogue," in *Modernism: Critical Concepts in Literary and Cultural Studies*, ed. Tim Middleton (London: Routledge, 2001), I: 281.
3 Pound, "Data," 104.
4 Mark S. Morrisson, *The Public Face of Modernism: Little Magazines, Audiences, and Reception, 1905–1920* (Madison: University of Wisconsin Press, 2001), 16.
5 Ezra Pound, "Small Magazines," *The English Journal* 19. 9 (November 1930): 701, 702.
6 Ezra Pound to Homer Pound, October 27, 1926, Ezra Pound Papers, 61:2692, Yale Collection of American Literature, Beinecke Rare Book and Manuscript Library.
7 Ezra Pound to Homer Pound, November 15, 1926, Pound Papers, 61:2692.
8 Ezra Pound to George Antheil, October 29, 1926, Antheil MSS, Lilly Library, Indiana University.
9 Pound, "Small Magazines," 701.
10 Pound, "Data," 107.
11 Moody, 169.
12 *Ibid.*, 133.
13 Ezra Pound, "The Exile," *The Exile* 3 (Spring 1928): 102.

14 Ira B. Nadel, *Ezra Pound: A Literary Life* (Basingstoke: Palgrave Macmillan, 2004), 111.
15 Ezra Pound to Homer Pound, November 15, 1926, Pound Papers, 61:2692.
16 Ezra Pound, "The Exile," *The Exile* 1 (spring 1927): 89.
17 *Ibid.*, 91.
18 Ezra Pound to John Price, October 29, 1926, John Price MSS, 2, Lilly Library, Indiana University.
19 Ezra Pound to John Price, October 29, 1926, Price MSS, 2.
20 Ezra Pound to John Price, December 11, 1925, Price MSS, 1.
21 John Price to Ezra Pound, December 22, 1925, Price MSS, 1.
22 Ezra Pound to John Price, January 8, 1926, Price MSS, 2.
23 John Price to Ezra Pound, December 22, 1925, Price MSS, 1.
24 Ezra Pound to John Price, December 11, 1925, Price MSS, 1.
25 John Price to Ezra Pound, January 22, 1926, Price MSS, 2.
26 Ezra Pound to John Price, January 22, 1927, Price MSS, 3.
27 Ezra Pound to John Price, December 2, 1926, Price MSS, 2.
28 Assistant Registrar of Copyrights, Washington to John Price, March 2, 1927, Price MSS, 4.
29 Ezra Pound to John Price, January 6, 1927, Price MSS, 3.
30 Ezra Pound to John Price, March 14, 1927, Price MSS, 4.
31 Ezra Pound to John Price, May 10, 1927, Price MSS, 4.
32 Ezra Pound, *Pound/The Little Review: The Letters of Ezra Pound to Margaret Anderson*, ed. Thomas L. Scott, Melvin J. Friedman, and Jackson R. Bryer (New York: New Directions, 1988), 4.
33 Ezra Pound to John Price, February 14/15, 1927, Price MSS, 3.
34 John Price to Ezra Pound, November 17, 1926, Price MSS, 2.
35 Ezra Pound to John Price, November 30, 1926, Price MSS, 2.
36 Ezra Pound, "Notice to Contributors," *The Exile* 2 (autumn 1927): 121.
37 Ezra Pound, "Bureaucracy," *The Exile* 4 (autumn 1928): 14.
38 Pound, "The Exile," *The Exile* 3, 106.
39 Pound, "Data," 116.
40 Pound, "Bureaucracy," 14.
41 Wendy Stallard Flory, *The American Ezra Pound* (New Haven: Yale University Press, 1989), 85.
42 Ezra Pound, "Prolegomena," *The Exile* 2 (autumn 1927): 35.
43 Pound, "The Exile," *The Exile* 3, 102, 105.
44 Ezra Pound, "Note Re 1st Number," *The Exile* 2 (autumn 1927): 120.
45 Ezra Pound to John Price, October 29, 1926, Price MSS, 2.
46 Ezra Pound to John Price, November 30, 1926, Price MSS, 2.
47 Pascal Covici to Ezra Pound, April 11, 1927, Pound Papers, 10:462.
48 Pascal Covici to Ezra Pound, September 29, 1927, Pound Papers, 10:462.
49 Ezra Pound to Isabel Pound, March 21, 1927, Pound Papers, 61:2693.
50 Ezra Pound, Letters to Ibbotson, ed. V. I. Mondolfo and M. Hurley (Orono, ME: National Poetry Foundation, 1979), 34.
51 Pascal Covici to Ezra Pound, April 11, 1927, Pound Papers, 10:462.

52 Pascal Covici to Ezra Pound, September 5, 1928, Pound Papers, 10:462.

53 Ezra Pound to Homer Pound, December 20, 1928, Pound Papers, 61:2696.

54 Catherine Turner, *Marketing Modernism between the Two World Wars* (Amherst: University of Massachusetts Press, 2003), 215, 218, 220.

55 Pound, "Small Magazines," 704.

56 Leon Surette, *Pound in Purgatory: From Economic Radicalism to Anti-Semitism* (Urbana: University of Illinois Press, 1999), 5.

CHAPTER 32

Publishing and publishers

Gregory Barnhisel

In the past twenty years, modernist studies has radically revised the conventional wisdom about modernism and its relationship to commerce, capitalism, and mass culture. Rejecting the claim that modernism was a mandarin movement, headed by highbrow reactionaries such as T.S. Eliot and Ezra Pound, the new modernist scholarship points to the many and forgotten links between modernism and mass culture. Certainly, links between the two had always been acknowledged, but they were connections of anathema: high modernist works such as *The Cantos*, "The Hollow Men," and even *Ulysses* were read as execrating mass culture, especially the kind of mass culture produced by capitalism. It followed, then, that modernist writers saw themselves as above the marketplace: to them mass popularity or success in the market was a sign of artistic failure.

But modernist writers such as Pound and Joyce were deeply involved in the marketplace and in the outlets of mass culture and not just to condemn them. This is nowhere clearer than in the relationship of modernist writers to their publishers. Throughout his career Pound published with very small presses as well as with large trade publishers in the USA and Britain, for whom he helped shape marketing and promotion campaigns for his books. Like modernism itself, Pound's publishing history describes an oscillation between coterie and crowd, between highbrow and middlebrow, between private presses and commercial establishments. And in this Pound becomes, perhaps, the signal example of modernism's ambivalence about commercial publishing, of the modernist desire to reach (and convert) a mass audience and its fierce insistence that it was aimed at the few.

In his early years as a publishing poet, Pound kept one foot in each camp, seeking out prominent or promising literary trade publishers while also publishing numerous limited edition books with small presses. From the 1920s on, he continued to publish with trade literary publishers and small presses, but at the same time published books with a university press and with publishers best known as political outlets (Stanley Nott, Henry Regnery). In these later years, Pound also inspired several young men (most notably James Laughlin of New Directions) to start their own publishing ventures.

Looking at Pound through the lens of his publishing history – recognizing that he worked simultaneously as a poet, a political/economic writer, and a prolific contributor to newspapers and magazines (Donald Gallup's bibliography lists over 1,800 such publications) – reinforces Pound's view that his poems, from *Cathay* to the *Cantos*, had a socio-political purpose and were part of a larger intellectual and artistic project. From the outset of his career until the mid 1920s, that project was close to what was the aesthetic mission of modernism: "make it new," also expressed as "*donner un sens plus pur aux mots de la tribu*," stripping away excess or inaccurate verbiage so as to let the image itself work in all of its power and purity.[1] But beginning in the 1920s, Pound's drive to purify poetry melded with his aim to purify society and politics through economic reform. From that point, Pound saw all of his works – from his "Ez Sez" newspaper columns to his literary-critical works to his poetry – as parts of a unified program. He approached the publication and promotion of his works always with this idea in mind.

From his earliest days as a professional writer, Pound attended to many of the typical concerns of a new writer: how his books looked, how much they cost, who read them, who reviewed them, where they were sold, where and how they were advertised.

Soon after arriving in London in 1908 after self-publishing *A Lume Spento* in Venice, Pound went to Elkin Mathews' bookshop and offered him several copies of the book to stock. Mathews was not just a bookseller, of course; with John Lane, his Bodley Head firm had until 1894 been a leading publisher of Decadents like Oscar Wilde and Lionel Johnson. By virtue of creative financial and production techniques, the Bodley Head was able to sell its books at significantly lower prices than most poetry books. In addition, Mathews also produced several series of inexpensive paperbacks intended to expose unknown writers to the public. The "Shilling Garland" series (1896–8) featured young experimental writers such as Robert Bridges, and the "Vigo Cabinet" series (1900–18) boasted Yeats, Synge, Masefield, and Max Weber among its authors.

Although Mathews declined to republish *A Lume Spento*, in December 1908 he did pay to print 100 copies of Pound's next collection, *A Quinzaine for This Yule* (which Pound had initially printed at his own expense), thus making him Pound's first real publisher. During the next decade Mathews put out some of Pound's most important early volumes of poetry – *Personae, Exultations, Canzoni, Cathay*, and *Lustra*, generally in printings of 1000 copies – as well as paying him to edit collections. But as Pound's work and vision grew more radical, Mathews got skittish. Upon seeing the scandalous poems and Catullan epigrams in his 1916 collection *Lustra*, Pound complained, "that idiot Mathews ... got in a panic and marked 25 poems for deletion" (*SL*, 80–1), fearing that *Lustra* would, like D.H. Lawrence's *The Rainbow* in 1915, be suppressed or that he would be prosecuted for obscenity. Mathews ultimately compromised, printing 800 sanitized copies for public sale and 200 unexpurgated copies that those in the know could specifically request. Mathews ended his association with the poet by publishing *Umbra*, a compilation of Pound's early poems, in 1920.

During this period, Pound's efforts to publish his work in the USA brought him in contact with a new generation of publishers, largely Jewish and based in New York rather than Boston. Horace Liveright's biographer Tom Dardis notes that because of the "basic conservatism" of the established American publishers, "most U.S. firms ignored the feverish wave of literary experimentation going on in Europe" in the 1910s and "it is for this reason that so many of the major works of the twentieth-century modernists were published by Jewish firms in the late teens and twenties."[2] Such publishers as Alfred A. Knopf, the Boni brothers, Horace Liveright, and Ben Huebsch, in their promotion of modern or experimental literature, combined contemporary techniques of marketing with such characteristically private-press techniques as snob appeal and the promotion of the object-value of an individual book. As Janice Radway has pointed out, in the late nineteenth century the growth of cheap mass-market books engendered anxiety among publishers and readers, who quickly began to associate poor literary quality with the cheap material quality of these books.[3] Turning that equation on its head, publishers such as Knopf and the Boni brothers stressed that the material quality of their books reflected their literary value.

After publishing a number of books with Small, Maynard and Company (a Boston firm influenced by the Bodley Head), Pound found that by late 1913 his books were no longer appearing in his home country. His agent in America, the New York lawyer and modernist sponsor John Quinn, shopped his manuscripts around, but got little interest from the established houses. Finally, in mid 1917, Knopf picked up the contract for an American edition of *Lustra*. In September 1917 Pound had sixty copies of a restored and expanded *Lustra*, including early versions of the first three Cantos, printed in the USA and circulated privately; a month later, Knopf published it commercially.

With his characteristic eye to promotion, Pound determined that he needed not only to reach influential reviewers, as he had been trying to do since *A Lume Spento*, but that an "introduction" to the work might also help. On Pound's suggestion, T.S. Eliot anonymously – "I want to boom Eliot, and one can't have too obvious a ping-pong match at that sort of thing," Pound explained to Quinn – wrote a short pamphlet entitled "Ezra Pound His Metric and Poetry," which Knopf published in 1917 to coincide with *Lustra*.[4] Sales were poor; writing to Harriet Monroe, he complained that "Knopf writes that he sold 323 copies *Lustra* in Oct. [1917] and 9 in Nov., and that no [reviewer] had offered any assistance" (*SL*, 127). Knopf then published the essay collection *Pavannes and Divisions* in 1918, anticipating a loss – he only agreed to publish it after John Quinn contributed $150. Angering Pound, Knopf later declined Pound's next collection of essays, *Instigations*, which came out, instead, from Boni & Liveright, another of New York's energetic new trade literary publishers.

Instigations inaugurated Pound's short collaboration with the flamboyant Roaring Twenties mainstay Horace Liveright. In the 1910s, Albert and Charles Boni, who ran the Washington Square Bookshop in Greenwich Village, had experimented with a series of cheap, leatherbound reprints (the Little Leather Library) that were initially included as premiums with other products, such as tobacco and Whitman's Samplers chocolates. Typical of this group of publishers, they also put out experimental work such as the 1914 anthology *Des Imagistes*. By 1916, however, the brothers were out of the publishing business until Albert and Horace Liveright found themselves working at adjacent desks at an advertising agency. They soon founded the Modern Library, which Boni envisioned as a larger-trim, higher-priced Little Leather Library. Boni and Liveright used the success of the Modern Library books to subsidize their other authors, but by 1920 the Boni brothers had both left the company and it was Liveright's alone.

Over the following years, the hard-partying, happily commercial Liveright would maintain an unlikely partnership and friendship with Pound, publishing significant works such as *Poems 1918–21* (including "Homage to Sextus Propertius" and "Hugh Selwyn Mauberley") and the revised *Personae*. In 1922 Pound squired Liveright around Paris, a trip that resulted in Pound's receiving a $500 annual retainer from Liveright in exchange for "scouting" and translating books for American publication, as well as agreements on the part of Liveright to publish *Ulysses* and *The Waste Land* in the USA (the latter came to fruition; the former, obviously, didn't).

Particularly notable in the three-way relationship between Pound, Quinn, and the American publishers is how Pound stands in the middle in terms of "commercialism." Quinn, as many scholars have noted, represents a model of patronage: buying Joyce's manuscripts to keep the author solvent, setting up the "Bel Esprit" fund for Eliot, and generally taking care of the financial needs of these authors in the USA. In this, he sought to protect them from the vicissitudes of the market and to limit the contamination that capitalist modes of book production and distribution brought to art. The publishers, from Huebsch to Knopf to Liveright, were largely creatures of the market, genuinely appreciating modernist literature but ultimately answering to commercial imperatives. Pound, in this model, is happy with either, as long as the end result is the publication of these works for a broad audience and the financial support of the writers. What bothered Pound wasn't commercialism but perceived personal affront.

Ironically, Pound may have had more "market success" – made more money – from small presses than from the trade publishing industry. Even though print runs were significantly smaller – a trade firm would usually order a first print run of 1,000 copies, while a small press might not exceed 350 total – private-press publication was often more remunerative for the author than commercial publication because of radically different arrangements for royalties. A typical royalty rate for trade publication was 15 percent to 20 percent on gross sales, but a private or limited edition (often sold by subscription) might offer royalties of up to 50 percent, and on the Shakespeare and Company edition of *Ulysses* Joyce received 66 percent of net profits.[5] Not only were the royalty terms more favorable, the books themselves were significantly more attractive and expensive: Bird's edition of XVI *Cantos* listed at 400 francs, with some of its ninety copies priced at 1,600 francs. (By way of comparison, the first edition of *Ulysses* sold at 150, 250, and 350 francs, depending upon the paper used, while a typical cover price for a French book at the time was 7.5 francs, or approximately sixty cents at the 1922 exchange rate of 12.2 francs to the dollar.) Describing such arrangements to William Carlos Williams in 1922, Pound wrote that "I got nearly as much from my little book [on Noh] with [the tiny Cuala Press] as from the big Macmillan edtn" (*EP/WCW*, 64).

Particularly while in Paris in the 1920s Pound worked extensively with small presses. John Rodker's London-based Ovid Press printed a few dozen copies of "The Fourth Canto" in 1919, then 200 copies (at 15 shillings) of *Hugh Selwyn Mauberley* in 1920. In Paris from 1923–5, the Three Mountains Press published several of Pound's works: *Indiscretions* (300 copies, 45 francs), *Antheil and the Treatise on Harmony* (440 copies, 10 or 40 francs), and *A Draft of* XVI *Cantos* (90 copies, 400 francs). The 65-page edition had elaborate illustrated initials by Henry Strater. The heiress and modernist patroness Nancy Cunard bought Bird's press and, in 1930, printed 200 copies of the first, limited edition of *A Draft of* XXX *Cantos* under the imprint of the Hours Press for 40 shillings or 5 guineas. Finally, in 1930 Pound published *Imaginary Letters* (50 copies on Japanese vellum; 300 copies on Navarre Paper; 25 copies hors-commerce at $5.00/$10.00 signed) with Harry and Caresse Crosby's Paris-based Black Sun Press.

The small-press books themselves present a different Pound than the poet and critic of his trade titles. These books were printed in small, often numbered runs and circulated privately, sold by subscription, or offered only by one bookstore. ("Trade publishing," on the other hand, indicates publishing books intended to be distributed widely to bookstores for retail sale.) Small-press titles were collectable art objects or investments, and implicated the purchaser in a relationship of patronage with the writer. At the same time, the physical appearance of these books – their typography, paper, binding and layout – elicited a different reading experience than one might have with a trade hardcover book. The Three Mountains Press edition of *A Draft of* XVI *Cantos* and John Rodker's 1928 edition of *A Draft of the Cantos 17–27*, for instance, are limited and numbered editions bound in vellum and with gold lettering and illuminated capitals; they intertwine design and text and binding. For today's readers, who generally encounter Pound's work in the aggressively spare typography of New Directions or Faber and Faber editions, encountering these books brings new dimensions to Pound's poetry, foregrounding the visual aesthetic of the work as well as the intellectual and historical content of *The Cantos*. They physically make clear the links Pound felt to the generation of the 1890s, of Morris and the Bodley Head.[6]

In the 1930s Pound moved away from small presses as the main outlet for his Cantos and ramped up his production of literary journalism, criticism, and political and economic work. In 1933, as his primary American publisher Boni & Liveright foundered, Pound chose to publish his Cantos with the new firm of Farrar & Rinehart, who issued three volumes (*A Draft of* XXX *Cantos*, 1933; *Eleven New Cantos* XXXI–XLI, 1934; *The Fifth Decad of Cantos*, 1937). Such books as *ABC of Economics* and especially *Jefferson and/or Mussolini*, though, were too controversial for John Farrar and Stanley Rinehart, forcing Pound to publish the latter work with the rump Liveright Publishing Corporation in New York and with the Social Credit-sympathizing Stanley Nott in London. Farrar & Rinehart's editions of *The Cantos* present us with the poems as they appear today: spare and unadorned, forbidding chunks of polyglot erudition. Because of the Depression, the difficulty of Pound's poetry, and Pound's increasing notoriety as a self-appointed spokesman for fascist Italy, the Farrar & Rinehart books sold poorly – in the second half of 1939, for instance, the firm sold a total of seventeen copies of the three Pound titles it had in print.

Pound did find a more amenable publisher in London: Faber and Gwyer (soon to become Faber and Faber), where T.S. Eliot was an editor. Beginning with *Selected Poems* (substantially the same text as Boni & Liveright's 1926 *Personae*) in 1928, Faber became (and remains) Pound's primary British publisher. The firm published installments of *The Cantos* through the 1930s, but also political works such as *ABC of Economics*, criticism in *Guide to Kulchur* and *Polite Essays*, other poetry such as the *Homage to Sextus Propertius*, and works edited by Pound such as the *Active Anthology*.

Pound's most important publishing relationship commenced in the early 1930s in part because of his manic energy and his compulsion to act as a mentor to young literary aspirants. In 1933 James Laughlin, Harvard freshman and scion of a Pittsburgh steel family, requested a meeting with Pound in Rapallo. Laughlin stayed briefly and returned the following year to the "Ezuversity," as Pound called his informal tutelage program. Between 1934 and 1938, the poet and the student corresponded frequently and often worked together – Laughlin as an agent or go-between for Pound and various American publications, and Pound as an exhorter and collaborator and source of inspiration for the young man. In 1936 Laughlin founded an annual – *New Directions in Prose and Poetry* – and two years later, with graduation money, incorporated a publishing company simply called "New Directions," with Pound and William Carlos Williams as his cornerstone authors.

In many ways the most significant development in Pound's publishing career was his 1939 agreement to allow the untested New Directions to become the American publisher of his *Cantos*. Fed up with Farrar & Rinehart's feeble marketing of his works, Pound signed a contract granting rights to *Cantos* LII–LXXI and future installments to Laughlin. In the negotiations for this contract, conducted transatlantically, Laughlin stood up to his idol and mentor, insisting that Pound include nothing libelous or anti-Semitic in his cantos. Pound balked at this but eventually acquiesced.[7] Because the war prevented him from seeing the book until 1945, Pound was unaware of Laughlin's inclusion of an insert in the first 500 copies of *Cantos* LII–LXXI, a pamphlet that sought to explain some of Pound's techniques and, more importantly, to "spin" his well-known endorsement of fascism. The pamphlet, authored anonymously by Laughlin and Laughlin's then-employee Delmore Schwartz, infuriated Pound when he saw that Laughlin had violated the spirit (if not the letter) of his 1939 demand that "Cantos can NOT have a preface IN the book."[8]

After 1945, when Pound was returned to the USA to face trial, Laughlin took control of publishing the poet's work in the USA and thereby transformed Pound's public and literary reputation. Faced with a poet whose work had ceased to sell and whose name had become synonymous with treason, Laughlin created a new public Pound, one stripped of political taint and who had, by 1960, indisputably joined the canon of American literature. Laughlin pursued this task on several fronts. In 1949 he produced an inexpensive edition of Pound's *Selected Poems* (again, without any political content) and set in motion a marketing campaign to get the book used in modern poetry classes in universities. In the late 1950s, he issued most of the New Directions Pound titles in the new "trade paperback" format, attractive to students because of its lower price (generally just over a dollar, as opposed to $3–$6 for hardcover titles). He published works by well-known New Critics insisting that a poet's biography and political views were irrelevant in the evaluation of poetry, advancing that method of interpretation, and worked with (although he did not publish) critics such as Hugh Kenner who were applying a formalist reading to Pound's work. And in advertisements in New Critical-oriented academic journals such as the *Hudson Review* and *Kenyon Review* – read by the very modern-poetry professors Laughlin sought to reach – literary celebrities such as Schwartz and Eliot celebrated Pound's work, giving the imprimatur of the literary establishment to a poet who had seemed, in 1945, doomed to ignominy.

Circumstances, of course, often conspired against Laughlin's "counter-swing," as he called it. Although the awarding of the initial Bollingen Prize to Pound in 1949 for *The Pisan Cantos* bolstered Laughlin's claims that Pound was still a vital poet, the resulting public controversy – conducted in part in the wide-circulation *Saturday Review of Literature* – dredged up Pound's wartime behavior, particularly his anti-Semitic slurs. Although Laughlin wanted to provide novices and student readers with introductions to or glosses of Pound's difficult poetry, Pound balked at this and refused to allow Rolfe Humphries' judicious preface to the *Selected Poems* to be included in the book. And as the 1950s wore on, Pound regained his voice, even from St. Elizabeths Hospital.

Among Pound's regular visitors at St. Elizabeths were two young admirers, John Kasper and T. David Horton. Pound, still very interested in promoting authors he considered underappreciated, urged Kasper and Horton to start their own firm to publish these authors – naturalist Louis Agassiz, for instance, and economist Alexander Del Mar. Kasper and Horton's Square Dollar Press eventually issued eleven titles, bound in gray paperback and priced at a dollar, all clearly chosen by Pound. Had it not been for John Kasper's 1957 arrest for bombing an integrated school in Clinton, Tennessee and the *New York Times'* exposure of Kasper's association with Pound, the poet's second-degree links to the Ku Klux Klan might never have become public knowledge. Fortunately for Pound, this revelation did not derail the efforts on the part of Laughlin, Robert Frost, Eliot, Archibald MacLeish, and others to free him from St. Elizabeths, and he returned to Italy in 1958.

After his release Pound continued to produce new Cantos, eventually publishing three installments with New Directions and Faber. The last – *Drafts and Fragments of Cantos CX–CXVII* (1968) – was a rush job, necessitated by the pirated publication *Cantos 110–116*. This book, "printed & published by the FUCK YOU press," compiled Cantos that had appeared in journals such as the *Paris Review* and *Agenda*. As Peter Stoicheff details, in Laughlin's mind this book threatened New Directions' claim to copyright on those Cantos, and so he summoned Ed Sanders – the Fuck You Press "head" and member of the underground band the Fugs – to the Russian Tea Room to express his displeasure.[9] A limited edition of 310 copies of *Drafts & Fragments* (printed by Iowa's Stone Wall Press) appeared in 1968, followed by a trade edition of 3,000 the following April.

Laughlin often used craft printers such as Stone Wall to produce limited editions of New Directions books, and in fact in the 1950s and 1960s Pound continued to work with small presses to publish many of his works. Pound's most important such relationship in this period of his life was with the Milanese publisher Vanni Scheiwiller, who put out Pound's translations and even produced the first edition of *Thrones* in 1959. (Although Pound had granted New Directions the American copyrights to his Cantos, his arrangements with small printers such as Scheiwiller – who exported their books to the USA – at times jeopardized this.) Although Pound had a strong relationship with Scheiwiller, the Italian edition of his complete *Cantos*, in a facing-page translation and with commentary by his daughter Mary de Rachewiltz, is published by Arnoldo Mondadori. During the 1950s and 1960s several other limited edition books, some of new material and some of reprints, appeared from small publishers in Germany, France, and the USA.

From Pound's return to Italy until after his 1972 death, his primary publishers – Faber and New Directions – filled in the gaps, republishing under their imprints many of the works (books, articles, and even correspon-dence) that had gone out of print or that had never been collected before. Until the 1970s, both publishers, wary of impeding their campaign to promote a depoliticized Pound, resisted making Pound's political and eco-nomic writings available, but in 1973 Faber produced a volume of "Selected Prose" that included some of Pound's most inflammatory writings, and by the mid 1970s a pirate press in Rotterdam published transcripts of Pound's World War II radio speeches. Today, New Directions has thirty Pound titles in print while Faber lists five. Even after Laughlin's death, Pound remains one of New Directions' cornerstone authors, and the editorial vision of the firm, shaped by Laughlin, continues to be characterized by Poundian values: internationalism, experimentation, an eclectic and dissenting view of literary history, and the conviction that literature possesses a profound social impact.

NOTES

1 The source of the French is Stephane Mallarmé's "Le Tombeau d'Edgar Poe," *Poésies* (1898).
2 Tom Dardis, *Firebrand: The Life of Horace Liveright* (New York: Random House, 1995), 51.
3 Janice Radway, *A Feeling for Books: The Book-of-the-Month Club, Literary Taste and Middle Class Desire* (Chapel Hill: University of North Carolina Press, 1997), 166.
4 Pound in B.L. Reid, *The Man from New York: John Quinn and His Friends* (Oxford: Oxford University Press, 1968), 280.
5 Lawrence Rainey, *Institutions of Modernism: Literary Elites and Public Culture* (New Haven: Yale University Press, 1998), 51.
6 See Jerome J. McGann, "Pound's *Cantos*: A Poem Including Bibliography," in *The Textual Condition* (Princeton: Princeton University Press, 1991), 129–52.
7 Greg Barnhisel, *James Laughlin, New Directions and the Remaking of Ezra Pound* (Amherst and Boston: University of Massachusetts Press, 2005), throughout.
8 Quoted *ibid.*, 84.
9 Peter Stoicheff, "The Composition and Publication History of Ezra Pound's *Drafts and Fragments*," *Twentieth Century Literature* 32.1 (Spring 1986): 78–94.

CHAPTER 33

Modernism

George Bornstein

When he looked back over the modernist experiment in the early 1950s
for his introduction to a collection of Ezra Pound's criticism, T. S. Eliot
did not doubt the role of his longtime friend and sometime antagonist in
helping to create an entire movement. "Mr. Pound is more responsible for
the xxth Century revolution in poetry than is any other individual," he
wrote (*LE*, xi). Eliot hastened to add that not merely Pound's own work
but his role as "a teacher and a campaigner" marked his contribution.
He noted Pound's insistence on conveying his own discoveries to others
and described his passion for communicating them as akin to that of
someone trying to convey to a deaf man the fact that the house is on
fire. Most of all, Eliot praised Pound because "he has cared less for his
personal achievement than for the life of letters and art" and that his
career yielded "the lesson to care unselfishly for the art one serves" (*LE*,
xii). Pound's promotion of literary art involved promotion of the men and
women who wrote it as well. Among others, he advanced the careers of
Hilda Doolittle (H.D.), William Carlos Williams, Marianne Moore, Eliot
himself, Richard Aldington, Robert Frost, Wyndham Lewis, James Joyce,
and Ernest Hemingway.

Pound's primary contributions lay in literary technique, though he produced plenty of ideas as well and grew increasingly strident about them. He
conceived of modernism originally in terms of reaction against nineteenth-
century poetry, especially late Victorians like Tennyson, Arnold, and the
derivative poets of the turn of the century like the Georgians. He had
a lifelong sympathy for Browning's experimentalism in diction, cadence,
and structure though, and generally though not always distinguished his
weaker contemporaries and immediate predecessors from their stronger
Romantic models like Keats. In his "Credo" of 1917 he expected modern poetry "to move against poppycock... to be harder and saner... it
will not try to seem forcible by rhetorical din and luxurious riot... fewer

painted adjectives . . . austere, direct, free from emotional slither" (*LE*, 12).
For Pound that meant stripping away unnecessary or florid diction, finding new rhythms to express the new formulations, and searching for new
ways of structuring verse. A learned poet, he called his "pawing" over
the past an attempt "to find out what has been done, once for all" and
"to find out what remains for us to do" (*LE*, 11). That "us" was significant and indicates Pound's drive not only toward individual achievement
but also toward promoting and organizing good work by others. Often
that involved championing groups and movements as much as individual
authors and works.

Pound found his first major coterie in one of the most successful student writing circles in modern literary history. Enrolling at the University of Pennsylvania in 1901, he met the medical student William Carlos
Williams, the artist William Brooke Smith, and at nearby Bryn Mawr the
classics student and aspiring poet Hilda Doolittle, whose father taught
astronomy in that college. Smith died young, but Williams and Doolittle
became lifelong friends and sometime literary allies. Doolittle was also
friendly with the young poet Marianne Moore, whom Pound apparently
did not meet at this time but who became an important if largely epistolary contact as well. Their student verse largely derived from late Victorian
models like Dante Gabriel Rossetti, but particularly Pound and Doolittle
knew classical and Continental works deeply. Each enduring relationship
went through multiple phases. Pound's early relationship with Doolittle
centered around the role of lover, with him presenting to her the vellum-
bound "Hilda's book" containing a selection of his early verse. Later in
London he would function as mentor and promoter, creating the signature
"H. D." for her and sending her imagist work to Harriet Monroe at *Poetry*
magazine. Though less close after his marriage to Dorothy Shakespear and
her marriage and divorce to Richard Aldington and companionship with
Bryher (Winifred Ellerman), they remained important to each other. And
she grappled with her tangled relationship to him, especially in *End to Torment: A Memoir of Ezra Pound*, where she wrote that "He gave, he took.
He gave extravagantly" (*End*, 49). The alliance with Williams likewise continued after Pound's move to London, with inclusion of Williams in the
imagist project and Pound's persuading his own publisher Elkin Matthews
to issue *The Tempers*, Williams' second book of verse. Responding to an
attack on native American poets by the English critic Edgar Jepson partly
arranged by Pound, Williams retaliated in the prologue to his *Kora in
Hell* volume by criticizing the "London Yankees" like Eliot, Pound, and

H. D. as too Europeanized, a disagreement that became an ongoing debate between them. The second issue was, of course, Pound's sympathy for fascism, which both Williams and H. D. condemned.

When Pound left America for Italy and then moved to London in December of 1908, he promptly sought contact with what he saw as the most lively parts of the literary scene. Among his elders, that meant particularly W. B. Yeats and Ford Madox Ford, then still using his Germanic last name Hueffer. "I went to London because I thought Yeats knew more about poetry than anybody else," he told interviewer Donald Hall. "I made my life in London by going to see Ford in the afternoons and Yeats in the evenings."[1] Pound rated Yeats the greatest living poet and said that he himself had come to London to find out how Yeats did it. In particular, Yeats had written poems with natural words in the natural order and without superfluous ornament, as in "The Folly of Being Comforted" from the *In the Seven Woods* (1903) volume. In contrast, Pound was still imitating troubadours like Bertrans de Born or the medieval prison poet Villon, though that would shortly change. Introduced to the Irish poet by Yeats' friend and sometime mistress Olivia Shakespear whose daughter Dorothy he himself would later marry, Pound quickly became a fixture at Yeats' Monday evening salons, where he handed out cigarettes and literary opinions with equal aplomb. After a few years the roles had become more even. "To talk over a poem with him is like getting you to put a sentence into dialect," Yeats confided to Lady Gregory while working on poems for his *Responsibilities* volume of 1914. "All becomes clear & natural."[2] That mutuality did not protect Pound when in his role as foreign editor of *Poetry* magazine he dared to make a few minor changes to poems of Yeats that he was transmitting to the magazine. Yeats exploded, though he eventually came around to Pound's suggestions, and in an essay for *Poetry* Pound labeled Yeats the only contemporary poet worth study. He happily served as Yeats' secretary for three winters beginning in 1913–1914 to carry out that study and in Canto LXXXIII left a memorable portrait of Yeats composing his poem "The Peacock."

When Pound came to London, he intended not to imitate what he found there but to critique it through expatriate eyes. For him "The common verse of Britain from 1890 to 1910 was a horrible agglomerate compost, not minted, most of it not even baked, all legato, a doughy mix of third-hand Keats, Wordsworth, heaven knows what, fourth-hand Elizabethan sonority" (*LE*, 205). Helping to organize the modernist revolt meant de-centering England as literary center, even if he continued to live in it until moving to Paris in 1921. But his alliances ran to Irish writers like Yeats and

Joyce or to Americans like himself, H.D., Williams, and shortly T. S. Eliot. "The language is now in the keeping of the Irish (Yeats and Joyce); apart from Yeats, since the death of Hardy, poetry is being written by Americans," he wrote in "How to Read." "All the developments in English verse since 1910 are due almost wholly to Americans" (*LE*, 34). Pound's explorations in time as he ransacked the past would match later postcolonial infusions and disruptions for Anglophone literature, including influences from foreign languages. The Englishmen with which he did ally himself included largely prose writers, among the older generation especially the novelist and critic Ford Madox Hueffer (later Ford), and these alliances again largely featured technique.

The grandson of the Pre-Raphaelite painter Ford Madox Brown and nephew of William Michael Rossetti, Ford reacted against the art of both in a productive career that included his masterpieces *The Good Soldier* (1915) and the *Parade's End* trilogy. Pound met him in early 1909 as Ford prepared to launch his important magazine *The English Review*, which published several of Pound's poems including "Sestina: Altaforte" along with other innovative work. Pound saw Ford as injecting the precision of French fiction into English literature (*The Good Soldier* is sometimes referred to as the finest French novel in English) and liked to quote Ford's aphorism that Wordsworth so liked the ordinary word that he never thought of looking for the exact word. Their thirty-year friendship lasted until Ford's death in 1939, the same year that Yeats died. As Pound pointed out in 1914, he found Ford "significant and revolutionary because of his insistence upon clarity and precision, upon the prose tradition, in brief, upon efficient writing – even in verse" (*LE*, 377). To that end Ford published in his magazine Thomas Hardy, H. G. Wells, Henry James, and Yeats among the older generation and Pound, Joyce, Hemingway, and Stein among the younger, along with staging debuts for Wyndham Lewis and D. H. Lawrence.

Ford's most memorable impact on Pound included the famous roll on the floor at Giessen in 1911. When Pound read Ford some of his derivative and florid early verse, Ford reacted by rolling on the floor in mock laughter. Pound told the story frequently, perhaps most memorably in his 1939 obituary notice for his old friend and ally. "And he felt the errors of contemporary style to the point of rolling . . . on the floor of his temporary quarters in Giessen when my third volume displayed me trapped, fly-papered, gummed and strapped down in a jejune provincial effort to learn, *merhecule*, the stilted language that then passed for 'good English' in the arthritic milieu that held control of the respected British critical styles," recalled Pound. "And that roll saved me at least two years, perhaps more.

It sent me back to my own proper effort, namely, toward using the living tongue" (*SPR*, 431–2). The shock of Ford's roll did wonders for Pound's awareness of throwing off a derivative recent past in order to write in a living syntax and vocabulary rather than a stilted and artificial one. And it prepared Pound to profit from the developing imagist school when he encountered it. As T. S. Eliot would later remark with only slight chronological wobble, "The *point de repère* usually and conveniently taken as the starting-point of modern poetry, is the group denominated 'imagists' in London about 1910."[3] Because this volume contains separate entries on both imagism and its successor vorticism, we may treat Pound's role in both movements only briefly here.

Imagism itself went through three phases as a movement. The first derived from the Poets' Club of 1909, loosely organized by the iconoclastic T. E. Hulme, fresh from his Cambridge expulsion and promoting a School of Images that avoided abstraction and verbosity. The second stage, organized by Pound itself, dates from the launch of the five brief lyrics ironically labeled "The Complete Poetical Works of T. E. Hulme" in Pound's *Ripostes* volume of 1912. As indicated by the *Des Imagistes* anthology of 1914, the group included principally H. D., Aldington, and Pound himself but also F. S. Flint, Amy Lowell, and more peripherally Williams, Joyce, Ford, and others. Pound had invented the epithet "imagist" to promote H. D.'s work when he sent it to Harriet Monroe for *Poetry* magazine and signed it "H. D. Imagiste." After that, the redoubtable Amy Lowell took over the movement, which Pound satirically dubbed "Amygism" and took little role in. By then, Pound had moved on to vorticism with Wyndham Lewis, the artist Henri Gaudier-Brzeska, and others in search of a more dynamic art and elaborate structure than imagism seemed to imply.

Imagism did help Pound to consolidate his break with the turn of the century rhetorical milieu. He proclaimed its three principles in an article for *Poetry* in March 1913 as including direct treatment, no superfluous words, and a musical rather than mechanical rhythm. That fit well with Pound's lifelong campaign to "make it new" for himself and for modernist literature generally. As he put it retrospectively in the Cavalcanti section of his *Make it New* volume of 1934, he had been "obfuscated by the Victorian language" and needed instead to make "a language to think in" (*LE*, 193–4). At the same time, he needed a new cadence as well. In another retrospective moment, this time from Canto LXXXI, he saluted the change in rhythm that matched the change in diction: "to break the pentameter, that was the first heave" (LXXXI/538). In that modernist makeover of derivative late Victorian verse Pound enlisted most of his friends and associates of his own age, including the Pennsylvania circle and the imagists. He could even see affinities with those who weren't imagists, such as the neo-traditional aesthete of the 1890s Lionel Johnson. "Johnson's verse is full of inversions, but no one has written purer Imagisme than he," declared Pound, and cited Johnson's line "Clear lie the fields, and fade into blue air" as example (*LE*, 362). On the other hand, he denied the label to Yeats, whom he always saw as a Symbolist instead. He hailed Yeats' *Responsibilities* volume (1914) but differentiated it from the work he and his friends were doing: "'Is Mr Yeats an Imagiste?' No, Mr Yeats is a symbolist," pronounced Pound, though he conceded that Yeats had included "*des Images*" in the volume (*LE*, 378). Pound remained firm in that conviction, and as late as Canto LXXXIII he offered the amusing yet provocative portrait of Yeats visiting Notre Dame in Paris and pausing "to admire the symbol / with Notre Dame standing inside it" (LXXXIII/548).

Pound did not have to worry about modernizing the next poet he discovered and promoted, T. S. Eliot. Meeting Eliot in September 1914, Pound described him to Harriet Monroe as "the only American I know of who has . . . trained himself *and* modernized himself *on his own*" (*SL*, 40). Considering "The Love Song of J. Alfred Prufrock" the best poem he had yet seen from an American, Pound promptly sent it to Monroe for publication in *Poetry* magazine, thus inaugurating a series of acts that included arranging publication of Eliot's eventual *Prufrock and Other Observations* from Egoist Press in London and his second volume of verse from Knopf in New York. Pound had to hector Monroe about "Prufrock," particularly its ending, but did succeed in getting into print Eliot's first poem since his undergraduate verse in the Harvard literary magazine *The Advocate*. The action typified both Pound's generosity to other modernists and his adroit manipulation of publishing venues to get them known in the first place. That included stints as subeditor of journals like *Poetry*, *The Egoist*, and *The Dial*, to which he steered important work by himself, Eliot, Moore, and Joyce among others. In parallel, he cultivated relations with a number of new commercial presses like Boni and Liveright, Alfred Knopf, or fine printing concerns like John Rodker's Ovid Press, often run by Jewish publishers who found their rise blocked at mainline commercial firms and who turned to modernist or minority writers to provide much of their lists. Pound, of course, also edited his own anthologies, including *Des Imagistes* of 1914 and *Catholic Anthology* of 1915, which sported five poems by Eliot, two by Williams, and ten by Pound.

If cycles follow the financial wizard Warren Buffet's "3 I"s rule – first innovators, then imitators, then idiots, itself a version of Pound's six-part

scheme for literary development in "How to Read" – by 1919 Pound thought
that the idiots had taken over again and conscripted Eliot to help him lead
the resistance. As Pound described "a movement to which no name has ever
been given" in Eliot's own magazine, *The Criterion*, in 1932: "two authors,
neither engaged in picking the other's pocket, decided that the dilutation of
vers libre, Amygism, Lee Masterism, general floppiness had gone too far and
that some counter-current must be set going. Parallel situation centuries
ago in China. Remedy prescribed 'Emaux et Camées' (or the Bay State
Hymn Book). Rhymes and regular strophes."[4] The remark encapsulates
much of Pound's poetic program for the second half of the 1910s, including injection of principles from Chinese poetry via the work of Ernest
Fenollosa, continued devotion to precision and conciseness, and critique
of the imagist and *vers libre* traditions originally intended to promote those
virtues but since subject to their own corruption. (Pound's resentment at
losing control of the imagist project shines through as well.) Most of all,
the remark situates both Eliot's quatrains from *Poems* and Pound's from
the Mauberley sequence as deliberate responses to slackening technique in
postwar modernist poetry.

Pound and Eliot reversed that trend toward smaller scale and overt
formalism yet again in their collaboration on perhaps the greatest work
of modernist poetry, *The Waste Land*, during 1921–2. Himself recovering from a mental crisis, Eliot sent Pound a draft of the poem roughly
twice as long as the eventual published version. True to the principle of
"dichten = condensare" that he delightedly found in a German/Latin
dictionary, Pound slashed words, lines, and even whole sections from
Eliot's packet. Along with praise like "echt" he included comments like
"too easy," "perhaps be damned," and "too loose." He also cut out entire
sections, like the opening bar crawl in Boston and a passage in Popean
couplets, and suggested individual phrasing like the word "demobbed" in
the pub scene. Not content with substantially revising the poem itself,
Pound arranged for its publication in *The Dial* in New York simultaneously with that in Eliot's own magazine *The Criterion* in London and
then its publication in book form by Boni and Liveright in New York.
He further exploited his new position as foreign correspondent for *The
Dial* to tout the book for the Dial prize, which along with the contract
from Boni brought Eliot considerable financial relief at a stressed time
for his own finances. No wonder that Eliot beginning in 1925 dedicated
the poem to Pound as "il migglior fabbro," Dante's laudatory phrase for
Arnaut Daniel. At a crucial moment Pound supplied the poetic craft that
the work demanded and Eliot needed. In a later essay Eliot saluted Pound

for turning *The Waste Land* "from a jumble of good and bad passages into a poem."[5]

The kind of poem that Pound turned *The Waste Land* into matched the principles that he used in his own epic *The Cantos* and reverberated hugely throughout modernist literature, as did the structural principles that Joyce developed for *Portrait* and *Ulysses*, which Pound also championed. His cuts resulted in a work of abrupt juxtapositions, often without connecting matter. That matched his own notion of "ideogramic method," which sought to build larger structures and meanings out of concrete particulars. He chose as one famous example the Chinese ideogram for "red," which he saw as composed of the signs for iron rust, cherry, rose, and flamingo. This condensed model of poetry resulted in his judging *The Waste Land* to be the longest true poem in the English language and even to confess his envy. Such structure dovetailed with what Eliot himself called "the mythic method" in his review of Joyce's *Ulysses*. Declaring Joyce's novel "the most important expression which the present age has found," Eliot found it a work to which all moderns were indebted and from which they could not escape. He called particular attention to Joyce's "mythic method" of extended parallels between Homer's *Odyssey* and the events of his own modern and urban work, a technique pioneered by Yeats. "In using the myth, in manipulating a continuous parallel between contemporaneity and antiquity, Mr Joyce is pursuing a method which others must pursue after him . . . It is simply a way of controlling, of ordering, of giving a shape and a significance to the immense panorama of futility and anarchy which is contemporary history," wrote Eliot.[6]

Pound's efforts to insert Joyce's work and techniques into the development of modernism far exceeded trumpeting a structural method, crucial though that was. From first learning of Joyce when at the Coleman's Hatch cottage Yeats suggested including some of his poems in the *Des Imagistes* anthology, Pound championed *Dubliners, Portrait of the Artist as a Young Man*, and *Ulysses* in turn. He helped get them published, encouraged Joyce to keep working, and helped Joyce make financial ends meet as well. The words he used to praise *Dubliners* and *Portrait* echoed those he valued in poetry of the period – "clear and direct," "free from sloppiness," and "hardness and gauntness" for example (*P/J* 24, 27, and 32). Yet his enthusiasm for *Ulysses* waned with its later chapters and despite loyally boosting *Finnegans Wake* (then called *Work in Progress*) at first, Pound grew increasingly critical and dubbed it a work "in regress" that displayed a "diarrhea of consciousness" instead (*SL*, 292, *P/J*, 257). As Pound grew more obsessed with contemporary politics and economics, he lost sympathy for stream of consciousness and interiority. In 1936 he exploded to Wyndham Lewis, another modernist associate with whom he had a sometimes stormy relationship, that "this flow of conSquishousness Girtie/Jimmee stuff has about FLOWED long enough" (*P/J*, 256).

The estrangement from Joyce exemplifies the ominous phrase "divergence later" that Pound used in describing his alliance with Eliot at the time of the quatrain poems of 1919. Over time he separated from many members of the modernist enterprise that he had once held dearest, often under the pressure of his growing devotion to increasingly right-wing political and economic ideas. The earlier Pound of the modernist heyday had valued precision and accuracy, taking a dim view of those whose rhetoric or views violated that standard. "Bad art is inaccurate art," he declared in 1913. "It is art that makes false reports" (*LE*, 43). But from the 1920s onward through World War II his increasingly strident tone caused him to do just that, and to estrange him from former allies. In the case of Joyce, he thought that a devotion to interior subjectivity and consciousness caused neglect of pressing social and political issues. He thought that Christianity had misled "Parson Eliot," as he teasingly called him, away from Confucian and later fascistic ideals. His own devotion to Italian fascism alienated Williams, H. D., Moore, and others, despite their personal devotion. Yet he had contributed so much to modernism and so generously to others that many of them rallied around him for the treason trial at the end of the war and the effort to release him from St. Elizabeths mental hospital after that.

In the late retrospective Cantos written from the collapse of Italian fascism onwards Pound increasingly mustered the modernists to populate his own greatest work, *The Cantos*. At Pisa he called them "these the companions" and among the recently deceased singled out Ford, Yeats, and Joyce: "Fordie that wrote of giants / And William who dreamed of nobility / And Jim the comedian singing" (LXXIV/452–3). Elsewhere he saluted Eliot ("Possum"), Wyndham Lewis, and more of his own generation and Blunt and others of an earlier one, all of whom had helped him gather from the air a live tradition. Racked by remorse, he sought humility. In the eighty-first Canto he rejects vanity and learns that "What thou love'st well is thy true heritage" (XXXI/541). Whatever his political and personal foibles, one thing that Pound always loved well was literature. Besides celebrating its usable past and creating his own works, he perhaps did more than any other single person to help create the movement we know as modernism. That is his true heritage, and our own.

NOTES

1 Interview "Ezra Pound," in *Writers at Work: The Paris Review Interviews*, second series, ed. George Plimpton (New York: Viking Press, 1965), 47.

2 W. B. Yeats to Lady Gregory, January 3, 1913, in *The Collected Letters of W. B. Yeats* (Oxford: Oxford University Press, Intelex Electronic Edition, 2002), Accession number 2053.

3 T. S. Eliot, *To Criticize the Critic* (New York: Farrar, Straus & Giroux, 1965), 58.

4 Ezra Pound, "Harold Monro," *The Criterion* 11. 45 (July 1932): 590.

5 T. S. Eliot, "On a Recent Piece of Criticism," *Purpose* 10. 2 (April–June, 1938), 92.

6 T. S. Eliot, "*Ulysses*, Order and Myth," *The Dial* 75 (November 1923): 480–3.

CHAPTER 34

Fascism

Serenella Zanotti

Pound's fascism has long been controversial. One point of agreement among critics, both detractors and enthusiasts, is that Pound's idea of Italian fascism should be distinguished, at least in part, from its reality.[1] As K. Ruthven stated, "Italian Fascism as a political practice, developed at a particular historical moment and in particular economic conditions, was related to Pound's 'Fascism' only by way of adjacency." The "Mussolini" of *Jefferson and/or Mussolini* was "a figment of Pound's imagination, the heroic agent of a 'fascism' as remote from Italian Fascism as 'Mussolini' was from Mussolini."[2]

The difficulty encountered by early Pound scholars in coping with this issue led to the creation of a divided image, as if the poet who helped create modernism were one thing, and the fascist who broadcasted in favor of Mussolini were another.[3] Studies carried out from the late seventies on helped recompose the fracture, demonstrating that Pound's poetry cannot be separated from his political beliefs.[4]

A common assumption has been that Pound came to fascism via economics, and that his adherence was motivated by a thorough examination of Mussolini's programs in the light of guild socialism.[5] But as recent studies have pointed out, the emergence of Pound's interest in fascism seems less indebted to economic theory than to the poet's aesthetic concerns.[6] The economic element was undeniably important, but it seems to have come in late. Pound's enthusiasm for Mussolini was rather rooted in his concern with the role of the artist in modern society and essentially bound to the project of his epic.

DREAMING A RENAISSANCE: PATRONAGE, PAGANISM, AND THE OUTSTANDING PERSONALITY

In 1921 Pound engaged in archival research on a Renaissance *condottiere*, Sigismondo Malatesta, which led him to visit Italy twice between 1922 and 1923. Sigismondo embodied the type of the Renaissance "entire man" (*GK*, 194) equally capable in war and art.[7] In the Malatesta Cantos he was celebrated as the great man of action who struggled "against the current of power" (*GK*, 159), both religious and economic, but also as the patron who gathered about him the best spirits of his epoch and built a "temple . . . full of pagan works" (1x/41).[8]

Inherent in Pound's celebration of Sigismondo was his "desire to invoke a new ethical-cultural order" in the modern world and his "aspiration to see this order embodied in (and through) a new type of man."[9] At this time, Pound's aesthetics had not yet merged into his politics. But the implications of his cult of the Renaissance patron are evident, for it was part and parcel with his cult of "the outstanding personality" (*SP*, 224).[10] Soon, he would look up to Mussolini, who seized power in late October 1922.[11]

As early as in 1924 Pound was planning to meet the Italian leader and convince him to pursue a program of cultural patronage which would make Italy "THE centre, not A centre" of European intellectual and cultural life, as it had been in the fourteenth and fifteenth centuries.[12] The meeting never took place. In the meantime, Pound moved to Rapallo. When asked about his choice, in 1931, he came up again with the same scheme, envisaging for Italy a "new Renaissance," "the return of an epoch . . . similar to the fifteenth century. An age in which . . . the summit of power coincided exactly with the summit of intelligence."[13] The dream of a new age as expressed in the Malatesta Cantos was thus fully accomplished in fascist Italy, where, in Pound's view, the myth of a resurgent past combined with the idea of a "continuing revolution" (*JM*, 28), and where a ruler existed who attracted and supported the best intelligence.[14]

JEFFERSON AND/OR MUSSOLINI: "THE DIRECTION OF THE WILL"

Pound's 1935 treatise on fascism aimed at indicating to America a way out of decadence with Mussolini the example to be followed. The originality of its operation was to present the Italian leader as the Thomas Jefferson of the modern world and the fascist revolution as a revival of the American one: "The heritage of Jefferson, Quincy Adams, old John Adams, Jackson, Van Buren is HERE, NOW, *in the Italian peninsula* at the beginning of the Fascist second decennio, not in Massachusetts or Delaware" (*JM*, 12). Like Jefferson, Mussolini was the Odyssean "*polumetis*" endowed with an exceptional intuitive genius (*JM*, 66). Unlike Jefferson, he had to cope with the "crusted conservatism" (*JM*, 23) of Italians and with "the cluttered rubbish and cluttered splendour of the dozen or more strata of human effort" (*JM*, 66) which was the Italian "cultural heritage" (*JM*, 127).

Mussolini was presented as a modern Malatesta whose "passion for construction" grew into a work of art: the fascist state.[15] Because he was an artist, his actions were to be judged according to aesthetic criteria:

> I don't believe any estimate of Mussolini will be valid unless it *starts* from his passion for construction. Treat him as *artifex* and all the details fall into place. Take him as anything save the artist and you will get muddled with contradictions. Or you will waste a lot of time finding that he don't fit your particular preconceptions or your particular theories. (*JM*, 33–4)[16]

This seems to suggest that the "Renaissance paradigm"[17] set up in the Malatesta Cantos was still fully at work. But with a difference: Pound's focus was now on the ethical aim of political action. The shift from Malatesta to Jefferson as a pre-figuration of Mussolini was a shift toward ethics: the view of the exceptional personality whose constructive impulse is directed toward imposing his will on the world, was replaced by the figure of the "great man" whose *will* is directed "toward order." Mussolini was not the "bos, bovis, the bull" who

> likes to order some fellow-human about.
>
> The "will to power" (admired and touted by the generation before my own) was literatureifyed by an ill-balanced hysterical teuto-polak. Nothing more vulgar, in the worst sense of the word, has ever been sprung on a dallying intelligentsia.
>
> Power is necessary to some acts, but neither Lenin nor Mussolini show themselves primarily as men thirsting for power.
>
> The great man is filled with a very different passion, the will toward *order*. (*JM*, 99)

Pound is confronting the tradition of Mussolini's iconography, which depicted him as a Nietzschean hero. The above passage addresses, in particular, a book by the German journalist Emil Ludwig, *Colloqui con Mussolini* (*Talks with Mussolini*, 1932), where the fascist leader was admiringly presented as an exceptional personality incarnating the Nietzschean man.[18] In contrast with Ludwig, Pound claimed that the Duce's was not a "will to power", but a "will toward order."

Pound firmly believed that Mussolini's will was directed toward the creation of a just and harmonious social order as the basis of a new civilization. "Order," for Pound, was a radiant word, whose meaning related to both ethics and aesthetics. Hence his claim that the Duce will stand not with despots and the lovers of power but with the lovers of

ORDER

τὸ χαλόν (*JM*, 128).

In Canto XXI the word *kalon* ("beautiful") was related to the actions of some Renaissance rulers who used their power "to create peace and prosperity, and to foster intellectual and artistic developments."[19] Now Pound had come to believe that that ideal had materialized in the fascist leader.

In its emphasis on political order as beauty and on the ruler as artist, *Jefferson and/or Mussolini* epitomizes the aestheticization of politics which Walter Benjamin attributes to fascist ideology.[20] It also shows Pound's enduring concern with stimulating a closer relation between art and power.[21] The importance of the book also lies in the underlying operation. In its almost exclusive focus on Mussolini, despite the promising binomial title, it publicizes and exalts Pound's new finding: a hero for his epic poem.

THE CONSTRUCTION OF THE MUSSOLINIAN MYTH:
ELEVEN NEW CANTOS

In accordance with the epic mode he had chosen for his poem, Pound's project in *Eleven New Cantos* was to show how the heroic individual could change the course of history by imposing new conditions.[22] The decade presents itself as an ascensional path starting with Jefferson, associated with Malatesta, and culminating in Mussolini. In between, a panorama of decay and corruption is depicted, which opposes both the "sanity and civilization" (*SP*, 154) of America before the Civil War and "the Mediterranean sanity" (*LE*, 154) embodied by Cavalcanti, Odysseus, Hanno, and of course Mussolini.

Scattered anticipations in the poem produce the climax of his appearance:

> And the watches kept time . . . Italian marshes
> been waiting since Tiberius' time . . .
> (xxxviii/188–9)

which prepares for Canto XLI:

> Having drained off the muck by Vada
> From the marshes, by Circeo, where no one else wd. have
> drained it   (xli/202)

An Odysseus-like figure who breaks the boundaries of his culture and opens up new possibilities for the wealth of his state, the Carthaginian navigator Hanno also anticipates the arrival of Mussolini in Canto XL.[23]

This complex set of motives projects Mussolini in a dimension which is both historical and mythical. In XLI/202 he is the political leader who drained the marshes, increased wheat productivity and water supply, and provided new homes. At the same time, Circeo links him to Circe/Venus (XXXIX/195) and the grain to Eleusis. The transformation of Mussolini into a mythic figure is fully achieved with the miraculous apparition of the imperial eagle:

> Una pace qualunque. Over Udine...
> wd. have called that eagle a portent
>
> (XLI/204)

The passage is a recollection of Sigismondo's speech at the end of Canto x: "And he said: The Romans would have called that an augury" (X/47). However, the main source for the passage, and for Mussolini's feats in general, is a classic of fascist propaganda: namely Margherita Sarfatti's *Dux*, a bestseller biography of the Italian dictator first published in 1926.[24] In Sarfatti's book, the prodigy of the eagle was an occasion to glorify "the man who revives omens and auspices – mysterious participations of the divine in human life."[25] The eagle as a symbol of the Roman Empire was a holy sign, as Dante explains in Paradiso VI.32.

A complex intertextual dynamic appears which denotes Mussolini, first, as a reincarnation of Sigismondo Malatesta and, second, as heir to the great Roman emperors. This is not just the parroting of a commonplace of fascist propaganda, but also an effect of Pound's Dantescan interpretation of fascism. As S. Sicari states, Mussolini is the just ruler who "has achieved a vision of a different social ordering whose highest expression is Dante's heavenly city."[26] This brings us back to the closing lines of Canto XL, when, "seeking an exit" from the confusion and evils of history, Pound's hero turns his eyes

> To the high air, to the stratosphere, to the imperial
> calm, to the empyrean, to the bally of the four towers
> the NOUS, the ineffable crystal
>
> (XL/201)

He has a vision of the ideal city: the fascist state Pound dreamed of, which tragically diverged from the actual one.

SIENA, CHINA, ADAMS: UTOPIAN PROJECTIONS FOR THE FASCIST STATE

Pound's achievement in Canto XLI is twofold: first, it presents Mussolini as the hero of the poem, thus transforming the real man into a character ("the Boss"); second, it openly states that Mussolini is the implied reader of the Cantos. The opening lines epitomize both elements while showing the Duce reading the poem:

> "MA QVESTO,"
> said the Boss, "è divertente."
> (XLI/202)

The implication of the scene is evident: "Mussolini acknowledges Pound's role as the visionary poet who grounds healthy and constructive political action."[27] In the following groups of Cantos, up to Canto LXXI, Pound will fulfill this task by providing the ideal ruler with historical examples of good government to be followed in the present time.[28] As Reed Way Dasenbrock rightly argues, this was implicit in the very choice of the epic mode, whereby "the prince is to be roused to emulate the epic hero of the poem." Mussolini is thus "the ideal reader" of the Cantos in that he is "the one who should learn from the array of exemplars Pound presents" and "should be guided by them in his action in the present."[29]

Accordingly, both the *Fifth Decad* and the China–Adams section provide parallels in the past and models for the fascist state. The former presents accomplishments of economic justice through anti-usurious politics which are clearly in parallel with those attributed to fascist Italy (XLIV/227–8). Pound's ideal fascist state is a social system which operates against usury and in harmony with nature. This is made clear in XLVI/231, where fascism, epitomized by Mussolini's "reconstructed office of Il Popolo" at the 1932 "Decennio exposition," is offered as a remedy to contemporary manifestations of what Canto XLV has presented as the perennial crime of usury.[30]

Canto XLVIII/242 presents us with what appears to be a popular feast resembling the rites of spring[31] rather than the mass events typical of Fascist celebrations. This interlude of human happiness projects us directly onto Canto XLIX, Pound's own vision of an earthly paradise:

> Sun up; work
> sundown; to rest
> dig well and drink of the water
> dig field; eat of the grain

> Imperial power is? and to us what is it?
>
> The fourth; the dimension of stillness.
> And the power over wild beasts
>
> (XLIX/245)

The description of a healthy humanity that is offered here exemplifies Pound's ideal of a social order based on perfect harmony with the natural world and on a perfect organization of power.

The illustration of the means by which that ideal is attainable is the object of Cantos LII–LXXI. This explains the openly didactic mode that is one of the most prominent features of the section. In the letter accompanying the copy of Cantos LII–LXXI he sent to Mussolini, Pound wrote: "I hope I have done *a useful job* in condensing some historical facts" (my emphasis).[32] This was Pound's own interpretation of the Confucian precept impelling the artist to "do something useful" (XIII/59). The historical situation was such that it required immediate and rapid action.[33]

At the same time, the letter gives us further evidence that Pound's condensation of the twelve volumes of de Mailla's *Histoire générale de la Chine* and of the ten volumes of *The Life and Work of John Adams* was done with one purpose among others: instructing the Duce.[34] Stephen Sicari suggests that Pound had come to regard himself as the Confucian "master of emperors" (LV/294).[35] Like Confucius, who had condensed "two thousand years of documented history . . . so as to render it useful to men in high official position," Pound offered to the "proponents of a world order" (Mussolini, and maybe Hitler) a "study of the only process that has repeatedly proved its efficiency as social coordinate" (TAH, 19).[36]

His method of operation was to align Confucian China and modern Italy[37] and references to fascism were displayed that made the identification undoubtable: the "rods in a bundle" of LIII/272; the Italian submarine maneuvers in honor of Hitler evoked in LIV/279–280; "the first Quindecennio" and the "charter of labour" of LIV/282 and 287; the "confino" and the "granaries / somewhat like those you want to establish" of LV/297–8 (a line which seems to address Mussolini directly), the policy of "AMMASSI" described in LXI/335.[38]

In terms of writing technique, the most outstanding feature of the section is the adoption of a documentary method based on the exclusive use of only one source, so that the polyphonic arrangement of voices that had characterized the previous Cantos gives way to a substantially monologic mode. This accompanies Pound's growing attraction to the "dogmatic and clear-cut statement," whereby the Cantos "moved from 'ideogram's' openness to the squeezing of slogans out of history read by program."[39] According to Massimo Bacigalupo, this kind of "reactionary operation" makes the China–Adams section "a glaring example of regime art or of what we could call 'fascist realism'."[40]

For similar reasons, *Guide to Kulchur* has been labeled "an overtly fascistic book."[41] Indeed, the book contains pure apologia.[42] But Pound did not embrace Mussolini's cause uncritically. One may read the omission of Augustus and the almost exclusive mention of Antoninus, Constantine, and Justinian among the Roman emperors as a subtle revision of the fascist myth of Rome (*GK*, 40). Those were the figures embodying "the responsible ruler" Pound wanted Mussolini to be.

In 1941 Pound started to broadcast in English from Radio Rome, while his writing was almost exclusively in Italian and for fascist publications. Besides concern for the cultural xenophobia manifested by the regime in the war years,[43] these contributions contain some fundamental thinking, which makes them an invaluable source for understanding Pound's fascism. As Caterina Ricciardi suggests, in the years between 1939 and 1943 Pound worked at constructing "his own pseudo-'Fascism'."[44] Mussolini's Italy thus underwent a process of radical transfiguration whereby it came to epitomize an ideal state grounded on a basically agrarian, even "evangelic" economy. In his vision of fascist Italy Pound merged his cult of Mediterranean culture, with its agrarian myths and rites (the Eleusian mystery of the grain), and his ideal of a just society, which now took on almost religious tones. For Pound, Italy embodied the agrarian and ethical values of the Latin civilization ("Animus italicus, ergo agricolus, inde heticus")[45] and Mussolini, the heir of that tradition, was as the Eleusian creator of a "sacred economics."[46]

Pound believed that Italy was, or could become, the Utopia he dreamed of:

On the 10th of September last, I walked down the Via Salaria and into the Republic of Utopia, a quiet country lying eighty years east of Fara Sabina. Noticing the cheerful disposition of the inhabitants, enquired the cause of their contentment, and I was told that it was due both to their laws and to the teaching they received from their earliest school days. (*SPR*, 306)

Idealized and transfigured as it was, fascist Italy happened to incarnate Pound's utopian dream. And when Italy's position in the war was clearly compromised, he decided on a full commitment to its cause. The almost exclusive Italianism of those years was but an effect of that choice.[47]

"THE SHATTERED DREAM": FASCIST ILLUMINATIONS
IN THE LATE CANTOS

The Pisan Cantos open with a requiem for Italian fascism:

> The enormous tragedy of the dream in the peasant's bent
> shoulders
> Manes! Manes was tanned and stuffed,
> Thus Ben and la Clara *a Milano*
>   by the heels at Milano
> That maggots shd/ eat the dead bullock
> DIGONOS, Δίγονος, but the twice crucified
>   where in history will you find it?
>
> (LXXIV/445)

The "enormous tragedy" is the failure of the fascist dream of social justice. But Pound is in no way repentant: he accepts full responsibility for his actions and remains firm in his beliefs. The dream will still come true since the poet's asserted purpose is "to build the city of Dioce whose terraces are the colour of / stars" (LXXIV/445).

Nevertheless, the impact of Mussolini's death on Pound's epic project was enormous. He had "staked the coherence of his poem on Mussolini's proving worthy of the role Pound had assigned him."[48] But things went differently: he ended up in a detention camp with a charge of treason, his hero brutally executed. Now he had to rethink the poem and his own role completely.

> "I believe in the resurrection of Italy   quia impossibile est
>   4 times to the song of Gassir
>   now in the mind indestructible
>
> (LXXIV/462)

The fascist dream, the ideal city of justice, will remain intact in the poet's mind.

Pound sees himself as the survivor of a wrecked civilization: "A lone ant from a broken ant-hill / from the wreckage of Europe, ego scriptor" (LXXVI/478). But like twelfth-century Provence, destroyed by the Albigensian crusade, fascist Italy, a civilization equally destroyed by the forces of usury, will survive through poetry.[49] Pound is now the survivor-historian who records and preserves the memory of Mussolini's words: " 'alla' non 'della' in il Programma di Verona / the old hand as stylist still holding its cunning" (LXXVIII/498).

> "definition can not be shut down under a box lid"
> but if the gelatine be effaced whereon is the record?

> "wherein is no responsible person
>> having a front name, a hind name and an address"
> "not a right but a duty"
>> those words still stand uncancelled,
> "Presente!"
>> and merrda for the monopolists   (LXXXVIII/499)

Like Aeneas, who brought "his Gods into Latium, / saving the bricabrac" (LXXVIII/498–9), Pound will save the ruined legacy of fascism, his "faith" still intact ("Amid the ruin, la fede" [LXXVIII/498]).[50]

The Pisan Cantos also mark a change in attitude, for Pound seems to distance himself from his hero. Thus, when he analyses Mussolini's "errors," elegy gives way to regret. Mussolini failed because he did not recognize the value of Pound's ideas on credit and taxation (LXXXVIII/501–2); because he chose the wrong advisors (LXXX/516–17); and, most importantly, because he did not follow the law of Confucius, as Pound had advised him to do:

> but on the other hand   emphasis
>> an error or excess of
>
>>> emphasis
>>> (LXXX/516)

In spite of this, Pound proudly asserts that his involvement in fascism and in the Republic of Salò was no error ("Here error is all in the not done" LXXXI/542). It is no surprise, thus, that the section concludes with the hailing of the "martyrs" of Salò – Alessandro Pavolini, Fernando Mezzasoma, and Mussolini, who were hanged head down in Milan:

> Wei, Chi and Pi-kan
> Yin had these three men full of humanitas (manhood)
>> or jên[2]
> Xaire Alessandro,
>> Xaire Fernando, e il Capo,
> Pierre, Vidkun,
>>> Henriot
>>>> (LXXXIV/559)

With the Pisan Cantos Pound composed his elegy for the "scattered dream" of Salò, haunted by the image of his Duce "hang'd dead by the heels" (LXXXVIII/502).

In *Section: Rock-Drill* and *Thrones*, Pound continued to use Italian fascism "as appropriate material for the epic."[51] But he was now "writing paradise" and fascist examples of political thought and action were presented as means for the reader to engage in the contemplation of ideal justice. Curiously enough, Mussolini is almost equaled in prominence to the blind veteran of the fascist revolution as well as lyric poet, Carlo Delcroix, who was recalled in *Guide to Kulchur* for saying "that poets ought 'to occupy themselves with these matters', namely credit, the nature of money, monetary issue, etc." (*GK*, 249).[52] And yet Mussolini emerges in the late Cantos as a sort of alter ego ("Muss wrecked for an error," cxvi/815). Although Pound's goal had changed, he did not abandon his fascism and continued to work at its metaphysics until silence overcame him.

According to Bacigalupo, "*The Cantos*...are, among other things, the sacred poem of the Nazi-Fascist millennium, which mercifully never eventuated."[53] Nevertheless, reading the poem solely as a "Fascist epic" would be too reductive.[54] Robert Casillo is right in claiming that "Pound wrongly dehistoricized and mythified fascism."[55] Indeed, Pound's political blindness and anti-Semitism are disturbing. Still, his work calls for an approach that cannot be merely ideological, for his fascism, as Ricciardi has suggested, was less an ideology than a vision;[56] it was a poet's projection of a new social order, both real and utopian, and thus directly connected to Pound's aesthetic concerns. His support of fascism came from his faith in the public function and utility of art. He thought that the artist's mission was to change the world: when he broadcast from Rome, he was more the poet speaking for himself than the agent of fascist propaganda. For Pound firmly believed that art could guide political action:

the artist, the maker is always too far ahead of any revolution, or reaction, or counter-revolution or counter-reaction for his vote to have any immediate result; and no party program ever contains enough of his program to give him the least satisfaction. The party that follows him wins; and the speed with which they set about it, is the measure of their practical capacity and intelligence. Blessed are they who pick the right artists and makers. (Pound, "The Exile," 1927)[57]

This is in no way to justify Pound's indisputable and tragic error, but rather to suggest that that error originated, in part, from his enduring sense of the artist's role in modern society.

NOTES

1 See for instance Robert Casillo, *The Genealogy of Demons. Anti-Semitism, Fascism, and the Myths of Ezra Pound* (Evanston, IL: Northwestern University Press, 1988), 200.
2 K. Ruthven, "'Ezra Pound' and 'F/fascism'," *Spunti e Ricerche: Rivista d'Italianistica* 3 (1987): 104.

3 See Tim Redman, *Ezra Pound and Italian Fascism* (Cambridge: Cambridge University Press, 1991), 3; Peter Makin, ed., *Ezra Pound's "Cantos." A Casebook* (Oxford: Oxford University Press, 2006), 20.

4 John Lauber, "Pound's *Cantos*: A Fascist Epic," *Journal of American Studies* 12 (1978): 3–21; Massimo Bacigalupo, *The Formèd Trace: The Later Poetry of Ezra Pound* (New York: Columbia University Press, 1980); Casillo, *Genealogy of Demons*; Peter Nicholls, *Ezra Pound: Politics, Economics and Writing: A Study of the Cantos* (London: Macmillan, 1984); Reed Way Dasenbrock, *The Literary Vorticism of Ezra Pound and Wyndham Lewis. Towards the Condition of Painting* (Baltimore: Johns Hopkins University Press, 1985); Peter Makin, *Pound's Cantos* (Baltimore: Johns Hopkins University Press, 1992); Charles Bernstein, *A Poetics* (Cambridge, MA: Harvard University Press, 1992).

5 See Hugh Kenner, "Ezra Pound," in Makin, ed., *Ezra Pound's "Cantos,"* 37. This view is questioned, among others, by Walter Baumann, *The Rose in the Steel Dust: An Examination of the Cantos of Ezra Pound* (Coral Gables: University of Miami Press, 1970), 165; Leon Surette, *Ezra Pound in Purgatory: From Economic Radicalism to Anti-Semitism* (Urbana and Chicago: University of Illinois Press, 1999), 283; Paul Morrison, *The Poetics of Fascism. Ezra Pound, T.S. Eliot, Paul de Man* (New York and Oxford: Oxford University Press 1996), 54; Lawrence Rainey, "'Between Mussolini and Me'," *London Review of Books* 21.6 (1999): 25.

6 See Reed Way Dasenbrock, *Imitating the Italians: Wyatt, Spenser, Synge, Pound, Joyce* (Baltimore: Johns Hopkins University Press, 1991) and Lawrence Rainey, *Ezra Pound and the Monument of Culture: Text, History, and the Malatesta Cantos* (Chicago: University of Chicago Press, 1991). See also Cairns Craig, *Yeats, Eliot, Pound, and the Politics of Poetry* (Pittsburgh, PA: University of Pittsburgh Press, 1982).

7 Rainey, *Monument of Culture*, 102.

8 This was also a prerogative of the Confucian prince (xiii/59).

9 Rainey, *Monument of Culture*, 47.

10 See Dasenbrock, *Imitating the Italians*, 156.

11 The parallel with Malatesta would become a *topos* of Pound's Mussolinian iconography. See *SL*, 239; *GK*, 159; and *SP*, 230.

12 See Rainey, "'All I Want You to Do Is to Follow the Orders': History, Faith, and Fascism in the Early Cantos," in Rainey, ed., *A Poem Containing History: Textual Studies in the Cantos* (Ann Arbor: University of Michigan Press, 1997), 100.

13 Text of an interview in *Belvedere* and later included in *Orientamenti* (1944). The translated text is quoted from Redman, *Italian Fascism*, 76–7.

14 Pound often referred to Fascism as "The New Era" (*GK*, 253). For him it meant *awakening* (*SP*, 54), *regeneration* (*EPCP*, vi: 27) and even *resurrection* (*GK*, 134).

15 This metaphor came to Pound via Burckhardt. See Kenner, "Ezra Pound," 42 and Robert Casillo, "The Italian Renaissance: Pound's Problematic Debt to Burckhardt," *Mosaic* 22.4 (1989): 13–29.

16 This idea also sprang from Mussolini, who thought of himself "as the artist of fascism, the artificer of a 'beautiful' system and a 'beautiful' doctrine."

See Simonetta Falasca Zamponi, *Fascist Spectacle: The Aesthetics of Power in Mussolini's Italy* (Berkeley: University of California Press, 1997), 16.

17 See Kenner, "Ezra Pound," 42, and Casillo, "The Italian Renaissance," 14.

18 Emil Ludwig, *Colloqui con Mussolini*, trans. Tommaso Gnoli (Milan: Mondadori, 1932). An English version appeared with the title *Talks with Mussolini*, trans. Eden and Cedar Paul (London: G. Allen & Unwin, 1932). See *JM*, 13 and *SP*, 261.

19 Peter Liebregts, *Ezra Pound and Neoplatonism* (Madison, NJ: Fairleigh Dickinson University Press, 2004), 186.

20 Walter Benjamin, "The Work of Art in the Age of Mechanical Reproduction," in *Illuminations* (New York: Harcourt, Brace & World, 1968), 243. On the role of aesthetics in Pound's politics see William Chace, *The Political Identities of Ezra Pound and T.S. Eliot* (Stanford, CA: Stanford University Press, 1973), 46–8.

21 See Reed Way Dasenbrock, "Pound and the Visual Arts," in *CCEP*, 233; and Surette, *Pound in Purgatory*, 283. In "Murder by Capital," also dated 1933, Mussolini was appointed as the ideal patron for the artists and writers marginalized by capitalism (*SP*, 230).

22 According to Leon Surette, by the time Pound wrote the third section of the *Cantos*, he had come to regard himself as "the court poet of the Fascist Era" (Surette, *Pound in Purgatory*, 99). A similar view is expressed by Casillo, "The Italian Renaissance," 28. See also Morrison, *The Poetics of Fascism*, 41, who reads the *Cantos* as "a poem dedicated to effecting a fascist revolution."

23 See Stephen Sicari, *Pound's Epic Ambition: Dante and the Modern World* (Albany, NY: State University of New York Press, 1991), 67, 91. The periplus of Hanno has also been read as a prefiguration of Italy's policy of African colonization. See Daniel D. Pearlman, *The Barb of Time: On the Unity of Ezra Pound's Cantos* (New York: Oxford University Press, 1969), 166 and Casillo, *Genealogy of Demons*, 154. On Pound's support of the Ethiopian invasion see also Stock, 435.

24 Margherita Sarfatti, *Dux* (Milan: Mondadori, 1926). According to Philip Cannistraro and Brian Sullivan (*Il Duce's Other Woman* [New York: Morrow & Co., 1993], 381), this aspect has been completely overlooked by Pound scholars.

25 *Ibid.*, 263; my translation.

26 Sicari, *Pound's Epic Ambition*, 95.

27 *Ibid.*, 98.

28 "History," Pound writes in LIV/280, "'is a schoolbook for princes'."

29 Reed Way Dasenbrock, "Why the Commedia Is Not the Model for the Cantos," in Makin ed., *Ezra Pound's "Cantos,"* 88.

30 Miranda Hickman, *The Geometry of Modernism: The Vorticist Idiom in Lewis, Pound, H. D., and Yeats* (Austin: University of Texas Press, 2005), 105. See also Baumann, *The Rose in the Steel Dust*, 110.

31 Terrell sees it as "an annual celebration for the founding of fascism." See Carroll Terrell, *A Companion to the Cantos of Ezra Pound* (Berkeley: University of California Press, 1993), 188.

32 In Niccolò Zapponi, *L'Italia di Ezra Pound* (Rome: Bulzoni, 1976), 53 (my translation).

33 See Peter Nicholls, "A Metaphysics of the State," in Makin, ed., *Ezra Pound's "Cantos,"* 151.

34 Bacigalupo, *The Formèd Trace*, 107–8.

35 See Sicari, *Pound's Epic Ambition*, 107–113.

36 The Rome–Berlin axis was hailed in LI/251, in a position that paralleled that of Mussolini at the close of the previous section.

37 One of Pound's tasks in the early forties was to create for Mussolini the mask of the Confucian ruler (see David Heymann, *Ezra Pound: The Last Rower* [London: Faber, 1976], 98–9). Almost in parallel, he worked to establish Confucius as a fascist author. He assimilated *Ta-Hio* to Mussolini's preface to the Statute of the Fascist National Party (*EPCP*, VIII: 149) and offered his translation to the Duce as a truly Fascist book ("un quaderno di fede fascista"). See Zapponi, *L'Italia di Ezra Pound*, 54.

38 See Nicholls, "Metaphysics of the State," 52.

39 Makin, ed., *Ezra Pound's "Cantos,"* 104, 11.

40 Bacigalupo, *The Formèd Trace*, 98.

41 Donald Davie, *Ezra Pound. Poet as Sculptor* (London: Routledge & Kegan Paul, 1965), 146.

42 *GK*, 105, 144, 159, 186.

43 See for instance *EPCP*, VIII: 166.

44 Caterina Ricciardi, *Introduzione*, in Pound, *Idee fondamentali* (Rome: Lucarini, 1991), xiii (my translation).

45 *EPCP*, VIII: 185.

46 Ricciardi, *Introduzione*, xviii. In *Idee fondamentali* Pound referred to Mussolini's "sacred and perfect autarchy" (*EPCP*, VIII: 170).

47 On Pound's Italian cantos see at least Robert Casillo, "Fascists of the Final Hour: Pound's Italian Cantos," in *Fascism, Aesthetics, and Culture*, ed. Richard Golsan (Hanover, NH: University Press of New England, 1992), 98–127; and Massimo Bacigalupo, "Ezra Pound's Cantos 72 and 73: An Annotated Translation," *Paideuma* 20 (1991): 9–41. On Pound writing cantos in Italian see Ronald Bush, "Modernism, Fascism, and the Composition of Ezra Pound's *Pisan Cantos*," *Modernism/Modernity* 2.3 (1995): 69–87 and Massimo Bacigalupo, "La scrittura dei *Cantos*," *Lingua e letteratura* 16 (1991): 56–77.

48 Dasenbrock, *Literary Vorticism*, 89. See also Makin, ed., *Ezra Pound's "Cantos,"* 233.

49 See Leon Surette, *The Birth of Modernism: Ezra Pound, T. S. Eliot, W. B. Yeats, and the Occult* (Montreal and Kingston: McGill-Queen's University Press, 1993), ch. 2.

50 See Sicari, *Pound's Epic Ambition*, 134.

51 *Ibid.*, 185.

52 See also James Wilhelm, *Ezra Pound: The Tragic Years, 1925–1972* (University Park: Pennsylvania State University Press, 1994), 131.

53 Bacigalupo, *The Formèd Trace*, x.
54 See Lauber, "Pound's *Cantos*."
55 Casillo, *Genealogy of Demons*, 28.
56 See Caterina Ricciardi, *Ezra Pound: Ghiande di luce* (Rimini: Raffaelli, 2006),
   123n.
57 In *EPCP*, IV: 379–80.

CHAPTER 35

Anti-Semitism

Alex Houen

Speaking on Radio Roma on April 27, 1943, Ezra Pound declared "I think it might be a good thing to hang Roosevelt and a few hundred yidds IF you can do it by due legal process" (*EPS*, 289). Such anti-Semitic, treasonous sentiment is found throughout the speeches that he broadcast for Radio Roma between 1941 and 1943. Refusing to speak anonymously (unlike other radio propagandists) Pound insisted on being introduced as an American citizen and, with the FBI investigating his activities, he was subsequently indicted in 1943 for treason – an offense that could carry the death penalty.

Detained by American forces in May 1945, Pound spent six months in the Army's Disciplinary Training Center near Pisa before being flown to Washington, DC. Much of the public outcry about his case was directed not so much at the treason charge as at the fervency of his anti-Semitism. In a *New Masses* article titled "Should Ezra Pound be Shot?" for example, a number of the contributors argued that in the context of the Jewish *Shoah* taking place, Pound's anti-Semitic pronouncements were themselves reason to execute him. As Norman Rosten stated the case, he "should be shot . . . as a fascist hireling [who] contributed to the murder of the innocent."[1] So when a Federal court declared the poet to be unfit to stand trial after a psychiatric examination deemed him to be insane, many people felt that Pound's anti-Semitism remained an unresolved issue.

Endeavoring to shed more light, Pound scholars have variously held his radio speeches and psychiatric records to be the linchpins on which to base arguments as to whether his anti-Semitism was heart-felt, transitory, or a symptom of insanity. In that respect, Robert Casillo's *The Genealogy of Demons: Anti-Semitism, Fascism, and the Myths of Ezra Pound* (1988) was the first major study to argue that the speeches' anti-Semitism was not an incidental phase nor a mental aberration but is indicative of a racism that underpins Pound's politics, economics, and aesthetics throughout his career. Leon Surette in *Pound in Purgatory: from Economic Radicalism to*

Anti-Semitism (1999) offers a necessary corrective to Casillo's study in arguing that what seems to be anti-Semitism in Pound's work is sometimes more a hatred of capitalist "usury" than of race. Yet such an argument has also been used to minimize the extent of Pound's overt anti-Semitism. In *Language, Sexuality, and Ideology in Ezra Pound's Cantos*, for example, Jean-Michel Rabaté cites the following 1935 statement by Pound as evidence that the poet's diatribes against usury are not racially motivated: "Usurers have no race. How long the whole Jewish people is to be sacrificial goat for the usurer, I know not" (*SPR*, 270). Yet by the time Pound was broadcasting his radio speeches, he was repeatedly issuing verbal attacks against "Jew usury," thereby pointedly turning economics into a racial matter.

In light of such shifts, I shall argue that we need to see Pound's anti-Semitism in terms of distinct stages. Surette, for his part, draws on the stages that Casillo outlines for Pound, the first being one of "suburban prejudice" that the poet would have witnessed in Pennsylvania as a youth stretching from 1885 to 1910. The second stage involves periodic expressions of overt anti-Semitism between 1910 and 1920. The third marks an increasingly vehement turn from 1920, followed by a fourth and final stage which Surette dates from 1934 (Casillo dates it from 1940) in which Pound's anti-Semitism intensifies further when he compounds biological racism with a conspiracy theory of usury. I agree with Surette's dating of the fourth stage, but I would add to it a fifth that runs from 1950 to 1958.

Incarcerated in St. Elizabeths after the collapse of his trial, Pound's racism took on a new lease of life in 1950 when he met John Kasper, a young man who became a fervent champion of the poet as well as a leading racial segregationist. Pound's dealings with Kasper show that the poet placed his racism on a new clandestine but active footing, secretly aiding Kasper's segregationist and anti-Semitic activities.[2] In my view, Pound's policy of dealing with Kasper – maintaining private correspondence with him along with public silence about his activities – amounts to a strategy that belies any insanity on Pound's part. By examining each of the stages of his anti-Semitism, I shall outline how it is only in the fourth stage that his racism takes on such proportions that it pervades the dynamic of his writing more generally. For Surette, this final expansion is more a matter of conspiracy theory than of "biological racism." In contrast, my position is that the two ultimately become wholly combined for Pound; indeed, the assistance he offered Kasper in fighting racial integration clearly evidences his convictions about the purity of race. It is thus the fifth phase that is crucial in determining the extent to which anti-Semitism ultimately was not an aberration for Pound but something which he fostered strategically as a battle over race.

The first instance of overt anti-Semitism in Pound's writing is in "Patria Mia" (1912). Discussing how the natural environment in America had influenced the national character of Americans, Pound cites an exception: "The Jew alone can retain his detestable qualities, despite climatic conditions" (*EPCP*, 1:78). Racist as it is, the comment can unfortunately be read as an example of the "suburban" anti-Semitism that was fairly common in the USA at this time. By 1914, though, we find him adopting a more belligerent version in the poem "Salutation the Third," which he contributed to *Blast*: "Let us be done with Jews and Jobbery, / Let us SPIT upon those who fawn on the JEWS for their money."[3]

Pound and Lewis were inspired by the syndicalist writings of Georges Sorel, and it is possible that Pound's twinning of Jews and money is partly influenced by Sorel's growing right-wing sympathies. Having advocated syndicalism as a left-wing activism favoring strikes as its main class weapon, by 1910 Sorel was embracing a nationalist stance that denounced capitalism while linking it to Jewish interests. The same cannot be said for Pound at this stage; despite the episodic outbursts that I have quoted, he was not combining anti-Semitism and ideas about usury into a theory of racial conspiracy. Nor was he injecting racism into the majority of his poetry, for there are no anti-Semitic comments in the first thirty Cantos which he published together in 1930. Canto XXII does cite a "nigger in the red fez, Mustafa" saying about a Jewish man, Yusuf, "Yais, he ees a goot fello. / "But after all a chew/," but this is in response to Pound reportedly saying "Yusuf's a damn good feller" (XXII/105).

That Pound in this second stage thought well of some Jews has been taken by critics as evidence that his anti-Semitism was more about certain aspects of Jewish culture and religion than about individuals. In a letter of 1926 to Richard Aldington, for example, Pound stated that "the root of evil is the monotheistic idea, JEW. JEW and again jew."[4] This is certainly anti-semitic, but it is also an instance of Pound presenting "jew" not in terms of actual individuals but as a theological "idea." And railing against Semitic monotheism did not prevent him from being friendly to particular Jewish people; in 1927, for example, he began corresponding with the Jewish poet Louis Zukofsky. With Pound living in Italy from 1924, their correspondence ceased when communications between Italy and the USA were severed because of the war, but the two poets began writing to each other again in the 1950s despite the public outcry about Pound's anti-Semitism. Indeed, Zukofsky never added his own voice to the throng of Pound's detractors – which is all the more remarkable given the insensitive nature of some of Pound's correspondence to him in 1934. In May that year Zukofsky sent Pound a recent issue of the right-wing Christian journal *Liberation* which contained an article by the journal's editor William Pelley entitled "The Mystery of the Civil War and Lincoln's Death." Pelley's argument was that the "mystery" of these events was that they had largely been orchestrated by a conspiracy of Jews. To Zukofsky, such an argument was an instance of the extremes to which anti-Semites could go, and he sent it to Pound as an instance of this. Unfortunately, it did not have the desired effect. Pound responded by stating that "Pelley is a stout felly. & obv. Onnerstans the murkn mind,"⁵ and so impressed was he by Pelley's argument that he took out a subscription to *Liberation*. Other letters that he sent to the openly anti-Semitic Hugo Fack show that Pound's acceptance of Pelley's conspiracy theory was hardening into anti-Semitic views about particular individuals. "What about JEWS Einstein is a god damn kike / a goddamn coward," he wrote to Fack after Albert Einstein had not responded to the "Volitionist Economics" handbill that the poet had sent him. As Pound elaborated: "have never been antisemite, but things do rile me. Is there any trace of jews in the abolitionist movement? I doubt it. They were all over the south foreclosing mortgages after 1865."⁶

1934 thus marks the point at which Pound begins to combine his convictions about conspiracy and economics into a compound theory of pervasive Jewish contagion, and this theory, in turn, starts to pervade his work more generally. To be sure, a good deal of his growing vehemence was rooted in beliefs about the evils of usury in general. Having moved to Italy in 1924, thinking that Mussolini's fascism was built on ideals of syndicalism and guildism, Pound became interested in the "Social Credit" theory of C. H. Douglas and then in Silvio Gesell's ideas about controlling monetary value in order to control the value of goods. If Pound was convinced that Douglas and Gesell proved the need for state control of the economy, it was largely because he increasingly viewed usury as responsible for undermining the values of state, culture, and nature in general. His "usura" Canto xlv, with its litany of invective, makes this patently clear – "with usura, sin against nature, / is thy bread ever more of stale rags"; "with usura is no clear demarcation / and no man can find site for his dwelling" (xlv/229). There are no anti-Semitic references in the Canto, however, and the 1935 statement that I have already cited – "Usurers have no race" – supports the view that the poet was still some way from reducing usury to "Jew usury."

But the seeds of this reductive shift are manifest in Pound's correspondence, as when he asked Zukofsky in 1934: "I spose Mr. Pelly will be annoyed wiff me fer askin if all bankers is jooz?"[7] Anti-Semitic statements also start to appear in the Cantos Pound wrote after 1934: Canto XLI makes reference to a "mezzo-yitt" (XLI /202), while Canto XXXV includes questionable comments about "the almost intravaginal warmth of / hebrew affections" (XXXV/ 172–3). And although the "usura" Canto contains no anti-Semitism, the preceding Canto XLIV alludes to problems of usury before referring to a 1799 uprising in Siena, Italy, that drove out French forces before going on "to sack and burn hebrews/ . . . with the liberty tree in the piazza" (XLIV/ 225). In Canto XLVIII Pound's growing interest in conspiracy theory also appears obliquely when he states that "Bismarck / blamed american civil war on jews; / particularly on the Rothschild" (XLVIII/ 240–1).

By 1938 Pound's growing investment in anti-Semitism was compounded by the Italian fascists' decision to follow Nazi examples and introduce a series of race decrees. These decrees were aimed in particular at Jews, and made provision for a host of anti-Semitic practices, including placing Jews in separate schools, banning them from various cultural and political associations, and forbidding them to enter into mixed marriages. A number of statements by Pound show that he readily approved of such racist policies. In his essay "Infamy of Taxes" (1938), for example, he wrote that "The Jew is excitable and given to excess. That is the sole reason there are any Aryan governments left on this planet" (*EPCP*, VII: 333). A second statement in his essay "Symposium – 1. Consegna" (1938) is more disturbing for the fact that it denies racism while being racist: "I am not anti-semite. I am AGAINST the aryio-kike. The aryio-kike is filthiness of whatever racial compost; he has all vices which the anti-semite attributes to the Jew" (*EPCP*, VII: 337).

Pound thus attempts to obviate charges of anti-Semitism by arguing that it is racial mixing and not the Jewish race that he is against, but he clearly shows his anti-Semitic colors in stating that the "filthiness" that is racial mixing *is* an attribute of "the Jew." Such an argument can stand only by supporting itself with the following invidious logic: racism against Jews cannot be racism if they are responsible for dislimning race. That is also the implicit logic with which he shrugged off a letter in 1937 from Lina Caico, informing him of Nazi persecution of Jews, as Pound's response shows: "They are the GREAT destroyers of value / the obliterators of all demarcations / the shifters of boundary stones."[8]

By the late 1930s, then, Pound clearly felt that usury and Jews somehow shared the same form of hateful origin. Indeed, Canto LII emphasizes this merger in a lengthy passage that links "jews, real jews, chazims" to "*neschek*" (the Hebrew word for usury), as well as "super-neschek or the international / racket specialité of the Stinkschuld [Rothschild]" (LII/ 257). Pound's editors refused to print much of the passage and any reference to "Stinkschuld," and the poem was published at Pound's insistence with the censored passages blacked out (they were restored in the 1986 edition of *The Cantos*). But although he had reconciled himself to censorship in his poetry, the radio speeches he began broadcasting in 1941 showed no such restraint.

The 110 published transcripts of Pound speeches are relentlessly anti-Semitic. Seventy-one percent of them make reference to Jews, and 48 percent call for some kind of action. By repeatedly linking Jews and usury, Pound invests in a new economics of anti-Semitism whereby Jewishness and loan capital are seen to increase in tandem as responsible for the demise of nations. Usury, he contends, is "WHY the JEW has been able to wreck one European country after another" (*EPS*, 30).

Admittedly, there are points where Pound states that it is the "LARGE kikes," Jews high up in finance, that he is targeting, as opposed to "the small kikes" (*EPS*, 247), but it is notable that he uses the same racist term here to denote both groups. There are also numerous other instances where no such distinction is made – as when he talks more generally of "the Jew's role in history" (*EPS*, 290) or states that "Talmudic Jews . . . want to kill off ALL the other races they cannot subjugate" (*EPS*, 140). The radio speeches thus show how the fourth stage of Pound's anti-Semitism is as volatile as it is vitriolic. On the one hand, the capacity of usury to generate loan interest becomes indexed, for Pound, to the spiralling inflation of his anti-Semitism. On the other hand, Pound's investment in valuing concrete particularities and putting ideas into action leads him to try and counter the "subnational" and "subhuman transmissions" (*EPS*, 159) of Jewish influence by pinioning these to individual Jews. By this fourth stage, then, the poet's anti-Semitism does not involve conspiracy theory more than race or individuals, it involves fighting on all three of these fronts simultaneously.

The Pisan Cantos that Pound subsequently composed while incarcerated in the US military detention camp show the poet mostly muting his racism. Devastated by fascist failures and collapse, these Cantos include some of the most beautiful lyric passages that Pound ever wrote. There are points, however, where meditations on cultural myth and spirituality lapse into denunciation of what undermines a culture. Only in the first of *The Pisan Cantos* does Pound link this to Jews generally: "the yidd is a stimulant, and the goyim are cattle" (LXXIV/459). Aside from this he mostly limits himself to denunciations of usury, usurers and "loan swine" in Canto LXXVIII/499, although there are also disparaging comments in Canto LXXX/508 about the French statesman Léon Blum. The fact that Pound never again openly advanced the kind of vehement anti-Semitism of his radio speeches has meant that when scholars have criticized Pound's stance at St. Elizabeths it has mostly been for the fact that he never recanted his statements from before and during the war. I would argue that during the fifth stage of Pound's anti-Semitism his anti-Semitic fervor was unabated and that moreover he found new ways of promoting it.

The degree to which Pound's racism remained a live issue after the foreclosure of his trial is evidenced by the renewed outcry against his anti-Semitism in response to his being awarded the Bollingen Prize in 1949 for *The Pisan Cantos*. Pound thus had clear reason to be cautious with his beliefs and public statements, and the fact that the treason charges still hung over him – they were not dismissed until April 1958, when he was finally released – was another potent incentive to tread extremely carefully. In light of that, his dealings with John Kasper are all the more remarkable. The correspondence between the two stretches from 1950 to 1963, and although the letters that Pound sent Kasper have not been located, Pound's investment in the relationship is clear from Kasper's letters (over 400 extant) as most of them respond to specific points of advice from the poet.

Kasper was just twenty years old when he first met Pound. His early letters show an intense identification with Pound, and it was not long before the young man was presenting himself to Pound and others as the poet's main disciple and middleman. Under Pound's direction, Kasper helped found the Square Dollar Press in 1951 to publish a range of works favored by Pound, and in 1953 he set up with his friends Paul and Lana Lett the Make It New bookshop in New York's Greenwich Village. In October that year Kasper wrote to Pound about the shop display he had made of an assortment of letters that Pound had sent him: "The letters are mainly concerned with education for a young man"; all potentially "compromising" remarks had, Kasper stated, been "pasted over."[9] Pound's angry response, as reported by Lana Lett, was that he had "no contact with the outside world," although Lett also reported that Pound was writing to Kasper up to "eight times a day."[10]

That Pound was maintaining a strategy of being privately voluble and publicly silent is also evident from a letter he wrote to Louis Dudek in 1953 when the latter openly discussed their correspondence: "SHUT UP," replied Pound; "You are not supposed to receive ANY letters from E. P. They are UNSIGNED [. . .]"[11] Another 1953 letter to Olivia Agresti shows just how compromising some of his correspondence could be: "Adolf [Hitler] clear on the bacillus of kikism... but failed to get a vaccine against that."[12] Such political views are unfortunately what Kasper began to act on in Pound's name. A series of letters between 1952 to 1955 from Kasper mention recruiting militant youths, one of whom is reported to be a "new gunman... ready to liquidate any 'big' hebrew,"[13] while another two are described as being "gunmen in need of a pogrom."[14] He also mentions organizing "some Afro-American vitality to break the Jew-Grip,"[15] which is precisely what Kasper proceeded to foment on a grander scale in Southern states after the US Supreme Court in 1954 ruled an end to the racial segregation of schools.

In line with the views Pound had expressed during the war about Jews and racial mixing, Kasper campaigned for segregation in the South on the basis that racial integration was fundamentally a Jewish plot. Not only did he incite race riots, he became chief executive of a Washington DC White Citizens' Council, he appeared at Ku Klux Klan rallies, he became involved in General Pedro Del Valle's quasi-militant "Defenders of the American Constitution" organization, and between 1955 and 1956 he managed Admiral John Crommelin's unsuccessful campaign to become an Alabama senator so as to save the state from Jewish subversion.

That Kasper fundamentally saw these activities as involving "the dissemination of Ezratic civilization"[16] is clear from the constant stream of letters he sent to Pound over these years. Moreover, that Pound was actively advising Kasper in his activities is incontrovertible. In April 1956, for example, Kasper wrote requesting "speeches" and "slogans" for Crommelin's campaign and went on to state that "the Admiral has taken up THE *Question* openly... The kike behind the nigger... Things look very good. The farmers are ON."[17] A subsequent letter thanking Pound for "summaries" and a "pome [poem]" show that the poet had been ready to contribute campaign material.[18] Two 1956 memos from Pound to Kasper also show that the poet was advising the segregationist on a range of campaign issues, from dealing with the Ku Klux Klan to undermining integration as a "local option."[19] Regarding the latter issue, one of the memos identified is particularly vehement:

"Nothing is more damnably harmful to everyone, black and white than miscegnation [*sic*], bastardization and mongrelization of EVERYthing... leave local option in principle but make it unbearable in fact... ostracize 'em, surround 'em, cut 'em off..."[20]

Kasper's willingness to act on this advice is evident not only from his letters but also from the regular national press coverage of his activities.

Repeatedly arrested for all kinds of activism – including the bombing of a school in 1957 – the segregationist managed to shake off the charges until December 1958, when he was finally convicted of inciting riots. With papers like the *New York Times* reporting Kasper's links with Pound, the poet came under intense pressure from friends campaigning for his release to renounce any relation with Kasper. Pound always refused to denounce him publicly, though, and for the most part he also continued to exercise restraint in the poetry he was writing at the time.

As Wendy Flory has pointed out, in *The Cantos'* last two decades, *Rock-Drill* and *Thrones* – both of which Pound wrote while in correspondence with Kasper – there are very few overt instances of anti-Semitism. As with *The Pisan Cantos*, in *Rock-Drill* Pound largely limits himself to denouncing usury, and there are mostly only oblique anti-Semitic references. Flory identifies six of these: an allusion in Canto XC to Hitler in "Evita, beer halls . . . /"; "furious from perception" (XC/626); two mentions of the anti-Semitic Sir Barry Domville (LXXXIX/619, and CII/749); a citation in Canto LXXXIX of a statement made to Pound by a Tyrolean, "Der Jud will Geld [The Jew wants money]" (LXXXIX/620); an implicit suggestion in Canto CV that troubadour Bertrans de Born's castle should now be owned by a Jew (CV/769); and the notorious passage in Canto XCI in which Pound lapses into overt anti-Semitism, "*Democracies electing their sewage / . . . and in this, their kikery functioned*"; "*Filth under filth*" (XCI/633–4). To these I would add the reference in Canto CVIII to the number of Jews that Edward I expelled from England in 1275 – "15 000 three score"; "Divers had banished / but the usuries no King before" (CVIII/785) – as well as the numerous references to Sir Edmund Coke (e.g. Cantos XCIV, CIV, CVII) who wrote favorably of this expulsion and of Edward's ban on usury. In addition, once we take into account Pound's advice to Kasper regarding such matters as local options for the racial integration of schools, then we surely need to look at the later Cantos' various references to pedagogy, curricula, and "local control of local purchasing power" (XCVI/ 669) in a different light.

Pound's willingness to admit Kasper's campaigning into his poetry is clear from Canto CV:

> a Crommelyn at the breech-block
> or a del Valle,
> This is what the swine haven't got.
>
> (CV/ 771)

In response to this passage Peter Dale Scott has argued that "If Pound's poetry could be shown to have instigated anyone like Crommelin or Kasper in their terrorism, the case for teaching it as literature would be tenuous."[21] The correspondence between Pound and the segregationist certainly shows that Kasper did take the above lines as encouragement. After Pound sent him a draft of Canto cv in 1956, Kasper replied: "New lines re Cromm / and D.V. [del Valle] mighty fine and much appreciate seeing contemporary hist/ fitted between the permanent."[22]

Such encouragement is obviously not enough to hold Pound wholly responsible for instigating Kasper's activities, but Kasper's written responses to Pound do show that the poet's directions and advice played an integral part in what Kasper was doing. My view is that this is all the more reason to continue teaching and researching Pound's poetry in order to question critically the degree to which his aesthetics, economics, and racism ultimately became mutually entangled. That Pound himself ultimately admitted and regretted his anti-Semitism is evident from his comment to Allen Ginsberg in 1967: "the worst mistake I made was the stupid suburban prejudice of anti-Semitism. All along, that spoiled everything." Ginsberg's reply to this was, "Ah, it's lovely to hear you say that."[23] Pound's admission came much too late, but the relief that Ginsberg nevertheless felt in hearing it has subsequently been shared by many others.

NOTES

1 Quoted in Wendy Stallard Flory, "Pound and Antisemitism," in *CCEP*, 285.
2 See the chapter "Ezra Pound: Anti-Semitism, Segregationism, and the 'Arsenal of Live Thought'," in my *Terrorism and Modern Literature: from Joseph Conrad to Ciaran Carson* (Oxford: Oxford University Press, 2002), 172–91.
3 Ezra Pound, "Salutation the Third," *Blast* 1, June 1914 (Santa Rosa, CA: Black Sparrow Press, 1997), 45.
4 Quoted in Leon Surette, *Pound in Purgatory: From Economic Radicalism to Anti-Semitism* (Urbana and Chicago: University of Illinois Press, 1999), 244.
5 Pound letter to Louis Zukofsky (6[–7] May [1934]), in Barry Ahearn, ed., *Pound/Zukofsky: Selected Letters of Ezra Pound and Louis Zukofsky* (New York: New Directions, 1987), 159.
6 Quoted in Surette, *Pound in Purgatory*, 245.
7 Pound letter to Zukofsky (May 6 [–7], [1934]), in Ahearn, ed., *Pound/Zukofsky: Selected Letters*, 158.
8 Ezra Pound letter to Lina Caico (March 15, 1937), quoted in Tim Redman, *Ezra Pound and Italian Fascism* (Cambridge: Cambridge University Press, 1991), 177.
9 John Kasper letter to Ezra Pound (October 23, 1953), Ezra Pound Papers, Yale University, Beinecke Library, Box 26, Folder 1124.

10 Lana Lett quoted in "Woman Tells of Financing Segregationist Shop," *New York Herald Tribune* (February 3, 1957): 21.

11 Quoted in Humphrey Carpenter, *A Serious Character: The Life of Ezra Pound* (London: Faber & Faber, 1988), 760.

12 Pound letter to Olivia Agresti (November 5, 1953), in *"I Cease Not to Yowl": Ezra Pound's Letters to Olivia Rosetti Agresti*, ed. Demetres P. Tryphonopoulos and Leon Surette (Urbana: University of Illinois Press, 1998), 132.

13 Kasper letter to Pound (September 4, 1955), Yale University, Beinecke Library, Box 26, folder 1129.

14 Kasper letter to Pound (September 2, 1955), Yale University, Beinecke Library, Box 26, folder 1129.

15 Kasper letter to Pound (May 18, 1955), Yale University, Beinecke Library, Box 26, folder 1128.

16 Kasper card to Pound ("Christmas '56"), Yale University, Beinecke Library, Box 26, folder 1131.

17 Kasper letter to Pound (April 10, 1956), Yale University, Beinecke Library, Box 26, folder 1130, Kasper's emphasis.

18 Kasper letter to Pound (April 13, 1956), Yale University, Beinecke Library, Box 26, folder 1132.

19 Pound memo to Kasper (June 1956), Yale University, Beinecke Library, Box 26, folder 1130. I identified this memo as being from Pound in *Terrorism and Modern Literature*, 180.

20 *Ibid.* The other Pound memo to Kasper (May 17, 1956) is in Yale University, Beinecke Library, Box 26, folder 1132. Carpenter, *ASC*, misdates this memo as being from May 17, 1959.

21 Peter Dale Scott, "Anger in Paradise: The Poetic Voicing of Disorder in Pound's Later Cantos," *Paideuma* 19.3 (Winter 1990): 58.

22 Kasper letter to Pound ("July 1, '71 E. P" [1956]), Yale University, Beinecke Library, Box 26, folder 1133.

23 Pound in Barry Miles, *Ginsberg: A Biography* (1989; London: Virgin, 2000), 398.

CHAPTER 36

Gender and sexuality

Helen Dennis

INTRODUCTION

Writing to his mother from London in 1908, the young aspiring poet, Ezra Pound, reflected on his attitudes toward her:

for some years past I have been so over busied contemplating abstractions of the marvelous working of my mental internal workings that I have not taken time to regard you as an individual with a certain right to think, hold ideas, etc. for yourself. & not necessisarily [*sic*] ideas in accord with my own. It seems to me that this action or rather lack of it on my part rather demands some sort of apology on my part which I here tender. (Moody, 72)

This endearing admission is paradigmatic: it balances the poet's attention to his "marvelous" imaginative inner life with the belated recognition of the woman's – in this case Isabel Pound's – right to individuated selfhood. And once the recognition occurs it leads to remorse and an apology. These three elements can be discerned in Pound's exchanges with women and in his depictions of "woman"; although we don't necessarily find all three in every case.

In the tradition of Dante Alighieri, often mediated by the Pre-Raphaelite poets such as Dante Gabriel Rossetti, Pound construed female friends as muses who nourished his internal workings. On occasion he would recognize their right to autonomy, treating them as equals, especially if they were poets he approved of, or editors, or publishers. And on occasion he would need to express remorse for failing to consistently acknowledge that his own agendas could cause them pain. However, it might also seem as if he sometimes continued to be "out of touch with his time" when it came to issues of gender and sexuality.

Pound's attitudes toward women and "woman" as depicted in his writings, and his masculine perceptions and formations of gender and sexuality were complex and problematic in the context of the New Woman, the struggle for universal suffrage, and the continuing effort of strong-minded women to achieve intellectual autonomy in modernist literary culture. Although many women facilitated Pound's career as poet and man of letters, and biographers and critics have discovered the traces of many beloved women in his poetry, this chapter shall concentrate on a few highly significant figures: the poet H.D., the musician Margaret Cravens, the artist Sheri Martinelli, his wife Dorothy Shakespear Pound, and his mistress Olga Rudge.

TREE YOU ARE

Hilda Doolittle was one of a growing band of young American women who attended university. She enrolled at Bryn Mawr, as a classmate of Marianne Moore, and later the University of Pennsylvania, where she befriended both Pound and William Carlos Williams. Upon graduation, like half of all college educated women, she appeared to bury ambitions, remaining in her father's house, and awaiting marriage. She was Pound's first love. The evidence of her *roman-à-clef*, entitled *Her*, is that she found Pound's proclivity to imaginatively transform her person into a mythological creature, which better suited his aesthetic stance, both seductive and profoundly disabling. During the first years of their friendship Pound wrote many poems to Hilda, some of which he gathered in a small, hand-bound, vellum-covered book called "Hilda's Book." He often addressed her as "Ysolt," or characterized her as a tree nymph. Rather than address her as an equal, he cast her in romantic versions of the archetypal feminine. The poem "A Girl" (published in *Ripostes* in 1912) exemplifies the nature of that relationship as Pound perceived and expressed it (*P*, 1990, 58).

"A Girl" uses a persona, and can be compared with H.D.'s "Oread." Its premise is the identification of the girl with the tree, as in the Ovidian myth of Daphne and Apollo. In H.D.'s "Oread" the speaker throughout is the mountain nymph of the title. In Pound's "The Girl" there is a shift in the speaking subject. In the first stanza it is the girl in the process of metamorphosis into the tree, in the second stanza "she" is addressed directly by the romantic poet.

"Tempora" (1914), also about H.D., is aware of the irony of mythologizing a modern woman, and allows H.D.'s contemporary voice to intrude into the male poet's artificial perceptions of her. Two worlds, that of modernist mythopoeia and that of modern times and economic exigencies, intersect here. In this poem Pound's humor is self-directed. He knows that he has been "so over busied contemplating abstractions of the marvelous working of [his] mental internal workings" that he has not regarded her as an autonomous contemporary poet in her own right (*P*, 1990, 113–14). However, one senses his disappointment at the crudeness of her request to have her poems published, as if he would prefer her to remain an atemporal muse.

Throughout nineteenth-century British and American poetry, the feminine is associated with landscape. Williams continues this tradition in his long poem *Paterson*; H.D.'s textual strategy is to enter this cultural locus but to speak from it. In Canto 11 of *The Cantos*, Pound seems to misunderstand her tactics, and writes what can be taken as a critique of the limitations of imagism. We can read this passage as Pound's definitive version of the "crystalline" H.D.:

> If you will lean over the rock,
>   the coral face under wave-tinge,
> Rose-paleness under water-shift,
>   Ileuthyeria, fair Dafne of sea-bords,
> The swimmer's arms turned to branches,
> Who will say in what year,
>   fleeing what band of tritons,
> The smooth brows, seen, and half seen,
>   now ivory stillness.
>
>   11/9

Pound writes this leading imagist poet back into the myth of Daphne, into the role of inspiring muse, a nereid version of the tree nymph who features in one of the Ovidian myths of the origin of poetry. It is not clear that Pound ever expressed remorse for crystallizing his first muse and fellow poet into a feminine archetype according to his own aesthetic necessity.

MARGARET

Margaret Cravens, a young American pianist living in Paris, was instrumental in supporting Pound at the start of his career, when her financial patronage made a crucial and enabling difference. She "on the basis of one or two days' acquaintance, offered him such a large sum of money that he was able to put everything out of mind except finishing *The Spirit of Romance* and getting on to new projects."[1] The arrangement was kept secret; Pound did not disclose his source of income to his parents nor to Dorothy's parents. The cause of Margaret Cravens' suicide in 1912 is usually adduced to be Walter Rummel's marriage; we cannot rule out the possibility that her despair was increased by Pound's unofficial engagement to Dorothy. Alone in a Paris flat she calmly took her own life after playing the tune that Pound and Rummel had written for her.[2]

She aspired to be a transformative patron, but it is unclear what she expected, if anything, in return. What Pound gave her, along with his gratitude, was the role of divine messenger or angel:

You have given me so much – I dont mean the apparent gift – but restorations of faith. Your "largesse" in all that a forgotten word should mean! – and then the apparent gift comes, as a sort of sign from beyond that my work is accepted. It couldn't have come unless there was some real reason, behind us all, for the work to go on unfettered. (*EP/MC*, 12)

Did Margaret Cravens give too much and demand too little in exchange? Their friendship was ambiguous enough for the editors of their letters to suggest the possibility that "Margaret asked Ezra to marry her and received a negative response of some sort" (*EP/MC*, 113). Again we find that the woman's role for the poet is that of angelic messenger from the divine beyond, confirming for the male artist the preordained validity of his individual enterprise. Characteristically, the woman functions as a intermediary with the "beyond," which it will be the poet's life's work to translate into song, while at the same time her function is to provide the material conditions which will make his artistic production possible.

DOROTHY/Δώρια

In January 1909, Pound met Olivia Shakespear at the salon of Mrs. Eva Fowler, an American living in London; she invited him to call for tea at the end of that month, where he met her daughter. Dorothy had been educated at a girls' boarding school, with a finishing year in Geneva, and then returned home in the Victorian manner. The evidence of her note-books is that she fell for Pound soon after they met, but his lack of a reliable and sufficient income was a major obstacle to official engagement and marriage. Despite the discretion of Dorothy's discourse, her letters to Pound reveal moments of anger and frustration, not only with the length of their unofficial engagement, but also with her having to abide by the constraints of social conventions whereas Pound was able to continue to range freely, both socially and geographically. Dorothy hardly ever complained; doubtless the so-called "aloofness" was her preservation, but one can read veiled criticism of Pound's sexual mores in some of her letters.[3]

The letters between Dorothy and Ezra which cover the four years of their courtship suggest that Dorothy was both dignified and discreet, and

Pound appears to have also been discreet in his inclusion of Dorothy in the poetic text. Her presence is not an overt one, and even when she is his muse the poet covers the traces. "Δώρια" (first published in *The Poetry Review* in February 1912) is a poem to Dorothy which captures something of the mood of their 1911 letters (*P*, 1990, 64). In "Δώρια" (meaning "gift" and punning on Dorothy's name), Dorothy is associated with a type of mythological landscape and the transcendental aspirations it evokes. However elusive and enigmatic this poem is, the impression the images convey is of emotional sincerity.

More concretely we can say that Dorothy influenced Pound's concentration on the visual arts, especially on the work of Lewis and Brezska during the First World War. She was also as influential on his insistence on the direct observation of the object as H.D.'s modern Hellenics were instrumental in helping him out of *fin-de-siècle* imitations of past masters and into the vanguard of twentieth century imagism and literary modernism.

A BIOLOGICAL PROCESS

In 1926 Pound published a translation of Rémy de Gourmont's *Natural Philosophy of Love*. He was drawn to its theme of eroticism crossed with Darwinian investigation of the relation between the human and other animal species. At the end of the chapter entitled "Love Organs," de Gourmont speculates that: "[t]here might be, perhaps, a certain correlation between complete and profound copulation and the development of the brain" (*NPL*, 55). In his "Translator's Postscript" Pound builds on this suggestion to contend that there is a physiological connection between copulation and ideation: "[I]t is more than likely that the brain itself, is, in origin and development, only a sort of great clot of genital fluid held in suspense or reserve" (*NPL*, 169). He argues that artistic genius is intimately connected with biological masculinity, whereas woman's role as conservator of culture is connected with her reproductive functions, and he draws authority for his argument from his own subjective experience of heterosexual passion: "There are traces of it in the symbolism of phallic religions, man really the phallus or spermatozoid charging, head-on, the female chaos; integration of the male in the male organ" (*NPL*, 170).

Pound's theory teases out a connection between the physiology of heterosexual desire, the image-making faculty, and the visionary experience of the mystic or initiate. It is a theory which confers glamor on women and elevates them to the status of divine muse, but which sits uneasily with a full consideration of the political rights of individual women to autonomy and equality. Woman is seen as biologically inferior to man, something of a biological mess at times. The masculinist theory of genius which he propounds in his translator's postscript informs Canto XXIX, which is problematic since its tone is unstable, possibly ironic. It can be read as a disguised "confessional" poem,[4] as it expresses similar views about gender formations as his "Translator's Postscript":

> Wein, Weib, TAN AOIDAN
> Chiefest of these the second, the female
> Is an element, the female
> Is a chaos
> An octopus
> A biological process
>
> > XXIX/144.

De Gourmont is not only the direct instigator of Pound's spurious, scientific argument for biological difference directly affecting intellectual capacity, but also an important source of his interest in Renaissance mysticism. He authored an interpretation of Dante's Beatrice which emphasizes the centrality of *l'idéal feminin*, the feminine ideal.[5] The medieval Provençal quote from Sordello, whom Dante placed in *Il Purgatorio*, captures the ethos of romance courtly love, with its emphasis, even reliance, on lack and absence. The male poet needs to be distanced from the female beloved object in order to transform and refine erotic desire into poetic utterance. In Canto XXIX the tension between Pound's desire to transform eroticism into mysticism and the messy realities of the war of the sexes emerges in a collage of different types of sexual encounters between men and women.

OLGA/LA CARA

Pound first met his lifelong mistress, Olga Rudge, in autumn 1922 at Natalie Barney's Paris salon. She was then at the Paris Conservatoire, a talented concert violinist at the start of a promising career. At the time, he was translating *The Natural Philosophy of Love*. The evidence of their letters suggests that he held profoundly conservative attitudes toward women, in life as in the poetic text. Anne Conover quotes from an exchange of letters written after Olga had spent a cold Christmas in a Venice pension on her own. When she complained, he retorted:

No, you God Dam fool, it is your vampirism. Your wanting more . . .

You have a set of values I don't care a damn for. I do not care a damn about private affairs, private life, personal interests. You do. It is perfectly right that you should, but you can't drag me into it . . . You want to be the centre of the circle. I can not [*sic*] be in perpetual orbit.[6]

Woman as vampire, sucking the life blood from the creative artist! Framed as avant-garde and bohemian, his assumption that she shouldn't complain, shouldn't assert her needs, shouldn't expect him to leave his wife just because she had an illegitimate child by him can be interpreted as a recurrence of Victorian attitudes toward sexuality: the wife has legal rights but remains "angelic"; the mistress has no rights but keeps her man by remaining an avatar of Venus/Aphrodite, the Great Goddess. However, their relationship weathered this and many more moments of critical tension, and there are traces of Olga's presence and indeed her perceptions and observations throughout *The Cantos*. Pound commemorates her as a divine icon of ideal femininity, whereas he berates her in their correspondence if her demands become too importunate.

When Olga discovered Pound was missing on May 3, 1945, taken to US Army headquarters at Genoa, she followed him and stuck with him during questioning. After his incarceration for thirteen years in St. Elizabeths, an asylum in Washington, he returned to Italy, with Dorothy as his legal guardian. But during the last decade of his life, it was Olga, not Dorothy, who looked after him, as the final fragment of *The Cantos* acknowledges and celebrates (Fragment [1966]/824).

Pound's recurrent enunciations of the archetypal feminine in association with subdued or erased allusions to Olga Rudge should be seen as expressions of love and admiration. Despite the apparent misogyny and narcissism Pound demonstrated, arguably *The Pisan Cantos* perform acts of contrition and thanksgiving toward the significant women in his life.

THAT FROM THE GATES OF DEATH

Pound's experience in the Disciplinary Training Center at Pisa was traumatic, precipitating visionary experiences and unleashing a welter of poetry whose source was buried deep in affection and memories. The lynx lyric in Canto LXXIX/508–12 is one such passage which mythologizes personal shades of emotion. It recreates a Bacchic ritual of transformation and distillation in which the mystery of the vine/wine and the mystery of woman in her archetypal manifestations are woven into lyrical evocation of the Dionysian dance. It contains these two lines, which H.D. was sure referred to their first demi-vierge embraces: "There is a stir of dust from old leaves/Will you trade roses for acorns" (LXXIX/511).

In "D.P. Remembered," Hugh Kenner tells us that Dorothy thought of the lynx lyric as her chorus.[7] Olga Rudge's presence could also be immanent. And Bride Scratton's. And Mary Moore of Trenton's (*ASC*, 325–444). *The Pisan Cantos* contain a series of visionary depictions of the ideal feminine arising from the flux of personal memories of several significant women, often placed within metamorphosed natural landscape. In some respects the *Pisan* poet saves himself from profound despair by "contemplating abstractions of the marvelous working of [his] mental internal workings." He also exhibits contrition. In Canto LXXVI he admits:

> J'ai eu pitié des autres
> probablement pas assez, and at moments that suited my own convenience
> Le paradis n'est pas artificiel,
> l'enfer non plus.   (LXXVI/480)

[I've felt pity for others / probably not enough, and at moments that suited my own convenience / Paradise isn't artificial / neither is hell.]

Within Christian worship, contrition or penance facilitates the washing away or cleansing of sins. In *The Pisan Cantos* images of weeping and of cleansing tears, repeated in a number of languages, recur as leitmotif, as for example, in Canto LXXX, expressed in three romance languages (French, Italian, and Latin), as well as American English (LXXX/533).

Despite being raised a Presbyterian, as a modernist poet, Pound explored many areas of Greek, Latin, and Egyptian mystery religions as well as Gnosticism, mysticism, and Neoplatonism, to construct a *paideuma* of different religious traditions. Even though the poetry may seem to foreground Hellenic traditions, we should not ignore the residual traces of the Presbyterian forms of common worship as practiced around the turn of the last century.

LA MARTINELLI

After his detention at the Disciplinary Training Center, Pound was taken to St. Elizabeths, where he would stay for the next thirteen years until his release into the care of "the Committee of Ezra Pound," Dorothy.[8] There, many acolytes came to visit, including Marcella Spann, who then accompanied Dorothy and Ezra back to Italy, and acted briefly as his secretary. The hipster painter, Sheri Martinelli, also visited there, and later claimed somewhat implausibly that they became lovers in St. Elizabeths. She certainly worshiped him as a type of "holy man" and Pound admired her and her paintings greatly (Stock, 439; *ASC*, 801–4, 829–30). She is the inspiration behind a passage in Canto XC which begins:

> from under the rubble heap
> > > m'elevasti
> from the dulled edge beyond pain,
> > > m'elevasti
> out of Erebus, the deep-lying
> > from the wind under the earth,
> > > m'elevasti
> > > > (XC/626)

Its repeated phrase, "m'elevasti" comes from Dante's *Paradiso* (1.75). The occasion of the Canto might have been Martinelli, but Pound transforms her, like his other women, into poetic utterance which aspires to transcend the merely personal.

CONCLUSION

The Women of Trachis (1954) depicts in a stylized "Noh" fashion the painful consequences of marital infidelity, and acknowledges that Kupris or erotic love controls human action and destiny:

> KUPRIS bears trophies away . . .
> Neath Her they must
> > > give way
> > > (*WT* 23)

Pound's errors were many. We might judge that, through his sins of hubris in relation to women, he deserved the pain and depression of his last years. And yet, his poetry expresses vividly and memorably the strength of eroticism as a force in human lives, the ongoing dialectic of relations between men and women in the twentieth century, and the extent of cultural work that has to be done to transform and transcend desire. Reading his notes toward Canto CXVII, it is difficult not to sympathize with the poet and man who could state so simply at the end of his life:

> Let the Gods forgive what I
> > have made
> Let those I love try to forgive
> > what I have made.
> > (Notes for Canto CXVII)

NOTES

1 "Introduction," *EP/MC*, 6.

2 *Ibid.*, [1]-7 and throughout; *ASC*, 180–1.

3 In *Ezra Pound: Poet*, Moody interprets the evidence somewhat differently to emphasize Dorothy's struggle to adhere to the role of spiritual muse that she felt Pound cast her in.

4 See Wendy Flory, *Ezra Pound and "The Cantos,": A Record of Struggle* (New Haven: Yale University Press, 1980), 115; Stock, 83, 243–4, 254, 284, 441–2.

5 Rémy de Gourmont, "La Béatrice de Dante: et l'idéal féminin en Italie à la fin du XIIIᵉ siècle," *La Revue du Monde Latin* (1885): 174–90, 286–96. See de Gourmont, *Le Latin Mystique: les poètes de l'antiphonaire et la symbolique au moyen age* (Paris: Mercure de France, 1930).

6 See Anne Conover, *Olga Rudge & Ezra Pound* (New Haven: Yale University Press, 2001), 1–2, 75, and throughout.

7 Hugh Kenner, "D. P. Remembered," *Paideuma* 2. 3 (Winter 1973): 491.

8 Conover, *Olga Rudge*, 215.

CHAPTER 37

Race

Michael Coyle

In February of 1952, from his room in St. Elizabeths mental hospital, Ezra Pound wrote to his old friend Olivia Rossetti Agresti – niece of poet Dante Gabriel Rossetti, one-time editor of the *fin-de-siècle* anarchist journal *The Torch*, and latterly – like Pound – an ardent supporter of Mussolini. But neither anarchism nor fascism was on the table at this moment; the question was race and culture:

Eropewns will NEBBER understan' deh Kulluᴅ race / marse blackman will most certainly NOT return to Africa to infect what the dirty brits have left there / with any more occidental hogwash / He will stay here . . . being human and refusing to be poured into a mould and cut to the stinckging patter[n] on the slicks and the weakly papers. An occasional upsurge of African agricultural heritage as in G. W. Carver, O.KAY but also marse Blakman him LAZY / lazy as Lin Yu Tang. thank god for it / AS a humanizing element most needed here / tho yr beloved kikes try to utilize him for purposes of demoralization / hell / he ain' nebber been moralized / thank God.[1]

Since the mid 1980s, scholars have been combing Pound's voluminous correspondence for this kind of pronouncement and have not surprisingly discovered the racism they expected. Indeed, Pound proves to have been as obsessed with race as everyone else in America.

But this passage offers an especially rich place for us to begin unpacking Pound's racial baggage. First, his widely remarked "cracker-barrel" pseudo-accent here shows itself unmistakably to be an imitation of "colored" speech – or, rather, of the "minstrel" speech long popular among both popular and cultivated American audiences; in particular, as the "Marse Blakman" [Master Blackman] bit makes clear, he is borrowing and expanding upon Joel Chandler Harris' *Uncle Remus: His Songs and His Sayings* (1881).[2] Second, whether or not Pound was racist he most definitely was "racialist": that is, he accepted race as a real and meaningful category and believed there to be profound differences among the races. In this particular instance Pound's pronouncements praise the humanity of black folks. The nature of this intended praise, however, takes unfortunate form. Third, like most racialists of his time, Pound was also a "primitivist," which is to say he regarded the darker races as more spiritual than the overcivilized, neurasthenic moderns of the Western world. Pound regarded black folks – and the word "folk" ("volk") matters here, owing as much to Pound's regard for German anthropologist Leo Frobenius as to his American upbringing – as superior, and generally counseled that "we" protect "them" from "us."

Fourth, Pound's lifelong anti-Semitism is evident here as something different in kind from his attitudes toward other races. Nevertheless, that well-documented and much-debated topic should be acknowledged as related to the question of Pound and race. Finally, despite its 4,000-year-old history, a history that Pound knew better than most Americans, China, too, seemed to him a participant in the deep spirituality of Africans and African Americans. This association owed more to Pound's primitivism than to his racialism – exemplifying the reaction against industrialized and mechanized life that is a distinct characteristic of the modernist imaginary.

These five points suggest a map and perhaps even a legend for Pound's journey through the fantasy land of race. Indeed, Aldon Lynn Nielsen has commented on the very passage with which I began, deploying it as part of his denunciation of what he sees as a pattern in modernist criticism:

> responses to criticism of racism in the works of prominent modernist writers often take the form of assertions that, while the statements under discussion may indeed be racist, they are not simply or merely racist, that they are considerably more complicated . . . What is sometimes overlooked in these discussions is that there has never been any such thing as a simple racism.[3]

Nielsen is right in principle. He is right, too, when he observes later in the same essay that Pound often "evidenced an appreciation of black cultural production even as he so often belittled black people."[4] In this last observation, however, is a distinction that merits further attention. Pound could admire the work even where he labored under prejudicial views of the makers.

Earlier generations of Pound scholars followed the lead of Hugh Kenner and T. S. Eliot: Kenner, in *The Poetry of Ezra Pound* (1951), and Eliot, in his selection of and introduction to *The Literary Essays of Ezra Pound* (1954), endeavored to separate the political and ethical failures of the man from the often astonishing brilliance of the poet. But in the 1980s, participating in and even leading the ideological turn of modernist criticism, some younger scholars contended that no such separation is either possible or desirable. In Pound studies this tendency reached its most totalizing form in Robert Casillo's *The Genealogy of Demons: Anti-Semitism, Fascism, and the Myths of Ezra Pound* (1988): "far from being adventitious or extraneous to Pound's texts, anti-Semitism is a characteristic manifestation of Pound's thought and language, a virtually inescapable response to the most pressing intellectual and poetic difficulties ... [It] belongs within his metaphorical system and is linked to the rest of his writing by a chain of metaphorical displacements and substitutions."[5]

Casillo was hardly the first to comment on Pound's anti-Semitism, but the nature of his argument opened the door to revisionist takes on Pound's other political and ethical commitments. And his move was soon repeated by scholars of other modernist writers close to Pound – most famously in 1995 when Anthony Julius drew on his legal background to indict T. S. Eliot, in terms analogous to Casillo's, for an anti-Semitism that was not marginal but central to his work. Soon enough there were numerous studies decrying Pound's sexism and racism.

Tellingly, as Nielsen notes, critical attention to "blackness" in Pound developed late – *long* after attention to his interests in China and Japan. Earlier generations of critics simply couldn't see why such issues mattered. But when critics did turn to the question of race, they did so with a vengeance. As Kevin Dettmar observes: "No sooner had race and gender become widely available analytical categories for literary studies than students of modernism rushed into the breach, proclaiming in less than nuanced terms the racism of Eliot, the misogyny of Lawrence and Joyce. The idols of Modernism were found (Surprise!) to have clay feet ... "[6]

In this revisionist atmosphere, no reputation suffered more than Pound's. To be sure, after the critics of the fifties and sixties had essentially attempted Pound's canonization in both senses of the word, some "correction" (as market analysts like to say) was both inevitable and necessary. If Hugh Kenner's *The Pound Era* (1972) – which framed Pound as the presiding genius of modernism – was the apotheosis of that impulse, Casillo's *Genealogy of Demons* was its negative counterpart. There is today no doubting Pound's racialism, which was always with him and which he sometimes consciously developed. Neither is there any doubt that his racialism sometimes led him to disturbingly racist formulations.

In the early twentieth Century, the question of "Pound and race" has developed into a tangled knot of interrelated questions:

(1) To what extent do Pound's racialist and racist "formulations" – most often overt pronouncements in his prose but sometimes individual lines in

his poetry – offer grounds for claims about the very *form* of his poetry (as Casillo and others would have it)?

(2) To what extent is Pound's "American Africanism," in Toni Morrison's phrase, analogous to his Orientalism? To what extent are both a function of what Marianna Torgovnik and others have identified as "modernist primitivism"?

(3) To what extent is the matter of Pound and race a function of the emergent and larger twenty-first-century dynamics of "globalism"?

(4) To what extent and in what ways do Pound's deployments of race necessarily inform what readers make of his poetry?

The moral issues here cannot, and should not, be disposed of. The engaging of literary texts being for our society a process immediately connected with questions of shared values, it will always be important for some readers not only to resist the racialist implications and imprecations of Pound's work but even perhaps to argue against its continued presence in the canon. For other readers, the object will be to resist literalizing Pound's racialist fantasies – or to work out ways of dealing with such aspects of the work that do not destroy what they might value. As Bob Perelman has said in *The Trouble With Genius*, there are trails in the *Cantos* that lead to racism and fascism, but readers do not have to take them: "there are other trails from most of Pound's words."[7] Given Pound's long insistence that reading is an activity, something pursued rather than passively experienced, Perelman's observation is important.

Never mind that for Pound himself all these trails relate. "Race, mind, culture, and nation": these are, as Edward Said famously noted, "hothouse formulations." Interrelated, perhaps inextricable, they represent less ideas than modes of thought. "Orientalism" and "primitivism" are both functions of, or maybe aspects of, the discourses of race and nation. As Said has observed, to the European mind "Orientals were almost everywhere nearly the same,"[8] and that same mind (to recur to Said's own reliance on that hothouse word) would have conceived of "primitives," too, as being outside of history.

It should occasion little surprise, then, that Pound saw both China and Africa in relation to his own ideas about Euro-American civilization. Thirty years after Said's *Orientalism*, and twenty years after Torgovnik's *Gone Primitive* or Toni Morrison's *Playing in the Dark*, asking whether Pound (or any other poet) was or wasn't racist or anti-Semitic seems less illuminating than asking how racialist/primitivist/Orientalist discourses function in his texts as dynamic and "productive" forces. Deploying essentially Foucauldian notions of "discourse," Said and Torgovnik demonstrate how terms like "oriental," "primitive" or "race" function as empty signifiers, capable of meaning a wide range of things, but serving always to define by opposition the modern (and white) west.

Morrison describes her own project, the exploration of what she calls "American Africanism," as "an investigation into the ways in which a nonwhite, Africanlike (or Africanist) presence or persona was constructed in the United States, and the imaginative uses this fabricated presence served."[9] What she finds is that its principal function is to define whiteness. To be sure, there has been a lag between the dissemination of these theories and the opening up of Poundian texts to such investigations, but such recent contributions as Richard Sieburth's exemplary introduction to his edition of *The Pisan Cantos*, or the essays collected in my own *Ezra Pound and African American Modernism*, are yielding exciting results. This work begins to move us from the topic of race/primitivism/Orientalism as content to race as an enabling discourse, giving shape to how Pound views history and himself.

Consider the opening of Canto LXXXII: "When with his hunting dog I see a cloud / 'Guten Morgen, Mein Herr' yells the black boy from the jo-cart . . . " The present tense of these lines situates us in Pound's present, mid to late May, 1945, and in a moment of successive surprises. In his cage at the Disciplinary Training Center (actually, a military prison) outside Pisa, Pound has been watching the clouds drift across the sky, observing a shape that reminds him of the hunter Orion. The opening "when" marks a first surprise at the sudden detection of meaningful form (or at least the appearance of form). Just then his reverie is broken by a greeting from a passing GI – a black soldier who crucially is identified by his race. The tone of the soldier's greeting is, like the passage itself, left open to interpretation: much depends on how one understands the relation between, on the one hand, the allusion to noble Orion with his chariot and, on the other, a black GI passing by Pound's cage with the coffee-wagon.[10] There's no missing the condescension of Pound's reference to "the black *boy*," nor perhaps the ironic reversal Pound felt in watching the free black man outside the cage that held the white poet prisoner.

But what of the soldier's cheeky greeting, which Terrell's *Companion* glosses simply as "good morning, Sir?" Is the soldier signifying (making fun of while carefully avoiding a direct insult) on Pound's loyalty to the Axis, or offering a friendly greeting to cheer the prisoner? Is the hot coffee the soldier brings after Pound's cold night in the cage the force that will drive the clouds from the poet's head, or an interruption to his reverie? Pound would seem here to be laughing at himself – but is that affirmation subsumed into his garden-variety primitivism, whereby the black man is happy-go-lucky and untroubled by political ideas? If so, is this image balanced by the reference, in Canto LXXIV, to the execution of Louis Till – a fate Pound initially expected to meet himself, and that he felt himself to be awaiting at the moment of his exchange with the black soldier?[11] Finally, since these are opening lines, we must ask in what ways they serve to frame the entire Canto: to what extent do they exemplify "American Africanism?"

Pound had developed similar passages earlier in the *Cantos*. Indeed, as Alec Marsh has shown, the original drafts of Canto XX (first published in the spring of 1927) contained a story about George Washington having been killed by one of his slaves, the slave having returned home to find the former President in bed with his wife.[12] In the *Cantos*, Pound's references to blackness most often take this kind of form, and they are invariably primitivist. It is no surprise then that typically they attempt humor, or at least a lightening of tone; typically, they serve in precisely the ways that Morrison theorizes. Blackness serves to define the condition of whiteness. It serves as a marker of modernity, always by contrast, never as a sign of the condition itself. The freedom of the black general-issue soldier functions to lend pathos to the incarceration of the white, self-consciously singular poet.

Indeed, the "black boy" who hails the poet in the opening of Canto LXXXII had already appeared in *The Pisan Cantos* – fourteen pages into the long, twenty-four-page Canto LXXX. And there, too, he spoke – and his speaking represents an act of defiance in more than one way. First, Pound was forbidden conversation with both other "trainees" or the guards; second, what the soldier has to say represents resistance to his assigned duties:

> There can be honesty of mind
> without overwhelming talent
> I have perhaps seen a waning of that tradition
> (young nigger at rest in his wheelbarrow
> in the shade back of the jo-house
> addresses me: Got it *made*, kid, you got it made.
> White boy says: do you speak Jugoslavian?)
> And also near the museum they served it mit Schlag
> in those days (pre 1914)
> the loss of that café
> meant the end of a B.M. era
> (British Museum era)
> (Canto LXXX/526)

Here, too, as in LXXXII, the reference to the black soldier is preceded by some cloud-gazing – cloud-gazing wherein an Italian mountain visible from Pound's cell merges with his imagined vision of the sacred Chinese mountain, Taishan: "and the clouds have made a pseudo-Vesuvius / this side of Taishan" (LXXX/515). This time the black soldier appears as a parenthetical illustration of "honesty of mind / without overwhelming talent." In the soldier's view, the jailed poet has "got it made" because – behind bars or in the medical tent – he doesn't have to work. Addressing the poet with the jocularly familiar "kid," he assumes an equality that Pound accepts. In fact, the only snide part of Pound's parenthesis is reserved for the reference to the "White boy" and his casual question about "Jugoslavian." Pound presents the juxtaposition without comment. The black soldier pretends to nothing; the white soldier by contrast reveals an ignorance of history and language in his very pretense to cultural interests. The white soldier disappears thereafter, but the black soldier's fraternity sparks a new reverie, in which Pound's memory returns to the Wiener Cafe on Oxford Street, a short walk from the British Museum.

As a veritable leitmotif in the Cantos, this café comes to stand for culture itself, for the conversation and exchange of ideas enabled by cultivated leisure. Obviously the young black man does not himself represent these things to Pound, but he provides the occasion for Pound to reconnect with old sources of strength. And precisely as he does so, Pound illustrates Morrison's thesis: "Africanism is the vehicle by which the American self knows itself as not enslaved, but free; not repulsive, but desirable; not helpless, but licensed and powerful; not history-less, but historical; not damned, but innocent."[13] The black soldier by the jo-cart is there to underscore the prisoner's freedom and perhaps his place in history. The black soldier thus appears at the head of a positive metonymic and Mnemosynic chain.

Reflecting on the framing of *Pisan Cantos*, Richard Sieburth observes that, "in this heart of darkness [the Disciplinary Training Center], with his fate and identity still uncertain, the prisoner casts his lot not with the American military victors but with their victims, not with the masters, but with their slaves." More than this, Sieburth proposes – almost as though echoing Casillo but resolving on a quite different note – that the references to these black faces are not coincidental but foundational to the poem:

Paternalistic though Pound's view of blacks might have been (and today's readers will no doubt wince at his insouciantly condescending use of the terms "coon" or "nigger"), these African-American "shades" nonetheless constitute the crucial informing presence (or absence, as the case may be) behind the *Pisan Cantos* – a poem whose conflicted attitude to race may well define its most profoundly American groundtone.[14]

Sieburth's reading is less interested in blackness as a function of discourse than my own, but like Morrison he reads Pound's attitudes toward blackness as signs of his irreducibly American identity.

Reading *The Cantos* necessarily means reading them actively – as Pound himself urges in *Guide To Kulchur*: "man reading shd. be man intensely alive" (*GK*, 55). And so, although Nielsen is right that "there has never been any such thing as a simple racism," it must nevertheless also be true that the racialist and racist elements in *The Cantos* (unlike perhaps such elements in his correspondence) are not simple but textualized. In other words, and with respect to Nielsen, critics are generally right that in *The Cantos* such materials "are not simply or merely racist, that they are considerably more complicated." However, Nielsen's charges about critical indifference to issues of race in Pound do not apply only to his intersections with African Americans. The letter to Olivia Rossetti Agresti quoted above exemplifies this point too.

The editors of that volume of letters offer this gloss to Pound's characterization of the "Blakman" being as "lazy as Lin Yu Tang": "Chinese emperor of the Tang dynasty proverbial for his indolence."[15] This reading resonates richly with Pound's primitivism – but the identification is incorrect. Lin Yutang was neither an emperor nor was he ancient. Born in Changchow in 1895 (d. Hong Kong 1976), he was instead a highly popular contemporary writer of both fiction and philosophy. His most famous book, *The Importance of Living* (1937), argues the importance of leisure: "all nature loafs, while man alone works for a living." Culture, he argued, "is essentially a product of leisure. The art of culture is, therefore, essentially the art of loafing."[16] All of which is to say that Lin was, not a primitive, but a primitivist, a modern who like Pound regretted the hectic and feverish pace of modern life. In this case, Pound's reference to Lin Yu Tang wasn't even itself necessarily primitivist – he was simply referring to Lin's celebration of leisure in a way he could have expected his correspondent to recognize. The tangled references of Pound's letter conflate Africa and China into one Orientalist "other," but do so to affirm a human commonality he fears the West is losing.

This commonality is a part of what Josephine Nock-Hee Park means when she describes "the two halves of Orientalism: one sets apart difference; the other enshrines a shared ideal." Pound's China, Park submits, "never devolved into rehearsals of difference; instead, he created a revelatory intimacy between China and America."[17] In the same way, we can see that the force of Pound's "subject rhymes" (*PE*, 92) generally depends on an initial experience of alterity, the recognition of wide separation in time and/or place, and thereafter on the closing of that distance. As Eric Hayot observes, "it was as though something in the Chinese permitted, or gave birth to, the Poundian unveiling of the universal."[18] In this way, Park notes that in Canto LVII Pound "casts Genghis Khan's Mongol invasion as a Western, specifically European, invasion," and in Canto LX rhymes Kang Hsi's embargo on European goods with Thomas Jefferson's 100 years later.[19] Indeed, the structural unity of the China Cantos with the Adams Cantos (Cantos LII-LXXI), Pound's framing them together as opposed to publishing them as distinct "decads," is a larger instance of the same impulse.

For similar reasons, Zhaoming Qian opens his *Orientalism and Modernism* by reconceiving orientalism against Said's model. Pound, Qian affirms, "did not believe in Western cultural superiority." On the contrary, "what attracted [him] to the Orient was really the affinities (the Self in the Other) rather than the differences (the Otherness in the Other)" between the two cultures. Mary Paterson Cheadle, investigating Pound's translations of – and embrace of – Confucius, reaches a comparable conclusion.[20] And Robert Kern characterizes "the relationship of orientalism and modernism in Pound's work" by affirming that Pound's modernizing of Orientalism was perhaps only an aspect of his orientalizing modernism.[21] Taken together, the work of these and other scholars suggests a conclusion that is, after all, consonant with one of Said's founding premises: Orientalism is not incidental to modernist literature but central to it. Here, that centrality is less about a particular theme than it is Pound's way of organizing his vision. Visions of the "other," particularly the racialized, exoticized other, serve principally as a kind of magic mirror wherein to see oneself. View can become vision, with consequences both for how we see the oriental other and how we see ourselves.

In the early twentieth century, the notion of "globalism," the expectation that the transformation of the entire world into one great marketplace would ultimately produce one global culture, is to say the least controversial. There are few, if any, voices in the arts that would today see such a development as a positive thing. But it would be a mistake to understand Pound's universalizing impulses as tending in such a direction. Most importantly, as the presence of so many un-translated phrases, ideograms, and even pictograms indicate, Pound regarded the variety of human

culture, the differences among cultures, as absolutely necessary for analo-
gies and parallels to be meaningful. Again, the very notion of "subject
rhyme" requires difference: the idea is rhyme between different words, and
not the collapse of the pair into one word. Pound's valorization of study,
his ambition to instigate activity, stands in antithetical relation to any such
easy identification.

Eric Hayot, Haun Saussy, and Steven Yao, treating modern writing about
China, propose that "the essays we have collected for this volume stage,
each in its way, an 'invention of China.' While a suspension of disbelief is
not necessary for the essays to take effect, the centers of their arguments
are situated 'beyond true and false,' so to speak in a China of meanings
rather than a China of facts."[22] This is something rather different from
what Eliot meant when he celebrated Pound as "the inventor of Chinese
poetry for our time," but it is hard today not to take his praise as meaning
something quite similar.[23] What Hayot, Saussy, and Yao say of a China
of meanings pertains, I have been arguing, to the question of Pound and
race. In both cases, Pound took his lead from scholars of the preceding
generation: Ernest Fenollosa (1853–1908) about Chinese heritage and Leo
Frobenius (1873–1938) about African heritage. With Fenollosa indebted to
Emerson, and Frobenius to Spengler, both of them charged Pound with a
vision of the racial other that was essentially Romantic – and romantically
essentializing at heart.

In 2001 David Roessel edited Pound's quarter-century correspondence
with Langston Hughes. Invaluable for anyone wanting to think further
about Pound and race, the correspondence began in 1931 with Pound trying
to interest Hughes in Frobenius' work: "Frobenius has done more than any
other living man to give the black race its charter of intellectual liberties."
Pound's lack of self-consciousness, his arrogance no doubt, when writing to
Hughes in the minstrel dialect noted above, is for us today embarrassing.
But in July 1932, praising Hughes' *Fine Clothes To The Jew*, he offered
two kinds of advice. The first was high modernist insistence that "every
word that don't work ought to be put out." The second has everything to
do with the racialism and primitivism we have been discussing here. As
another means of learning compression, Pound advises Hughes to study
the "Negro Songs of Protest" collected by Lawrence Gellert – but then
warns him that there is "nothing harder than to do a folk song once one
has touched any sort of sophistication."[24] That attitude (the same position
we saw in Pound's letter to Olivia Rossetti Agresti) we now can recognize
as modernist, and as American, but also as primitivist and American-
Africanist. That race in Pound is less a condition of being than a condition

of writing is both cause for our regret and an originary point of his powerful imagination.

NOTES

1 Letter of February 19, 1952, in *"I Cease Not To Yowl": Ezra Pound's Letters To Olivia Rossetti Agresti*, ed. Demetres P. Tryphonopoulos and Leon Surette (Urbana: University of Illinois Press, 1998), 85.

2 This connection was first made by Michael North in "Old Possum and Brer Rabbit: Pound and Eliot's Racial Masquerade," in *The Dialect of Modernism: Race, Language and Twentieth Century Literature* (New York: Oxford University Press, 1994), 77–99.

3 Aldon Lynn Nielsen, "Ezra Pound and 'The Best-Known Colored Man in the United States,'" in *Ezra Pound and African American Modernism*, ed. Michael Coyle (Orono, ME: National Poetry Foundation, 2001), 151.

4 *Ibid.*, 154.

5 Robert Casillo, *The Genealogy of Demons: Anti-Semitism, Fascism and the Myths of Ezra Pound* (Evanston, IL: Northwestern University Press, 1988) 16–17.

6 Kevin Dettmar, "Review of *The Dialect of Modernism: Race, Language and Twentieth-Century Literature* by Michael North," in Coyle, ed., *Ezra Pound and African American Modernism*, 257.

7 Bob Perelman, *The Trouble With Genius: Reading Pound, Joyce, Stein and Zukofsky* (Berkeley: University of California Press, 1994), 39.

8 Edward Said, *Orientalism* (New York: Vintage, 1979), 148, 38. Also of importance is Marianna Torgovnik's *Gone Primitive: Savage Intellects, Modern Lives* (Chicago: University of Chicago Press, 1990).

9 Toni Morrison, *Playing in the Dark: Whiteness and the Literary Imagination* (New York: Vintage, 1993), 6.

10 Reference is unglossed in Carroll F. Terrell, *A Companion to the Cantos of Ezra Pound* (Berkeley: University of California Press, 1984), but the definition of "jo" with coffee can be found in the *Dictionary of Service Slang*, compiled by Park Kendall (New York: M.S. Mill, 1944).

11 This trope is the subject of Milton L. Welch's " 'Till was hung yesterday': Louis Till as Lynching Topos in the *Pisan Cantos*," in *Ezra Pound And Education*, ed. Michael Coyle (Orono, ME: National Poetry Foundation, forthcoming).

12 Alec Marsh, "Letting the Black Cat Out of the Bag: A Rejected Instance of 'American Africanism' in Pound's *Cantos*," in Coyle, ed., *Ezra Pound and African American Modernism*, 125–42.

13 Morrison, *Playing in the Dark*, 52.

14 Richard Sieburth, "Introduction," *The Pisan Cantos* (New York: New Directions, 2003), xix, xxi.

15 Tryphonopoulos and Surette, eds., *"I Cease Not To Yowl,"* 85–6. There is today abundant information about Lin available on the web; one particularly informative site is http://idler.co.uk/idle-idols/idle-idols-lin-yutang/.

16 Lin Yutang, *The Importance of Living* (New York: Reynal & Hitchcock, 1937), 145, 150.

17 Josephine Nock-Hee Park, *Apparitions of Asia: Modernist Form and Asian American Poetics* (New York: Oxford University Press, 2008), 24.

18 Eric Hayot, *Chinese Dreams: Pound, Brecht, Tel quel* (Ann Arbor: University Michigan Press, 2004), 33.

19 Park, *Apparitions of Asia*, 43–4.

20 Zhaoming Qian, *Orientalism and Modernism, The Legacy of China in Pound and Williams* (Durham, NC: Duke University Press, 1995), 2; Mary Paterson Cheadle, *Ezra Pound's Confucian Translations* (Ann Arbor: University of Michigan Press), 1997.

21 Robert Kern, *Orientalism, Modernism, and the American Poem* (New York: Cambridge University Press, 1996), 155.

22 Eric Hayot, Haun Saussy and Steven Yao, *Sinographies: Writing China* (Minneapolis: University of Minnesota Press, 2008), xix.

23 T. S. Eliot, Preface to *Selected Poems of Ezra Pound* (London: Faber and Gwyer, 1928), 14.

24 In Coyle, ed., *Ezra Pound and African American Modernism*, 207–42 (212, 221).

CHAPTER 38

Travel

Daniel Katz

"And then went down to the ship" (1/3) begins *The Cantos*, opening not only *in medias res*, but also, as it were, on the road, in the midst of a journey which immediately proceeds to chart a series of liminal, shifting spaces. For Canto 1 moves not only between land and sea, but also between Greek, Latin, and English – as Pound translates Andreas Divus translating Homer – and finally between life and death: most of the Canto is devoted to the "Nekuia," that is, Odysseus's descent to the underworld in search of Tiresias. Indeed, if *The Cantos* have no real model, it is worth noting that among the venerable precursors for them which Pound had in mind, perhaps the two most important – *The Odyssey* and *The Divine Comedy* – are obviously also both travel poems, organized entirely according to tropes of exile, journey, arrival, and restoration.

As Robert Crawford has pointed out, motifs of homecoming and return were central to the strategies by which many high modernist texts attempted to assert the "structural unity" they might seem to lack, but he quite rightly distances *The Cantos* from the gestures of circularity by way of arrival and return visible in *Ulysses*, *Finnegans Wake*, and *The Waste Land*.[1] Whatever Pound's plans and intentions may have been, *The Cantos* distinguish themselves from these works by their consistent deferral of destination, their sacrifice of progression for digression, becoming less a "travel poem" than perhaps a "road poem." In this light (though certainly not in others), they can seem more analogous to the work of Kerouac, for example, than to that of Pound's modernist friends. Again, to gauge the extremity of *The Cantos'* errance and drift, it is worth noting that three of the poems which most clearly work out of the poetics and precedent of Pound's epic – William Carlos Williams' *Paterson*, Charles Olson's *The Maximus Poems*, and Basil Bunting's *Briggflatts* – all rely heavily on the structural anchoring of a particular site or place, in contradistinction to the wanderings which occur on every level in *The Cantos*, and perhaps in counterbalance.

For in addition to being a travel poem or a road poem, Jahan Ramazani points to *The Cantos* as his first example of what he calls "traveling poetry": poetry able to "leap across national and cultural boundaries" as well as to "travel" via "the imaginative enactment of geographic movement, as in the rapid-fire transnational displacements"[2] which Ramazani sees in the *Pisan Cantos*. As this description makes clear, "traveling poetry" is likely also to be "translating poetry"; in Pound's case at least, the leaps across cultural boundaries transpire, above all, through his dedication to a multilingual text, content to cite copiously from foreign tongues and even silently reproduce the marks of other graphic systems, while also producing a seemingly endless series of rhetorics which, when they translate foreign texts, do so in a manner to highlight and magnify interferences and differences, rather than to erase and incorporate them inside a comforting, uniform, cleanly bounded idiom. Crawford is right to point out that *The Cantos* are a "work that revels in 'translatorese'"[3] and perhaps the work's most salient stylistic trait is its stressing of this properly *linguistic* traveling, the disjunctions of "displacements" both of geography and of idiom.

One instance where the link between travel and translation in Pound can be seen is in his evaluation of Henry James, for Pound the supreme example of the expatriated American artist. Not only did he characterize James' achievement as above all a "labour of translation," but among James' works he also singled out for special praise a piece of travel writing, *The American Scene*: a "triumph of the author's long practice . . . I know of no such grave record, of no such attempt at faithful portrayal as *The American Scene*" (*LE*, 327). Clearly, for Pound, travel writing as seen in James' experiment in auto-ethnography is as "serious" an artistic and intellectual undertaking, on every level, as the writing of poetry or fiction.

At the same time, to praise James as a "translator" is to imply that "translation" in its usual acceptation is only one element in a broader form of cultural, social, and geographic "translation" of which James is the outstanding figure, dedicated as he was to "making it possible for individuals to meet across national borders" and to "the research of the significance of nationality, French, English, American" (*LE*, 296). If James, along with Chaucer "Le Grand Translateur," is crucial for Pound's figuring of translation in this sense, Pound extended the lessons of the master well beyond the entirely Eurocentric scope of these investigations, using openings provided by Fenollosa and Frobenius, again via translation and "rapid-fire transnational displacements," to attempt to assay, probe, and redraw the borders between European cultural and linguistic practice and that of parts of Asia and Africa.

However, if this sense of border-crossing as productive displacement and interference rather than seamless assimilation is crucial for the entire Poundian project, it is very largely in relation to James that Pound thinks these ideas through. In fact, one of Pound's two extended forays into travel writing per se, his *Patria Mia*, is modeled on *The American Scene* to a significant degree. James had extensively toured the United States in 1904 and 1905 after more than twenty years of absence, collecting the "impressions" of the "restless analyst," as he calls himself throughout, that would constitute the basis of his book. Pound would repeat James' gesture, with characteristic imagist compression, as it were, spending about eight months mostly in New York and the Philadelphia area in 1910 and 1911, after around two years based in London.

Both texts follow the perceptions and impressions of a "restored absentee," to use another of James' favored expressions, while in an early serialized version of *Patria Mia*, Pound described his task as follows: "I am . . . to set forth the simplicity of America, in such fashion that not only will all foreigners understand implicitly America and its people – all its people; but I am expected simultaneously to bring my fatherland to self-consciousness, to cause America to see its face in the glass" (*EPCP*, 1: 77). Not surprisingly, his attempts to define the American character tend to proceed by way of contrast with that of the English. Pound wryly tweaks both countries, for example, in this comment on national character and the effect of immigration: "We get from every village the most ruthless and the most energetic. The merely discontented stop in England" (*EPCP*, 1: 77). But more important are a series of linked observations on family, kinship, friendship, and economy. In London, Pound explains, "A new acquaintance is an experiment, a new friend a peril" (*EPCP*, 1: 104), whereas "No American ever knows all the interesting people he wants to know. The American is constantly rushing into intimacies" (*EPCP*, 1: 104). This is because "Our family bond [in America] is so slight that we collect another family, not bound to us by blood but by temperament. And I think it is very hard for Europeans to understand our process of doing this" (*EPCP*, 1: 104). But prophetically of his future interests, Pound also sees the rootedness of the English family bond as ultimately linked to the relationship to capital: "So far as I can make out, there is no morality in England which is not in one way or another a manifestation of the sense of property" (*EPCP*, 1: 104). To be noted here are not only Pound's particular constructions of Englishness, but also that like James, Pound posits himself as able to see what makes America distinctive precisely through contrast to the different forms of social organization he has witnessed abroad.

Pound banks on the premise that an alienated gaze is most pertinent when applied to the homeland – as the title makes clear, his book is about America, not England. In other words, if touristic travel relies on exoticization and defamiliarization, *Patria Mia*, like *The American Scene*, turns this touristic gaze upon one's homeland and oneself, implying that "travel" is not only about the "other" and the "foreign," but about how such encounters re-elaborate the "self" and the "domestic." As in James' case, a "labour of translation" also implies auto-translation and a reconfiguration of the domestic, which becomes the central question as soon as one is absented from it. It is precisely this emphasis in James which allows Pound to insist on the latter's essential "Americanness," a position which means Pound can posit expatriation not as a retreat from American identity, but on the contrary as a heightened modality of it.

This reading of James is but one interesting instance of how translation, textual travel, and geographical travel each imply the other for Pound. Another is the walking tour of French troubadour country he undertook in 1912. The genesis of the project is worth pausing over, and says much about the relationship between travel and "traveling poetry" in Pound. In Greenwich Village in 1910, while absorbing the radical modernity of Manhattan on which he was to comment in *Patria Mia*, Pound was largely engaged in a literary undertaking which could seem diametrically opposed: translating the thirteenth-century Tuscan poet Guido Cavalcanti. That this sort of constructive dissonance was cultivated by Pound is evident, and moreover, in the coming decades Cavalcanti will for Pound increasingly be valued for nothing so much as his own intellectual "modernity" as Pound saw it. In any event, by the time he returned to Europe in 1911, Pound had decided to extend his work on Dante's precursors by adding to his Cavalcanti renderings new translations of the troubadour poet Arnaut Daniel – the famous "*miglior fabbro*" of Eliot's later dedication of *The Waste Land* to Pound. Pound's approach to the Arnaut texts was a fascinating mix of formalism and historical materialism, in a combination which in some ways prefigures the mix of translation, pastiche, lyric flights, and presentation of something meant to be taken as documentary evidence which is so characteristic of *The Cantos*.

Pound clearly prizes Arnaut above all as a master of rhyme and a creator of forms – characteristically on the move, Pound writes his future mother-in-law Olivia Shakespear from Sirmione in 1910, asking her to go to the British Museum to copy "single stanzas" of different Arnaut canzoni (*EPDS*, 19) – all he cares about is the cadence and rhyme schemes. But this seeming indifference to content will be increasingly counterbalanced by an obstinately hard-nosed belief in the referent, most saliently, the landscape of the troubadour country. Indeed, by 1912, Pound's sense of Arnaut has evolved to the point where he feels that the significance of the formal mastery which won Arnaut the epithet of "better craftsman" from Dante can only be appreciated in light of certain material contexts in which the troubadours worked. As Pound was to put it, "There are three ways of 'going back,' of feeling as well as knowing about the troubadours, first, by way of the music, second, by way of the land, third, by way of the books themselves, for a manuscript on vellum has a sort of life and personality which no work of the press attains" (*WTSF*, 84). All of these implied travel.

First of all, Pound went to see the manuscripts: in the spring of 1911, shortly after his return from the United States, Pound betook himself to the Ambrosian Library in Milan, to examine and have photographed the only known manuscript with musical settings of Arnaut (*WTSF*, x); this was killing two birds with one journey, acquiring both the musical notation and the feel of the entire cultural space radiating out in traces from the luminous detail of a manuscript on vellum. Not only a research trip in the scholarly interests of textual accuracy, and hardly a pilgrimage to the aura of the sacred object, Pound's visit to the manuscript book is consonant with the most contemporary materialist, genealogical forms of historical inquiry: Arnaut's poetry could not be understood apart from the context of a social space in which manuscript books like these was its mode of transmission.[4] As Jack Spicer has written, "Words are what sticks to the real,"[5] and Pound's metonymic interest in what "stuck" to the words of Arnaut and the troubadours instigated the walking tour he undertook in the summer of 1912.

Though the notes Pound took on the journey were only published in 1992, under the title *A Walking Tour in Southern France*, Pound had initially hoped to amortize his poetically indispensable investigative journey as a commercially viable piece of travel writing, at one point envisaging publishing the never completed "Gironde" in a diptych alongside *Patria Mia* (*WTSF*, xii).[6] In his introduction to the volume, Richard Sieburth has magnificently sketched the extent to which "the imagistic notations of place scattered throughout the *Walking Tour* unmistakably prepare the palette for the *Cantos*" (*WTSF*, xvi), as Pound finds the language to mirror his full physical immersion in a palimpsestic historical density at once geological, climatic, and cultural. In this vein, in terms of Pound's relationship to travel and travel writing, it is crucial again to sketch how much Pound distances himself from the guidebook account of monuments and attractions, in order to use travel as a form of historical, psychological, and even psycho-geographical inquiry.

Shunning the train as much as possible and traveling on foot is the essence of the project. Pound strives to approximate the pace of the troubadours, to take in the landscape at the rate their eyes would have perused it, to suffer and glory in the climate and weather as one would have been forced to do in the twelfth century. As Pound put it, "It is undeniable that if one wishes to see objects instead of to realize conditions, he had better travel by rail" (*WTSF*, 31). But in addition to getting inside the troubadours' sensibility and metric by inhabiting their gaze and their gait, one of the "conditions" Pound was interested in throughout was precisely the condition of travel, travel *as* a condition, the productive refusal to ever quite be anywhere. As he put it about Henry James: "The essence of James is that he is always 'settling in,' it is the ground-tone of his genius" (*LE*, 332).

Ungroundedness as ground-tone rings familiar not only in terms of Pound's writing, but also his biography. Ira B. Nadel has emphasized the extent of Pound's youthful urge to keep on the move, and noted how many acquaintances, from T. S. Eliot to Charles Doolittle – H. D.'s father, and therefore Pound's potential father-in-law – thought Pound to be, as Doolittle put it, "nothing but a nomad."[7] And indeed, a cursory look at Pound's movements between his arrival in Gibraltar in March, 1908, having quit his post at Wabash College in Indiana, and the outbreak of the First World War in 1914, is dizzying: aside from the long journey to the United States in 1910–11, every few months one finds him leaving his London base for Paris, or the south of France, or sites in Italy like Milan, Venice, and Sirmione, or Stone Cottage in Sussex, where he would winter as Yeats' secretary from 1913 to 1915, or even Giessen in 1911, where he met up with Ford Madox Hueffer (later to change his surname to Ford), and took a detour to Freiburg to unknot a Provençal crux with the help of the specialist Emil Lévy, as famously recounted in Canto xx.

This propensity for "nomadism" is one Pound comments on in *Guide to Kulchur*, a peripatetic book not only because of its long section on Aristotle. The passage must be quoted at some length, to convey the density of the complex of issues in which nomadism is imbricated for Pound:

Obviously the need of nutriment indicates incompleteness in the moving animal. It is not self-sustaining, it is not completely autonomous.

The tree picks up its roots and turns them inward to walk. How convenient to stick one's foot into the earth and be nourished? At sacrifice of the freedom to be nomadic?

Frobenius' lists of characteristics of races leave one with inability to accept, for oneself unconditionally, either a patriarchal or a matriarchal disposition. I prefer a lex Germanica to a lex Salica. My predisposition (at least in youth) being nomadic. It is not for me to rebuke brother semite for similar disposition. Happy the man born to rich acres, a saecular vine bearing good grapes, olive trees spreading with years. (*GK*, 243).

Numerous things are noteworthy in this passage, and not least that his nomadic "predisposition" leads Pound to assert kinship with his "brother semite" here in the late thirties, just when his anti-Semitism is reaching its most horrific pitch. At the same time, nomadism finds itself balanced precariously in an entirely ambivalent construction of lack. On the one hand, nomadism is seen as a consequence of incompletion, here figured as hunger, or the "need of nutriment." On the other hand, Pound's musings here and elsewhere on the opposition of "Salic" to "Germanic" law imply that the most salutary position is that of the disinherited, forced to wander from the patriarchal hearth. This becomes clear when one remembers that the Salic Law which Pound discounts here is notable for its provision of agnatic succession, which prohibits female descendants from inheriting a throne or fief.

Although a detailed examination of these issues is beyond the scope of this discussion, it seems that Pound's major objection to "lex Salica" is its imposition of property through its insistence on primogeniture. As Pound puts it in a roughly contemporaneous letter: "Ownership is often a damnd nuisance, and anchor. It was my parents' owning a house that put me wise, and I struggled for years to own nothing that I can't pack in a suitcase. Never really got it down to less than *two* cases" (*SL*, 279). As opposed to these constraints, in his short text "Aux Etuves de Wiesbaden," Pound imagines a "lex Germanica" that would feature a polyandrous matrilineal kinship structure, in which men wander among different women, untethered to family: "a woman kept whatever man she liked, so long as she fancied: the children being brought up by her brothers, being a part of the female family, *cognati*" (*PDD*, 100). This circulation of men between various women, with no binding paternal ties except to the children of their sisters, would have been eminently convenient for Pound, an only child.

Interestingly, in his somewhat anomalous autobiographical prose sketch of 1923, "Indiscretions," Pound also uses "lex Salica" as a kind of shorthand for patrilineal descent, in order to emphasize its lack of authority within his own maternal ancestry (*PDD*, 21, 25), and this within a text which tightly interleaves artistic self-engendering, maternal kinship, and travel. Pound pointedly tells us at the very outset that he deliberately chose to write his life history from Venice because Venice itself is nothing if not a place of inceptions and origins for him: "some sort of salvo must be allowed the habitat where one's first recueil was printed" (*PDD*, 5). Indeed, Pound had had *A Lume Spento* privately printed in Venice in 1908, shortly before leaving to seek his literary fortune in London.

But if Venice is the site of his poetic beginning, the origin of his ever being in Venice in the first place is his "Aunt Frank," his mother's father's brother's wife, who first took him to Europe in 1898, when he was twelve: "Without her I might not have been here" (*PDD*, 6). For Pound, a displacement of geographical, national, cultural, and linguistic space goes along with a displacement of maternal debt and filiation, in this parable of the birth of the poet. "It is peculiarly fitting that this manuscript should begin in Venice" (*PDD*, 3) are the first words of this text, in which the surrogate mother brings the nomad to the surrogate birthplace, and autobiography is couched from the inception explicitly in terms of travel writing, of the "Harzreise" (*PDD*, 5).

The distancing effected by travel, the Grand Tour, or "Europe or the Setting" as he was to phrase it in *Guide to Kulchur*, are thus all unequivocally associated with the artistic birth of a writer who remains all the more American for the fact of discovering his symbolic birthplace elsewhere. And Venice – where Pound settled following his release from St. Elizabeths in 1958 – was also to become the site of his death, and the place of his burial. But returning to James, it is legitimate to posit that the artistic "Harzreise" and expatriate self-engenderment begin within death from the outset. In *Italian Hours* James wrote: "Venetian life, in the large old sense, has long since come to an end, and the essential present character of the most melancholy of cities resides simply in its being the most beautiful of tombs. Nowhere else has the past been laid to rest with such tenderness . . . Nowhere else is the present so alien, so discontinuous."[8]

If it is precisely Pound's genius for the discontinuous that makes him a master of traveling poetry and translating poetry generally, then the point here is not only that Pound is "a poet whose progress begins and ends in the realm of the dead,"[9] as Daniel Tiffany has put it, but that Pound also manages to posit Venice and the realm of the dead as discontinuous themselves. This accomplishment might be due in part to the ironic displacement that expatriation imposes on the concept of "travel" in the first place: if one comes finally to recuse the idea that any particular place of residence one is at the moment "settling into" might be one's home, then one can never stop traveling either. This in turn means domestic routine and the everyday provoke nothing so much as the deciphering, defamiliarized, and fetishistically mystified gaze of the travel writer, as in the case of Henry

James' return "home," chronicled in *The American Scene*, or in Gertrude Stein's *Paris France*, in which her adoptive hometown "is not real but it is really there."[10]

William Stowe has emphasized how for Americans traveling to Europe in the nineteenth century, the journey was often conceived as a ritual separation after which "more-than-ordinary benefits" could be cashed in upon "reintegration into the home society."[11] What must be noted is that in Pound's case, this moment of reintegration, like the ending of *The Cantos*, is perpetually deferred. The cultural plunder of the land of the dead is never returned to America, to whose "Renaissance" or "Risvegliamento" (*EPCP*, 1: 139) about half of *Patria Mia* is dedicated. Rather, the final "Drafts and Fragments" begin at Torcello, in the Venetian lagoon, before navigating through familiar European histories of usury, but also Na-Khi ritual in China: "can you see with eyes of coral or turquoise / or walk with the oak's root?" (cx/797) Pound asks, instigating a sustained reflection on rootedness which rhymes the Na-Khi rites for the dead with a more familiar Greek myth of "Laurel bark sheathing the fugitive" (cx/799) and "Daphne afoot in vain speed" (cxiii/810). The great port city becomes the site of the final reflections on the "not self-sustaining" moving animal as opposed to the non-nomadic tree; reflections which go back to *Guide to Kulchur*. Indeed, almost as echo of the originally motivating "need of nutriment," these Cantos laconically note, "war is the destruction of restaurants" (cx/800).

In the end, then, Venice is not only the mother lode of cultural capital delivered by Aunt Frank, nor the site where the young poet ponders whether to print his first volume or "chuck the lot" of his proofs into the canal (lxxvi/480). It is also the place where, Pound remembers: "I sat on the Dogana's steps / For the gondolas cost too much, that year" (iii/11), the impoverished young poet unable to afford the "traghetto" across the Grand Canal. But "Dogana," translated, is customs-house – the site at the tip of the Grand Canal where entrances and exits are registered, recorded, and controlled; where the taxes to be paid for the privilege of border crossings are assessed and imposed. And, despite its seeming distance, it is a distinctly American site, as evidenced by those other great travelers, travel writers, and customs-house sitters, Hawthorne and Melville.

NOTES

1 Robert Crawford, *Devolving English Literature*, 2nd edn. (Edinburgh: Edinburgh University Press, 2000), 242–3.

2 Jahan Ramazani, "Traveling Poetry," *Modern Language Quarterly* 68.2 (June 2007): 281–3.

3 Crawford, *Devolving English Literature*, 243.

4 Although the *chansonniers* he consulted were largely posterior to the heyday of the troubadours, as Pound would have known.

5 Jack Spicer, *My Vocabulary Did This To Me: The Collected Poetry of Jack Spicer*, ed. Peter Gizzi and Kevin Killian (Middletown, CT: Wesleyan University Press, 2008), 123.

6 Such a commercial venture can hardly have seemed far-fetched; travel writing was a "cash cow" for such prominent and successful American writers of the previous generation as Mark Twain, Edith Wharton, and W. D. Howells, as well as James. For a full account of the phenomenon, see William Stowe, *Going Abroad: European Travel in Nineteenth-Century American Culture* (Princeton: Princeton University Press, 1994), pp. 3–15.

7 Ira Nadel, "'Nothing but a nomad': Ezra Pound in Europe (1898–1911)," in *Ezra Pound and Europe*, ed. Richard Taylor and Claus Melchior (Amsterdam: Rodopi, 1993), 24, 19.

8 Henry James, *Collected Travel Writings: The Continent* (New York: Library of America, 1993), 314.

9 Daniel Tiffany, *Radio Corpse: Imagism and the Cryptaesthetic of Ezra Pound* (Cambridge, MA: Harvard University Press, 1995), 81.

10 Gertrude Stein, *Paris France* (London: Peter Owen, 2003), 2.

11 Stowe, *Going Abroad*, 21–2.

PART III

Critical reception

CHAPTER 39

Pound before Paris: 1908–1920

Barry Ahearn

Anyone needing a chronological survey of Pound's critical reception in the early years of his career should consult Eric Homberger's introduction to his *Ezra Pound: The Critical Heritage*. He amply covers the year-by-year comments on the early poetry, translations, and criticism. This chapter takes a different, synchronic approach. It examines the key terms that were brought to Pound's work between 1909 and 1921. Such an approach highlights the dominant critical standards of his day, some of which remain in the vocabulary of today's reviewers. Others have altered, dwindled, or faded from use. As has often been said, it was partly due to Pound's influence, and the influence of his associates, that critical discourse changed.

"ALL THINGS SAVE BEAUTY ALONE"

T. S. Eliot played a major role in that alteration. His slim volume, *Ezra Pound: His Metric and Poetry* (1917), was clearly the most important consideration of Pound's work to that point. It was significant because of the arguments Eliot made in Pound's favor and because of those he declined to consider. He observed at the start that his essay would "not dilate upon 'beauties'."[1] The remark may be lost on those who are unaware how frequently critics of the period praised or faulted an author for the presence (or absence) of beauty in the work. We find, for example, *Personae* (1909) welcomed because it contained "true beauty" and was "unquestionably beautiful." F. S. Flint similarly delighted in the "fresh beauty." Ford Madox Ford discerned in the poems of *Cathay* "a supreme beauty" (*EPCH*, 44, 46, 108).

"Beauty," however, remained undefined. It clearly signified approval, but readers were left to wonder what precisely it meant. The critics seemed to know beauty when they saw it, but apparently one had to take their word for it. The term was just as useful to those who found fault with Pound. A reviewer of *Ripostes* announced that he "could not see the art or beauty of it" (*EPCH*, 95). John Gould Fletcher examined *Quia Pauper Amavi* and regretted that its contents were "the patchwork and debris of a mind that has never quite been able to find the living, vivid beauty it set out to seek" (*EPCH*, 173). Those who faulted Pound for being unable to produce beauty were not forthcoming about the exact nature of his failure. They were just as vague as those who praised his manifold beauties. On rare occasions a reference to "beautiful lines" might be taken to refer to skillful use of meter, assonance, and consonance, but for the most part "beauty" remained a nebulous signifier.

"HE STROVE TO RESUSCITATE THE DEAD ART / OF POETRY"

In his essay on Pound, Eliot noted that an artist intent on improving his craft runs the risk of losing part of his audience. Alterations in his art are "disconcerting to the public which likes a poet to spin his whole work out of the feelings of his youth." The public did not like "that constant readjustment which the following of Mr. Pound's work demands." Eliot pointed to specific elements in Pound's craftsmanship. For example, he noted that the verse was the result of an "intensive study of metre."[2] Eliot carefully avoided the phrase "*extensive* study," which might have implied a high degree of erudition on Pound's part. To say that it was "intensive" suggested originality and virtuoso command.

Eliot was amplifying what other critics had already noted. It was common for Pound's volumes to be greeted respectfully as embodiments of "craft and artistry" and even applauded as containing "effects . . . exquisitely designed and exactly carried out" (*EPCH*, 47, 70–1). Commentators as different as Carl Sandburg and A. R. Orage were in agreement (respectively) about Pound's manifest "art and craftsmanship" and "deliberate craftsmanship" (*EPCH*, 115, 140). Richard Aldington tried to sum up just what it was about that devotion and craft that made it so remarkable when he stressed certain aspects of Pound's style: "Its simplicity, its masterly use of words, the absence of cliché of thought and phrase, are obvious."[3] Reference to the absence of cliché suggested an artistic independence and toughness dissatisfied with anything less than perfection. Ford Madox Ford further illuminated the originality in Pound's art by observing that the poems deployed "concrete objects [so] that the emotions produced by the objects shall arise in the reader" (*EPCH*, 108).

There were, however, numerous dissenters when it came to the question of Pound's artistry. One reviewer of *Personae* warned his readers that "Mr. Pound sometimes is incoherent in order to seem original" (*EPCH*, 43).

Similarly, another commentator discovered "abrupt, discontinuous and meaningless exclamations" (*EPCH*, 56). Louis Untermeyer found fault with Pound's prose, which displayed a "disorderly retreat into the mazes of technique and pedantry" (*EPCH*, 142). Untermeyer was seconded by Conrad Aiken, who objected to the "disjointed and aimless prose" that Pound offered, a prose style characterized by "ugliness and awkwardness" (*EPCH*, 146). Aiken also faulted Pound's poetry. In comparison with some other writers, Aiken was rather benign. Even he did not go so far as to refer to Pound's "Jerked English" and "erratic lines," as some did.[4] Edward Garnett slashed away at *Personae*, condemning it as a "specimen of false poetic mosaic-pseudo-medieval *tesserae* set in sticky, modern cement that can never harden. Such stand condemned as style, by their adulterate jargon."[5] The mosaic-and-cement metaphor seemed to imply that Pound was doubly wrong, not only in his choice of materials but in his delusion that he could meld them into a coherent work.

Perhaps it was fortunate for Pound that many of his critics found him hard to understand. Otherwise they might have discovered what a handful of their peers discerned: not obscurity, but obscenity. One of them alleged that Pound's verse was likely to attract those readers who were "frankly lascivious" (*EPCH*, 100–1). Another reviewer rang the alarm bell, warning that some of Pound's "lines seem written for indecency's sake" (*EPCH*, 105). Generally, however, these allegations were infrequent. Pound was not in danger of being banned in Boston.

"BORN / IN A HALF SAVAGE COUNTRY"

But he was soon in danger of making himself the subject of his poems. From the beginning, everyone agreed that Pound exhibited a vivid presence. He had been in residence in London for only a few months when *Punch* noticed that "Mr. Ton . . . has left America . . . to impress his personality on English editors, publishers and readers" (*EPCH*, 6). At times it seemed that possession of a striking personality was considered un-English, and that only Americans and other foreigners were guilty of this sin. John Felton, when parodying "Portrait d'une Femme," snootily observed that Pound "has the average American's respect for the latest novelty."[6] But as Richard Aldington said of *Quia Pauper Amavi*, "he has evolved a poetry of his own . . . so stamped with his own personality, that he has made it something new."[7]

In *Ezra Pound: His Metric and Poetry*, Eliot was notably silent about the presence of Pound in his work. By doing so he was already implying what he would make explicit in "Tradition and the Individual Talent" (1919): the necessity of regarding the work of art as a product of impersonality. Clearly Eliot was swimming against the contemporary critical tide. Almost everyone else who looked at Pound's work saw manifestations of Pound. As one reviewer said of *Quia Pauper Amavi*, "More and more as we read we become aware of the Poundian personality" (*EPCH*, 167). This reviewer and others came to the conclusion that a little bit of self-display should be welcomed, but that Pound had run to excess. A commentator said of *The Spirit of Romance* that, "He relies . . . as much upon his personality as upon his learning" (*EPCH*, 68).

One has an intimation, when reading such comments about Pound's alleged egotism, of the background of *Mauberley* and Pound's reasons for his eventual departure from London. Surely it was not pleasant for him to read in the pages of *The Egoist*, a journal usually receptive to his work, that "He is too lost in the bog of personal vanity."[8] Nor could he have been happy to read that *Gaudier-Brzeska* suffered from having "too much Pound in the book and too little Gaudier-Brzeska."[9] Pound's decision to move to Paris, rather than to return to the United States, was probably influenced by such comments as these by Lewis Worthington Smith in the influential pages of the *Atlantic Monthly:* "That egotistic self-consciousness is a primary motive in the new movement appears sufficiently in the demand on the part of Mr. Ezra Pound, the self-appointed high priest of the coterie, that poets be endowed so that they may escape the need of writing to please the public." [10]

"A DURABLE PASSION"

Somewhat paradoxically, the chorus of critics who detected and deplored the exorbitant amount of Pound's personality in his work was joined by others who faulted him for showing insufficient emotion. He was charged with a display of "hard thinking" but "very little emotion" (*EPCH*, 84). Even when emotion was observed, it was found to be the wrong sort: "his sensations are secondary, aesthetic, not pure, primary and direct" (*EPCH*, 127). Somehow Pound failed to satisfy contemporary emotion detectors. Louis Untermeyer deplored his "gradual withdrawal from life." As Untermeyer saw it, Pound, despite his aggressive presence in his art, was a shrinking violet: "contact with the actual world is feared . . . he shrinks back into literature" (*EPCH*, 130). Pound, according to this view, had retreated to pedantry. A reviewer of *Lustra* suggested that Pound might be incapable of displaying feeling: "In craftsmanship, viewed unnaturally as a thing isolated, there is sometimes improvement, but native heat is lacking."[11]

When Eliot scrutinized Pound's work in *Ezra Pound: His Metric and His Poetry*, he was almost as reluctant to discuss emotion as he had been to list beauties. Yet he did point it out, insisting that "Pound's verse is always definite and concrete, because he always has a definite emotion behind it." Eliot refrained from saying precisely whose emotion was in question. He was already moving toward his argument in "Tradition and the Individual Talent" that true poets dealt not with their personal feelings but with "art emotions." In correcting those reviewers who were unable to discern emotion in Pound's poems, he added, "Many readers are apt to confuse the maturing of personality with desiccation of the emotions." Furthermore, Eliot remarked, readers might be looking for the emotions that they were used to finding in an author, and thus not recognizing novel ones: "Any poet, if he is to survive as a writer beyond his twenty-fifth year, must alter; he must seek new literary influences; he will have different emotions to express."[12]

"INCAPABLE OF THE LEAST UTTERANCE OR COMPOSITION"

One of the issues that arose when critics considered Pound's craftsmanship was his originality; this created a rift between critics. An early review of *A Lume Spento* and *Personae* hailed them as containing "The most original note struck in English verse, since the publication of Ernest Dowson's poems some three or four years ago."[13] A notice of *Provença* singled out Pound's "fine and original genius."[14] Eliot praised Pound's "original use of language."[15] An example of extreme praise came from Carl Sandburg, who declared that Pound had "done more of living men to incite new impulses in poetry" (*EPCH*, 112). Echoing Sandburg, the Belgian critic Jean de Bosschere indicated that one of Pound's notable strengths was "the bold line he takes after he has cleared everything away in revolt. Even if his manner of way of thought be influenced, he is new, and his vision is his own." [16]

There were, nevertheless, others who took the quite contrary view. These critics discerned in Pound absolutely no "originality of thought" (*EPCH*, 104). This dearth of originality was attributed by one reviewer to the fact that Pound was too steeped in the work of previous generations of poets: "If Mr. Pound could only forget his literature" (*EPCH*, 65). Marguerite Wilkinson, who faulted Pound for his lack of emotion, seemed willing to allow that there might be some novelty but that "Most of his poems are no better than clever." [17]

Originality was one facet that reviewers inspected carefully. They also scrutinized what appears to be its opposite: the degree to which Pound was influenced by other poets. Two names were often repeated: Browning and Whitman. Much of the time the critics considered their influence to be simply worth mentioning. One of them, however, thought Pound's work revealed a "twisted Browningesque personality" and the "dangerous influence of Whitman" (*EPCH*, 58–9). Here and there we find a critic who expands the list of influences to include Rossetti and Yeats (*EPCH*, 62). Eliot, however, limited the names of recent influences to Browning and Yeats. Since some of Pound's more notable poems took the form of dramatic monologues, and since he handled traditional meters rather freely, Browning's presence was frequently discerned. Eliot, though, found Whitman's presence to be negligible or nil. [18] In fact, Eliot found the influence of other poets to be limited mostly to Pound's earliest work. Thereafter, Eliot stressed, what was central to the development of Pound's art was his inventiveness.

"THE CLASSICS IN PARAPHRASE"

Invention, many critics recognized, was also necessary when it came to translation. Pound's presentation of specimens of translation in *The Spirit of Romance* were called "in the main admirable" (*EPCH*, 68). As his career developed, he was even considered "so excellent a translator" (*EPCH*, 136). Another reviewer judged that *The Sonnets and Ballate of Guido Cavalcanti* offered "admirable translations." [19] Pound, however, sometimes ran afoul of academic experts. After inspecting *Cavalcanti*, one professor charged that Pound had chosen for his text one that was "obsolete and unworthy" (*EPCH*, 86). Compounding this error, the translations revealed an "ignorance of some of the commonest rules of syntax, grammar and metrics" (*EPCH*, 86). One did not have to be an inmate of the classroom, however, to find fault. Another reviewer, not a member of the academy, dismissed Pound as a bungler: "He is sometimes clumsy, and often obscure, and has no fine tact about language" (*EPCH*, 91).

Pound's version of Propertius was the most controversial of his translations. Of course to call it a translation is already to miss the point. Professor William G. Hale assumed that Pound was attempting to cleave to standard notions of how a text in another language should be made into English. Pound's defenders retorted that such an assumption was misplaced. One of them argued that "It is . . . hardly fair to judge the 'Homage to Propertius' by reference to Propertius. It is obviously not meant as a translation" (*EPCH*, 161). Such critics, although they were more perceptive about Pound's ambitions than was Hale, suffered under the disadvantage of being unable to name what it was that Pound was trying to put on the page. (Pound called it an "homage," but no one else seemed happy to repeat the term.) It was much easier for his detractors to accuse him of simply making bad translations.

His translations (if that is what they were) from the Chinese drew almost unanimous praise. As we have seen, Ford Madox Ford raved about the beauties of *Cathay*. A. R. Orage attested to their power when he wrote, "they delight and astonish me" (*EPCH*, 110). Later, Pound also convinced some reviewers that his skill with Chinese was matched by his command of Japanese. A *TLS* reviewer praised Pound's renditions of Japanese. He wrote of *"Noh," or Accomplishment* that "Mr. Pound succeeds in conveying some hint of otherwise unfamiliar allusions, by the lyrical structure of pictorial prose" and demonstrated a "mastery of beautiful diction" as well as "cunningly rhythmical prose."[20] We should add, however, that it seems that no professors of Chinese or Japanese were asked to review the results of his excavations from the Fenollosa papers. This may have spared him raps on the knuckles similar to those dealt by professors steeped in Latin and Italian.

"john ruskin produced / 'kings treasuries'"

The treatment of Pound the critic repeated the divided opinions about Pound the poet and Pound the translator. From the beginning it was recognized that he was no ordinary critic. But were his extraordinary opinions declarations of genius or just hogwash? Even early in his career a single review could contain sharply divided assessments. A notice of *The Spirit of Romance* called it a "delightful book" that shed light on a little understood segment of European literature. The reviewer declared that "There is a deal of brilliant if a little disjointed criticism." So far so good. But the reviewer then complained that "Mr. Pound retains the stupid little affectations that mar so much of his poetry."[21] This early review sounded a note that would recur over and over again: Pound had flashes of insight, but he could also be extremely irritating.

There were, unfortunately, some who doubted he had anything worthwhile to impart. "Auceps" derided him for producing an essay ("The New Sculpture") in which Pound revealed "his own offensive incompetence."[22]

Even James Sibley Watson, who might have been expected to appreciate Poundian insights (he was one of the backers of *The Dial*), found fault with him. Reviewing *Instigations*, he deplored Pound's apparent inability to go beyond merely impressionistic views. "Well, Mr. Pound is a poet. He doesn't write prose . . . His destructive remarks are limited to funny oaths and insults; no reasoned attack" (*EPCH*, 192). Looking at the same collection of essays, Padraic Colum argued that Pound had indeed helped others to make progress: "the *Instigations* of Ezra Pound have this virtue – they badger and bully us out of a state of intellectual backwardness." Colum saw a discriminating and illuminating visionary, one who "is constantly striving . . . to make current some compelling portion of the reality of the day."[23]

Almost all of Pound's reviewers were sensitive to the liveliness of his criticism, whether they responded to it warmly or abusively. The exception that proves the rule is Conrad Aiken's commentary on *Pavannes and Divisions*. His perception was that "the outstanding feature of this book of prose is its dullness."[24] Far more receptive was another American, Ben Hecht, who saw in Pound one of the foremost critics of the age. "Cultured Pound is, and more than that, sane and clear visioned. His reflections upon the art of others are based upon shrewd, definite understandings . . ." Although Hecht defended Pound's intellectual acumen, he, too, found the style troubling. So far as Hecht could determine, Pound had not yet forged a style of his own: "He does not present to me a style – but a series of portrayals."[25]

It was left to Eliot to point out one value in Pound's criticism that most other commentators ignored, namely, that "His critical writings are the comments of a practitioner upon his own and related arts; and in this type we have very little since Dryden's Prefaces of any permanent value." Eliot's quite laudatory comments on *Pavannes and Divisions* made it clear that he thought Pound's insights were indeed of permanent value. As Eliot had already emphasized, Pound had a gift for focusing on the essential element in a work. Eliot underscored Pound's "insistence upon technique: it is only a study of technique which can widen our understanding of different types of art, for excellence of technique . . . is the only thing that all types of arts have in common."[26] For Eliot, the Poundian style was a matter of little or no interest. It seems that any style would do so long as the critic steadily gazed at technique. Of course, Eliot was aware of the unusual nature of Pound's prose style, but he thought it irrelevant. The insight mattered however it was transmitted. Even though Eliot's own style was markedly different from Pound's, he declined to find fault with it.

"SOMETHING FOR THE MODERN STAGE"

Assessors of Pound's contribution to culture sometimes speculated on his place in literary history. Eliot pointed out that he was "turning to more modern subjects" recently.[27] It was a hint that those who were interested in the meaning of modernity might well look at Pound's treatment of it. A young Babette Deutsch, writing about the same time as Eliot, emphasized this aspect of Pound: "He is a modern of the moderns, whose credo it is that a study of comparative literatures of many epochs and races is essential to that keen critical faculty which is part of an artist's equipment" (*EPCH*, 132). By calling him a "modern of the moderns," Deutsch placed the spotlight on Pound as the leader, or at least one of the leaders, of the modern movement in the arts.

Whatever literary criteria were used to evaluate Pound, he was a truly controversial figure about whom the most contrary things were written. For some he was the herald of a new age in poetry; others regarded him as a hatchet man bent on mutilating sacred traditions. It is hard to find anyone indifferent to Pound. He had succeeded in making his presence felt. His was a name one could not ignore. But it is clear that by the end of his London years he had not acquired as distinguished and unalloyed a reputation as he desired when he first arrived.

NOTES

1 T. S. Eliot, "Ezra Pound: His Metric and Poetry," in *To Criticize the Critic* (New York: Farrar, Straus & Giroux, 1965), 163.

2 *Ibid.*, 177–8, 165.

3 Richard Aldington, "The Art of Poetry," *The Dial* 69 (August 1920): 175.

4 Wallace Rice, "Ex Libra Et Libris," *The Dial* 54 (June 1913): 449.

5 Edward Garnett, "Critical Notes on American Poets," *Atlantic Monthly* 120 (September 1917): 367.

6 Felton, James. "Contemporary Caricatures: Mr. E*** P****," *The Egoist* 1 (August 1, 1914): 297.

7 Richard Aldington, "A Book for Literary Philosophers," *Poetry* 16.4 (July 1920): 215.

8 Felton, "Contemporary Caricatures," 297.

9 Anonymous, "Gaudier-Brzeska," *New York Times Review of Books* (August 13, 1916): 324.

10 Lewis Worthington Smith, "The New Naivete," *Atlantic Monthly* 117 (April 1916): 491–2.

11 M. T., "Ezra Pound and Others," *New Republic* 13 (January 19, 1918): 352.

12 Eliot, *Ezra Pound: His Metric and Poetry*, 170, 173, 177.

13 Curtis Hidden Page, "Recent Verse," *Book News Monthly* 28.1 (September 1909): 51.
14 Anonymous, "A Triad of American Poets," *New York Times Review of Books* (March 12, 1911): 134.
15 Eliot, *Ezra Pound: His Metric and Poetry*, 167.
16 Jean de Bosschere, "Ezra Pound," *The Egoist* 4 (April 1917): 44.
17 Marguerite Wilkinson, *New Voices: An Introduction to Contemporary Poetry* (New York: Macmillan, 1919): 183.
18 Eliot, *Ezra Pound: His Metric and Poetry*, 167.
19 William Stanley Braithewaite, "Guido Cavalcanti," *New York Times Review of Books* (June 16, 1912): 371.
20 Anonymous, "Japanese Mysteries," *Times Literary Supplement* 784 (January 25, 1917): 41.
21 Anonymous, "The Spirit of Romance," *English Review* 5 (July 1910): 757, 758.
22 Auceps, "The New Sculpture," *The Egoist* 1 (April 1, 1914): 137.
23 Padraic Colum, "Studies in the Sophisticated," *New Republic* 25 (December 8, 1920): 54, 52.
24 Conrad Aiken, *Scepticisms: Notes on Contemporary Poetry* (New York: Knopf, 1919): 137.
25 Ben Hecht, "Pounding Ezra," *The Little Review* 5 (November 1918): 39, 40.
26 T.S. Eliot, "Studies in Contemporary Criticism," *The Egoist* 5 (November–December 1918): 132.
27 Eliot, *Ezra Pound: His Metric and Poetry*, 173.

CHAPTER 40

Pound before Pisa: 1920–1945

John Xiros Cooper

Ezra Pound's career comes in three acts. This chapter deals with Act Two, the period between his forsaking of London in 1920 and before he is returned to the United States from the Italian city of Pisa as a traitor in 1946. There is no doubt that tragedy dominates Act Three in Pisa and beyond, but Act One, the London years, can be cast in epic terms, as a heroic struggle to rid Mount Helicon of both the beefy bluster left over from the Victorians and the genteel prissiness of Edwardian and Georgian literary culture. The undercurrent of aestheticism that runs from the Pre-Raphaelites in the 1850s, through Walter Pater, to the nineties, the Rhymers Club, and, finally, to the martyrdom of Oscar Wilde on the altar of Victorian moralism, is still, in Pound's London years, in very bad odor. "Yeux Glaques," the sixth lyric in *Hugh Selwyn Mauberley (Life and Contacts)*(1920) captures precisely the soft, sexualized underside of aestheticism and the bullying Victorian response:

> Foetid Buchanan lifted up his voice
> When that faun's head of hers
> Became a pastime for
> Painters and adulterers.
>
> (*P*, 1990, 189)

It was easy to dismiss the Buchanans and to proclaim a new kind of heady, virile aestheticism that apologized for nothing and gave back as good as it got.

Act Two, the middle years, are neither tragic nor heroic. They are not so easy to characterize. Perhaps they have elements of the tragic and comic about them. Or perhaps they constitute a kind of Purgatorio, but they do not, as in Dante, lead to Paradiso. In a reversal of Dante's plot, the London years may have been more of a paradise than what follows after 1920. And certainly at Pisa in 1945 Pound entered a real Inferno. In the London years, Pound seemed to be in heaven, to borrow the words of William

447

Wordsworth in another context, "Bliss was it in that dawn to be alive" (*The Prelude*, 11.108). His poetry, critical interventions, his masterminding of a number of literary schemes to promote the new literary and artistic culture of modernism are still spoken of as something of a triumph of keen intelligence, shrewdness, energy, and unbridled optimism. The Men (and Women) of 1914 – Lewis, Joyce, Eliot, H.D., and Pound – were going to change the world.

The world may have been bemused, even taken aback, by the brash brio emanating from *Blast* in 1914, but it wasn't about to beat a path to Pound's triangular sitting room in Kensington Church Walk. Instead, the world in 1914 was marching to a different beat and heading for a rather different vortex. The carnage of the Great War put an end to the hopes of the first generation of modernists. The jingoism, political stupidity, profiteering, blood-drenched sacrifice of so many young men and women including several of his closest friends and colleagues stunned Pound. He would never really recover his composure after the catastrophe. Indeed, his interest in economics and the question of social and political order emerged during the war as a way of understanding both how Europe could have descended into such barbarity and what one could do to prevent it in the future. It was difficult to imagine in 1918 that an even more stupefying barbarism lay ahead.

When Pound removed himself to Paris in late 1920, London and England had become the "ultimate urinal, middan, pisswallow without a cloaca" (xv/64). But by moving to Paris there were losses. For one thing, Pound removed himself from a literary scene which was immediately present. That sense of immediate engagement with friends and foes in the intellectual commerce of lively, many-faceted literary struggles suddenly vanished. One wrote or spoke there and one was immediately noticed, one's work was received straight away, was answered without delay. In the French capital, there was an English or "murkan licherture" scene, what came to be known as the Lost Generation, but it was a community of expatriate exiles (*SL*, 201). They were together as a group of foreigners among foreigners. There were a few ties with French writers and artists, Pound admired Jean Cocteau and Francis Picabia for example, but these did not lead to the kind of collaborations and activities that had characterized the London maelstrom. Beyond the expatriate community there was mostly silence in the immediate vicinity.

The give and take of continuing debate in newspapers, journals, small magazines, manifestos that had made of London a literary vortex suddenly grew more still. The critical reception of Pound's work, criticism, and publicity campaigns which had been immediate and forceful in London, suddenly withdrew into a strange silence. Now he communicated with his friends and colleagues principally by letter. What others thought of him and their responses to his work were muted by distance, by the inevitable lag time of snail mail. And, worse, a kind of ominous impersonality and for someone who was always a vivid "character," this new remoteness must have seemed at times like a near death experience. This he tried to overcome by a constant stream of letters to far-flung correspondents. He tried to connect by a number of rhetorical stratagems, staging fake and comical American or Cockney accents in his missives, taking on flamboyant personas for the amusement of correspondents he now, of necessity, needed to deal with at arm's length. In Paris, he had important literary friends, such as Ernest Hemingway and James Joyce, but it was minor talents such as William Bird and Robert MacAlmon who operated small literary presses that kept Pound going with any kind of critical or intellectual feedback.

This wasn't enough for a personality in need of a more vibrant community. By May 1923, he could see that communication at a distance was not working. He wrote to Kate Buss in the United States on May 12 that "my communication with America is over . . . The last link severed" (*SL*, 186). He had been "sacked" by one of his financial lifelines and an outlet for his writing, *The Dial*. It seemed that absence did not make the heart grow fonder; indeed, by the early 1920s the Pound flame that had burned so brightly in London was guttering and about to go out. By early 1924 he'd had enough of Paris. There was America of course, but as "to establishing any sort of milieu in America: it is not my job" (*SL*, 199).[1] Instead Italy beckoned and so did the deeper exile to which he now withdrew on the northwestern coast at Rapallo.

It was his years in Rapallo, a city he has made famous for English and American literature, that gives Act Two its specific setting. He lived there from 1924 to 1945, twenty-one years when he was around but not in view. He was still writing letters, publishing small editions of his books, and being kept in print in Britain by his friend T. S. Eliot, who had landed on his feet in a publishing company, Faber and Faber, and by new American friends like James Laughlin, founder and guiding intelligence of New Directions books in the United States. Both firms were eager to brand themselves as "modern" and "modernist" and Pound's reputation as a young lion from the early days was an important element in that strategy. But Pound was no longer news in the way he had been when he was at the nerve center of the London vortex. He grew increasingly cranky and petulant. Another side of his personality began to emerge that had only been visible fitfully in Act One as a robust, and even charmingly Yankee, combatitiveness. But an uglier side had already shown itself in the Hell Cantos, a side as ugly as the war madness Cantos XIV, XV, and XVI described.

> Profiteers drinking blood sweetened with sh[i]t,
> And behind them [Zaharof] f and the financiers
>   lashing them with steel wires.
>
> (XIV/61)

On July 8, 1922, in a very long letter to an old university teacher, Felix E. Schelling, this crankiness crackled for a moment as out and out misanthropy, "Humanity is malleable mud . . . Victoria was an excrement, Curtis, Lorrimer, *all* British journalism are excrement" (*SL*, 181). It was difficult at times to tell if Pound was exaggerating the misanthropy as a comic effect or was something that he really believed. Later, during the war years in the 1940s, the resentment and malevolence would lose its generality and spill over as a virulent anti-Semitism. There was absolutely nothing funny about this turn of events. It had perhaps always been there but, by 1941, Pound would no longer be able to keep it in check. It would hang out in all its naked ferocity on Roman radio.

After 1920, as Pound's literary engagements grew to depend more and more on the postal systems of western Europe and the USA, his reception among his contemporaries changed. His early work was slowly being absorbed into the evolving canon of twentieth-century poetry and criticism. This was aided by a younger generation who now began to write the history of early modernism, especially the events at ground zero in London. Many of his letters from Rapallo all through the 1920s and 1930s were responses to queries from those who were trying to piece together the story of modernism's heroic years (see especially letters to Glenn Hughes, René Taupin, and James Vogel in *SL*, 212, 216, 222 respectively). There were queries from a younger generation of American scholars as well, such as R. P. Blackmur (*SL*, 189) and John Crowe Ransom (*SL*, 318). They represented new tendencies in American higher education that had begun to absorb some of the new teaching about literature and criticism by the early modernists.

These critics shared much of Pound's low opinion of humanities university education in the USA and saw themselves as helping to launch a new era in which the example of the modernists both as critics and scholars would make the universities more vital centers of culture and learning. In this regard, the 1930s saw the arrival of a new kind of academic literary criticism with Eliot and Pound as its principal instigators. It was called the "new criticism" or occasionally the "new formalism." Cleanth Brooks, Robert Penn Warren, Blackmur, Ransom were at the forefront in the USA of this modernist legacy. New criticism dominated the academic study of English literature in American universities right up until the 1960s when it was supplanted by the great theory revolution we associate with the name of Jacques Derrida.

A second generation of poets also began to contact Pound during the 1920s and 1930s. Louis Zukofsky and his Objectivist colleagues, Basil Bunting, Ronald Duncan, Mary Barnard, and others looked to Pound for advice and help in getting their work published. In addition, as a great and innovative translator and adapter of the work of poets in ancient Greece and Rome, medieval Provence and Italy, and China and Japan, Pound was sought out by those involved in bringing over into English the great literary works in other languages. His detailed correspondence with W. H. D. Rouse on translating Homer and with Laurence Binyon on translating Dante can still be read with profit more than half a century later.

Of course, Pound did not only busy himself with writing letters to far-flung friends and colleagues. He published a collection of his literary essays in *Make It New* (1934) and four years later the pedagogic rant, *Guide to Kulchur*, an irritable (and some might say irritating) revaluation of Western cultural values. In addition, he continued to research and to write about economics as the Great Depression extended deep into the 1930s. Work on *The Cantos* continued and their publication as a sequence of "Some Length"[2] began with the appearance from Faber of *A Draft of xxx Cantos* in 1933. Groups of Cantos followed in relatively quick succession, *Eleven New Cantos, xxxi–xli* in 1934, the *Fifth Decad of Cantos* (1937), and *Cantos lii–lxxi* (1940). But if we gauge a writer's standing among his contemporaries by the alacrity with which his work is put into circulation, Pound's place in the literary pecking order in the 1920s and 1930s began to slip. The *enfant terrible* of the London years became the "lion in winter" of the Rapallo years. He was finding it more and more difficult to get his work noticed and sometimes even getting it published.[3]

These difficulties made for a fuming leitmotif in his correspondence. If it hadn't been for T. S. Eliot at Faber and Faber in London, and the rich, young, Harvard man James Laughlin who founded New Directions publishing as a venue for the new literature, Pound would have been limited to small, avant-garde publishing enterprises on the margins of a literary culture that by the 1930s and early 1940s was beginning to leave him behind. It is true that his espousal of an unorthodox economic system known as Social Credit did not help his cause. Coming at a time when a variety of economic panaceas, many of them decidedly the work of oddballs and ideologues, were being proposed to deal with the collapse of the global financial system during the Great Depression, Social Credit, for better or worse, was cast into the same crank mold. Even Pound's young American benefactor, "Jas" Laughlin, ended up ditching his mentor's economic theories and quipping that Pound the economist would not "lead the world," but perhaps Pound the poet could (*ASC*, 531).

Poetry, unfortunately, seemed the least of Pound's concerns in those years. He still worked away at *The Cantos* but the new ones after the first thirty seemed unable to sustain either the lyric radiance or the historical vigor of the earlier ones. The long stretches of fragments and quotations from documents, letters, and memoirs were occasionally vivified by lyric intensities that recalled the vibrancy of his best work from the London years. Canto xxxvi, "A lady asks me" – a marvelous translation of Guido Cavalcanti's "Donna me prega" – returns us for a moment to the Pound that excited a generation of poets hungry for the dawn of a new era. It is a fertile shower amidst the thirst-inducing aridity of, for example, "'Thou shalt not,' said Martin Van Buren, 'jail 'em for debt.' / 'that an immigrant shd. set out with good banknotes / and find 'em at the end of his voyage / but waste paper . . .'"(xxxvii/181). The attempt to catch the voice of a straight-talkin', cartoon frontiersman, "jail'em," etc. is mildly amusing at first but then little more than an annoying mannerism. He was still capable of wonderfully virile plangencies, such as the opening of Canto xxxix

> Desolate is the roof where the cat sat,
> Desolate is the iron rail that he walked
> And the corner post whence he greeted the sunrise.
> In hill path: "thkk, thgk"
>   of the loom
>   . . .
>   Fat panther lay by me
> Girls talked of fucking, beasts talked there of eating,
> All heavy with sleep, fucked girls and fat leopards,
> Lion's loggy with Circe's tisane . . .
>   (xxxix/193)

But this potency could just as easily go limp in lines that occasionally resemble badly recorded minutes from a very dull committee meeting:

> '62, report of committee:
> Profit on arms sold to the government: Morgan
> (Case 97) sold to the government the government's arms . . .

I mean the government owned'em already
at an extortionate profit
Dollars 160 thousand, one swat, to Mr. Morgan
for forcing up gold.   (XL/197)

There are probably no more beautiful Cantos in *The Fifth Decad* than XLIX, the Seven Lakes Canto (XLIX/244–5), and LI, "Shines / in the mind of God" (LI/250–2). But to follow up these triumphs with some nasty swipes at Jews in LII/257 and then pages and pages of ill-digested, barely coherent fragments drawn from the dynastic histories of China are a bit of a letdown. To then fuse a series of Cantos about the founding of the American republic via more documentary fragments that are cherry-picked to prop up Pound's own somewhat eccentric assignments of praise and blame, good guys against the bad, in early US history becomes increasingly tiresome. At one point in Canto LXX, the speaker asks, "Will the french refuse to receive Mr. Pinckney?" (LXX/409). The reader's response? Probably only a weary sigh and a whispered "who cares."

The fusing of Chinese and American history in *Cantos LII–LXXI* (1940) seems to effect an argument of considerable historical weight. But the argument is so well hidden from view by the approach that it required years and years of scholarly exegesis to bring it to the surface. The result? The disappointing discovery that there is no actual argument there at all, simply a series of quotations and references to shore up fixed ideas and prejudices in Pound's mind, ideas arrived at *a priori* rather than derived from the evidence to hand, and ideas, in fact, that no amount of contrary data could shake.

Pound's obsessive return to the political and economic issues that began to dominate his thinking from about the mid 1920s on erected a wall between the poet and his readers more impenetrable than even the cognitive detonations of *Blast*. The impenetrability of much of his thought was the result of his relative isolation from a vigorous daily dialogue with those who disagreed with him. Without the back and forth of argument, response, and reformulation, Pound's thought seemed more and more frozen and incomprehensible as the years passed. Contemporaries indulged him, some listened politely, some thought him comical, but very few paid him the serious attention he felt he deserved. F. R. Leavis, the Cambridge critic, famously opined in 1932 that no one need read Pound after *Hugh Selwyn Mauberley* (ASC, 469). Leavis, of course, was exaggerating, but as the Cantos appeared in the 1930s they were acknowledged by contemporaries and, then, often dismissed. Their descent into conspiratorial theories of economic and cultural history seemed more and more unbalanced. When embedded in poems, these seemed harmless enough, but in his prose works his eccentric theories led to more serious dismissals. His problem in finding a publisher for *Jefferson and/or Mussolini* might serve to illustrate the point. Was it simply the result of a conspiracy among financiers, liberals, and Jews to keep him out of print or was it primarily because the book is a farrago of balderdash, economic simplifications, and seething rage?

Faber and Faber did publish *Guide to Kulchur* in 1938, hoping that it might have the success of the earlier *ABC of Reading* (1934), a work that was more accessible and made a clear, defensible argument about what constituted excellence in verse composition. *Guide to Kulchur*, however, was another matter. The poet and translator Dudley Fitts found that the "scolding pitch" of the writing radiates the persona of "the bad boy strutting and shocking" (quoted in *ASC*, 543). The book's pedagogical promise vanishes in a cloud of rhetorical bluster and exaggeration ("Never in my 12 years in Gomorrah [London] on the Thames did I find an Englishman who knew anything" [*GK*, 280–1]). Many acute observations (see comments on Chaucer's "verbal melody," *GK*, 280–1) get lost in geysers of references and allusions that one could only accumulate by having done precisely the same reading as Pound for the previous twenty plus years.

To gain the maximum meaning from *Guide* a reader would need to have read not only Pound's own works but all of his favorite authors and authorities as well. And, beyond that, to independently come up with precisely Pound's own interpretations of what they had to say. In other words, the only competent reader of *Guide to Kulchur* was Pound himself. No wonder most of the responses to the book ended much like Dudley Fitts in amused and/or irritated mystification. After all, what could one make of the following, "An instant sense of proportion imperils financiers" (*GK*, 281)? In truth, what really imperils the freedom of financiers to enrich themselves and fleece their investors, as the Great Depression of 1929 and the more recent one in 2008–9 have shown, is a greater degree of government regulation, not a more acute aesthetic sensibility. Needless to say, *Guide to Kulchur* was not well received in its time and has been, as far as its "argument" is concerned, largely ignored subsequently. Yet it is an interesting document, a symptom of Pound's isolation in the years between London and Pisa, and a warning of what was to come during the war years.

The war in Europe did not at first affect Pound directly. He was still an American and the USA would not enter the war for two years after the start of hostilities in 1939. He tried to return to his homeland several times during this period but was stymied by bad timing, limited transport, and bureaucracy. When the USA did enter the war after Pearl Harbour, Pound suddenly found himself in very dangerous circumstances. As a US citizen in what was now enemy territory, he could not afford to take any risks. But he was never a risk-averse individual and he had developed not only a personal liking for Benito Mussolini, the Italian dictator, whom he met on one occasion for a half-hour chat (XLI/202) but also an ideological affinity as a political master and man of action. Pound was so convinced of Mussolini's superiority to the leaders of the democracies that he was intellectually self-immunized to resist the prevailing Western perception of the Italian "Boss" as a loud-mouthed buffoon.

The successes of Mussolini's fascist government in peacetime were almost immediately squandered by his ill-fated military campaigns in North Africa and against the Greeks. Unable and perhaps even unwilling to leave Italy and wanting to do his bit for the "Boss," Pound began to broadcast on Radio Rome. The talks were his typical jumble of economics, history, and literature, but now with a poisonous admixture of anti-Semitism and anti-Allied propaganda. When word got out that he was broadcasting from Rome, his US friends were deeply shocked and, some, like William Carlos Williams and Nancy Cunard, deeply angered.[4] Some were not surprised. His outbursts in the 1930s had become so erratic and extreme that this new turn of events was not out of character, or at least the character or caricature that he had become. It was, in effect, the last straw. In the years between the two wars, Pound had slowly alienated many of his former friends and colleagues, but with this new escapade, he was now more alone, more isolated, than at any time in his life. He even turned against his wife, Dorothy, when she dared to suggest to him that some of his radio talks seemed to lack coherence. Even his Italian hosts had their doubts; either he was deranged, they thought, or he was an American spy using his radio talks as a cover for espionage.

Even *The Cantos*, his *magnum opus*, did not escape the fray. Cantos LXXII and LXXIII were written in Italian during the war but were thought to be so infected with the poison of those years, especially LXXIII with its dreadful celebratory imagining of twenty Allied soldiers being led to their bloody deaths in a minefield by a peasant girl, that, for many years after, the two poems were missing from the sequence. The symbolism was apt: a ruptured text mirroring a ruptured life. One disfigurement leading to another. On Thursday May 3, 1945, while Pound was sitting quietly at his desk working on a translation of Confucius, two Italian partisans, probably young communists, arrived at his door and arrested him. They took him to the nearest American military post, which was in Lavagna, a small town near Rapallo, and handed him over to the US authorities. He had already been indicted for treason in Washington two years before. After some confusion among the American officers about who he was and what to do with him, it was decided he should be sent to the military detention center at Pisa. Act Three was about to begin.

NOTES

1 Returning to the United States remained a persistent theme. When moving from London to Paris, he considered gravitating "to a New York which wants me as little now as it did ten and fifteen years ago" (*SL*, 158).
2 *A Draft of* XVI *Cantos for the Beginning of a Poem of Some Length* (1925) was published by the Three Mountains Press in Paris, a small literary press operated by the American ex-pat William Bird. But it had limited circulation. Individual or small groups of Cantos had also been published in various small press editions and literary periodicals before 1933, but *A Draft of* XXX *Cantos* as a trade publication brought the sequence to a larger readership, although sales figures were never very high.
3 His brief Foreword to *Jefferson and / or Mussolini* (1935) tells the whole story: "The body of this ms. was written and left my hands in February 1933. 40 publishers have refused it. No typescript of mine has been read by so many people or brought me a more interesting correspondence." *Jefferson and / or Mussolini* (New York: Liveright Paperbound Edition, 1970), p. iv.
4 J. J. Wilhelm, *Ezra Pound: The Tragic Years, 1925–1972* (University Park: Pennsylvania State University Press, 1994), 195.

CHAPTER 41

Pound after Pisa: 1945–1972

Stephen Sicari

On May 3, 1945, American soldiers took Ezra Pound into custody and began the process that would bring him by the end of the month to the Detention Training Center outside of Pisa. According to his several biographers, Pound had spent the preceding months engaged in various propagandistic activities on behalf of the fascist cause, as if completely ignorant of the events signaling its imminent demise.[1] He even traveled to Salo (after a visit to his daughter Mary in Gais), where he met with the minister of foreign affairs for the puppet regime the Nazis had set up for Mussolini. Not only did he continue to write articles and pamphlets in support of the new government, he wrote letters to leading Salo officials and to Mussolini himself. He even went on the radio once more, this time in Milan, and wrote radio broadcasts for Milan radio even after he no longer was on the air himself. I sketch this "pre-Pisa" activity in order to underscore the depth of his commitment to Italian fascism in general, and to Mussolini in particular, right up to the moment of his arrest and internment in Pisa.

Mussolini was arrested and executed by Italian partisans in late April, and his body (as well as that of his mistress, Clara Petacci) was brought to Milan in the early hours of April 29, 1945, where they were hung by the feet from a scaffold in a brutal image of revenge. Only days later, on May 3, partisans arrested Pound and handed him over to American troops the following day. These two events – the very public death of Mussolini and Pound's more private incarceration – are nearly simultaneous, and they dominate the poems Pound writes while in custody at the Pisan Detention Training Center. In fact, the image of Mussolini's corpse famously opens these Cantos. For Pound, the death of Mussolini and the defeat of Italian fascism constitute "[t]he enormous tragedy of the dream" (LXXIV/445) and *The Pisan Cantos* may be read as the poet's attempt to continue his epic poem under radically new and enormously trying conditions. Pound does not relinquish his allegiance to the ideal of the fascist State, nor does he apologize for any of the views he has expressed, even those infamous tirades over Rome radio; but the poems written while in the Detention Training Center under arrest for treason do reflect a powerful and substantial shift toward the personal, and in this shift we may see a new poetic project unfolding.

The earliest reviews of *The Pisan Cantos* did not miss this fact, although it has taken decades to be fully appreciated. The dust jacket that accompanied the first editions explained to the potential reader that these poems are a "revelation of the poet's personal tragedy," and in his review from November 1948 Hugh Whittenmore noted that Pound, "having in fact despaired of his Program (without rejecting it for a minute)," can regard it now "with the kind of detachment so effective in his earlier treatment of reformers" (*EPCH*, 370). Pound indeed had been writing poems that can be considered a "Program" with a capital P, and Whittenmore's comment anticipates the careful and useful distinction Roger Griffen has recently made between two distinct types of modernism, "programmatic" modernism and "epiphanic" modernism. The former is categorized by its desire "to change society, to inaugurate a new epoch, to start time anew," while the latter focuses on "the cultivation of special moments, the spiritual kind with no revolutionary, epoch-making designs."[2] *The Cantos* up to Pisa may indeed be seen as perhaps the epitome of a "programmatic" modernism that, under the pressure both of the public fall of Mussolini and the personal threats against his life, undergoes reassessment.

The Pisan Cantos do indeed continue what we can call Pound's Enlightenment project, based as it is on the belief that the proper education can bring the alert reader to an understanding of basic economic and political truths the poet has already grasped. But the public and personal events have called into question the efficacy of rational thought and pedagogical commitment, and in these poems he situates himself squarely at the center of the project. No longer can he remain mainly behind the scenes, providing the reader with historical insights;[3] we must see the poet, this poet now turning sixty, with a name and a personal past and above all a unique and highly dramatic predicament, as he struggles to continue his poem. In bringing in the personal dimension in *The Cantos* so dramatically, these poems constitute a radical shift.

Which is why it was always a hard case to separate "Pound the poet from Pound the man,"[4] as so many defenders of *The Pisan Cantos* sought to do. Pound makes the case untenable by the daring presentation of himself as the organizing figure of the poems, having survived the wreckage of the war and struggling to maintain his status as poet of the dream, "now in the mind indestructible" (LXXIV/450). One of the most perceptive early reviews was by Robert Fitzgerald, who noticed that "in certain passages Pound is for the first time expressing a personal desolation and a kind of repentance, that is enormously moving: 'Tard, très tard, je t'ai connue la Tristesse / I had [*sic*] been hard as youth sixty years'" (*EPCH*, 363). This passage is a confession of personal culpability, of having been too hard, of not having compassion, of not having loved enough. It comes just after an immersion in which he "drinks of the bitterness" (LXXX/533) and feels that he has been overwhelmed by the tears he now sheds. And it comes just pages before one of the great lyric moments in the poem, which Fitzgerald also cites:

> What thou lovest well remains,
>   the rest is dross
> What thou lov'st well shall not be reft from thee
> What thou lov'st well is thy true heritage
>   (LXXXI/540–1)

This might indeed be the key to *The Pisan Cantos*, Pound's acknowledgement that he had been too hard in his thinking, that he had lacked compassion and had lacked love. In Pisa, under the enormous pressure of both personal and public disaster, he rewrites the cogito, so much at the heart of any Enlightenment project: now it's "Amo ergo sum, and in just that proportion" (LXXX/513).[5]

The Pisan Cantos were withheld for publication by James Laughlin until the summer of 1948, allowing some of the negative feelings against a poet accused of treason to fade. But public furor was ignited when the next year the Library of Congress awarded the first ever Bollingen Award, a national poetry award, to Pound for *The Pisan Cantos*. The awards committee was comprised of fifteen Fellows of the Library of Congress, and included eminent writers such as Eliot, Conrad Aiken, Allen Tate, Robert Lowell, Katherine Anne Porter, Theodore Spencer, and Louis Martz. Part of the announcement of the award read, "To permit other considerations than that of poetic achievement would destroy the significance of the award and would in principle deny the validity of that objective perception of value on which civilized society must rest." A special symposium in *Partisan Review* in May 1949 allowed other eminent writers of the day – among them W.H. Auden, Clement Greenberg, and George Orwell – a public forum where they could attack the Fellows for awarding the prize to a poet who had espoused vicious anti-Semitic views. Later that year, *Poetry* issued a pamphlet defending the award, which included a letter written by John Berryman and signed by seventy-three equally prominent figures.

So fierce and public was the controversy that the government refused to issue a second award, and Yale University took over the Bollingen in 1949. Pound was for a while front-page news.

At the heart of the controversy was whether one can separate politics from poetry, whether one can read these poems in particular without attention to the writer's loud, frequent, and very public views on matters such as banking practices, the Axis nations, and a world-wide conspiracy of the Jews against Western civilization. A review from September 1949 struggles to make this attempt:

> We must forget Pound's politics and his war-record; we must also forget his disagreeable personality on paper, his cockiness and offensiveness, his pretences to scholarship of which he is almost totally deficient (even in *Pisan Cantos* most of the Greek quotations are ungrammatical), his contempt for anything that might be thought pretty or warm-hearted or ordinarily human. If we can make this effort, we may turn to *Pisan Cantos*. (*EPCH*, 373)

But such a separation is not possible in Pound's case, if it is ever possible for any poet under any circumstances; for the point of these Cantos is for Pound to emerge still intact after the public and personal failures he had experienced, still recording fascist slogans as models for future activism (" 'wherein is no responsible person / having a front name, a hind name, and address' / 'not a right but a duty' / those words still stand uncancelled," LXXVIII/499). He may indeed be "a man on whom the sun has gone down" but one still called upon to record the dream "now in the mind indestructible" (LXXIV/450). No one, perhaps with the exception of Dante, has so intertwined poetry and politics as has Pound, and no poem has made more of its writer's political views and politically determined fate as has *The Pisan Cantos*.[6] No poet to my knowledge ever made his own personal predicament, which was after all a consequence of his political views, so much a part of the poems he wrote. Any attempt to disentangle the personal from the political does injustice to the poem. William Carlos Williams, in a review from Spring 1949, saw how the two are inextricably linked and offered this melodramatic compromise: "Give him the prize and hang him if you like, but give him the prize" (*EPCH*, 372).

Much had happened to Pound between his internment in Pisa and the Bollingen controversy. Pound left Pisa on November 16, 1945 and arrived in Washington, DC two days later, where he was incarcerated as lawyers and psychiatrists met to determine his fate. A few days before Christmas he was remanded to Howard Hall, the prison ward of St. Elizabeth's hospital, where he came under the care of Dr Winfred Overholser, an eminent psychiatrist who had much to do with keeping Pound from ever standing trial for treason[7] and who in 1947 was able to get Pound transferred from the "hell hole" of Howard Hall to the much more humane setting of the Chestnut Ward, where Pound could be said to have actually flourished, as Nadel contends.[8] There was a tremendous outpouring of published material, both old and new, in these years: in addition to revising *The Pisan Cantos*, Pound was able to finish his work on Confucius, published in 1947; a new and enlarged edition of *Personae* appeared, as did *Selected Poems*; Harcourt Brace published *The Letters of Ezra Pound*, edited by D.D. Paige, in 1950; a new edition of *Guide to Kulchur* was published in 1952; and in 1953 *The Translations of Ezra Pound* and in 1954 *Literary Essays of Ezra Pound* were published. New sections of *The Cantos* also appeared: in 1955 *Section: Rock-Drill* and in 1959, the year after his release, *Thrones de los Cantares*. All this production, which was widely and often positively reviewed, did much to rehabilitate Pound's reputation after the scandal of his arrest and incarceration.

Two items apart from the new Cantos deserve special attention for their role in this calculated project of rehabilitation. T.S. Eliot edited and wrote the introduction to *Literary Essays*, and the collection of his literary criticism did much to remind the world of Pound's famed ability to see and promote others' talent, as well as his role in having shaped modernist poetics. Eliot's introduction was useful propaganda in the mission to rehabilitate Pound: "I hope . . . that this volume will demonstrate that Pound's literary criticism is the most important contemporary criticism of its kind . . . Pound has said much . . . that is permanently valid and useful. Very few critics have done that" (*LE*, 10). Much of the critical reception to this volume followed Eliot's lead. Charles Tomlinson begins his review in the February number of the *Spectator* with the assertion that "Our debt to the greatness and generosity of Ezra Pound is a vast one and in the essays on his contemporaries in this volume we are reminded of it most forcibly" (*EPCH*, 422). Roy Fuller castigates Pound's criticism as "repetitive, narrow, often annoying, ill-considered, and rude, sometimes dated, egotistic" but can, just a paragraph later, find something to praise: "It is from Pound . . . that the hard, sharp critical view has stemmed in the last thirty years" (*EPCH*, 430–1). In 1966, reviewing another book of essays (*Ezra Pound Perspectives*), Louis Simpson sums up the way Pound was coming to be viewed as a critic: Pound's "ideas are responsible for most of the good writing in verse in the 20th century, and for a good deal of the prose too" (*EPCH*, 466).

Perhaps as important as anything published in Pound's name in this part of his life was the appearance in 1951 of the first major scholarly account of Pound's work, Hugh Kenner's *The Poetry of Ezra Pound*.[9] Kenner was able to bring a critical approach to Pound's poetry, especially *The Cantos*, that allowed other scholars to begin serious appreciation of the body of his work.[10] James Laughlin reflects in an introduction he writes for a reprinting of Kenner's book, "it was the beginning, and the catalyst, for a change in attitude toward Pound on the American literary and educational scenes"; "I can't *prove* that it was *The Poetry of Ezra Pound* that turned the tide for Pound, but I think it was."[11] By the end of the decade there were other scholarly treatises on Pound, as well as the *Annotated Index to The Cantos of Ezra Pound*. What the Bollingen prize could not do these efforts accomplished: it now seemed possible again to sever the politics from the poetry, or at least the man from the poet. The Pound industry had begun.

Meanwhile, Pound had continued to work steadily on *The Cantos*, and in 1955 *Section: Rock-Drill* was published. As critics have long noticed, having access to the Library of Congress allowed him to renew his research on historical and economic themes, and the sheer amount of historical material in this and the following section – *Thrones de los Cantares*, mostly written in St. Elizabeths but published in 1959, the year after his release – is new even for this poem. But it would be an error to see these late Cantos as a simple return to his former project, for both in the method of presentation and in the foregrounding of a visionary capacity on the poet's part, these sections have more in common with *The Pisan Cantos* than the earlier sequences. A. Alvarez, in a review from 1957, noted the new method and even seemed to be using Kenner's insights to explain it:

As the work has grown, the references . . . have become more and more condensed and oblique. In the beginning Pound used the method of the ideogram as a shorthand to save himself a great deal of tedious explanation. By the time he reached *The Pisan Cantos* the shorthand had become a code; the ideograms had broken down into heaps of fragmentary half-references. Now, in the opening cantos of *Rock-Drill*, the obliqueness has led him to the disappearing-point of poetry. (*EPCH*, 442)

Donald Davie invites certain readers "to write him off again" because "much of the new sequence of eleven cantos presents Pound at his most forbidding, stringing together 'gists' from unfamiliar works that he thinks wrongly neglected" (*EPCH*, 443). But Davie ends his review with what might be considered the challenge to readers of *The Cantos*: "In short, the great gamble continues. The method is being pressed to its logical conclusion. Either this is a waste of a prodigious talent, or else it is the poetry of the future" (*EPCH*, 444).

Such comments seem important in assessing how critical reception was being shaped by the various efforts aimed at rehabilitating Pound's reputation: even those who were highly dubious of what Pound was now doing felt obligated to give him the benefit of the doubt and search out something deeper or more worthwhile in what might have otherwise been dismissed as an overwhelming jumble of oblique references to unimportant texts. Delmore Schwartz, reviewing *Thrones* in late 1959, calls the new sequence "self-indulgent and personal in the worst way" (*EPCH*, 449); nevertheless, he hastens to praise the poem in a way that tries to see deeply the implications of Pound's method:

it must immediately be added that what is bad and self-indulgent . . . is inseparable from Pound's poetic genius at its best: in other passages, the suddenness of transition and apparent randomness of historical juxtaposition and range are necessary to create the historical perspective of the Cantos, the sense that all history is relevant to any moment of history, and the profound belief that the entire past, at any moment and in any place, is capable of illuminating the present and the whole nature of historical experience. (*EPCH*, 450)

It seems important to note that, as the poem became increasingly difficult and more susceptible to being dismissed as the work of someone officially deemed mentally incompetent, important readers, such as Davie and Schwartz, worked harder than ever to understand and learn from it. The reputation of *The Cantos*, and its author, now seemed secure.

Pound was finally released from St. Elizabeths on May 7, 1958 and arrived back in Italy to stay with his daughter Mary in Brunnenburg on July 9. But this change in circumstances did not bring peace or happiness to the aging poet. His personal life became infinitely more complicated, with Dorothy now competing for his attention with Olga and Mary (and for a time with a young woman who was acting as an aid and secretary to the poet, Marcella Spann, as well). His physical health began breaking down, and he became visibly depressed, manifested most dramatically in his descent into an almost utter silence. Pound was able to work slowly and sporadically on some new poetic material for *The Cantos*, but no definitive version of these late poems was ever published.[12] Pound sent two separately edited groups of Cantos from draft material to Donald Hall, who had offered Pound payment for an interview if the poet allowed *The Paris Review* to publish new material. Hall lent his copy of the sequence of poems to a graduate student, which then eventually surfaced as a pirated edition of *Cantos 110–116* published in 1967 by the FuckYou / Press. This then led James Laughlin to write to Pound for an authorized edition, and after some difficult exchanges between the poet and the publisher *Drafts*

& Fragments eventually appeared with the New Directions imprint in 1969. Even then, there was still confusion about the way the sequence was arranged, especially about what should constitute the final words of this seemingly interminable poem. Nadel summarizes the problem, "*Drafts and Fragments* remains the least authorial sanctioned portion of the poem; not even the title was Pound's choice."[13]

The poems of this last sequence may not bring *The Cantos* to any clear or certain closure, but they do provide a final assessment of some of the purposes of the poem, as well as a towering sense of haunting grandeur as the poem does finally come to an end. Perhaps the clearest and most powerful moment of retrospection occurs in Canto CXVI:

> but about that terzo
> > third heaven,
> > > that Venere,
> again is all "paradiso"
> > a nice quiet paradise
> > > over the shambles,
> and some climbing
> > before the take-off,
> to "see again,"
> the verb is "see," not "walk on"
> i.e. it coheres all right
> > even if my notes do not cohere.
> > > (CXVI/816–17)

The error was that he had tried to make an earthly paradise to walk on, a utopian project that led him to an engagement with reactionary politics; the proper poetic goal was visionary, bringing the reader to see glimpses of heaven. The poem may have become a jumble of notes that do not cohere, but paradise coheres; it's there to be seen and *The Cantos* can be said to have achieved moments of sublimity if the reader has had such glimpses.

Different final lines have "ended" *The Cantos*: a poem originally titled "Canto CXX" told us clearly that he had "tried to write Paradise" and asked for forgiveness from those he loves for what he had made (notes for Canto CXVII *et seq.*, 822); another ending presented a poignant plea that humanity make the effort "To be men not destroyers" (823); followed by a fragment in memory of Olga Rudge that ends with these words:

> These lines are for the
> > ultimate CANTO
> whatever I may write
> > in the interim.
> [*24 August 1966*] (824)

The case may be made for any of these endings as appropriate, but the present configuration has the virtue of acknowledging that *The Cantos* may have no logical ending while at the same time insisting on a most personal final gesture.

The year before Pound's death Hugh Kenner published *The Pound Era*, a masterful account of literary modernism as best approached with Pound at its center. And in 1972, Pound died and *Paideuma* ("a journal devoted to Pound scholarship") was born, signaling a new phase in the history of the poet's place in the academy, a place that at his death was perhaps the highest it would ever be.

NOTES

1 For the biographical information in this chapter I rely on John Tytell's *Ezra Pound: The Solitary Volcano* (New York: Doubleday, 1987); C. David Heymann's *Ezra Pound: The Last Rower* (New York: Seaver Books, 1977); and Ira B. Nadel's *Ezra Pound: A Literary Life* (New York: Palgrave Macmillan, 2004).

2 Roger Griffen, *Modernism and Fascism* (New York: Palgrave Macmillan, 2007), 62.

3 There are a handful of exceptions in the pre-Pisa Cantos where Pound does present himself: in Canto III on the Dogana's steps attaining a vision of the gods and goddesses who "float in the azure air"; in Canto XXII, where he recalls an interview he and Major Douglas had with John Maynard Keynes on economics, a conversation which ended in his exasperated exclamation, "Jesus Christo!/ Standu nel paradiso terrestre / Pensando come si fesse compagna d'Adamo!!"; and in Canto XLVI, where he presents himself as a detective on a case searching for evidence against the usurers. These are so few that they stand in stark contrast to the Cantos written in Pisa, where a page does not go by without a depiction of the poet and his predicament.

4 This is a phrase from the note to the 1950 edition of the Modern Library's *Anthology of Famous English and American Poetry* that explained why it was now including some poems by Pound after having delightedly kept them out from the first edition. See Heymann, *Ezra Pound*, 217–18.

5 As Ira B. Nadel reports, "when Pound could order his own stationery in 1946, printed as a crescent at the top was this statement: 'J'AYME DONC JE SUIS' ('I love, therefore I am')" (Nadel, *Ezra Pound, A Literary Life*, 170).

6 Malcolm Cowley argued, in a review entitled "The Battle over Ezra Pound," published in *The New Republic* in Fall 1949, that the Fellows did not intend to advance "the false principle that art is entirely separate from life." Rather, they simply exercised poor judgement in awarding the Bollingen prize to *The Pisan Cantos* because the poem is "spoiled work" and "the weakest of his books, the most crotchety and maundering." "My chief grievance against the Fellows is that by giving a prize to Pound they forced him back into the limelight, thus destroying the symmetry and perfect justice of his fate." Nonetheless, Cowley registers grudging respect for the Fellows for battling the tendency in

the postwar period to award inferior writers for merely being what we have learned to call "politically correct": "Too many second-rate authors had been given prizes for expressing right opinions . . . The Fellows insisted that there are other virtues in literary works than those of the good citizen." It seems fitting that Pound was the lightning-rod for a controversy over such issues and a powerful test for the New Criticism.

7 E. Fuller Torrey rather famously takes Overholser to task in *The Roots of Treason* (New York: Harcourt Brace Jovanovich, 1984), arguing forcefully but hardly objectively that Pound should have stood trial and been found guilty.

8 Nadel, *Ezra Pound: A Literary Life*, 165.

9 Hugh Kenner, *The Poetry of Ezra Pound* (New York: New Directions, 1951).

10 For instance, Kenner in *The Pound Era* devotes three chapters to the ideogram in Pound's work, advancing a way of understanding Pound's experimental method that would soon become axiomatic in Pound studies.

11 Introduction to Kenner, *The Poetry of Ezra Pound*, xii, xiii.

12 Ronald Bush gives the definitive account of the publication history of *Drafts and Fragments* in his essay on "Late Cantos LXXII–CXVII", in *CCEP*, 109–38. In *Ezra Pound: A Literary Life*, Nadel also recounts the story, and I rely on his version for the summary here.

13 Nadel, *Ezra Pound: A Literary Life*, 184.

CHAPTER 42

Influence

James Longenbach

"I have done more log rolling and attending to other people's affairs, Joyce, Lewis, Gaudier, etc. (don't regret it)," wrote Pound to Margaret Anderson, the editor of the *Little Review* in 1921. "But I am in my own small way, a writer myself" (*EPLR*, 266).

This is not a tone one often hears from the mastermind of the Great English Vortex, who thought of himself as an inventor, an instigator, an artist who caused the careers of other artists to flourish because he himself was flourishing. But by the time his London years were drawing to a close (he would move to Paris at the end of 1920), Pound was deeply worried that he was known not primarily as an artist but as a patron, a facilitator, an influencer. Although he had offered crucial aesthetic and economic support to T. S. Eliot, Ford Madox Ford, H. D., Robert Frost, James Joyce, Wyndham Lewis, Marianne Moore, William Carlos Williams, and W. B. Yeats, his early *Cantos* were languishing.

"I am wracked by the seven jealousies," wrote Pound to Eliot after they had worked together on the manuscript of *The Waste Land*, "and cogitating an excuse for always exuding my deformative secretions in my own stuff, and never getting an outline" (*SL*, 169). Eliot took pains to honor Pound's crucial contribution to *The Waste Land*, not only dedicating the poem to him but with the phrase "*il miglior fabbro*" (the phrase Dante used to describe the Provençal poet Arnaut Daniel) associating Pound with an artist whom Pound himself considered one of the greatest inventors in Western literature. Privately, however, Eliot was worried. "He is becoming forgotten," he wrote of Pound to a mutual friend. "I am worried as to what is to become of him."[1]

What became of Pound is all too familiar. Given the political and moral debacle of his later years along with the intractable difficulty of the later *Cantos*, many people have latched onto the legend of Pound's generosity. To remember how he rejuvenated the careers of older writers whom he revered (Yeats and Ford), hustled endlessly for writers who were his contemporaries (Eliot and Joyce), and offered unstinting support to younger writers who learned, however equivocally, from his work (Oppen and Hemingway) is to find a way to feel good about Pound. And such generosity, however compromised by self-promotion or self-blindness, deserves our admiration. But we also need to be wary of the slightly too available legend of Pound's generosity, for behind it lurks a small voice only occasionally willing to admit that "I am in my own small way, a writer myself." The dynamic of Pound's influence is not easily described in general terms, for it took different shapes with different writers, and those shapes were sometimes occluded by the very generosity for which Pound remains so well known.

Pound himself was in large part responsible for the creation of the nearly mythic sense of his importance to other writers; many passages in *The Pisan Cantos* look back to his associations with a variety of artists from his London years, some prominent, some obscure.

> Lordly men are to earth o'ergiven
> 　　　　these the companions:
> Fordie that wrote of giants
> 　　　and William who dreamed of nobility
> 　　　　　and Jim the comedian singing:
> 　　　"Blarrney castle me darlin'
> 　　　　you're nothing now but a Stowne"
> and Plarr talking of mathematics
> or Jepson lover of jade
> Maurie who wrote historical novels
> And Newbolt who looked twice bathed
> are to earth o'ergiven.
>
> 　　　　　　　　(LXXIV/452–33)

The brief accounts of these companions are meticulous: Yeats was of course everywhere preoccupied with nobility, Ford quite literally wrote about giants, Joyce was renowned for his fine tenor voice, and one assumes that the qualities associated with Victor Plarr, Edgar Jepson, Maurice Hewlett, and Henry Newbolt are chosen with similar precision. Most tellingly precise is the line that frames this passage – "Lordly men are to earth o'ergiven" – a line Pound quotes from his own translation from the Anglo-Saxon "Seafarer," first published in London in 1911. Pound the influencer, the companion of the living, was also Pound the influenced, the companion of the dead, and he wants his readers to remember him as the central vehicle through which the past was made new. Whatever his political failures, whatever the ultimate value of his work, he wants to be remembered as the maker of modernism. Hugh Kenner, Pound's greatest critic, expanded this sense of Pound's importance into *The Pound Era* (1971), one of the very few works of literary criticism that offers the permanent seduction of a work of art, regardless of the plausibility of its conclusions.

Today, few people would position Pound quite so centrally in modernist literature, if only because we now see modernism as a much larger and more conflicted arena, an arena that rightly includes artists whom Pound disdained or was ignorant of. Not even Robert Frost, whom Pound respected, has a place in *The Pound Era*, much less Gertrude Stein, Wallace Stevens, or Jean Toomer. But the need to preserve Pound's position as a centralizing figure – Pound's own need – remains fascinating; the need is itself one of the many overdetermined factors that come together to make what we think of, less confidently than Kenner might have, as literary modernism.

Even as a very young man, Pound craved the aura of the impresario. While still a student at the University of Pennsylvania, he exerted considerable power over his friends Hilda Doolittle (whom he would christen H. D. in *Poetry* magazine) and William Carlos Williams. And as Pound's work developed over the next decade, these poets followed, torquing Pound's imagism to their own needs. Williams, who began writing poems that sounded like the weakest possible imitations of Pre-Raphaelite imitations of Keats –

> I've fond anticipation of a day
> O'erfilled with pure diversion presently,
> For I must read a lady poesy
> The while we glide by many a leafy bay[2]

– was transformed by the example of Pound's imagist work, especially his insistence that poets must adhere to a "direct treatment of the 'thing'" (*LE*, 3):

> It was an icy day.
> We buried the cat,
> then took her box
> and set match to it
> in the back yard.
> Those fleas that escaped
> earth and fire
> died by the cold.[3]

This poem, "Complete Destruction," does not sound at all like Pound, but it exists not only because of the polemical power of Pound's imagist manifestoes but more precisely because of the charismatic example of Pound's imagist poems. Yet by the time Williams published it in *Sour Grapes* in 1921, imagism was for Pound a thing of the past. What was a phase for Pound became a career-long mission for Williams, since he connected imagist concision (as Pound did not) to a sense of domestic locality, the pared-down language in service of a sensibility that honored American locality. "No ideas but in things," intoned Williams in *Paterson*, the long poem that constitutes his response to the *Cantos*.[4]

"I am late at my singing," said Williams in the first poem in *Sour Grapes*.[5] Williams lived his entire life feeling that he was catching up to Pound, whose ministrations to Williams never lost a faintly pedagogical taint. With other writers, however, Pound's desire to make himself indispensable took different forms – most prominently with writers whose reputations he coveted, writers who made Pound himself feel like a late singer. "He is full of the middle ages and helps me to get back to the definite and the concrete away from modern abstractions," wrote Yeats about Pound in 1913. "All becomes clear and natural. Yet in his own work he is very uncertain, often very bad though very interesting sometimes."[6]

For many years this statement played a prominent role in the stories that got told about modern poetry, especially those stories that depended on the polemical notion that modern poetry represented an improvement over Victorian poetry. Having been born in 1865, two decades earlier than Pound, Eliot, or Joyce, Yeats supposedly had to be dragged into the twentieth century. Neither was he strong enough to drag himself: Pound supposedly applied the muscle, pushing the dreamy Yeats toward a starker, meaner sound. But while Pound did make some minor revisions in poems that Yeats had submitted to *Poetry* magazine late in 1912, Yeats himself called the changes "misprints – Ezra's fault."[7] A transformation of style is not based on misprints. Yet Yeats' praise of Pound's editorial acumen (along with his justly negative assessment of Pound's early poems) sounds sincere. How should Pound's influence on Yeats properly be described?

When Pound first arrived in London in 1908, he considered Yeats the greatest living poet, a poet who stood above the contemporary scene as Theocritus stood above Alexandria. Pound still believed that Yeats' crowning achievement was *The Wind among the Reeds* (1899), but when Pound was finally introduced to Yeats in 1909, he met a different poet, the poet soon to publish *The Green Helmet and Other Poems*, a poet whose stark new style baffled most readers. In "Reconciliation," one of these shockingly new poems, Yeats addresses his long-time love-interest Maud Gonne, suggesting that her repeated rejection of him had produced the new barrenness of his verse.

> Some may have blamed you that you took away
> The verses that could move them on the day
> When, the ears being deafened, the sight of the eyes blind
> With lightning, you went from me, and I could find
> Nothing to make a song about but kings,
> Helmets, and swords, and half-forgotten things.[8]

These lines feel willfully condensed, at war with their own formal expectations, argumentative rather than suggestive – the kind of writing that Pound would soon champion himself. But when Pound first read "Reconciliation," he was writing poems that sound like weak imitations of the early Yeats, the dreamy poems of *The Wind among the Reeds*. Pound wrote excitedly that Yeats had "come out of the shadows & has declared for life. Of course there is in that a tremendous uplift for me – for he and I are now as it were in one movement, with aims very nearly identical" (*EP/MC* 41).

Yeats' transformation transformed Pound in turn – not only stylistically but emotionally, since the younger poet felt suddenly that he was participating in an unprecedented moment in literary culture. In response to Yeats' poem, Pound quickly wrote a poem called "The Fault of It," quoting the first line of "Reconciliation" as an epigraph ("Some may have blamed you –") before declaring his allegiance with the new Yeats.

> Some may have blamed us that we cease to speak
> Of things we spoke of in our verses early,
> Saying: a lovely voice is such and such;
> Saying: that lady's eyes were sad last week,
> Wherein the world's whole joy is born and dies;
> Saying: she hath this way or that, this much
> Of grace, this little misericorde;
> Ask us no further word;
> If we were proud, then proud to be so wise
> Ask us no more of all the things ye heard;
> We may not speak of them, they touch us nearly.
> (*CEP*, 207)

Pound's diction is not yet as concrete as Yeats', his syntax not yet as pressurized; but what was for Yeats a personal transformation became, in Pound's adoption of its metaphors, the beginning of the larger conundrum we now call modernism: Yeats' "I" became Pound's "we." If Pound was in a few years able to push Yeats toward the definite and the concrete, he was able to do so because Yeats had already shown him how.

Even when Pound mocked the early Yeats in his imagist poems, turning on familiar lines from "The Lake Isle of Innisfree" –

> O God, O Venus, O Mercury, patron of thieves,
> Give me in due time, I beseech out, a little tobacco-shop,
> With the little bright boxes
> piled up neatly upon the shelves.
>
> (*P*, 1990, 121)

– he was nonetheless expressing his deep camaraderie with the new Yeats, the Yeats who turned against himself more violently than any subsequent poet could turn against him. Pound's influence on Yeats was conducted on psychically complicated levels, not merely on the level of style alone, for what Pound gave Yeats was an image of himself in a younger artist – a feeling that he shared something with a generation of artists whose work he did not always understand: an adamant disregard for expectation, a refusal to countenance the accepted terms of taste. Yeats' "Reconciliation" feels both tender and arrogant in its stalwart defense of change, and Pound echoed this tonal complexity through the imagist manifestoes and poems: "Will people accept them? / (i.e. these songs)," begins the first poem in *Lustra* (*P*, 1990, 83).

Pound himself thought about influence in a classical way: an artist cultivates his influences, imitating important models, gathering the past around him in order to honor it by changing it, making it new. But Pound's relationship with Yeats actually adheres to the pattern of romantic influence described most profoundly by Harold Bloom in *The Anxiety of Influence* and other related books.[9] As Williams was to Pound (a belated poet always catching up to a grandeur he could never quite match), so was Pound to Yeats. Pound would not have described the relationship with Yeats in this way, but his inability truly to perceive his relationship with his precursor is an integral part of the dynamic of influence itself. Neither was Yeats any more capable of accurate perception in this regard. "What is astonishing is that you do not see what Ezra is to you," wrote a mutual friend in 1916.[10]

With T. S. Eliot (a poet who was neither Pound's malleable junior, like Williams, nor Pound's august senior, like Yeats) Pound achieved a more equitable exchange, a literary relationship that was for a brief time conducted truly on the level of diction, rhythm, and syntax – without those poetic elements standing for the terms of power and prestige. Pound first met Eliot in 1915, and (as would so often be the case with artists he admired) Pound shepherded most of Eliot's early poems into print; he also concocted far-fetched schemes attempting to ameliorate Eliot's financial situation. But it was not until early in 1922, when Eliot handed over to Pound the chaotic manuscript of the poem that would become *The Waste Land*, that Pound exerted his most profound and long-lasting influence – an influence long-lasting not only for Eliot but for modern and postmodern literature at large.

As is well known, Pound persuaded Eliot to cut fully a third of what was then called *He Do the Police in Different Voices*; three long narrative passages were scuttled, and, more importantly, the remaining parts of the poem became increasingly fragmentary, so that *The Waste Land* emerged not a sequence of discrete poems (like Tennyson's *In Memoriam* or even Pound's own *Hugh Selwyn Mauberley*) but as an expression of what the critic Roland Barthes would call the "syntagmatic" imagination, a poem "whose fabrication, by arrangement of discontinuous and mobile elements, constitutes the spectacle itself."[11]

For instance, when we reach these lines in the second movement of *The Waste Land*, "A Game of Chess" –

> "Do
> "You know nothing? Do you see nothing? Do you remember
> "Nothing?"
> > I remember
> Those are pearls that were his eyes.[12]

– our attention is drawn to the line quoted from *The Tempest* (and its suggestion of the possibility of resurrection and transfiguration) because we recall its earlier appearance in the Madame Sosostris passage in "The Burial of the Dead": "Those are pearl that were his eyes." The connection is associational, a matter of considering the implications of connections made both within and without the poem.

But had Eliot retained an earlier version of these lines –

> I remember
> The hyacinth garden. Those are pearls that were his eyes, yes![13]

– the connection would be made on the level of narrative, since we would be encouraged to think of the "I" speaking these lines as the same "I" that could not speak to his beloved in the hyacinth garden in "The Burial of the Dead." This particular excision from the manuscript of *The Waste Land* was Eliot's doing, but as Pound and Eliot worked together on the manuscript, Pound pushed Eliot to cut the suggestion of such continuities from *The*

Waste Land. The poem would not be bound together by narrative tissue
or continuity of voice, and neither would the negotiation of the poem's
variously juxtaposed pieces be aided by a strong sense of the boundaries of
those pieces.

Pound did admit, when Eliot completed *The Waste Land*, that he was
jealous; he had been unable to achieve such integrity of form in his own
long poem. But it's telling that Pound could make this statement; he never
openly expressed jealousy of Yeats or Joyce, whose achievements were to
him far more overwhelming. For by working on Eliot's long poem, Pound
was in fact working on his own: having helped Eliot to see how the structure
of a long poem could depend on discretely interconnected fragments, a
structure that becomes apparent not immediately but over time, Pound
returned to the languishing Cantos. He added two crucial lines to the
end of Canto IV – "And we sit here . . . / there in the arena" (IV/16) –
as if to emphasize that he had witnessed the Canto's concatenation of
historical events. Then, adopting the structural procedures he'd developed
while working on the manuscript of *The Waste Land*, he repeated versions
of these lines in Canto XI – "I have sat here / For forty four thousand
years" (XI/ 50) – and again in Canto XII – "And we sit here / under the
wall" (XII/ 53). These procedures would help to determine the shape of
subsequent long poems not only by Williams, H. D., George Oppen,
and Lorine Niedecker, poets who have a place in *The Pound Era*, but
also poets whom we don't so readily associate with a Poundian tradition,
poets like John Berryman, Charles Wright, and Adrienne Rich. Even more
profoundly, Pound discovered the shape of his own work through the task
of influencing the work of other people.

As a result, Pound's influence on subsequent writers is often filtered
through the work of other writers whose work he helped to shape, particularly Eliot's. For while it's often said that *The Waste Land* is a hierarchical,
myth-centered poem, it was at the time of its conception the most radically decentered poem that had ever been written, thanks in part to Pound.
Listen to the opening lines of a poem written self-consciously in its wake.

> The
> Voice of Jesus I. Rush singing
>   in the wilderness
> A boy's best friend is his mother,
> It's your mother all the time.
> Residue of Oedipus-faced wrecks
> Creating out of the dead, –
> From the candle flames of the souls of dead mothers

Vide the legend of thin Christ sending her out of the temple, –
Books from the stony heart, flames rapping the stone,
Residue of self-exiled man
By the Tyrrhenian.
            Paris.
But everywhere only the South Wind, the sirocco, the broken Earth-face.
The broken Earth-face, the age demands an image of its life and contacts,
Lord, lord, not that we pray, are sure of the question,
But why are our finest always dead?[14]

These are the opening lines of Louis Zukofsky's *Poem beginning "The"* (1928). Line by line, the poem leaps, folds back on itself, simultaneously establishing tentative lines of continuity while also disrupting them. The poem lurches from the lyrical to the broadly comic, from high to low, spooky to dorky. Zukofsky's notes for just these opening lines of *Poem beginning "The"* send us to Sophocles, Aldous Huxley, James Joyce, Norman Douglas, the Bible, and popular songs. Zukofsky also refers to Pound's *Hugh Selwyn Mauberley* ("the age demands an image of its life and contacts"), but *Poem beginning "The"* is not, like *Mauberley*, a sequence of well-made individual poems. A few lines later, the poem references Zukofsky's crucial, more challenging model: "And why if the waste land has been explored, traveled over, circumscribed, / Are there only wrathless skeletons exhumed new planted in its sacred wood."[15]

Zukofsky wanted his readers to think of his poem as a corrective response to *The Waste Land*. But however different Zukofsky's vision may be from Eliot's, especially in its inclusion of ethnic and social tones to which Eliot was deaf, Zukofsky's formal procedures are unthinkable without Eliot's precedent. At the time Zukofsky was writing *Poem beginning "The,"* Pound's *Cantos* had not yet accrued the prestige or widespread circulation of *The Waste Land*, so Pound's influence spread to later writers in part through Eliot's achievement. Because of the ways in which the literary history of modernism usually gets told, however, we assume that Zukofsky's project is merely opposed to Eliot's, but in fact, Zukofsky's difference from Eliot is the mark of his debt not only to Eliot but also to Pound.

"The success of *The Cantos*," says the contemporary poet Charles Bernstein, "is that its coherence is of a kind totally different than Pound desired or could – in his more rigid moments – accept. For the coherence of the 'hyperspace' of Pound's modernist collage is not a predetermined Truth of a pancultural elitism but a product of a compositionally decentered multiculturalism."[16] A similar argument could be made about *The Waste Land*, and the task of poets devoted to both Pound and Eliot has been to discover ways of harnessing their formal innovations without necessarily reinforcing their ideological positions. The more bombastic and sometimes offensive passages of *The Cantos* are as crucial to the poem's effect as its passages of lyric beauty: the power of the poem depends on the interaction of these different kinds of language, the choices that such interaction provides for a reader. And a poet like Zukofsky, while in no way sharing Pound's convictions, wanted similarly to create poems that allow readers to discover their own way through a barrage of strategically conflicted kinds of language.

But not every poet open to Pound's influence has chosen – or has needed to choose – to replicate this high-wire heteroglossia. Listen to Charles Wright, who began to write poetry in the 1950s when he began reading Pound.

> The limbs of a leafless chestnut tree are back-combed by the wind.
> The English mind, he said, the cold soup of the English mind.
> At Pisa it all came back
> > in a different light
> In the wind-sear and sun-sear of the death cages,
> Remembering Christmases in the country, the names
> Of dead friends in the Tuscan twilight
> > building and disappearing across the sky.
> Cold soup, cold soup,
> Longwater color of pewter,
> > late grass green neon.[17]

Walking through Kensington, where Pound lived during his London years, Wright remembers how Pound remembered, recalling those passages in *The Pisan Cantos* in which Pound intoned the names of his dead friends: Ford, Yeats, Joyce, Plarr, Jepson, Hewlett, Newbolt – "Lordly men are to earth o'ergiven." More profoundly, Wright's image-littered, spondee-freighted line is derived from Pound's ("In the wind-sear and the sun-sear of the death cages"), and his homage to Pound moves with the unpredictable gravity of *The Pisan Cantos* themselves.

Very few readers interested in a poet like Zukofsky (who is associated with staunchly experimental writing) are also interested in a poet like Wright (whose work is not aggressively disjunctive or political). But to limit our sense of Pound's influence to a proscribed canon of Poundian poets is to resist what is most valuable about Pound – his extraordinary catholicity of taste, his uncanny ability to perceive the greatness in poets who could not reliably perceive the greatness in each other. Even today, many readers still need to choose between Williams and Eliot, but for

Pound there was no choice to be made. "I am worried as to what is to become of him," said Eliot of Pound in 1921: to know what has become of Pound we have only to read the widest possible variety of poets writing today.

NOTES

1 T. S. Eliot, *Letters*, ed. Valerie Eliot (New York: Harcourt, 1988), 50.
2 William Carlos Williams, *Collected Poems*, ed. A. Walton Litz and Christopher MacGowan, 2 vols. (New York: New Directions, 1986), 1: 21.
3 *Ibid.*, 159.
4 William Carlos Williams, *Paterson*, ed. Christopher MacGowan (New York: New Directions, 1992), 6. For a reading of *Paterson* as a response to the *Cantos*, see Michael Andre Bernstein, *The Tale of the Tribe: Ezra Pound and the Modern Verse Epic* (Princeton: Princeton University Press, 1980).
5 Williams, *Collected Poems*, 137.
6 W. B. Yeats to Lady Gregory, January 3, 1913; quoted in A. Norman Jeffares, *W. B. Yeats: Man and Poet* (New Haven: Yale University Press, 1949), 167.
7 W. B. Yeats to Lady Gregory, January 8, 1913; quoted in James Longenbach, *Stone Cottage: Pound, Yeats, and Modernism* (New York: Oxford University Press, 1988), 19.
8 W. B. Yeats, *The Poems*, ed. Richard Finneran (New York: Macmillan, 1989), 91.
9 See Harold Bloom, *The Anxiety of Influence* (New York: Oxford University Press, 1973) and *A Map of Misreading* (New York: Oxford University Press, 1975).
10 See George Mills Harper, *W. B. Yeats and W. T. Horton: The Record of an Occult Friendship* (New York: Macmillan, 1980), 129.
11 Roland Barthes, *Critical Essays*, trans. Richard Howard (Evanston, Il: Northwestern University Press, 1972), 211. In the terms of Joseph Conte, one can say (though Conte would not) that *The Waste Land* is a poetic series rather than a sequence: see *The Forms of Postmodern Poetry* (Ithaca, NY: Cornell University Press, 1991).
12 T. S. Eliot, *Complete Poems and Plays* (New York: Harcourt, 1971), 41.
13 T. S. Eliot, *The Waste Land: A Facsimile and Transcript of the Original Drafts Including the Annotations of Ezra Pound*, ed. Valerie Eliot (New York: Harcourt, 1971), 13.
14 Louis Zukofsky, *Selected Poems*, ed. Charles Bernstein (New York: Library of America, 2006), 3.
15 *Ibid.*, 4.
16 Charles Bernstein, *A Poetics* (Cambridge, MA: Harvard University Press, 1992), 122–3.
17 Charles Wright, *Zone Journals* (New York: Farrar, Straus and Giroux, 1988), p. 11.

Further reading

TEXTS

Fenollosa, Ernest and Ezra Pound. *The Chinese Written Character as a Medium for Poetry: A Critical Edition*. Ed. H. Saussy, J. Sterling, and L. Klien. New York: Fordham University Press, 2008.

Pound, Ezra. *A Draft of xxx Cantos*. New York: New Directions, 1990.

ABC of Economics. London: Faber and Faber, 1933.

ABC of Reading. 1934. New York: New Directions, 1960.

Cantos. 13th Printing. New York: New Directions, 1995.

Certain Noble Plays of Japan. Intro. William B. Yeats. Churchtown, Dundrum: The Cuala Press, 1916.

Collected Early Poems of Ezra Pound. 1976. Ed. Michael John King. New York: New Directions, 1982.

Early Writings, Poems and Prose. Ed. Ira B. Nadel. New York: Penguin, 2005.

Ezra Pound and Music. Ed. R. Murray Schafer. New York: New Directions, 1977.

Ezra Pound and the Visual Arts. Ed. Harriet Zinnes. New York: New Directions, 1980.

How to Read. London: Harmsworth, 1931.

I Cantos. Ed. Mary de Rachewiltz. Milan: Mondadori, 1985.

Idee fondamentali, Meridiano di Roma 1939–1943. Ed. Caterina Ricciardi. Rome: Lucarini Editori, 1991.

Impact, Essays on Ignorance and the Decline of American Civilization. Ed. Noel Stock. Chicago: Henry Regnery Company, 1960.

Literary Essays. Ed. T.S. Eliot. New York: New Directions, 1968.

"Noh" or Accomplishment. London: Macmillan and Company, 1916.

The Pisan Cantos. Ed. Richard Sieburth. New York: New Directions, 2003.

Patria Mia. Chicago: Ralph Fletcher Seymour, 1950.

Poems and Translations. Ed. Richard Sieburth. New York: Library of America, 2003.

Polite Essays. London: Faber and Faber, 1937.

Selected Prose 1909–1965. Ed. William Cookson. London: Faber and Faber, 1978.

Social Credit. London: Stanley Nott, 1935.

Translations. Intro. Hugh Kenner. London: Faber and Faber, 1953.

BIOGRAPHY

Ackroyd, Peter. *Ezra Pound and His World*. New York: Scribner's, 1980.

Carpenter, Humphrey. *A Serious Character, The Life of Ezra Pound*. London: Faber and Faber, 1988.

Conover, Anne. *Olga Rudge & Ezra Pound*. New Haven: Yale University Press, 2001.

Cornell, Julien. *The Trial of Ezra Pound*. New York: John Day, 1966.

Heymann, C. David. *Ezra Pound, The Last Rower, a Political Profile*. New York: Richard Seaver/ Viking Press, 1976.

Hutchins, Patricia. *Ezra Pound's Kensington*. London: Faber and Faber, 1965.

Meacham, Harry M. *The Caged Panther, Ezra Pound at St. Elizabeths*. New York: Twayne, 1967.

Moody, A. David. *Ezra Pound: Poet, A Portrait of the Man and his Work. Vol. 1: The Young Genius 1885–1920*. Oxford: Oxford University Press, 2007.

Nadel, Ira B. *Ezra Pound. A Literary Life*. London: Palgrave Macmillan, 2004.

Stock, Noel. *The Life of Ezra Pound*. London: Penguin, 1974.

Torrey, E. Fuller. *The Roots of Treason: Ezra Pound and the Secret of St. Elizabeths*. New York: Harcourt, Brace, Jovanovich, 1984.

Tytell, John. *Ezra Pound: The Solitary Volcano*. New York: Doubleday, 1987.

Wilhelm, J. J. *The American Roots of Ezra Pound*. New York: Garland, 1985.

Ezra Pound in London and Paris 1908–1925. University Park: Pennsylvania State University Press, 1990.

Ezra Pound, The Tragic Years, 1925–1972. University Park: Penn State University Press, 1994.

LETTERS

Ezra Pound and Margaret Cravens, A Tragic Friendship 1910–1912. Ed. Omar Pound and Robert Spoo. Durham, NC: Duke University Press, 1988.

Ezra Pound to Alice Corbin Henderson. Ed. Ira B. Nadel. Austin: University of Texas Press, 1993.

Ezra Pound's Economic Correspondence, 1933–1940. Ed. Roxana Preda. Gainesville: University Press of Florida, 2007.

The Letters of Ezra Pound to James Joyce. Ed. Forrest Read. New York: New Directions, 1970.

The Selected Letters of Ezra Pound, 1907–1941. Ed. D.D. Paige. New York: New Directions, 1971.

MEMOIRS

Aldington, Richard. *Life for Life's Sake*. New York: Viking, 1941.

de Rachewiltz, Mary. *Discretions*. Boston: Little Brown, 1971.

Doolittle, Hilda ("H.D."). *End to Torment: A Memoir of Ezra Pound*. New York: New Directions, 1979.

Laughlin, James. *Pound as Wuz: Recollections and Interpretations.* London: Peter Owen, 1989.

Olson, Charles. *Charles Olson and Ezra Pound: An Encounter at St. Elizabeths.* Ed. Catherine Seelye. New York: Grossman, 1975.

BIBLIOGRAPHY AND CRITICISM

Alexander, Michael. *The Poetic Achievement of Ezra Pound.* Berkeley: University of California Press, 1979.

Bacigalupo, Massimo. *The Formèd Trace: The Later Poetry of Ezra Pound.* New York: Columbia University Press, 1980.

Bernstein, Michael André. *The Tale of the Tribe: Ezra Pound and the Modern Verse Epic.* Princeton: Princeton University Press, 1980.

Bischoff, Volker. *Ezra Pound Criticism 1905–1985, A Chronological Listing of Publications in English.* Marburg, Germany: Universitatsbibliothek Marburg, 1991.

Bornstein, George, ed. *Ezra Pound Among the Poets.* Chicago: University of Chicago Press, 1985.

Bush, Ronald. "Excavating the Ideological Faultlines of Modernism: Editing Ezra Pound's Cantos," In *Representing Modernist Texts, Editing as Interpretation.* Ed. George Bornstein. Ann Arbor: University of Michigan Press, 1991. 67–98.

Dasenbrock, Reed Way. *Imitating the Italians, Wyatt, Spenser, Synge, Pound, Joyce.* Baltimore: Johns Hopkins University Press, 1991.
  The Literary Vorticism of Ezra Pound and Wyndham Lewis. Baltimore: Johns Hopkins University Press, 1983.

Davidson, Peter. *Ezra Pound and Roman Poetry: A Preliminary Survey.* Amsterdam: Rodopi, 1995.

Davie, Donald. *Ezra Pound: Poet as Sculptor.* New York: Oxford University Press, 1964.

Fisher, Margaret. *Ezra Pound's Radio Operas, The BBC Experiments 1931–1933.* Cambridge, MA: The MIT Press, 2002.

Flory, Wendy Stallard. *The American Ezra Pound.* New Haven: Yale University Press, 1989.

Froula, Christine. *To Write Paradise: Style and Error in Pound's Cantos.* New Haven: Yale University Press, 1985.

Gallup, Donald. *Ezra Pound: A Bibliography.* Charlottesville: University Press of Virginia, 1983.

Hesse, Eva, ed. *New Approaches to Ezra Pound.* Berkeley: University of California Press, 1969.

Homberger, Eric, ed. *Ezra Pound: The Critical Heritage.* London: Routledge, 1972.

Hughes, Robert and Margaret Fisher. *Cavalcanti: A Perspective on the Music of Ezra Pound.* Emeryville, CA: Second Evening Art Publishing, 2003.

Kaye, Jacqueline, ed. *Ezra Pound and America.* London: Macmillan, 1992.

Kenner, Hugh. *The Poetry of Ezra Pound.* 1951. Lincoln: University of Nebraska Press, 1985.

The Pound Era. Berkeley: University of California Press, 1971.

Longenbach, James. *Stone Cottage: Pound, Yeats and Modernism*. New York: Oxford University Press, 1988.

McDonald, Gail. *Learning to be Modern: Pound, Eliot and the American University*. Oxford: Clarendon Press, 1993.

Makin, Peter, ed. *Ezra Pound's Cantos, A Casebook*. New York: Oxford University Press, 2006.

Nadel, Ira B., ed. *The Cambridge Companion to Ezra Pound*. Cambridge: Cambridge University Press, 1999.

  The Cambridge Introduction to Ezra Pound. Cambridge: Cambridge University Press, 2007.

North, Michael. *The Political Aesthetic of Yeats, Eliot and Pound*. New York: Cambridge University Press, 1991.

O'Connor, William Van and Edward Stone, eds. *A Casebook on Ezra Pound*. New York: Thomas Y. Crowell, 1959.

Paideuma, Studies in American and British Modernist Poetry. 1972–

Rainey, Lawrence. *Ezra Pound and the Monument of Culture. Text, History, and the Malatesta Cantos*. Chicago: University of Chicago Press, 1991.

Rainey, Lawrence, ed. *A Poem Containing History: Textual Studies in The Cantos*. Ann Arbor: University of Michigan Press, 1997.

Read, Forrest. *'76 One World and The Cantos of Ezra Pound*. Chapel Hill: University of North Carolina Press, 1981.

Reck, Michael. *Ezra Pound: A Close-Up*. New York: McGraw-Hill, 1968.

Redman, Tim. *Ezra Pound and Italian Fascism*. Cambridge: Cambridge University Press, 1991.

  "Pound's Library, a Preliminary Catalogue," *Paideuma* 15 (1986): 213–37.

Ruthven, K.K. *A Guide to Ezra Pound's Personae (1926)*. Berkeley: University of California Press, 1969.

Sieburth, Richard. *Instigations: Ezra Pound and Rémy de Gourmont*. Cambridge, MA: Harvard University Press, 1978.

Singh, G. *Ezra Pound as Critic*. London: Macmillan/ St. Martin's Press, 1984.

Società Letteraria Rapallo, ed. *Il Mare Supplemento Letterario 1932–1933*. Rapallo: Comune di Rapallo, 1999.

Stoicheff, Peter. *The Hall of Mirrors, Drafts & Fragments and the End of Ezra Pound's Cantos*. Ann Arbor: University of Michigan, 1995.

Sullivan, J.P., *Ezra Pound and Sextus Propertius: A Study in Creative Translation*. Austin: University of Texas Press, 1964.

Sullivan, J.P., ed. *Ezra Pound, A Critical Anthology*. Harmondsworth: Penguin, 1970.

Tate Gallery. *Pound's Artists, Ezra Pound and the Visual Arts in London, Paris and Italy*. London: Tate Gallery, 1985.

Taylor, Richard and Claus Melchior, eds. *Ezra Pound and Europe*. Amsterdam: Rodopi, 1993.

Terrell, Carroll F. *A Companion to the Cantos of Ezra Pound*. 2 vols. Berkeley: University of California Press, 1980.

Thomas, Ron. *The Latin Masks of Ezra Pound.* Ann Arbor, MI: UMI Press, 1983.

Tiffany, Daniel. *Radio Corpse, Imagism and The Cryptaestheic of Ezra Pound.* Cambridge, MA: Harvard University Press, 1995.

Tryphonopoulos, Demetres P. and Stephen J. Adams, eds. *The Ezra Pound Encyclopedia.* Westport, CT: Greenwood Press, 2005.

Wilson, Peter. *A Preface to Ezra Pound.* London: Longman, 1997.

Witemeyer, Hugh. *The Poetry of Ezra Pound, Forms and Renewal 1908–1920.* 1969; Berkeley: University of California Press, 1981.

Witemeyer, Hugh, ed. "Ezra Pound and American Identity," Special Issue, *Paideuma* 34, 2 and 3 (Winter 2005).

Zukofsky, Louis. "Ezra Pound." In *Prepositions: The Collected Critical Essays of Louis Zukofsky.* Expanded edition. Berkeley: University of California Press, 1981. 67–83.

Index